Conceptions of Truth

Conceptions of Truth

WOLFGANG KÜNNE

CLARENDON PRESS · OXFORD

This book has been printed digitally and produced in a standard specification
in order to ensure its continuing availability

OXFORD
UNIVERSITY PRESS

Great Clarendon Street, Oxford OX2 6DP

Oxford University Press is a department of the University of Oxford.
It furthers the University's objective of excellence in research, scholarship,
and education by publishing worldwide in

Oxford New York

Auckland   Cape Town   Dar es Salaam   Hong Kong   Karachi
Kuala Lumpur   Madrid   Melbourne   Mexico City   Nairobi
New Delhi   Shanghai   Taipei   Toronto
With offices in
Argentina   Austria   Brazil   Chile   Czech Republic   France   Greece
Guatemala   Hungary   Italy   Japan   South Korea   Poland   Portugal
Singapore   Switzerland   Thailand   Turkey   Ukraine   Vietnam

Oxford is a registered trade mark of Oxford University Press
in the UK and in certain other countries

Published in the United States
by Oxford University Press Inc., New York

ISBN 978-0-19-928019-3

FOR PETER STRAWSON

Preface

This book is organized around a set of conceptual questions about truth which are charted in the introductory chapter, and it argues for what I take to be the most reasonable answers. It is partly due to my philosophical upbringing in Gadamer's Heidelberg, I suppose, that the history of philosophical reflections on the key questions I have selected will play a far larger role in these pages than it does in books on truth from the pen of other analytical philosophers. I am deeply convinced that, as Strawson once put it, 'the progress of philosophy, at least, is dialectical: we return to old insights in new and, we hope, improved forms'. A more specific reason why I have gone to some lengths to trace answers to my key questions is that I cannot help thinking that nowadays too many analytical philosophers neglect even the English classics of their own tradition. (As the reader will soon notice, I take this tradition to have originated already in the early nineteenth century in Prague, in the heart of what my Anglophone colleagues tend to call 'the Continent'.) I hope that, as a result of my scholarly ambitions, this book will also serve as a reliable guide to the vast literature, both 'ancient' and contemporary, on its topic(s). As to the questions I shall go into, a confession at the outset might spare my prospective readers at least one disappointment: I have nothing enlightening to say about, let alone to contribute to, the debate on the semantic antinomies. Bracketing this deep problem about truth, apart from a few asides and a brief guide to the literature, might well be the most glaring of the omissions from which this book suffers. (But then, there is also something to be said in favour of not entering this arena: in antiquity, at least one philosopher died prematurely because he had worried too much about the 'Liar'.)

The book is based on courses of lectures, and I have deliberately retained some features of those lectures: the use of tables and flow charts, a certain amount of rhetorical emphasis and recapitulation, the prodigality of examples, and even one or two serious attempts at making a joke. I hope all this will make for greater readability. The very rich supply of sometimes fairly extensive quotations is meant to give the reader a chance to assess my interpretations of other philosophers on the spot. The book has been long in the making. Various earlier versions of my lectures were delivered at my home university. The first (more or less) English versions of my Hamburg lectures were presented in the mid-1990s in Oslo and in Venice. It was on those occasions that I began thinking that it might be worthwhile to transform my lectures into a book. Material from what are now the two final chapters was used in 'Simple Truth and Alethic Realism', which was my Gareth Evans Memorial Lecture in Oxford in May 1998. Parts of the penultimate draft of this book formed the text of the Dasturzada Dr Jal Pavry Lectures which I delivered at Oxford in Hilary Term 1999. Drafts of many sections of this book were read as occasional papers in Berlin, Bertinoro, Bielefeld, Fribourg, Heidelberg, Kirchberg, London, Munich, New York, Oldenburg, Oxford, Padua, Reading, Saarbrücken, San Marino, Siena, Toruń, Zielona Góra, and, most recently, at the Moral Sciences Club in Cambridge. Many of the questions and objections of my audiences have contributed greatly to the clarification of my thoughts.

I am indebted to my students in Hamburg for much feedback over the years, especially to Simon Dähnhardt, David Filip, Ben Höfer, Miguel Hoeltje, Niels Kröner, Vincent Müller, Michael Oliva-Cordoba, Stefanie Richter, Severin Schröder, Christian Stein, Armin Tatzel, Christian Tielmann, Elisabeth Wienberg, and above all, to Benjamin Schnieder. I am also grateful to Maik Sühr, who helped prepare the manuscript for the publisher. I consider myself lucky that, many years ago, Kevin Mulligan, Peter Simons, and Barry Smith infected me with their enthusiasm for Austro-Polish philosophy, and I hope to have added a distinctly Bolzanian tone to their singing. I benefited especially from meetings with Peter in those years, when he had occasion to speak Austrian German most of the time. In Norway, Italy, and Poland exchanges with Dagfinn Føllesdal, Olaf Gjelsvik, Paolo Leonardi, Ernesto Napoli, and Jan Woleński were very stimulating. At different stages I was helped by comments on various chapters of the book, which I received from Ansgar Beckermann, Ali Behboud, Emma Borg, Bill Brewer, Pascal Engel, Hartry Field, Manuel García-Carpintero, Thomas Hofweber, Andrea Jacona, David Kaplan, Andreas Kemmerling, Holger Klärner, Max Kölbel, David Oderberg, Hilary Putnam, Tobias Rosefeldt, Ian Rumfitt, Stephen Schiffer, Mark Siebel, Markus Stepanians, Mark Textor, David Wiggins, and Ed Zalta.

Very special thanks must go to Sir Michael Dummett, who commented incisively on my Evans Lecture, and to Jonathan Dancy, Hanjo Glock, Peter Hacker, Paul Horwich, John Hyman, Christopher Peacocke, and the anonymous referees commissioned by Oxford University Press for taking the trouble to go through drafts of the entire book and to provide me with generously detailed and pointed written comments. Their searching questions and constructive suggestions have prompted much needed clarification and revision (and for very different reasons they will presumably all be disappointed by my inability to follow their good advice on every point).

I am particularly indebted to Chris Peacocke and David Wiggins, who opened many doors for me at Oxford. I have to thank various British institutions for support of my work. (In view of the nationality of the author of this book, the second adjective should be stressed.) I am grateful for the hospitality of three Oxford Colleges, St Catherine's, St John's, and Wolfson, during the terms when I held Visiting Fellowships. I am much obliged to The Leverhulme Trust, which awarded me a Visiting Professorship, and to the members of the very lively Department of Philosophy at Reading University, who made my time as Leverhulme Visiting Professor extremely rewarding and very enjoyable indeed. I also wish to thank my editor at OUP, Peter Momtchiloff, for his unfailing interest in my project, his constant support, and his admirable efficiency in all matters editorial. I have also been very fortunate to have Sarah Dancy as copy-editor, to whom I am most grateful for her careful work. For many months, when my thoughts were occupied by the content of this book to the exclusion of most other things and when my spirits often flagged, my wife Malakeh and my son Sebastian must often have found life with me less than easy, to put it mildly. I thank them very much for their forbearance.

With admiration, gratitude, and affection I dedicate this book to Sir Peter Strawson. Whenever I met him in Oxford, he gave me the greatest possible encouragement. 'Under certain circumstances', a great novel has it, 'there are few hours in life more agreeable than the hour dedicated to the ceremony known as afternoon tea.' For me, these circumstances are defined by his entirely unceremonious presence and the opportunity to enjoy the perceptiveness, self-irony, and dry humour of his remarks on philosophy, philosophers, and much else. Thirty years ago, his work drew me into analytical philosophy, and his lasting influence will be visible, or so I would like to think, on many pages of this book.

Hamburg, 14 July 2002   W. K.

Contents

Some Questions about Truth

> To the lay mind it is a perplexing thing that the nature of truth should be
> a vexed problem. That such is the case seems another illustration of
> Berkeley's remark about the proneness of philosophers to throw dust into
> their own eyes and then complain that they cannot see.... The plain man
> ... has learned, through hard discipline, that it is no easy matter to discover
> what the truth is in special instances. But such difficulties assume that the
> nature of truth is perfectly understood.... Whence and why the pother?
>
> (John Dewey, 'The Problem of Truth', 12)

There are at least two ways of asking the question, 'What is truth?' One of them is
commonly attributed to Pilate: is there ever any hope that we might disclose the
truth if the problem is a really delicate one? As is well known, 'jesting Pilate...
would not stay for an answer'.[1] Another way of putting that question is the way
Socrates asked, 'What is courage, what is piety, what is knowledge?' Many great
philosophers took the question 'What is truth?' in a Socratic spirit, and the answers
given through the ages are what the title of this book alludes to as 'conceptions of
truth'. In advocating a conception of truth, philosophers may pursue different,
though internally related, goals. Some of them try to explain the concept of
truth—or to demonstrate the futility of all attempts at explaining this concept.
Some of them mean to tell us what being true consists in (assuming that this may
very well not be written into our concept, as it were). Most of them endeavour to
specify (conceptually) necessary and sufficient conditions for something's being
true. All of them aspire to be faithful to our workaday concept of truth, which is
employed by Dewey's 'plain' men and women who have 'learned, through hard
discipline, that it is no easy matter to discover what the truth is in special instances'.

The phrase 'the concept of truth' or, equivalently, 'the concept of being true',
like all locutions of the type 'the concept of being F' or 'the concept of F-ness'
(where 'F-ness' is a placeholder for the appropriate nominalization of the general

---

[1] Francis Bacon, 'Of Truth', 377 (alluding to John 18: 38). Austin echoes Bacon's remark in his 'Truth', 117.

term replacing 'F'), must be handled with care. Having a concept is having a cognitive capacity: you have the concept of being thus-and-so, I take it, if and only if you are able to think of something *as* thus-and-so (or as not thus-and-so). The concept of being F differs from the concept of being G if it is possible that somebody thinks of something as F without thinking of it as G. This may be the case even if (the property of) being F *is* (the property of) being G. An example or two will do no harm. A girl may be able to think of her father as having spent half of his salary on drink without being able to think of him as having spent 50 per cent of his salary on drink, notwithstanding the fact that having spent half of one's salary on drink *is* having spent 50 per cent of it for this purpose. Two concepts, one property. Thinking of a dish as needing some salt was something we often did long before our first lessons in chemistry, but at that stage we were not yet able to think of a dish as needing some sodium chloride. Nevertheless, needing some salt *is* needing some sodium chloride. Two concepts, one property. Of course, having the concept of being F differs vastly from having the property of being F: fortunately, you do not have to commit a murder in order to acquire the concept of a being a murderer.[2]

I shall try to defend a (decidedly non-startling) answer to the Socratic question, 'What is truth?', understood as a request for an elucidation of the concept, but I also invite the reader to a journey through the ages. The focus is clearly on the analytical tradition, but I think there is still a lot to be learned from pondering over conceptions of truth which grew on different soils. Michael Dummett once remarked, as an aside, that 'philosophical theories of truth have usually been intended as contributions to delineating the outlines of some theory of meaning'.[3] I am taken aback by the adverb. Generations of philosophers, from Plato and Aristotle to Bolzano and Brentano, Peirce and Bradley, had no such intention, and quite a few analytical philosophers and logicians of the twentieth century who struggled with the concept of truth did not dream of thereby contributing to the theory of meaning; neither Moore nor Tarski did, to mention just two examples.[4]

In this introductory chapter I shall present a kind of flow chart. It is meant to give a bird's-eye view of a fairly large theoretical landscape and to provide a guide to the overall structure of this book. The chart comprises sixteen *quaestiones de veritate*. They draw attention to some of the main junctions of the many roads which lead through this landscape. I shall describe these intersections, explain

---

[2] Cf. Strawson, 'Concepts and Properties', 88–9. '*Having*' is used differently in 'having (= having command of, being able to use) a concept' and 'having (= exemplifying) a property'.

[3] Dummett, *Frege—Philosophy of Language* (henceforth *FPL*), 457; cf. 462–3.

[4] As far as Tarski is concerned, Dummett himself is clearly aware of this.

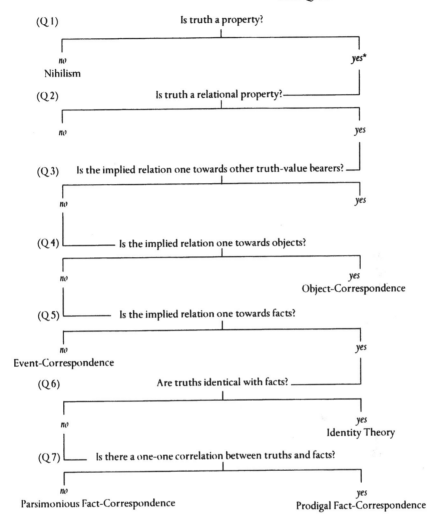

(Q1)   Is truth a property?

no   *yes**
Nihilism

(Q2)   Is truth a relational property?

no   *yes*

(Q3)   Is the implied relation one towards other truth-value bearers?

no   *yes*

(Q4)   Is the implied relation one towards objects?

no   *yes*
                                                 Object-Correspondence

(Q5)   Is the implied relation one towards facts?

no   *yes*
Event-Correspondence

(Q6)   Are truths identical with facts?

no   *yes*
                                                     Identity Theory

(Q7)   Is there a one-one correlation between truths and facts?

no   *yes*
Parsimonious Fact-Correspondence   Prodigal Fact-Correspondence

Figure 1.1. QUESTIONS 1–7

some key terms, mention some of the philosophers who took either this road or that one, and mark those answers I intend to examine as well as those which I am going to put aside. I will announce which answers I shall endorse. (On the chart they are marked by asterisks.)

Is truth a relational or a non-relational property? Is it a naturalistic property or a non-naturalistic one? Is it epistemically constrained or unconstrained? Some philosophers give the same answer to all three questions: it is neither one nor the other. Truth isn't any kind of property, so nothing has the property of being true. I call this view (tongue in cheek) 'nihilism'. In a way this is the most radical stance one can take in our field, so in Chapter 2 ('A Bogus Predicate?') I shall devote quite a lot of critical attention to the negative answer to QUESTION 1 in Figure 1.1. One strand in Gottlob Frege's reflections on truth points in this direction. The question when, according to Frege, two sentences express one and the same proposition will loom large in this chapter, and some lessons will be drawn from Bernard Bolzano's rather different answer to that question. In his very first essay on truth Peter Strawson drew nihilist conclusions from certain observations concerning the performative potential of the expression 'is true'.[5] Frank Ramsey's so-called Redundancy Theory and its refinement in the work of Arthur Prior have been a fertile source of inspiration for nihilism in the last three decades. Detailed expositions of nihilism were given by Christopher Williams and by Dorothy Grover, and the most recent version is Robert Brandom's. I shall scrutinize their views at length, and I shall reject all of them.

Suppose, truth *is* a property: is it a *relational* property (QUESTION 2)? In order to get a grip on this question, some terminological preparations will be useful. A predicate is an expression which takes one or more singular terms to make a sentence, in other words, it is a sentence-forming operator on singular terms. So from 'Rachel is married to Jacob' you can obtain two different monadic predicates, depending on which singular term you delete; when you remove both singular terms, the result is a dyadic predicate. A property which is *designated* by a singular term of the type 'F-ness' (or 'being F') is, as I shall put it, *signified* by the corresponding predicate 'is F'. (This predicate *applies* to all, and only to, F-things, if there are any, and if one fully understands it, one possesses the concept which is *expressed* by it.) So if truth is a property, then the singular term 'truth' (or 'being true') designates it, and the monadic predicate 'is true' signifies it. Being F is a *relational property*[6] if and only if (the property of) being F is (the property of) being related in such-and-such a way to something/somebody. Thus, (i) being married to Jacob and (ii) being a spouse (that is, being married to somebody) are relational properties of Rachel. Both properties are signified by monadic predicates, 'is married to Jacob' and 'is a spouse' respectively. Only polyadic predicates signify relations. The dyadic predicate 'is married to' signifies the relation that is implied, as it were, by (i) and (ii). In case (i) a member of the right field, or counter-domain, of the implied relation is identified, in case (ii) it is not.

---

[5] In his post-1950 writings on our topic Strawson unequivocally abandoned what is nowadays still referred to in the literature as 'Strawson's Performative Theory of Truth'.

[6] Moore seems to have introduced this term: see his 'External and Internal Relations', 281–2.

So if truth is a relational property, then, in analogy with case (ii), being true is being related in a certain way to something. In giving a negative answer to QUESTION 2 one denies the consequent of this conditional. Nihilism is bound to give a negative answer to QUESTION 2. Prima facie at least, several other conceptions of truth are not committed to a positive answer, thus disquotationalism, minimalism, and the account I favour. (We will soon have occasion to give a provisional description of these views when we confront a different set of questions.[7])

But suppose truth *is* a relational property: is the implied relation one in which truth-candidates stand to other truth-value bearers (QUESTION 3)? Yes, say those who embrace a Coherence Theory. (This, too, is a view we shall encounter again when posing a different kind of question.) Philosophers who opt for a Correspondence Theory answer QUESTION 3 negatively. Strangely enough, only one of the varieties of correspondence which are distinguished under QUESTIONS 4–7 tends to be registered in the literature, namely the Cambridge variety, which I call 'Fact(-based) Correspondence'.[8] A central aim of Chapter 3 ('Varieties of Correspondence') will be to restore the balance. Aristotle paved the way for 'Object(-based) Correspondence', the affirmative answer to QUESTION 4, which was to be the prevailing view for many centuries. Paradigmatic elements of the right field of the correspondence relation thus understood are material objects such as mountains and people. In the first decades of the twentieth century some philosophers in Cambridge took *facts* to be what truths correspond to. The entries under QUESTION 7 allude to a sort of economical difference between the Cambridge friends of correspondence: George Edward Moore was rather lavish with facts, whereas Bertrand Russell, pushed by Ludwig Wittgenstein, came to be rather stingy with them. More recently, John Searle is hardly less generous than Moore was: 'If it is true that if the cat had been on the mat, then the dog would have had to have been in the kitchen, then it must be a fact that if the cat had been on the mat, then the dog would have had to have been in the kitchen. For every true statement there is a corresponding fact.'[9]

---

[7] See below, (Q 10) and (Q 14).

[8] Here are two representative examples from the recent literature. In his comprehensive survey, Richard Kirkham takes the following thesis to be the common denominator of *all* correspondence theories of truth: a truth-bearer is true if and only if it corresponds to a state of affairs and that state of affairs obtains (*Theories of Truth* (henceforth *ThT*), 131–3). David Lewis, who advises us to 'Forget About the "Correspondence Theory of Truth" ' (henceforth 'Correspondence') describes it as the theory which 'says that truth is correspondence to fact' (281).

[9] Searle, *The Construction of Social Reality*, 219.

In the course of weighing up the main objections against Fact-based Correspondence, we will see that there is yet another option for correspondence theorists. Under the left branch of QUESTION 5 it is registered as 'Event(-based) Correspondence'. Here and elsewhere in this book, the term 'event' is meant only to cover one-off happenings that could not be repeated, such as the eruption of Vesuvius which buried Pompeii, or the death of a particular cat. (Even if a cat had nine lives, none of its nine deaths could be repeated.) By contrast, the Venice Carnival, which is celebrated year after year, is not an event, but an event-kind. Russell, never at a loss for a new answer to his old questions, pleaded for Event-based Correspondence in 1940. Let me briefly illustrate the three options for friends of correspondence which have to be canvassed. Suppose I have the true belief that Vesuvius erupted in 79. Does the correspondence obtain (i) between the concept expressed by the predicate 'erupted in 79' and the mountain my belief is about? Or between (ii) my belief as a whole and the fact that Vesuvius erupted in 79? Or between (iii) my belief and an event which took place in 79? On the whole, my verdict on correspondence accounts of truth will be less than favourable.

Nowadays there is much talk about '*making true*'. Making sense of this talk turns out to be rather difficult. In the long final section of Chapter 3 I shall try to convince you that several readings, with very different credentials and ranges, should be carefully distinguished.

The limiting case of a relational conception of truth is referred to under the right branch of QUESTION 6. According to the so-called Identity Theory, something is true if and only if it is (identical with) a fact. This contention makes sense only if one does not regard linguistic or mental entities as truth-value bearers, but, rather, propositions, something which can be expressed by declarative sentences and which can be the content of certain mental acts and states.[10] So the tenet is

(*Idem*)   For all x, x is a true proposition iff (if and only if) there is a fact with which x is identical.

Between 1899 and 1906 Moore and Russell upheld the Identity Theory (which by 1910 they were to renounce in favour of fact-based correspondence views).[11]

---

[10] Contrast Kirkham, *ThT*, 138: '[F]acts, they say, are not really anything different from true sentences.' I wonder who 'they' are.

[11] As for Russell, compare his 'Meinong's Theory of Complexes and Assumptions' (III). For documentation, explanation and discussion of the early Moore–Russell view, see Richard Cartwright, 'A Neglected Theory of Truth', and Julian Dodd, *An Identity Theory of Truth* (henceforth *ITT*), 159–66.

Around the turn of the century they complained that correspondence theorists suffer from double vision:

> It is commonly supposed that the truth of a proposition consists in some relation which it bears to reality; and falsehood in the absence of this relation. The relation in question is generally called a 'correspondence' or 'agreement'.../... It is essential to the theory that a truth should differ in some specific way from the reality, in relation to which its truth is to consist.... It is the impossibility of finding any such difference... which refutes the theory.... A truth differs in no respect from the reality to which it was supposed merely to correspond: e.g. the truth that I exist differs in no respect from the corresponding reality—my existence. (Moore, 'Truth', 20, 21)

The derived nominal phrase at the very end of this passage is to be understood, I take it, as in a sentence like 'Not many people are aware of my existence', which comes to the same thing as 'Not many people are aware (of the fact) that I exist'. Alexius Meinong characterized truths as 'subsisting objectives [*bestehende Objektive*]', 'factual objectives [*tatsächliche Objektive*]', or 'facts [*Tatsachen*]'. Implicitly, this provides identity theorists with an account of falsity as well. Analysing the notion of a fact as that of a state of affairs [*Objektiv*] which obtains [*besteht*], an advocate of (*Idem*) can say: x is false iff for some y, y is a state of affairs and y does not obtain and x is identical with y. However, Meinong's agreement with the identity theorists is only partial: he accepted only the left-to-right half of (*Idem*), because he took only those facts to be truths which are contents of acts of judgement.[12] Frege, who referred to the truth-evaluable contents of utterances as thoughts, embraced (*Idem*) without any reservation when he wrote in his paper 'The Thought':[13]

> '*Tatsachen! Tatsachen! Tatsachen!*' *ruft der Naturforscher aus... Was ist eine Tatsache? Eine Tatsache ist ein Gedanke, der wahr ist.* ['Facts, facts, facts', cries the scientist... What is a fact? A fact is a thought that is true.] ('*Der Gedanke*', 74)[14]

---

[12] Meinong, *Über Annahmen*, ch. 3. As can be seen from his writings in those years, Moore did accept the biconditional in both directions.

[13] The Fregean identification has been endorsed by philosophers of very different stripes: for example, by Ducasse ('Propositions, Truth, and the Ultimate Criterion of Truth', 154); Prior (*Objects of Thought*, 5, 11); Armstrong (*Belief, Truth and Knowledge*, 113); Chisholm (*Theory of Knowledge*, 2nd edn., 88); Tugendhat (*Logisch-semantische Propädeutik*, 232); Strawson ('Reply to John Searle', 403); Brandom (*Making It Explicit*, 327–8); and Schiffer ('Pleonastic Fregeanism', 2, 6). According to Carnap, only *contingently* true propositions are facts (*Meaning and Necessity*, 28). Such a restriction is suggested by Leibniz's distinction between 'truths of reason' and 'truths of fact', and by Hume's cleavage between 'relations of ideas' and 'matters of fact'. In §3 of *Die Grundlagen der Arithmetik*, Frege too used a narrower notion of 'fact': according to his less than perspicuous explanation, it is meant to cover all and only 'unprovable truths devoid of generality which contain predications of particular objects'.

[14]. Frege's articles are cited by page number of the original publication, since the original pagination is given both in the German collection, *Kleine Schriften*, and in the English translation in *Collected Papers on Mathematics, Logic, and Philosophy*. Whenever I refer to one of Frege's articles just by title and page number, it is contained in these collections. The preface to Frege's *Grundgesetze der Arithmetik* is cited by the page

Frege, Moore and Russell are agreed that for a correspondence theory it is essential that the relata of the correspondence relation are distinct. (That's why I introduced the Identity Theory as the limiting case, not of a correspondence view, but of a relational conception of truth.[15]) But unlike Moore and Russell in their early writings, Frege never dreamt of saying that reality, or the world, consists of true propositions (and their components): his 'first realm', the physical world, and his 'second realm', the mental world, do not contain any proposition (nor any constituent of propositions), and the 'third realm', with its somewhat unfortunate German name, harbours not only *true* propositions, but also false ones. In the correspondence between Russell and Frege the reason for this disagreement became clear. Both take propositions to be structured entities, but whereas the components of Fregean propositions are 'modes of presentation' ('senses'), Russellian propositions are composed of the things represented, objects and properties. For Frege, the proposition that Mont Blanc is more than 4,000 metres high consists of the sense of 'Mont Blanc' and the sense of 'is more than 4,000 metres high'; Russell, on the other hand, takes that proposition to contain the mountain with all its snowfields and the property of being 4,000 metres high as constituents.[16] The claim that true propositions (and their components) are the building-blocks of the world is surely more palatable if one thinks of Russellian propositions.

There is, however, at least one adherent of (*Idem*) who does take the world to consist of true Fregean propositions, namely John McDowell:[17]

[T]here is no ontological gap between the sort of thing ... one can think, and the sort of thing that can be the case. When one thinks truly, what one thinks is what is the case. So since the world is everything that is the case (as [Wittgenstein] once wrote), there is

number of the original publication which is also given in the translation, *The Basic Laws of Arithmetic*. Unfortunately, the English translations of *Nachgelassene Schriften* (henceforth *NS*) and of *Wissenschaftlicher Briefwechsel* (henceforth *WB*) do not indicate the pagination of the German editions. References to these collections are to the German versions, followed, in brackets, by the page number of *Posthumous Writings* or *Philosophical and Mathematical Correspondence*. (Responsibility for translations from German, Latin, and Greek is mine, even when I refer to, benefit from, or simply echo published translations.)

[15] Cf. the above extract from Moore, and Frege, '*Der Gedanke*', 60. By contrast, Roderick Chisholm contends, 'There is no question ... about the sense in which true propositions may be said to "correspond with" facts. They correspond with facts in the fullest sense that is possible, for they *are* facts' (*Theory of Knowledge*, 88); and Lewis maintains: if one takes a fact to be 'nothing other than a true proposition', then '*of course* truth is correspondence to fact: each truth corresponds to a fact by being identical to that fact' ('Correspondence', 277).

[16] Compare Frege, *NS*, 203–4 (187), 243 (225), 250 (232), 275 (255); *WB*, 127 (79), 245 (163) [letter to Russell, 13/11/1904], with Russell's reply to Frege, *WB*, 250–1 (169) [12/12/1904], and his *Principles of Mathematics*, §§47, 51.

[17] McDowell's conception is spelled out and enthusiastically endorsed by Jennifer Hornsby, 'Truth: The Identity Theory'. Dodd, *ITT*, 174–86, raises formidable objections.

no gap between thought, as such, and the world.... But to say that there is no gap between thought, as such, and the world is just to dress up a truism in high-flown language. All the point comes to is that one can think, for instance, *that spring has begun*, and that the very same thing, *that spring has begun*, can be the case. That is truistic, and it cannot embody something metaphysically contentious... / ...

Given the identity between what one thinks (when one's thought is true) and what is the case, to conceive the world as everything that is the case (as in *Tractatus Logico-Philosophicus*, 1) is to incorporate the world into what figures in Frege as the realm of sense. The realm of sense (*Sinn*) contains thoughts in the sense of what can be thought (thinkables) as opposed to acts or episodes of thinking. The identity displays facts, things that are the case, as thoughts in that sense—the thinkables that are the case. (*Mind and World*, 27, 179)

Is (*Idem*) really truistic, as McDowell wants us to believe? It is indeed a truism that one and the same that-clause can be used to single out a true thinkable (a true proposition) and a fact. But does it follow from this that facts are nothing but true thinkables?[18] Suppose we accept

(P1)   What Ben first thought was that Ann survived the accident.

(P2)   That Ann survived the accident is a miracle.

If the identity of the that-clauses in (P1) and (P2), provided that the context is kept constant, were to guarantee that 'the very same thing' is introduced into discourse, then we would have to conclude from these premisses:

(C)   Therefore (?), what Ben first thought is a miracle.

We can avoid this slide into nonsense by treating that-clauses as systematically ambiguous. Then we can say: only in (P1) does the that-clause single out a thinkable (and a true one, provided that Ann survived the accident), hence the displayed argument commits the fallacy of equivocation.[19] We do not have to dwell on the question (which we will face in due course[20]) what the that-clause singles out in (P2): what matters here and now is only the explanatory potential of assigning different 'things' to the that-clauses in (P1) and (P2). The unacceptability of the argument to (C) shows that McDowell cannot simply conclude from the identity of his italicized that-clauses that 'the very same thing' can be both a true thinkable (a true proposition) and a fact.

Of course, even if McDowell's argument is weak, (*Idem*) may be correct. But a former advocate of (*Idem*) seems to have refuted it a long time ago:

[Suppose I have the true belief] that a given tree, which I see, is an oak.... [T]he proposition that the tree is an oak is something which is and equally is whether the belief is true

---

[18]   The question is raised, in passing, in Dodd, *ITT*, 179.
[19]   Cf. Terence Parsons, 'On Denoting Propositions and Facts', sect. 3.   [20]   In Ch. 5.1.1.

or false.... But... the fact that the tree is an oak is something which *is*, only if the belief be true; and hence it is quite plain that... the fact that the tree is an oak is quite a different thing... from what I believe, when I believe that it is one.... (Moore, *Some Main Problems of Philosophy*, 308 [21])

Let 'p' express some contingently true proposition. Somebody could think that p even if it were false that p; what our thinker thinks, the *proposition* that p, exists whether or not he is right. But the *fact* that p would not exist if it were false that p. Therefore, Moore argues, the proposition that p is not identical with the fact that p.

But is this refutation really cogent?[22] An advocate of (*Idem*) can reply: 'Socrates' designates Socrates in every possible world in which he exists, regardless of whether he is married or not. By contrast, 'Xanthippe's husband' designates him only in those possible worlds in which he is married. Obviously this does not prevent Socrates from being identical with Xanthippe's husband. Now, similarly, the adherent of (*Idem*) continues, 'the proposition that p' designates the proposition that p in all possible worlds, whereas 'the fact that p' designates that proposition only in those worlds in which it is true. So why, he asks, should this observation refute the identity claim?[23]

But I think there are good reasons for rejecting (*Idem*). If facts are nothing but true propositions, why is it that 'True propositions are true' expresses a trivial truth, whereas 'Facts are true' has an awkward ring?[24] Why is it that 'The Pythagorean Theorem is true' makes sense, whereas 'The Pythagorean Theorem is a fact' does not? Why is it that 'The victory of the Labour Party in 2001 is a fact' is significant, whereas 'The victory of the Labour Party in 2001 is a true proposition'

---

[21] Henceforth *SMPP*. Cf. ibid., 260.

[22] As A. J. Ayer, in *Russell and Moore*, 211, and Kit Fine, in 'First Order Modal Theories III—Facts', 46–7, maintain. Cf. also Parsons, 'On Denoting Propositions and Facts', 454–5.

[23] The counter-argument is due to Cartwright, 'A Neglected Theory of Truth', 77–8. Dodd offers a reconstruction which assumes that the subject-term in a sentence of the form (F), 'The fact that p is well known', is a (referentially used) *definite description* (*ITT*, 87–8). This assumption, which can also be found in Timothy Williamson, *Knowledge and Its Limits*, 43 (henceforth *KL*), and in Stephen Neale, *Facing Facts* (henceforth *FF*), 87 n., is not a matter of course. As it stands, an expression of the form 'the fact that p' does not seem to contain any part which signifies a condition that could be met by exactly one fact. Since we can scarcely make sense of the pseudo-predicate 'is *a* fact that p', the putative Russellian analysans of (F), 'For some x, x is *a* fact that p, and for all y, if y is *a* fact that p then y = x, and x is well known', looks very fishy. In English, that pseudo-predicate makes sense only if prefixed by the pseudo-subject 'it': the resulting sentence can be construed either as the output of the application of the operator 'it is a fact that' to a sentence or as a stylistic variant of 'that p is a fact'. (I owe this point to Jonathan Lowe, *The Possibility of Metaphysics*, 231.) Perhaps one can circumvent this problem by assigning more structure to the locution 'the fact that p' than meets the eye, something like 'the unique x such that x is a fact and x = that p'. (The same problem arises, of course, with respect to the phrases of the form 'the proposition that p': it will be discussed in Ch. 5.1.1.)

[24] Austin declares 'A fact is a truth' to be absurd ('Unfair to Facts', 173).

is nonsense? If you think that the doubtful propriety or undeniable impropriety of certain forms of speech cannot bear much weight as evidence against a philosophical thesis like (*Idem*),[25] recall that McDowell at least did not offer any other support *for* that thesis than a linguistic observation. But this is only an *ad hominem* argument.

By reminding us of an earlier use of 'fact' and offering an alternative explanatory hypothesis, Julian Dodd has tried to show that the kind of linguistic observations I adduced does not rebut the identification of facts and true propositions. Once upon a time, he tells us, 'fact' was used as a synonym for 'event'. John L. Austin has conveniently summarized the evidence collected in the Oxford English Dictionary, so let me insert his summary here:

For the first 200 years of [the] use of ['fact'] (sixteenth and seventeenth centuries) it meant (cf. 'feat') a deed or action, either the thing done or the doing of the thing, and more especially a criminal action; during the eighteenth century this use gradually died out in favour of a more extended meaning which began to appear already in the seventeenth century: a fact is now *something that has really occurred* (even classical Latin extended *factum* to mean '[actual] event' or '[actual] occurrence'). ('Unfair to Facts', 164)

Nowadays this use is no longer predominant, but, Dodd argues, if there were still occasional hangovers from that earlier usage in our 'fact' talk, this would explain why the expressions 'fact' and 'true proposition' are sometimes not interchangeable, although facts, in the currently dominant use of this term, *are* true propositions. For then we could say that 'this [substitution-resistent] part of our discourse concerning "fact" is still stained with its old meaning.'[26] But consider the following expansion of one of my examples: 'The victory of the Labour Party in 2001 is a fact which no British citizen denies.' Dodd's hypothesis cannot explain why the substitution of 'true proposition' is not acceptable therein. One can deny only what can be stated, but no *event* can be stated. So although 'fact' does *not* have its earlier meaning in this sentence, it cannot be replaced by 'true proposition', and Dodd's alleged inference to the best explanation evaporates.

At any rate, the next observation should carry conviction: we individuate facts less finely than true propositions. The fact that you never met Cassius Clay is the same as the fact that you never met Muhammad Ali, the fact that I am

---

[25] We would badly affect rhythm, rhyme, and reason in Schiller's *Ode to Joy* if we were to replace the final word of 'All men become brothers' by 'male siblings'. Nevertheless, brothers *are* male siblings, and 'brother' even *means* MALE SIBLING.

[26] Dodd, *ITT*, 84. This book contains a careful exposition and defence of the Fregean reading of (*Idem*). Dodd rightly takes it to be an answer to the question what facts are rather than to the question what truth is (120), but he wrongly takes it to be the correct answer to the former question, or so it seems to me. He makes a very convincing case for his claim that the Fregean identification is compatible with what he calls a deflationist view of truth.

German is identical with the fact that WK is German, the fact that three-quarters of the electorate went to the polls is the same as the fact 75 per cent of the electorate went to the polls, and the fact that for cooking we often need some common salt is identical with the fact that for cooking we often need some sodium chloride. But (as Frege would be the first to insist[27]) in each of these cases my utterances of the embedded sentences express different propositions.

Criticizing his teacher Husserl and other members of the Brentano school, Adolf Reinach once said: 'All Austrians constantly confuse proposition [*Satz*] and state of affairs [*Sachverhalt*].'[28] Philosophers who quite explicitly identify facts (obtaining states of affairs) with true propositions cannot be accused of *confusing* them, but I think they, too, are confused. So I shall not revisit (*Idem*) in the following chapters.

Let us now consider the next three questions on my flow chart (see Figure 1.2). Suppose truth is a property of sentences (QUESTION 8), of type-sentences perhaps or of token-sentences (or of acts of producing such tokens):[29] then the next question is whether the concept of (sentential) truth is explainable (QUESTION 9). I call those philosophers who answer 'No' adherents of 'sentential primitivism'. You will not hear 'primitivism' as a term of abuse once you realize, or recall, that Donald Davidson has maintained, for many years now, that our general notion of truth is a 'primitive concept':

[T]ruth is as clear and basic a concept as we have.... Any attempt to explain, define, analyse or explicate the concept will...either add nothing to our understanding of truth or have obvious counter-examples. Why on earth should we expect to be able to reduce truth to something clearer and more fundamental? After all, the only concept Plato succeeded in defining was [the concept of] mud. ('Afterthoughts', 155–6)

(The sarcastic allusion is to Plato's *Theaetetus*: in this dialogue 'mud' gets defined as 'earth mixed with water', whereas the attempt at defining 'knowledge' is the first of a long series of failures.) The very title of Davidson's paper, 'The Folly of Trying to Define Truth', epitomizes the theme.[30] Of course, primitivism does

---

[27] See Ch. 2.1.3 below.

[28] Reinach, '*Zum Begriff der Zahl*', 526. As to 'the Austrians', cf. Edgar Morscher's lucid overview, 'Propositions and States of Affairs in Austrian Philosophy'.

[29] The standard reference for the type–token distinction is Peirce, *Collected Papers* (henceforth *CP*), vol. 4, sect. 537: 'There will ordinarily be about twenty *the*'s on a page, and of course they count as twenty words. In another sense of the word "word", however, there is but one word "the" in the English language; and it is impossible that this word should lie visibly on a page or be heard in any voice.' This distinction obviously also applies to whole sentences.

[30] Cf. also Davidson, 'A Coherence Theory of Truth and Knowledge', 139, 'Introduction' to his *Inquiries into Truth and Interpretation* (henceforth *ITI*), xiv. David Wiggins concurs: see especially his crisply titled paper, 'An Indefinibilist cum Normative View of Truth and the Marks of Truth' (henceforth 'Indefinibilist').

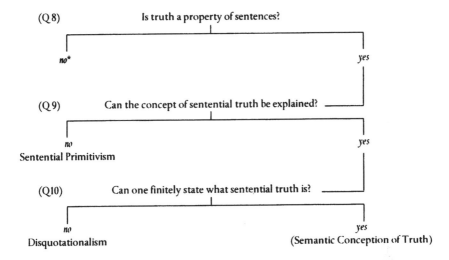

Figure 1.2. QUESTIONS 8–10

not exclude that a lot of what we know a priori involves the concept of truth essentially. Thus we know a priori, for example, that a set of truths is always consistent.

Note how quickly Davidson moves, in the passage quoted above, from 'explanation, definition' to 'reduction to something more fundamental'. Perhaps this is too quick. Why shouldn't a concept resist the latter and yet allow for the former?[31] Johann Heinrich Lambert (much admired by Kant) was perhaps the first German philosopher who declared truth to be a simple concept. (We will soon see that he wasn't the last.) But he conceded that a concept may defy reduction or dismantling analysis without resisting explanation:

[*Wahrheit*] *ist ein einfacher Begriff, welcher sich folglich, da er nicht mehrere innere Merkmale hat, höchstens nur durch Verhältnisse zu andern Begriffen definieren oder kenntlich machen läßt.* [Truth is a simple concept which, as it does not have several internal marks, can at best be defined or elucidated only through its relations to other concepts.] (*Anlage zur Architectonic*, vol. I, §305)

In the course of this book I shall confront sentential primitivism only indirectly, by arguing (a) that propositions are the primary truth-value bearers, and (b) that the notion of truth can be adequately explained.[32]

---

[31] Cf. Strawson, *Analysis and Metaphysics*, chs. 1 and 2, on the difference between 'reductive (dismantling) analysis' and 'connecting analysis (elucidation)'.

[32] For (a), see Ch. 5.1; for (b), see Ch. 6.2.

Alfred Tarski's elaboration of the so-called semantic conception of truth has often been read as if it were an attempt to answer the philosophical question 'What is truth?', an attempt which should be entered under the right branch of QUESTION 10. Whether this is a correct reading is a matter of controversy, and we will have to enter this debate, which has been raging now for six decades. What can hardly be doubted is that Tarski provides us with a recipe for systematically specifying the truth-conditions of sentences in languages which have a certain tightly circumscribed structure. If L is such a language, then the complete specification of the truth-conditions of all sentences in L is what Tarski calls a definition of a truth-predicate for L. Without much deference to Tarski's own words, various claims and counter-claims have been made, sometimes by one and the same philosopher, on behalf of such truth-definitions, and only very few of his critics and admirers (outside of Poland) ever take his background in Austro-Polish philosophy into account. Trying to make up for these omissions will turn out to be particularly helpful, or so I would like to think, when it comes to determining the relation between Tarski's conception of truth and correspondence views.

Tarski offered a touchstone for definitions of truth-predicates which has been a source of inspiration for the view registered under the left branch of QUESTION 10. According to Tarski's criterion of material adequacy, a definition of 'true' for a regimented part of English which contains the sentence 'Snow is white' is materially adequate only if it allows for the derivation of the biconditional: *'Snow is white' is true if and only if snow is white.* Here, the sentence quoted on the left-hand side is disquoted[33] (shorn of quotation-marks) on the right-hand side. The biconditional is a substitution-instance of the Disquotation Schema

(Dis)   'p' is true if and only if p,

where both occurrences of the letter 'p' are to be taken as place-holders for occurrences of the same declarative sentence. In other words, we are not to understand the left-hand side of (Dis) as ascribing truth to the sixteenth letter of the Roman alphabet.[34] Starting from the observation that we are generally inclined to accept as a matter of course any instance of (Dis), save for those that engender paradox,[35] champions of disquotationalism go a step further and

---

[33] This term was coined by Quine.

[34] Incidentally, if you have a close look at the German translation of the snowy biconditional, you will realize that not all languages permit the use of a syntactic replica of the quoted sentence on the right-hand side: *'Schnee ist weiß' ist wahr genau dann, wenn Schnee weiß ist.* ('So much the worse for German', you may say. Well, there are a few other languages which suffer from the same disease.)

[35] The cautionary restriction will be explained in Ch. 4.1.2.

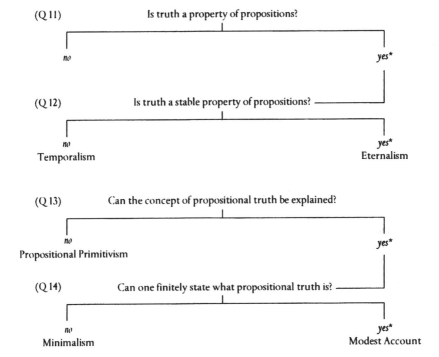

(Q 11)   Is truth a property of propositions?

no   *yes**

(Q 12)   Is truth a stable property of propositions? ————

no   *yes**
Temporalism   Eternalism

(Q 13)   Can the concept of propositional truth be explained?

no   *yes**
Propositional Primitivism

(Q 14)   Can one finitely state what propositional truth is? ————

no   *yes**
Minimalism   Modest Account

Figure 1.3. QUESTIONS 11–14

maintain that what is said remains unaffected whether we append the predicate 'is true' to the quotational designator of a sentence or whether we simply erase the quotation marks. But then, why use such a predicate at all? Because it turns out to be a priceless gift, so the disquotationalists' answer runs, when we want to talk about truth-candidates that we cannot present verbatim. Disquotationalists like Hartry Field claim that in the mouth of a certain speaker of English at a certain time x *is true* abbreviates an infinite disjunction: $(x = `p_1$', and $p_1$), or $(x = `p_2$', and p_2), or $(x = `p_3$', and p_3), or..., where 'p_1', 'p_2', 'p_3', etc. are all the declarative sentences which that speaker at that time understands. I have put this conception of truth under the left-hand branch of QUESTION 10, since it is not only for medical reasons (as Russell might have put it) that this disjunction cannot be written down. I shall devote Chapter 4 ('In and Out of Quotation Marks') to the semantic conception of truth and to disquotationalism. We shall see that, for different reasons, both approaches provide us, not with an explanation of our workaday concept of truth, but rather with a multitude of surrogates.

The penultimate sequence of questions on my flow chart is given in Figure 1.3. Suppose truth is primarily a property (not of sentences but) of what sentences can be used to say, of propositions (QUESTION 11): then my next question is whether truth is a stable property of propositions (QUESTION 12). Is there such a thing as *the* proposition that today is Tuesday, which (if today *is* Tuesday) will become false tomorrow and will regain truth next week? Or is the proposition which is today expressed by 'Today is Tuesday' different from the proposition which will tomorrow be expressed by this sentence? In Chapter 5 ('Propositions, Time, and Eternity') I shall first elucidate the concept of a proposition and argue that truth is primarily a property of the things which fall under that concept. Then I will confront the question whether it is a property that can be lost. I shall mark some divisions within the opposing camps of temporalists and eternalists and plead for a version of eternalism. As is to be expected, indexicality is a topic which will loom large in that chapter.

With respect to sentential truth, there was no counterpart to QUESTION 12 on my flow chart, because if type-sentences can be said to be true at all, then it is a matter of course that some sentences *have* shifting truth-values, and if utterances of type-sentences can be said to be true at all, then they do *not* have shifting truth-values. QUESTION 13, on the other hand, echoes question QUESTION 9. Propositional primitivism is an important ingredient in Frege's reflections on truth, from his early to his late work:

Was wahr sei, halte ich für nicht erklärbar. [What is true, I hold to be not explainable.] ('*Kernsätze zur Logik*' [1880], in *NS* 189 (174))

Wahrheit ist offenbar etwas so Ursprüngliches und Einfaches, dass eine Zurückführung auf noch Einfacheres nicht möglich ist. [Apparently truth is something so primitive and simple that a reduction to anything still simpler is not possible.] ('*Logik*' [1897], in *NS*, 140 (129))

Hiernach ist es wahrscheinlich, daß der Inhalt des Wortes 'wahr' ganz einzigartig und undefinierbar ist. [Hence the content of the word 'true' is probably quite unique and indefinable.] ('*Der Gedanke*' [1918], 60)

As can be seen from the beginning of the last statement, Frege thinks he has a good argument for his primitivism. (It is actually a very puzzling argument which is not above the suspicion of sophistry.[36]) Looking back at our discussion of the Identity Theory above, the three extracts from Frege put it beyond any doubt that, by assenting to (*Idem*), Frege did not mean to explain the concept of truth. Rather, he took (*Idem*) to explain the notion of a fact.

Note that Frege moves from 'explanation' to 'reduction to something still simpler'. The similarity to Davidson's move is striking, and once again the question arises why a concept couldn't defy the latter while permitting the former.

---

[36] I shall comment on it in Ch. 3.3.2.

Moore and Russell, too, were adherents of propositional primitivism—as long as they identified truths with facts. As in the case of Frege, this throws some light on the status of the Identity Theory in their thinking. They did not take it to be an explanation of the meaning of 'true',[37] but, rather, as a metaphysical claim. Reality, Moore and Russell then thought, is the totality of all true propositions; it consists of true propositions and their components. Here is Moore's own characterization of the theory that he once pleaded for:

[The] theory which I myself formerly held . . . adopts the supposition that in the case of every belief, true or false, there is a proposition which is what is believed. . . . But the difference between a true and a false belief, it says, consists simply in this, that where the belief is true the proposition believed . . . has a . . . simple unanalysable property which is possessed by some propositions and not by others. The propositions which don't possess it, and which therefore we call false . . . just have not got this . . . property of being *true*. (*SMPP* 261)

Certainly, the young Moore would have been ready to say of truth what he actually did say of goodness and yellowness:

'[G]ood' is a simple notion, just as 'yellow' is a simple notion. . . . Definitions . . . which describe the real nature of the . . . notion denoted by a word . . . are only possible when the . . . notion in question is something complex. . . . But yellow and good, we say, are not complex: they are notions of that simple kind, out of which definitions are composed and with which the power of further defining ceases. (*Principia Ethica*, 6–8)

Here again, primitivism with respect to a concept does not exclude that a lot of what we know a priori involves that concept essentially. Thus we know a priori that no surface that is yellow all over is black all over, that personal affection is intrinsically good, and that whatever follows from what is true is itself true. The colour example makes it plain that the following comment on the early Moore's conception of truth is misguided: propositional primitivism, we are told, 'gives a sense of impenetrable mysteriousness to the notion of truth'.[38] Does Moore give a sense of impenetrable mysteriousness to the notion of *yellowness* by declaring it to be indefinable? As Davidson's example shows, one can be a primitivist with respect to truth and yet contend that 'truth is as clear a concept as we have'. The entailment example ('Whatever follows from what is true is itself true') helps us to see why Frege's primitivism does not prevent him from maintaining, a few lines before making his indefinability claim that 'it is the task

---

[37] Nor does Hornsby (and presumably the same applies to McDowell): see her 'Truth: The Identity Theory', n. 5.

[38] Horwich, *Truth* (references always to the revised second edition unless otherwise stated), 10.

of logic to discover the laws of truth.... In the laws of truth the meaning of the word "true" is spelled out.'[39] Of course, talk of spelling out is very misleading here, since it almost inevitably suggests the idea of dismantling analysis. The point must be rather that of uncovering a system of principles concerning truth, such as 'Every logical consequence of a truth is itself a truth', 'The conjunction of a truth with its own negation is a falsehood', or 'The negation of a truth is a falsehood.' In this book I shall confront propositional primitivism only indirectly.[40] It is a conception of truth which should only be resorted to, I think, when one has made sure that 'the decent alternatives have been exhausted',[41] and I will try to show that there is a decent alternative, a non-reductive explanation.

In Chapter 6 ('Two Pleas for Modesty') I shall confront QUESTION 14. At the centre of Paul Horwich's highly influential reflections on truth[42] stands a schema which I propose to call the Denominalization Schema

(Den)   It is true that p, if and only if p,

since the sentence nominalized in the left branch of the biconditional is denominalized in the right branch.[43] Most authors call this schema either 'T-schema' or, following Dummett, 'Equivalence Schema'. The obvious drawback of both titles is that they suit the Disquotation Schema equally well. Note that the crucial feature of the biconditionals covered by (Den) and by its translations into other languages is that the sentence-nominalization on the left-hand side is cancelled on the right-hand side. Not all languages are so obliging that the nominalization of a sentence literally contains an occurrence of that very sentence. Thus, in the Latin translation of 'It is true that snow is white, iff snow is white', the nominalization of '*nix est alba*' needed in the left-hand branch is an accusative-cum-infinitive construction: '*nivem albam esse* verum est'. This difference notwithstanding, '*verum est*' shares with 'it is true' the feature that is captured by (Den) and enshrined in my title for this schema.

---

[39] '*Der Logik kommt es zu, die Gesetze des Wahrseins zu erkennen.... In den Gesetzen des Wahrseins wird die Bedeutung des Wortes "wahr" entwickelt*' (Frege, '*Der Gedanke*', 58–9). This contention, too, is already to be found in much earlier writings: NS [between 1879 and 1891], 3 (3); *Grundgesetze* [1893], xvi. Cf. also NS [1897], 139 (128).

[40] The only latter-day advocate of propositional primitivism I have come across (and on whose presentation I have drawn) is Ernest Sosa: see 'Epistemology, Realism, and Truth', 10–15 (= 'Epistemology and Primitive Truth', 653–9, 661 n. 8).   [41] As Horwich puts it in *Truth*, 10.

[42] The first edition of his book *Truth* was published in 1990, the revised second edition in 1998.

[43] I will treat 'it is true that p' and 'that p is true' as synonymous, and 'the proposition that p is true' as a pleonastic variant. Justification of this treatment will have to wait until Chs. 5.1.1 and 6.2.3. Incidentally, the comma in (Den), though usually omitted, serves to distinguish (Den) from 'It is true that (p iff p)' which, though praiseworthy in itself, is irrelevant here.

Horwich's 'minimal theory' of truth contains all and (almost) only those propositions which are expressed by (non-pathological) instances of (Den).[44] According to Horwich's 'minimalist conception' of truth, the content of the concept of truth is completely captured by the minimal theory. Since one cannot write down the minimal theory, I have put this view in the left-hand branch under QUESTION 14. Finally, I shall explain the contrasting conception of truth that I favour: the Modest Account. 'A new theory of truth?'—Heaven forbid. I shall unearth the roots of this account in earlier works; but I will introduce, motivate, and develop it in my own way, and I will be at pains to defend it against various objections.

Let me insert here a remark on terminological policy. I shall steadfastly refrain from using the term 'deflationism', which has been applied to various entries on my flow chart (in particular to nihilism, disquotationalism, and minimalism). What deflationism comes to varies with the target that is alleged to be inflated. So we find a confusing multiplicity of uses in the literature.[45] According to Field, ' "Deflationism" is the view that truth is at bottom disquotational.'[46] This implies that deflationists must take truth to be a property of something that can be put between quotation marks. But then Horwich's minimalism cannot be called deflationist, since he takes truth to be a property of *propositions*. Yet he is very keen to promote his conception of truth under the label 'deflationism'. Nihilists, too, would lose the right to call themselves deflationists,[47] since they deny that truth is a property *at all*. Marian David links deflationism with a metaphysical distaste for non-physical entities.[48] Again, minimalism is out, and so is every conception according to which truth is a property of type-sentences. According to Paul Boghossian, Crispin Wright, and William Alston, deflationism is the view that 'it is a mistake to suppose that there is a *property* of truth (falsity) that one attributes to propositions, statements, beliefs, and/or sentences'.[49] Once

---

[44] The cautionary restrictions in parenthesis will be explained in Chs. 4.1.2 and 6.1.1.

[45] Isaiah Berlin's paper 'Logical Translation' (1950) contains what is perhaps the earliest philosophical use of this pair of terms. Berlin used them ('for want of a better label') to characterize opposite vices in metaphysics, ontological stinginess (of the logical positivist type), and ontological prodigality (of the Meinongian type): 'deflationists' condemn much that is significant as nonsensical because their ontology admits *too few* entities; 'inflationists', on the other hand, accept as significant much that is nonsensical because their ontology admits *too many* entities. When Cartwright borrowed Berlin's terms a decade later in his 'Negative Existentials', he also used them for labelling two ontological positions which he deemed to be equally unacceptable. Cf. also his 'Propositions of Pure Logic', 225–6.

[46] See, 'Disquotational Truth and Factually Defective Discourse' (henceforth 'Disquotational'), 405.

[47] Claimed by Grover in Ch. 9 of her collection *A Prosentential Theory of Truth* (henceforth *PrTh*).

[48] David, *Correspondence and Disquotation* (henceforth *C&D*), 53–60.

[49] See Boghossian, 'The Status of Content', 161; C. Wright, *Truth and Objectivity* (henceforth *T&O*), 16. A few pages later Wright acknowledges that at least one 'deflationist' *does* take truth to be a property (*T&O*, 21 n. 15). The quotation is from Alston, *A Realist Conception of Truth* (henceforth *RCT*), 41; cf. p. 2. In Kirkham, *ThT*, 307 ff., 'the Deflationary Thesis' is explained along the same lines.

again, minimalism turns out to be inflationist, and so does disquotationalism, because they take truth to be a *property* of propositions or of certain linguistic objects. A few pages later Wright tells us that it is deflationism's 'most basic and distinctive contention that "true" is merely a device for endorsing assertions'.[50] But this characterization only fits the position that Strawson took in 1949. Horwich himself seems to mean by 'deflationism' the denial of the claim that 'the property of truth has some sort of underlying nature,'[51] but why not call the minimalist account an attempt at disclosing the nature of truth? In view of this terminological chaos, I propose to put the term 'deflationism' on what Otto Neurath once called, tongue in cheek, the *Index Verborum Prohibitorum*.

The last two questions to be considered in this book are given in Figure 1.4. The term 'alethic realism' (which I have borrowed from Alston[52]) is not only a very ugly Greco-Latin concoction. It also tends to be mispronounced or mis-printed as 'athletic realism', which is very unfortunate because the doctrine for which I use this title is not a very muscular affair. Its one and only contention is this: *some true propositions which human beings are able to comprehend can never be contents of any justified human beliefs.* Truth, alethic realists contend, outruns rational acceptability; it is not epistemically constrained.[53] (Notice that in my mouth these slogans are intended to abbreviate the italicized statement.) Alethic realism, thus understood, calls attention to a kind of *inevitable ignorance* on our part, but it is not committed to allowing the possibility of *undetectable error*: it does not imply that even a 'theory that is "ideal" from the point of view of operational utility, inner beauty and elegance, "plausibility", "simplicity", "conservatism", etc. might be false.'[54] (Since it lacks this implication, alethic realism differs vastly from the doctrine Putnam calls 'metaphysical realism'.) Furthermore, alethic realism is *not* wedded to the princi-ple of bivalence, according to which every truth-candidate is either true or false.

According to alethic *anti*-realism, on the other hand, every truth that is com-prehensible to human beings can become the content of a justified human

---

[50] C. Wright, *T&O*, 33; cf. p. 21. Somewhat ironically, Wright's justified complaint that 'deflationism is actually something of a potpourri' (30) is confirmed by the use of this term in *T&O*.

[51] Horwich, *Truth*, 120.

[52] Alston, *RCT*. As to the doctrine associated with this term, the definition in *RCT*, 1, 6, and 231 dif-fers widely from my own explanation in the text above.

[53] I have adopted the second term from C. Wright, 'Can a Davidsonian Meaning-Theory be Construed in Terms of Assertibility?' (henceforth 'Assertibility'), 426. In *T&O* Wright uses 'not evidence-transcendent' with the same intent, but the latter phrase is less felicitous: most justified beliefs 'go beyond' the evidence because they are not strictly entailed by the evidence.

[54] Putnam, *Meaning and the Moral Sciences*, 125; cf. *Realism and Reason*, 13. The kind of realism that Davidson rejects is also characterized by the admission of undetectable error: see his 'A Coherence Theory of Truth and Knowledge', 140, 'Epistemology and Truth', 188–9; and 'The Structure and Content of Truth' (henceforth 'Structure'), 298, 308.

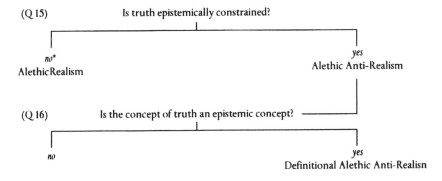

Figure 1.4. QUESTIONS 15–16

belief. (The term 'anti-realism' is Dummett's coinage. Its paleness is intended: 'idealism' carries too many connotations which are irrelevant to the point at issue.) Truth, alethic anti-realists claim, does *not* outrun rational acceptability, it *is* epistemically constrained: whatever is true *could be* rationally accepted.

Taking the variables in the following universally quantified biconditionals to run over acts or states or propositions (as the case may be) which human beings can perform or be in or comprehend, we can say that alethic anti-realism is correct if (the left-to-right half of) any of these biconditionals expresses a truth about truth.

Brentano	∀x (x is true ↔ x is, or has the same content as, an evident judgement)
Bradley	∀x (x is true ↔ x belongs to a maximally coherent set of beliefs)
Peirce	∀x (x is true ↔ x is a belief that all investigators would finally share if investigation were pursued long enough)
James	∀x (x is true ↔ ∃t (x is a belief acquired at time t & x meets all experiences at t and after t satisfactorily))
Goodman	∀x (x is true ↔ ∃t (x is credible at time t & x remains credible at all times after t))
Putnam	∀x (x is true ↔ it would be rational to accept x if epistemic conditions were good enough))
Dummett	∀x (x is true ↔ x can in principle become a content of knowledge)
(*Wright*)	∀x (x is true ↔ ∃y (y is an actually accessible state of information & x is warrantedly assertible in y & x remains warrantedly assertible no matter how y is enlarged upon or improved)).

I've put the last name in brackets, because Wright offers this biconditional in an exploratory spirit. In Chapter 7 ('Truth and Justifiability'), the final chapter of this book, I shall explain, and brood on, the above anti-realist biconditionals.[55]

I have spelt out the anti-realist slogan, 'Truth does not outrun rational acceptability', in such a way that 'it is rationally acceptable that p' abbreviates 'it is in principle possible that some *human being* or other is justified in believing that p'. Let me now motivate this anthropocentrism by considering certain features of traditional theism and of Dummett's portrayal of the realist. The God of the Philosophers cognitively surpasses us to such an extent that He literally knows *everything*. Which impact would this doctrine, if it were true, have on the alethic realism/anti-realism issue? Bolzano marks one respect in which it would have no impact:

Aus der Allwissenheit Gottes folgt zwar, daß eine jede Wahrheit, sollte sie auch von keinem anderen Wesen gekannt, ja nur gedacht werden, doch ihm, dem Allwissenden, bekannt sey . . . Daher gibt es eigentlich nicht eine einzige, durchaus von Niemand erkannte Wahrheit. Dieß hindert uns aber doch nicht, von Wahrheiten an sich als solchen zu reden, in deren Begriffe noch gar nicht vorausgesetzt wird, daß sie von irgend Jemand gedacht werden müßten. Denn wenn dieß Gedachtwerden auch nicht in dem Begriffe solcher Wahrheiten liegt: so kann es gleichwohl aus einem anderen Umstande (nämlich aus Gottes Allwissenheit) folgen, daß sie, wenn sonst von Niemand, wenigstens von Gott selbst erkannt werden müssen. [It follows indeed from God's omniscience that each truth is known to him, even if it is not recognized nor even thought by any other being. . . . Consequently, there actually is no truth that is recognized by nobody at all. This, however, should not keep us from speaking of truths in themselves, since their concept does not presuppose that they must be thought by someone. It is not contained in the concept of such truths that they are thought, but it can nevertheless follow from some other circumstance (in this case the omniscience of God) that they must be recognized by God himself, if by no one else.] (*Wissenschaftslehre*, I, 113[56])

As we shall soon see, only *definitional* anti-realists take the concept of 'recognizability' to be 'contained in the concept of truth'. But in any case one does not forsake alethic realism by conceding that an omniscient deity would not miss any truth. If it were the case that a deity who is essentially omniscient exists necessarily, it would be *impossible* for there to be any truth beyond rational acceptability, but even that would not settle the issue of alethic realism,[57] for the constraint that realists deem to be misplaced is characterized in terms of 'recognizability by cognitively *finite* beings'.

---

[55] I did not enter in the above catalogue of anti-realist pronouncements Rorty's off-hand remark that true is whatever is accepted by our cultural peers, for I cannot help thinking that this is just an attempt at being provocative (at playing Nietzsche?). In any case, Putnam has said all that needs to be said about it (see his *Renewing Philosophy*, 68–9), and Rorty himself has come to regret it.

[56] References to Bolzano's *WL* (as I shall hereinafter abbreviate the title of his *magnum opus*) are always to the original pagination, which is reproduced in all later editions as well as in the (abridged) English translations.   [57] *Pace* Alvin Plantinga, 'How to Be an Anti-Realist'.

Now even cognitively finite beings might be much superior to *us* (and other beings with our modes of sensory awareness and our conceptual resources), and this possibility is relevant for the way Dummett conceives of alethic realism. According to the Dummettian anti-realist biconditional, it is true that p, iff it is in principle possible to *know* that p. But the difference between knowability and, say, rational acceptability is not important for the point that is now at issue. There is another worry that can be safely put aside here. The modal expression '*can*' in the Dummettian biconditional is to be understood in such a way that the following holds: if it is not true that p, then it cannot be known that p. Under the standard reading of 'possible' in alethic modal logic, the right-to-left half of that biconditional would be clearly incorrect: some contingent falsehoods *are* possible contents of knowledge, since a proposition that p which is false in the actual world but true in other possible worlds may be such that in some of those possible worlds somebody knows that p.[58] So Dummett needs a reading of 'knowable' in which the possibility of knowledge implies truth. (Thus understood, the right-to-left half of his biconditional is a matter of course. Contrast, for example, Putnam's equivalence, read in the same direction: 'If under epistemically optimal conditions it would be rational to believe that p, then it is true that p' is a substantial claim, as can be seen from the fact that it has been seriously debated.[59]) But what we are interested in here is the left-to-right half of Dummett's biconditional.

Somewhat surprisingly, Dummett maintains that even a *realist* has to concede that the concept of truth is governed by the principle of knowability: 'If a statement is true, it must be in principle possible to know that it is true.'[60] A realist is bound to reject this principle, of course, if 'in principle possible' is supposed to mean: in principle possible for beings with our modes of sensory awareness and our conceptual resources. But his attitude towards the principle of knowability will change, Dummett contends, as soon as it is taken also to cover hypothetical beings endowed with super-human (yet sub-divine) perceptual and conceptual abilities. Why is the realist's attitude towards the principle of knowability supposed to change if it is given this reading? Dummett challenges him to explain how we can understand answers to questions that we do not know how

---

[58] This warning is due to Georg Henrik von Wright: see his *Logical Studies*, 183–4. Cf. also Richard Routley, 'Necessary Limits to Knowledge', 96–7, 105, 112 n. 27. (Could one avoid this trouble by prefixing the indexical modal operator 'actually' to 'p', i.e. by formulating the principle of knowability thus: 'It is true that actually p iff it is possible to know that actually p'? There are grave problems with making real sense of such a formula; that was the upshot of the discussion of a paper by Dorothy Edgington, referred to below on p. 443 n. 206.)   [59] Cf., for example, J. J. C. Smart, 'Realism vs Idealism'.
[60] Dummett, 'What is a Theory of Meaning? II' (henceforth 'Meaning'), 61; cf. 'Truth', 23–4; *FPL*, 465; *The Logical Basis of Metaphysics* (henceforth *LBM*), 345.

to decide, and the hypothesis of a super-human (yet finite) verifier seems to enable the realist to give such an explanation:

The realist holds that we give sense to those sentences of our language which are not effectively decidable[61] by appealing tacitly to means of determining their truth-values which we do not ourselves possess, but which we can conceive of by analogy with those which we do. ('Truth', 24)

[The realist] concedes the absurdity of supposing that a statement could be true if it was in principle impossible to know that it was true. The anti-realist's mistake, he thinks, is to apply this proposition in such a way that 'impossible' is taken to mean 'impossible *for us*'. Our... observational and intellectual faculties are, contingently, limited, so that there is no reason to suppose that any true statement will be able to be known to be true by us. All that is necessary is that there could be a subject capable of knowing it, if only with greater perceptual or cognitive powers than ours. (*LBM* 345)

In the case of questions we do not know how to decide, the realist is supposed to think of a super-human, but not omniscient, verifier, of a being with cognitive abilities which transcend our own, but which we can conceive of by analogy with those we do possess. This being, just to mention a few of its most remarkable achievements, is *per hypothesin* able to inspect not only each cup in his or her cupboard individually but also all elements of an infinite totality, and it can 'directly see' into the remote past and future as well as into your soul. Dummett then goes on to reject this appeal to a hypothetical super-human cognitive subject as an *obscurum per obscurius*. After all, what is dubious is whether the realist correctly ascribes to *us* an ability to understand answers to questions we do not know how to decide. How could this ascription be legitimized by appealing to the idea of an ability which we—undoubtedly—do not possess?[62] Realists will be well advised to lock out this Trojan Horse before Dummett can jump out with the sword of his criticism. But then they must find a more plausible way of answering Dummett's hermeneutical challenge: how can we understand sentences that allegedly express truths beyond justifiability?

---

[61] Statements of a certain class are 'effectively decidable' iff there is a standard procedure which can be applied in any given case and which is guaranteed to lead to a correct verdict as to the statement's truth-value. A statement may lack this property, although under certain circumstances we may be able to tell whether the condition for its truth is fulfilled or not. Take Goldbach's Conjecture that every even number greater than two is the sum of two prime numbers. If it is false, we might one day be confronted with a counter-example and recognize it for what it is; if it is true, we might one day stumble upon a proof of it and recognize this proof for what it is. But there is no standard procedure of bringing about a situation of either kind.

[62] Cf. Dummett, *FPL*, 467–8; 'Meaning', 62; and, especially, *LBM* 346–8. Cf. also McDowell, 'On "The Reality of the Past" ', §5. Gareth Evans cautioned against 'ideal verificationism' in *The Varieties of Reference*, 94–100.

Alethic anti-realists never present empirical evidence for their biconditionals, and they never restrict the alleged co-extensiveness of truth and a certain epistemic property to the actual world. So we may assume that they take their biconditionals to express *conceptual* (necessary and a priori knowable) truths about truth. They do not thereby incur an obligation to identify the sense of 'true' with that of any epistemic predicate. But some of them make such an identification and thus answer QUESTION 16 affirmatively. Charles Sanders Peirce, for example, seems to do so when he says:

If your terms 'truth' and 'falsity' are taken in such senses as to be definable in terms of doubt and belief and the course of experience . . . well and good. ('What Pragmatism Is' (1905))[63]

The distinction registered under QUESTION 16 and the implications of calling a claim 'conceptual' are of great importance for the enquiry to be undertaken in this book. So let me pause to elaborate. The demands on 'is F' in tenets of the form 'for all x, x is true iff x is F' can be of various strengths, ranging from absolutely minimal to absolutely maximal. This predicate may be required to express

(I)   a concept that is *co-extensive* with the truth concept;
(II)   a concept that is *necessarily co-extensive* with it;
(III) a concept that *can be known a priori to be co-extensive* with it;
(IV)   a concept that is *self-evidently co-extensive* with it;
(V)   *the same concept* as is expressed by 'true'.

If a predicate expresses a concept C, fully understanding that predicate suffices for possessing C. Satisfaction of condition *n* is a necessary but not sufficient condition for satisfying condition *n* + *1*. Here are some philosophically neutral examples of predicate pairs, arranged in the same order, in which the second predicate meets the pertinent requirement with respect to the concept expressed by the first. (These examples will serve us at various points in the course of our reflections on truth.[64]) For all x,

(1)   (a)   x is a vertebrate with a heart iff x is a vertebrate with a liver
      (b)   x was written by the author of *Middlemarch* iff x was written by the author of *Silas Marner*

---

[63] In *CP* 5.416. (Peirce pleads here for a definition of truth in terms of what he calls an *inquiry*: we embark on an inquiry whenever we seek to transform a state of doubt by means of a course of experience into a state of belief.) As for the question whether he really is a definitional anti-realist, cf. Peirce. *CP*, 5.407 [1905], cited below on p. 679, as well as my cautionary remark in the accompanying footnote.

[64] As for (1a), I take it on faith that Kirkham knows his biology here: *ThT*, 4–5. As for the modal status of (2), I accept Kripke's and Putnam's view of such statements.

(2) (a) x is a lump of common salt iff x is a lump of sodium chloride

    (b) x was written by George Eliot iff x was written by Mary Ann Evans

(3) (a) x is a triangle iff x is a closed plane rectilinear figure whose internal angles add up to 180°

    (b) x is an equiangular triangle iff x is an equilateral triangle

    (c) x has a hundred inhabitants iff x has $1^3 + 2^3 + 3^3 + 4^3$ inhabitants

(4) (a) x is a closed three-sided plane rectilinear figure iff x is a closed three-angled plane rectilinear figure

    (b) x is a glass which is half-full iff x is a glass which is half-empty

(5) (a) x is a triangle iff x is a plane figure bounded by three straight lines

    (b) x is an equiangular triangle iff x is a triangle with equal angles

    (c) x is a drake iff x is a male duck

    (d) x is a serpent iff x is a snake.

The property of being F is identical with the property of being G only if *necessarily* all and only F's are G.[65] So properties are more finely individuated than extensions. The concept of being F is the same as the concept of being G if and only if 'F' and 'G' are *synonymous*. So concepts, too, are more fine-grained than extensions. If two predicates need not have the same sense in order to signify the same property (as many philosophers plausibly assume[66]), then properties are more coarsely individuated than concepts. The predicates paired in (5b), for example, unlike those in (3b), are synonymous, hence they express the same concept.

No philosopher who tries to define 'true' is aiming to graft a new meaning upon an old word. So the notion of a definition which my rubric 'definitional alethic anti-realism' invokes is not that of a 'constructive definition' or a *stipulation*, which either introduces a new expression for purposes of abbreviation (such as 'pi-meson' in physics) or forces an old expression into a new, tightly circumscribed service (e.g., 'model' in mathematical logic), but rather that of an *'analytic* definition' which purports to capture, by means of a compound expression, the sense of an atomic expression already in use.[67] The predicate on

---

[65] If this condition is also sufficient, there can be neither two or more necessarily co-exemplified properties nor two or more necessarily unexemplified properties.

[66] e.g. Putnam, 'On Properties'; Armstrong, *A Theory of Universals*; Peacocke, *A Study of Concepts*. Carnap used 'concept' to cover properties and relations, and he took F-ness to be the same property as G-ness iff 'F' and 'G' are logically equivalent (*Meaning and Necessity*, §4). This is to individuate concepts too coarsely, I think. Nowadays Horwich regards F-ness and G-ness as identical iff 'F' and 'G' have the same meaning, so it is not surprising that he sees 'no good reason not to identify properties with concepts' (*Meaning*, 21). In *Abstrakte Gegenstände*, 245–8, I took the same view. I now think that this is to individuate properties too finely.

[67] The terminology in quotation marks is Frege's: see *NS*, 224–9 (207–11) on definitions that are *aufbauend* (lit., 'building up') and those which are *zerlegend* (lit., 'dissecting').

the right-hand side of (5c), for example, could serve as definiens in an analytic definition of the predicate on the left-hand side. As can be seen from (5d), a non-analytic definition need not be a stipulation.

Tenets of strengths (III), (IV), and (V), if correct, articulate *conceptual* truths about truth. Acquiring the knowledge that is described in (III) may be a strenuous undertaking (as your school-day memories concerning the examples under (3) may confirm). By contrast, the knowledge alluded to in (IV) is just a matter of lexical competence: two predicates express self-evidently co-extensive concepts if and only if nobody who fully understands both predicates (knows their conventional linguistic meanings) can believe that one of them applies to a certain entity x (doesn't apply to x) without believing that the other one applies to x as well (doesn't apply to x either). Meeting this requirement is also a necessary condition for two predicates' expressing the same concept. It isn't a sufficient condition, though, for otherwise we would have to declare the predicates paired in (4), or the predicates 'is true' and 'is true and either denied by someone or not denied by anyone' to express the same concept.

Let us now consider, in the light of these distinctions, two attempts at refuting all epistemic conceptions of truth. They both brandish the Denominalization Schema

(Den)   It is true that p, iff p

as an allegedly lethal weapon. It is commonly thought that advocates of very different views about truth—including alethic anti-realists—can, with the greatest equanimity, accept as conceptually true all propositions expressed by (non-pathological) instances of this schema. But Alston and Lewis disagree with the common lore. Let us start with Alston's argument. How does he reach the heterodox conclusion that 'epistemic accounts of the concept of truth...are incompatible with an acceptance of the T-schema [i.e. (Den)]'?[68] The core of his argument is this:

[T]he fact that sugar is sweet is both necessary and sufficient for its being true that sugar is sweet. It is true that p if and only if p.... Any such biconditional is necessarily, conceptually true.... Since the fact that p is (necessarily) both necessary and sufficient for its being true that p, that leaves no room for an epistemic necessary or sufficient condition for truth. Nothing more is required for its being true that p than just the fact that p; and nothing less will suffice. How then can some epistemic status of the proposition...that p be necessary and sufficient for the truth of [the proposition that] p? It seems clear that the imposition of an epistemic necessary and sufficient condition for truth runs into conflict with the T-schema. (*RCT*, 209)

---

[68] Alston, *RCT*, 217; cf. 3, 209.

Since there is no reference to facts in the schema, I assume that Alston's talk of facts here is just a manner of speaking: as soon as one replaces the binary connective 'if and only if' by the dyadic predicate 'is necessary and sufficient for', one has to grope for' noun phrases. (Actually, it isn't a very felicitous way of speaking, for if it is *not true* that p, talk of 'the fact that p' is inappropriate.)

As Alston recognizes, the argument will not yet do by itself.[69] Why shouldn't *two* non-synonymous sentences equally succeed in specifying a (necessarily) necessary-and-sufficient condition for a certain proposition's being true? Substitution-instances of our examples (3a) and (5a) contain on their right-hand sides two non-synonymous sentences which equally succeed in specifying such a condition for a certain figure's being a triangle.

Before we turn to Alston's reaction to this reply, let us look at Lewis's (more recent and apparently independent) attempt to show how acceptance of instances of (Den), which he somewhat misleadingly calls 'redundancy biconditionals', conflicts with any 'epistemic theory of truth'.[70] Consider the following derivation. Its first premiss is a substitution-instance of (Den), its second premiss results from applying an anti-realist ('epistemic') conception of truth to a particular truth-candidate, and the conclusion is obtained via transitivity of 'iff':

(P1)   it is true that cats purr, iff cats purr;
(P2)   it is true that cats purr, iff it is (knowable) that cats purr;
(C)   therefore, cats purr iff it is (knowable) that cats purr.

I have kept Lewis's feline example, but I have replaced his 'it is useful to believe' with 'it is (knowable)'. This is legitimate because Lewis explicitly claims that his reflections on what he calls the 'pragmatic theory' of truth apply with equal force to 'epistemic theories'. The locution 'is (knowable)' is just a place-holder for a predicate that is alleged to signify an epistemic necessary-and-sufficient condition for truth. (You find serious candidates in my list of anti-realist biconditionals.) Now Lewis rightly says about the premisses of the derivation that 'these two biconditional are meant to be a priori', he declares the conclusion to be 'manifestly not a priori', and he concludes that a conception of truth which embraces (P1) is incompatible with an account which endorses something like (P2). How is this supposed to follow? A logically valid derivation, the premisses of which are all a priori, cannot have a conclusion that is not a priori. The above derivation is logically valid. So if (C) is not a priori, then (P1) and (P2) cannot both be a priori, and, consequently, the two theories which assign apriority to the premisses cannot both be true. This is incontestable. Unfortunately, Lewis does not

[69] *RCT*, 211.   [70] Lewis, 'Correspondence', 275. Cf. Colin McGinn, *Logical Properties*, 88–90.

say *why* he takes (C) to be manifestly not a priori. An alethic anti-realist who thinks otherwise is not refuted by being told that he is obviously wrong.

Alston substantially agrees with Lewis. He explicitly says that all (non-pathological) instances of (Den) express 'necessary, conceptual, analytic' truths,[71] so by his lights, too, it is a priori knowable that P1. His argument from (Den) is directed against definitional alethic anti-realists who 'identify the concept of truth with the concept of a positive epistemic status'[72] and who are thereby committed to maintain that it is a priori knowable that P2. When confronting the anti-realist reply to his core argument cited above, Alston argues that the biconditional connecting the two allegedly necessary-and-sufficient conditions for the truth of a given proposition must itself also be taken to express a conceptual truth.[73] Thus

(C*)   sugar is sweet iff it is (knowable) that sugar is sweet

would have to formulate a conceptual truth. And at this point Alston believes himself to have shown what he had set out to show, for 'what should we say about that [i.e. about the assumption that it is conceptually true that C*]? So far as I can see, it is totally lacking in plausibility.'[74] So he concurs with Lewis's comment on (C).

Alston does tell us why he finds this assumption about the status of (C*) totally implausible. The proposition expressed on the left-hand side of (C*), he says, 'attributes sweetness to sugar. It says nothing whatever about [any epistemic condition]. It asserts a fact about a substance, a foodstuff.'[75] This reasoning presupposes that a biconditional cannot express a conceptual truth if one side of it 'says something about' something about which the other side is silent. Is this presupposition plausible? A truth (about truth, or whatever) is either conceptual or non-conceptual, and if it is non-conceptual then it is either contingent or necessary. Alston duly registers these distinctions, but he neglects the differences, within the field of conceptual truths, between (III), (IV), and (V). He takes it for granted that an anti-realist biconditional can only express a conceptual truth about truth if an epistemic condition is, as it were, *written into* the concept of truth; in other words, if the epistemic predicate in its right branch spells out the sense of the truth-predicate.[76] This explains why Alston takes it to be an objection against anti-realist biconditionals that we are not 'saying anything about [any epistemic condition] when we say that a proposition is true' (unless, of course, that proposition itself happens to be about an epistemic condition).[77]

---

[71] *RCT*, 1.   [72] Ibid., 219. We will soon see that this seriously restricts the scope of his argument.
[73] His argument for this contention is less perspicuous than that of Lewis: see ibid., 211–14.
[74] Ibid., 214.   [75] Ibid., 218.   [76] Ibid., 219.   [77] Ibid., 214.

Alston is keenly aware that advocates of an epistemic conception of truth are not obliged to identify the concept of truth with any epistemic concept. In any case, one may wonder whether any appeal to (Den) is needed to refute the conceptual identity claim: as the ongoing philosophical debate amply illustrates, the concept of truth is not self-evidently co-extensive with any of the concepts expressed in the anti-realist biconditionals, hence it is a fortiori not identical with any of them. When Alston characterizes the alternative option (which he then goes on to reject as well) he uses biconditional (2a) as a model:

There may be necessary and sufficient conditions for [a proposition's being true] that are not embodied in the concept [of truth]. Having a chemical composition of sodium chloride is necessary and sufficient for a substance's being salt, even though that is different from the conditions embedded in our (ordinary) concept of salt (looking and tasting a certain way). (*RCT*, 229–30)[78]

If alethic anti-realists really had to rely on the model of equivalences like (2a), then one should scold them as follows: 'A necessary but non-conceptual truth can only be discovered a posteriori. But you never offer empirical evidence for your claim about truth. Hence your contention is just a wild speculation.' But does alethic anti-realism depend on that model? A biconditional may very well express a conceptual truth even though on its right-hand side something is said about something, about which nothing is said on the left-hand side. Recall our examples for pairs of concepts that can be known a priori to be co-extensive: (3a) something is a triangle iff it is a closed plane rectilinear figure whose internal angles add up to 180°; (3b) something is an equiangular triangle iff it is an equilateral triangle; (3c) something has a hundred inhabitants iff it has $1^3 + 2^3 + 3^3 + 4^3$ inhabitants. Nothing is 'said about' a sum of angles on the left-hand-side of (3a), or about sides of equal length on the left of (3b), or about a sum of numbers on the left of (3c). Nevertheless, all three biconditionals formulate conceptual truths. So an alethic anti-realist can consistently claim to teach us a conceptual truth about truth and deny that 'true' has the same sense as any epistemic predicate.

For all that, I confess to finding the assumption that (C) and (C*) express conceptual truths as implausible as Alston and Lewis do. But Lewis does not pause to argue for this verdict, and I have tried to show that Alston's argument from 'aboutness' does not succeed. Suppose a version of alethic anti-realism implies that (even if there is no omniscient being) it can never be true that things are thus-and-so unless there (actually) is at least one thinking being. Advocates of this view who also subscribe to (Den) are committed to a kind of idealism

---

[78] His argument for this contention is less perspicuous than that of Lewis: see *RCT*, 37–8.

according to which things can never be thus-and-so if no thinker exists. So if you believe that the moon would be round even if there were no thinkers around, you would be well advised not to embrace such a variety of alethic anti-realism. Still, acceptance of (Den) can consistently be combined even with this view of truth, provided the latter is in itself consistent.

So it seems that the common lore got it right: the Denominalization Schema is not a lethal weapon against every conception of truth which takes truth to be epistemically constrained. It may, however, provide ammunition against some such accounts. Thus, Spinoza, who seems to favour a coherentist conception of truth,[79] comes dangerously close to denying the right-to-left half of a (non-pathological) instance of (Den) when he writes in his *Treatise on the Emendation of Human Understanding*:

Si aliquis dicit, Petrum ex. gr. existere, nec tamen scit, Petrum existere, illa cogitatio respectu illius falsa est, vel, si mavis, non est vera, quamvis Petrus re vera existat. Nec haec enunciatio, Petrus existit, vera est, nisi respectu illius, qui certo scit, Petrum existere. [If somebody says, for instance, that Peter exists, although he does not know that Peter exists, then his thought, with regard to him, is false, or, if you prefer, not true, even though Peter really does exist. Nor is this statement, 'Peter exists,' true except with regard to somebody who knows for certain that Peter exists.] (*Tractatus de intellectus emendatione*, 26 (trans. 31))

These reflections, I daresay, scarcely contribute to the emendation of our understanding of *truth*.

Russell attributes to William James the tenet that, for all p, it is true that p, iff it makes for happiness to believe that p. His critique of this contention relies on (Den):

Take the question whether other people exist. . . . It is plain that it makes for happiness to believe that they exist—for even the greatest misanthropist would not wish to be deprived of the objects of his hate. Hence the belief that other people exist is, pragmatically, a true belief. But if I am troubled by solipsism, the discovery that a belief in the existence of others is 'true' in the pragmatist's sense is not enough to allay my sense of loneliness: the perception that I should profit by rejecting solipsism is not alone sufficient to make me reject it. For what I desire is not that the belief in solipsism should be false in the pragmatic sense, but that other people should in fact exist. And with the pragmatist's meaning of truth, these two do not necessarily go together. The belief in solipsism might be false even if I were the only person . . . in the universe. ('Transatlantic "Truth" ', 122)

The core of Russell's argument (using 'p$_1$' as abbreviation for 'There are other people' and 'p$_2$' for 'I am alone') is this: (A) It may be pragmatically-true that p$_1$, although not-p$_1$, and (B) it may not be pragmatically-true that p$_2$, although p$_2$. Hence 'pragmatically-true' is not equivalent with 'true'. Why does this follow? Well, if we replace 'pragmatically-true' in the first conjunct by 'true', we see that

---

[79] Cf. Ralph Walker, *The Coherence Theory of Truth*, 48–60.

it does not comply with the right-to-left half of (Den), and if we make the same substitution in the second conjunct, we recognize that it offends against the left-to-right half of (Den).[80] (In his reply James hastens to assure his critic that the pragmatist conception of truth, properly understood, does not allow for (A). He forgets to tackle (B).[81])

For more than a decade Hilary Putnam, partially under Dummett's influence, advocated what may very well be the most liberal variety of (non-definitional) alethic anti-realism. At that time he was convinced that

> every truth that human beings can understand is made true by conditions that are, in principle, accessible to some human beings at some time or other, if not necessarily at all times or to all human beings. ('Reply to David Anderson', 364)

By the early 1990s he had given up this position. After rehearsing his reasons, I shall offer an argument from blind spots in the field of justification, which refutes all varieties of anti-realism at one stroke—or so I would like to think. I shall try to show how the alethic realist can cope with Dummett's hermeneutical challenge if this challenge is directed at the starting-point of that argument.

Before embarking on the long exploratory voyage on which I have invited you to join me in this chapter, some of my readers may want to know where they will come across my own (positive) views. So I'd better tell them right now that in

- Chapter 2, sections 1.3–5, 2 (Introduction), and 3,
- Chapter 5, sections 1, 3.3, and 4,
- Chapter 6, section 2, and
- Chapter 7, section 3.

I shall argue for the answers that are 'starred' in the flow charts in Figures 1.1–1.4, and explain the principles and notions that are required for those arguments. I hope this hint will not be misunderstood. I would have written a book that comprises not much more than the sections just mentioned, if I were not thoroughly convinced that much is to be learned from engaging with the opposite answers.

---

[80] Whereas Lewis takes 'It is useful to believe that cats purr, iff cats purr' to be 'manifestly not a priori', Russell declares 'It is useful to believe that there are other people, iff there are other people' to be manifestly false. Lewis's verdict could be correct even if Russell's is not.

[81] James, 'Two English Critics', 148. Putnam is convinced that Russell was unfair to James, but at the end of his paper, 'James's Theory of Truth', it turns out that under his reading, too, the theory is 'disastrous'. Interestingly, his objection is structurally the same as Russell's: James's view, as understood by Putnam, implies that a judgement that p may not be pragmatically-true, although p; so pragmatical 'truth' isn't truth. Putnam's 'p' is a past-tense sentence (which doesn't ring any bells with me): 'Lizzie Borden committed [didn't commit] the famous axe murders.' See Putnam, op. cit., 182–3. For my own reading of, and objection to, James, see Postscript to Ch. 7.1.3 below.

2

A Bogus Predicate?

Truth, to coin a phrase, isn't a genuine predicate.
(Grover et al., 'A Prosentential Theory of Truth', 94)

The noun 'truth' was not to John Austin's liking. At the beginning of his contribution to the famous debate with Strawson, he remarked: '*In vino*, possibly, "*veritas*", but in a sober symposium "*verum*".'[1] Bearing this advice in mind, let us glimpse only at the different uses of the noun 'truth', lest we get drunk. When Jane Austen writes, 'It is a truth universally acknowledged, that a single man in possession of a good fortune, must be in want of a wife', she uses 'truth' as a count noun. When you comment upon a lecture, 'There was not much (some, a lot of) truth in what he said', you use the noun as a mass term, the pertinent 'mass' consisting of truths. When somebody declares, 'Improbability does not exclude truth', he uses 'truth' as a singular term: truth in this sense seems to be a property (quality, attribute, characteristic, feature) shared by all truths.[2] One seems to ascribe this property to thinkables and sayables when one calls them 'true'. (At last we have arrived at the adjective the Oxford symposiast wants us to concentrate upon.) If grammatical appearances are not deceptive, we can now go on and ask: is the property of being true relational, is it epistemically constrained? etc.

But perhaps appearances *are* deceptive: some philosophers squarely deny that truth is any kind of property. They pursue what Kotarbiński and Tarski called 'the nihilistic approach to the theory of truth'.[3] This conception is registered under the left branch of QUESTION 1 on the flow chart in Figure 1.1. A. J. Ayer, who took his cue from Frank Ramsey,[4] presented truth-theoretical

---

[1] Austin, 'Truth', 117. I shall take up part of this debate in sect. 3.3.4.
[2] Cf. Bolzano, *WL*, I. 107–11.
[3] Kotarbiński, 'On the Concept of Truth', 85–6; Tarski, 'Truth and Proof' (henceforth 'Proof'), 410.
[4] Ramsey, 'Facts and Propositions', esp. 38–9. I shall have occasion to recur to this passage in sect. 2.2.1 and again in Ch. 6.2.

nihilism with characteristic drive:

[T]here is no problem of truth as it is ordinarily conceived. The traditional conception of truth as a 'real quality' or a 'real relation' is due, like most philosophical mistakes, to a failure to analyse sentences correctly. There are sentences . . . in which the word ['true'] seems to stand for something real. [But] our analysis has shown that [it] does not stand for anything. (*Language, Truth and Logic*, 119)

According to one strand in Gottlob Frege's numerous (and not easily reconcilable) reflections on the sense of 'true', truth is at best a very strange kind of property. I shall scrutinize this aspect of Frege's views on truth in section 2.1. My criticism will be inspired in part by Bernard Bolzano, the 'great-grandfather' of analytical philosophy.[5] In section 2.2, I shall give a critical exposition of several (two British and two American) varieties of truth-theoretical nihilism. As a whole, the chapter is an attempt to defend the affirmative answer to the question whether truth is a property.

2.1 Frege's Identity Thesis

2.1.1 *Redundancy and omnipresence*

Here is a very telling passage from Frege's 1918 paper 'The Thought', in which he declares truth to be a 'property' in shudder-quotes, so to speak:[6]

[A] *[Es gibt] zu denken, daß wir an keinem Dinge eine Eigenschaft erkennen können, ohne damit zugleich den Gedanken, daß dieses Ding diese Eigenschaft habe, wahr zu finden. So ist mit jeder Eigenschaft eines Dinges eine Eigenschaft eines Gedankens verknüpft, nämlich die der Wahrheit.* [It is worth pondering that we cannot recognize a property of a thing without at the same time taking the thought that this thing has this property to be true. So with every property of a thing there is tied up a property of a thought, namely truth.]

[B] *Beachtenswert ist auch, daß der Satz 'ich rieche Veilchenduft' doch wohl denselben Inhalt hat wie der Satz 'es ist wahr, daß ich Veilchenduft rieche'. So scheint denn dem Gedanken dadurch nichts hinzugefügt zu werden, daß ich ihm die Eigenschaft der Wahrheit beilege . . .* [It is also worth noticing that the sentence 'I smell the scent of violets' has just the same content as the sentence 'It is true that I smell the scent of violets.' So it seems, then, that nothing is added to the thought by my ascribing to it the property of truth . . .]

[C] *Die Bedeutung des Wortes 'wahr' scheint ganz einzigartig zu sein. Sollten wir es hier mit etwas zu tun haben, was in dem sonst üblichen Sinne gar nicht Eigenschaft genannt werden kann?* [The meaning of the word 'true' seems to be altogether unique. May we not be dealing here with something which cannot, in the ordinary sense, be called a property at all?] ('*Der Gedanke*', 61)

---

[5] As Dummett calls him: *Origins of Analytical Philosophy* (henceforth *OAP*), 171.

[6] Capital letters in brackets are inserted for ease of reference.

The logically strongest contention of this passage is the statement at the beginning of [B] which is surely meant to generalize. Thus understood Frege claims that every substitution instance of

(IDENTITY)   The proposition that $p =$ the proposition that *it is true that p*

is correct.[7] We should beware of mistaking the displayed identity schema for the biconditional Denominalization Schema

(Den)   It is true that p, if and only if p.

If you accept an instance of IDENTITY you are committed to endorsing the corresponding instance of (Den), but there is no such obligation in the other direction.[8]

In [A] Frege maintains that you cannot take an object a to be F without thereby taking the proposition that a is F to be true. (If one 'recognizes' that a is F, one takes a to be F, that is, one believes that a is F. Just as taking Helen to be beautiful is believing that she is beautiful, so taking a proposition to be true is believing that it is true; hence one doesn't explain the notion of belief by saying 'to believe a proposition is to take it to be true'.[9]) The tenet in [A], which is weaker than and entailed by IDENTITY, is certainly not meant to be restricted to those propositions that are expressible by simple subject-predicate sentences, and presumably it is not meant to hold only for belief.[10] So let us put it this way: *necessarily, if somebody Vs that (whether) p, she Vs that (whether) it is true that p,* where 'V' is a placeholder for verbs that are used to ascribe propositional attitudes/acts (such as 'believe' and 'wonder') or speech-acts (such as 'assert' and 'ask'). If one endorses this schema one subscribes to what I shall call Frege's *Omnipresence* Thesis.[11]

In the second statement in [B] Frege highlights the *Redundancy* Thesis which is implicit in IDENTITY: when you say that the proposition that things are thus-and-so is true, you say no more than if you had just said that things are thus-and-so.[12]

---

[7] Cf. Frege, *Nachgelassene Schriften* (henceforth *NS*), 153 (141).

[8] Many philosophers maintain that believing that p *is* believing that it is true that p, that asserting that p *is* asserting that it is true that p, and so on, for all substitution-instances of the schema 'Ving that (whether) p *is* Ving that (whether) it is true that p'. If one endorses IDENTITY, one is committed to accepting this claim. Following Simon Blackburn (*Spreading the Word*, 227), C. Wright calls this claim the Transparency Platitude: see 'Truth: A Traditional Debate Reviewed' (henceforth 'Debate'), 227 (= 'Minimalism, Deflationism, Pragmatism, Pluralism' (henceforth 'Minimalism'), 761). He says that the Transparency Platitude is 'tantamount to the validity of [(Den)] for all propositional contents' ('Debate', 233). I cannot see this. Somebody who endorses (Den) but denies that its two sides express the same proposition will not accept the Transparency Platitude.

[9] Dummett, 'The Two Faces of the Concept of Truth', 260. (I do not mean to suggest that Dummett is under any illusion here.)   [10] In *NS*, 140 (129) Frege upholds it for assertion.

[11] Cf. ibid., 140 (129).   [12] Cf. ibid., 211, 251, 271 (194, 233–4, 251); idem, *WB*, 245 (163).

Consider a philosophically uncontentious example of redundancy:[13] you would not add anything to the claim you can make by uttering, 'I foretold that', if you were to say instead, 'I foretold that beforehand': the adverb is content-redundant. Frege upholds a similar thesis for 'true'. What can be said to be redundant in 'It is true that I smell the scent of violets' is certainly not the predicate 'is true', but (at best) the sentential operator, or unary connective, 'It is true that'. (If you remove a predicate from a sentence, the remaining fragment is no longer a sentence.) So one way of capturing Frege's point is this: the result of prefacing a sentence with the operator 'It is true that' expresses the very same proposition as the original sentence. Alternatively, treating 'It is true that...' as a stylistic variant of 'That... is true',[14] we can render the Redundancy Thesis as follows. Attaching the predicate 'is true' to the nominalization of a sentence ('that I smell the scent of violets') cancels the effect of the nominalization: one and the same proposition is expressed whether we attach 'is true' to a that-clause or whether we simply erase the word 'that'.

In the final section [C], Frege claims that in view of the preceding reflections it is very dubious whether truth is a property at all.[15]

After Frege, and apparently quite independently of him, Ramsey (arguably) and Ayer (unequivocally) advocated the so-called 'Redundancy Theory of Truth':[16]

[T]he question 'What is truth?' is reducible to the question 'What is the analysis of the sentence "p is true"?' And it is plain that this question raises no genuine problem, since... to say that p is true is simply a way of asserting p. (*Language, Truth and Logic*, 118–19)

---

[13] Borrowed from Moore, *Lectures on Metaphysics*, 115. Readers who do not (yet) suffer from terminal melancholia will be grateful to Quine for preserving this poignant exchange: 'Help, Ma, I'm drowning to death.' 'Don't be redundant, dear' (*Quiddities*, 177).

[14] For a defence of this treatment, see pp. 350–1 below.

[15] Cf. Frege, *NS*, 251–2 (233–4). In view of this clear textual evidence, Wright should reconsider his allusion to Frege as the archetype of 'those philosophers who ... hold that truth is a substantial ... characteristic of the items—be they sentences, propositions, or attitudes—which have it' (Wright, 'Response to Commentators', 911). In *'Der Gedanke'* there is no trace of the assumption that truth-values are objects which are the designata of declarative sentences. Scott Soames takes *'Über Sinn und Bedeutung* (On Sense and Reference)', 34–5, to contain an argument for Frege's Identity Thesis which uses this assumption as a premiss, and he has no difficulty in showing that the alleged argument is unsuccessful even if one accepts the premiss (Soames, *Understanding Truth* (henceforth *UT*), 46–7). However, I am not sure that his reading of that tantalizing passage is correct. Cf. Tyler Burge, 'Frege on Truth', 98–123; Markus Stepanians, *Frege und Husserl über Urteilen und Denken*, 93–103.

[16] The term was coined by William Ernest Johnson: see his *Logic*, vol. I, ch. IV, 52. The Redundancy Theory of Truth has also been called 'No-Truth Theory' (Prior), 'Disappearance Theory' (Sellars), or 'Logical Superfluity Theory' (Austin, White). (Readers of Gerald Vision's *Modern Anti-Realism and Manufactured Truth* might get the impression that the theory takes truth to be a kind of liquid, for it is always referred to as the 'Logical Superfluidity Theory' (9, 39, 112).)

On this view, the concept of truth can be explained just by appealing to IDENTITY.[17] This is definitely *not* Frege's view. He thought that the notion of truth cannot be explained at all, and he even took himself to be in possession of a proof that this is so.[18] One can consistently accept what I have called the Redundancy Thesis and refuse to accept the Redundancy Theory.[19] But since the Theory depends on the Thesis, by attacking the latter I shall also be attacking the former.

2.1.2 *An internal conflict within Frege's theory?*

At least prima facie there is a tension between Frege's Identity Thesis and another doctrine you find in his work. Like Geach and Strawson some decades after him, Frege held that (un-embedded) sentences containing (unquoted) 'empty', i.e. non-designating singular terms express propositions that are neither true nor false.[20] If somebody were to utter the conjecture,

(K)   *Kant's wife* was Protestant,

then, according to Frege, what is said falls into a truth-value gap. In his famous 1959 paper 'Truth', Michael Dummett argued that acceptance of all (non-pathological) instances of (Den) is incorrect if Frege's doctrine of truth-value gaps

---

[17] In order to make grammatical sense of the quotation from Ayer, we must assume that he uses the letter 'p' as a place-holder for sentence-*nominalizations* (whereas I have adopted in this book the more common practice of using it only as a place-holder for *sentences*). With respect to the 'absolute' ('non-semantical') concept of truth, Rudolf Carnap seems to be an adherent of the Redundancy *Theory*: '(The proposition) p is true = $_{\text{Df}}$ p' (*Introduction to Semantics* (henceforth *IS*), 90). As it stands, this definition is unfortunately ungrammatical, for 'p' is first a place-holder for a sentence-nominalization and then for a sentence. So let us rewrite it: (The proposition) that p is true = $_{\text{Df}}$ p.

[18] The classification of Frege as a Redundancy Theorist is unfortunately rather common in the literature: see, for example, Blackburn, *Spreading the Word*, 258; Horwich, *Truth*, ix, 122. It is also seriously misleading to represent Frege as contributing to 'Early Minimalist Theories of Truth', as is done in Blackburn and Simmons (eds.), *Truth*, 83–5.

[19] Putnam has always been opposed to the Redundancy Theory, but he subscribes to the Redundancy Thesis: 'What is right in deflationism is that if I assert that it is true that p, then I assert the same thing as if I simply assert [that] p' ('Sense, Nonsense, and the Senses', 56; I have taken the liberty of deleting misused quotation-marks and restoring syntactical orderliness by adding 'that').

[20] This amounts to a rejection of the principle of *tertium non datur*, if we follow Dummett's regimentation of the confusing terminology in this area: see his *Truth and Other Enigmas* (henceforth *TOE*), xix. See Frege '*Über Sinn und Bedeutung*', 33, 40; *NS*, 211 (194); Geach, 'Russell's Theory of Descriptions'; Strawson, 'On Referring'. The sentence 'Vulcan is a planet in Mercury's orbit' contains a non-designating *proper name* that came into circulation because of an astronomical error; and in the mouth of hallucinating Macbeth 'This is a bloody dagger' contains a non-designating *demonstrative*. The problem arises with such terms as well, hence it cannot be solved simply by accepting Russell's theory of definite descriptions which makes (K) come out as false.

is correct. If this verdict of inconsistency is well-founded, then it will apply a fortiori to the combination of IDENTITY with the latter doctrine. Since Dummett is certainly above any suspicion of rashly accusing Frege of inconsistency, we'd better look closely at his argument:

[A] Suppose that P contains a singular term which has a sense but no reference: then, according to Frege, P expresses a proposition which has no truth-value. This proposition is therefore not true, and hence the statement ⌈It is true that P⌉ will be *false*. P will therefore not have the same sense as ⌈It is true that P⌉, since the latter is false while the former is not. [B] It is not possible to plead that ⌈It is true that P⌉ is itself neither true nor false when the singular term occurring in P lacks a reference, since [C] the *oratio obliqua* clause ⌈that P⌉ stands for the proposition expressed by P, and it is admitted that P does have a sense and express a proposition; the singular term occurring in P has in ⌈It is true that P⌉ its indirect reference, namely its sense, and we assumed that it did have a sense. [D] In general it will always be inconsistent to maintain the truth of every instance of ⌈It is true that p if and only if p⌉ while allowing that there is a type of sentence which under certain conditions is neither true nor false. ('Truth', 4–5) [21]

The plea that is rejected in [B] looks very reasonable indeed: if the proposition I now express by (K) really is the *same* as the proposition I could have expressed now by

(TK)   It is true that Kant's wife was Protestant,

then, of course, the truth-value status of what is expressed by (TK) (true, false, or neither) has got to be the same as the truth-value status of what is expressed by (K). This is just an application of the Leibnizian Principle of the Indiscernibility of Identicals. So, contrary to [A], what is said by (TK) cannot possibly be false if what is said by (K) falls into the truth-value gap.

The argument given in [C] for rejecting this reply assumes that the that-clause in (TK) designates the proposition expressed by the embedded sentence (K). This assumption may be entirely correct (and I think it is). But if Frege were to accept it, then he would have to acknowledge, without any reservation, that being true is a *property* of some propositions, just as he takes being an axiom, or containing the sense of 'the Morning Star', to be properties of some propositions. But as we saw, this is exactly what Frege refrains from doing. Hence we have not been shown that the *consistency* of Frege's views is threatened by his adopting both the identity claim and the truth-value gap thesis.

---

[21] Cf. also Dummett, *TOE*, xx; *FPL* 445; and Geach, 'Truth and God', 87. Capital letters in brackets are inserted for ease of reference. 'P' is a place-holder for a quotational designator of a sentence, and ⌈It is true that P⌉ designates the result of applying 'It is true that' to that sentence.

As to the second half of [C], it is by no means clear that the subject-term of (K) has its indirect reference in (TK). Frege ascribes indirect reference to a term in a context if its replacement by another term with the same ordinary reference in that context can affect the truth-value of the proposition expressed.[22] But there is no such risk if the replacement takes place in the context of 'It is true that—'. Replacing 'Kant's wife' in (TK) by another empty singular term, e.g. 'the King of Switzerland in 1905', cannot affect the truth-value status of what is said.

But there are more data to be accounted for than this. If you replace the italicized singular term in either of the following sentences by another term with the same ordinary reference

(S1)   That *the Morning Star* is a planet is true, but Ben does not believe it

(S2)   Ben does not believe that *the Morning Star* is a planet, but it is true,

you might affect the truth-value of what is said. We can budget for this if the anaphoric pronoun 'it' in the second conjunct goes proxy for its antecedent, the nominalized sentence in the first conjunct, understood in the same way.[23] At first sight, this is evidence in favour of the claim Dummett makes in the second half of [C]. But it is far from conclusive. For consider the following 'reversal' of the argument concerning (S1). The anaphoric pronoun in the second conjunct of

(S3)   Ben does not believe that *the Morning Star* is a planet, but it is a planet

refers to the ordinary referent of its antecedent, the italicized term in the first conjunct, for surely the second half of (S3) does not declare the indirect referent, i.e. the sense, of 'the Morning Star' to be a planet. Prima facie this is evidence in favour of the contention that this term must have its ordinary reference in the first conjunct. If we do not trust this (anti-Fregean) argument, we should not put much confidence in its precursor either.

The following reflection carries more conviction.[24] Argument (A) is certainly valid:

(A)   That *the Evening Star* is a planet is believed by Ben.

That *the Evening Star* is a planet is true.

Therefore, there is something which is both believed by Ben and true.

But its validity is unproblematic only if the italicized singular term makes the same contribution to the content of *both* premisses, for otherwise the two

---

[22] In order to keep the formulation straight, I assume that 't and t* have *no* ordinary reference' is a borderline case of 't and t* have the *same* ordinary reference'.

[23] See Dummett, 'Is the Concept of Truth Needed for Semantics?', 4.

[24] It is also due to Dummett: 'Of What Kind of Thing is Truth a Property?' 271, and 'Sentences and Propositions', 12.

that-clauses would have to be understood differently, and the argument would not instantiate the form 'Fa, Ga ∴ ∃x (Fx & Gx)'. But of course, if one defends Dummett's remark about indirect reference in [C] along these lines, or in the style of the last paragraph, one treats the that-clauses in (A), or in (S1) and (S2), as designating objects to which properties are being ascribed.[25]

Several philosophers have presented an argument against combining the endorsement of the schema IDENTITY with the admission of truth-value gaps that does not depend on taking 'It is true that p' to be an ascription of a bona fide property.[26] This objection, too, does not invoke IDENTITY directly, but the weaker schema (Den), and it assumes a similar equivalence schema for falsity:[27]

(Den)   It is true that p, iff p
(Falsity)   It is false that p, iff it is not the case that p.

In the next lines of the putative proof I shall abbreviate 'it is not the case that' by 'not-'. Now let us assume that the proposition that Kant's wife was Protestant falls into a gap:

(Gap)   It is neither true that K nor false that K.

Applying (Den) to the left half and (Falsity) to the right half of (Gap), we obtain:

(C1)   Therefore, neither K nor not-K,

and from this we can immediately derive what looks like a flat contradiction:

(C2)   Therefore, not-K and not-(not-K).

So it seems that we are bound to accept the verdict that (Den), (Falsity), and (Gap) form an inconsistent triad.

But perhaps this is a bit too quick. For one thing, it is by no means clear that (C2) is really *false*: as (K) is supposed to fall into a truth-value gap, one could claim that its (simple or double) negation, and hence the conjunction (C2), do the same. But this is small consolation, for under the standard understanding of validity an argument that starts from true premisses is not valid unless it has a *true* conclusion. So far the argument still seems to show that the three premisses cannot be jointly true. But there is a way of preserving the consistency of Frege's triad. The step from (C1) to (C2) is only correct if we interpret the conjunctive denial 'Neither A nor B' in such a way that its truth requires the *falsity* of the components 'A' and 'B'.[28] But this interpretation is not obligatory.[29]

Lest this move seem entirely ad hoc, consider the role that conjunctive denials sometimes play when philosophers try to draw a line between falsehoods and cases of *Sphärenvermengung* [confounding of types[30]] or category mismatch. When Gilbert Ryle wants to drive home the point that two sentences 'F's are G' and 'F's are H' (where 'G' and 'H' are lexical antonyms) are both 'category mistakes', he tends to say, 'F's are neither G nor H'. Here is a philosophically uncontentious example: some words are more difficult to spell than others, but letters are not the sort of things that can be spelled: 'letters are neither easy to spell, nor insuperably hard to spell.' Or, slightly less uncontentiously: why is it a category mistake to say that Napoleon is the meaning of 'Napoleon'? Well, Napoleon sometimes wore boots, whereas 'meanings...never wear boots—or go barefoot either'. Obviously, Ryle does not take 'Neither A nor B' to mean 'It is false that A, and it is false that B'. Wanting to reject both components as non-significant, he must assume that the truth of the conjunctive denial requires only that its components *lack truth*. Another of Ryle's examples brings us even closer to the case at hand: 'Most epithets...are not appropriate to linguistic expressions....Reptiles do or do not hibernate; adverbs neither do nor do not.'[31] Clearly, he takes the last sentence to be tantamount to 'It is not true that adverbs hibernate, and it is not true that adverbs do not hibernate.' This suggests that there are two ways of rejecting 'Adverbs hibernate': asserting the internal negation, namely 'Adverbs don't hibernate', and asserting the external negation, viz. 'It is not true that adverbs hibernate', where the latter, but not the former, is taken to be compatible with 'It does not even make sense to say that adverbs hibernate'. If we can avail ourselves of the distinction between internal and external negation, we can define falsity as truth of the internal negation rather than as absence of truth. If the right-hand side of (Falsity) is understood as the external negation of 'p', then the schema (Falsity) amounts to 'It is false that p, iff it is not true that p', and the alleged refutation asumes at the outset that there are no truth-value gaps. After all, advocates of gappiness believe that a proposition may lack truth *without* being false. If Ryle is right, then one way of

---

[28] This interpretation is adopted by Frege: '*Gedankengefüge* [Compound Thoughts]', 41. But note his restriction, ibid., 40.

[29] See Anil Gupta and Nuel Belnap, *The Revision Theory of Truth* (henceforth *RTT*), 22 n. 40; Dorothy Grover, *PrTh*, 200–1, 232–3; and, especially, Timothy Smiley, 'Sense without Denotation'.

[30] Carnap, *Der logische Aufbau der Welt*, §§30–1.

[31] The three quotations come from Ryle, *The Concept of Mind*, ch. VII, sect. 2; 'Theory of Meaning', 355; and 'Heterologicality', 251 (in this order).

being void of truth-value is being a category mistake.[32] If Frege, Geach, and Strawson are right, then suffering from a radical reference-failure is another way. 'Kant's wife was Protestant' expresses a falsehood only if its internal negation, to wit 'Kant's wife wasn't Protestant', yields a truth. Since Kant was a bachelor, it is neither true that Kant's wife was a Protestant, nor true that she wasn't. Or so those philosophers could say.[33]

2.1.3 Conditions of propositional identity

Frege's Identity Thesis may be compatible with his admission of truth-value gaps (as I have just now tried to convince you), and yet it may be implausible. So our question must be: is Frege's contention in itself plausible? Let us first look for Frege's *general* criterion of propositional identity. (This enterprise may be destined to the same frustration as looking for the philosophers' stone.) In a manuscript of 1906, entitled '*Kurze Übersicht meiner logischen Lehren* [A Brief Surview of My Logical Doctrines]', Frege says:

Zwei Sätze A und B können in der Beziehung zueinander stehen, dass jeder, der den Inhalt von A als wahr anerkennt, auch den von B ohne weiteres als wahr anerkennen muss, und dass auch umgekehrt jeder, der den Inhalt von B anerkennt, auch den von A unmittelbar anerkennen muss (Äquipollenz), wobei vorausgesetzt wird, dass die Auffassung der Inhalte von A und B keine Schwierigkeit macht. [Two sentences A and B can stand in such a relation that anyone who recognizes the content of A as true must straightaway recognize the content of B as true, and conversely . . . anyone who recognizes the content of B as true must immediately recognize that of A as true (equipollence). It is here being assumed that there is no difficulty in grasping the content of A and B.] (in *NS*, 213 (197))

I prefer to call the relation which obtains between two sentences if and only if this condition is satisfied '*cognitive equivalence*' (this being a more tell-tale term than 'equipollence'), and I suggest the following rendering of Frege's conception of this relation:

(CognE)   Two sentences are cognitively equivalent if and only if, for any context c, nobody who fully understands them can take one of them to express a truth with respect to c without immediately being ready to take the other to express a truth with respect to c as well.

I have inserted a reference to contexts in order to ensure the applicability of (CognE) to indexical sentence pairs (such as {'I am now observing a drake',

---

[32] More on this topic in Ch. 7.3.2.
[33] We shall return to this issue in Ch. 6, sects. 3 and 2.3 *sub* [C] and [D].

'I am now observing a male duck'}, where a certain speaker and a certain time would be the relevant components of c).[34]

Now what is the relation between being cognitively equivalent and expressing the same proposition? According to Dummett, we have already found what we were looking for: Frege, he says, claims cognitive equivalence 'as a sufficient as well as necessary condition for identity of sense'.[35] Such a claim would indeed account for Frege's verdict on pairs such as {'Snow is white', 'It is true that snow is white'}, for their members are certainly cognitively equivalent. But if cognitive equivalence were to guarantee identity of sense, Frege would have to swallow some intuitively bizarre consequences which are certainly not acceptable to him. The sentences 'A rose is a rose' and 'No woman is her own mother' are cognitively equivalent, since the content of either sentence is such that (to use Frege's own words) 'it would have to be immediately recognized as true by anyone who had grasped it properly'.[36] Hence, if cognitive equivalence were a sufficient condition of propositional identity, then our two sentences would express the same proposition. *All* sentences the contents of which simply defy disbelief would express one and the same proposition. In other words, there would be only one proposition which is 'self-evident [*unmittelbar einleuchtend*]'.[37] Surely Frege's conception of an axiom does not allow him to accept this result. Furthermore, any conjunction containing one such sentence would express the same proposition as the other conjunct by itself.[38]

None of these consequences is forthcoming if Frege takes cognitive equivalence only to be a necessary condition for identity of sense. After all, as Dummett observes, Frege 'never applies [the cognitive equivalence criterion] save to prove that two expressions do not have the same sense.'[39] Henceforth I shall endorse

---

[34] (CognE) allows us to classify pairs of instantiations of 'p' and 'it is true that p' as cognitively equivalent, regardless of whether the proposition that p has a truth-value or not. This would no longer be so if we were to reformulate (CognE) in such a way that it also covers taking a sentence to express a *falsehood*. Suppose that the proposition that p falls into a truth-value gap. Then somebody who understands 'It is true that p' (and hence also 'p') may take the former to express a falsehood but refuse to take the latter to express a falsehood as well. This is why I prefer (CognE) to the following formulation in Dummett: 'Anyone who grasps the thought expressed by the one sentence and that expressed by the other must immediately recognize ... that both must have the same truth-value' (*Frege—Philosophy of Mathematics* (henceforth *FPM*), 171). By contrast, the formulation in Dummett's 'More about Thoughts', 294, is equivalent to (CognE).

[35] Dummett, *FPM*, 171; cf. 'More about Thoughts', 298, 301.   [36] Frege, *NS*, 213 (197).

[37] Ibid., 242 (224).

[38] e.g. {'Kant was a bachelor, and a rose is a rose', 'Kant was a bachelor'}. As we shall see in sect. 3.3.3, the early Wittgenstein does not find this consequence repulsive, but his conception of sense is vastly different from Frege's.

[39] Dummett, *FPM*, 171. As to the claim criticized in the last paragraph, cf. now Dummett, 'Comments on WK's Paper', 247–8.

Frege's Necessary Condition for propositional identity, which I shall also refer to as the *Cognitive Equivalence Criterion:*[40]

(F-Nec)   Two sentences express the same proposition (with respect to c) *only if* they are cognitively equivalent (in c).

Propositions must be at least as fine-grained as is required by (F-Nec) if we want to make sense of our practice of ascribing attitudes and reporting speech by means of that-clauses. 'Ann believes that the Big Dipper consists of seven stars, but she does not believe that the Plough consists of seven stars' may very well be a correct report, and the same holds for 'Ben said that there was some water in the vicinity, but he did not say that there was some H_2O in the vicinity.' If the embedded sentences were to express the same proposition, such reports would be inconsistent.[41]

Cognitive equivalence is only a component of what Frege takes to be a sufficient condition for identity of sense. We find the second component in the very same 1906 manuscript from which I took the passage cited on p. 42:

[Two sentences A and B express the same Thought *if*]
(i) anyone who recognizes the content of A as true must straightaway recognize the content of B as true, and conversely . . . anyone who recognizes the content of B as true must immediately recognize that of A as true (equipollence). It is here being assumed that there is no difficulty in grasping the content of A and B . . . [and]

(ii) [*V*]*on jedem der beiden äquipollenten Sätze A und B* [*gilt*], *dass in seinem Inhalte nichts ist, was von jedem, der es richtig erfasst hat, sofort unmittelbar als wahr anerkannt werden müsste.* [There is nothing in the content of either of the two equipollent sentences A and B that would have to be at once immediately recognized as true by anyone who had grasped it properly.] (*NS* 213 (197))

Frege insists on both (i) and (ii) when he says (a few lines later): the proposition expressed by two sentences is the same in 'equipollent' (cognitively equivalent) sentences 'of the kind given above [*der oben erwähnten Art*].' By adding clause (ii) Frege forestalls the intuitively bizarre results I mentioned. So what Frege takes to be a Sufficient Condition for propositional identity is this:

(F-Suff)   Two sentences express the same proposition (with respect to c), *if*
            (1) they are cognitively equivalent and
            (2) neither of them is, or contains a part which is,[42] such that one cannot understand it without realizing that it expresses a truth.

---

[40] (F-Nec) is close to what Evans calls Frege's Intuitive Criterion of Difference (see *The Varieties of Reference*, 18–19). The criteria do not coincide for the same reason that (CognE) does not coincide with Dummett's formula in *FPM*, 171.

[41] The theoretical assumptions which some philosophers adduce as reasons for denying this consistency claim seem to me to be far less trustworthy than the claim.

[42] This restriction ensures that (F-Suff) does not declare, e.g., instantiations of 'p & a rose is a rose' to express the same proposition as their first part.

Table 2.1. *One proposition, or two?*

	zero	plus
(1)	p	It is true that p
(2)	p	p and p
(3)	p	p or p
(4)	p	Not-not-p

There is, of course, a price to be paid for shielding off the various odd consequences of identifying cognitive equivalence with propositional identity:
(F-Suff) is silent on sentences the content of which is, or contains a part which
is, self-evidently true.[43]

Now let us apply Frege's Sufficient Condition to pairs of sentences which
exemplify the schemata presented in Table 2.1: do 'plus' sentences express the
same proposition as their 'zero' counterparts? If we consider only those materi-
alizations of the schemata in Table 2.1 that can be understood *without* being
assented to, then we can apply (F-Suff), and in all three cases it yields the
verdict: *yes*, 'plus' sentences do express the same proposition as their 'zero' counterparts.[44] Hence the four 'plus' sentences also have one and the same propositional content. (Because of the structural similarity between (1) and (4),
Davidson calls the redundancy theory 'the double-negation theory of truth'.[45])

In all four cases Bolzano's answer is an adamant 'no'. Here is what he says
about the first pair:

*Wenn der Satz: A ist B, wahr ist: so ist unläugbar auch [der Satz:] daß A B sey, ist wahr, ein wahrer Satz;
und dieser ist seinen Bestandtheilen nach schon ein anderer, als der Satz: A ist B.* [If the proposition *A is
B* is true, then the proposition *It is true that A is B* is undeniably also true, and since the
latter has different parts, it is a different proposition from *A is B*.] (*WL* I, 147)

---

[43] Neale comments on our quotation from Frege's *NS* as follows: 'This characterization [of equipol-
lence] invites the thought that mutual entailment is at the heart of the notion', and then he goes on to
object: 'There is an obvious problem with all of this: if logically equivalent sentences have the same
sense, then such sentences ought to be intersubstitutable *salva veritate* in contexts of propositional attitude. But this is simply not the case according to Frege' (*FF*, 82). The very obviousness of this problem
should have prevented him from ascribing to Frege the view that co-entailment guarantees identity of
sense. It is only in a letter to Husserl (*WB*, 105–6 (70–1)) that Frege comes indeed 'fairly close' to endorsing this view, but charity demands that this be put aside as a momentary aberration.

[44] The evidence for the identity claims concerning (2)–(4) comes from Frege's 1923 paper
'*Gedankengefüge* [Compound Thoughts]': for (2) and (3), see 39 n. and 49, for (4), see 44. On the last page of
his 1918 paper '*Die Verneinung* [Negation]', Frege seems to takes 'p' and 'not-not-p' to express different
propositions.   [45] Davidson, 'True to the Facts', 38; cf. his 'Structure', 282.

[Wir finden], daß der Satz, welchen die Worte 'A ist wahr' ausdrücken, ein von A selbst verschiedener sei; denn jener hat offenbar ein ganz anderes Subjekt als dieser. Sein Subjekt ist nämlich der ganze Satz A selbst. [We see that the proposition expressed by the words 'A is true' is different from the proposition A, for the former obviously has quite another subject than the latter. The subject of the former is the whole proposition A.] (*Paradoxien des Unendlichen*, §13)

So, according to Bolzano, (1 plus) sentences have senses that contain the concept of truth, and this concept is (normally) absent from the senses of their less wordy counterparts. (Of course, the shorter sentence may itself already contain 'true'.) This non-identity thesis is presupposed in an important section of Bolzano's 'Theory of Science'. In his theory of the ground-consequence relation [*Abfolge*] he repeatedly asserts that the proposition that *it is true that things are thus-and-so* is a consequence [*Folge*] of the proposition that *things are thus-and-so*.[46] This contention could not consistently be combined with the Fregean claim that 'it is true that' is propositionally redundant, since the ground-consequence relation is irreflexive.[47] Bolzano would also contend that the propositions expressed by the other 'plus' sentences in Table 2.1 contain the concepts of conjunction, disjunction, or double-negation, which may very well be absent from the propositions expressed by the corresponding 'zero' sentences.[48]

Russell repeated Bolzano's non-identity thesis when he wrote (in 1904 and 1910):

Consider . . . what it is that we mean when we judge. At first sight, we seem to mean that a certain proposition is true; but '*p* is true' is not the same proposition as *p*, and therefore cannot be what we mean. ('Meinong's Theory of Complexes and Assumptions', 62)

The notion of truth is not part of the content of what is judged. (*Principia Mathematica*, 41)

In recent years Alston and Horwich also took Bolzano's side in this issue. (Like Russell, they did not know that they had been anticipated by Bolzano.) About the pair of sentences which Ramsey had used to illustrate the Redundancy Thesis,

(S⁰)   Caesar was murdered
(S⁺)   The proposition that Caesar was murdered is true,

Alston says, '[S⁺] includes in its content the concept of a proposition, which it uses to set up a subject of predication; and the concept of truth is used in that predication. While [S⁰] is about Caesar, [S⁺] is about a proposition.'[49] Replacing 'proposition' in (S⁺) by 'statement', Horwich writes in the same vein, the claim

---

[46] Bolzano, *WL*, II. 357, 370, 374. Cf. pp. 151–2 below.   [47] Ibid., *WL*, II. 356.

[48] The reasons for Bolzano's 'no' in response to case (1) apply here as well. Cf. ibid., I. 206, 447.

[49] Alston, *RCT*, 47. (I have inserted the bracketed letters.)

that (S^0) and (S^+) 'have exactly the same meaning ... is implausibly strong; for after all, the words "true" and "statement" do have meanings, and those meanings would appear to be, in some sense, "components" of the meaning of $[S^+]$ but not of $[S^0]$.'[50]

The argument for non-redundancy should not make too much of the presence of the noun-phrase 'the proposition' in (S^+). We should, rather, delete it, because the point at issue is whether 'p' and 'It is true that p' (or 'That p is true') express the same proposition.[51] Nor should the argument rely on the contention that the subject of (S^+) differs from that of (S^0). There are two reasons for this. First, the opponent can retort, '(S^+), purged of the first two words, is formed by applying a unary connective to (S^0). As the case of the negation operator shows, such an operation does not always engender a change of subject. Why shouldn't the truth operator resemble the negation operator in this respect?' Secondly, even if (S^+) and (S^0) do have different subjects, that alone does not guarantee that their contents differ. Consider '*He* is of unknown origin' and '*His origin* is unknown': do these sentences not have the same content in spite of having different subjects?

From Bolzano's theory of *Sätze an sich* (propositions) and their constituents,[52] one can distil the *Bolzanian Necessary Condition* for propositional identity, which I shall also refer to as the *Conceptual Balance Requirement*:

(B-Nec)   Two sentences express the same proposition *only if* there is no concept whose mastery has to be exercised only in understanding utterances of *one* of them.

As used in (B-Nec), the term 'concept' applies to pieces of cognitive equipment a thinker may have or lack. To possess the concept of (an) F is to be able to think of something as being, or as not being, (an) F. I accept the Conceptual Balance Requirement, and I shall repeatedly invoke it in the course of this book. (I am not the first to appeal to such a principle in a discussion of Frege: (B-Nec) is a variant of a principle that Dummett invokes in his criticism of certain identity claims in Frege's *Grundlagen*.[53]) Notice that by appealing to (B-Nec), one does not incur a commitment to Bolzano's 'structuralist' thesis that concepts are components of propositions.

As to the question how concepts are to be individuated, the following *necessary* identity condition will do for the purposes of this book:[54] the concept of (an) F is identical with the concept of (a) G only if every sentence combining 'is (an) F'

---

[50] Horwich, *Truth*, 124; cf. 38. (I have inserted the bracketed letters.)

[51] I shall return to this topic in Ch. 5.1.   [52] Cf. my 'Propositions in Bolzano and Frege', esp. 235.

[53] 'If one sentence involves a concept that another sentence does not involve, the two sentences cannot express the same thought or have the same content' (Dummett, 'More about Thoughts', 295). Talk of a *concept's* being involved in a *sentence* is a bit confusing.

[54] Recall the reflections on strengths (IV) and (V) on pp. 25–7 above, and the remark on the meaning of 'the concept of F-ness' on pp. 1–2.

with a singular term is cognitively equivalent with a sentence combining 'is (a) G' with the same singular term. (Sometimes, even a far weaker condition will suffice: the concept of (an) F is identical with the concept of (a) G only if 'is (an) F' and 'is (a) G' have the same extension.) If the cognitive equivalence condition were also sufficient, there could not be several self-evidently co-applicable concepts. But surely we do not want to declare the concept of an object that is identical with itself to be the same as the concept of an object that is rectangular if it is square. (Consequently, we should not accept the thesis that concepts are discriminatory capacities.)

Of course, two sentences may meet the Conceptual Balance Requirement without expressing the same proposition: take '3 > 2' and '2 > 3', or the negation and the double negation of any sentence. So this criterion no more provides us with a sufficient condition for propositional identity than does its Fregean counterpart (F-Nec), the Cognitive Equivalence Criterion. But (B-Nec) is more demanding than (F-Nec) in that sentences which satisfy the latter may not satisfy the former. 'She has ten fingers' and 'The number of her fingers equals ten multiplied by one' comply with the Cognitive Equivalence Criterion. But mastery of the concept of multiplication is only required for understanding an utterance of the second sentence, so they do not comply with the Conceptual Balance Requirement. Propositions must be at least as fine-grained as is required by (B-Nec) if we want to make sense of our practice of ascribing attitudes and reporting speech by means of that-clauses: 'Our youngest daughter believes (said) that she has ten fingers, but she does not believe (did not say) that the number of her fingers equals ten multiplied by one' may be a correct report, but if the embedded sentences were to express the same proposition, such a report would be inconsistent.

Unfortunately, we cannot decide simply by appealing to (B-Nec) whether Frege's propositional identity claim concerning 'p' and 'It is true that p' is correct, because according to Frege such pairs actually fulfil that condition: for all utterances of declarative sentences, mastery of the concept of truth has to be exercised in understanding them. So the question remains:

2.1.4 *Who is right, Frege or Bolzano?*

Frege maintains that 'It is true that p' expresses the same proposition as the plain 'p'. He also points out that prefacing an utterance of a declarative sentence with 'It is true that' (or a synonym thereof) is neither sufficient nor necessary for making an assertion.[55] And he suggests that there is a close connection between

---

[55] Not sufficient: see Frege's frequent references to the actor's use of declarative sentences on the stage ('*Der Gedanke*', 63; *NS*, 211 (194), 251–2 (233–4). Not necessary: cf. ibid. and *NS*, 140 (129), 271–2 (251–2). Frege's insight will play a critical role in sect. 2.2.1.

content redundancy and *force* redundancy.[56] But his point about force, which should be conceded on all sides, does not justify his controversial tenet about content. Surely one can acknowledge Frege's observation that adding the truth operator to an utterance of a declarative sentence does not change its force, or give it one if it had none, without thereby incurring a commitment to endorse his propositional identity claim.

Can one justify Frege's verdict on 'p'/'It is true that p' pairs (and the other sentence pairs in Table 2.1 above) by appealing to his Sufficient Condition? If one accepts (F-Suff), one has to concede that sentences like

(H)   *Hemlock is poisonous*

(TH)   It is true that *hemlock is poisonous*

express the same proposition, but then one must also grant that (H) and (BH) do so as well:

(BH)   Anyone who were to believe that hemlock is poisonous would be right in so believing.

These three sentences are cognitively equivalent, and none of them has a content that is self-evidently true or self-evidently false. But is the complex operator surrounding (H) as it occurs within (BH) propositionally redundant? Even if Davidson were right in claiming that one cannot believe anything without having the concept of a belief (which I find hard to believe),[57] surely you can understand an utterance of (H) without actually exercising your mastery of the concept of a belief, whereas you certainly cannot understand an utterance of (BH) without doing just that. (In my formulation of the Conceptual Balance Requirement I presuppose an *occurrent* sense of 'understand':[58] in this sense you cannot understand an utterance of (H) without actually entertaining the thought that hemlock is poisonous, whereas, in the *dispositional* sense, you can at any time correctly be said to understand the type-sentence (H) provided your English is good enough.) The Bolzanian requirement seems to deliver the intuitively correct answer. After all, somebody might very well believe that H without believing that BH. By refusing to regard utterances of (H) and (BH) as expressing the same proposition, we give up Frege's Sufficient Condition of propositional identity. Hence we can no

---

[56] At one point Frege seems to suggest that the independence of the assertoric force of an utterance from the presence or absence of the truth operator explains the latter's propositional redundancy: '*Der Gedanke*', 63. In *NS*, 271–2 (251–2) the order of explanation seems to be the reverse.

[57] Cf. Davidson, 'Thought and Talk', 170.

[58] Dummett has convincingly argued that, *pace* Wittgenstein, such a sense of 'understand' is indispensable: *OAP*, 58–60, 101–3, 109, 133.

longer base a justification of Frege's treatment of the pair (H) and (TH) on his principle.

Here is another example which discredits (F-Suff).[59] Suppose the next two sentences are uttered at the same time, while the same blackboard is being pointed at:

(D)   On that blackboard there is a diagram that is square.

(P)   On that blackboard there is a parallelogram that is square.

Two propositions, or only one? 'Only one' is the answer delivered by Frege's Sufficient Condition. 'Two' is the answer delivered by the Conceptual Balance Requirement: you can understand the utterance of (D) without knowing what a parallelogram is, but without bringing this conceptual knowledge into play you cannot understand the utterance of (P). (Obviously our weaker identity condition suffices to demonstrate that the concept of a diagram is not identical with that of a parallelogram.[60]) Again, the Bolzanian requirement seems to deliver the intuitively correct answer. After all, somebody might very well believe that D without believing that P.

If Frege's verdict on 'p'/'It is true that p' pairs cannot be justified by an appeal to his insight concerning force, and if his allegedly Sufficient Condition for propositional identity which would indeed legitimize his identity claim can be shown to be implausible anyway, one starts wondering why one should accept that claim.

As we saw, Frege upholds not only a Redundancy Thesis, but also an Omni presence Thesis. Here is another piece of evidence for this:

[Das Prädikat 'wahr'] unterscheidet sich von allen anderen Prädikaten dadurch, dass es immer mit ausgesagt wird, wenn irgend etwas ausgesagt wird. [What distinguishes 'true' from all other predicates is that predicating it is always included in predicating anything whatever.] (*NS*, 140 (129))[61]

Now if 'true' (or rather, 'It is true that') were senseless, then, Frege argues, sentences containing it (unquoted) would be senseless too.[62] Unless, one should add, 'It is true that p' and 'p' were to differ only with respect to what Frege calls 'colouration'.[63] Consider an example: Frege maintains that elimination of 'alas' from, say, 'I've studied philosophy, jurisprudence, and medicine, and, alas, theology as well' would not affect the identity of the proposition that is expressed in

---

[59] Cf. my *Abstrakte Gegenstände*, 262.   [60] See p. 48 above.

[61] From his 1897 manuscript 'Logic'.

[62] Frege, *NS*, 272 (252). Naturally, Frege doesn't want to put 'It is true that 2 is prime' into the same boat as gibberish such as 'It is eurt that 2 is prime'. Cf. Moore, *Lectures on Metaphysics*, 115–17.

[63] Cf. Frege, '*Der Gedanke*', 63–4; *NS* 151–3 (139–41).

Faust's monologue. So an expression's lack of Fregean sense, which is not a lack of conventional linguistic meaning ('alas' means the same as '*leider*' in Goethe's original), does not always condemn utterances containing it (unquoted) to senselessness. But what a colouring feature of a sentence contributes to the complete content of an utterance of the sentence can be removed: there is no such thing as an ubiquitous colouration. So Frege's Omnipresence Thesis precludes characterizing the relation between 'It is true that' and 'p' (only) in terms of colouration. Unlike 'alas', the truth operator does have a sense, but, Frege claims, this sense somehow annihilates itself:

Das Wort 'wahr' hat einen Sinn, der zum Sinne des ganzen Satzes, in dem es als Prädikat vorkommt, nichts beiträgt. [The word 'true' has a sense that contributes nothing to the sense of the whole sentence in which it occurs as a predicate.] (*NS* 272 (252))[64]

If Frege's contention were correct, then one cannot understand any declarative sentence whatsoever without grasping the (mysteriously self-effacing) sense of 'true' (or rather, of 'It is true that').[65]

I find this doctrine hard to swallow. Isn't it possible to entertain the thought that *it is raining* without exercising one's mastery of the concept of truth? (When we say that the cat, or the baby, has noticed that it is raining, do we presuppose that the cat, or the baby, has mastered the concept of truth?) Young children can certainly understand lots of sentences without understanding the word 'true' or any synonym thereof. We can, and we often do, I think, explain to children what 'true' means by giving them instructions such as: 'If you say, "It is raining", and it is raining, then what you say is true. But if you say, "It is raining", and it isn't raining, then what you say is not true. Or if you say, "It is snowing", and it is snowing, then what you say is true. But if you say, "It is snowing", and it isn't snowing, then what you say is not true. Got it?' To understand such an explanation, the child must of course already understand sentences such as 'It is raining' and 'It is snowing'. Whether the child has 'got it' will become manifest in her or his future use of 'true'. (In Ch. 4.2.3, I shall argue that by 'getting' it the child has not yet *completely* mastered our concept of truth: she has not yet learned to envisage the possibility that an utterance she doesn't understand conveys a truth.)

Do we have to assume that in such lessons the child only acquires a word to express a concept which is already in his or her repertoire? The 'say' in such

---

[64] From Frege's 1915 manuscript '*Meine grundlegenden logischen Einsichten* [My Basic Logical Insights]'.

[65] Using a bit of jargon introduced by John O'Leary-Hawthorne and Graham Oppy (and confirming their conjecture), we can say that Frege's conception of truth is anything but 'minimalist along the dimension of width of conceptual role' (see their 'Minimalism and Truth', 178).

lessons seems to amount to the same thing as 'assertorically utter'. So one might argue: 'As a person who makes assertions, you must be aware that you are expected to aim at *truth*. So you cannot make assertions if you lack the concept of truth.' But is the premiss of this argument really correct? Can a child not recognize her obligation as an asserter by coming to realize that she is expected to assert something only if she is *justified* in doing so? (After all, the injunction to make only true assertions cannot call for acts that are not already called for by the injunction to make only warranted assertions.[66]) Of course, this reply needs to be supported by an argument to the effect that one can have the concept of justification without yet having acquired the concept of truth. Towards the end of this book, in Chapter 7.3.5, I shall present such an argument. So let us tentatively join Bolzano in denying Frege's Identity Thesis.

2.1.5 *Two kinds of truth talk*

It has often been complained, and rightly so, that Frege gives us no hint whatsoever how his reflections on the allegedly self-annihilating sense of 'true' are to cover its use in *propositionally unrevealing* truth declarations such as 'Everything the Pope says *ex cathedra* is true' or 'Pythagoras' Theorem is true'—i.e. in sentences in which the relevant truth candidates are not revealed (expressed) by an embedded sentence.[67] This problem is an urgent one, for we would hardly welcome the conclusion that 'true' as used in 'Pythagoras' Theorem is true' has a different sense than as used in a *propositionally revealing* truth declaration like 'The proposition that the square on the hypotenuse is equal to the sum of the squares on the other two sides is true.' After all, there are intuitively valid arguments connecting both kinds of truth talk:[68]

(P1) Pythagoras' Theorem is true.

(P2) Pythagoras' Theorem = the proposition that the square on the hypotenuse is equal to the sum of the squares on the other two sides.

(C)   Therefore, the proposition that the square on the hypotenuse is equal to the sum of the squares on the other two sides is true.

Surely we do not want to condemn this nice little argument as an example of the fallacy of equivocation. As it stands, Frege's Redundancy Thesis can at best

---

[66] This is a point on which Davidson and Rorty agree: cf. Rorty, 'Is Truth a Goal of Enquiry? Davidson vs. Wright', 287; and Davidson, 'Is Truth a Goal of Inquiry? Discussion with Rorty', 17–18.

[67] Notice that here, and in the remainder of this chapter, I use the term 'truth declaration' to refer to sentences whose surface grammar suggests that they are ascriptions of truth. Unfortunately, 'truth declaration' has a certain ceremonial air which makes it less than ideal, but it may help us to avoid begging the question against those who deny that truth is a property.

[68] Cf. Davidson, 'True to the Facts', 38–9; Horwich, *Truth*, 39, 125, 141–2.

hold of the conclusion, not of the first premiss, and I hope to have convinced you that there are good reasons to doubt its plausibility even there. Ramsey was acutely aware that the use of 'true' in propositionally unrevealing contexts provides adherents of the Redundancy Thesis with a serious challenge. (We will consider his way of meeting the challenge in Chapter 6.2.2.) The nihilists who I am now about to interrogate are also ready to face this problem. We can bring the task they have set themselves into focus by completing the Frege quotation I gave on p. 34. It is worth completing for another reason as well: the continuation of [B] in that passage contains Frege's own example for propositionally unrevealing truth talk.

[B] . . . *Und doch! ist es nicht ein großer Erfolg, wenn nach langem Schwanken und mühsamen Untersuchungen der Forscher schließlich sagen kann: 'was ich vermutet habe, ist wahr'?* [. . . And yet is it not a great result when the scientist after much hesitation and laborious research can finally say 'My conjecture is true'?]

[C] *Die Bedeutung des Wortes 'wahr' scheint ganz einzigartig zu sein. Sollten wir es hier mit etwas zu tun haben, was in dem sonst üblichen Sinne gar nicht Eigenschaft genannt werden kann? Trotz diesem Zweifel will ich mich zunächst noch dem Sprachgebrauch folgend so ausdrücken, als ob die Wahrheit eine Eigenschaft wäre, bis etwas Zutreffenderes gefunden sein wird.* [The meaning of the word 'true' seems to be altogether unique. May we not be dealing here with something which cannot, in the ordinary sense, be called a property at all? In spite of this doubt I want first to express myself in accordance with ordinary usage, as if truth were a property, until something more adequate is found.] (*'Der Gedanke'*, 61)

The nihilists' task is exactly this: to find something more adequate.[69]

2.2 Truth-Theoretical Nihilism

Nihilists declare that, even under the most generous reading of 'property', truth is not a property. Under that reading, (almost) every genuine predicate is such that its nominalization can be used to refer successfully to a property. Let me explain. A *predicate*, whether genuine or not, is a sentence-forming operator on

[69] Let me add a few comments on the role of the concept of truth in Frege's Concept Script as explained in *Grundgesetze der Arithmetik*. In the formulation of *every* assertion in this language the horizontal, or content stroke, is present. It can be read as 'is the True' (see *Grundgesetze* I, §5). (An assertoric use of 'The moon is round', for example, is formulated thus: ⊢The moon is round. The prefixed vertical, or judgement stroke, represents assertoric force.) Hence one cannot understand any assertion in this language without understanding 'is the True'. The horizontal does not add to the sense of what follows it, *provided that* it is followed by a sentence. It can also be applied to singular terms like 'the moon'. (In Frege's Concept Script '——the moon' expresses a false proposition, and the conditional with '——the moon' as antecedent and '——the sun' as consequent expresses a true proposition.) But, of course, the sense of 'the moon' is not the same as that of '——the moon': the former term does not express a thought. So not even 'is the True' as used in Frege's logical notation complies with *all* his claims about the concept of truth. Cf. Burge, 'Frege on Truth', esp. 128–31, 144–6; Stepanians, *Frege und Husserl*, chs. 2–3.

singular terms. By *nominalizing* a predicate, one transforms it into an abstract singular term, e.g. 'is stupid' into 'stupidity', 'is courageous' into 'courage', 'is a friend of' into 'friendship', 'is a philosopher' into 'being a philosopher', 'exist(s)' into 'existence', or 'is true' into 'truth'. A fragment of a natural language sentence S is a *genuine* predicate, a predicate in the logical sense, just in case a formalization of S in the language of first-order predicate logic would be correct if that fragment were replaced by a predicate letter. Properties that are designated by nominalizations of genuine polyadic predicates are relations.[70]

Focusing on syntactically simple monadic predicates, we can explain the prodigal conception of properties as follows: From a premiss of the form

(P)   a is (an) F,

in which 'F' is replaced by an adjective or a noun, we can infer its pleonastic equivalent

(C)   a has the property of being (an) F,

and similarly, from a premiss of the form

(P*)   a Vs,

in which 'V' is replaced by a verb, we can infer its more verbose counterpart

(C*)   a has the property of Ving (of being an entity that Vs),

provided the predicates in (P) and (P*) are genuine (and don't engender paradox[71]). Thus, from a sentence in which no property is designated, one deduces a sentence that contains a designator of a property.[72] If one is inclined to take such steps to be a conceptual matter of course, one endorses the prodigal conception of a property that is pertinent in this chapter.

The concept of a property which is explained in terms of a predicate's being genuine is very broad indeed. The expression 'is red or green' is a genuine predicate.[73] But to Australian ontologists it seems laughable to say that blood and grass share

---

[70] If a predicate is indexical (e.g. 'will arrive tomorrow', 'is in love with you', 'is a foreigner'), its nominalization designates a property only with respect to a given context. I suppress relativization to context, since it is not pertinent in the case that interests us.

[71] The bracketed proviso, and the '(almost)' at the beginning of the previous paragraph, will be explained in a minute.

[72] Apart from the 'genuineness' proviso, this is what Stephen Schiffer calls a 'something-from-nothing transformation': from a sentence in which no entity of kind K is designated we deduce a sentence in which such an entity is designated (Schiffer, 'A Paradox of Meaning', 304–8, *The Things We Mean* (henceforth *TWM*), ch. 2.3).

[73] We can replace it by a predicate letter when formalizing, for example, the following argument: 'Whatever is red or green is coloured. The sheet is red or green. Therefore, the sheet is coloured.'

the property of being red or green.[74] Or take the expression 'is grue', defined à la Nelson Goodman: 'x is grue = Df. x is green before t_0, or x is blue at or after t_0'.[75] This is a genuine predicate, so grueness is a property. But friends of a more parsimonious conception of a property tend to find this rather gruesome. Suppose 'grue' applies to a certain screen because, before t_0, it was green all over. Then 'grue' remains true of the screen even if it has been white ever since. Certainly, there is a reading of 'property' under which it would be bizarre to claim that the screen's still being an instance of 'grue' entails that it has preserved at least one of its (accidental) properties.[76] Finally, a property in the broad sense is something you may first have and then lack without yourself having changed. Take the expression 'is sadly missed': it is a genuine predicate, so being sadly missed is a property. But you may acquire and lose this property without yourself changing, and this development might even occur at a time when you are no longer alive.[77]

But since not every predicate is a genuine predicate, even this prodigal notion of a property excludes some contenders, most famously existence: the predicate in 'Tame tigers exist' isn't a genuine predicate, because in the formalization of this sentence it would be replaced by the existential quantifier; hence the term 'existence' (taken as the nominalization of the predicate 'exist' as used in this sentence) does not designate a property. (It is to Kant's famous dictum that 'existence is not a real predicate' that Grover, Camp, and Belnap are alluding in their tongue-in-cheek remark which serves as the epigraph to this chapter. That remark even mimicks what is potentially confusing in the original: for us, the point at issue is whether the *expressions* 'exist(s)' and 'is true' are genuine predicates.[78]) Here is a very different kind of example. The expression 'was so-called because of his size' clearly is a predicate: it takes a singular term, such as 'Little John' (the name of one of Robin Hood's companions), to form a sentence. But it is not a genuine predicate, because it could not correctly be replaced by a predicate letter. So there is no such thing as the property of being so-called because of his size. Let us postpone (for a while) the question for what reasons logicians refuse to treat either of these predicates as a genuine predicate.

I still owe you an explanation of the bracketed proviso concerning paradox-infected predicates. In the overwhelming majority of cases, whenever 'is F' is a genuine predicate, the step from (*P*) to (*C*) is valid.[79] But, notoriously, some instances

---

[74] David Armstrong, *A Theory of Universals*, 20.

[75] Cf. Goodman, *Fact, Fiction, and Forecast*, pt. III, sect. 4.   [76] Armstrong, *A Theory of Universals*, 31.

[77] This is a topic that will occupy us in Ch. 5.2.3.

[78] For the dictum, see Kant, *Kritik der reinen Vernunft*, B 626 ('*Sein ist offenbar kein reales Prädicat*'); for the punctilious comment, see Moore, 'Is Existence a Predicate?', 115–16.

[79] Advocates of a more parsimonious conception of properties may want to replace this move by an inference of the form: *a is F ∴ a is F because of some property, or some properties, a has*. But we are here concerned with the prodigal conception.

of this move lead into trouble. Some people are courageous, but, whatever Plato may have thought, courage is not the sort of thing that could be courageous. Some properties, such as imperceptibility and self-identity, do exemplify themselves, but

(P₁)   Courage is a property that does not exemplify itself.

Applying the standard move to this premiss, we obtain the innocent-looking conclusion

(C₁)   Therefore, courage has *the property of being a property that does not exemplify itself.*

But what are we to say about the property apparently designated by the italicized description in (C₁)? Does it exemplify itself? If it does, it doesn't, and if it doesn't, it does; which is logically equivalent to a contradiction. This result is standardly taken to show that the predicate in (P₁) does not signify a property.[80] The very paradoxicality of the paradox is due to our inclination to endorse all inferences of the form '(*P*) ∴ (*C*)' as a conceptual matter of course. In problematic cases we may have to resist this inclination, but this does not discredit standard inferences of that form as invalid. So let us bracket this problem, and return to nihilism.

According to nihilists, the predicate 'is true' is not a genuine predicate. So, in a way, they want to convince us that nothing, no thing, is true. Nihilists deem any attempt to tell us what all and only truths have in common to be fundamentally misguided: if 'is true' isn't a genuine predicate, we cannot explain truth talk by a universal biconditional '∀x (x is true ↔ …x…)', for the left-hand side is only well formed if 'is true' is a genuine predicate. Let us now look at an early version of truth-theoretical nihilism.

2.2.1   *The performative potential of 'true'*

'Truth is…not a property', Peter Strawson maintained in his first paper on the concept of truth.[81] His point of departure was Ramsey's propositional identity claim:

'It is true that Caesar was murdered' means no more than that Caesar was murdered, and 'It is false that Caesar was murdered' means that Caesar was not murdered. They are

---

[80] Two examples out of many: my *Abstrakte Gegenstände*, 100, following the footsteps of Castañeda and Wolterstorff; and Schiffer, *TWM*, ch. 2.3. Perhaps one could also take the paradox to show that the predicate in (P₁) signifies a property with respect to which the attempt to answer an apparently reasonable question leads to inconsistency. In any case, assuming that the predicate in (P₁) does not signify a property no more *solves* the paradox than assuming that 'Liar' sentences do not express propositions solves the 'Liar' antinomy. For both these points, see Hofweber, 'Inexpressible Properties and Propositions', sect. 3.3. (Actually, Kurt Grelling's original 1908 version of the paradox can be spelt out in a way that does not take recourse to properties: cf. its elegant rendering in the title essay of Quine's *The Ways of Paradox*, 4–5.)

[81] Strawson, 'Truth' (1949), 262.

phrases which we sometimes use for emphasis or for stylistic reasons, or to indicate the position occupied by the statement in our argument. (Ramsey, 'Facts and Propositions', 38)[82]

Like Ramsey, the early Strawson held that a speaker who assertively utters either of the following three sentences

(A)   Caesar was murdered
(B)   It is true that Caesar was murdered
(C)   That is true [said in response to an assertoric utterance of (A)]

does not make a statement to the effect that something has the property of being true: in assertively uttering (B) or (C), we state nothing over and above what is stated in an assertive utterance of (A). But then, why are we not always ready to tolerate substitution of (B) for (A)? Surely it would be rather odd to use (B) when one wished to inform somebody about the way Caesar died or to answer a query on this matter. Strawson's positive account of 'the actual use of the word "true" '[83] can be described as spelling out what is only hinted at in the second half of Ramsey's remark.

Let us start with (C). Suppose you assert (A). If I were to react by (assertively) repeating (A), I would be open to the charge of parroting. I can easily avoid it by using (C). But no matter whether I use (A) or (C), Strawson contended, I am not talking about what you said. What then *am* I doing, over and above asserting what you asserted, in responding to your utterance by saying (C)?

I am agreeing with, endorsing, underwriting what you said; and, unless you had said something, I couldn't perform *these* activities, though I could *make the assertion* you made. ('Truth' (1949), 269)

If this is correct, then under certain circumstances

(C⁵)   I endorse that

is an entirely appropriate substitute for (C). Now to *say* 'I endorse that' (in the right circumstances) *is* to make an endorsement. So here the performative potential of 'true' comes to the fore: sometimes the point of the utterance of a truth declaration can be captured by the utterance of an *explicitly performative* formula in Austin's

---

[82] Putting this into Fregean terms, it amounts to the claim that 'p' and 'It is true that p' differ only with respect to *colouration*. On pp. 50–1 we saw why this is no option for Frege: if the truth operator contributes only a 'colouration' to the content of an utterance, its contribution is not *always* present when an assertoric sentence is uttered. Being in principle eliminable is a defining feature of colouration.

[83] 'Truth' (1949), 260. (Unlike Strawson's second essay with the same title, in 1950, which was his contribution to the symposium with Austin, the first one is not contained in his *Logico-Linguistic Papers*. The homonymy of these essays has caused some confusion in the literature.)

sense, a first-person present-tense sentence with the main verb 'V', whose utterance (under appropriate circumstances) *is* an act of Ving.

It is due to his account of (C) that Strawson's early position has been dubbed 'the *amen* theory of truth'. This nick-name is rather appropriate: the expression 'amen' does not consist of a grammatical subject and a grammatical predicate, so there is hardly any temptation to say that in ending a prayer by saying 'amen', one is talking about what was said before. In the case of (C), because of its grammatical surface-structure, the temptation is far stronger, but Strawson wants us to resist it here, too.

Other uses of 'true' call for a different description. Assertive utterances of sentences like (B) are often followed by a but-clause. What is the producer of such an utterance of (B) doing, over and above asserting that Caesar was murdered?

> The words 'It's true that...but...' could, in these sentences, be replaced by the word 'Although'; or alternatively, by the words 'I concede that...but...' This use of the phrase, then, is concessive. ('Truth' (1949), 275)

In a manuscript (which was to be published many years after Strawson wrote his article), Ramsey had made the very same point about the use of this binary connective:

> We can use it rather like 'although' in conceding a point but denying a supposed consequence. 'It is true that the earth is round, but still...' (*On Truth*, 12)

If this is correct, then (B) could be replaced (in the context under discussion) by

(B^s)   Caesar was murdered. I concede that.

Since to *say* 'I concede that' (in the right circumstances) *is* to make a concession, this is another manifestation of the performative potential of 'true'. So far, Strawson's main positive contention is this: in assertively uttering truth declarations like (B) or (C), we are not *just* asserting that things are thus-and-so (e.g. that Caesar was murdered); we are also doing something else—endorsing what somebody said, for example, or conceding what somebody might say. (The claim that one and the same utterance is an instance of two different kinds of speech-act is not in itself problematic: after all, an utterance of 'There is a bull in that field' may be both an assertion and a warning.) The performative aspect which distinguishes an assertive utterance of (B) from an assertive utterance of (A) explains, Strawson would contend, why it would be odd to use (B) when one wished to inform somebody about the way Caesar died or to answer a query on this matter.

There is a striking resemblance between Strawson's account of the use of 'true' in (B) and (C) and the expressivist account of moral discourse as presented by Ayer:[84]

The presence of an ethical symbol in a proposition adds nothing to its factual content. Thus if I say to someone, 'You acted wrongly in stealing that money,' I am not stating anything more than if I had simply said, 'You stole that money.' In adding that this action is wrong I am not making any further statement about it. I am simply evincing my moral disapproval of it. (*Language, Truth and Logic*, 142)

Here is one possible way of developing this claim: in assertively uttering sentences like

(E) You acted wrongly in stealing that money
  You acted rightly in giving him some money

or, paratactically,

  You stole that money. That was wrong
  You gave him some money. That was right

I only seem to be ascribing the property of wrongness, or of rightness, to somebody's action, for I might just as well say:

(Eª) You stole that money. I reprove you for this.
  You gave him some money. I praise you for this.

This theory has been called the *boo-bravo* theory of (what seem to be) ascriptions of wrongness or rightness. Again, the nick-name is quite apt: 'Boo!' and 'Bravo!' do not consist of a grammatical subject and a grammatical predicate, so there is hardly any temptation to say that in finishing my report on your deed by using one of these interjections, I should be ascribing a property to what you did.

How did Strawson account for truth talk in which what is said to be true is *not revealed*?[85] His paradigm case was

(D) What the policeman stated is true.

---

[84] This analogy has been noticed before. See Boghossian, 'The Status of Content', 162. (Boghossian goes on to argue that there is a tension between Ayer's nihilist account of truth and his expressivist view of moral discourse: op. cit. 163–6. But it is hard to see why the contrast Ayer wants to draw between moral and 'factual' discourse can *only* be drawn if one takes the truth operator as applied to the latter type of discourse to be propositionally non-redundant.)

[85] As we shall see in Ch. 6.2.2, at this point Strawson moved far away from Ramsey. Contrary to what Horwich says (*Truth*, 39), the performative theory does not 'address only' propositionally revealing truth ascriptions. (This error is less surprising when one notices that Horwich does not refer to Strawson's pertinent 1949 article, but only to the homonymous paper of 1950 (cf. *Truth*, 38, 153).)

As a first step he maintained that assertive utterances of such a sentence 'may be regarded as involving an implicit meta-statement':[86]

(d)   The policeman made a statement.

Apart from making this meta-statement, what else may a speaker be doing by assertively uttering (D)?

> What is this additional performance? Consider the circumstances in which we might use the expression [(D)]. . . . Uttered by a witness, the sentence is a *confirmation*; wrung from the culprit, it is an *admission*. No doubt there are other cases. . . . To complete the analysis, then, of the entire sentence [(D)], we have to add, to the existential meta-assertion [i.e. (d)], a phrase which is not assertive. . . . We might, e.g., offer, as a complete analysis of one case, the expression:
>
> (D^s)   'The policeman made a statement. I confirm it';
>
> where, in uttering the words 'I confirm it', I am not describing something I do, but doing something. Cf. also 'I admit it.' To *say* this *is* to make an admission. ('Truth' (1949), 272–3; bracketed letters inserted)

Is Strawson's so-called 'performative theory of truth' adequate?[87] Let us split this question into three: (1) Are Strawson's descriptions of (some of) the uses of 'true' correct as far as they go? (2) How much light do they throw on the concept of truth? Do they elucidate the linguistic meaning (conventional significance) of 'true'? (3) Can they only be accommodated if one denies that truth is a property?

[1] There is some reason to doubt that Strawson's account of the uses of 'true' (even in unembedded sentences) casts the net wide enough. All the speech-acts he mentions as activating the performative potential of truth declarations— endorsing, conceding, confirming, admitting, etc.—share the following

---

[86]   Strawson, 'Truth' (1949), 273.

[87]   Alluding to 'Truth' (1950), Brandom describes Strawson's performative theory, somewhat confusingly, as an account focusing on 'the redundancy of force', where 'force' is supposed to mean what it means in Frege (*Making It Explicit* (henceforth *MIE*) 288, 299, 682). He then goes on to ascribe the performative theory to William James (287–90). Now admittedly, James's conception of truth is rather hard to pin down, but Brandom does not bother at all to back up his rather idiosyncratic reading. On p. 681 the reader is simply given a reference to '*Pragmatism* (Cambridge: 1978), bound with its sequel, *The Meaning of Truth*' and to Rorty's paper 'Pragmatism, Davidson, and Truth'. If you look up this article, you find that Rorty does not support the 'performative' reading by referring to any specific passages in James either, but rather by a respectful allusion to Brandom's forthcoming work which 'saves Dewey's [sic] intentions' (335). I get dizzy from this merry-go-round, I must confess. (For my own, far less creative, effort to understand James, cf. Ch. 7.1.3, Postscript. For a well-documented attempt at combining early Strawson and Dewey, cf. Gertrude Ezorsky, 'Truth in Context'.)

feature: if you perform such an act, you *commit* yourself to the content of a certain (actual or merely envisaged) utterance. Now, when you assertively utter (D), you may, unlike the witness and the culprit described by Strawson, not know what the policeman stated. You may state that D because you believe, strangely enough, that policemen always speak the truth, or because you think, what is more likely, that the policeman you are referring to always speaks the truth, or that a policeman in those circumstances could not but have spoken the truth. Suppose you now learn, to your surprise, that the policeman actually said, 'Most immigrants are potential criminals', and (as is to be hoped) this discovery immediately makes you withdraw your rash statement that D. You do not thereby withdraw your commitment to what the policeman said, since you were not committed to it in the first place.[88]

[2] The 'performative theory of truth', on the assumption that it was intended to give an account of the linguistic meaning of 'true', multiplies meanings beyond necessity. First, (D⁵) does not have the same meaning as '. . . I admit it', but it is very implausible to assume that (D) has a different meaning in the mouth of the culprit than it has in the mouth of the witness. The same holds, *mutatis mutandis*, for sentences like (B) and (C). Secondly, the theory applies at best to uses of the word 'true' within a declarative sentence. But this word occurs also as part of *non-declarative* sentences:

(F)   Is it true that Caesar was murdered?
(G)   If only it were true that Caesar was murdered!

In utterances of (F) or (G) one does not activate the performative potential of 'true': one does not endorse, concede, confirm, admit, etc. what is stated in an assertive utterance of (A). But if 'true' had different linguistic meanings in (F) and (B), say, then it would be hard to understand how an utterance of (B) can serve as an answer to a question expressed by (F). Finally, and this is the standard objection,[89] the theory cannot even account for all uses of 'true' in utterances of declarative sentences, since 'true' also occurs in *embedded* sentences, as in

(H)   If it is true that Caesar was murdered, then a civil war is most likely
(I)   Most historians believe that it is true that Caesar was murdered.

---

[88] This was Paul Grice's argument in 'Logic and Conversation', 55–6. For further worries about Strawson's early account of unrevealing truth talk, cf. Soames, *UT*, 235–6.

[89] This objections has its roots in Frege (see, e.g., '*Der Gedanke*', top of p. 63), and it was applied to the 'performative theory' by Geach (in 'Ascriptivism', 252–3) and Searle (in 'Meaning and Speech Acts'). Cf. Brandom, *MIE*, 297 ff., and Soames, *UT*, 237–8. The latter points out that David Ross used an analogous argument against the 'expressivist' view of moral discourse: *The Foundations of Ethics*, 33–4.

Certainly we do not activate the performative potential of 'true' in assertively uttering (H) or (I). Again, on the assumption that the theory was intended to give an account of the meaning of 'true', it multiplies meanings of 'true' beyond endurance: it is forced to condemn clearly valid arguments like

> If it is true that Caesar was murdered, then a civil war is most likely.
> It is true that Caesar was murdered.
> Therefore, a civil war is most likely.

as committing the fallacy of equivocation, because the same truth declaration occurs first embedded and then free-standing.

[3] The anti-nihilist assumption that truth *is* a property is perfectly compatible with an acknowledgement of the fact that many uses of 'true' really have the performative aspect Strawson attributes to them. In asserting 'You are an idiot', one may insult somebody, and such a feat is performed *by ascribing to the addressee a certain property.* Similarly, in an assertive utterance of sentences such as (C) or (B), one endorses, concedes, confirms, admits, etc. something *by ascribing to it the property of being true.*[90] This marks an important *difference* between those sentences and their counterparts (C^s) and (B^s), which should be as carefully registered as the similarity pointed out by Strawson. (I think the same holds, *mutatis mutandis*, in the case of moral discourse: in asserting 'You acted wrongly in stealing that money', the speaker reproves the addressee *by* ascribing the property of being wrong to his action, and this marks an important difference between that sentence and 'You stole that money. I reprove you for this.') So one can consistently acknowledge the performative potential of 'true' while rejecting truth-nihilism.

Let me summarize (part of) this criticism by using Strawson's own words:

In my earliest writings on this subject I made a mistake which I excluded from subsequent ones.[91] The mistake arose from confining my attention to positive assertions to the effect that some proposition was true and thus being trapped into declaring that all uses of 'true' were instances of such speech-acts as confirming or endorsing or conceding etc. It was not wrong to draw attention to these uses of the word, but it was wrong not to distinguish this aspect of the *use* of the word from the question of its *sense* (thus perhaps encouraging confusion between them). This can be seen clearly enough, as

---

[90] See Austin, 'Truth', 133; Geoffrey Warnock, 'A Problem about Truth', 57–8. (Alston repeats this point: *RCT*, 43.)

[91] See Strawson, 'A Problem about Truth', 214 ff. The paper 'Truth' (1950) still contains some vestiges of the 'performative theory'.

several commentators have pointed out, from the fact that 'true' can also occur, without any change of sense, in, e.g., a conditional clause or in one of the limbs of a disjunction. ('Reply to Manricio Beuchot', 28)

[I have long come to admit that] truth is a genuine property, 'true' a genuine predicate. ('Reply to John Searle', 402)

It is noteworthy that neither Frege's reservations, nor Strawson's early opposition, against taking truth to be a property, were coupled with a metaphysical aversion against propositions. Strawson's point was not that in an utterance of 'I endorse (concede, confirm, admit, etc.) that' no reference to a proposition is made, but rather that in such an utterance we do not attribute a property to the proposition designated by the demonstrative (and the same was supposed to hold for 'That is true').

By contrast, the varieties of truth-theoretical nihilism to be considered in the remainder of this chapter are *reductionist*. We are offered (what these nihilists deem to be) content-preserving translations or paraphrases of our ordinary truth talk which neither contain a component designating a truth-value bearer (a proposition) nor a component signifying the property of being true.[92] The paraphrasability is taken to show that in truth declarations, contrary to surface appearances, no proposition is referred to and hence no property is ascribed to a proposition. But why should we suppose that the translation proffered by a nihilist is to be given priority over the original when it comes to characterizing the content they allegedly share? After all, the relation of having the same

---

[92] Reductionist truth-theoretical nihilism is sometimes seriously misrepresented in the literature. According to Horwich, 'self-styled "prosententialists" such as Grover et al. and Brandom...tend to suppose that "is true" should be analysed using substitutional quantification—roughly speaking, that "x is true" means "$\forall p ((x = \text{the proposition that } p) \rightarrow p)$".' (*Truth*, 125; cf. 26). A brief look at the epigraph at the start of this chapter suffices to see that this is not even a 'roughly' correct representation of a 'tendency' on their part. Horwich describes prosententialists, of all people, as champions of the claim that 'true' is an analysable genuine predicate of propositions. As to substitutional quantification 'SQ' for short, Christopher Williams, who is not mentioned by Horwich, *says* he champions it (*What is Truth?* (henceforth *WIT*), 11), but as a matter of fact he doesn't, for he allows an existential quantification to be true even if it has no true substitution-instance (ibid., 14). Grover explicitly calls the SQ-reading of sentential quantifiers a 'version of the prosentential theory' to be compared with other versions (*PrTh*, 26 n. 34, 222, 231). Brandom comes out strongly in favour of what he calls SQ (see *MIE*, chs. 6–7), but he proposes a rather non-standard variant: cf. his 'From Truth to Semantics' and 'Reply to Tomberlin'. According to Alston's account of Williams's theory, a statement such as 'What Percy said is true' is analysed as 'There is exactly one p such that Percy said that p, and p.' Alston adds that such formulations 'clearly...use substitutional quantification' (*RCT*, 45). I do not find this clear at all. Substitutionally understood, the alleged analysans can only be true in the very unlikely case that there is exactly one English sentence that captures what Percy said. But what Percy said may very well be true, even though 'Percy said that Ben and Ann are happy' and 'Percy said that Ann and Ben are happy' capture equally well what he said. The interpretation of SQ will become an issue in Ch. 6.2.3.

content is symmetrical. So why shouldn't we say that when the proffered paraphrase is used to make a statement the speaker is really, contrary to surface appearances, attributing the property of being true to a proposition?[93] At this point, the nihilists we are now going to confront tend to praise the demythologizing power of their translations. They break the spell of some age-old metaphysical mysteries, we are told. Brandom gives voice to an attitude that is common to all advocates of reductionist truth-nihilism when he says about the camp he himself belongs to:

> A feature dear to the hearts of the prosententialists is the metaphysical parsimony of the theory. For what in the past were explained as attributions of a special and mysterious property (truth) to equally mysterious bearers of truth (propositions) are exhibited instead as uses of grammatical proforms anaphorically referring only to sentence tokenings that are their antecedents. (*MIE* 302–3)[94]

(The technical details here alluded to will be explained in due course.) We should keep the promise of demythologization firmly in mind when we consider the way adherents of reductionist nihilism try to elucidate our common truth talk.

2.2.2 *Introducing 'somewhether' and 'thether'*

The central tenet of Christopher Williams's variety of nihilism is this:[95]

> [NIHILISM$_W$] A certain *variant* of English, which contains neither 'true' nor any synonym thereof but which is enriched by a prosentence and a sentential quantifier, has the same expressive power as English.

As we shall see, Dorothy Grover also builds her account of truth around the concept of a prosentence. She even calls her account 'A Prosentential Theory of Truth', but the title would be equally appropriate for Williams's rather different view. (In Chapter 6.2 it will turn out that the concept of a prosentence is important not only for nihilists.)

In order to introduce this concept, I need some grammatical stage-setting. (On the whole, questions of grammar have to loom large in the remainder of this chapter, for nihilists claim to have traced a fundamental philosophical mistake to a grammatical confusion. So I ask the reader to bear with me when it seems as though I am embarking on nothing more than exercises in grammar.) If in your utterance of the sentence

(1)   Ann is fond of *Vienna*, and Ben is fond of *Vienna*

---

[93] This question is posed in Alston, *RCT*, 48–51.

[94] Cf. Williams, *WIT*, 1, 32, 55; Grover, *PrTh*, 103, 137.

[95] Williams, *WIT*, and (more easily digestible) *Being, Identity, and Truth* (henceforth *BIT*), ch. 5.

you refer twice to the same town, you could have saved a bit of breath or ink by using (what Geach calls) a pronoun of laziness:[96]

(1a)   Ann is fond of *Vienna*, and Ben is fond of *it*.

The pronoun picks up the referent of its antecedent for which it deputizes. (As we shall see, this talk of pronouns of laziness is a bit too lazy. But the refinement can wait till the last section of this chapter.)

The pronoun 'it' plays a very different role when we infer from (1) by existential generalization:

(2)   Ann is fond of *something*, and Ben is fond of *it*.

Here the word 'it' is a quantificational pronoun. According to (2) it is not only the case that there is something Ann is fond of and something Ben is fond of, but that there is at least *one* thing they are *both* fond of. A semiformal paraphrase makes this abundantly clear:

(2*) $\exists x$ (Ann is fond of x & Ben is fond of x).

Now in (1) we are not only told that Ben has an attitude towards the same object as Ann, but also that she has the same attitude towards that object. So we can easily save even more breath and ink by saying

(1b)   Ann is *fond of Vienna*, and *so* is Ben.

Here the proform 'so' deputizes not for a name, but for a predicate: it is not a pronoun, but rather a pro-predicate of laziness. (For the sake of euphony, and only in the present context, I am using 'predicate' in the pre-Fregean sense of 'general term'.) Now in ordinary language we can also quantify into predicate position: (1) implies not only (2) but also

(3)   Ann is *something*, and Ben is *so*, too

where 'so' is a quantificational propredicate. According to (3) there is something Ann and Ben both are. Semiformally this becomes

(3*) $\exists F$ (Ann is F & Ben is F).

Let us terminologically distinguish the quantifiers in (2*) and (3*) by calling the former 'nominal' and the latter 'predicational'. This terminology alludes to the substitution range of the variables bound by the quantifier in question: in

---

[96] Initially characterized by Geach as 'a grammatical dodge to avoid inelegant repetition of words' (*Logic Matters*, 89)

(2*) names and other singular terms, and in (3*) predicates.[97] (Once again, 'predicate' is used in the old-fashioned sense, for in (3) and (3*) the copula 'survives' the quantification.)

All this was only by way of prelude. It is time to get closer to truth talk. Consider

(4)   Ann says that Vienna is large, and Ben says that Vienna is large.

Assuming that both speakers are talking about the same Vienna, we can shorten this to:

(4a)   Ann says that Vienna is large, and Ben says so, too.

And by existential generalization we can infer from (4):

(5)   Ann says something, and Ben says so, too.

If we understand the lazy 'so (too)' and the quantificational 'so (too)' in the last two sentences along the lines of (1a) and (2), then the proform is again a pronoun, the quantification is into name (singular term) position, and consequently the semiformal rendering would have to use what I have called a nominal quantifier:

(5*) $\exists$x (Ann says x & Ben says x).

But then, remember, in (3) we also used 'something' plus 'so', and yet *there* the quantification was clearly *not* into singular term position. So perhaps the nominal reading of the English sentence (5) is not obligatory. And even if it is, we may be able to reformulate (5) in a certain variant of English in such a way that the quantification is definitely not nominal.

In order to provide a paraphrase of (5) that is unmistakably a quantification into sentence position, we need a further kind of proform, a pro*sentence*, and another kind of quantifier, a *sentential* quantifier. In search of a helpful analogy, Williams considers quantifications into adverbial positions. From 'Ann lives in Oxford, and Ben lives in Oxford' we can infer 'Ann lives somewhere, and Ben lives there', and from 'Ann left at midnight, and Ben left at midnight' we can infer 'Ann left somewhen, and Ben left then.' In these conclusions we have quantificational pro-adverbs ('there', 'then') which are bound by non-nominal, adverbial quantifiers ('somewhere', 'somewhen').[98] Notice that these adverbial proforms and adverbial quantifiers rhyme

---

[97] In the following argument 'everything' is used as a predicational quantifier: 'Ann is everything Ben wants a friend to be. Ben wants a friend to be reliable. Therefore Ann is reliable.'

[98] Cf. Strawson, 'Singular Terms and Predicates', 72 n. 2; 'Positions for Quantifiers', 73–5; Prior, *OT*, 37. In 'A lives in Oxford, but B does not live *there*' and 'B left at midnight, but S did not leave *then*', we have pro-adverbs of *laziness*.

with certain interrogatives: 'there' and 'somewhere' with 'where?', 'then' and 'somewhen' with 'when?'. This observation inspired Arthur Prior to a neologism.[99] Declarative sentences can be used to answer yes-no questions. In English such questions are not introduced by a particular word, but are expressed by an inversion of word order. But in indirect speech we report such questions by using the word 'whether', and in Latin the word '*an*' is used both to ask such a question and to report it. So we could simply *concoct* the sentential quantifier 'somewhether' and the prosentence 'thether', which rhyme with the (indirect) interrogative 'whether?'. Exploiting Prior's playful suggestion, Williams reformulates sentences such as (4a) and (5) in a variant of English I shall call 'Prior-English'—or 'Prenglish' ('Pr') for short. The vocabulary of Prenglish includes neither 'true' nor any synonym of 'true', but it has two entries that are not to be found in any English dictionary: the prosentence 'thether' and the sentential quantifier 'somewhether'.

If we translate (4a) and (5) into this target-language, we obtain:

Pr(4a)   Ann says that *Vienna is large*, and Ben says that *thether*.

Pr(5)   Ann says that *somewhether*, and Ben says that *thether*.

In the former sentence 'thether' is a prosentence of laziness, in the latter a quantificational prosentence. (Again, laziness should not be overdone, but, as before, I postpone the needed refinement till the end of this chapter.)

In his 1976 book Williams used a variant of Prenglish which does not shy away from logical symbols. In that semiformal target-language, to which I shall refer as 'Loglish' ('L'), the message of Pr(5) is conveyed by

L (5) $\exists$p (Ann says that p .&. Ben says that p).[100]

Like Prior,[101] Williams wrote this in Polish notation, but I thought I should spare you this additional torment.

In Prenglish we can have quantification into all sentence positions, no matter whether free-standing or embedded. Thus from

(6)   Vienna is large, but Ann does not know that Vienna is large

we can infer that Ann is not omniscient:

Pr(7)   Somewhether, but Ann does not know that thether.

L (7) $\exists$p (p & $\neg$ (Ann knows that p)).

---

[99] Prior, 'Definitions, Rules and Axioms', 41; cf. *OT*, 37.

[100] On these pages I use the notation '.&.' in order to remove scope ambiguity. Thus in the case of L(5) it is meant to preclude the reading 'A says that (p & S says that p).

[101] In his use of sentential variables Prior followed the precedent of Leśniewski's 'Protothetic'.

Incidentally, contrary to what Williams says, it wasn't Prior who first used the term 'prosentence'.[102] Ramsey anticipated him,[103] and Franz Brentano had anticipated Ramsey.[104] Brentano also pointed out that in German '*ja*' is used as a prosentence (*Fürsatz*), and this observation can be easily adapted to (real) English as well. Here are two examples: 'Is it raining?' 'Yes.' (Notice that in this, and in the the the next, example, the prosentence acts as deputy for the declarative counterpart of its antecendent.) '*Regnet es? Wenn ja, so bleibe ich lieber hier*': in other words: 'Is it raining? If so, I'd rather stay here.' The advantage of Prenglish over English is that, unlike 'yes' and 'so', the prosentence 'thether' can be substituted for sentences (of the declarative type) in any context, and, unlike 'so', it can be substituted only for sentences.[105]

Williams burdens his theory with a certain syntactical hypothesis about English which Prior put forward. This hypothesis concerns sentences in which a verb of saying or thinking is followed by a that-clause. According to Prior[106] sentences like 'Ben said that it was snowing' are not to be parsed as 'Ben said / that it was snowing' but rather as 'Ben said that / it was snowing.' By thus shifting the parsing line a bit to the right we take such sentences to be formed from a syntactically heterogenous operator like '[ ] said that ( )' by inserting a name and a sentence (in this order). Since such operators are 'as it were predicates at one end and connectives at the other',[107] one might call them prenectives. According to Prior's parsing, the word 'that' goes with the verb, and the that-clause dissolves (thereby suffering from a somewhat similar fate as definite descriptions do under Russell's treatment). If Prior gets the syntax of English right, the sentence 'Ben said that it was snowing' contains the clause 'that it was

---

[102] Williams, *BIT*, 94 n. 2.   [103] Ramsey, *On Truth*, 10.

[104] Brentano, *Wahrheit und Evidenz*, 76 (65) [Sept. 1904]. This precursor is duly acknowledged in Grover et al., 'A Prosentential Theory of Truth' (henceforth 'Prosentential'), 85. (Unfortunately Brentano's German wording is misquoted, so the point of the acknowledgement gets completely lost.) Brentano's pupil Kazimierz Twardowski emphasized the fact that when asked whether p, one can always voice the judgement that p by saying, 'Yes'. See his 'On So-Called Relative Truths', 40–1. (The English translation does not quite preserve the point: 150.)

[105] As to the advantage of greater mobility, it suffices to recall Pr(4a), where 'yes' or 'so' could not do the job of 'thether', and as to the advantage of univocity, just remember our (1b) '. . . , and *so* is Ben', or consider 'She twitched *violently*, and while *so* twitching, expired' (Grover et al., 'Prosentential', 84).

[106] In the opening pages of 'Berkeley in Logical Form' Prior seems to have presented his syntactical hypothesis for the first time, but see especially 'Oratio Obliqua' and *OT* 16–21. Quine toys with the idea in *Word and Object* (henceforth *W&O*), 216, which earns him a somewhat backhanded compliment from Prior: 'This is . . . one of the two points in the philosophy of logic where Quine seems to me dead right' (*OT* 20). What is the other point? For a guess, see below p. 256 n. 19.

[107] Prior, *OT*, 19. Cf. Williams, *WIT*, ch. 1; *BIT*, sects. 1–2. Somewhat absurdly, Hugly and Sayward answer the question whether 'said that' is a predicate or a connective by saying: 'It is both' (*I&T*, 136).

snowing' not as a syntactical unit (let alone as a singular term designating a proposition), but only in the sense in which it also comprises the word-sequence 'said that it'. Consider a connective which results from inserting a name into the left slot of a prenective, e.g. 'Prior believes that'. In Prior's eyes the deep grammar of this phrase is the same as the surface grammar of 'in Prior's eyes': both belong to the category of sentence adverbials.

I think there are fairly strong syntactical objections against taking Priorese Syntax to be faithful to English.[108] Passive and cleft transformations preserve the attachment of 'that' to the sentence following it: we have 'That it was snowing was said by Ben' (but not 'It was snowing was said-that by Ben'), and 'What Ben said was that it was snowing' (but not 'What Ben said-that was it was snowing'). Furthermore, the insertion of parenthetical expressions between verb and 'that' is possible, but it is not acceptable immediately after 'that': we have 'Ben said—as you very well know—that it was snowing' (but not 'Ben said-that—as you very well know—it was snowing'). Nihilists like Williams would presumably retort that people who put forward this kind of consideration are in the grip of 'superficial grammar'. But taking things really to be as they seem to be is not always a symptom of shallowness. Williams correctly observes that the 'that' of *oratio obliqua* can often be removed without loss of sentencehood.[109] But he fails to notice that it is bound to reappear in passive and cleft transformations: thus 'Ben said it was snowing' does not go into 'It was snowing was said by Ben' nor into 'What Ben said was it was snowing'.

All this speaks in favour of the standard treatment of that-clauses in current linguistic theory: the word 'that' functions as a *complementizer*, i.e. it combines with a sentence to produce a special kind of syntactical unit, a *complement*. If that-clauses are not torn apart, then taking their replacement by 'it', 'everything', or 'something' to be a replacement by a pronoun and a nominal quantifier is a real option, and consequently an argument like

(A) Ann believes that Vienna is large,
      but Ben does not believe it;
      so Ben does not believe everything Ann believes

can be regarded as valid in the predicate calculus, for now we can assign to the conclusion of (A) the same quantificational structure as to 'Ben does not touch everything Ann touches,' namely $\neg\forall x\,(aRx \to bRx)$.[110] But then the quantificational structure of (5) can also be represented by (5*).

---

[108] Alan White, 'What We Believe', 80; Bede Rundle, *Grammar in Philosophy* (henceforth *GP*), 286–7; Kent Wilson, 'Some Reflections on the Prosentential Theory of Truth', 24.   [109] Williams, *BIT*, 88, 95.

[110] Cf. Parsons, 'On Denoting Propositions and Facts', 442–4, and the references to the linguistic and logical literature given there.

Actually, nihilists should not, and need not, rest their case on the assumption that Priorese Syntax is correct for English. They should, rather, take it as correct for that *variant* of English which they claim to have the same expressive power as English with its predicate 'true'.

The question whether *English* also permits quantification into sentence position is entirely independent of the question whether it complies with Priorese Syntax. Taking that-clauses to be genuine syntactical units does not, by itself, prevent you from quantifying into the position of the embedded sentence. After all, unity does not imply atomicity. Here is an analogy: Frege, unlike Russell, takes definite descriptions like 'The capital of Austria' to be genuine singular terms, so the inference 'The capital of Austria is a charming town, therefore $\exists x$ (x is a charming town)' is formally valid. But that does not stop Frege from quantifying into the position of the embedded name and to deduce from the same premiss '$\exists x$ (the capital of x is a charming town)'. Similarly, from 'A believes that Vienna is large' we may derive not only '$\exists x$ (A believes x)', but also '$\exists p$ (A believes that p)', if we can make sense of sentential quantification.

For the first three of these quantified conclusions we can easily provide translations from Loglish into English which preserve the quantificational structure, but can this be done at all for the last conclusion? I shall confront this question twice: with critical intent in the next sub-section 2.2.4 and with a positive proposal in the course of defending my own view in Chapter 6.2.3. For the moment, the question whether there is such a thing as sentential quantification in English can be put to one side.

Here, at last, is the crucial question: is Williams right in contending that Prenglish (or Loglish) has the same expressive power as English? Philosophers who deny the very intelligibility of sentential quantification would claim that Prenglish is at bottom incomprehensible. I suspect that this is an unjustified dogma of Quineanism. In any case, the alleged problem is not peculiar to nihilism, and I shall postpone its discussion, too, until it threatens to undermine my own position. Taking the comprehensibility of Prenglish for granted, let us examine Williams's main contention by considering a few test cases, first a propositionally revealing truth declaration and then some propositionally unrevealing ones. Of course, nihilists will not like my description of such test cases, since it suggests that truth talk is about propositions. Never mind the description: just look at the test cases. How do they fare with Williams?

When confronted with a propositionally *revealing* truth declaration such as

(R)   It is true that snow is white.

Williams first gives an English paraphrase which moves the that-clause behind a verb:

> What anyone who was to say that snow is white would thereby be saying is true.

Then he gets rid of 'true' by translating this into Prenglish or Loglish:

Pr(R)   Anyone who was to say that snow is white would thereby be saying that somewhether, and thether.

L (R)   ∃p (Anyone who was to say that snow is white would thereby be saying that p .&. p).

Somewhat surprisingly, Williams also embraces the Redundancy Thesis: 'we can simply lop off "It is true that" from [(R)] and it will make no difference to what we want to say',[111] But surely we do not have to exercise our concept of same-saying in order to understand an utterance of 'Snow is white.' So the content of such an utterance is not the same as that of an utterance of Pr(R) or L(R). Since nothing can be identical with two different things, Williams must make up his mind here. Let us assume that his considered view is that it makes no difference to what we want to say whether we use the English sentence (R) or its Prenglish or Loglish counterpart. Is this correct? The locution 'thereby say' makes for a problem. It seems that every speaker who was to say that Joyce wrote *Ulysses* but not *Dubliners* would thereby be saying, among other things, that Joyce wrote *Ulysses*. But then Williams's paraphrastic strategy is in trouble, for although it is not true that Joyce wrote *Ulysses* but not *Dubliners*, the alleged paraphrase is true, for there is a true substitution-instance of the matrix 'anybody who was to say that Joyce wrote *Ulysses* but not *Dubliners* would thereby be saying that p, and (indeed) p'. Williams could avoid this objection if he were to modify L(R) by inserting 'and vice versa' before '&'.[112] So let us proceed to our next question.

How does Williams explain propositionally *unrevealing* truth declarations? Explicitly quantified truth talk like

(Q)   Ann said something true

is not much of a challenge:

Pr(Q)   Ann said that somewhether, and thether

L(Q)   ∃p (Ann said that p .&. p).

---

[111] Williams, *BIT*, 101. Cf. Prior, *OT*, 11–12.

[112] As we will see a few pages further down, this emendation would be in tune with his use of the same-saying connective in L(T).

What about truth declarations that have a *name* (like 'Pythagoras' Theorem') for their grammatical subject? In Williams's books of 1976 and 1992 you will not find a single line about them.[113] But in an earlier paper he did consider this kind of truth talk briefly:

[E]xpressions like 'Utilitarianism' and 'the doctrine of transubstantiation'...function more or less like proper names. We do not, or should not, allow that a person understands what an expression of this sort refers to unless he can produce a proposition [sentence] which can express what it refers to: the sense of 'Tom believes in a', where 'a' is a referring expression of this sort, must also be expressible by a sentence of the form 'Tom believes that p.' Accordingly, with this sort of referring expression 'a is true' is always paraphrasable by a proposition [sentence] of the form 'It is true that p.' ('What does "X is true" say about X?', 124)[114]

If this were correct, then names of propositions would have the same sense as nominalizations of sentences expressing those propositions. Every substitution-instance of the following schema would yield a truth:

If a is the proposition that p then to say that *a is true* is to say that *it is true that p*,

and the problem with name-involving truth declarations would boil down to that of accounting, in Prenglish, for propositionally revealing ones. But is it correct? Let us for a moment put truth talk aside. Williams seems to be right in maintaining that you cannot 'believe in' the First Law of Thermodynamics, say, without believing that p_1 (where 'p_1', something like 'Energy is never created or destroyed', expresses that law). But as soon as we consider other examples, we see that Williams's contention jars with our practice of attitude (and indirect speech) reports. Suppose that in her teens Ann had listened to public lectures by Helmholtz. Half a century later, in 1930, she is willing to tell anyone who might be interested in her reminiscences: 'The First Law of Thermodynamics was often referred to in Helmholtz's lectures', but now she is unwilling to assert, 'The law that p_1 was often referred to in Helmholtz's lectures.' One could truly say about her:

(8)   Ann believes that the First Law of Thermodynamics was often referred to in Helmholtz' lectures, but she does not believe that the law that p_1 was often referred to in his lectures.

---

[113] The same glaring omission mars the authoritative study of Prior's work on truth and propositional attitude ascriptions: See Hugly and Sayward, *I&T*, cf. especially 60–1, 164, 333 (see 'category 3'), 340–5. Only once, forced by a quotation from Davidson, do they try their hands on a paraphrase of a sentence which contains the name 'the Pythagorean theorem' (164–5), and the result of their paraphrastic endeavours is equivalent to (Y), to be considered a few pages hence.

[114] Geach concurs: '[A]pparent names as "Fermat's Last Theorem"... are not names but mere abbreviations for *that* clauses' ('Truth and God', 94).

So the proposition that the First Law of Thermodynamics is thus-and-so is different from the proposition that the law that p_1 is thus-and-so.

Soames would disagree, and Evans's views about abstract singular terms suggest a question, so let me briefly digress here. Soames's argument is based on two premises: he takes names of propositions as well as that-clauses to be 'directly referential' terms, and he assumes that directly referential terms designating the same thing are intersubstitutable, outside quotational contexts, *salva veritate.* If 'logicism' and '(the proposition) that mathematics is reducible to logic' designate the same proposition, then, Soames maintains,[115] the truth of (9), taken as a *de dicto* belief-ascription, guarantees the truth of (10):

(9)   Ben believes that logicism was defended by Russell
(10) Ben believes that the proposition that mathematics is reducible to logic
      was defended by Russell.

I find Soames's comments on (9) eminently plausible: '[A] student attending his first lecture in the philosophy of mathematics... may be told that logicism is a proposition about the relationship between mathematics and logic, that formalism is a doctrine about the interpretation of mathematics, and so on. At this stage, the student may not be able to distinguish logicism from other propositions about the relationship between logic and mathematics.... Nevertheless, he may acquire beliefs about logicism. For example, he may be told, "Russell was a defender of logicism," and thereby acquire the belief that Russell defended logicism.'[116] The student described by Soames may also ask, 'What does logicism say about the relationship between mathematics and logic?' and thereby give voice to his curiosity concerning logicism. But he may not yet be able to grasp the proposition that mathematics is reducible to logic, because he has not yet acquired the concept of reducibility. But then, *pace* Soames, this student cannot be the Ben of (10): nobody can grasp the proposition Ben believes according to (10) without grasping the proposition that mathematics is reducible to logic, and nobody can grasp this proposition without having the concept of reducibility.[117] So something must be wrong with either or both of Soames's premises.

According to Evans, one has a 'fundamental Idea of an object' if and only if one knows a true answer to the question 'What differentiates that object from others?' Do I contradict Evans's contention that 'proper names of abstract objects are typically such that understanding them requires a fundamental Idea

---

[115] Soames, 'Semantics and Semantic Competence', 585.
[116] Ibid., 586. Cf. Saul Kripke, *Naming and Necessity*, 95; David Kaplan, 'Afterthoughts', 603.
[117] Cf. the reflections on 'mixed cases': See Ch. 5.1.2, example (R).

of the referent'?[118] In one respect, this is hard to say, since among his examples for such names there is none that (purportedly) designates a proposition, and one doesn't know which proper names of abstract objects Evans would regard as 'typical'. At any rate, Ben does have 'distinguishing knowledge' of logicism: it is that doctrine about the relationship between mathematics and logic which was referred to in yesterday's lecture as logicism. But this name-involving bit of knowledge seems to be parasitic rather than 'fundamental'. Ben, as described by Soames, is not able to distinguish logicism from other doctrines about the relationship between mathematics and logic *as regards their content.* So presumably Evans would have said that for the time being Ben has only a non-fundamental Idea of logicism. (Perhaps he would have regarded that-clauses as 'typical proper names' of propositions.) But this is compatible with my claims that (9) and (10) might differ in truth-value, or that (8) might be true.

Let us return to Ann and put truth into the picture. If in 1930 somebody had said about her:

(11)   Ann is convinced that *the First Law of Thermodynamics is true,* but she is not convinced that *it is true that* p_1,

he would have been right, for at that time (let us assume) she was still willing to use the first italicized sentence assertively, but no longer ready to use the second italicized sentence assertively. So, contrary to Williams's contention, to say that the First Law of Thermodynamics is true is *not* to say that it is true that p_1.

Williams's claim that one cannot understand the name of a proposition unless one is able to express this proposition seems to me as implausible as the contention that one cannot understand a man's name unless one is able to recognize him when one sees him.[119] But what cannot plausibly be said about names of propositions does hold of another type of terms that (ostensibly) designate propositions: whenever a sentence 'p' is free of context-sensitive elements, one cannot understand the term '(the proposition) that p' without being able to express the proposition it (apparently) stands for. As Russell might have put it, such a term is a *logically proper name* of a proposition, understanding it provides one with *knowledge by acquaintance* of a proposition. In this respect, 'the First Law of Thermodynamics' and 'logicism' are related to '(the proposition) that energy is never created or destroyed' and '(the proposition) that mathematics

---

[118] Evans, *Varieties of Reference,* 107.

[119] As to the normative variant of this claim (delicately intimated in the Williams quotation on p. 72 above), I cannot see a good reason for accepting it either. (Surely the fact that by following this recommendation we would spare Williams's theory some trouble does not count as a good reason.)

reduces to logic' respectively as 'alpha' is related to ' "α" '. You cannot understand the quotational designator without *eo ipso* knowing which object is
designated by it.[120]

In his later writings Williams no longer pursues the line he took in his 1969
paper, perhaps because he no longer accepts it. Unfortunately, in these writings
he is entirely silent on the topic. But his book on truth is (from the first to the
last page, mind you!) about another propositionally unrevealing truth declaration, namely

(T) What Percy says is true.

So I shall try to extrapolate from what he does say about (T) to what he might
say about those truth declarations that we are after. Let us take (T) to entail
uniqueness: 'The one and only thing Percy says (at the pertinent time) is true.'
Williams first offers a provisional paraphrase of this:

(X) $\exists$p (Percy says that p &
      $\forall$q (Percy says that q $\rightarrow$ (that p $=$ that q)) & p).

(Since Prenglish as described by Williams has only one prosentence and one sentential quantifier, its Loglish counterpart is better equipped to cope with sentences like (T). But of course, if we were to introduce a general quantifier and
subscripts into Prenglish, 'everywhether$_1$', 'somewhether$_2$', 'thether$_1$',
'thether$_2$', the resources would be equalized.) Now for Williams, (X) can be only
an intermediate step: in substitution-instances of the identity clause in (X) the
combination 'that' plus sentence seems to function rather as a bona fide singular term which, together with a bona fide predicate, could form a truly predicative truth declaration. For the nihilist, this appearance must be deceptive. So he
is bound to paraphrase the identity clause in (X) away. Williams suggests that
the point, which is made in identity clauses of the form 'that p $=$ that q' by
nominalization and the identity operator, can be captured by a connective:
'anyone who was to say that p would thereby be saying that q, and anyone who
was to say that q would thereby be saying that p.' Since this is rather cumbersome, let me abbreviate it thus: 'p $\Leftrightarrow$ q' (read: 'To say that p is to say that q').
Finally then, (T) goes into Loglish as

L(T) $\exists$p (Percy says that p & $\forall$q (Percy says that q $\rightarrow$ (p $\Leftrightarrow$ q)) & p).

Now let us try to cope along these lines with

(U) Pythagoras' Theorem is true.

---

[120] More about the topic of this paragraph in my *Abstrakte Gegenstände*, 170–96. See also Ch. 5.1.1.

As a first step, (U) would be transformed into

(Y) $\exists p$ (Pythagoras' Theorem $=$ that p .&. p).

Now a theorem cannot *say* anything, at least not in the way Percy does. And (U) is true although Pythagoras never said anything to the effect that the square on the hypotenuse is equal to the sum of the squares on the other two sides.[121] The trouble is that, unlike the definite description in (T), the grammatical subject of (U) does not contain any verb. In order to capture the point of identity clauses of the form 'x $=$ that p', where 'x' is a placeholder for names, Williams needs a syntactically heterogenous operator, something like 'anyone who was to express x would thereby be saying that p, and anyone who was to say that p would thereby be expressing x'. Abbreviating this prenective by 'Δ (x, p)', we obtain the following paraphrase of (U) into semiformal Prenglish:

L(U) $\exists p$ [Δ (Pythagoras' Theorem, p) & p].

This is scarcely a result an advocate of reductionist truth-theoretical nihilism can be happy with. After all, William contends:

> The word 'true' has the job . . . of satisfying the need of bogus subject-expressions for a bogus predicate. (*BIT* 85)

But L(U) obviously still contains a singular term which stubbornly resists Williams's paraphrastic endeavours. So there is nothing bogus about subject-expressions such as 'Pythagoras' Theorem'. Nor, it seems, about predicate-expressions such as 'is true'. We obtain a predicate from L(U) if we replace the singular term by a gap (or by a variable). So it rather looks as if L(U) saves the appearances: (U) really is what it seems to be—an application of a genuine predicate to a proposition, and L(U) is an honourable attempt to elucidate this predicate. Williams wanted his account of truth to steer clear of, as he puts it, mysterious entities called 'Propositions' or '*Sätze an sich*'.[122] But isn't this a bogus mystery by Williams's own lights? After all, in his attempt at explaining his favourite sentence 'What Percy says is true', he is ready to use the 'same-saying' connective '$\Leftrightarrow$'. So presumably he understands it. Now this connective is obviously hyper-intensional. (Necessarily, ABC is an equilateral triangle iff it is an

---

[121] Although they look like definite descriptions, substantival phrases like 'the Big Apple', which 'have grown capital letters', are proper names (Strawson, 'On Referring', 21). Thanks to Walter Burkert's work on ancient Pythagoreanism, the singular term in (U) has retired as a definite description and become a name. Pythagoras did believe in the transmigration of the soul, he did promote precepts like 'Abstain from beans!', but he did not discover the geometrical theorem that was named after him (nor any other).   [122] Cf. Williams, *WIT*, 1, 32, 55, *et passim*.

equiangular triangle, but surely it is not the case that anyone who was to say that ABC is an equilateral triangle would thereby be saying that it is an equiangular triangle.) If Williams understands this connective nevertheless, he must have already overcome most, if not all, Quinean worries about the lack of criteria of identity for propositions. But then, where is the mystery?

So in the end it seems to me that Williams made somewhat heavy weather of 'somewhether' and 'thether'. Perhaps we will find the American varieties of nihilism more convincing. So let us turn first to Grover and then to Brandom (whose theory is an offshoot of Grover's).

2.2.3 'True' as a syncategorematic expression

The central claim of Dorothy Grover's version of nihilism is this: [123]

[NIHILISM_G]   A certain *fragment* of English, in which the word 'true' occurs only within prosentences and within some sentential operators, has the same expressive power as English.

Grover's and Williams's varieties of nihilism were developed independently of each other, but, considering my representations of their views, one can imagine Grover telling Williams: 'You did not look hard enough, there *are* prosentences available in English that can be substituted for sentences in any context.' Well, where are they?

This time, our target language is a fragment of English in which 'true' does not appear *as a predicate* (general term). So sentences like 'What Ann says is true' or 'Ben's favourite hypothesis is true' are excluded. As you might have expected, or feared, I shall call Grover's target-language 'Grenglish' ('Gr'). Notice that the characterization of Grenglish I just gave does not imply that the word 'true' does not appear *at all* in the sentences of this language.

Suppose, Ann says,

(1)   Vienna is large,

and Ben agrees,

(2)   That is true.

One is inclined to hear Ben's remark as an utterance of a subject-predicate sentence. Thus understood, the demonstrative 'that' in his utterance of (2) is used

---

[123] The seminal paper 'A Prosentential Theory of Truth' was co-authored with Joseph Camp and Nuel D. Belnap. So, as far as 'Prosentential' is concerned, my references to her should be taken as *pars pro toto*.

to refer to what Ann said (the proposition that Vienna is large), and 'is true' is employed to ascribe truth to this object. Hence, under this reading, (2) is not a sentence of Grenglish. Now Grover pleads for a different reading of (2). She regards *the whole sentence* 'That is true' as a generally available prosentence of laziness.[124] If we understand this sentence as a prosentence, it no longer requires a subject-predicate analysis. Using the terminology of late medieval logicians, we might say that by Grover's lights 'true' is only a *syncategorematic*, or *consignificative*, component of 'that is true'. In Ben's utterance of (2) the prosentence deputizes for its antecedent, i.e. Ann's utterance of 'Vienna is large'. Hence nothing is referred to in the utterance of the prosentence which is not also referred to in its antecedent. After all, under Grover's reading of 'that is true', its utterance acquires all its content from its antecedent, so there cannot be any additional reference in 'that is true'.[125] (Here again, talk of laziness can be misleading, as we shall see in the last section.)

Notice two major differences between the prosentences in Prenglish and in Grenglish. In Prior's target-language the prosentence is atomic and an addition to English, whereas the prosentence in Grover's target-language is neither. Her insistence that 'true' is not an *isolable* part of prosentences[126] should not be mistaken for the claim that prosentences are semantically seamless wholes. (A comparison might help. The suffix of the name 'Mikhail*ovich*' isn't isolable either, and yet it makes a distinct contribution to what is grasped in understanding Russian patronyms.)

It is not easy to believe what Grover tells us about 'That is true.' Consider the following comments on a claim that has come under attack:

(T1)   That is true, so it cannot be inconsistent

(T2)   That is true, even if it is incompatible with a dogma of the church.

In (T1) and (T2) a predicative reading of the second sentence is obligatory. So how does the anaphoric subject-expression 'it' acquire its referent? From

---

[124] Grover points out that in many contexts '*it is true*' has an equal claim to be conceived of as a prosentence of laziness. For ease of exposition, I shall neglect this here.

[125] Horwich's sketch of Grover's idea of prosentences of laziness runs as follows: 'Just as one might use the pronoun "he" instead of repeating a name (as in "John said he was happy"), so one might say "That's true" instead of repeating the sentence just asserted. Evidently this is a perfectly correct observation as far as it goes. However ...' (*Truth*, 125). The comparison with pronouns of laziness is apt (and echoes Grover's own procedure), but the example chosen is inept. Since John may suffer from amnesia, 'John said he was happy' may express a truth, while 'John said John was happy' yields a falsehood. This kind of divergence is excluded when 'That is true' goes proxy for a declarative sentence just uttered. When Grover introduces the comparison, she uses examples like the pair (1)/(1a) in the previous section.

[126] Cf. 'Prosentential', 90.

the demonstrative in the first sentence of (T1) and (T2), one feels inclined to answer. But then, that sentence, too, is a predication, and its grammatical appearance does *not* belie its logical structure.[127]

Furthermore, is it really beyond doubt that an utterance of 'That is true' has the very same content as the utterance of its antecedent? Suppose Ann says, 'Atlantis was engulfed by the Atlantic Ocean', and Ben confirms, 'That's true'. If what she said falls into a truth-value gap, then, according to Grover's theory (and Leibniz's Law), what he said cannot but share the same destiny. But one might reasonably doubt this: didn't he say something *false*? In the case of the concocted prosentence of Prenglish, such doubt can be excluded by stipulation. More interestingly, in the case of the uncontroversially authentic prosentence 'Yes', it simply does not arise: if Ann asks, 'Was Atlantis engulfed by the Atlantic Ocean?' and Ben replies, 'Yes' (or 'Yes, it was'), his answer must receive the same valuation as the proposition expressed by the interrogative.[128] This difference can be explained if 'That's true' is used to ascribe a property to what is designated by the demonstrative. But of course, this explanation is not available to Grover.

Let us subdue all nagging doubts, at least for a while, and try to obtain a more complete picture of Grover's theory. So far, we have focused on one feature of Grenglish: its prosentence of laziness. What about quantificational prosentences? If Ben's comment on Ann's remark (1), 'Vienna is large', was correct, we may conclude:

(Q)   Ann said something true.

This conclusion is rendered into Grenglish as

Gr(Q)   There is a proposition such that Ann said that it is true, and it is true.

But here we stumble at once over another difficulty. Is this really a sentence of Grenglish? It is very hard to resist the temptation to read the word 'it' in Gr(Q) as a quantificational pronoun. After all, the quantifier phrase 'There is a proposition such that' contains the count noun 'proposition', and doesn't that impose on the following occurrences of 'it' a pronominal reading?[129] This hits you in the eye if you translate Grover's formulation into a language with a gender

---

[127] This sharpens, I think, a similar objection raised in Graeme Forbes, 'Truth, Correspondence and Redundancy', 37, 51–2 n. 6, and Dodd, *ITT*, 40–2. Both authors turn it against 'Prosentential', 101–3.

[128] Yes/no interrogatives express the same proposition as the corresponding declarative sentences: see Ch. 5.1.1.

[129] This problem is treated far too cavalierly in 'Prosentential', 86–7 (and in Grover, *PrTh*, 59–60). Peter van Inwagen is right in taking this to be a major difficulty for Grover's theory: cf. his 'Generalizations of Homophonic Truth-Sentences' (henceforth 'Truth-Sentences'), 220–2.

system for nouns: '*Es gibt eine* (!) *Proposition, von der gilt: Ann sagte, dass sie* (!) *wahr ist, und sie* (!) *ist wahr.*' But truth-nihilists should carefully avoid formulations that suggest, at least to the untrained eye, that propositions as truth-value bearers are here to stay. If the pronominal reading is obligatory, then 'is true' is a predicate, and if it is a genuine predicate, then we have to take $Gr(Q)$ for the counterpart of the nominal quantification over propositions, '$\exists x$ (Ann said that x is true .&. x is true)'. But Grover wants us to read the whole sentence 'it is true' as a quantificational prosentence. The quantificational prosentence in Grenglish is no more susceptible to a subject-predicate analysis than the Grenglish prosentence of laziness. So in effect we are asked to interpret $Gr(Q)$ as the counterpart of a *sentential* quantification in Loglish:

L (Q) $\exists p$ (Ann said that p .&. p).

But invoking the assistance of $L(Q)$ in order to understand $Gr(Q)$ would be putting the cart before the horse. Grover began her pertinent work in philosophical logic with reflections on what she called 'propositional quantifiers', and originally she had been under the impression that 'there appear to be no faithful and perspicuous readings in English' for sentences such as $L(Q)$. For the sake of making sense of quantifiers like the one in $L(Q)$, she first thought of adding to English an atomic prosentence (apparently without realizing that Prior had already done this).[130] But then, so she reports, 'Joe Camp pointed out that "That is true" seemed to do the work in English that I had described [the concocted prosentence] as doing.'[131] So we are back with an unresolved tension between the intended reading of the quantificational prosentence in $Gr(Q)$ and the prefixed quantifier phrase which binds it. But let us move on.

In English (as opposed to Grenglish) the verb in 'that is true' and 'it is true' is often modified, as for example in

(3)   Ben denies that Vienna is large, but it might be true.

In order to cope with such cases, another bit of English is incorporated into Grenglish, namely sentential operators in which the word 'true' appears, e.g. 'it might be true that', 'it was true that', 'it is not true that', etc. An utterance of 'It might be (was) true that' followed by the sentence 'Vienna is large' has the same content as the internally modalized (tensed) variant of that sentence: 'Vienna might be (was) small.' Prefixing 'It is not true that' to a sentence S, you obtain the contradictory of S, in the sense that they can be neither true together nor

---

[130] See *PrTh*, ch. 1 ('Propositional Quantifiers' [1972]), quotation from p. 47.
[131] Ibid., 'Introductory Essay', 17; cf. 56–7.

false together. Sometimes there is a less verbose contradictory of S available in English ('Nobody is perfect', if S is 'Somebody is perfect'), sometimes there isn't ('If Ben were to leave her, Ann would be very unhappy').[132]

If you apply a truth operator to a prosentence, the result has the same content as the result of applying the operator to the antecedent of that prosentence. Let me try to insinuate the intended interpretation by writing the Grenglish translation of (3) like this:

Gr(3)   Ben denies that *Vienna is large*, but IT MIGHT BE TRUE THAT *it is true*.

Like prosentences, truth operators in Grenglish contain the word 'true' only as a syncategorematic component. In the case of these operators, and only in their case, Grover marks this feature by using hyphens.[133] This is misleading. After all, 'true' is supposed to be non-isolable in prosentences, too. If truth operators were atomic, then the presence of 'true' in all of them (as well as in prosentences) would be just an orthographic accident. (Realizing that 'able' occurs both in 'stable' and in 'table' is no help in understanding either of these expressions.) In the remainder of this section, truth operators will play no role. But in Chapter 5.3.2 we shall have a close look at grammatically tensed truth operators like 'It was true that', 'It will be true that'.

Let me repeat what Grover calls the 'principle claim' of the nihilist theory of truth, this time using her own words (and her own sobriquet for Grenglish):

English can be translated without significant residue into its fragment English* ... Such a translation is perspicuous and explanatory ... / ... Truth talk is wholly intelligible without truth bearers and truth characteristics. ('Prosentential', 90, 105)

Is Grover right in contending that Grenglish has the same expressive power as English? As with Williams, I shall assume that questions about the intelligibility of sentential quantification can be given satisfactory answers. Grover's treatment of the propositionally *revealing* truth declaration

(R)   It is true that snow is white

is rather confusing.[134] She says that in a translation into Grenglish it 'could be treated ... by making the truth predicate disappear entirely'. (Obviously, she means that the truth operator could be made to disappear in the translation.) She then goes on to say that in some cases, which syntactically also admit of an

---

[132] 'Prosentential', 93–6; *PrTh*, 123.   [133] 'Prosentential', 90, 93–6.   [134] Ibid., 90–1; cf. 71.

eliminative treatment, the translation into Grenglish 'can be improved'. Her melancholy example is a sentence which contains (R):

(R+)   It is true that snow is white, but it rarely looks white in Pittsburgh,

and she offers the following treatment:

Gr(R+)   Snow is white. *That is true*, but it rarely looks white in Pittsburgh.

So in this environment (R) is given a paratactic treatment. Why is this supposed to be an improvement? Because the presence of the prosentence allows the speaker of Gr(R+) to do what the speaker of (R+) does, or can do, with the truth operator: explicitly grant someone's point. (Here Grover appropriates Strawson's description of the performative potential of 'true', which was examined in section 2.2.1 above.) But the performative potential which is thus preserved in Gr(R+) is not activated when (R) occurs as the antecedent of a conditional. Hence, we are confronted with an embarrassing ambiguity: sometimes (R) means the same as 'Snow is white', sometimes it doesn't. Surely a theory would be preferable which avoids this multiplication of senses.

Does propositionally *unrevealing* truth talk fare any better with Grover than with Williams? Her paradigm of a truth declaration which has a *name* for its grammatical subject is

(U*)   Goldbach's Conjecture is true.

'In order to get the effect' of such truth talk in Grenglish, she writes,

we need to invoke a connective like 'that—is-the-same-conjecture-as-that—', which we abbreviate by '⇔', and we need also some device to keep straight the cross-referencing of our quantificational prosentences, on pain of syntactical ambiguity. Perhaps we should have an infinite stock of prosentences 'It is true', 'It is true₁',... plus a bunch of quantifying expressions with subscripts (for example). Then we would say

Gr(U*)   *There is a proposition₁ such that Goldbach conjectured that it is true₁, and for every proposition₂, if Goldbach conjectured that it is true₂ then it is true₁ ⇔ it is true₂, and it is true₁.*

That's messy, but the idea is obvious enough. ('Prosentential', 95)[135]

Notice that this translation of (U*) into Grenglish has the same structure as Williams's more easily digestible translation of 'What Percy says is true' (T) into Loglish.[136] By adding subscripted prosentences, Grover has extended Grenglish,

---

[135] Cf. 'Prosentential', 73. I have changed Grover's numbering of the example.
[136] See L(T) on p. 75 above.

of course. But she has a good reply to those who would take this fact to falsify the principal claim of her theory:[137]

Nothing is going on here that is not already necessary for reading ordinary first-order quantifications into English.... No one has ever provided a thorough translation of first-order quantification into English *as it is*, as opposed to English with a denumerable family of distinct pronouns and quantifiers. (ibid.)

Ardent extensionalists will take offence at the 'same conjecture'-connective '⇔'. Grover is ready to admit that this connective awaits explanation, but she adds that 'those who set themselves the task of analyzing language must also account for such usage'.[138] That's fair enough. But quite a few pressing questions remain. First of all, there is our complaint about Grover's use of the count noun 'proposition' in the quantifier phrase. Secondly, does Grover really want to have a special connective for each such noun-phrase as 'Goldbach's Conjecture', e.g. 'A.'s notorious contention', 'B.'s last statement', 'C.'s most cherished belief', etc.? Adoption of Williams' 'same-say' connective '⇔' would spare her such a crowd of operators. Thirdly, the admission that Gr(U*) is messy is somewhat disarming, but it should not make us forget that we were promised 'perspicuous' translations. The very messiness of the paraphrase arouses the suspicion that the availability of the sentence to be paraphrased might be a precondition of our thinking the thought which the nihilist then tries to capture in another idiom. (In a similar context Strawson has put such a suspicion into words which I cannot resist quoting: 'Committed in thought to what we shun in speech, we should then seem like people seeking euphemisms in order to avoid explicit mention of distasteful realities.'[139]) Fourthly, it is extremely unlikely that Goldbach conjectured only one thing in his life, as Gr(U*) has it, and even if he did, the transformation of the grammatical subject of (U*) into the operator 'Goldbach conjectured that' is very dubious: the grammatical subject of (U*) is, so to speak, a retired definite description which has become a name, so (U*) could express a truth even if Goldbach had never entertained any thought to the effect that every even number greater than 2 is the sum of two prime numbers.[140] Finally, often it is simply impossible to recover a verb from the noun-phrases which form

---

[137] Cf. *PrTh*, 171.   [138] 'Prosentential', 98.   [139] Strawson, 'Universals', 58.

[140] This is the proposition that 'Goldbach's Conjecture' designates in present-day mathematical (and philosophical) parlance. In a letter, dated 27 May/7 June 1742, Christian Goldbach told Leonhard Euler (in a charmingly Frenchified German) that he wanted 'to risk a conjecture [*eine conjecture hazardieren*]': that every whole number greater than 2 is the sum of three numbers that are either prime or 1. The editors of the correspondence refer to this proposition as Goldbach's Conjecture (Juškevič and Winter (eds.), *Euler und Goldbach*, 104, 106 n.).

the grammatical subject of a propositionally unrevealing truth declaration. Just recall

(U)   Pythagoras' Theorem is true.

There are many more examples of this kind: 'the First Law of Thermodynamics', 'logicism', 'the doctrine of eternal recurrence', 'the principle of sufficient reason', 'Church's thesis', etc. So Williams's deadlock reappears. We seem to be stuck with singular terms which obstinately resist the nihilists' paraphrastic endeavours. So in spite of their hard labour, we still cannot help thinking that in (U) and (U*) a singular term is combined with a genuine predicate to form a predicative truth declaration. Contrary to what nihilists want us to believe, truth talk just doesn't seem to be wholly intelligible without truth-bearers and truth characteristics. This verdict can also be upheld, I think, in the face of the most recent version of nihilism.

2.2.4 *'Is True' as a prosentence-forming operator*

Robert Brandom largely agrees with Grover's approach. Interestingly, he parts company with her when it comes to sentences like

(U*)   Goldbach's Conjecture is true.

What matters in our context is this partial disagreement, but let me just mention in passing that Brandom's characterization of what he takes to be common ground starts with a blunder: 'So "Snow is white is true" is read as a prosentence of laziness, having the same semantic content as its anaphoric antecedent, perhaps the token of "Snow is white" that it contains.'[141] The first string of words mentioned here isn't a prosentence of any kind, but plain nonsense, and I cannot for the life of me see how a proform could possibly *contain* its antecedent. Brandom accepts Grover's treatment of truth declarations which wear their quantifiers on their sleeves ('Ann said something true'). 'But it is not clear that it is a good idea to assimilate what look like straightforward predications of truth to this quantificational model.... Otherwise almost all sentences involving "true" must be seen as radically misleading as to their underlying logical form.'[142] Now in the mouth of a nihilist, this objection against Gr(U*) sounds rather strange: isn't the central claim of truth-theoretical nihilism that the grammatical form of truth declarations *is* radically misleading in each and

---

[141] Brandom, *MIE*, 302. If you suspect that this might be a misprint, have a look at p. 328.
[142] Ibid., 304.

every case? But let this pass. What modification of Grover's theory does Brandom propose in order to avoid a quantificational account of statements like (U*)?

'It would be preferable', he writes, 'to follow the treatment of sentence nominalizations suggested by disquotational generalizations of redundancy theories.'[143] Since (U*) does not contain any sentence nominalization, let alone any quotation, you might well wonder how the treatment alluded to could possibly help. But we shall soon see that Brandom's use of the term 'sentence nominalization' is decidedly non-standard (and that the adjective 'disquotational' is best ignored). He starts with the observation, repeatedly made in the course of this chapter, that 'simple redundancy accounts will not offer a correct reading of sentences like "Goldbach's conjecture is true." For this sentence is not interchangeable with "Goldbach's conjecture". For instance, the former, but not the latter, appears as the antecedent of well-formed and significant conditionals.' We hardly need such a substitution test in order to find out that a term isn't a sentence, but let us see how the so-called 'disquotational generalization' of 'simple redundancy accounts' is supposed to deal with (U*):

In the case of sentences such as 'Goldbach's conjecture is true', the claim with respect to which the truth-taking is content redundant must be determined by a two-stage process. First, a sentence nominalization is discerned. This may be a description like 'Goldbach's conjecture'.... Next, a sentence is produced that is nominalized by the locution picked out in the first stage. This is the sentence expressing Goldbach's conjecture.... It is this sentence that is then treated by theory as intersubstitutable with the truth-attributing sentence, whether occurring embedded or freestanding. (*MIE* 300)

Brandom now integrates this into his own brand of prosententialism by maintaining that the function of the term 'Goldbach's Conjecture' is 'just to pick out the antecedent on which the whole prosentence formed using "true" [i.e. U*] is anaphorically dependent, and from which it accordingly inherits its content.'[144] So the idea is that '. . . is true' is neither a predicate, i.e. a sentence-forming operator on singular terms, nor a syncategorematic fragment of a prosentence, as Grover has it, but rather a '*prosentence-forming operator*'.[145]

When all the dust has settled you will experience a certain déjà vu. According to Brandom's version of prosententialism (U*) has the same content as

(S)   Every even number greater than 2 is the sum of two prime numbers.

This contention is obviously close to Williams as cited on p. 72.[146] Confusingly (S) is described as what is nominalized by the term 'Goldbach's Conjecture', but

---

[143] Ibid.   [144] Ibid.   [145] Ibid., 305.

[146] But it is worth marking the difference, too: Williams had maintained, at least for a while, that (U*) has the same content as 'It is true that' plus (S).

this can be put aside as a terminological aberration. Certainly Brandom's account of (U*) is less messy than Grover's Gr(U*). Actually it is not messy at all, but it has the decisive disadvantage of being utterly implausible. It is open to the same kind of objections as those made against Williams. Suppose Ben has recently heard about Goldbach's Conjecture in his first lecture in the philosophy of mathematics. He is not yet able to distinguish it from other theorems about prime numbers, but he is able to acquire beliefs about it. This morning he read in a newspaper: 'American Mathematician Proves Goldbach's Conjecture', so he feels authorized to claim that U*. How could this claim possibly have the same content as an assertion that S? Ben might even deny that every even number greater than 2 is the sum of two prime numbers, while maintaining that U*. If Brandom were right, Ben could not possibly fail to realize that these contentions cannot both be true.

Brandom calls the grammatical subject of (U*) a description. In section 2.2.3 I expressed my reservations about this. Let me conclude this section by inspecting Brandom's account of truth declarations, which really have definite descriptions for their grammatical subjects. He asks us to consider such examples as

(X)   Hegel's most notorious remark about truth is true.

Suppose I assert this, relying on Brandom's authority in matters arcane. According to his theory, in order to understand (X), 'one *must* process the noun phrase to determine what sentence tokening (or class of such tokenings) it picks out as anaphoric antecedent(s)'.[147] Let us assume, again following Brandom, that Hegel's most notorious remark about truth is '*Das Wahre . . . ist der bacchantische Taumel, an dem kein Glied nicht trunken ist.*' Do I really not understand (X) unless I am able to identify Hegel's remark? Do I really fail to comprehend (X) if, in assertively uttering it, I do not take myself to 'endorse', as Brandom has it, 'the claim that truth is a vast Bacchanalian revel with not a soul sober'?[148] A sober reader may very well suspect that these consequences rebut Brandom's theory. Suppose I had taken a deeper breath and said

(X+)   Hegel's most notorious remark about truth is true, but I have no idea what that remark is.

Can I only understand (X+) by falsifying the second conjunct of my utterance? Brandom's version of prosententialism does not seem to improve upon the original.

---

[147] Brandom, 'Explanatory vs. Expressive Deflationism about Truth', 106; my italics.
[148] Ibid., 106–7 (and Hegel, *Phänomenologie des Geistes*, preface, 39).

2.3 A Real Predicate, After All

Recall our earlier example of an intuitively valid argument in which propositionally revealing, and propositionally unrevealing, truth declarations are interlocked:

(P1) Pythagoras' Theorem is true.

(P2) Pythagoras' Theorem = the proposition that the square on the hypotenuse is equal to the sum of the squares on the other two sides.

(C) Therefore, the proposition that the square on the hypotenuse is equal to the sum of the squares on the other two sides is true.

The nihilists vainly tried to dispel the impression that we need the predicate 'true' for making sense of the propositionally unrevealing first premiss. If we take the propositionally revealing conclusion also to have a predicative structure, we can easily budget for the intuition that the argument is *formally* valid: it exemplifies the valid argument-pattern 'Fa, a = b ∴ Fb'. In view of this striking advantage of taking grammatical appearances at face value, one needs very strong reasons for investing any further labour into the nihilists' project. But the reasons they give for declaring 'is true' not to be a genuine predicate are far weaker than the reasons one can give for saying this about 'exist' and 'was so-called because of his size'.

Let us put the philosophically contentious first case aside[149] and content ourselves with asking: why is the predicate 'was so-called because of his size' not a genuine predicate? If an expression is a genuine predicate, it applies to an object regardless of how this object is designated. So if we were to treat 'was so-called because of his size' as a genuine predicate, we would have to declare the following argument to be valid:[150]

(P1) Giorgione was so-called because of his size.

(P2) Giorgione is identical with Giorgio da Castelfranco.

(C) Therefore (?), Giorgio da Castelfranco was so-called because of his size.

This argument is invalid. (So the logician does not want it to be an instance of the valid argument-pattern 'Fa, a = b ∴ Fb'.) Hence our predicate is not a

---

[149] As to the first case, cf. the brief summary of the standard arguments in Alston, *RCT*, 50–1; the brief criticism of the standard arguments in Dummett, *FPL*, 278–80; and the discussion in Strawson, 'Is Existence Never a Predicate?'.

[150] The example is Quine's, of course (cf. *W&O*, 153), but I have taken the liberty to replace (what art-historians deem to be) a rather dubious claim as to Giorgione's identity by a less controversial one.

genuine predicate, and consequently there is no such thing as the property of being so-called because of his size. If there were, then Giorgione could not have it without Giorgio da Castelfranco having it.[151] How strong are the reasons for reductionist nihilism, as compared with this case? Williams prides himself upon 'making many of the traditional problems about Truth disappear'.[152] (Presumably the capital T is to surround the word with a kind of disreputable metaphysical aureole.) What are the riddles that can only, or best, be solved by embracing nihilism? The only 'traditional problems' which receive some critical attention in Williams's books are connected with correspondence theories of the Cambridge variety.[153] Certainly NIHILISM$_W$ cannot claim to be the one and only truth-theoretical option which avoids those problems. In the pioneering paper that served as my main text, Grover contends that the prosentential theory, 'eliminates some of the problems about truth',[154] without specifying any of these alleged problems. In a later paper, though, she argues that her theory blocks the semantic antinomies.[155] Whether it really succeeds is a matter of controversy,[156] but in any case, NIHILISM$_G$ cannot, and does not, claim to be the one and only defence against the menace of the 'Liar'.

As we saw above, the problem-solving power of the reductionist versions of truth-theoretical nihilism is supposed to consist, to a large degree, in its helping us to get rid of 'mysterious bearers of truth (propositions)'.[157] I wonder whether the nihilists' reliance on the notion of anaphora is compatible with their ritual complaint about propositions' being mysterious. In earlier sections I have announced a certain reservation concerning lazy talk of proforms of laziness. The reservation I had in mind is this: we should not be misled by this kind of talk into thinking that simple repetition of the antecedent of the proform will always preserve the message. This affects already ordinary pronouns. Look at this little dialogue:

Ann: My *favourite male colleague* is a philosopher with a snub-nose.
Ben: *He* seems to be made in the image of Socrates.

---

[151] There is no '*concept* of being so-called because of his size' either. So Wright is not quite right when he says: 'All truths have at least the following property in common: the property of falling under [the] concept [of truth]... *that is*, the property of having "true" correctly predicable of them' ('Minimalism', 753 and n. 5; my italics). The predicate 'is so-called because of his size' is correctly predicable of Little John and Giorgione, but that does not mean that they share the property of falling under 'the concept of being so-called because of his size'.   [152] Williams, *WIT*, xiv.

[153] Ibid., 74 ff.; *BIT*, 106 ff. See below, Chap. 3.2.1, on Moore.   [154] Grover, 'Prosentential', 70.

[155] Cf. the chapter 'Inheritors and Paradox' in her book *PrTh*.

[156] See Jerry Kapus, 'The Liar and the Prosentential Theory of Truth'.

[157] Cf. the passage from Brandom cited above on p. 64.

If one were to exchange the pronoun in Ben's rejoinder for its antecedent in Ann's remark, reference might not be preserved. Here the pronoun of laziness goes proxy for the second person counterpart of its antecedent.[158] This observation also affects prosentences of laziness, as can be seen from the following exchanges in Prenglish and in Grenglish:

Ann: *I am ill.*
Ben: Sorry, I did not know that *thether.*

Ann: *I am ill.*
Ben: Sorry, I did not know that *that is true.*

If either prosentence were replaced verbatim by its antecedent, these dialogues would be of doubtful coherence. By taking each proform to act as deputy for the second person counterpart of its antecedent, we preserve the propositional content of the antecedent.[159] So it seems that nihilists cannot explain the notion of anaphora that is relied upon in their accounts of truth without appealing to a prior notion of propositional content as what is inherited by a prosentence of laziness from its antecedent. This notion allows for the possibility that sentences which differ in linguistic meaning are used to express one and the same proposition. Since the nihilists' accounts of truth depend on the notion of anaphora, they cannot without circularity explain the notion of propositional content in terms of truth. (Of all nihilists, only Brandom clearly faces the charge of giving an alternative account of this notion. This makes it all the more surprising that in the passage quoted on p. 64 he joins in the anti-propositionalist singing.) What matters here and now is that truth-theoretical nihilists have no right to complain about the mysteriousness of the concept of a proposition if their own theories rely on that very concept.

The predicate 'is true', I have argued, is a genuine predicate, hence truth is a *property*, under that prodigal reading under which whatever is ascribable by a genuine predicate is a property. In so arguing, one does *not* incur a commitment to a 'realist' view of such properties. In this respect the position defended in this chapter is metaphysically neutral: whatever ontological status properties prodigally conceived may have, truth has the same status. Furthermore, one can accept the central tenet of this chapter and yet deny that truth is a property in a more demanding sense. Philosophers who want to deny this are not always at

[158] The reason why simple repetition won't do is not always that the antecedent contains an indexical element. Sometimes the antecedent does not even have the right 'shape'. Take 'Columbus was not the first European to reach America, though many people still believe *it* (believe *so*)': here, the anaphoric pronoun goes proxy for a that-clause which does not surface in the preceding sentence.

[159] Cf. pp. 287–9 below. As can be seen from 'Prosentential', 75, 98, Grover is clearly aware of all this, and on pp. 110–11 she comes close to anticipating the objection I am about to make.

their best when it comes to characterizing a more demanding sense. Truth is not, Wright avers, 'a property of intrinsic metaphysical *gravitas*'.[160] The meaning of this locution, I have to confess, completely escapes me. I have found some consolation in Wiggins's comment: 'Intrinsic metaphysical *gravitas* sounds heavy and bad. So no doubt the reader who wants to avoid it, if only because he doesn't know what it is, is reassured to find that what he will be offered is truth ... without that.'[161] Horwich writes:

> [I]t is not part of the minimalist conception to maintain that truth is not a property. On the contrary, 'is true' is a perfectly good English predicate—and (leaving aside nominalistic concerns about the very notion of 'property') one might well take this to be a conclusive criterion for standing for a property of *some* sort. What the minimalist wishes to emphasize, however, is that truth is not a *complex* or *naturalistic* property but a property of some other kind. (Hartry Field suggests the term '*logical* property'.) ... According to minimalism, we should ... beware of assimilating *being true* to such properties as *being turquoise, being a tree*, or *being made of tin*. Otherwise we will find ourselves looking for its constitutive structure, its causal behaviour, and its typical manifestations—features peculiar to what I am calling '*complex*' or '*naturalistic* properties.' (*Truth*, 37–8)

Being a perfectly good English predicate may not be good enough for signifying a property, as witness 'is so-called because of his size'. But apart from this caveat, I agree with the spirit of Horwich's affirmative contention.[162] What about his negative tenet? A philosopher who defines 'true' in terms of some kind of correspondence with some kind of entities apparently regards the *concept* of truth as complex: he does not think that it resists analysis. Does he take the *property* of being true to be complex? Pending an explanation of 'complex property', this is hard to tell.[163] (Couldn't a complex concept be a concept of a 'simple property'? Couldn't a predicate signify a 'simple property' even though it has a complex sense? After all, the sense of the singular term 'the centre of mass of the solar system' is fairly complex, but that doesn't seem to be a good reason for taking the designated object to be complex. A structured designator of a property need not designate a 'structured property'. Is the *property* of being married somehow part of the property of being unmarried just because the sense of 'unmarried' contains that of 'married'? And for that matter, couldn't an unanalysable concept be a concept of a 'complex property'? Maybe the concept expressed by a certain colour predicate is simple, whereas the property of having that colour is 'complex'.)

---

[160] Wright, 'Truth in Ethics', 213.   [161] Wiggins, 'Objective and Subjective in Ethics', 254.
[162] Horwich highlights the point again in *Truth*, 141–2.
[163] Not by Horwich's own lights, of course, for as we saw in Ch. 1 n. 66, he *identifies* concepts and properties. Like many other philosophers I have pleaded for keeping them distinct, so the questions posed above become pressing.

At any rate, a correspondence theorist may have reasons to deny that truth is a naturalistic property. First, he might regard it as a property *sui generis*.[164] Secondly, he may have a view about the bearers of this property which enforces that denial. 'Naturalistic' properties, I take it, are causal powers of, or bestow causal powers upon, their instances.[165] (This nicely fits being made of tin, etc.) Now if truth is primarily a property of propositions, of sayables and thinkables (as I shall argue in Chapter 5.1 and as Horwich would be the first to admit), then truth-bearers are causally inert and, consequently, truth cannot be a naturalistic property. Even though the proposition that p is not causally efficacious, a propositional act like realizing that p may cause a heart-attack. This is no more mysterious, I think, than the fact that two earthquakes may completely destroy a town, although the number 2 has no causal impact on anything. But the observation that truth, unlike being made of tin etc., isn't a naturalistic property seems to leave it still in the wrong neighbourhood, as it were, for being a Wednesday and being a meridian do not seem to be naturalistic properties either.[166]

Horwich also emphasizes that truth is a property which has no 'underlying nature'.[167] What does having an underlying nature come to? Judging from Horwich's examples (such as having diabetes and being magnetic), the idea seems to be something like this. The property of being F has an underlying nature if and only if, for some G, the observable characteristics in virtue of which we identify something as F can be explained by a scientific theory according to which all and only F's are G. Certainly, truth does not comply with this condition (and one may wonder whether anybody ever thought otherwise), but the property of being a chair, and that of having a chair, do not comply with it either, so again the characterization is not very distinctive of truth. In Chapter 6.2 I shall argue that truth is a *(broadly) logical property*; which brings me close to Field's suggestion. Whatever '(broadly) logical property' may mean exactly (and we will of course have to go into this), hardly anyone would be inclined to apply this label to being made of tin, being a meridian, or being a chair.

---

[164] See Dodd, *ITT* 136–7.

[165] Cf. Armstrong, *A Theory of Universals*, ch. 16.1, and Sydney Shoemaker's paper in Mellor and Oliver (eds.), *Properties*, ch. XV.

[166] On the final pages of '*Der Gedanke*' Frege argued that propositions, though incapable of being acted upon, are capable of (indirectly) acting upon something else. His argument goes like this: Ben's coming to believe that p caused his excitement, his excitement caused an accident; hence (?) the proposition that p had an (indirect) causal impact on the traffic. You might as well argue for the causal efficacy of Baal from the premiss that someone's praying to Baal on the middle of the road in Baalbek caused a traffic jam. Frege should have said about propositions what he said (in *Grundlagen der Arithmetik*, §26) about the axis of the earth, the equator, and the centre of mass of the solar system: that they have no causal power. Cf. my *Abstrakte Gegenstände*, 64–75, 141–9.

[167] Horwich, *Truth*, 2, 125.

One thing should be conceded to Frege, and in accepting the central tenet of this chapter one is not prevented from doing so: truth is a *very peculiar* property indeed. It is the one and only property of any proposition to the effect that things are thus-and-so which allows us to infer directly that things really are thus. Truth is unique among all the properties propositions may have in being, so to speak, by itself transparent, enabling us to look through the *proposition* right to the (non-propositional) *world*.[168] Note that the modifiers 'directly' and 'by itself' are needed to shield off apparent counter-examples which would otherwise be real counter-examples. Here is a list of properties of the proposition that the moon is round which also allow us to infer how things stand with the moon:

- being such that anyone who were to believe it would be right in so believing
- being held true by an omniscient God, if there is any such being
- being deducible from truths
- being true and referred to in this book.

Obviously, all these properties are truth-entailing, in the sense that if a proposition has any of them, it follows that it is a true proposition. They owe their transparency to the property of being true. The latter is the only property of propositions that is transparent in its own right.[169] One can, and should, acknowledge the uniqueness of the property of being true rather than go to the nihilists' extreme of denying its propertyhood.

---

[168] Several paintings by René Magritte, such as *La Condition humaine* and *Les Promenades d'Euclide*, can be seen to illustrate this.

[169] McGinn highlights this feature of truth in *Logical Properties*, 96–104. Some of his formulations muddy the water a bit, I am afraid. Is truth 'a device of ontological leapfrog' (103)? Maybe we'd better leapfrog over this remark, granting it a kind of poetic licence. 'Truth is essentially a method for deducing facts from propositions' (102): whatever truth may be, it is certainly not a method, and there is no need to deploy the category of facts in order to make the point about the underrived transparency of truth McGinn is rightly keen to make. He says about this point: 'no one (to my knowledge) has ever thought to defend it before—or even to formulate it explicitly' (100). So let me set the record straight: Alston (*RCT*, 53–5) and Horwich (*Truth*, 126–7; *Meaning*, 140; 'A Defense of Minimalism', 566) did explicitly formulate and defend the same point.

3

Varieties of Correspondence

It takes two to make a truth.

(John Austin, 'Truth', 124)

In this chapter I want to contrast and to assess three fundamentally different ways of conceiving truth as correspondence. So we turn now to QUESTIONS 2–7 on our flow chart.[1] In the final section I shall enquire whether a kind of Correspondence Intuition (hinted at in the above epigraph) can be upheld even if the concept of truth cannot be explained, in either of those three ways, in terms of correspondence.

Let it be clear at once that you do not become a partisan of a correspondence conception of truth simply by assenting to the slogan that what somebody thought or said is true if and only if it agrees with reality.[2] It all depends on whether you take the expression 'agrees with' in sentences like 'What Ann said agrees with reality' to be *'seriously dyadic'*.[3] A comparison may be helpful. From the premiss 'Ben fell into oblivion', nobody would seriously conclude 'There is something into which Ben fell', but everybody would be ready to infer this from 'Ben fell into the swimming-pool': only in the latter context is 'fell into' seriously dyadic. If you do *not* allow the step from 'What Ann said agrees with reality' to 'There is something with which it agrees', you have not committed yourself to a correspondence view of truth. But if you accept that inference, then assenting to the slogan is the first step towards adopting such a conception. Let us listen to a famous opponent of any such view:

Eine Übereinstimmung ist eine Beziehung. Dem widerspricht aber die Gebrauchsweise des Wortes 'wahr', das kein Beziehungswort ist. [An agreement is a relation. But this is incompatible with the use of the word 'true', which is not a relation word.] ('*Der Gedanke*', 59)

I quote this, not because I consider it to be a strong objection, but because I think that it reveals how the correspondence slogan is to be taken if it is to have any

---

[1] See above, Ch. 1, Fig. 1.1.

[2] The slogan is, as Dewey puts it, 'sufficiently bromidic to be acceptable to common sense' ('The Problem of Truth', 33.)

[3] The phrase is Wright's: see *T&O*, 83.

philosophical bite: it must be understood as declaring truth to be a relational property (and as taking the implied relation to be irreflexive[4]). As an objection, Frege's argument is rather weak. To be sure, unlike 'agrees with' or 'corresponds to', the predicate 'is true' is a one-place predicate, hence it does not signify a *relation*. But the predicate 'x is a spouse' is also a one-place predicate, hence it does not signify a relation either, and yet it is correctly explained as 'There is somebody to whom x is married'. It signifies a *relational property*.[5] Perhaps the predicate 'x is true' can be similarly explained: 'There is something to which x corresponds'. If this explanation is correct, then, as Russell once put it, 'the difference between a true belief and a false belief is like that between a wife and a spinster'.[6]

3.1 Classical Correspondence

It is noteworthy how Frege describes the conception of truth he wants to demolish, and how he illustrates it. He describes it thus: '*wahr ist eine Vorstellung, wenn sie mit der Wirklichkeit übereinstimmt* [an idea is true if it agrees with reality].'[7] As to the domain, the left field, of the correspondence relation, Frege goes on to argue that ideas are 'improperly [*mißbräuchlich*]' called true,[8] but let us put this aside here. For the topic of this chapter, it is more important to draw attention to Frege's example for the counter-domain, the right field. It is Cologne Cathedral.[9] According to his description of the correspondence view, a truth about Cologne Cathedral is said to agree with a thing, not with a fact (about that thing): the correspondence is alleged to obtain between a mental item and a chunk of reality, and reality is not taken to be the totality of all facts. We should not be surprised at Frege's illustration of the correspondence view. For centuries, 'correspondence' had been wedded to 'thing', or 'object', rather than to 'fact'. Nevertheless, in the vast amount of literature on our topic this very tenacious union is hardly so much as even mentioned.[10] So the first section of this chapter is about the entry under the right branch under QUESTION 4.

---

[4] 'When truth is defined as agreement of an idea with something real . . . it is essential that the reality be distinct from the idea' (Frege, '*Der Gedanke*', 60).

[5] In my usage, as explained above, monadic (polyadic) predicates 'signify' the properties (relations) their nominalizations can be used to refer to.

[6] Russell, *Human Knowledge—Its Scope and its Limits*, 165.

[7] Frege, *Logik* (1897), in: *NS*, 137 (126); cf. '*Der Gedanke*', 59.   [8] Frege, '*Der Gedanke*', 60.

[9] Frege, *NS*, 140 (129), '*Der Gedanke*', 60. By the end of this paper, Frege's use of the term '*Wirklichkeit*' changes: now it denotes the *property* of being *wirksam*, i.e. of being capable of acting upon something ('*Der Gedanke*', 76–7). The latter usage is also to be found in Bolzano. Cf. my 'Propositions in Bolzano and Frege', 204, 208.

[10] Notice how the conviction that truth-constituting correspondence has got to be a relation to facts can make latter-day readers blind to obviously recalcitrant features of Frege's exposition. Commenting

3.1.1 *From Aristotle to Aquinas*

In his *Metaphysics* Aristotle presents an explanation of falsity and truth which is almost obsessively quoted in most discussions of the topic. So here it is again:

[W]e first define what truth and falsity are. To say [λέγειν] of what is that it is not, or of what is not that it is, is false [ψεῦδος], while to say of what is that it is, and of what is not that it is not, is true [ἀληθές]. (*Met. Γ* 7: 1011b 26–7; [A.1])[11]

The first half of this explanation is actually borrowed, without any acknowledgement in the footnotes, from Plato's *Sophist*.[12] The explanation is stunningly monosyllabic and far from transparent. When 'a famous and forceful religious leader assured [Russell] that philosophy is only difficult because of the long words that it uses', he could have presented [A.1] as counter-evidence: 'It cannot be said that it is long words that make this sentence difficult.'[13]

Let us start with two minor problems. One concerns the frame of [A.1], as it were: 'To say (…) is true'. This seems to be a predication about acts of saying, but can acts of saying correctly be called true? In a similar vein Jean Buridan objects to the statement 'To say that a man is an animal is true':

Taken literally, [this] is false, though I admit that when we are speaking loosely statements of this kind are sometimes taken to do duty for the ones that would really be true. This one, for example, *is* true: … To say that a man is an animal is to say something true. (*Sophismata*, ch. VIII, 6th Soph., lines 42–7)

One might also think of another emendation: 'It is true to say (…).' But Buridan would not approve of this either. And indeed, if it is nice to meet you, then meeting you is nice, but can (the act of) saying such-and-such correctly be called true?

With respect to his own example, Buridan suggests also this rephrasal: 'That a man is an animal is true.' But [A.1] does not allow for such a reformulation, at least not in my translation, for it does not contain the *de dicto* construction 'to say that…' but the *de re* construction 'to say of… that…'. This brings us to the second minor problem. The Greek original does also have a *de dicto* reading. This would give us, 'To say that *that which is not is* (*that which is is not*) is false, and to say

---

on '*Der Gedanke*' Dodd writes, 'Frege [argues] against someone who holds that truth consists in the obtaining of a relation between a thought and an item from the real world: a *state of affairs*, in other words' (*An Identity Theory of Truth*, 116; his italics). Dodd does not need to be told that cathedrals are not states of affairs.

[11] This quotation will be referred to henceforth in the text as [A.2]. Subsequent Aristotle quotations in this section will be labelled, and referred to, as [A.2], [A.3], etc. Incidentally, most philosophers who quote [A.1], including Aquinas, Tarski, and Davidson, actually misquote: the text has 'and', not 'or', in the *definiens* of truth. This is not much of a complaint, however, because the difference has no impact on the interpretation.   [12] Plato, *Sophistes*, 240 e 10–241 a 1.

[13] Russell, *My Philosophical Development*, 63.

that *that which is (not) is (not)*, is true,' and here the frame would grammatically allow for Buridan's second rephrasal, '(...) is true'. But the *de dicto* interpretation cannot really be intended, for under this reading [A.1] would declare all falsehoods to be glaringly inconsistent and all truths to be self-evident. So we should stick to the *de re* interpretation as presupposed in the above translation, and expand the final 'is true' into 'is to say something true' to obtain a smooth reading.

The most pressing question concerns the meaning of the key word, 'is'. Prima facie there are three options: it can be used in the sense of 'exists', or of 'is the case', or of 'is so-and-so'. Davidson, commenting upon Tarski's somewhat qualified approval of Aristotle's explanation, opts for the 'existential' reading (without giving any argument for it).[14] Kirwan, in his commentary on the passage, favours the 'factual' reading (for the reason that it alone 'makes the definitions cover all truths and falsehoods').[15] Williams prefers the 'predicative' or 'dummy verb' interpretation (trying to alleviate the generality worry by the observation that a restriction to subject-predicate sentences is 'unlikely to have been felt as a restriction by Aristotle').[16]

Which reading is the correct one? Or is the textual evidence indecisive? The 'factual' interpretation might seem to be the most charitable, but actually the hope that it would give passage [A.1] more generality than its competitors is illusory: under this reading, [A.1] would claim that every true affirmative statement says *of* a fact *that* it is a fact; but our statements very seldom have the structure of 'That Socrates drank the hemlock is the case (is a fact)'.[17] I shall now try to show

---

[14] Davidson, 'The Folly of Trying to Define Truth' (henceforth 'Folly'), 267. Cf. Chisholm, *Theory of Knowledge*, 1st edn., 105.

[15] See his *Aristotle's Metaphysics Γ, Δ, E*, 117. Cf. Nuchelmans, *Theories of the Proposition*, §3.3; Tugendhat, *Vorlesungen zur Einführung in die sprachanalytische Philosophie*, 249–50, 264 n. 3; and Simons, 'Aristotle's Concept of States of Affairs', 107–8. Blackburn and Simmons move from [A.1] without any further ado ('in other words') to Fact-based Correspondence (*Truth*, 'Introduction', 1).

[16] C. J. F. Williams, *WIT*, 67. Cf. Fred Sommers, 'On Concepts of Truth in Natural Languages', 282. In the course of lecturing on the concept of existence, Austin is reported to have said: 'When God called out to Moses from the burning bush, "I am", the only proper reply for Moses to have made was "You are what?" ' (see *Proc. Aristotelian Soc.* 61 (1961) 57). This is to plead for a 'predicative reading' of the verb in God's cryptic utterance (or rather, in its rendering into English).

[17] Peter Geach seems to me to be absolutely right when he says that it is 'quite clearly anachronistic' to 'ascrib[e] to Aristotle a metaphysic that admits "facts" as entities' ('Aristotle on Conjunctive Propositions', 21). The point at issue is not whether Aristotle ever refers to facts or states of affairs, but whether a reference to them enters into his account of truth. The former question is to be answered affirmatively. Thus in *Met. Δ* 29: 1024^{b}17–21, 24–5, he says, 'this, that the diagonal is commensurable' and 'this, that you are sitting' are 'falsehoods' in the sense of 'things [πράγματα] that are not'—the former always, the latter sometimes. Here the best translation of 'things that are not' would be 'states of affairs that do not obtain'. In *Cat.* 10: 12^{b}13–16, he says, 'In the way in which an affirmation is opposed to a negation, e.g. "he is sitting" to "he is not sitting", so are opposed also the things underlying each: this, that he is sitting, to this, that he is not sitting.' Here, too, the 'things' referred to are states of affairs.

that the predicative interpretation is the correct one. But let me first spell out (step by unhurried step) what the predicative interpretation comes to. Using the traditional notation 'S is P' we can convey the point of [A.1], predicatively understood, by means of the following set of schemata:

(1a) If S is P, then it is true that S is P.
(1b) If S is not P, then it is true that S is not P.
(2a) If S is P, then it is false that S is not P.
(2b) If S is not P, then it is false that S is P.

Now if it is false that things are thus-and-so, then it is not true that things are thus-and-so. Hence (2a) and (2b), in virtue of the transitivity of 'if-then', entail, respectively,

(3a) If S is P, then it is not true that S is not P.
(3b) If S is not P, then it is not true that S is P.

Applying to (3b) the inference rules of contraposition and of double negation,[18] we obtain

(4) If it is true that S is P, then S is P.

From (1a) and (4) follows

(5) It is true that S is P, iff S is P.

Similarly, applying contraposition and double negation to (3a), we obtain

(6) If it is true that S is not P, then S is not P.

From (1b) and (6) follows

(7) It is true that S is not p, iff S is not P.

So what [A.1], predicatively understood, tells us about truth is perspicuously captured by

(SCHEMA A) It is true that S is [not] P, iff S is [not] P.

Apart from the bracketed 'not', this is what the Denominalization Schema amounts to if you assume that every declarative sentence has a subject-predicate structure.

But now back to our exegetical question: is the predicative reading correct? Both the context of the quoted passage and some of Aristotle's own less

---

[18] I am assuming here that 'It is not the case that (. . . is not —)' is tantamount to ' . . . is —'.

monosyllabic statements about truth point clearly in this direction. A first, if somewhat enigmatic, hint is to be found in *De Interpretatione*:

Falsity and truth have to do with combination [σύνθεσις, *compositio*] and separation [διαίρεσις, *divisio*] (*De Int.* 1: 16ª12–13; [A.2])[19]

Readers of this text get a chance to understand [A.2] when Aristotle comes to distinguish two kinds of predication [ἀπόφανσις, *enuntiatio*]: [20]

An affirmation [κατά-φασις] is a predication of something '*towards*' something, a negation [ἀπό-φασις] is a predication of something '*away from*' something. Now it is possible to predicate

[a]   what does belong [ὕπαρχον] [to s.th.] as not belonging [to it], and

[b]   what does not belong as belonging, and

[c]   what does belong as belonging, and

[d]   what does not belong as not belonging. (*De Int.* 6: 17ª25–9; [A.3])

Obviously Aristotle is criss-crossing here between two distinctions: [a] and [d] characterize the structure of negations, [b] and [c] the structure of affirmations; false predications are characterized by [a] and [b], true predications by [c] and [d].[21] In this context 'belongs to' signifies the converse of the relation signified by 'exemplifies'. Tentatively replacing 'x belongs to y' by 'x and y are combined', and 'x does not belong to y' by 'x and y are separate', we begin to see what might be meant in [A.2].

Before we collect more evidence for this reading, let us register a point that is relevant for the interpretation of [A.1]. Affirmation and negation as defined in [A.3] constitute what Aristotle, a few lines later, calls an ἀντίφασις or 'contradictory pair', i.e. a pair of predications in which 'the same thing is both affirmed and denied of the same thing'.[22] Now Aristotle's account of truth and falsity in [A.1] is to pave the way for his answer to the question whether there could be anything 'in the middle of a contradictory pair', understood in the same way.[23]

---

[19] The Latin insertions are meant to facilitate comparison with Aquinas' views [which will demand our attention a few pages hence].

[20] The standard translation of 'ἀπόφανσις' is 'statement'. If this captured Aristotle's intention, then he could not say, e.g., that in the antecedent of the conditional 'If Socrates is (not) wise then Plato is right (wrong),' wisdom is affirmed (negated) of Socrates. Following Geach, 'Ascriptivism', 252–3, I take 'predication' in such a way that the antecedent is an affirmative (negative) predication of wisdom. Though important in itself, the distinction between stating and predicating will not loom large in this chapter. Nor will the distinction between believing (or judging) that p and merely entertaining the thought that p.

[21] Cf. Aquinas, *Sententia super Peri hermeneias*, §110: '*prima divisio: ex ipsa forma vel modo enunciandi. secunda divisio: per comparationem ad rem.* [The first division is taken from the form or mode of predicating, the second division is with respect to the comparison with the object.]' Aquinas' way of describing the second division is of course highly pertinent to the topic of this chapter.   [22] *De Int.* 6: 17ª33–5.

[23] *Met.* Γ7: 1011ᵇ23–4.

But in neither context does Aristotle offer *being existent* as an example of 'things' both affirmed and denied in such pairs. His examples are rather being pale or being a man. Hence Davidson's existential reading of the 'is' in [A.1] squares rather badly with the context, whereas the predicative reading fits it perfectly.

What are the relata of the relation signified by 'x belongs to y' in [A.3]? We can take our clue from the following passage:

> Of things [πράγματα, *res*] some are universal [καθόλου], some are particular [καθ' ἕκαστον]. I call universal that which is by its nature capable of being predicated of several things, and particular that which is not.... So necessarily, the thing of which something is predicated as belonging or as not belonging is sometimes a universal, sometimes a particular. (*De Int.* 7: 17ª38–b3; [A.4])

Helen and Thersites are particulars, beauty and ugliness are universals. Beauty belongs to Helen; they are 'combined'. Beauty does not belong to Thersites, the ugliest of all Greeks before Troy; they are 'separate'. Universals can themselves instantiate universals. Excellence belongs to beauty; they are 'combined'. It does not belong to ugliness; they are 'separate'.[24] (If Aristotle had seriously considered the category of facts, he would presumably have noticed that [A.4] would commit him to misclassify them as particulars because they are logical subjects which are not predicable.) Against this background the following two passages from the *Metaphysics* become transparent. They throw far more light on Aristotle's conception of truth and falsity than the notorious quotation [A.1], and they show that our conjecture about the message of [A.2] pointed in the right direction:

> [Of the members of a contradictory pair] the true [one] has the [character of an] affirmation in the case of what is combined and the [character of a] negation in the case of what is separate, while the falsehood has the contradictory of this apportionment. (*Met.* E 4: 1027b20–3; [A.5])

> The true and the false depend, as far as things [πράγματα] are concerned, upon their being combined or separate; so that somebody who takes what is separate to be separate, or what is combined to be combined, has a true thought; while somebody who is in disagreement with things [ὁ ἐναντίως ἔχων ἢ τὰ πράγματα] has a false thought. (*Met.* Θ 10: 1051b1–5; [A.6])

Taking Helen and beauty to be combined amounts to thinking of Helen that she is beautiful, and taking Helen and ugliness to be separate is thinking of Helen that she is not ugly. So this confirms the predicative reading of [A.1] which I

---

[24] Cf. *Prior Analytics* I 27, where the πράγματα of [A.4] are called ὄντα (43ª25, 32). We 'predicate of a universal *universally*', Aristotle claims (*De Int.* 7: 17b5–6), when we say that every F (no F) is G. The idea seems to be that in such utterances we ascribe to the universal signified by 'F' the property of having only instances which are G (not G).

tried to capture by SCHEMA A. Phrased in a way that is close to the language of [A.2–6], the *Aristotelian* conception of truth (and falsity) comes to something like this:

(A-TRUTH)   ∀x (x is a *true* predication / belief ↔ the object and the property which are combined [separate] according to x *are* combined [separate])
∀x (x is a *false* predication / belief ↔ the object and the property which are combined [separate] according to x are *not* combined [*not* separate]).

As to the definiendum, there is a problem, which I shall put aside for quite a while. In this chapter I shall just register that the accounts of truth under discussion, at least prima facie, take different kinds of entity to be truth-value bearers. In section 5.1, we shall pore over this (apparent or real) variation. A-TRUTH puts down for the record that in Aristotle truth and falsity can be ascribed to a statement or predication [λόγος (sc. ἀποφαντικός), ἀπόφανσις] as in [A.1] and [A.5], or to a thought, judgement, or belief [δόξα] as in [A.6].[25]

The notion of an *object* used in the definiens is as broad as can be: if '*a*' is a singular term, then *a* is an object. So Helen, her beauty, the fading of her beauty, the fact that she was beautiful, and beauty are all objects. The notion of a *property* used in the definiens is the liberal one that was specified in the previous chapter. Let us confine our attention to those cases that are structurally most favourable to Aristotle's account, i.e. statements that are made, and beliefs that could be voiced, by utterances of sentences that are composed of n singular terms and an n-place predicate, and briefly consider how the account copes with (1) 'empty' singular terms, (2) 'inappropriate' singular terms, and (3) the multiple decomposability of sentences.

(1) Suppose Ann, seeking an explanation for Ben's melancholy state, acquires the belief that Ben's wife is a shrew, but, as a matter of fact, Ben is an unhappy bachelor. How is Ann's belief to be evaluated in the light of A-TRUTH? Since X and Y are not combined if only X exists, her belief is to be classified as false, for the property of being a shrew which she takes to be combined with Ben's wife is not so combined. Or suppose that in the situation described, Ann asserts, 'Ben's wife is not kind'. Assuming that X and Y are separate if only X exists, her assertion is to be classified as true, for kindness is indeed separate from Ben's wife. Both verdicts coincide with those Aristotle gives for 'Socrates is sick' and 'Socrates is not sick' under the counterfactual assumption that Socrates does not exist.[26]

[25] On pp. 295–6, I shall quote two passages from Aristotle in which this duplicity of truth-candidates is quite explicit.
[26] *Cat.* 10: 13ᵇ27–35. (Unfortunately this passage is not easy to reconcile with *De Int.* 11: 21ᵃ25–8.)

(2) Suppose Ben asserts, 'Ann's husband is a very kind man', pointing to the man standing beside Ann, and that man really is very kind. Now as it so happens, Ann is unmarried: the man in question is her lover. In such a case we may not wish to say that Ben's statement is simply *true*, even though we would concede that he succeeds in saying something *true of* the man he is pointing to. [27] That man really has the property which he has according to Ben's statement, or, in the language of [A.1], Ben said of a man who is kind that he is kind. But then Aristotle's account covers such cases as well as their more felicitous counterparts where the definite description used by the speaker is descriptively adequate, yet it is only in the latter kind of case that we feel it entirely appropriate to say that the statement is (simply) true.

(3) The object–property distinction leaves some free play when we apply it to relational predications and thoughts. Let x be the statement that Meletus accuses Socrates. Which entity is 'the' object and which is 'the' property which are combined according to x? Is the relational property of accusing Socrates ascribed to Meletus? Or is Socrates said to have the relational property of being accused by Meletus? Or (although this is not likely to have occurred to Aristotle) is the relation of accusing attributed to Meletus and Socrates (in this order)? Obviously these are three different (n-place) properties, for they do not even have the same extension, and the objects to which they are assigned in x are different. Or let x be the belief that Socrates defends Socrates. What is the property that someone who holds x thereby takes Socrates to have? Is it the property of defending Socrates, or the property of being defended by Socrates, or the property of being a self-defender? Again, we have three different properties which are not even co-extensive. [28] But these consequences of multiple decomposability do not affect the evaluation of a predication or thought as regards truth and falsity.

At present, it is far more urgent to face the following question. Should we follow tradition in calling A-TRUTH a *correspondence* conception of truth? Davidson argues that Aristotle 'ought not to be considered as giving comfort to serious partisans of correspondence theories'. [29] His reason is that the Aristotelian definition does not introduce facts or states of affairs for truth candidates to correspond to. This is confirmed not only by [A.1], the passage Davidson relies on, but also by [A.5] and [A.6]. If the introduction of facts or states of affairs really is a *necessary*

---

[27] Cf. Keith Donnellan, 'Reference and Definite Descriptions', §VIII.

[28] The problem is due to the multiple decomposability of sentences, which was pointed out by Frege. The striking exemplification by 'aRa' sentences is due to Geach, *Reference and Generality*, §43: 'aRa' can be obtained by saturating '( )Ra', 'aR( )', or '( )R( )'.   [29] Davidson, 'Folly', 268.

condition for being a 'serious' correspondence theorist, then Davidson is right, of course: Aristotle does not belong to this camp. But as we shall soon see, this restriction looks rather arbitrary if one considers what was the dominant under-standing of truth as correspondence for many centuries. Yet a problem remains: even if there can be a correspondence view of truth without *facts*, there can hardly be a correspondence view without *correspondence*. But the Aristotelian explanations of 'true' contain no word or phrase which could be translated by 'corresponds to', 'squares with', 'agrees with', or 'fits'. So how does a two-place predicate get into the picture?

A key role in this story is played by Thomas Aquinas. He explains 'truth' in terms of *adaequatio, commensuratio, concordia, conformitas* or *convenientia* with an object. So here we have a rich supply of (nominalized) two-place predicates. About his favourite formula, 'Truth is the agreement (*adaequatio*) between intellect and object', Aquinas says that it is to be found in the *Book of Definitions* by Isaac Israeli, a Neoplatonist who lived in the early tenth century in North Africa.[30] This seems to be an error on Aquinas' part. The definition one finds in that treatise is very different from that formula, but the latter has been traced back to the Persian philosopher-scientist Ibn Sina (Avicenna) who flourished in the early eleventh century.[31] But no matter where Aquinas picked it up: the formula is actually far older than Israeli's and Ibn Sina's works. In the second half of the sixth century a commentator on Aristotle's Categories wrote that 'the *concordance* of statement and thing yields truth, whereas their discordance yields falsity [ἡ συμφωνία τῶν δύο—i.e. τοῦ λόγου καὶ τοῦ πράγματος—ποιεῖ τἀληθές, ἡ δὲ ἀσυμφωνία τὸ ψεῦδος]'.[32] Early in the sixth century Johannes Philoponus, also commenting on the Categories, claimed that truth consists 'in the *adjustment* (agreement) of state-ments to things [ἐν τῇ ἐφαρμογῇ τῶν λόγων πρὸς τὰ πράγματα]'.[33] Mid-fifth century Proclus maintained that truth is 'the *adjustment* of the knower to the known [ἡ πρὸς τὸ γιγνωσκόμενον ἐφαρμογὴ τοῦ γιγνώσκοντος]'[34] which is the least felicitous of all these phrases, since a knower cannot sensibly be called true. In the middle of the third century, Plotinus used a correspondence formula, if only to deny its applicability to the realm of 'primary beings' (whatever that may mean

---

[30] See Aquinas, *Quaestiones disputatae de veritate*, q. 1, a. 1; *Summa contra gentiles* I, c. 59; and *Summa theologiae* Ia, q. 16, a. 2, 2.   [31] Cf. translation and comments in Altmann and Stern, *Isaac Israeli*, 58–9.
[32] Elias [?], *In Aristotelis Categorias commentarium*, 184: 19–20. Like Philoponus before him, the author com-pares *'adjusting' a statement to a thing* with *fitting a sandal to a foot* (ibid., 20–2). We shall have occasion to return to this comparison in the next section.
[33] Philoponus, *In Aristotelis Categorias commentarium*, 81: 29–34. His teacher Ammonius had used the corresponding verb, ἐφαρμόζειν to explain the notion of truth (*In Aristotelis De Interpretatione commentarium*, 21: 10–13).   [34] Proclus, *In Platonis Timaeum commentaria*, II, 287: 3–5.

exactly): 'there truth is not a *concordance* with something else [συμφωνία πρòς
ἄλλο]'.[35] Carneades, head of the sceptical Academy, is reported to have taught
that a 'presentation [φαντασία]' is 'true when it is *in accord with* the object presented [σύμφωνος τῷ φανταστῷ], but false when it is in discord [διάφωνος]
with it'; which gets us to the second century BC.[36]

Now Aquinas is far from considering (what I shall henceforth call) the *correspondence formula* to compete with Aristotle's explanation. He takes the second
term of the relation to be the object [res] the true thought is about, and immediately after having explained truth in terms of agreement he goes on to explain
the correspondence formula with the help of Aristotle's definiens of 'true'
in [A.1]:

*[V]eritas intellectus [est] adaequatio intellectus et rei; secundum quod intellectus 'dicit esse quod est vel non
esse quod non est'.* [The truth of the intellect is the agreement between intellect and thing;
insofar as the intellect 'says of that which is that it is or of that which is not that it is not'.]
(*Summa contra gentiles* I, c. 59)[37]

Hence the explanation in terms of the intellect's agreement with the object
ultimately boils down to A-TRUTH, for Aquinas, too, understands Aristotle's
conception of truth along these lines:

*Intellectus... dicit verum... componendo et dividendo: nam in omni propositione aliquam formam significatam
per praedicatum, vel applicat alicui rei significatae per subjectum, vel removet ab ea.* [The intellect...
says what is true...by combining and separating, for in every proposition the intellect
either applies a form which the predicate stands for, to a thing which the subject
stands for, or it withholds the former from the latter.] (*Summa theologiae* Ia, q. 16, a. 2, resp.)

So an affirmation (or a negation) agrees with its object just in case the object
picked out by its subject-part meets the condition signified by the predicate 'is
(not) such-and-such'. The fit Aquinas has in mind is *not* that of the complete
predication to a fact. The fact that Socrates was wise is what the subject of the
following predication stands for: 'The fact that Socrates was wise is well known.'
Facts are normally not what true predications are *about*.[38]

---

[35] Plotinus, *Enneads*, III.7, 4: 11–12.

[36] I have picked up the reference to Carneades from Bolzano (*WL*, I. 127), who quotes Sextus
Empiricus, *Adversus Mathematicos*, VII. 168. Surprisingly Bolzano does not mention Aquinas in his historical sketch at all (although Aquinas was surely the most influential propagator of the correspondence
formula), but jumps from Carneades to philosophers of the Enlightenment.

[37] Like the Greek original (see above on [A.1]), the Latin translation of Aristotle has a *de dicto* reading
under which all truths are declared to be tautological (in the ancient sense). In *Q. de veritate*, q. 1, a. 1, ad
1, Aquinas articulates the intended *de re* reading: something true is said 'if one says about something
which is that it is [*cum dicitur esse de aliquo quod est*]. [38] Strawson, 'Truth' (1950), 196.

3.1.2 *Interlude: non-propositional truth*

Let us pause, to ask why Aquinas is so fond of the correspondence formula—in spite of the fact that he endorses the Aristotelian explanation. The only reason I can see is that he believes the correspondence formula to be applicable to truth in what is said or thought as well as to what he calls *'truth in things [veritas in rebus]'*.[39] Consider one of Aquinas' paradigms for which talk of 'truth in things' is most easily understood: an artefact of kind F is a 'true F' if it perfectly complies with its *praeconceptio* in the mind of the standard-setting F-designer. Hence if intellect and object do not agree with each other, then this might be either the intellect's or the object's fault. Either the *object* serves as 'measure and rule *[mensura et regula]*' for our thinking: the belief or statement should be in agreement with the object it is about. Or the *thought* serves as 'measure and rule' for the object: the object should be in agreement with its design.[40] Thus, although *agreement with* is a symmetrical relation, there are different 'directions of fit'.[41] The following example may help to alleviate the worry that there is a conflict here: 'If Cinderella goes into a shoe store to buy a new pair of shoes, she takes her foot size as given and seeks shoes to fit [the foot as *mensura et regula*]. But when the prince seeks the owner of the shoe, he takes the shoe as given and seeks a foot to fit the shoe [the shoe as *mensura et regula*].'[42] The onus of match may fall on either side.

The notion of *veritas in rebus*, of 'objectual truth' as one might call it[43] (as opposed to truth in what can be thought or said, 'propositional truth' for short) fell into disrepute with Hobbes, Descartes, Spinoza, and Locke.[44] Even Leibniz, who was prone to a charitable treatment of traditional philosophy, condemned it as *'bien inutile et presque vuide de sens* [thoroughly useless and almost senseless]'.[45] Kant declared the scholastics' use of 'true' as a 'predicate of things' to be mistaken.[46] It was left to Hegel to make an attempt at breathing new life into the moribund notion of objectual truth. He even regarded it as philosophically more important than the concept of propositional truth or correctness (as he called it):

Die Wahrheit ist dies, daß die Objektivität dem Begriffe entspricht.... Dieser tiefere Sinn der Wahrheit ist es, um den es sich handelt, wenn z.B. von einem wahren Staat oder von einem wahren Kunstwerk die Rede ist.

---

[39] Cf. *Summa theol. Ia*, q. 16, a. 1, resp. (last sentence).

[40] Cf. Aquinas, *Summa theol. Ia*, q. 16, a. 1; q. 21, a. 2. With respect to the intellect of the *divine* designer and creator, Aquinas maintains, *every* contingently existing thing is 'true': *Q. de veritate*, q. 1, a. 10.

[41] This is a concept which Austin (in 'How to Talk') introduced into the theory of speech-acts.

[42] Searle, *Intentionality*, 8. Latin embellishments are mine.

[43] Traditionally also referred to as 'metaphysical' or 'transcendental' truth.

[44] Hobbes, *De corpore*, ch. III, sect. 7; Descartes, *Regulae ad directionem ingenii*, rule VIII, 396 (tr. 30); Spinoza, *Cogitata metaphysica*, pt. I, ch. 6, 247 (tr. 312–13); Locke, *An Essay concerning Human Understanding*, bk. IV, ch. 5, sect. 11.   [45] Leibniz, *Nouveaux essais sur l'entendement humain*, bk. IV, ch. 5, sect. 11, 397 (tr. ditto).

[46] Kant, *Kritik der reinen Vernunft*, B 113–14; cf. B 350.

Diese Gegenstände sind wahr, wenn sie das sind, was sie sein sollen, d.h. wenn ihre Realität ihrem Begriff entspricht . . . / . . . Richtigkeit und Wahrheit werden im gemeinen Leben sehr häufig als gleichbedeutend betrachtet . . . / . . . [Doch] findet sich die tiefere (philosophische) Bedeutung der Wahrheit zum Teil auch schon im gewöhnlichen Sprachgebrauch. So spricht man z.B. von einem wahren Freund und versteht darunter einen solchen, dessen Handlungsweise dem Begriff der Freundschaft gemäß ist. . . . In diesem Sinne ist ein schlechter Staat ein unwahrer Staat. . . . Von einem solchen schlechten Gegenstand können wir uns eine richtige Vorstellung machen, aber der Inhalt dieser Vorstellung ist ein in sich Unwahres. Solcher Richtigkeiten, die zugleich Unwahrheiten sind, können wir viele im Kopf haben. [Truth consists in the conformity of objectivity with the notion. . . . It is in this deeper sense of truth that we speak of a true State, or of a true work of art. Objects are true, if they are as they ought to be, i.e. if their reality conforms to their notion. . . . / . . . In common life correctness and truth are very often taken to be synonyms . . . / . . . [But] traces of the deeper (philosophical) meaning of truth may be found even in ordinary language. Thus we speak of a true friend; by which we mean a friend whose behaviour is in accordance with the notion of friendship. . . . In this sense a bad State is an untrue State. . . . Of such a bad object we may form a correct conception, but the content of this conception is something inherently untrue. Such correctnesses, which are at the same time untruths, we may have many in our heads.] (*Enzyklopädie, Wissenschaft der Logik* [1830], §213 and n.; §172; §24 n. 2)

The final remark is confused: if a thinker is right in taking State X to be a bad State, then it is his thought that X is bad which is correct (propositionally true), whereas it is State X which is untrue (bad). So there is not one thing, within our heads or wherever, which is both correct and untrue. (Philosophers who favour an Identity Theory of truth make a contention about what Hegel prefers to call correctness.[47] But as far as correctness is concerned, Hegel just repeats the traditional correspondence account. So in spite of rumours to the contrary,[48] he clearly does not belong to the ranks of Identity Theorists.) Hegel's proposal to use '*Richtigkeit* [correctness]' for propositional truth has not won many adherents even in the German-speaking world—apart from Heidegger and his followers, and, for all I know, it did not win any adherents in the anglophone world. Be that as it may, a rose by any other name will smell as sweet: propositional truth is the topic of this book.[49] In the passages quoted, Hegel does not give any reason why he takes the notion of objectual truth to be 'deeper' than that of propositional truth. At any rate, the two notions are vastly different. Something is a true F, in Hegel's acceptation of this phrase, if and only if it satisfies the

---

[47] See the discussion of (*Idem*) in Ch. 1.   [48] Thomas Baldwin, 'The Identity Theory of Truth', 49.

[49] *Within* the field of what I call propositional truth there seem to be subtle differences in actual usage between 'true' on the one hand and 'correct' and 'right' on the other: as a reply to the question 'You are married?' We expect 'That's right' rather than 'That's true,' and when assessing the result of a calculation, 'That's correct' is more natural than 'That's true' (Rundle, *GP*, 365–6).

highest standards for being an F.[50] Hence the verdict that something which has been called a work of art is not a true work of art throws some doubt on its claim to the title 'work of art'. By contrast, the verdict that something which has been called a statement is not true leaves its claim to the title 'statement' entirely unaffected. Furthermore, in its objectual use the adjective 'true' is not a predicate in its own right but substantive-hungry or syncategorematic.[51] A true work of art is not a work of art which is true, and since Ann's friend, the amateur painter Ben, may be a true friend without being a true artist, it does not make sense to say that he is true, full-stop, or to acknowledge his truth. A true statement, on the other hand, is both a statement and true, and its truth can sensibly be acknowledged.

For many years Martin Heidegger maintained that propositional truth is ontologically dependent on a kind of non-propositional truth. Before Plato, he claimed, the Greeks thought of truth, in accordance with the alleged etymology of *ἀ-λήθ-εια* as *Un-verborgen-heit* [un-hidden-ness, unconcealedness, disclosedness] of things rather than as *ὀρθότης*, as *Richtigkeit der Aussagen oder Urteile* [correctness of statements or judgements], and he tried to show that the possibility of correctness (and of incorrectness, for that matter) is due to unhiddenness. After *Sein und Zeit*, drawing on an analogy with what happens when things become visible at dawn, Heidegger came to conceive of *Unverborgenheit* rather as *Entbergung*, as a process [*Geschehnis*] of things unveiling themselves, as an unconcealment or disclosure which comes to pass without any kind of human intervention.[52] It is only because this (metaphorically described) process takes place, he argued, that statements have the property of being true (or of being false), hence 'what first makes correctness [of the statement] possible must with more original right be taken as the essence of truth.'[53] This argument is less than persuasive. For one thing, if the possibility of true statements is due to the same process as the possibility of false statements (as we are told), why is that process the essence of being true rather than the essence of being *true or false*? And then, why is that to which propositional truth owes its possibility to be taken as the *essence* of truth?

---

[50] Cf. Bolzano, *WL*, I, 110; Frege, '*Der Gedanke*', 59; White, *Truth*, 3–6. I do not claim that this biconditional covers all non-propositional uses of 'true'. In 'true to the cause', for example, 'true' means something like *faithful*. (Cf. Verdi, *Otello*, III. iii. 278: 'If she be false, O, then heaven mocks itself.')

[51] Cf. Geach, 'Good and Evil', on 'good'; Austin, *Sense and Sensibilia*, Ch. 7, on 'real'; and Quine, *W&O*. 132 (and 103) on 'false prophets' and 'true artists'.

[52] See, for example, Heidegger, '*Der Ursprung des Kunstwerks* [The Origin of the Work of Art]', 42 (176).

[53] Heidegger, '*Vom Wesen der Wahrheit* [On the Essence of Truth]', 12 (124–5): '*muß das, was die Richtigkeit [der Aussage] erst ermöglicht, mit ursprünglicherem Recht als das Wesen der Wahrheit gelten.*'

You might as well argue, 'Seeing becomes possible only through light; therefore light must be taken as the essence of seeing.'[54]

In the early 1960s Heidegger came round to conceding that, long before the alleged Platonic decline, the Greeks took ἀλήθεια to be a property of statements[55] and that it was a mistake to describe the history of conceptions of truth as a (philosophically deplorable) transition from conceiving truth as unhiddenness to conceiving truth as correctness.[56] But although he had come to admit, '*Die Frage . . . nach der Unverborgenheit als solcher ist nicht die Frage nach der Wahrheit* [The question, What is unhiddenness as such?, is *not* the question, What is truth?]',[57] he kept on claiming that truth as correctness somehow depends upon the process of things unveiling themselves. But as far as I can see (which may not be very far), Heidegger's descriptions of that process always rely on metaphors and a play on words, and he never succeeds in clarifying how correctness (as opposed to incorrectness) is to be accounted for in terms of its alleged dependency on that process.

3.1.3 *Variants and limits of the Aristotelian conception*

Let us return to Aquinas' rendering of the Aristotelian conception of (propositional) truth and falsity in terms of the correspondence formula. In the centuries to follow, most philosophers, Hegel and Heidegger included, continue to use Aquinas' relational predicates in their characterizations of (propositional) truth, and they always take the second term of the relation to be an object. Thus, for example, Christian Wolff writes:[58]

Si praedicatum . . . subiecto . . . convenit, propositio dicitur vera; si minus, falsa. Est itaque veritas consensus iudicii nostri cum obiecto, seu re repraesentata; falsitas vero dissensus eiusdem ab obiecto. [If what is

---

[54] There is a predecessor of this glaring non sequitur in §44.b of *Sein und Zeit*. For detailed exegesis and criticism, cf. part II of Tugendhat, *Der Wahrheitsbegriff bei Husserl und Heidegger*.

[55] As Charles Kahn puts it, 'even in the earliest use, in Homer, there is no trace of "the things themselves" emerging from their hiddenness or showing themselves', and insofar as archaic usage reflects the alleged etymology of 'ἀλήθεια' at all, it concerns 'truthfulness or sincerity in one man's speaking openly to another, *sans arrière-pensée*' (*The Verb 'be' in Ancient Greek*, 365). Cf. Dorothea Frede, '*Wahrheit*', §4, and the references to earlier research by Boeder, Heitsch, and Krischer.

[56] Heidegger, '*Das Ende der Philosophie und die Aufgabe des Denkens*', 77 (390).

[57] Ibid., 77 (389). As to 'correctness', Heidegger goes on to give a very rough sketch of two different (and historically consecutive) conceptions, *adaequatio* and *certitudo*. Varieties of the former are currently our topic; a version of the latter will be discussed in Ch. 7.1.1.

[58] What follows is just a particularly clear statement of what you will also find in Descartes, Spinoza, and Leibniz. Thus Descartes, in a letter to Mersenne, 597 (tr. 139): the word 'truth', properly understood, means *la conformité de la pensée avec l'objet* (the conformity of thought with its object); Spinoza, in *Korte Verhandeling . . .* , 78 (tr. 119): truth is 'an affirmation (or denial) that one makes concerning a thing [*zaak*] and which agrees [*overeenkomende*] with the thing itself'; Leibniz, in *Nouveaux Essais*, IV, 5, §11, 398 (tr. ditto): truth is to be found in '*la correspondance des propositions qui sont dans l'esprit avec les choses dont il s'agit* [correspondence of propositions that are in the mind with the things that they are about]'.

predicated fits the subject, the proposition is called true; in the case of a misfit, it is called false. Hence truth is the agreement of our judgement with the object or the thing represented, and falsity is its disagreement with the object.] (*Philosophia rationalis sive Logica*, §505)

Kant concurs, both in his 'Inaugural Dissertation':

Veritas in iudicando consist[i]t in consensus praedicati cum subiecto dato. [Truth in a judgement consists in the agreement of its predicate with the given subject.] (*De mundi ... forma et principiis*, sect. II, §11)

and in the first Critique:

Wahrheit [besteht] in der Übereinstimmung einer Erkenntnis mit ihrem Gegenstande.... Eine Erkenntnis ist falsch, wenn sie mit dem Gegenstande, worauf sie bezogen wird, nicht übereinstimmt, ob sie gleich etwas enthält, was wohl von anderen Gegenständen gelten könnte. [Truth consists in the agreement of a judgement with its object.... A judgement is false if it does not agree with the object it is about, even if it contains something which may hold of other objects.] (*Kritik der reinen Vernunft*, B 82–3)[59]

The judgement that Königsberg is a metropolis, for example, is false, but it contains something which holds of, or fits, St Petersburg, namely (the predicable) *that it is a metropolis*. Hence the corresponding judgement about St Petersburg is true.

All these philosophers take a mental or verbal predication to 'agree with its object' if and only if what is predicated fits (holds of) the object it is predicated of, hence they explain the concept of truth in terms of *object-based correspondence*:

(ObjC) $\forall x$ (x is a true mental or verbal predication $\leftrightarrow$ what is predicated in x fits the object it is predicated of).

Clearly this formula inherits all the problems we made out for A-TRUTH.[60]

In 1837 Bolzano's explanation of truth is still in the same spirit, but he painstakingly avoids any appeal to the correspondence formula.[61] Taking *Sätze an sich*, thinkables and sayables which can be singled out by that-clauses, to be truth-value bearers, he writes:

Ein Satz [ist] wahr, wenn er ... von seinem Gegenstande aussagt, was demselben zukommt. [A proposition is true if [and only if] it ascribes to its object something that belongs to it.] (*WL* I. 124)[62]

---

[59] Cf. ibid., B 236, 296, 670, 848; *Logik*, Introduction, sect. VII. B, init. The phrasing in the second quotation above and in several other passages in the *Kritik* is rather unfortunate, since '*wahre Erkenntnis*' is pleonastic, and '*falsche Erkenntnis*' is a contradiction in terms. Kant should have used the (German counterpart of) the word he used in the first quotation above: '*Urteil* [judgement]'. My translation is meant to spare the reader this embarrassment.   [60] See above, pp. 100–1.

[61] Bolzano criticizes the correspondence formula, mainly because of the 'shifting meaning [*schwankende Bedeutung*]' of 'agreement' and its suggestion of similarity: see *WL* I. 127–32, 179–80, 200; and '*Verbesserungen und Zusätze zur Logik*', 128, 163.

[62] The explanation suggested in Alston, *RCT*, 26 formula (vii), is equivalent to this.

This is obviously very close to the Aristotelian account. But why does Bolzano not add, like Aristotle, a clause for true negations, 'or denies of its object something that it lacks'? Unlike many of his predecessors, Bolzano does not leave us in the dark as to why he drops it: he maintains that 'Thersites is not beautiful' is used either to ascribe lack of truth to the proposition that Thersites is beautiful (external negation) or to ascribe lack of beauty to Thersites (internal negation).[63]

The quotation above does not contain Bolzano's last word on the concept of truth. Under the heading '*Definition der Wahrheit* [definition of truth]', he wrote in a manuscript:

Ein Satz ist wahr, wenn jeder Gegenstand, der dem Subjecte des Satzes untersteht, eine Beschaffenheit hat, die dem Prädicate untersteht. [A proposition is true if [and only if] every object which falls under its subject has a property which falls under the predicate.] ('*Verbesserungen*', 105)

Compared with the previous passage, this has the advantage of no longer saying of propositions that they 'ascribe' something to something (which would be more appropriately said of speakers and thinkers). The terms 'subject' and 'predicate' here can be easily misunderstood. Bolzano assumes that every proposition X can be expressed by a sentence of the form 'a has F-ness', where the sense of 'a' is what he calls the subject(-part) of X, and the sense of 'F-ness' is what he calls the predicate(-part) of X. Bolzano reads 'Socrates is mortal' as 'Socrates has mortality', and 'All men are mortal' as 'Man has mortality'. So his explanation is meant to cover immediately both the proposition that Socrates is mortal and the proposition that all men are mortal. In the former case, every object falling under the subject-part of the proposition is identical with Socrates. In 'a has redness' (which is the canonical reformulation of 'a is red') Bolzano takes the predicate-expression to express a sense (concept) under which *many* properties fall, namely all maximally specific shades of redness.[64] Finally, we should register that in Bolzano's (as in Aristotle's) eyes, the quantifier 'every' has existential import.[65] So we can render the *Bolzanian* conception of truth (and falsity) in the following way:

(B-Truth) $\forall$x [x is a *true* proposition $\leftrightarrow$

$\exists$y (y falls under the subject-part of x) &

$\forall$y (y falls under the subject-part of x $\rightarrow$

$\exists$z (z falls under the predicate-part of x & y has z))].

A proposition which is not true is *false*.

---

[63] Bolzano, *WL*, II. 45–7, 269.   [64] Bolzano, *WL* II. 26–7; cf. Moore, *Philosophical Studies*, 22.

[65] Cf., *inter alia*, Bolzano, *WL* II. 114, no. 3.

This account[66] enjoins an assessment of the use of (1) 'empty' and (2) 'inappropriate' subject-terms that differs markedly from that which was recommended by its Aristotelian predecessor:[67] according to B-Truth, (1) a proposition is always false if nothing falls under its subject-part, and (2) what the subject-part of the propositional content of a thought represents is independent of what the thinker *takes* it to represent. The fact of multiple decomposability, (3), is embarrassing for B-Truth, for this account presupposes a unique decomposition for each proposition. (Do 'Socrates has the property of being as tall as Theaetetus' and 'Theaetetus has the property of being as tall as Socrates' express different propositions?)

Let us leave Prague for Vienna. Half a century later, Franz Brentano delivered a lecture, 'On the Concept of Truth'. His point of departure was (as was to be expected from an Aristotelian scholar of his rank) Aristotle's conception of truth. Actually, it is the formulation of this account given in passage [A.6] above. What is most interesting is that Brentano lays claim to Aristotle's authority for the correspondence formula:

Hören wir . . ., wie der mächtigste wissenschaftliche Geist, der je auf die Geschicke der Menschheit Einfluß genommen hat, den Terminus 'Wahrheit' erklärt. . . . Wann ist nach ihm ein Urteil wahr?, wann falsch? Aristoteles antwortet darauf, wahr sei es, wenn der Urteilende sich den Dingen entsprechend, falsch, wenn er sich ihnen entgegengesetzt verhalte. 'Wenn Einer, was geschieden ist, für geschieden, was verbunden ist, für verbunden hält, urteilt er wahr, und er irrt, wenn er sich entgegengesetzt verhält.' Damit war . . . Wahrheit für die Übereinstimmung des Urteils mit den wirklichen Dingen erklärt. [Let us recall how the most powerful scientific mind ever to influence the fate of mankind explained the term 'truth'. . . . When—according to Aristotle—is a judgement true, when is it false? His answer is this: a judgement is true if the person who is making the judgement is in agreement with things, and it is false, if he is in disagreement with things. 'If somebody takes what is separate to be separate, or what is combined to be combined, he judges truly, and he is in error if he does the opposite.' Thereby truth was declared to be the agreement of the judgement with real things.] ('*Über den Begriff der Wahrheit*', §§7, 11–12)[68]

'Being in disagreement with things' was Aristotle's abbreviation, in [A.6] above, for 'taking what is combined to be separate, and taking what is separate to be combined'. Brentano invents a positive counterpart to this abbreviation, '*being in agreement with things*' and then transfers it from persons to judgements. Thus he is

---

[66] On pp. 200–1 I shall give in passing a 'semanticized' version of Bolzano's conception.

[67] See above, pp. 100–1.

[68] Cf. Brentano, *Von der mannigfachen Bedeutung des Seienden nach Aristoteles*, 26 ff., where he quotes both [A.5] and [A.6].

able to connect Aristotle's definition almost seamlessly with the correspondence formula of later centuries. *This* is the tradition Tarski defers to when he declares again and again (much to Davidson's annoyance) that he wants to remain faithful to 'the intentions which are contained in the so-called classical conception of truth ("true—agreeing with reality")'.[69]

But like Brentano before him,[70] and for a very similar reason, Tarski is not satisfied with the Aristotelian explanation. In 1944 he merely complains that it is 'not sufficiently precise and clear', though he prefers it to two others which are cast in more 'modern philosophical terminology'.[71] In his last paper on truth he explicitly states why he is dissatisfied:

[The Aristotelian explanation] is not general enough; it refers only to sentences that 'say' about something 'that it is' or 'that it is not'; in most cases it would hardly be possible to cast a sentence in this mold without slanting the sense of the sentence and forcing the spirit of the language. ('Truth and Proof', 402)

Let us call this worry the Procrustes Problem. If we understand [A.1], the passage that Tarski refers to, along the lines suggested in A-TRUTH, the situation may not be quite as hopeless as he makes it appear. Atomic sentences are obviously the paradigm cases for the Aristotelian explanation, and here we can easily find for each true utterance an object to which a property is ascribed in that utterance. But conditional and other molecular sentences can be covered, too, if they contain a singular term. Thus, saying 'Ann is happy if she is able to come' can be construed as ascribing to Ann the property of *being happy if able to come*.[72] But the more complex our truth-candidates are, the more convoluted such construals become. Furthermore, it is hard to see how one could tame along these lines a feature-placing sentence such as

(S) As it was rather cold, it may have been snowing for many hours.

---

[69] Tarski, *Der Wahrheitsbegriff*...(henceforth *WB*), 153. (Quoted as [T.11] on p. 209 below, Bolzano's *Theory of Science* was a source of inspiration for Twardowski, whose teacher was Brentano; Twardowski was a teacher of Kotarbiński, and Kotarbiński was Tarski's philosophy teacher in Warsaw. This will not be our last encounter with Brentano's legacy in Poland.)

[70] Cf. Brentano, '*Über den Begriff der Wahrheit*', §42, on 'There are no dragons'; and his pupil Carl Stumpf, *Erkenntnislehre*, 58, on 'It is raining'. Which property, they asked, do we ascribe to which object when we utter such a sentence? Bolzano would have replied: In the first case, what is said is about the concept of a dragon, and the property of lacking 'objectuality' (of not being instantiated) is ascribed to it (*WL*, ii. 212–13). In the second case, he would continue, what is said is about the concept of a rainfall occurring at the time of the utterance in the vicinity of the speaker, and the property of being 'objectual' (of being instantiated) is attributed to it (*WL*, ii 5. 215).

[71] Tarski, 'The Semantic Conception of Truth', §3; see Ch. 4.1.5 below.

[72] Cf. Alston, *RCT*, 25.

Take any utterance of (S): which property could be said to be ascribed in this utterance to which object(s)? We could prefix 'The world is such that' to (S), to be sure, but that could be done with every declarative sentence, and Aristotle certainly does not assume that all truth-candidates ascribe a property to one and the same object, the universe. It would not help here to resort to Tarski's own recursive strategy and to take A-TRUTH as a base clause for atomic sentences only. (S) contains two non-extensional connectives ('as', '[it] may [be the case that]'), a feature-placing construction (with dummy 'it'), tenses, and a non-standard quantifier ('many'). As we shall see in Chapter 4.1, none of this is provided for by Tarski's machinery. Obviously, (ObjC) and B-TRUTH are in trouble here as well, since they, too, depend on the assumption that every truth-candidate has a subject-predicate structure. Can we paraphrase (S) in this style 'without slanting its sense and forcing the spirit of the language'?

The Procrustes Problem may not be unsolvable, but should our explanation of the concept of truth depend on its solvability? In any case, it can be evaded by theorists of fact-based correspondence (of *one* of two varieties, as we shall see). So let us turn now to the right branch under QUESTION 5 (see Figure 1.1).

3.2 Cambridge Correspondence

It was in about 1910 in Cambridge that G. E. Moore and Bertrand Russell married 'correspondence' with 'fact', and Ludwig Wittgenstein was soon to give his blessing to this union.[73]

Do agreement with reality and correspondence to the facts come to the same thing? That depends on how grand terms like 'reality', '*Wirklichkeit*' (or 'the world', '*die Welt*') are to be understood. Of course, if we take reality to be the totality of facts, the answer is, Yes, and we all know by heart the most famous recommendation of the latter option: '*Die Welt ist alles, was der Fall ist. Die Welt ist die Gesamtheit der Tatsachen, nicht der Dinge.* [The world is everything that is the case.

---

[73] The story of their betrothal in the work of German and Austrian philosophers between 1879 and 1911 is told in Barry Smith, '*Sachverhalt*', and Simons, '*Tatsache*'. An incidental earlier meeting of these notions in British philosophy is registered by Prior in *The Doctrine of Propositions and Terms*, 19. Geach's somewhat defamatory contention that it was largely due to 'journalism' that 'facts came to be counted among the entities in the philosopher's world' does not square with the facts, if I may say so ('Aristotle on Conjunctive Propositions', 21–2). Incidentally, one senses a certain tension between Geach's many eulogies of 'Cambridge philosophers of the great days, like Russell and McTaggart' ('What Actually Exists', 71), not to mention the author of the *Tractatus*, and his sneering remarks about 'this philosophy's journalistic origins'.

The world is the totality of facts, not of things.]'[74] But if we take reality or the world to be the spatio-temporal order, the totality of locatables and datables, then the answer is, No, and obviously Wittgenstein even relies on this natural, 'Heaven and Earth' understanding of the term 'the world' in order to lend poignancy to the opening sentence of the *Tractatus*. But isn't the natural understanding the only correct one? If so, the *Tractatus* starts with a category mistake. This is the point of Strawson's slightly ironic transformation of Wittgenstein's pronouncements: 'The *facts* are everything that is the case',[75] and 'The world is the totality of *things*, not of facts'.[76] I take it that 'things' in the latter remark is not meant to exclude events, states, and particularized qualities.[77] The actual world, the universe, is not just the totality of all continuants that actually exist, because these continuants are common to many possible worlds. (This may be the point of Russell's remark that the universe 'is not completely described by a lot of "particulars"',[78] or, rather, by a list of many particulars. And it would not be completely described by a list of many particulars and universals either, because in different possible worlds these may be differently combined.) Anti-Cantabrigians like Strawson must take the universe to comprise continuants as well as the events they are actually involved in, the states they are actually in, and the particularized qualities they actually have.

One can easily get the impression that the Cambridge union of truth and fact is firmly based on a truism. Austin, for one, seems to be a victim of this impression when he writes:

When is a statement true? The temptation is to answer (at least if we confine ourselves to 'straightforward' statements): 'When it corresponds to the facts'. And as a piece of standard English this can hardly be wrong. Indeed, I must confess I do not think it wrong at all: the theory of truth is a series of truisms. ('Truth', 121)

Notice that the piece of standard English has 'facts' in the plural. What Crispin Wright is fond of calling the 'Correspondence Platitude',[79] i.e. the schema

'P' is true if and only if 'P' corresponds to the facts,

---

[74] Wittgenstein, *Tractatus Logico-Philosophicus*, 1, 1.1. In *Mind and World* McDowell follows in his footsteps when he calls the world 'a constellation of facts'.   [75] Strawson, 'Reply to Mauricio Beuchot', 30.

[76] Strawson, 'Truth' (1950), 198. Simons concurs: see 'How the World Can Make Propositions True' (henceforth 'World'), 115.

[77] An instance of the last category (which will receive some attention in Ch. 3.5.1) is the red with which Ann's face was suffused when she blushed and which faded gradually away.

[78] Russell, 'The Philosophy of Logical Atomism' (henceforth 'PLA'), 183.

[79] Wright, *T&O*, 25, *et passim*. But notice that Wright's Correspondence Platitude, as formulated here, takes sentences rather than statements to be truth-value bearers, which does not conform with Austin's piece of standard English. (At least so I shall argue in sect. 5.1.) By contrast, in 'Debate', 227, = 'Minimalism', 760, Wright offers a fact-free non-sentential formulation of what he apparently regards as the same platitude.

reproduces this feature (without Austin's parenthetical restriction to 'straightforward' statements[80]). But as we shall soon see, (some) theorists of fact-based correspondence would maintain, for example, that the suspect's statement that he was at home at the time of the crime corresponds, if true, with *the fact that he was at home at the time of the crime*. Yet in standard English his true statement would rather be said to correspond with (square with, tally with, fit, be borne out by) *various* facts known to the police, e.g. that he was seen by a neighbour, answered the phone, described accurately the TV film on at that time, etc. So the piece of standard English is at one remove from any particular conception of truth.[81]

The title 'Fact-based Correspondence' actually covers two different conceptions which are registered on our flow chart under QUESTION 7 (see Figure 1.1). If two philosophers seem to answer the question 'What is it that truth-bearers correspond to?' unanimously by saying: 'Facts', this consensus might conceal fundamental differences between their views. And so it does already in the case of Moore, Russell, and the early Wittgenstein.

3.2.1 *Moorean prodigality*

In his 1910–11 lectures in London, published some decades later under the title *Some Main Problems of Philosophy*, Moore presents his version of a correspondence theory of truth. First he notes a constraint on definitions of truth and falsity:

Suppose that . . . my friend believes that I have gone away for my holidays. There is, I think, no doubt whatever that there is at least one ordinary sense of the words 'true' and 'false', such that the following statements hold [:] [i]f this belief of his is true then I must have gone away for my holidays . . . and, conversely . . . if I have gone away, then this belief of his certainly is true. . . . In other words, my having actually gone away for my holidays is both a necessary and a sufficient condition for the truth of his belief. . . . And similarly . . . my not having gone away is both a necessary and a sufficient condition for the falsehood of this belief. . . . If, therefore, we are to find a correct definition of these senses of the words 'true' and 'false' it must be a definition which does not conflict with the statement that these conditions are necessary and sufficient conditions. (*SMPP*, 274–5; [M.1])

---

[80] Austin hints at his reason for this restriction in a later footnote: 'If space permitted, other types of statements (existential, general, hypothetical, etc.) should be dealt with: these raise problems rather of meaning than of truth, though I feel uneasiness about hypotheticals' ('Truth', 123). On the same page it becomes clear that Austin sympathizes with (what I shall call) the parsimoniousness of Logical Atomism. See below, sect. 3.2.2.

[81] Cf. Austin, 'Unfair to Facts', 160; Zeno Vendler, 'Facts and Events', 146; White, *Truth*, 107–8; Rundle, *GP*, 340–1. White also maintains that it should be 'corresponds *with*' rather than 'corresponds to' (*Truth*, 105–6). 'Truths correspond to (with) the facts' does not imply that for each truth there is exactly one fact to which it corresponds, any more than 'Spiders give her the willies' implies that for each spider she comes across there is exactly one willy such that the former gives her the latter.

This is a sadly neglected (propositionalist) precursor of Tarski's famous Criterion T.[82] The that-clause in 'the belief that p' specifies what it takes for the belief to be true: nothing more is required for its truth, and nothing less will suffice. Surely a good way to demonstrate the absence of a conflict between statements of the form 'The belief that p is true if and only if p' and an alleged definition of 'true' would be to show that the latter entails the former. (The right-to-left direction of the biconditional is only plausible if we understand the locution 'the belief that p' as it is to be understood in 'Nobody holds the belief that p, and yet it may be true.'[83]) Moore immediately goes on to insist that 'the statement that these conditions are necessary and sufficient does not *constitute* a definition' (not even a 'partial definition' of 'true' as applied to a particular belief, as Tarski might say). For all substitution-instances of 'p', Moore observes, the *satisfied* necessary and sufficient condition for the truth of the belief that p can be referred to as '*the fact that p*': in each and every case one and the same that-clause can serve to specify both the true belief and the pertinent fact.[84] In order to define truth, Moore needs a name for the relation that obtains between a belief and a fact whenever the belief is true:

[E]very true belief has some peculiar relation to one fact, and one fact only—every *different* true belief having the relation in question to a *different* fact ... / ... The relation I mean is the relation which the belief *that I have gone away*, if true, has to the fact *that I have gone away*, and to no other fact.... [T]he difficulty of *defining* truth and falsehood arises chiefly from the fact that this relation ... has no unambiguous name; it has no name which is just appropriated to it alone, and which may not also be used for other relations, which are perhaps quite different from it.... I propose to call it the relation of 'correspondence'.... [U]sing the name 'correspondence' *merely* as a name for this relation, we can at once assert 'To say that this belief is true is to say that there is in the Universe a fact to which it corresponds; and to say that it is false is to say that there is *not* in the Universe any fact to which it corresponds.' And this statement, I think, fulfils all the requirements of a definition—a definition of what we actually mean by saying that the belief is true or false. (*SMPP* 256, 276–7; [M.2])

The long sentence between quotation marks formulates the central claim of the Moorean conception of truth as *fact-based correspondence*:[85]

(M-FactC) $\forall x$ [x is a true belief $\leftrightarrow$ $\exists y$ (y is a fact & x corresponds to y)]

---

[82] See Ch. 4.1.1. Cf. also Ramsey: '[A] belief that p is true if and only if p. We may deride this as trivial formalism, but since we cannot contradict it without absurdity, it provides a slight check on any deeper investigations that they must square with this obvious truism' (*On Truth*, 14). So, *pace* Anil Gupta, 'Tarski's Definition of Truth', 265, and many others, Tarski was *not* the first to use such an equivalence as a touchstone for explanations of 'true'.   [83] Cf. my 'Some Varieties of Thinking', 372.

[84] *SMPP*, 256–7.

[85] In 1912 Russell also accepted (M-FactC), as can be seen from ch. 12 of *The Problems of Philosophy*, last page: 'a belief is true when there is a corresponding fact, and is false when there is no corresponding fact'.

But (M-FactC) does not yet fully capture Moore's conception as formulated in [M.2], since it leaves open the possibility that *more than one fact* might correspond to one and the same true belief. So the following principle has to be added:

(P) $\forall x$ [x is a true belief $\rightarrow \exists_1 y$ (y is a fact & x corresponds to y)].

However complex a true belief may be, there is exactly one ('$\exists_1$') fact to which it owes its truth. Thus a true belief expressed by an utterance of a disjunction of conjunctions such as 'Either Ben goes out, and Ann stays at home, or Ann goes out, and Ben stays at home' has its own fact corresponding to it.

This feature of Moore's account reappears in one of the latest pleas for an explanation of truth as fact-based correspondence. Without ever mentioning the philosopher who is closer to his position than anyone else, Searle writes:

What fact corresponds to the true statement that the cat is not on the mat? Obviously the fact that the cat is not on the mat. What fact corresponds to the true statement that if the cat had been on the mat the dog would have bitten it? Obviously the fact that if the cat had been on the mat the dog would have bitten it. And so on for every case. For every true statement there is a corresponding fact. ('Truth: A Reconsideration of Strawson's Views', 395)[86]

So far, our characterization of Moore's position still leaves open the possibility that *different beliefs* might correspond to one and the same fact. You might think, for example, that the belief that George Eliot wrote *Middlemarch* differs from the belief that Mary Ann Evans wrote *Middlemarch*, yet both beliefs correspond to the same fact. But according to [M.2], if we have two true beliefs here, then we also have two facts in virtue of which they are true. In order to record the prodigality of Moore's correspondence view, a further principle has to be added:[87]

(P*) $\forall x$ [Fx $\rightarrow \forall y \, \forall z$ ((By & y C x & Bz & z C x) $\rightarrow$ y = z)]

(where the three predicate letters abbreviate 'is a *fact*', 'is a *belief*' and 'corresponds to' respectively). Again we must be careful not to misread Moore's talk of belief. If Ben's tentative belief that George Eliot wrote *Middlemarch* corresponds to a fact, then this fact is surely identical with the fact to which Ann's firm belief that George Eliot wrote *Middlemarch* corresponds. But there is not one item that is both tentative and firm. So if this is not to refute (P*), we must take the belief

---

[86] Cf. Searle, *The Construction of Social Reality*, 211, 214, 219.

[87] In this respect Searle does not follow Moore: 'The same fact may be stated by different statements. For example, the same fact is stated by "Cicero was an orator" and "Tully was an orator" ' (ibid., 220). Application of the Cognitive Equivalence Criterion (see (F-Nec) on p. 44) shows that these sentences do not express the same *proposition*.

which is *shared* by Ben and Ann, and not their different believings, to be what falls under the notion of belief that is used in [M.2].[88]

Moore's conception of truth fares rather well when we apply to it the criterion of adequacy he gives in [M.1]. Whatever 'p' may be, the belief that p is true, according to [M.2], if and only if there is such a thing as the fact that p. Now the following assumption looks plausible: there is such a thing as the fact that p, iff p. Hence, by transitivity of 'iff', the belief that p is true iff p. Similarly, the belief that p is false, according to [M.2], iff there is no such thing as the fact that p. Again, it seems safe to assume: there is no such thing as the fact that p, iff not-p. Hence, by transitivity of 'iff', the belief that p is false iff not-p. So if we grant Moore those two assumptions,[89] we must agree with him:

It follows from these definitions that the condition which we saw to be necessary and sufficient for the truth and falsehood of this belief [i.e. the belief that I have gone away] *are* necessary and sufficient for it: there is not only no conflict between these definitions and the statement that these conditions are necessary and sufficient, but it actually follows from the definitions that they are so. (*SMPP*, 278; [M.3])

Moore dismisses any attempt to explain the meaning that 'corresponds' is supposed to have in his definition by appealing to the ways this word is used in other contexts (such as 'His expenses do not correspond to his income', 'The American Congress corresponds to the British Parliament', or perhaps 'That key corresponds *with* this keyhole', 'One half of a torn piece of paper corresponds *with* the other half'[90]). This saves Moore from the accusation of relying on misleading analogies. He seems to hold that the relevant notion of correspondence is just too basic to admit of any illuminating explanation. He thereby weakens the elucidatory power of his account, of course, for as to the meaning of the term 'corresponds' in [M. 2], we only know that in this usage it signifies the relation that obtains between a belief and a fact whenever the belief is true. Moore's account would become flatly circular if we took this to be a dismantling analysis of the pertinent concept of correspondence, for then it would read: x is a *true* belief iff there is a fact to which x stands in that relation which obtains between a belief and a fact whenever the belief is *true*. If we want to know which fact a given true belief corresponds with, Moore's recipe is rather simple: take a sentence that expresses that belief and insert it into the singular-term-forming operator 'the

---

[88] In *SMPP*, 62–3 Moore contrasts these two uses 'belief', explains the one that is pertinent in (P*) by '*what is believed*', and subsumes what is believed under the concept *proposition*. Later in the lectures he gets confused about this concept. In the 1953 preface to the book, p. xii, he comments upon this tension.

[89] As we shall soon see, Logical Atomists do not grant either of these assumptions.

[90] White, *Truth*, 105.

fact that...' (or its counterpart in the language of that sentence). Surely one can grasp these notions of correspondence and fact only if one already has the concept of truth. Since the notions that Moore's *definiens* appeals to are not independent of the concept of truth, his definition is not *reductive*. But in the case of a concept as basic as that of truth, asking for a reductive definition may be asking for too much in any case, and then this observation cannot be held against Moore.

3.2.2 *Logical atomist parsimony*

> Whatever corresponds in reality to compound propositions must not be more than what corresponds to their several atomic propositions.
>
> (Ludwig Wittgenstein, 'Notes on Logic', 98)

Let us now compare the Moorean conception of truth as fact-based correspondence with its early competitor. In 1918 Russell delivered a course of lectures, 'The Philosophy of Logical Atomism', which were, as he says, 'very largely concerned with explaining certain ideas which I learnt from my friend and former pupil Wittgenstein'.[91] (Wittgenstein's explanation of his ideas, the *Tractatus Logico-Philosophicus*, appeared only three years later in print.[92])

> When I speak of a fact—I do not propose to attempt an exact definition, but an explanation, so that you will know what I am talking about—I mean the kind of thing that makes a proposition true or false.../...A proposition...is a sentence in the indicative.../... Suppose it is a fact that Socrates is dead. You have two propositions: 'Socrates is dead' and 'Socrates is not dead'...corresponding to the same fact, there is one fact in the world which makes one true and one false. (*PLA* 182, 185, 187)

Here we can notice at once two rather superficial differences between Moore on the one hand and the Logical Atomists on the other. First, Russell (in spite of using the term 'proposition') takes sentences as truth-value bearers, at least some of the time,[93] whereas Moore never does. Secondly, Russell maintains that not only true sentences, but also false ones correspond to facts. In the case of 'Socrates is dead' the correspondence is an accordance with the fact that Socrates is dead, in the case of 'Socrates is not dead' it is a discordance with the same fact.[94] (For Russell in 1918 the difference between a true belief and a false belief is not

---

[91] *PLA*, 177.

[92] I will stick, most of the time, to Russell's more comprehensible version of Logical Atomism. Like many other readers, I find both Wittgenstein's use of the terms '*Tatsache* (fact)', '*Sachverhalt* (state of affairs)' and '*Sachlage* (situation)' in the *Tractatus* and his occasional comments on this use very confusing.

[93] For a thorough account of Russell's fluctuations, cf. White, 'Propositions and Sentences'.

[94] Cf. Wittgenstein, 'Notes on Logic', 95; *Tractatus* 4.0621 c (and the reflections on Johnson and Broad in Moore, *Lectures on Metaphysics*, 145–7, 157–9).

like that between a wife and a spinster but rather like that between friend and foe—of the same person.) Hence, what Moore calls 'correspondence to a fact' can at best be identical with what Russell calls 'being made *true* by a fact'. I shall continue to use 'correspond' in the 'accordance' or 'agreement' sense. Its opposite number as characterized by Russell above could be called 'counter-correspondence'. But so far we have not even touched on what makes the Logical Atomists Logical Atomists.

On their view, one and the same fact can make several sentences (which express different propositions) true, and several facts can collectively render one and the same sentence true. Here, a distinction becomes decisive which is entirely irrelevant for Moore's account of truth: the distinction between 'atomic' and 'molecular' sentences. In Russell, an atomic sentence is a concatenation of one ('simple') n-place predicate with n ('logically proper') names. At this point we can safely ignore the additional demands imposed on predicates and names.[95] What matters now is only that atomic sentences contain neither sentential operators nor quantifiers. In the case of 'truth-functional molecular propositions' such as conjunctions and disjunctions, the truth-value of the whole sentence is determined by the truth-values of its component sentences. Hence Russell can voice what might be called an Occamite Complaint against Moore and plead for ontological parsimony: the fact which makes an atomic sentence S true will *eo ipso* make any disjunction containing S true. And as regards true conjunctions of atomic sentences, there does not have to be a fact, over and above the two facts which render the conjuncts true, in virtue of which the conjunction is true.

I do not see any reason to suppose that there is a complexity in the facts corresponding to these molecular propositions. ... [In such cases one is] dealing only with a new form of proposition and not with a new form of fact. (*PLA* 211, 216)[96]

Nor do we need a special kind of truth-donors for existential generalizations: whatever makes an atomic sentence 'a is F' true will also render 'There is at least one object which is F' true.[97] The kernel of the *Russellian* conception of truth as *fact-based correspondence* is this:

(R-FactC) $\forall x$ [x is a true atomic sentence →
$\exists_1 y$ (y is a fact & x corresponds to y)].

---

[95] For predicates meeting the Russellian demand amounts to resisting reductive analysis, and for names it amounts to not abbreviating a definite description. (You might very well wonder whether this excludes many predicates or any names.)

[96] This is one of the main ideas of his friend and former pupil which Russell set out to explain. See the epigraph to this section.

[97] I take it that the remark to the contrary in *PLA*, 236, cannot be his considered view.

We must beware of replacing the arrow in (R-FactC) by a double-arrow, for Russell thought that there are (at least) two types of *non-atomic* sentence for which the right-hand side of the conditional in (R-FactC) also holds: negations of atomic sentences and general sentences. He was convinced that we could not do without negative and general facts. The author of the *Tractatus* was more radical:[98]

Die Angabe aller wahren Elementarsätze beschreibt die Welt vollständig. [If all true atomic sentences are given, the result is a complete description of the world.] (*Tracatus Logico-Philosophicus*, 4.26)

Why did Russell think that we cannot describe the world completely without general sentences and negations of atomic sentences? When he argued at Harvard that there are negative facts, this 'nearly produced a riot'.[99] One can sympathize with the audience, for his argument is anything but perspicuous,[100] and he makes no convincing case against the following strategy: (1) The negation of an atomic sentence S is true iff for some x, x is a fact and S counter-corresponds to x. (2) For some x, x is a fact and S counter-corresponds to x iff there is an atomic sentence S* such that S and S* are incompatible (i.e. cannot be true together) and S* corresponds to x. It may even seem that one can extract an illustration of this proposal from Russell's text (as cited above on p. 118), replacing S by 'Socrates is alive' and S* by 'Socrates is dead'. But in this case Russell would reply: the sentence 'Socrates is dead' abbreviates 'Socrates was alive & ¬ (Socrates is alive)', hence it is not really atomic, but contains a 'hidden' negation operator.[101] Let us rather substitute 'A (this little patch) is red' and 'A is green' for S and S*. In the second lecture of *PLA* Russell treats them as atomic sentences, so he allows for unanalysable predicates that cannot be jointly true of the same thing. Since his version of Logical Atomism, unlike Wittgenstein's,[102] concedes that atomic sentences can be incompatible, he is not in a position to dismiss (2) out of hand.[103] At any rate, and this move may be acceptable even to the author of the *Tractatus*, rioters can say: (1*) The negation of an atomic sentence S is true iff there is no fact to which S corresponds. Absence of a fact, they should add, is not itself a (higher-order) fact for the negation of S to correspond to.[104]

---

[98] When coming across talk about negative facts in the *Tractatus* (see 2.06 or 4.063), one must remember that Wittgenstein's ontological inventory contains facts *and* states of affairs, and he seems not to acknowledge negative states of affairs. Of course, this would be inconsistent if Tractarian facts were obtaining states of affairs.   [99] *PLA*, 211.

[100] Cf. *PLA*, 211–16, and the discussion in Ayer, *Russell and Moore*, 86–90.   [101] See *PLA*, 215.

[102] See *Tractatus*, 4.211, 6.3751.

[103] Contrast the defence of the *PLA* position on negative facts in Mark Sainsbury, *Russell*, 221–3.

[104] Cf. Simons, 'World', 122–3 (as against his earlier 'Logical Atomism and its Ontological Refinement', 164). Taking falsity to be truth of the negation, one recognizes that proposal (1*) is a partial return to Moore: see passage [M.2] above, on false beliefs.

In the case of the general sentences, Russell's argument is crystalline. About 'All men are mortal', he says:

When you have taken all the particular men that there are, and found each one of them severally to be mortal, it is definitely a new fact that all men are mortal; how new a fact, appears from [the observation] that it could not be inferred from the mortality of the several men that there are in the world. (*PLA*, 236)

Now Russell is certainly right when he claims that from the premisses 'Adam is a mortal human', 'Eve is a mortal human',—allow me to skip a few, 'Ultimus is a mortal human', 'Ultima is a mortal human', it does not follow that all humans are mortal.[105] Only by adding the sentence 'Adam, ..., and Ultima are all the humans' do we obtain a set of premisses from which that conclusion can be logically inferred,[106] and this additional premiss is itself a general sentence. But does this insight really justify Russell's thesis that we have to admit general as well as particular facts?[107] Russell's argument is based on the assumption that if the facts $f_1, f_2, \ldots, f_n$ make the sentences $S_1, S_2, \ldots, S_n$ true, then they can only render a further sentence R true if the conjunction of the S_i *entails* R. But he does not explain why this is required. Why does it not suffice that the general sentence is, in Russell's sense, 'materially equivalent' with (i.e. has the same truth-value as) the conjunction of all its confirming instances? If they are materially equivalent, the truth of the conjunction is sufficient, as it so happens, for the truth of the general sentence. Of course, our 'from Adam to Ultima' conjunction *could* be true while the general sentence is false: there might exist an additional human being who never dies. But why is this possibility relevant? Why should not the general sentence be rendered true in the actual world by something that fails to do so in another possible world?[108]

Let us now consider the second fundamental difference between Moore's conception of truth and the Logical Atomist view. Russell thinks that true atomic sentences and the facts that make them true have the same 'structure':[109] the atomic sentence 'Fa', if true, 'mirrors' a fact which has as its 'components' the

---

[105] For the sake of the argument, I follow Russell in neglecting the fact that none of the premisses in the original set is genuinely atomic: 'a is a mortal human' seems to abbreviate something like 'a is human & $\exists t$ (a is alive till t & $\neg$ (a is alive after t))'.

[106] Exceptions to this are easily accounted for. From 'Last January was bad, and last February was bad, ... and last December was bad', it does follow that last year every month was bad, since whoever understands both premiss and conclusion thereby knows that the conclusion cannot fail to be true if the premiss is.

[107] Cf. the critique of Russell's position in Ayer, *Russell and Moore*, 91, and Simons, 'Logical Atomism and Its Ontological Refinement', 166–8, and its defence in Sainsbury, *Russell*, 220–1.

[108] Russell's insistence on entailment may be epistemologically motivated: if there is no entailment, then we cannot know for sure that things are as R says they are merely on the basis of knowing all the f_i. In sect. 3.5.3, I will present a different reason for that insistence.   [109] *PLA*, 197 ff.

object that 'a' stands for and the property that is signified by 'F'. This conception is fraught with difficulties. First of all, in the case of facts talk of components is very problematic: both a and F-ness may exist, although it is not a fact that Fa, so the existence of the 'components' does not imply the existence of what they allegedly 'compose'. Adding the tie of instantiation as a third 'component' will not help.[110] Furthermore, if the fact that aRb 'contains' the objects a and b (in a certain order) and if a and b have a location in time, then that fact is itself time-bound: it can exist at a time t only if all its constituent objects exist at t. This is cause for serious categorial worries (which I will articulate in section 3.3.4), but even if they could be laid to rest, an embarrassing question remains:[111] when does the fact represented by 'Socrates lived long before Wittgenstein' exist? It did not exist before Socrates was born; it did not exist when Socrates was alive, because then Wittgenstein was not yet around; it did not exist when Wittgenstein was alive, because then Socrates was no longer around; and, for a doubly sad reason, it does not exist now nor will it ever exist in the future. And yet, what is now said by 'Socrates lived long before Wittgenstein' is as true as can be.

Secondly, the relation that correspondence is said to consist in also makes for trouble. *Having the same structure as* is a relation which certainly obtains in other areas: between texts, their copies, and their recitations, for example, between scores and their correct performances, or between maps and the areas they represent. Hence, the Logical Atomists' account of truth does not run the risk that the key term 'correspondence' itself cannot be explained except in terms of truth. But it does, of course, run the risk of false assimilations. In all the other areas I mentioned, the relation obtains between items jointly belonging to the spatio-temporal order. So one may very well wonder how the correspondence relation, which is alleged to obtain between a sentence truly ascribing certain geographical features to Vienna and the *fact that* Vienna really has those features, could possibly be the same correspondence relation as that between an accurate map of Vienna and *Vienna*. After all, there is a vast categorial gulf between what is corresponded to in the first case and in the second. A fact concerning Vienna cannot, unlike Vienna, be moonlit or invaded by tourists, and Vienna cannot, unlike a fact concerning Vienna, be stated, communicated, or controverted.

---

[110] This is by no means a minor problem. See David Lewis, 'A World of Truthmakers?', 218, for a statement of the difficulty. For attempts at circumventing it by taking facts to be 'irreducible entities in their own right' and assuming a 'non-mereological mode of composition', cf. Kenneth Olson, *An Essay on Facts*, 60–1; David Armstrong, *A World of States of Affairs* (henceforth *WSA*), 118–22. For well-taken criticisms of these attempts, see William Vallicella, 'Three Conceptions of States of Affairs', 245–9, and Jonathan Lowe, *The Possibility of Metaphysics*, 243–4.

[111] Posed, in a different context, by Joseph Almog: see 'The Subject-Predicate Class I', 604–7.

These and similar worries about the assimilation of true sentences to accurate maps etc. have often been voiced in the literature, but we can leave them aside here, since an advocate of Fact-based Correspondence (no matter whether he is in favour of the ontological parsimony of Logical Atomism or not) does not have to cash 'correspondence' in terms of identity of structure. This is an optional extra, and a correspondence theorist may ardently oppose it:[112]

[A] statement no more needs, in order to be true, to reproduce the 'multiplicity', say, or the 'structure' or 'form' of reality, than a word needs to be echoic or writing pictographic. To suppose that it does, is to fall once again into the error of reading back into the world the features of language. (Austin, 'Truth', 125)

It is noteworthy that the optional extra can severely restrict the range of applicability of 'true'. It does so in the case of Wittgenstein's version of Logical Atomism (whose 'picture theory' is far more complex than the Russellian one just sketched[113]). The dialectical background of this restriction is Wittgenstein's dissatisfaction with Russell's view of logic. Russell takes 'logical propositions' to be maximally general truths in which there is 'no mention of any particular things or particular qualities or relations'.[114] An example would be: 'Whatever qualities x and y may be, if all things that have x also have y, then all things that do not have y do not have x either.' (Apparently what is signified by 'have' is not to be regarded as a 'particular relation', and there is a very good reason for this: if we were to take the tie of exemplification as a relation, we would be drawn into a vicious infinite regress.[115]) Logical propositions, Russell seems to think, are made true by what he calls 'completely general facts', i.e. by facts that

---

[112] Kirkham, following Pitcher, usefully distinguishes between 'Correspondence as Correlation' and 'Correspondence as Congruence' (*ThT*, 199 ff.). Austin, for one, accepts the former and rejects the latter.

[113] One important difference is that the author of the *Tractatus* takes the left field of the relation of depicting to consist of *facts*. More important for us is that the isomorphism is supposed to obtain between atomic sentences, no matter whether true or false, and possible states of affairs, the latter being identified with the senses of those sentences. Of course, if an atomic sentence is true, then, according to this theory, the pertinent possible state of affairs obtains (4.25) and the sentence *is* isomorphic with one of those items the Tractarian world consists of. But Wittgenstein regards the concept of isomorphism as an ingredient of the explanation of the concept of *sense*, not of truth. (This is rightly emphasized by Ansgar Beckermann in '*Wittgenstein. Neurath und Tarski über Wahrheit*', sect. II.3.) Hence, he could consistently maintain in the *Tractatus* what he had maintained before and what he did maintain ever after, namely that a complete explanation of the concept of *truth* is provided by pointing out that in saying that 'p' is true (or that it is true that p) one says neither more nor less than in saying that p. For documentation, see sect. 4.2.1 below.

[114] *PLA*, 184; cf. 237–41. The idea appears already in Russell's 1914 lectures, published as *Our Knowledge of the External World* (53, 66). Wittgenstein convinced him that complete generality is at any rate not *sufficient* for being a logical proposition: the proposition that there is at least one thing that is identical with itself *is* completely general, but its truth is 'merely an accident, so to so speak' (*PLA*, 240).

[115] Cf. Ryle, 'Plato's Parmenides', 9–10, and Strawson, *Individuals*, 167.

contain no particular things or particular qualities or relations as components.[116] Wittgenstein totally disagrees. He denies that 'logical propositions' have to be completely general ones (in Russell's sense): 'If all humans are mortal then all non-mortals are non-human' and 'It is either raining or not raining' are perfectly respectable specimens.[117] He denies that there are any 'logical facts' in virtue of which logical propositions are true. There is no need to postulate such facts, he maintains, because strictly speaking there are no logical truths. All truths are *vérités de fait*. The so-called *vérités de raison* are not really truths, any more than toy ducks are ducks. Wittgenstein's reasons for this audacious claim are contained in the following mosaic of quotations:

[A] *Um zu erkennen, ob [ein] Bild wahr oder falsch ist, müssen wir es mit der Wirklichkeit vergleichen. Aus dem Bild allein ist nicht zu erkennen, ob es wahr oder falsch ist. Ein a priori wahres Bild gibt es nicht.* [In order to tell whether a picture is true or false, we must compare it with reality. We cannot tell from the picture alone whether it is true or false. There are no pictures that are true a priori.] (*Tractatus*, 2.223–5)

[B] *Tautologien . . . sind nicht Bilder der Wirklichkeit.* [Tautologies . . . are not pictures of reality.] (ibid., 4.462)

[C] *Nur dadurch kann der Satz wahr oder falsch sein, indem er ein Bild der Wirklichkeit ist.* [Only by being a picture of reality can a proposition be true or false.] (ibid., 4.06)

The reasoning in [A] is intuitively compelling (just think of portraits or maps) and lends strong support to [B]. From [B] and [C] we can infer that tautologies are neither true nor false.[118] Now even if one rejects Wittgenstein's contention that *all* logical (let alone all analytical) propositions are tautologies,[119] one cannot but admit that, with respect to pictoriality, all logical propositions, and all other traditional candidates for the title '*vérité de raison*', are in the same boat as tautologies. The argument is clearly valid; but is it sound? That entirely depends on contention [C], i.e. on the picture theory. Without the backing of the picture theory, the

---

[116] *PLA*, 184. In his book *Introduction to Mathematical Philosophy*, also written in 1918, Russell says, 'Logic . . . is concerned with the real world, just as truly as zoology, though with its more abstract and general features' (169). There are traces of Wittgenstein's new conception of logical propositions as tautologies both in *PLA*, 240, and in this book (205), but in each case Russell confesses that he does 'not know how to define "tautology"'.   [117] Cf. *Tractatus*, 6.1231–2.

[118] Wittgenstein endorses this conclusion explicitly when he maintains, '[L]ogical propositions are neither true nor false' ('Notes Dictated to G. E. Moore in Norway, April 1914', 109). '*Man kann von einer Tautologie nicht sagen, daß sie wahr ist.* [One cannot say of a tautology that it is true]' (*Notebooks* (6.6.1915)). Cartwright has convincingly argued that Russell confused the above-mentioned 'completely general' proposition with the proposition that *each proposition of the form* '$\forall x\, (Fx \rightarrow Gx) \rightarrow \forall x\, (\neg Gx \rightarrow \neg Fx)$' *is true*; which has a better claim to be one of the 'Propositions of Pure Logic' (see Cartwright's paper of this name). Cartwright agrees with Russell that instances of that schema *are* true, and he does not share Wittgenstein's pre-Tarskian scruples against semantic ascent.   [119] *Tractatus*, 6.1.

contention that tautologies are not true looks rather arbitrary. One of its unappealing consequences is that nobody can truly be said to know, for example, that it is not both raining and not raining, for one can only know that p if it is true that p.[120] Actually, Wittgenstein himself wavers in his resolution to refrain from attributing truth to tautologies:

[D] *Die Tautologie hat keine Wahrheitsbedingungen, denn sie ist bedingungslos wahr.* [A tautology has no truth-conditions, since it is unconditionally true.] (*Tractatus*, 4.461)

[E] *Es ist das besondere Merkmal der logischen Sätze, daß man am Symbol allein erkennen kann, daß sie wahr sind.* [It is the peculiar mark of logical propositions that one can recognize that they are true from the symbol alone.] (ibid., 6.113)

The reasoning in [D] is rather feeble: if a tautology is unconditionally true, then it is a fortiori true, as is conceded in [E].[121] But then, why not say that a tautology is true under *all* conditions (and that, consequently, all tautologies have the same truth-conditions)?[122] [E] also discredits the earlier verdict against 'A knows that p' in case 'p' is a tautology: if one can recognize that it is true that p, then one can come to know that it is true that p. But how can one come to know that it is true that p, without coming to know that p? A Logical Atomist, who can be persuaded, along these lines, to admit that tautologies (and other analytic propositions) are true, but rightly refrains from postulating 'completely general facts' for them to correspond to, should be ready to admit that his version of a correspondence theory of truth is too narrow. (The Disquotation Schema is as hospitable to 'All bachelors are bachelors' and 'All bachelors are unmarried' as it is to 'Kant was a bachelor.')

Logical Atomism relieves correspondence theorists of the need to find a unique truth-conferrer for each truth. If we can account for the truth of atomic sentences, we can dispense with special truth-conferrers for various kinds of molecular sentence. But whenever the truth-value of a logically complex sentence is *not* determined by the truth-values of atomic sentences, the Logical Atomist is still stuck with non-atomic facts as truth-donors. Sentences containing causal, subjunctive, counterfactual, or modal connectives, ascriptions of beliefs or of other propositional attitudes all make the feasibility of the general reductive

---

[120] Wittgenstein calmly accepts this consequence in *Tractatus*, 5.1362 b; cf. 'Notes on Logic', 104. To be sure, '*Ich weiß . . . nichts über das Wetter, wenn ich weiß, daß es regnet oder nicht regnet* [I do not know anything about the weather when I know that it is either raining or not raining]' (*Tractatus*, 4.461c), but that does not imply that I don't know *anything* when I know that it's either raining or not raining.

[121] As it stands, [E] does not succeed in determining the peculiarity of logical propositions, for one would hardly want to classify the final (token-) sentence of this footnote as a logical proposition: *This sentence inscription is written in italics.*

[122] Cf. Christopher Peacocke, 'How Are A Priori Truths Possible?', 183–4.

programme rather doubtful. Furthermore, the Logical Atomist can only be confident that no empirical truth will fall through his net if every logically simple, empirical sentence has the structure needed for applying his recursive machinery. But what justifies this structural presumption? (Recall our example 'It is snowing'.) So, on the whole, we should not overestimate the gains a correspondence theory can expect from adopting the parsimonious Logical Atomist approach.

3.3 A Battery of Objections

By now I think I have provided enough evidence for my claim that even fact-based correspondence is not as monolithic a position as it is all too often represented in the literature.[123] We noticed local difficulties with both versions—and with their long-lived predecessor: the Moorean variety provokes the Occamite Complaint, but the feasibility of the reductionist programme of its Atomist rival is not beyond doubt either, and in the first section of this chapter we saw that Object-based Correspondence suffers from the Procrustes Problem. Let us now weigh some more sweeping objections, two against any account of truth in terms of correspondence, two against all versions of Fact-based Correspondence.

3.3.1 *The comparison objection*

Many philosophers have complained that a correspondence account is epistemologically barren. In his ('pre-critical') lectures on logic, Kant ridiculed an epistemological reading of the explanation of truth as object-based correspondence. Under this reading I would have to *compare* my judgement with the object

---

[123] Davidson asks us to consider when sentences of the form *The statement that p corresponds to the fact that q* hold, and his reply begins as follows: 'Certainly when "p" and "q" are replaced by the same [true] sentence [of English]' ('True to the Facts', 41; my additions). This is far from certain, Russell would retort—we obtain a false instance if we substitute for the sentence letter a true conjunction or a true disjunction. Horwich (*Truth*, 1st edn., 112) says that all adherents of Fact-based Correspondence subscribe to the schema *For some x, x = the fact that p, if and only if p*. The if-part of this biconditional is *not* accepted by Logical Atomists. Neale writes, 'Obviously *The fact that (φ) = the fact that (φ)* is true (for fact-theorists)' (*FF*, 221). Presumably, what is supposed to be obvious is that all substitution-instances of that identity schema in which the sentence letter is replaced by a true sentence (of English) are true (for fact-theorists). Again, partisans of parsimonious Fact-based Correspondence will object that this is not even true, let alone obviously so. (Elsewhere in *FF* Neale duly registers the Logical Atomist point: see, for example, p. 87 n.)

it is about in order to find out whether it is true. But how is this feat to be accomplished? Kant writes:

[*Ich kann*] *das Objekt nur mit meine[r] Erkenntni[s] vergleichen, dadurch daß ich es erkenne. Meine Erkenntnis soll sich also selbst bestätigen, welches aber zur Wahrheit noch lange nicht hinreichend ist. Denn da das Objekt außer mir und die Erkenntnis in mir ist: so kann ich immer doch nur beurteilen: ob meine Erkenntnis vom Objekt mit meiner Erkenntnis vom Objekt übereinstimme.* [I can only compare the object with my judgement[124] by making a judgement about the object. Thus my judgement is supposed to be confirmed by itself, which is not at all sufficient for its truth. For since the object is external to my mind and my judgement is in my mind, I can only judge whether my judgement about the object agrees with my judgement about the object.] (*Logik*, Introduction, sect. VII. B, init.[125])

Generally, Brentano considered Kant to be the father of the 'German School of Common Nonsense Philosophy', i.e. of German Idealism, but this is one of the few points where he basically agreed with him.[126] But whereas Kant took the alleged comparison to be a pseudo-comparison of a judgement with itself, Brentano argued that any attempt at a comparison becomes entirely pointless as soon as a necessary condition for the alleged comparison to yield knowledge is fulfilled:

Es ist ... ersichtlich, daß man sich einer großen Täuschung hingab, wenn man meinte, daß [die Übereinstimmungstheorie] den Weg angebe, auf welchem ich selbst in den Besitz der Wahrheit gelange. Manche glaubten, das geschehe, indem ich mein Denken mit dem Ding vergleiche, und sahen nicht, daß ich, um diesen Vergleich machen zu können, schon ... wissen müßte, wie es mit ihm [dem Ding] in Wirklichkeit steht. Dies wissen heißt aber schon im Besitze der Wahrheit sein. [Clearly, those philosophers were entirely deluded who thought that [the correspondence account of truth] specifies a procedure which enables me to get hold of the truth. Some maintained that I could get hold of it by comparing my thought with the object. They did not realize that in order to make such a comparison I would already ... have to know what the object is really like. Yet to know this is to be already in possession of the truth. (*Wahrheit und Evidenz* (11.5.1915), 133 (117))

Accounts of truth as fact-based correspondence have also been taken to fall victim to this kind of objection: 'It would be odd, wouldn't it, to test whether the proposition that Toby sighed was true by taking the fact that Toby sighed and seeing whether the proposition fitted it?'[127] Taking both variants of the objection together, the challenge to the correspondence view is that it enjoins upon us an epistemic performance which is either unfeasible or pointless. The epistemological objection has been upheld by the Oxford pragmatist

---

[124] Cf. p. 108 n. 59.

[125] Bolzano puts this kind of argument into the mouth of a sceptic and then goes on to defuse it (*WL*, I. 179–80).

[126] Cf. Brentano, '*Über den Begriff der Wahrheit*', §58 b; *Wahrheit und Evidenz* (5.3.1915), 137 (120).

[127] C. J. F. Williams, *WIT*, 76.

F. C. S. Schiller,[128] by Logical Empiricists such as Neurath and Hempel, by idealists such as Blanshard, and, more recently, by M. Williams and by Davidson (for a while).[129]

If we do not understand a correspondence account of truth as an answer to the question 'How can we *find out* which truth-value a proposition has?', both variants of the objection misfire. As the continuation of the text from which I took the Kant quotation above shows, Kant thought of his objection as applying only to those who mistook correspondence for a *criterion* of truth, and Brentano quite explicitly called the epistemological reading a *misreading*.[130] Correspondence views allow for the possibility that some truths are beyond our ken, but they do not put all truths beyond our ken: finding out whether the statement that p corresponds with an object or a fact is as easy or difficult as finding out whether p. No correspondence account of truth makes any pretensions to tell us how to proceed with that job.

One may also wonder whether the epistemological misreading of Object-based Correspondence really leads to the absurdity that every judgement has to confirm itself, as Kant contends. Let us consider this contention in the light of a concrete example.[131] Before her first perceptual encounter with Cologne Cathedral, Ann had the tentative belief (based on hearsay) that it has two steeples. Now, looking at the cathedral, she makes the perceptual judgement that it has two steeples, and thereby she gains the conviction that, at least as far as the number of its steeples is concerned, the cathedral is as she thought it to be. Perhaps she betrays this conviction by exclaiming: 'The cathedral *really* has two steeples.' In this story no judgement is supposed to confirm *itself*: rather, a

---

[128] In his richly documented discussion of the Comparison Objection, Douglas McDermid claims, 'Even if not peculiar to pragmatists, [it] has been absolutely central to their case against correspondence from the time of classical pragmatists down to the present day' ('Pragmatism and Truth', 776–7). But apart from self-styled latter-day pragmatists, his only piece of evidence is a quotation from Schiller: '"Truth" ... cannot be defined as the agreement or correspondence of thought with "reality", for how can thought determine whether it correctly "copies" what transcends it?' (ibid., 777; cf. 775). As we will see on the last pages of this chapter, both James and Dewey (*pace* McDermid) *accept* the definition that Schiller rejects.

[129] Davidson, 'A Coherence Theory of Truth and Knowledge', 144; 'Empirical Content', 164. As to Neurath, cf. the quotation on p. 381 below. Pertinent passages from Hempel, Blanshard, and M. Williams are quoted, and thoroughly discussed, in Alston, *RCT*, ch. 3. Davidson has come round to denying the soundness of the Comparison Objection (as is duly registered by Alston): see Davidson, 'Afterthoughts', 155; 'Epistemology and Truth', 183 (= 'Structure', 302–3).

[130] The correspondence formula was '*irrig gedeutet* [misinterpreted]' by advocates of the comparison objection (Brentano, *Wahrheit und Evidenz*, 133 (117)).

[131] Actually, it is Frege's cathedral and Schlick's scenario: see the latter's 'Facts and Propositions'. (Unfortunately Schlick's use of 'fact' is thoroughly confused, and his critics from the 'coherentist' wing of the Vienna Circle inherited this confusion: unlike Frege, they have to be reminded that a cathedral isn't a fact.)

perceptual judgement is taken to confirm a tentative belief which has the same (conceptual) content. Certainly, such a confirmation is no *guarantee* of truth, but why should a perceptual encounter with the object our belief is about provide us with such a guarantee? Davidson, like many others before him, declares any attempt to 'confront our beliefs... with what they are about' to be an 'impossible feat'.[132] But what's wrong with saying that in Ann's perceptual encounter with the cathedral a belief was confronted with what it is about? Presumably, Michael Williams is right in condemning the idea that justification 'terminates... with our confronting raw chunks of reality' as 'incoherent'.[133] But there is nothing incoherent about the contention that the justification of a belief about a cathedral may terminate in a perceptual judgement about that cathedral, and surely it would be an insult to the medieval master builders to call their cathedrals raw chunks of reality.

3.3.2 *The treadmill*

As we saw in Chapter 1, Frege identified facts with true thoughts, and he correctly assumed that it is essential for a correspondence theory that the 'correspondents' are distinct. So if he had conceived of his opponents as advocates of Fact-based Correspondence, one would expect him to criticize them (as Dummett actually does[134]) by appealing to that identification. But in Frege's own criticism it plays no role whatsoever. Rather, he tries to show, in part [A] of his argument, that the predicament of an advocate of Object-based Correspondence is that of 'a man in a treadmill who makes a step forward and upwards, but the steps he treads on keep giving away and he falls back to where he was before'.[135] If his argument were convincing, it would also refute all varieties of Fact-based Correspondence, for, as Frege himself registers in part [B] of his argument, it is actually an objection against *any* attempt at defining the concept of truth. Suppose we define truth as a kind of correspondence:[136]

[A] *Was müßten wir... tun, um zu entscheiden, ob etwas wahr wäre? Wir müßten untersuchen, ob es wahr wäre, daß—etwa eine Vorstellung und ein Wirkliches... übereinstimmten. Und damit ständen wir wieder vor einer Frage derselben Art, und das Spiel könnte von neuem beginnen. So scheitert dieser Versuch, die Wahrheit als eine Übereinstimmung zu erklären.* [B] *So scheitert aber auch jeder andere Versuch, das Wahrsein zu definieren. Denn in einer Definition gäbe man gewisse Merkmale an. Und bei der Anwendung auf einen besonderen Fall käme es dann immer darauf an, ob es wahr wäre, daß diese Merkmale zuträfen. So drehte man sich im Kreise. Hiernach ist es wahrscheinlich, daß der Inhalt des Wortes 'wahr' ganz einzigartig und undefinierbar ist.*

---

[132] Davidson, 'Empirical Content', 174; 'A Coherence Theory of Truth and Knowledge', 140.
[133] Quoted after Alston, *RCT*, 86. [134] Dummett, *FPL*, 442.
[135] Frege, '*Logik*' (1897), in *NS* 146 (143).
[136] The argument appears for the first time in ibid., 139–40 (128–9).

[A] [What ought we to do so as to decide whether something is true? We should have to enquire whether it is true that an idea and something real, say, correspond.... And then we should be confronted with a question of the same kind, and the game could begin again. Thus the attempted explanation of truth as correspondence breaks down. [B] And so does any other attempt to define truth. For in a definition certain marks would be specified. And with respect to any particular case the point at issue would always be whether it were true that those marks applied. So one would be going round in a circle. Hence the content of the word 'true' is probably quite unique and indefinable.] (*'Der Gedanke'*, 60; bracketed letters added)

In spite of the penultimate sentence many have taken this passage to contain a *vicious regress* objection.[137] Let us try to spell it out in some detail and then ask whether it is reasonable to ascribe it to Frege. His regress argument (which may only be a figment of the imagination of some of his readers) relies on the following principle:[138]

(Dec)   Each substitution-instance of the following schema expresses a truth: *one cannot decide whether p without deciding whether it is true that p.*

Let us use 'Δ' as a dummy for an alleged definiens of '(is) true', e.g. for 'agrees with reality'. The argument starts with the putative definition and an assumption concerning a thinker a and a truth-candidate P:

(Df) $\forall x$ (x is true iff x is Δ)

(1)   a decides whether P is true.

From (Df) and (1) we derive

(2)   a decides whether P is Δ.

Applying principle (Dec) to (2) we obtain

(3)   a decides whether it is true that P is Δ.

Appealing to (Df) we replace 'true' in (3) by the proposed definiens:

(4)   a decides whether it is Δ that P is Δ.

We then apply (Dec) to (4) and transform the result by appealing to (Df), etc. ad nauseam.

(5)   So if 'true' is definable by 'Δ', whatever 'Δ' may be, then nobody can decide whether a given truth-candidate is true without, *per impossibile*, deciding for infinitely many distinct truth-candidates whether they are true.

---

[137] e.g. Dummett, *FPL* 443; Carruthers, 'Frege's Regress'.

[138] If one endorses Frege's Identity Thesis, one is committed to accepting (Dec) and its ilk: see p. 35 above.

(6)   But sometimes one can decide whether a given truth-candidate is true.

(C)   Hence 'true' is indefinable.

This argument is not convincing at all: step (5) is a non sequitur of numbing grossness.[139] Step (5) would follow only if one of the following contentions were true:

(Dec*)   Each substitution-instance of the following schema expresses a truth: One cannot decide whether p without *first* deciding whether it is true that p.

(Dec†)   Each substitution-instance of the following schema expresses a truth: One cannot decide whether it is true that p without *first* deciding whether it is *Δ* that p.

(Dec*) is utterly implausible. It is different from principle (Dec), which does not maintain that one decision has to be *preceded* by another. If (Dec*) were correct, one could establish a vicious regress without appealing to the alleged definition of 'true' at all. Furthermore, (Dec*) clashes with Frege's contention that 'p' expresses the same proposition as 'It is true that p'.[140] If that thesis is correct then (3), for example, is just a more verbose report of the very same decision that is reported in (2). By contrast, (Dec) follows from Frege's Identity Thesis.

(Dec†) is equally implausible. As Aquinas said when defending his correspondence formula:

Per conformitatem intellectus et rei veritas definitur. Unde conformitatem cognoscere, est cognoscere veritatem. [Truth is defined as the agreement of intellect and thing. Hence recognizing that such an agreement obtains *is* recognizing that something is true.] (*Summa theol. Ia*, q. 16, a. 2, resp)

Generally, if 'true' and '*Δ*' really have the same sense, the proposition that P is true is identical with the proposition that P is *Δ*, hence deciding whether P is true is deciding whether P is *Δ*. Can Frege, of all people, have overlooked this? In any case, the regress established in the above argument is entirely innocent: there is no question of our having to take infinitely many distinct steps in order to decide whether P is true. The vicious regress objection is a failure.[141]

---

[139]   The insult is lifted from Strawson's *The Bounds of Sense*, where it is also aimed at a great philosopher.

[140]   See Ch. 2.1.1.

[141]   My reconstruction, and assessment of, the vicious regress objection largely coincides with that in Soames, *UT*, 25–6. But I have far more scruples than Soames in ascribing it to Frege.

We should hesitate to ascribe a fallacy to Frege which not only provokes the strong language I used above, but also relies on a contention that glaringly contradicts one of his basic claims about the concept of truth. A more charitable interpretation, suggested by the metaphor of the treadmill and strongly supported by the penultimate sentence in the passage cited on p. 130, sees him driving rather at a kind of *vicious circle* objection.[142] So far, we have not paid any attention to the term 'marks' in part [B] of that quotation. According to Frege's official use of this word, M is a mark of the concept expressed by the predicate 'F' iff the following condition is fulfilled: M is a concept, M is expressed by a component of an analytic definition of 'F', and nothing can fall under the concept F without falling under M. This condition is met if and only if the definiens of 'F' is *conjunctive*. Thus, in virtue of the definition 'For all x, x is a drake iff (x is a duck and x is male)', the concepts expressed by 'male' and by 'duck' are marks of the concept expressed by 'drake'.[143] Such a definition pays epistemic dividends, for it allows us to answer the question whether the definiens applies to an object via answering two simpler questions. So let us suppose, for argument's sake, that the alleged definiens of 'true' has this structure. From

(df) $\forall$x (x is true iff (x is δ_1, and x is δ_2))

(1)   a decides whether P is true

we derive

(2)   a decides whether (P is δ_1, and P is δ_2).

Relying on the plausible inference rule that 'decides whether' distributes across conjunction we obtain

(3a)   a decides whether P is δ_1.   (3b)   a decides whether P is δ_2.

This seems to be real progress, for a complex question is apparently dissected into more easily tractable sub-questions. But now we invoke Frege's Identity Thesis:

(4)   'P is δ_1' expresses the same proposition as 'It is true that P is δ_1'.

From (3a), (4), and the plausible assumption that

(5)   One cannot decide whether it is true that things are thus-and-so without activating one's mastery of the concept of truth

---

[142] See Stepanians, *Gottlob Frege*, 157–60, 184 n. 51.

[143] For exegetical evidence and further explanation, see my 'Constituents of Concepts', 274–8. I employ the word 'concept' for what Frege would have called the sense of a concept-word. On Frege's conception of *analytic* (as opposed to stipulative) *definitions*, see p. 26 above.

it follows that

(6)   a activates his mastery of the concept of truth.

So the progress was more apparent than real.

(7)   But an analytic definition is adequate only if one can decide whether one of its predicative components applies *without* activating one's mastery of the concept expressed by the definiendum.

(C)   So no analytic definition of 'true' is adequate.

Is this argument convincing? One problem lurks in the presupposition behind (df). An analytic definition need not have this structure, and clearly 'x agrees with reality' does not have it. But Frege's vicious circle argument is supposed to cover it as well as any other candidate for the role of an analytic definiens of 'true', whatever its structure. So his talk of 'marks' in the passage under discussion can amount to no more than the requirement that the alleged definiens is *not atomic* (unlike that in 'For all x, x is a serpent iff x is a snake').[144] It is far from clear how the argument would have to be modified in order to obtain the required scope. At any rate, the argument depends on Frege's Identity Thesis. If our critique of this thesis, begun in Chapter 2.1.4 and to be completed in Chapter 7.3.5, is successful, the vicious circle objection must also be declared to be a failure. In view of this diagnosis, it is worth drawing attention to a word in the last sentence of our quotation, which seems to have been overlooked by most commentators: doesn't Frege's 'probably' betoken that he himself does not regard his argument as a watertight proof of (C)?

3.3.3   *The spectre of fact monism*

What Davidson calls 'the real objection to correspondence theories' is an argument which is supposed to show that

if true sentences correspond to anything, they all correspond to the same thing. But this is to trivialize the concept of correspondence completely; there is no interest in the *relation* of correspondence if there is only one thing to which to correspond, since, as in any such case, the relation may as well be collapsed into a simple property: thus, 's corresponds to the facts' can less misleadingly be read 's is true'. ('Structure', 303)[145]

Davidson's argument for this conclusion is nowadays often referred to as (his version of) 'The Slingshot', presumably because philosophers like David(son)

---

[144]   As the example shows, a definition can be non-analytic without being stipulative.

[145]   Cf. Davidson, 'Epistemology and Truth', 184.

take it to be a very simple but lethal weapon against quite a few philosophical Goliaths.[146] The argument allegedly shows that the multitude of facts collapses into one, 'The Great Fact'. As spelt out by Davidson, the argument assumes that

a true sentence cannot be made to correspond to something different [A] by the substitution of co-referring singular terms, or [B] by the substitution of logically equivalent sentences. ('Structure', 303; bracketed letters added)

Let us call the two prongs of this assumption the principle of *Term Substitution* [A] and the principle of *Sentence Substitution* [B]. If one takes facts to be more coarse-grained entities than truths, one is easily driven towards acceptance of both principles: isn't the fact that Charles Dodgson is an Oxford don really the same as the fact that Lewis Carroll is an Oxford don, and isn't it also identical with the fact that it is not the case that Charles Dodgson is not an Oxford don?

The catapult is set to work as follows.[147] Let 'S' abbreviate some true sentence. Then surely, Davidson says,

(I) 'S' corresponds to the fact that S.

Surely? Logical Atomists are bound to object here that this depends on what kind of sentence 'S' is—but let that pass. According to Sentence Substitution we may substitute for the second 'S' in (I) the logically equivalent sentence 'the unique x such that $(x = $ Diogenes & S) is identical with the unique x such that $x = $ Diogenes,' which gives us

(II) 'S' corresponds to the fact that the unique x such that $(x = $ Diogenes & S) is identical with the unique x such that $x = $ Diogenes.

Now the definite descriptions 'the unique x such that $(x = $ Diogenes & S)' and 'the unique x such that $(x = $ Diogenes & T)' both stand for Diogenes, provided 'T' also abbreviates a true sentence. So applying Term Substitution to (II), we obtain

(III) 'S' corresponds to the fact that the unique x such that $(x = $ Diogenes & T) is identical with the unique x such that $x = $ Diogenes.

Finally, applying Sentence Substitution to (III), we conclude

(IV) 'S' corresponds to the fact that T.

---

[146] Davidson's Slingshot is a variant of an argument first used in Alonzo Church's 1943 'Review of Carnap's *Introduction to Semantics*' and repeated in Church, *Introduction to Mathematical Logic*, 24–5. Following Church, Davidson claims that the Slingshot ultimately 'derives from Frege' ('True to the Facts', n. 6). The alleged source is Frege's argument (in *Über Sinn und Bedeutung*, 34–5) that all true declarative sentences designate one and the same object, the True. But there is a vast methodological difference between Frege's reflections and (all versions of) the Slingshot, as Burge has pointed out: 'Frege on Truth', 104, 108–11, 151.

[147] Davidson, 'True to the Facts', 42.

If this argument is sound, it demonstrates that *any* two true sentences correspond to the same fact. Davidson aptly calls the conclusion 'the redundancy theory of facts'.[148]

Let us examine the two principles on which Davidson's Slingshot relies. Term Substitution can only too easily be refuted if there are true sentences in which co-designative singular terms cannot be exchanged *salva veritate*. There seem to be lots of such sentences. Surely, the truth 'Alec believes that Charles Dodgson is an Oxford don' does not correspond to the same fact as 'Alec believes that Lewis Carroll is an Oxford don' if, as a matter of fact, Alec does not have the latter belief. Sentence Substitution, too, can very easily be refuted if there are true sentences in which logically equivalent sentences cannot be exchanged *salva veritate*. Again, belief ascriptions provide us with ammunition, since the belief operator seems to be not only non-extensional, but also non-intensional: surely, the truth 'Ann believes that $2 + 2 = 4$' does not correspond to the same fact as 'Ann believes that $312 + 317 = 629$' if Ann does not have the latter belief. So Davidson's Slingshot only has a chance of setting the stone in motion if he succeeds in showing that there are no true sentences in which co-designative singular terms or logically equivalent sentences cannot be exchanged *salva veritate*. (His paratactic theory of *oratio obliqua* is a step in this direction.[149]) But perhaps this extremely ambitious enterprise is doomed to failure. So for the sake of our discussion, let us take the principles of Term Substitution and Sentence Substitution to be restricted to those truths that are free of purportedly non-extensional operators. The argument does not thereby become worthless, for the conclusion that all truths of this type correspond to one and the same thing is still bad enough for the friends of Fact-based Correspondence.

If Sentence Substitution, restricted to extensional contexts, is correct, then we have to admit that the fact represented by

(S1)   Oxford has many spires

is identical with the fact represented by

(S2)   Oxford has many spires & ¬ (London is large & ¬ London is large).

Barwise and Perry refuse to accept Sentence Substitution.[150] They would maintain that the simpler truth does not correspond to the same fact as the more complex one, since they differ in subject-matter: only the latter is partly about

---

[148] 'True to the Facts', 43. (The possible suspicion that the definite description used in this argument is somewhat fishy is dispelled by Neale, *FF*, 53–4, 171.)

[149] Cf. pp. 205–8 ff. and 328–31 ff. below.

[150] *Situations and Attitudes*, 24–6. Searle follows the same line: see *The Construction of Social Reality*, 221–6.

London. (Certainly (S2) does not tell us anything specific about London: after all, no object is both large and not-large. But why should aboutness depend on non-triviality?) Nevertheless, for cases like (S2) not all correspondence theorists can welcome this defence. According to the *Tractatus* tautologies are not made true by any facts. So friends of Fact-based Correspondence who follow this line cannot maintain that (S2) is made true by a pair of facts one of which by itself renders (S1) true.[151] Hence, for cases like (S2) they have to accept the identity claim reached via Sentence Substitution. (In any case, we will soon get to know another version of the Slingshot which does not rely on Sentence Substitution, so rejection of this principle does not really help.)

Let us instead ponder over Term Substitution. As Davidson's application of this principle to line (II) in the Slingshot shows, he regards definite descriptions as singular terms. By contrast, Russell takes definite descriptions ('the man who cheated Esau', 'Rachel's husband') to be quantificational noun phrases and thus in the same boat as 'every man', 'some man', 'no man'. According to Russell's Theory of Descriptions, (S3) 'Rachel's husband is fond of Joseph' is not an atomic sentence, since its logical form is quantificational: 'Every husband of Rachel is fond of Joseph, and there is exactly one husband of Rachel.' Nowadays, advocates of Russell's theory would add that (S3) does contain two genuine singular terms, namely 'Rachel' and 'Joseph'. So the principle of Term Substitution, as used by Davidson, might better be called LIBERAL TERM SUBSTITUTION:[152]

(LTS)   Within extensional contexts names *and* definite descriptions can be exchanged *salvo facto* if they are co-designative.

Does an exchange of co-designative singular terms (liberally conceived) in a true sentence that is free of putative non-extensional operators never affect the identity of the fact to which it corresponds? Consider this example. Jacob was both Rachel's and Leah's husband, and he was very fond of his son Joseph. But is the fact stated in an utterance of

(S3)   Rachel's husband is very fond of Joseph

---

[151] Wittgenstein, *Notebooks* (3.10.1914): *'Das logische Produkt einer Tautologie und eines Satzes sagt nicht mehr noch weniger aus als dieser allein* [The logical product of a tautology and a proposition says neither more nor less than the latter by itself]'. Cf. (12.12.1914), (25.5.1915) and *Tractatus*, 4.465 and 5.513 c. (Of course, according to the Conceptual Balance Requirement, (S1) and (S2) do *not* have the same propositional content, and I have argued that the Tractarian identification would not be welcome to Frege either: see p. 47 on (B-Nec) and p. 43.

[152] A definite descriptions 'the F' and a name 'N' are 'co-designative singular terms' (in the liberal sense) iff there is an object to which 'F' uniquely applies and which 'N' designates, and 'the F' is co-designative with 'the G' iff there is an object to which both 'F' and 'G' uniquely apply.

identical with the fact stated in an utterance of the next sentence?

(S4)   Leah's husband is very fond of Joseph.

These utterances have different truth-conditions: (S3) can only be true if Rachel is married, but this is not a condition of (S4)'s being true. (S4) could be true while (S3) is not, and vice versa. We do not need to seek far for the explanation of this difference: both utterances express contingent truths, both use a definite description that 'catches its man, so to speak, in a certain relation',[153] and the second *relatum* is different in both cases. Or take the following pair of sentences:

(S5)   Rachel's husband is Rachel's husband
(S6)   Rachel's husband is Leah's husband.

Their utterances, too, have different truth-conditions: for (S5) to yield a truth, it is sufficient that Rachel has exactly one husband, but in the case of (S6) more is asked for. Finally, (S5) gets us close to a logical truth, so let us transform it into such a truth and compare

(S5$^+$)   If there is exactly one husband of Rachel, then Rachel's husband is Rachel's husband

(S6$^+$)   If there is exactly one husband of Rachel, then Rachel's husband is Leah's husband.

While (S5$^+$) is unconditionally true, (S6$^+$) is not. Surely these sentences cannot be used to state the same fact. (The author of the *Tractatus* would have said that (S5$^+$) does not represent a fact at all.) Generally, friends of Fact-based Correspondence would be well advised to uphold the following principle as a necessary condition for fact-identity: two assertoric utterances state the same fact only if there is no object that is referred to in only one of them. Call it the *No Additional Object* principle. (Figuratively speaking, Rachel is not 'contained in' the fact that Leah's husband was very fond of Joseph, and a fact that does *not* contain Rachel cannot be identical with a fact that *does* contain her. But notice that the present attack on Davidson's assumption does not depend on taking facts literally to be structured entities somehow containing objects as parts.[154]) So the correspondence theorist can maintain that Davidson's principle of Liberal Term

---

[153] The phrase is Strawson's: see *Subject and Predicate in Logic and Grammar*, 45.

[154] As was mentioned in our discussion of the isomorphism theory of correspondence (see pp. 121–3 above), talk of facts being composed of parts cannot be understood in terms of mereological composition: the existence of the attribute F-ness, the object *a*, and the tie of instantiation does not ensure that it is a fact that F*a*.

Substitution turns out to be false whenever at least one of two co-designative singular terms contains a singular term that does not designate the same object as the containing term. (The relative clause is to exclude singular terms like 'the square-root of 1' or 'the person whom Narcissus loves most'.) So far, accounts of truth as fact-based correspondence seem to survive Davidson's variant of the Slingshot.

Let us finally consider an earlier version of this argument. It was sketched in 1944 by Kurt Gödel.[155] His Slingshot does not rely on Sentence Substitution. Slightly modified to fit into our discussion of Fact-based Correspondence, Gödel's argument runs as follows. Let

(1)   Fa
(2) $a \neq b$
(3)   Gb

abbreviate three true atomic sentences (containing no purportedly non-extensional operator). According to adherents of Fact-based Correspondence, each of our three truths corresponds to some fact or other; call these facts f_1, f_2, and f_3 respectively.

The argument appeals to two principles. We know one of them from Davidson's Slingshot: (LTS), i.e. LIBERAL TERM SUBSTITUTION. (So we know already that friends of facts can evade this Slingshot, too.) The second principle is far less sweeping than Davidson's principle of Sentence Substitution (which takes any two logically equivalent sentences, if true, to correspond to the same fact). Let us call it GÖDELIAN INTERCHANGE:

(GI)   An atomic sentence of the form 'Φa', if true (and free of purportedly non-extensional operators), always corresponds to the same fact as its expansion into 'a is the unique x such that $(x = a \ \& \ \Phi x)$'.

According to (GI), sentences (1) and

(4)   a is the unique x such that $(x = a \ \& \ Fx)$

both correspond to the fact f_1. Similarly, sentences (2) and

(5)   a is the unique x such that $(x = a \ \& \ x \neq b)$

both correspond to the fact f_2. Now the definite descriptions in (4) and (5), taken as singular terms, both designate the same object, namely a. So, relying on (LTS)

[155] 'Russell's Mathematical Logic', 128–9. Cf. Olson, *An Essay on Facts*, 93 ff.; Perry's reply, 'Evading the Slingshot'; García-Carpintero and Otero, '[T]he Frege-Gödel-Church Argument'; and, especially, Neale's comprehensive and thorough study of Gödel's Slingshot. Apart from some adaptations to my discussion of Davidson's Slingshot, I echo Neale's reconstruction: see *FF*, 128–36, 183–5, 220–2.

we conclude that (4) and (5) correspond to the same fact, i.e. f_1 is identical with f_2.

Once again, according to (GI), sentences (3) and

(6)   b is the unique x such that $(x = b \ \& \ Gx)$

both correspond to the fact f_3. Similarly, the sentences (2) and

(7)   b is the unique x such that $(x = b \ \& \ x \neq a)$

both correspond to the fact f_2. The definite descriptions in (6) and (7), taken as singular terms, both designate the same object, namely b. So, relying on (LTS) we conclude that (6) and (7) correspond to the same fact, that is to say: f_3, too, is identical with f_2. Thus f_1, f_2, and f_3 are identical, so (1) and (3) correspond to the same fact. Obviously the same argument can be run for any pair of atomic truths about two different objects, and a similar argument in which premiss (2) is replaced by '$a = b$' can be run for any pair of atomic truths about the same object. So *all atomic truths correspond to one and the same fact.*[156]

(GI) does *not* offend against the No Additional Object principle, since there is no object which is referred to in an utterance of 'Jacob is the unique person who is both identical with Jacob and very fond of Joseph' which is not also referred to in an utterance of 'Jacob is very fond of Joseph', and vice versa.[157] But we know that (LTS) does offend against that principle. Thus in (5) an object is designated which is not designated in (4), and the same applies to (7) and (6).

Advocates of Fact-based Correspondence can, and I think should, accept a principle which might be called STRICT TERM SUBSTITUTION:

(STS)   Within extensional contexts co-designative *names* can be exchanged *salvo facto.*

They can concede that 'George Eliot wrote *Middlemarch*' and 'Mary Ann Evans wrote *Middlemarch*' correspond to the same fact, while denying that 'The author of *The Mill on the Floss* wrote *Middlemarch*' and 'The author of *Silas Marner* wrote

---

[156] Gödel actually assumes that 'every proposition...can be brought to the form $\phi(a)$' ('Russell's Mathematical Logic', 129 n.). On pp. 111–12 above, we have seen reason to question the assumption that every sentence can be squeezed into this Procrustean bed. (Neale's suggestion, on Gödel's behalf, that 'All men snore' can be transformed into 'Socrates is an x such that all men snore' (*FF* 130) is rather odd, for one would have thought that the truth of the general statement is independent of the existence of Socrates. Aristotle's suggestion in *De Int.*, as explained on p. 99 n. 24 above, looks more attractive.) At any rate,' without [Gödel's Procrustean] assumption, his Slingshot will show only that all true *atomic* sentences stand for the same fact—of course, this conclusion would be every bit as devastating for most friends of facts' (ibid.; cf. 186).

[157] In this respect, the first sentence is related to the second, as 'The person whom Narcissus loves most is looking into the mirror' is related to 'Narcissus is looking into the mirror'.

Middlemarch' do so as well.[158] Gödel clearly recognized that the Russellian retreat to (STS) blocks the Slingshot.

Now consider the following question: is the fact stated in an utterance of

(S7)   Jacob is Rachel's husband

identical with the fact stated in an utterance of the next sentence?

(S8)   Jacob is the only man who made love to Rachel.

These utterances have different truth-conditions: (S7) can only be true if Rachel is married, but this is not a condition of (S8)'s being true. (S7) could be true while (S8) is not, and vice versa. Intuitively, those utterances do not state the same fact. But this time the No Additional Object principle is *not* violated. So why are the definite descriptions in (S7) and (S8) not interchangeable *salvo facto*? One cannot plausibly maintain that definite descriptions which apply to the same object can *never* be exchanged *salvo facto*. As one can see from the following pair

> Esau is Jacob's elder brother
> Esau is Israel's elder brother,

such a general prohibition would be incompatible with accepting (STS).[159] But friends of Fact-based Correspondence can motivate their refusal to assign the same fact to (S7) and (S8) by arguing that two definite descriptions which apply to the same object are not intersubstitutable *salvo facto* if one of them introduces a *property* (e.g. being a husband) into discourse which is not introduced by the other. Two assertoric utterances, they can plausibly maintain, state the same fact only if there is no property which is introduced in only one of them. Call this the *No Additional Property* principle. (Figuratively speaking, the property of being a husband is not 'contained in' the fact that Jacob is the only man who made love to Rachel, and a fact that does *not* contain that property cannot be identical with a fact that *does* contain it. But notice, once again, that the rejection of (LTS) does not

---

[158] (STS) is in agreement with our everyday use of 'fact', I think, and with Russell's conception of facts, and it is in disagreement with Moore's view in *SMPP*: see pp. 116 and 121–2 above. In 'Substitution and Simple Sentences' Jennifer Saul has presented examples that might be taken to show that even (STS) is not correct. Here is a variant of one of her examples. Suppose that 'The Strange Case of Dr Jekyll and Mr Hyde' is a correct historical report. Then (S) 'Jekyll is more pleasant than Hyde' can be used to convey a truth, whereas (S*) 'Jekyll is more pleasant than Jekyll' cannot. The most reasonable reaction to such examples, I take it, is the one that Saul also seems to favour: what is literally said by (S) is as false as what is literally said by (S*), but an utterance of (S) can have the true pragmatic implicature that Jekyll is more pleasant in those phases of his life when he is referred to as Dr Jekyll than in those periods when one refers to him as Mr Hyde. (Cf. the discussion of Saul's paper in *Analysis*, 1997–2000.)

[159] According to Genesis 32, Jacob is Israel.

depend on taking facts literally to be structured entities somehow containing properties as parts.) Interestingly, the No Additional *Property* principle can even be turned against (GI): after all, the property of being identical with a is introduced in (4), but not in (1). All this would be congenial to Russell,[160] but in order to defend this treatment of pairs like (S7) and (S8), or of pairs like (1) and (4), one does not have to follow Russell in denying that definite descriptions are singular terms (or in regarding atomic facts as composed of objects and properties).[161]

A conception of truth in terms of fact-based correspondence, I conclude, can survive both variants of what Davidson calls 'the real objection to correspondence theories'.

3.3.4 *The unworldliness objection*

Let us now consider (one aspect of) Strawson's famous attack on Austin's version of a correspondence theory. Austin tried to explain truth (or at least empirical truth) as a relation between truth vehicles and parts of the spatio-temporal world which he called 'facts'. In order to show that this attempt fails, Strawson asks us to consider a true statement made by first referring to a part of the spatio-temporal world ('That cat...') and then characterizing or describing it ('... has mange'). Notice that in Strawson's reflections 'the world' designates the totality of whatever can be dated or located.

That... to which the referring part of the statement refers, and which the describing part of the statement fits or fails to fit, is that which the statement is *about*.

Before we continue reading, let me insert a reminder. The notion of fitting that Strawson employs here is the very notion that was used as long as 'correspondence' was wedded to 'object' rather than to 'fact': the describing (predicative) part of an atomic statement S 'fits' what is referred to in S if and only if the *object* S is about has the *property* that S ascribes to it. Strawson goes on to say:

[T]here is nothing else in the world for the statement itself to be related to either in some further way of its own or in either of the different ways in which these different parts of the statement are related to what the statement is about.... What 'makes the statement' that the cat has mange 'true', is not the cat, but... the fact that the cat has mange. The only plausible candidate for the position of what (in the world) makes the statement true is the fact it states; but the fact it states is not something in the world...∕... Events can

---

[160] See Neale, *FF*, 204.   [161] Here I seem to disagree with Neale.

be dated and things can be located. But the facts which statements (when true) state can neither be located nor dated. ('Truth' (1950), 194–5, 199)[162]

Hugh Mellor disagrees with Strawson's final verdict. The fact which is stated in a true utterance of 'Don dies', he argues, does have a 'location in space and time':

[N]ote first that we can and often do identify facts by their location. Thus 'it rains in Paris on March 1998' and 'it rains in London on 9 July 2001', if atemporally true, state different facts, located at those places and times. And whether we say so or not, the fact is that Don dies somewhere and at some time: say in the Lake District in June 1988— not in London and not in May. Similarly for any other located fact P. (*The Facts of Causation*, 9)

To be sure, rainfalls and deaths occur somewhere and somewhen, but how is that supposed to show that the facts stated in true weather reports and death notices are located in space and time? That our identifications of facts sometimes include reference to times and places is scarcely a good reason for assigning a spatio-temporal location to those facts. For otherwise the following argument would be sound: our identifications of mathematical theorems sometimes include reference to times and places (as witness 'the mathematical theorem which Hilbert proved in Göttingen in 1909'), therefore (?), those theorems have a spatio-temporal location.

Does Austin's reply to his co-symposiast fare any better? He complained that Strawson was 'Unfair to Facts':

Strawson admits that events are ['genuinely-in-the-world']. Yet surely of ... these we can say that they *are facts*. The collapse of the Germans is an event and is a fact. ... Strawson, however, seems to suppose that anything of which we can say '. . . is a fact' is, automatically, *not* something in the world. ('Unfair to Facts', 156)

This reply contains a glaring mistake. Ramsey had put his finger on this mistake some decades before the Austin–Strawson debate. 'A phrase like "the death of Caesar" can be used in two different ways':[163] it is *either* used to refer to an event which took place in Rome on the Ides of March, 44 BC, *or* to refer to a fact which

---

[162] In his 1931 manuscript entitled '*Komplex und Tatsache*' Wittgenstein criticized his own earlier self along the same lines (in *Philosophische Grammatik*, 200–1): '*Man sagt freilich auch: "auf eine Tatsache hinweisen", aber das heißt immer: "auf die Tatsache hinweisen, daß . . .". Dagegen heißt "auf eine Blume zeigen (oder hinweisen)" nicht, darauf hinweisen, daß . . . Auf eine Tatsache hinweisen heißt, etwas behaupten, aussagen. "Auf eine Blume hinweisen" heißt das nicht.* [Of course we also say: "to point out a fact", but that always means: "to point out the fact that . . .". Whereas "to point (or point out) a flower" does not mean to point out that . . . To point out a fact means to assert something, to state something. "To point out a flower" does not mean this.]'

[163] Ramsey, 'Facts and Propositions', 37. Ryle made the same point forcefully in his 1932 paper 'Systematically Misleading Expressions', 57; cf. Vendler, 'Facts and Events'.

might be denied or controverted but which can be neither dated nor located. Ramsey's point holds for all derived nominals. Consider

(1)   The collapse of the Germans is a fact
(2)   The collapse of the Germans began in 1944.

If the identity of the derived nominals in (1) and (2) were to guarantee that the very same entity is introduced into discourse, then we would have to conclude from these premisses:

(3)   Therefore (?), a fact began in 1944.

We can avoid this slide into nonsense by treating derived nominals as systematically ambiguous. Then we can say: only in (2) does the subject-term designate an event, hence the displayed argument commits the fallacy of equivocation.[164] So Austin's reply to Strawson fails: '*The collapse of the Germans* is both an event and a fact' is a zeugma like '*Anna Karenina* is both a beautiful woman and a great novel', forcing one expression into two conflicting services.[165]

(Ramsey's argument to the same conclusion is less than satisfactory. It goes essentially like this: suppose that (S) 'Ben is aware of the fact that Caesar was murdered' expresses a truth. If the locution (a) 'the fact that Caesar was murdered' were to designate an event, namely the murder of Caesar, then (b) 'the fact that Caesar was assassinated' would designate the same event, since the murder of Caesar was an assassination. So substitution of (b) for (a) in (S) should not alter its truth-value. But of course, it does: Ben might have no idea, or a false idea, about the motives of the murderers. Hence, Ramsey concludes, the fact that Caesar was murdered is not identical with the event in the Senate House. This argument, so an advocate of the (mistaken) identity claim could reply, only shows that the operator 'Ben is aware of the fact that . . .' is not extensional.)

Austin's mistake was recently repeated by Searle. In order to combat Frege's identification of facts with true propositions (an identification which, by 1998, is actually endorsed by Strawson[166]), Searle argues:

For Frege, facts just are true propositions. But that must be a mistake because, for example, facts can function causally in a way that true statements cannot. Consider: 'The fact

---

[164] You find this systematic ambiguity not only with derived nominals, but also with verbal gerunds: 'Ann's dancing with Ben' may be used to refer to an event, or to a fact. Embedded in '. . . lasted 30 minutes', it designates an event; embedded in 'He was informed of . . .' it designates a fact. In Ch. 1 I argued, as against McDowell's defence of (*Idem*), that even that-clauses are systematically ambiguous, and in Ch. 5.1 I shall return to this observation.

[165] At one point Austin assimilates facts even to objects: 'Suppose that we confront "France is hexagonal" with the facts, in this case, I suppose, with France . . .' (*How to Do Things With Words*, 142).

[166] Strawson, 'Reply to Searle', 403. In 'Truth' (1950), 196, Strawson had rejected this identification; which justifies Searle's claim on p. 389 of his paper.

that Napoleon recognized the danger to his left flank, caused him to move his troops forward.' You cannot make a parallel claim about the true statement. The true statement that Napoleon recognized the danger to his left flank, didn't cause anything. ('Truth: A Reconsideration of Strawson's Views', 389)[167]

Speech-acts are certainly not causally inert: somebody's statement (= stating) that Napoleon recognized the danger to his left flank might cause a lot of surprise. So charitable readers will take 'statement' in our quotation to mean *what is stated* rather than the act of stating it. Now Searle's sample sentence does not show at all that facts can be causally *efficacious*. As Strawson points out in his reply,[168] it is only evidence for the claim that facts can be causally *explanatory*. The remark about Napoleon invokes one fact in explanation of another, and the point of this remark can be less misleadingly conveyed by saying: 'The reason why Napoleon moved his troops forward was that he recognized the danger to his left flank', or 'Napoleon moved his troops forward *because* he recognized the danger to his left flank'. What is causally efficacious, on the other hand, is not the fact which is stated after the 'because' but rather the *event* which is reported by that statement: the event of Napoleon's recognizing the danger to his left flank at a certain location on a certain date. What is causally efficacious belongs to the natural order of datables and locatables, but the explanans in an explanation (even if it is a causal explanation) does not belong to this order.[169]

None of this shows that Frege and Strawson are right in *identifying* facts with true propositions, but it exempts this identification from the charge of mistaking something spatio-temporal for an abstract entity. Facts are indeed, like propositions and unlike events, abstract entities. (They resemble propositions also in being *non-extensional* abstract entities: 'The fact that Fa is the same as the fact that Ga' is only true if the predicates 'F' and 'G' signify the same property, and they may fail to do that even if they are co-extensive. Thus the fact that Ben has a liver is different from the fact that he has a heart, even though the predicates

---

[167] The same argument against the Fregean identification can be found in Vision, *Modern Anti-Realism*, 57; Kirkham, *ThT*, 138.

[168] 'Reply to Searle', 404. Actually Searle could have found this reply already in 'Truth' (1950), 197: 'Being alarmed by a fact is not like being frightened by a shadow. It is being alarmed because . . .', and in 'Causation and Explanation'.

[169] In the Napoleon example we can extract from the causal explanation a description of the causally efficacious event. Various examples presented by Mellor (*The Facts of Causation*, 132–5) show that this is not always possible. But these examples do not show that in such cases there is no causally efficacious event (or state), hence they lend no support to the thesis that at least some causes are facts. To take just one of Mellor's mountaineer examples: 'Don's fall is the first because his rope is the weakest' (ibid., 117, 135). This explanation can hardly be correct if an (admittedly less informative) statement like 'The breaking of Don's rope caused his fall' were not also true.

'has a liver' and 'has a heart' are co-extensive.) In the course of putting the Identity Theorists' answer to QUESTION 6 on our flow-chart aside (see Figure 1.1), I have argued against the contention that facts are nothing but true propositions.[170] In any case, if true (empirical) statements are supposed to be 'made true' by something within the spatio-temporal world, then (non-extensional) abstract entities such as facts are unavailable for this role.

3.4 A Neglected Alternative

But is there really *no* 'plausible candidate for the position of what (in the world) makes the statement true', as Strawson says? When I quoted Russell's 'preliminary explanation' of what he meant by 'fact' (in 1918), I quietly dropped one of his examples. Let me now make good for this omission:

When I speak of a fact...I mean the kind of thing that makes a proposition true or false.... If I say 'Socrates is dead,' my statement will be true owing to a certain physiological occurrence which happened in Athens long ago. (*PLA*, 182)

Clearly, Russell overlooks here the categorial distinction between events (occurrences) and facts: the thing that happened in Athens isn't a fact. This confusion might be responsible for his claim that facts, 'just as much as particular chairs and tables, are part of the real world'.[171] (Facts have hardly ever been assimilated more closely to the '*furniture* of the universe' than in this remark.[172]) But perhaps Russell's confusion contains the germ of a different kind of correspondence theory. Isn't the event that took place in Athens in 399 BC a plausible candidate for the position of what in the real world makes the historical statement true? When Russell in 1940 delivered the William James Lectures at Harvard University, later published as *An Inquiry into Meaning and Truth*, he still adhered to a correspondence view of truth, and he still called the entities in the right field of the correspondence relation 'facts'. But now this is no more than a rather unfortunate terminological relic:

As to 'facts': they are not to be conceived as 'that grass is green' or 'that all men are mortal'; they are to be conceived as occurrences... /... When an empirical belief is true, it is true in virtue of a certain occurrence which I call its 'verifier'. I believe that Caesar was assassinated; the verifier of this belief is the actual event which happened in the Senate House long ago... /... We...define 'truth' by reference to 'events'. (I am speaking of non-logical truth.) (*IMT*, 268, 227, 288)

---

[170] See the arguments above on pp. 10–12.   [171] *PLA*, 183.
[172] I wish I had said that, but the joke is Olson's: *An Essay on Facts*, 1.

Let us just register in passing that with respect to general beliefs Russell has by now come to agree with Wittgenstein that

> the world can, in theory, be completely described without the use of any logical words.... If 'all men are mortal' is to be true, there must be an occurrence which is A's death, another which is B's death, and so on throughout the catalogue of men.... There is no *one* verifier for 'All men are mortal'. (*IMT*, 241; cf. *PLA*, 236, cited above on p. 121)

He also rejects negative facts, or, rather, negative events.[173] However, talk of negative events seems to be deplorable for reasons which have nothing to do with 'over-populating the universe' but rather with transgressing the bounds of sense. 'Eruption of a volcano' applies to events, so presumably 'non-eruption of a volcano' would apply to negative events if there were any, and the putative verifier of the statement that Vesuvius did not erupt at midnight would have to be a particular non-eruption of Vesuvius if only there were such things. Now if something is a (past) event, then we can sensibly ask 'When did it take place?' and, barring point-events, 'How long did it last?' But questions like 'When did the last non-eruption of Vesuvius take place?' or 'How long did it last?' do not make sense at all. It's not that we can very well do without such things: we do not know what to do with them.

Russell's use of 'verifying' in 1940 is just a latinized echo of his former use of 'making true'. Obviously, in his mouth 'verifying' does not mean what it meant in Vienna: finding out that (or checking whether) something is true. Russell reactivates here a fairly old use of this verb. We find it in Aquinas when he says that statements implying a flat contradiction 'cannot be veri-fied even by divine intervention [*nullo miraculo verificari possunt*]'.[174] Logical Positivists tended to confuse both uses. In the course of arguing that among empirical propositions some are only 'weakly verifiable' whereas others are in a better position, Ayer wrote:

> There is a class of empirical propositions of which it is permissible to say that they can be verified conclusively. It is characteristic of these propositions ... that they refer solely to the content of a single experience, and what may be said to verify them conclusively is the occurrence of the experience to which they uniquely refer. (*Language, Truth and Logic*, 2nd edn., 13.)

Thus understood, being conclusively verified is being made true. It is hard to see why this property should be the prerogative of those first-person present-tense reports of experiences which Ayer has in mind. Anyway, unlike being 'weakly verified', it is certainly not a property that a proposition achieves after having been submitted to a certain procedure.[175] So what is the generic sense of 'verification'

---

[173] Russell, *Human Knowledge*, 520.   [174] Aquinas, *Expositio super librum Boethii De trinitate*, 151.

[175] This was pointed out by Morris Lazerowitz in 'Strong and Weak Verification, II'.

which is common to 'weak' and 'strong (conclusive) verification' thus understood?

Back to Russell, who was certainly not a Logical Positivist. The first passage from *IMT* quoted above contains a plea for what was registered, under the left branch of QUESTION 5, as *Event-based Correspondence*. We can codify Russell's 1940 view thus:

(EventC) $\forall x$ (x is a true empirical belief $\leftrightarrow$ x is made true by one or more events severally or jointly).

The adverb 'severally' is meant to cover disjunctions and existential quantifications (where there may be more than one veri-fier but none of them needs the help of the others to do its job), and 'jointly' is to take care of conjunctions and, according to our second excerpt from *IMT*, of universal quantifications. Obviously this cannot be a *definition* of 'true' as applied to empirical beliefs, for the right-hand side contains this very word. But it might be an adequate account of what, in the case of empirical beliefs, being true consists in.

Whenever one acquires a true '*basic*' empirical belief, Russell claims, the occurrence that makes the belief true is the *cause* of the belief acquisition. If, dazzled by a flash of lightning, I cannot help thinking that there is now a flash of lightning, then the meteorological event that, according to Russell, renders my judgement true is the cause of my judging. In such cases, Russell claims, making true *is* causing: for true basic beliefs 'a causal connection ... constitutes the correspondence' in which their truth consists.[176] Even if we bracket problems with deviant causal chains, this cannot possibly hold for all empirical beliefs. If I truly judge now that in a few seconds there will be a flash of lightning within my field of vision, the future event can hardly be the cause of my present mental act. And the trouble is by no means confined to prognostic judgements. I may truly think that a few seconds ago an explosion was occurring a million light-years away, but no such explosion can be the cause of my act of judging. (If Einstein got things right, no causation could cross distances faster than light.) So, again, we are not offered a plausible general account of correspondence for empirical beliefs in terms of a relational predicate with which we are familiar. As to the meaning of 'making true', Russell leaves us in the dark.

In any case, assuming that *events* are veri-fiers (in a sense still awaiting articulation) seems not even to suffice for explaining what it is for singular empirical statements to be true. We may believe truly (a) that Bucephalus is a horse, (b) that Hesperus is Phosphorus, and (c) that the planet Venus exists. No occurrences seem

---

[176] *IMT*, 283; cf. 231.

to be reported by assignments to natural kinds, identity statements, or singular existentials. What are they made true by? In the next section I will outline a conception of making true that is more articulate than Russell's and that answers this question as follows: (a) is made true by Bucephalus (since he is essentially a horse); and Venus (Hesperus, Phosphorus) is the veri-fier of (b) and (c). Suppose this reply is well motivated. Then (EventC) can only be upheld if one pleads for a revisionary ontology that declares horses, planets, and all other continuants to be nothing but strings of contiguous and causally related events. But then the account of (empirical) truth becomes saddled with a major conceptual revision whose feasibility is rather doubtful. How are non-circular identity criteria for (strings of) events to be provided, without compromising their allegedly fundamental status? (We will see that the post-Russellian view I alluded to preserves the spirit of (EventC) but abandons its mono-categoriality.)

A further reason for complaint is a built-in limitation of the whole enterprise: the restriction to empirical truth. The theory does not even try to tell us what being true in general consists in. The problem of range has been with us in this chapter since we left Moore. Neither adherents of the Tractarian version of Fact-based Correspondence nor proponents of Event-based Correspondence face the general question that the other correspondence theorists considered in this chapter at least tried to answer: what do all truths have in common?

3.5 Varieties of Making True

Notwithstanding major disagreements about the right field of the correspondence relation and about the character of this relation, almost every correspondence account that we discussed was intended, to use Moore's words, as 'a definition of what we actually mean by saying that [a truth candidate of such-and-such a kind] is true'.[177] But one can advocate a correspondence theory of truth without aspiring to give a definition. 'Equilateral triangle' does not *mean* EQUIANGULAR TRIANGLE, and yet it is a conceptual truth that all and only equiangular triangles are equilateral triangles. Arguably, being an equilateral triangle and being an equiangular triangle are one and the same property, but the concepts are definitely different. So a philosopher who takes truth to be a relational property (where the implied relation is not one towards other truth-value bearers) can consistently claim to

---

[177] See passage [M.2] on p. 115. Kant famously called the explanation quoted on p. 108 a '*Namenserklärung* (nominal definition) of truth': see *Kritik der reinen Vernunft*, B 82. I say 'almost every correspondence account' because of (R-FactC), which obviously does not make any claim to being a definition (see p. 119 above).

teach us a conceptual truth about truth and deny that 'true' has the same *sense* as any predicate which signifies that relational property. The property of being true, she can say, is the same as the relational property signified by 'F', whereas the concept expressed by 'true' is not identical with the concept expressed by 'F'.[178]

In any case, even if the concept of truth cannot be defined in terms of correspondence, there may be something to the intuition behind such failed definitions. Putnam illustrates what might be called the Correspondence Intuition when he writes:

[T]here is a realist intuition, namely that there is a substantive kind of rightness (or wrongness) that my statement that I had cereal for breakfast this morning possesses *as a consequence of* what happened this morning ... which must be preserved. ('On Truth', 329; my italics)

(I shall comment on the label 'realist intuition' in the final section of this chapter. For the time being, think of it as a stylistic variant of 'Correspondence Intuition'.) Dummett articulates this intuition as a principle:[179]

(Principle C)   If a statement is true, there must be something *in virtue of which* it is true

and he comments upon it as follows:

This principle underlies the philosophical attempts to explain truth as a correspondence between a statement and some component of reality, and I shall accordingly refer to it as principle C. The principle C is certainly in part constitutive of our notion of truth. ('Meaning', 52)

Advocates of Principle C would certainly also accept the *bi*conditional: necessarily, a statement is true if and only if there is something in virtue of which it is

---

[178] In Ch. 11 I have argued that this distinction can help to protect epistemic theories of truth against the objection Alston mounts against them in his book *RCT*. In Alston's recent paper, 'Truth: Concept and Property', the distinction is carved out, and it is used to show that there is room for combining a 'minimalist' explanation of the concept of truth with a correspondence theory of the property of being true. He is not exactly loquacious as to the content of such a theory.

[179] Dummett, 'Meaning', 52; cf. 'Truth', 14, and *FPL*, 464. Wiggins concurs with Dummett in taking it to be one of the 'Marks of Truth' that 'every truth is true in virtue of something': cf. his 'What Would be a Substantial Theory of Truth?' (henceforth 'Substantial'), 211; 'Truth, and Truth as Predicated of Moral Judgements' (henceforth 'Moral'), 148; and 'Indefinibilist', 329. He adds that this statement 'simply condenses the statement' of three other 'marks' ('Moral', 150). Since he does not explain this contention, it is difficult to fathom, and one wonders, anyway, why something is listed as one of five marks of a concept if it only 'condenses' others that have already been mentioned. (In the postscript to Ch. 7.3.1, we will look at one of the other 'Marks of Truth' on Wiggins's list.) Searle repeatedly invokes Principle C, and he also takes it to articulate 'the fundamental intuition behind the correspondence theory' (see 'Truth: A Reconsideration of Strawson's Views', 387).

true. It is not implausible to maintain that this biconditional, like Principle C, articulates a conceptual truth about truth, but of course, one cannot sensibly offer it as a definition of 'true'. Russell seems to subscribe to Principle C when he insists (in 1918 and in 1940) that true statements are *made true by* something, and of course, he was not the first philosopher who endorsed Principle C, or something like it.

3.5.1 *Aristotle and the Principle C*

Aristotle appears to make a claim to the effect that a truth owes its truth to something, is true in virtue of something, is rendered or made true by something, when he says:

> It is not because of [διά] our having the true thought that you are pale, that you *are* pale; rather it is because of your *being* pale that we who say so have a true thought. (*Met.*, Θ 10: 1051ᵇ6–9)

> It is because of the thing's being, or not being, thus-and-so [τῷ … τὸ πρᾶγμα εἶναι ἢ μὴ εἶναι] that the predication is said to be true or false … (*Cat.* 5: 4ᵇ8–10)[180]

On one interpretation of these remarks (the other readings will have to wait for a while), the intended message is best conveyed if we replace the preposition 'because of' by the connective 'because' and accordingly substitute a sentence for the gerund phrase. Then we obtain: 'The statement that you are pale is true, because you are pale,' and the general point can be captured by

(Schema P) If *the statement that p* is true, then *it* is true because p.

Is Aristotle's contention (thus understood) plausible? Certainly it would be ridiculous to answer the question 'Why is Socrates pale?' by saying: 'Because it is true (to think or say) that he is pale.' We would rather expect answers like 'Because he is ill' or 'Because he has just received bad news.' But do things really look better the other way round? If our question is 'Why is it true that Socrates is pale?' we would normally be annoyed if we were told: 'Because he is pale.' (This looks more like an answer to questions like 'Why does Xanthippe feel sorry for Socrates?') Again, we would rather expect answers like 'Because he is ill' or

---

[180] The second passage continues: '…not because it is itself able to receive contraries'. So the Greek phrase in brackets should not be taken to mean: in virtue of the thing's existence or non-existence (as Ackrill assumes in his translation): the point of the passage is that substances can *really* 'receive contraries'—Aristotle's example is one and the same man receiving paleness and darkness—whereas predications only *seem* to be able to receive contraries. (*Cat.*, 12: 14ᵇ18–22, on the other hand, seems to demand an existential reading because of the example given in line 14.)

'Because he has just received bad news.' The reason for this is, I think, that 'It is true that p' and 'p' are cognitively equivalent. But then, how *are* we to understand the question 'Why is it true that p?' if 'Because p' is supposed to be a *proper* answer? Chisholm once called this answer 'Aristotle's basic insight' concerning truth, but unfortunately he did not pause to explain it.[181]

One might be tempted to explain this alleged insight by an argument that invokes (an instance of) the Denominalization Schema:

(Den)   It is true that p, if and only if p.

After all, Aristotle himself was very well aware that

If it is true to say that so-and-so is pale... then necessarily he is pale; and if he is pale... then it was true to say that he is. (*De Int.* 9: 18^a39–42)[182]

This is clearly meant to generalize, and if we do so we obtain (the universal closure of) the (modally strengthened) Denominalization Schema. Jean Buridan calls this principle *regula Aristotelis*.[183] Let 's' abbreviate 'Socrates is pale'. Why is it true that s? An appeal to Aristotle's Rule and a look at the man would seem to deliver the answer:

(1)   It is true that s, if (and only if) s.   Aristotle's Rule
(2)   s.   perceptual judgement
(3)   Therefore, it is true that s.   1, 2 *modus ponens.*

But this immaculate little deduction does not really capture Aristotle's alleged insight. The following argument appealing to the other direction of Aristotle's Rule is equally sound:

(1*)   It is true that s, (if and) only if s.   Aristotle's Rule
(2*)   It is true that s.   perceptual judgement
(3*)   Therefore, s.   1, 2 *modus ponens.*

Certainly this reasoning does *not* answer the question why s. But if the soundness of the second argument does not rationalize the bizarre claim, 's because it is true that s', it is hard to see why the soundness of the first argument should legitimize the contention 'It is true that s, because s'.

In Bolzano's philosophy of logic, propositions of the form 'The truth that q is a consequence of the truth that p' are treated as logically equivalent with

---

[181] Chisholm, *Theory of Knowledge*, 1st edn., 113; 2nd edn., 101.
[182] Aristotle makes the same point in *Cat.* 12: 14^b14–18. Here he immediately goes on to formulate his 'basic insight': see n. 180.   [183] Buridanus, *Sophismata*, ch. VIII, 2nd Soph., 45, 47.

'q because p'. The relation signified by 'is a consequence of' is an *asymmetrical* relation which obtains between true propositions.[184] Hence, when Bolzano says:

Es sey ... A was immer für eine Wahrheit: so ist die Wahrheit, daß der Satz A wahr sey, eine echte Folge aus ihr. [Let A be any truth you like: then the truth that A is true is a proper consequence of A. (*WL* II. 357)

he accepts Aristotle's point, and he does not fail to notice either that 'from any given proposition *A* the proposition *A is true* is deducible [*ableitbar*], and the latter proposition is in turn deducible from the former'.[185]

By endorsing Principle C, Dummett seems to confirm Aristotle, and he clearly distinguishes this principle from the Denominalization Schema when he writes:

[T]he correspondence theory expresses one important feature of the concept of truth which is not expressed by the law 'It is true that p if and only if p' ... that a statement is true only if there is something in the world *in virtue of which* it is true. ('Truth', 14)

As we saw, (Den) really fails to capture this alleged feature of the concept of truth. For the same reason, (Den)'s sibling, the Disquotation Schema

(Dis)   'p' is true if and only if p,

does not capture it either. Quine thinks otherwise:

[T]ruth should hinge on reality, and it does. No sentence is true but reality makes it so. The sentence 'Snow is white' is true, as Tarski has taught us, if and only if real snow is really white. (*Philosophy of Logic* [henceforth *PL*] 10)

But surely this will not do. The predicates 'x is made true by y' and 'x is true in virtue of y' signify asymmetrical relations, so we cannot preserve the point of the slogan 'No sentence is true but reality makes it so' by using a 'symmetrical' (commutative) connective even if we embellish the right-hand side of the biconditional by a generous use of 'real(ly)'. The Disquotation Schema is no substitute for the principle which that slogan incapsulates.[186]

Elizabeth Anscombe finds talk of 'making true' intelligible only if one truth is said to be made true by a different truth. As we saw in section 3.2.2, Logical Atomists have presented one kind of example which meets this condition. Suppose somebody asserts that either Socrates or Seneca drank the hemlock. Then the question may arise who did, and if somebody answers that Socrates did, he can intelligibly be said to have told us what makes that disjunction

---

[184] Bolzano, *WL*, II. 362; cf. above, Ch. 2.1.3.

[185] Bolzano, *WL*, IV. 114. He explains his conception of deducibility [*Ableitbarkeit*] in *WL*, II. 113 ff.

[186] Nor can it do duty for the sentential counterpart of SCHEMA P: if [the contextually stable and unambiguous English-sentence] 'p' is true, then 'p' is true because ('p' means that p, and p).

true.[187] By contrast, Anscombe finds statements, to the effect that a certain proposition is made true, but *not* by the truth of any other proposition, hard to understand:

[A] proposition can't make itself true: we have to gloss the statement and say '[the proposition that] p is made true by the *fact that* p.' If we have a Tractatus-like metaphysic of facts this would be possible: we would have reached an elementary proposition, made true by the existence of an atomic fact. But without such a metaphysic we are only saying [that the proposition that] p is made true by its being the case that p, or by its being true! That is an empty statement, with only a false air of explanation. And so in the end we'd have to accept...propositions which are true without being made true. If this seems shocking, that is because of a deep metaphysical prejudice. ('"Making true"', 8)

Now we are in a quandary. Does Aristotle give voice to a basic insight or to a deep prejudice?

And there is a further question which needs to be considered: does Principle C really articulate Aristotle's alleged insight if we take the latter to be captured by SCHEMA P? Consider the locution 'true in virtue of something' in Principle C. There are uses of 'something' in which it does not subserve quantification into singular-term position ('There is something that Solomon and Socrates both are, namely wise'),[188] but in Principle C the prepositional phrase 'in virtue of' enforces such a reading: the open sentence '...is true in virtue of...' is, so to speak, singular-term hungry on both sides. It goes well with this that in some of his formulations of the principle Dummett expands 'something' into 'something in the world' or 'some component of reality'. So apparently the point of Principle C can be conveyed by

(SCHEMA X)   If *the statement that p* is true, then for some x, x makes *it* true.

By contrast, SCHEMA P does not contain any quantification over objects in the world or components of reality. Davidson seems to contest Principle C and SCHEMA X, when he writes:

Nothing, no thing, makes sentences and theories true: not experience, not surface irritations, not the world, can make a sentence true. *That* experience takes a certain course, *that* our skin is warmed or punctured, *that* the universe is finite, these facts, if we like to talk that way, make sentences and theories true. But this point is put better without mention of facts. ('On the Very Idea of a Conceptual Scheme', 194)[189]

---

[187] Anscombe, '"Making true"', 1–2.   [188] See Ch. 2.2.2 above.

[189] Davidson might have included in his negative list 'cosmic distributions of particles over space-time'; which are said by Quine to make sentences true (*PL*, 4).

But does he thereby deny 'Aristotle's basic insight'? One would hope not, if the latter deserves its laurel. But if not, then there must be at least two varieties of making true.

3.5.2　*A propositional reading of 'making true'*

In order to clear the ground for an attempt at explaining the first variety of making true, let us stand back for a while and ask: how are sentences of the type 'x makes y such-and-such' to be understood? Often we use them to ascribe a *causal connection*: 'Sunshine makes the flowers grow;' 'Ann's arrival made Ben happy, her departure will make him sad.' Some ordinary applications of 'x makes y *true*' are also to be understood causally: 'She had announced in advance that she would visit him, and yesterday she made her announcement true.' Here, something is made true by the efforts of an agent.[190] Perhaps the Almighty, by a remarkably efficient illocutionary act, made it true (brought it about, saw to it) that there was light. But obviously this use of 'making true' is far away from the philosopher's use: by assenting to Aristotle's, or to Dummett's, tenet one is not committed to endorsing any, let alone each, instance of the schema. If it is true that p, then some agent or other brought it about that p. (Surely one does not incur a commitment to theism by subscribing to Schema P, or to Schema X, for that matter.)

But then, sentences of the type 'x makes y such-and-such' are not always to be understood causally. Look at the following example: 'This molecule consists of two hydrogen atoms and one oxygen atom, which makes it a water molecule.' We might just as well say: 'This is a water molecule because it consists of two H-atoms and one O-atom.' This is not the 'because' of causal explanation, but rather that of *theoretical reduction*: chemical theory tells us that being water is having a certain molecular structure. But obviously the 'because' in Schema P is not that of theoretical reduction either. So we are still in want of a model for understanding it.

Happily, talk of x's making y such-and-such is not confined to these two kinds of use. Consider

(R)　He is a child of a sibling of one of your parents,
　　　which makes him your first cousin.

---

[190] In Schiller's drama Don Carlos (IV. 21) the best friend of the heir to the throne expects him to 'make the bold vision of a new State true' ['*er mache ... das Traumbild wahr, | Das kühne Traumbild eines neuen Staates*']. In Annette von Droste-Hülshoff's novelette *Die Judenbuche* we are told, about the boastful negative hero, that he sometimes tried hard 'to avoid possible exposure by making true what had originally only been vain pretence on his part [*um durch Wahrmachung des Usurpierten möglicher Beschämung zu entgehen*]'. Compare Henry James, *The Wings of the Dove* (bk. X, ch. 1): ' "If I had denied you", Densher said with his eyes on [Kate], "I'd have stuck to it." ... "Oh you'd have broken with me to make your denial a truth? You'd have 'chucked' me"—she embraced it perfectly—"to save your conscience?" '

In other words,

(R*)   He is your first cousin
      because he is a child of a sibling of one of your parents.

This is the 'because' of *conceptual explanation*: the second part of (R*) elucidates the sense of the first part. If we take the use of 'make' which is exemplified by (R) as our model for understanding philosophical pronouncements like

(S)   The fact that snow is white makes the statement that snow is white true,

then they do not affirm a relation of any kind between a truth vehicle and something in the world.[191] There is no reason to ban claims of type (S), but their point can be made without mention of facts:[192]

(S*)   The statement that snow is white is true, because snow is white.

And we can understand (S*) along the same lines as (R*). Why is it correct to say of him that he is your first cousin? The second clause of (R*) gives the answer. Why is it correct to say of the statement that snow is white that it is true? The second clause of (S*) gives the answer. Of course, there are differences as well: unlike the sense of 'first cousin', that of 'true' can be elucidated (at least partially) by a sentence that contains *no* component expressing it. And by contrast with the 'first cousin' case, (S*) does not give us a *full* account of the sense of 'true'. To be sure, Schema P, whose consequent is instantiated by (S*), is equally hospitable to all propositionally revealing truth-ascriptions, but as it stands it does not elucidate propositionally unrevealing applications of 'true' ('The Pythagorean Theorem is true', 'Everything the witness said was true').

The intelligibility of sentences like 'It is true that either Socrates or Seneca drank the hemlock, because Socrates did' or 'It is true that somebody drank the hemlock, because Socrates did' is conceded on all sides. Will Anscombe's doubts concerning the comprehensibility of substitution-instances of 'It is true that p, because p' be allayed by pointing out that one can make sense of (S*) without invoking a 'Tractatus-like metaphysic of facts'? Presumably not, for she thinks that (apart from a few 'quite particular situations') ascribing truth to the proposition that snow is white, or even to the sentence 'snow is white', comes to the very

---

[191] See Rundle, *GP*, 345–8. I disagree with him, however, on one point. In claiming that the fact that p makes it true that p, Rundle contends, we affirm 'no more than a deductive connection between one proposition and another' (348). This cannot be the whole story, for the entailment between 'p' and 'It is true that p' runs in both directions, whereas 'makes true' signifies an asymmetrical relation.

[192] Just as Davidson says in the passage quoted on p. 153 above. Unfortunately, he then goes on to claim that the point can be made by saying, e.g., 'The sentence "My skin is warm" is true if and only if my skin is warm' (ibid.). This repeats Quine's mistake.

same thing as saying that snow is white,[193] and if these identity claims are correct, then one might think that (S*) is, as Anscombe puts it, 'an empty statement, with only a false air of explanation'. I have argued in Chapter 2.1 against the first identity claim, and I shall argue against the second in Chapter 4.2.1. Apart from those identifications, Anscombe offers no reason for her harsh verdict on statements like (S*). Furthermore, even if two sentences 'p' and 'q' have the same conventional linguistic meaning, uttering 'q because p' with assertoric force may *not* be making an empty statement, with only a false air of explanation: examples like (R*) above show this.[194]

Let me contrast my attempt to vindicate Aristotle's basic insight with the efforts made by Horwich and Wright. According to Horwich, that insight (he calls it 'the "Correspondence" Intuition') can be accounted for by an appeal to 'the minimal theory' of truth and certain further facts (which are not facts about *truth*). The so-called minimal theory consists of whatever is expressed by (non-pathological) substitution-instances of the Denominalization Schema.[195] But Horwich's appeal to Aristotle's Rule is not the direct one which we deemed to be unilluminating a few pages ago. He takes the following argument to vindicate (S*):

In mapping out the relations of explanatory dependence between phenomena, we naturally and properly grant ultimate explanatory priority to such things as the basic laws of nature and the initial conditions of the universe. From these facts we attempt to deduce, and thereby explain, why, for example,

(1)   *snow is white.*

And only then, invoking the minimal theory, do we deduce, and thereby explain, why

(2)   *the proposition that snow is white is true.*

Therefore, from the minimalistic point of view, (1) is indeed explanatorily prior to (2), and so (S*) [is] fine. Thus we can be perfectly comfortable with the idea that truths are made true by elements of reality. Since this follows from the minimal theory (given certain further facts), it need not be an explicitly stated part of it. (*Truth*, 105)[196]

Even if this treatment were plausible for the case at hand, it is far too limited in scope. As long as we are not told which other things are 'such things as the basic laws of nature and the initial conditions of the universe', we have no idea how

---

[193] Anscombe, ' "Making True" ', 4–5; cf. Dummett's critique: 'Sentences and Propositions', 14–17, 'Is the Concept of Truth Needed for Semantics?', 7.

[194] Contrast 'He is your first cousin because he is your first cousin'.

[195] For explanations, refinements, and discussion see Ch. 6.1.

[196] Within the brackets I have renamed the three sample sentences.

to apply Howich's strategy to a statement such as: 'It is true that Davidson's Slingshot can be evaded, because Davidson's Slingshot can be evaded.' The treatment we are offered is not even applicable to all statements of physics.[197] First, physicists (I have been told) maintain that the truth that this tritium atom will decay in the next minute, for example, cannot be deduced from laws of nature and initial conditions. If they are right, then 'The proposition that this tritium atom will decay in the next minute is true, because this tritium atom will decay in the next minute' cannot be accounted for along Horwich's lines. Secondly, what about those propositions that specify basic laws of nature and those that specify the initial conditions of the universe? Surely the alleged Aristotelian insight is meant to cover them just as well as it does the proposition that snow is white.

Now what about the case at hand? Does Horwich's strategy answer the challenge to legitimize (S*), 'The proposition that snow is white is true because snow is white'? Wright has shown, I think, that it does not:[198]

[A]ll that Horwich points to is the possibility of explaining why *1* in terms of basic physical laws and the initial conditions of the universe, and then transferring that explanation, across (Den), into an explanation of why *2*. That is, evidently enough, not to explain why *2* in terms of *snow's being white*; it is rather (quite a different thing) to explain why *2* in terms of the physical laws and initial conditions which also explain snow's being white. The challenge, however, was to provide an account of the explanatory relationship adverted to by (S*)—a relationship which would obtain...even if there was no possible physical explanation of snow's being white at all. (*T&O*, 27)

Wright's own account avoids this mistake only at the expense of not throwing any light whatsoever on the relevant sense of 'explain'. He tries to account for the 'because' in (S*) by appealing to the 'platitude' that *P is true if and only if things are as P says they are*:

[T]he question why things are as the proposition that *1* says they are is quite properly—if rather trivially—answered by citing its being the case that *1*. Whence, given |the platitude], the truth of the proposition that *1* can quite properly be explained by citing the fact that *1*. (Ibid.)

This is not very illuminating, since the 'because' in 'Things are as the proposition that *1* says they are, because *1*' stands as much in need of clarification as the 'because' in (T*). This is glaringly obvious if, as I shall argue in Chapter 6.2, to claim that things are as P says they are just *is* to claim that P is true.

So much for the first variety of making true.

---

[197] See Igor Douven, 'Minimalism and the "Correspondence Intuition" ', 168–9.
[198] I have taken the liberty of implanting my abbreviations into this and the next excerpt from Wright.

3.5.3 *An ontic reading of 'making true'*

In my attempt at spelling out the Aristotelian insight along the lines of SCHEMA P, I took it for granted that the same sentence can be used both in the specification of what *is* true and in the specification of what *makes* it true. No such presupposition is visible in Principle C or in SCHEMA X. David Armstrong implicitly denies that presupposition when he says:

> [E]very truth has a truthmaker. The truthmaker for a particular truth is that object or entity in the world in virtue of which that truth is true.... The truthmaker is the 'correspondent' in the [?] Correspondence theory of truth, but with the repudiation of the view that the correspondence involved is always one–one. The discovery of what are in fact truthmakers for a particular truth can be as difficult and controversial as the whole enterprise of ontology.... A truthmaker must ... necessitate the truths that it is a truthmaker for. It must not be metaphysically possible for the truthmaker to exist and the truths not to be true. ('Difficult Cases in the Theory of Truthmaking', 150)[199]

This reading of 'making true' is common among Australian and Austrian (self-styled) realists. What renders a truth-candidate true, they are prone to call a 'truth-maker'.[200] I shall model my discussion on the Austrian variant of the theory. According to this theory, no truth-maker is a fact, and all truth-makers for empirical truths are parts of the natural (spatio-temporal causal) order.[201] Suppose the statement that p is an atomic empirical statement which is true. Then you specify its Truth-Maker, if you answer the following question:

(TM)   Which part of the natural order, x, is such that

(i)   the existence or occurrence of x ensures that the statement that p is true, and

(ii)   x is what that statement is about or what it reports on?

---

[199] As to the question-mark I have inserted, remember that of all the correspondence accounts we discussed, only Moore's is committed to one–one correspondence.

[200] The Austrian contributions I have in mind (which are Austrian by inspiration rather than by nationality) are Kevin Mulligan, Peter Simons, and Barry Smith, 'Truth-Makers', and Simons's paper 'World'. In Australia, the basic idea was first presented in print, as far as I know, by John Fox in 'Truthmaker', 189, 204–7, and in John Bigelow's *The Reality of Numbers*, esp. 122–34. The most elaborate antipodean version is to be found in Armstrong's book, *WSA*. It is not only the use of the hyphen that separates Austrians and Australians. Incidentally, to my ear, for what it is worth, 'truth-donor' (designed after the model of 'blood-donor') or 'truth-conferrer' would be stylistically less unpleasant. '*Wahrmacher*' in German is acceptable, '*Wahrheitsmacher*' sounds discordant. Is the English counterpart any less cacophonous?

[201] By contrast, Armstrong takes facts (which he calls states of affairs) to be truth-makers. This is not easy to reconcile with Armstrong's naturalism according to which the world consists of, and is exhausted by, whatever stands in spatio-temporal and causal relations. Facts, being abstract (non-extensional) entities, are not parts of the natural (spatio-temporal causal) order. (I could not discover a rebuttal of this objection in the passage in which Armstrong faces it: *WSA*, 135–8.) At any rate, not all truth-makers can be facts. Certainly there are entities which are not facts (even if they were somehow constituents of facts). So the truth that there are non-facts is made true by those non-facts severally. See Lewis, 'Correspondence', 278.

Let me first run through some examples before I try to motivate the details of this formulation. Substituting for the sentence letter in (TM) (a) 'Caesar was assassinated', (b) 'Philip of Macedonia begot Alexander', (c) 'Alexander was angry', (d) 'Bucephalus is a horse', (e) 'Bucephalus is an animal', (f) 'Hesperus is Phosphorus', and (g) 'Venus exists', reasonable answers to that question will specify the following truth-makers: for (a) Caesar's assassination, for (b) the pertinent royal procreation, for (c) the king's anger at the contextually relevant time, for (d) and (e), the king's war horse (being essentially a horse and an animal), and, for (f) and (g), the planet Hesperus (alias Phosphorus alias Venus). In the last two pairs, two different truths are made true by the same thing. And the truth-maker is never specified by means of a sentence, let alone by means of the same sentence which is, or expresses, what is made true. The schematic letter 'x' in (TM) is a place-holder for singular terms, and the same holds for its role in SCHEMA X. So let us call this interpretation of 'making true' the *non-propositional*, or *ontic*, reading.

The truth-maker for the statement that Caesar was assassinated is an event.[202] In the case of events, one feels more at ease with '*occurrence*' than with '*existence*', so I have formulated clause (i) of (TM) accordingly. 'The existence or occurrence of x ensures (guarantees, necessitates) that...' is equivalent with 'That x exists or occurs entails that...' (where 'entails', as I shall soon argue, is best read as 'relevantly entails'). As to the disjunction in clause (ii), let aboutness be tied to identifying reference, so statements (a)–(c) are about the persons referred to, whereas (a) and (b) report on an event and (c) reports on someone's state.[203] Clause (ii) as a whole restricts the range of claimants for the title 'truth-maker'. Take (a), the statement that Caesar was assassinated. Someone's witnessing Caesar's assassination could not occur if Caesar had not been assassinated, hence that witnessing ensures the truth of (a). But it does so only indirectly, as it were, in virtue of the event witnessed, and it is shut out by clause (ii). Thanks to this clause, neither the History of the Universe nor the (slightly less colossal) totality of events that consists of Caesar's assassination and everything that happened before, nor the sum of all events that occurred at the time of his assassination, is the truth-maker of (a). Or consider (g), the statement that the planet Venus exists. Clause (ii) prevents the Universe and the (less gigantic) collection of all heavenly bodies from playing the role of the truth-maker for (g).

If we drop the second clause of (TM), the remaining question has a truly global (if boring) answer: 'the world', or 'world-history'. In this connection,

---

[202] Recall Russell, *IMT*.

[203] As far as temporally extended events and states are concerned, one could, perhaps, regard states as monotonous events (or events as variegated states).

Davidson's regret about 'three little words' in the passage we quoted on p. 153 is worth registering:

I was right about experience and surface irritations, but I gave no argument against saying [that] the world makes some sentences true. After all, this is exactly as harmless as saying that a sentence is true because it corresponds to The One Fact, and just as empty.... Maybe we can't locate a part of the world that makes an individual sentence true, but the world itself makes the true sentences true.../...[T]hose three little words ('not the world') were seriously misleading. ('Reply to Neale', 668–9)

Advocates of (TM) will find no comfort in Davidson's concession: they are looking for discriminative truth-makers for individual statements, and, since our true statements seldom have the whole world for their topic, it rarely meets the requirements set up in (TM). Was Davidson right about experience and surface irritations? Whether such states and events can play the role that some epistemologists assign to them (roughly, whether they can serve as *evidence* for all empirical beliefs, or for any) is an issue that is orthogonal to the question pursued by truth-maker theorists.[204] At any rate, Davidson did not rebut the claim that *some* statements are *made true by* experience or by surface irritations. And if we say, 'The statement that Ann's surface is being irritated, if true, is made true by an irritation of her ever so irritable surface', or 'It is one of Ben's experiences which makes the statement that he is feeling nausea true, if it is true', do we not 'locate parts of the world', passing events or states, that make two individual statements true? After all, on the last page of the very essay from which our earlier quotation was taken, Davidson allowed himself to say: '[By giving up the idea of a conceptual scheme] we do not give up the world, but re-establish unmediated touch with familiar objects whose antics make our sentences and opinions true or false' ('On the Very Idea of a Conceptual Scheme', 198). What are the antics (i.e., according to my dictionary, the clownish movements, the grotesque performances) of familiar things, if not events? Truth-maker theorists take Davidson's turn of phrase here to be more than just a *façon de parler*, and the Slingshot alluded to in his 'Reply to Neale' (see above) has not shown this to be a mistake.[205]

---

[204] Davidson is alluding to Quine. In 'Two Dogmas of Empiricism', §6, Quine took sense experiences, and later (in 'The Scope and Language of Science', §1, and *W&O*, 22, for example) he took surface irritations, triggerings of our nerve endings, to be 'the tribunal which our beliefs about the external world collectively face'. But Quine never claims that those beliefs, if true, owe their *truth* to such events, but only that their warrant, if they are warranted, is due to them. The latter contention may be implausible enough, but it is very different from the former. See Quine's protest in 'On the Very Idea of a Third Dogma'.

[205] There are many passages like our last extract in his *Essays in Actions and Events*: see 6, 110, 117, 134, 170, 190–1. (In some of these passages, Davidson calls events, as Aquinas and Russell did before him, 'verifiers' of statements.) The tension recurs in 'Epistemology and Truth': cf. 184 and 189. As for the Slingshot, see sect. 3.3.3 above.

How is the question posed in (TM) to be answered if we replace the sentence letter with (h) 'Socrates is wise' or any other property attribution which, unlike (c), cannot be read as a report on a thing's state? According to the Austrian theory I am outlining, the statement that (h) is made true by the wisdom of Socrates. The definite description in this answer is not meant to refer to a shareable quality (for that would exist even if Socrates were a fool), nor to a fact, of course, but to an individual accident or a particularized quality. Thus understood, Socrates' wisdom cannot be identical with Solomon's, since Solomon is not identical with Socrates; his wisdom is subject to change, and it can no more survive Socrates than the grin of the Cheshire cat can linger on after the Cheshire cat has died.[206]

Notice that this provides us with an alternative interpretation of Aristotle's claim that the statement that you are pale is true because of your being pale. Perhaps we are to take the gerund as designating an individual accident, your paleness—something that is different from my paleness even if I am just as pale as you are. (For our purposes it is not important to decide this exegetical issue.[207])

A truth expressed by a substitution-instance of 'If it is true that p, then x makes it true' does not have to be knowable a priori, let alone be self-evident. If I am now putting salt on my omelette, then that statement is made true by WK's currently putting sodium chloride on his omelette, but this conditional truth cannot be known a priori. If physicalism is correct, then every empirical

---

[206] The term 'individual accident' is borrowed from Leibniz (who inherited it from the scholastics), and 'particularized quality' is Strawson's term. The entities in question have been variously named 'modes' (Descartes, Locke, Lowe), '*Adhärenzen*' (Bolzano), '*individuelle Momente*' (Husserl, Mulligan et al.), 'abstract particulars' (Stout, Campbell) or 'cases' (Wolterstorff). Nowadays, the least appropriate title of all, 'tropes' (due to D. C. Williams), has become the common coin. For discussion of the category, cf. Mellor and Oliver (eds.), *Properties*, chs. 9–11. In his comments on the Austrian truth-maker theory, Dodd contends that individual accidents are 'transferable', and by this he means that an individual accident which in the actual world is a moment of *a* may be a moment of *b* in another possible world in which *a* does not exist. He concludes, correctly, that individual accidents, *thus conceived*, cannot be truthmakers, for the existence of *a*'s F-ness would no longer ensure that the statement that *a* is F is true (*ITT*, 8–9). Dodd's admission that his way of conceiving individual accidents is 'controversial' is a vast understatement. All friends of this category whom I have mentioned in this footnote take it to be a defining feature of individual accidents that they are *not* transferable. (For Leibniz and Bolzano, cf. my '*Substanzen und Adhärenzen*'.) Dodd concurs with Mulligan et al. that the grin of the Cheshire cat is an individual accident which can be seen. Does he really think that this very grin can be seen in possible worlds in which the Cheshire cat does not exist? (Incidentally, Dodd also fails to register that the Austrian theory does not take the realm of truth-makers to be monocategorial, as was illustrated by my eight examples.)

[207] If we paraphrase 'because of your being pale' as 'because of the fact that you are pale' and then refrain from taking the latter to be a verbose variant of 'because you are pale', we hit on a third interpretation of Aristotle's remark. Unsurprisingly, this is the way Armstrong reads Aristotle when he enrols him as an early advocate of a 'factualist' truth-maker theory (*WSA*, 13). The evidence Armstrong himself provides is just a bad translation of *Categories* 12: 14^{b}14–22. (I have argued in sect. 3.1.1 that one should not invoke the category of facts when trying to understand Aristotle's conception of truth.)

truth is made true by something that can be specified in the language of (an ideally completed?) physics, but the correct physical specification of those truth-makers would not be a matter of a priori knowledge.

When a truth-maker theorist claims that the statement that Caesar was assassinated is true because of Caesar's assassination, the 'because' is neither that of causal explanation nor that of theoretical reduction nor that of conceptual explanation. It could be called the 'because' of *ontological grounding*. (You may be pleased to hear that this intimidating unexplained phrase will not occur again on the following pages.)

Using 'T' and 'M' as short for 'It is true that' and 'makes it true that', respectively, we can abbreviate our

SCHEMA X: If Tp, then $\exists$ x (x M p).

To be on the (comparatively) safe side, let us preserve the restriction of the substitution-class of 'p' to singular non-compound empirical statements. Additional intuitively plausible schematic principles governing 'M' will include

(P1)   If $\exists$ x (x M p), then Tp
(P2)   If a M p and that p entails that q, then a M q.

According to (P1), the operator 'M' is factive: if a proposition is made true by something, then it is true. From SCHEMA X and (P1) as premisses we obtain

(T1)   Tp iff $\exists$ x (x M p)

as a theorem. From (P1) it follows that if a proposition is made true by something then nothing makes its negation true:

(T2)   If $\exists$ x (x M p), then $\neg \exists$ y (y M $\neg$ p).

For suppose that for some x and some y, x makes a certain statement true whereas y makes its negation true. Then, by (P1), both the statement and its negation are true, which is absurd. Therefore (T2).[208]

According to the entailment principle (P2) different atomic truths can have the same truth-maker. Intuitively, the truth that this page is less than 20 centimetres broad entails the proposition that it is less than 21 centimetres broad, and so on, for all n greater than 20. Hence, the truth-maker of the former proposition makes all the latter propositions true at one fell swoop. Now if we endorse the orthodox conception of entailment which underlies both classical and

---

[208] In Mulligan et al., 'Truth-Makers', sect. 6, principles (P1) and (P2) are registered under (1) and (14). In Simons, 'World', 120, they are given as (1) and (4), and what is there given as (2) follows from theorem (T1), hence from Principle C and (P1).

intuitionistic logic, (P2) has a consequence that may be less easy to swallow. Suppose that a certain event X makes some empirical truth true. Then whatever that truth may be, each logical truth is entailed by it, according to the orthodox conception.[209] Hence, by (P2), X makes each logical truth true. The death of Socrates, for example, makes it true that a rose is a rose, that nobody is both married and unmarried, etc. This very consequence may stimulate the search for a different conception of entailment.[210] One will look for the formal implementation of such a conception in systems of Relevant Logic, for they contain no theorems of the form $A \rightarrow B$ where A and B do not share any parameter, and consequently they do not validate the claim that a logically necessary proposition is entailed by every proposition. Let us suppose that the truth-maker theory is supplemented by a conception of entailment which absolves us from maintaining that the death of Socrates, or any other particular, makes any conceptual truth (whether logical or not) true.

As a result of this supplementation, the truth-maker theory, as it stands, does not answer the question what it is for a truth-candidate, *any* truth-candidate, to be true. (The Austrian variant on which my sketch was based did not aspire to answer this question in the first place.) But eventually an adherent of such a theory has to face the question whether conceptual truths are made true by anything, and if so, by what. Let me hint at one way he could begin to answer it.[211] Take atomic conceptual truths such as the propositions (j) that beauty is an excellence and (k) that ten is even. If we refrain from identifying the world with the natural (spatio-temporal causal) order and subscribe to Platonism,[212] we can

---

[209] According to the orthodox conception, A entails B iff it is impossible that (A is true, and B is false). Now if B is a logical truth then it is impossible that B is false. So take any A you like, if B is a logical truth, A entails B.

[210] As several authors have pointed out: cf. Romane Clark, 'Facts, Fact-correlates, and Fact-surrogates', 9 (and the reference to Van Fraassen given there), and Greg Restall, 'Truthmakers, Entailment and Necessity' (who pleads for a conception of entailment which is close to, but not quite as restrictive as, relevant implication). The passing appeal to 'the entailment of Anderson and Belnap' in Mulligan et al., 'Truth-Makers', 313, may be similarly motivated, and Simons explicitly rejects a truth-maker theory according to which logical truths are made true by something in the natural order ('World', 114). By contrast, Quine argues: 'Any sentence logically implies the logical truths. Trivially, then, the logical truths are true by virtue of any circumstances you care to name—language, the world, anything' (*PL*, 96). Quine takes this to demonstrate that the doctrine that logical truths are true by virtue of meaning is vacuously true. But isn't the doctrine rather that logical truths are true by virtue of meaning *alone*? So if his 'anything you like' thesis were correct it would show the doctrine to be *false*. One also senses a certain tension between this thesis and the invocation of Tarski's paradigm in Quine, *PL* 10 (cited above on p. 152): there, Quine's suggestion seems to be that every truth is true in virtue of its satisfied disquotational truth-condition.

[211] I took my cue for this move (which down-to-earth Austrians would hardly approve of) from Strawson: see his 'Universals', 61–2.

[212] By opposing naturalism, the Platonist also rejects physicalism, of course, but a naturalist does not have to be a physicalist.

easily specify the truth-makers for (j) and (k). Remember Bucephalus: since he is essentially a horse, his existence ensures the truth of the statement that he is a horse. Similarly, or so the Platonist truth-maker theorist could say, beauty is essentially an excellence, hence its existence guarantees the truth of (j), and the number ten cannot fail to be even, so its existence entails that (k) is true.

This outline of a truth-maker theory goes some way, I hope, to give substance to Principle C under the ontic reading captured by Schema X, and it may suffice to highlight its difference from the conception of making true conveyed by Schema P. But, of course, it invites questions. One of them concerns the whole enterprise. Is the concept of truth essentially involved in it? Take any particular claim to the effect that the existence or occurrence of x ensures that the statement that p is true (and that x is what the statement that p is about or what it reports on). We would save breath without losing anything essential to this claim if we were to say instead: 'The existence or occurrence of x ensures that p.' So to all intents and purposes we can, as it were, subtract truth from Schema X:

(Schema X–) If p then for some x, the existence or occurrence of x (topic-specifically) ensures that p.

The use of 'true' in Principle C allows us to subscribe to all instantiations of (Schema X–) in one breath. It seems to have fallen into oblivion that some early Australian truth-maker theorists saw this clearly:

[What the Truthmaker axiom says] is this: Whenever something is true, there must be something whose existence entails that it is true.... The term 'truth' makes its appearance here largely to facilitate generality of exposition. If we focus on just one particular truth, then the guts of Truthmaker can be stated without even using the term 'truth' or any equivalent. (*The Reality of Numbers*, 125, 127)[213]

The idea that truth talk provides us with expressive facilities will loom large in Chapters 4.2.2 and 6.1.1.

Other questions invited by the truth-maker theory sketched above point at various kinds of recalcitrant empirical truths: what are the truth-makers for general statements, for example, or for negative existentials? In view of the controversy between Russell and Wittgenstein concerning general statements, it is worth mentioning that the truth-maker theory supports the view Russell took in 1918.[214] For

---

[213] Exactly the same tenet is upheld by Fox: see 'Truthmaker', 189. It must be due to oblivion that D. Lewis makes the point that 'truth is mentioned in the truth-maker principle only for the sake of making a long story short' with an air of novelty: 'Correspondence', 278–9; 'Truthmaking and Difference-Making', 604–6.   [214] See p. 121 above.

the sake of the example he used, let us assume that mortality is not written into the concept of a human being. An advocate of the theory sketched above has to maintain that the many human deaths which occur in the history of the universe do not jointly ensure that all humans are mortal, for there *could* exist a Methuselah who successfully refuses ever to die. But then, what makes that general statement true? Furthermore, what about negative existentials?[215] Which part of the natural order, if any, makes it true that Martians do not exist, or that Vulcan does not exist? Such truths do not seem to owe their truth to the existence of any veri-fier, but rather to the non-existence of any falsi-fiers. (If it were true that there is nothing, no contingent thing, rather than something, then that truth would certainly not be due to the existence or occurrence of something.) So we are back with instances of Schema P: if the statement that there are no Martians is true, then it is true because there are no Martians. This claim explains why 'true' is correctly applied to a certain statement if it applies to it all, but truth-maker theorists are not aiming at conceptual explanation. And it is a claim about a particular truth in which 'true' occurs essentially, for surely 'There are no Martians because there are no Martians' does not pass muster as an explanation in any sense of this word.

3.5.4 *Another propositional reading*

Dummett's formulations of Principle C strongly suggest that he agrees with the Austr(al)ians in favouring an ontic reading of 'true in virtue of' or of 'made true by'. But perhaps the agreement is merely verbal.

[The principle] that a thought can be true only if there is something in virtue of which it is true ... is not easily explained, particularly in the absence of any ontological realm of facts to constitute that in virtue of which thoughts may be true. (*FPL* 464)[216]

By itself, this only excludes an ontic reading in terms of *facts*, but Dummett not only denounces facts as truth-conferrers,[217] he also never argues in favour of any

---

[215] See D. Lewis, 'Armstrong on Combinatorial Possibility', 204, 'Truthmaking and Difference-Making', 610–12. Putnam also presents negative existentials as evidence when he maintains that the principle, 'if a statement is true there must be a *something* which "makes" it true', is a 'picture' which does not fit all empirical statements, let alone all statements. He does think that it fits some empirical statements, but his advice is to '[break] free of the grip of the picture'. (The wording of this advice comes as no surprise in a paper 'On Wittgenstein's Philosophy of Mathematics', 251–2.) The problem is recognized as such in Mulligan et al., 'Truth-Makers', 315.

[216] Cf. Dummett, *The Interpretation of Frege's Philosophy* (henceforth *IFP*), 444.

[217] Provided that they are regarded as different from truths! Dummett often mentions Frege's tenet that facts are nothing but true thoughts, and as far as I can see he never raises any objection to it. (On pp. 10–12, 144–5, some doubt was cast on that tenet.) If he accepts the Fregean identification, then his

other kind of entities as being better equipped for this role (be they continuants, events, states, or particularized qualities). So what is the point *he* attempts to make by invoking Principle C? I suspect that the difficulty of explaining this principle in the way Dummett wants it to be understood ultimately stems from an infelicity of phrasing: he talks of 'something (in the world)' or of 'some component of reality'; he asks 'what sort of things count as rendering a given type of statement true?'[218]—and all this inevitably suggests quantification into singular term position, as represented in SCHEMA X. But that is precisely what is not intended. This becomes obvious as soon as one considers Dummett's distinction between truths that are 'barely true' and those that are not:[219]

> Let us say of a true statement that it is 'barely true' if there is no other statement or set of statements of which we can say that it is true in virtue of their truth. This formulation suffers...from reliance on the obscure, if compelling, notion of a statement's being true in virtue of the truth of another. [Here is] one way of avoiding this.... [W]e may call a class of statements 'irreducible' if there is no disjoint class such that a necessary and sufficient condition for the truth of any statement in the first class is that of some set of statements of the second class. It is then clear that any specific way of construing the notion of a statement's being true in virtue of the truth of other statements will require that some true statements be barely true. (*LBM* 328)

Notice that (at least) in the case of truths that are not 'barely true' Dummettian truth-donors are themselves *truths*. So in this respect Dummett's conception resembles Anscombe's. But Dummett does subscribe to the unrestricted Principle C: for *every* truth there is a correct affirmative answer to the (somewhat misleadingly phrased) question, 'In virtue of what is it true?' So Dummett's understanding of that principle may be best captured by something like

(SCHEMA Q)   If the statement that p is true, then
                 for some q, the statement that p is true, because q.[220]

Sometimes the answer to the question in virtue of which truth a certain truth is true is bound to be lame, since it can only be given either in the homophonic manner, 'The statement that p is true, because p', or by an instance of 'The

---

occasional references to facts as truth-donors (e.g. in 'The Reality of the Past', 361, or 'Realism' (1982), 248) are compatible with his dismissal of facts, as different from truths, cited above, and, as we shall soon see, in harmony with his understanding of Principle C.

[218] Dummett, *LBM*, 328.

[219] Cf. Dummett, 'Realism' (1963), 148–50; 'The Reality of the Past', 360; *FPL*, 464; 'Meaning', 52–7; 66–7; *IFP*, 447–8, 'Realism' (1982), 247–8.

[220] Questions concerning the viability of sentential quantification will be faced in Ch. 6.2.3.

statement that p is true, because q' in which 'q' just paraphrases 'p'. ('It is true that Kaa is a serpent, because Kaa is a snake' would be an example of allophonic lameness.) Whenever we are in this predicament, the truth in question is 'irreducible'. If we go in for neither phenomenalism nor physicalism, we will take the truth that THIS HERE is a book to belong to such a class. True disjunctions are not barely true, of course.[221] And the true counterfactual conditional that this sugar cube would have begun to dissolve if it had been immersed in water is true in virtue of the truth of an (at least prima facie) categorical proposition to the effect that this sugar cube has such-and-such a molecular structure. In this case, too, the homophonic answer would not be incorrect, *pace* Anscombe, but it can be superseded by a more informative answer. The 'truth-free' variant of a homophonic answer is always incorrect, since 'because' is not commutative. So our SCHEMA Q really is about truth.

There is a difference between my two examples for non-lame answers, which is relevant for assessing appeals to the theory of linguistic understanding in determining truth-conferrers. Such appeals are as alien to the 'directly' metaphysical project pursued by Austr(al)ian realists,[222] as they are essential to Dummett's project of settling, or dissolving, metaphysical issues by first constructing a systematic account of linguistic understanding. Important though the difference in logical form between SCHEMATA X and Q is, the fundamental contrast between the projects associated with these schemata comes to the fore when Dummett says:

The theory of meaning determines what makes a statement true, if it is true. (*IFP* 446)

[T]he specific content of any assertion is given by what is taken as rendering . . . true the sentence used to make the assertion. (*LBM* 166)

Thus a meaning-theory for a given language L would have to determine, among other things, which classes of sentences of L are such that understanding their members is not based upon understanding sentences that belong to a disjoint class: they are the sentences that are barely true (if true at all). Now recall my

---

[221] 'On the explanation given', Dummett says, 'no universal statement can be barely true. . . . A true universal statement will be true in virtue of the truth of all its instances' ('Meaning', 67). But in which sense does the truth of all instances of a general statement S 'determine' S 'as true'? Of course, the statement that all instances of S are true entails that S is true. But it is possible that these instances are all true although S is not true, and doesn't this refute the determination thesis?

[222] '[T]ruthmakers are one thing, meanings are quite another' is the war-cry of Austr(al)ian realists against approaches to metaphysics that are driven by semantics (Armstrong, 'Difficult Cases . . .', 153).

two examples for reducible truth-candidates. If somebody does not know that the truth of 'Either Socrates or Seneca drank the hemlock' is due to the truth of one of the disjuncts, his or her knowledge of English is deficient. But in the case of our counterfactual conditional no such claim could be upheld: here, the 'reductive' answer does *not* 'reflect the way we do, or the only way in which we can, acquire an understanding of statements of the given class'.[223] Or take statements to the effect that it is true that a certain vessel contains some F, because it contains some G, where 'F' is a non-scientific mass-noun like 'water' or 'salt' and 'G' specifies the chemical composition of the F-stuff: certainly, such statements do not show that our comprehension of 'F'-sentences rests upon our understanding of 'G'-sentences. Several of Dummett's own examples clearly exemplify reductions that are in this sense hermeneutically sterile. To be sure, he describes such cases always in a non-committal way: some philosophers (might) think, we are told, that statements about a person's character, linguistic abilities, or mental acts, if true, are rendered true by neurophysiological truths about that person.[224] Still, one wonders whether such examples (however plausible or implausible they may be in themselves) are at all compatible with the following tenet:

It is essential...that the reductive thesis be advanced, not as a mere observation concerning a connection between the truth-conditions of statements of the two classes, but as part of an account of the meanings of the statements of the given class: the proponent of the thesis holds that an understanding of those statements involves an implicit grasp of their relations to statements of the reductive class. ('Realism' (1982), 242)

This worry does not affect Dummett's observation that reducibility does not imply eliminability. Sometimes truths in the 'reductive class' will contain truths of the 'given class' as constituents. Take intrafictional truths: in virtue of what is it true that Anna Karenina committed suicide? It seems to be reasonable to answer: well, it is true because *in Tolstoy's novel* Anna Karenina committed suicide. Quite generally, I would suggest, whenever 'p' expresses an intrafictional truth, it is true that p because there is a work of fiction according to which p.[225] So the expression of what makes true contains an expression of what is

---

[223] Dummett, *TOE*, xxxiv.

[224] Cf. 'Realism' (1963), 148–50; 'The Reality of the Past', 359; 'Meaning', 53–7; 'Realism' (1982), 245–7, *LBM*, 324.

[225] I call the example 'intrafictional' as opposed to (a) interfictional statements ('Anna Karenina did not live in the same country as Madame Bovary'), (b) transfictional statements ('Many readers pity Anna Karenina'), and (c) 'ontological' statements ('Anna Karenina never existed'). A Fregean approach to this minefield is pursued in my '*Fiktion ohne fiktive Gegenstände*', 141–62.

made true as a subordinate clause. (By contrast, Meinong takes intrafictional truths to be barely true.) One of Dummett's own examples is mathematical constructivism: in virtue of what is Lagrange's Theorem true? It is true, constructivists maintain, because *we possess a proof which demonstrates that* every natural number is the sum of four squares. (Platonists disagree, of course.) In the constructivists' answer, an expression of what is made true is embedded in the expression of what makes it true.[226] If non-eliminativist reductionism of this type holds for the sentences of a given class, one's understanding of an assertion made by uttering a sentence *s* of this class is deficient unless one knows that this assertion, if true, owes its truth to the truth of what is expressed by the appropriately prefixed counterpart of *s*.

Let us take stock. I have distinguished sharply between *ontic* and *propositional* readings of 'making true'. Austr(al)ian realists favour the ontic reading. I have argued, as others did before, that many empirical statements are true without the benefit of a 'truth-maker' and that 'truth-maker' principles are at bottom not really about truth. Aristotle, on one interpretation, and Dummett both opt for the propositional reading. But Aristotle, understood along the lines of SCHEMA P, can be seen as making an attempt at illuminating the *sense of 'true'* as applied to given truth-candidates, while Dummett takes substitution-instances of SCHEMA Q to be contributions to a meaning-theory for a given language. Those instances, when they are not lame, throw light on the *sense of the truth-candidates* mentioned in their antecedents, and so does the fact that sometimes those instances are bound to be lame.[227] I have remarked on a certain tension between this role of SCHEMA Q and some of Dummett's examples for full-fledged reductionism.

3.5.5 *Correspondence and alethic realism*

I certainly don't reject realism, at least not until I know what it is I am rejecting.

(Davidson, 'Reply to J. J. C. Smart', 123)

As far as I know, all advocates of the ontic reading wave the flag of *realism*; that is why I have referred to them by their favourite name. But the philosophical use

---

[226] Cf. Dummett, 'The Reality of the Past', 361; 'Realism' (1982), 243–5; *LBM*, 324.

[227] Strictly speaking, this requires replacing the sentence-nominalizations in SCHEMA Q by quotational designators of sentences, for what has a sense is not the statement that snow is white, say, but the sentence 'Snow is white'. But then, sentences are not true (or false) *simpliciter*, so some relativizations would have to be put in. Although these issues are important, and will demand much of our attention in Chs. 4–6 below, I do not think that they matter for the contrasts that I wanted to emphasize in the present context.

of the term 'realism' is, to put it mildly, underconstrained. So let us focus on *alethic realism* as explained in the first chapter of this book, according to which truth outruns rational acceptability. Now does the claim that certain, or all, truths are true in virtue of something (in any of the senses we distinguished above) commit one to alethic realism? I cannot see that it does. First, one can consistently maintain both that all (non-pathological) substitution-instances of SCHEMA P are true and that in principle all truths are epistemically accessible to us. Secondly, somebody who thinks that every true empirical statement is made true by one or more parts of the natural order severally or jointly may also believe that in principle we can always know whether something is true: an Austr(al)ian alethic *anti*-realist may be an unlikely figure, but his position could scarcely be accused of inconsistency. Thirdly, one can consistently maintain that no irreducible truth and no reducible truth is in principle beyond our ken. (In particular, the truth-donors in our examples for non-eliminativist reductionism are not recognition-transcendent: we can find out whether according to a certain novel things are thus-and-so, and constructivists say the same about the question whether we have a proof for a certain mathematical theorem.) Thus, one can accept the Correspondence Intuition in *any* of the varieties I took pains to distinguish without thereby incurring an obligation to embrace alethic realism.

Dummett disagrees; or, rather, he disagreed for a while. In his classic paper of 1959, immediately after his introduction of Principle C, he goes on to say:

Although we no longer accept the correspondence theory, we remain realists *au fond*; we retain in our thinking a fundamentally realist conception of truth. ('Truth', 14)

This is obviously meant to give voice to a conviction shared by all advocates of Principle C, and in his first book on Frege, Dummett calls this principle a 'realist thesis'.[228] One might suspect that this divergence results from a fundamentally different understanding of the slippery term 'realism'. But that doesn't seem to be the case, for a few pages later he says:

The fundamental tenet of realism is that any sentence on which a fully specific sense has been conferred has a determinate truth-value independently of our actual capacity to decide what the truth-value is. (*FPL*, 466)

To be sure, there are subtle differences between this characterization of realism and my definition of 'alethic realism'. But we do not have to go into them here, for the question recurs: why shouldn't a philosopher who adopts SCHEMA P, X,

---

[228] Dummett, *FPL*, 464.

or Q *reject* realism as characterized by Dummett? Each of these principles permits, of course, that some sentences on which a fully specific sense has been conferred may have a determinate truth-value independently of our actual capacity to decide what the truth-value is, but none of those principles *requires* that there are such sentences. So Dummett's retraction is to be welcomed:[229]

It is [a] mistake to regard the principle that, if a statement is true, there must be something in virtue of which it is true, as peculiar to realism. On the contrary, it is a regulative principle which all must accept. (*LBM*, 331)

One does not even incur an obligation to endorse alethic realism if one accepts a *definition* of truth in terms of correspondence.[230] Of course, such an explanation of the concept of truth *tolerates* truths beyond verifiability. But it does not *require* that there are such truths. An advocate of Object-based Correspondence is not committed to deny that in principle we can always find out whether the object a proposition is about really is as it is said to be by someone who expresses that proposition. An adherent of Fact-based Correspondence can consistently maintain that in principle each fact can be recognized by us.[231] And a partisan of Event-based Correspondence would not to be convicted of inconsistency if he were to claim that in principle we could always come into the possession of information which would justify accepting a true statement to the effect that such-and-such an event occurred (will occur).

We are not moving here in the realm of mere possibilities. Nobody will suspect William James of subscribing to alethic realism, and yet he maintains:

Truth, as any dictionary will tell you, is a property of certain of our ideas. It means their 'agreement', as falsity means their disagreement, with 'reality'. Pragmatists and intellectualists both accept this definition as a matter of course. They begin to quarrel only after the question is raised as to what may precisely be meant by the term 'agreement,' and what by the term 'reality,' when reality is taken as something for our ideas to agree with. (*Pragmatism*, 96)

---

[229] Actually he retracted already in his 1972 'Postscript' to 'Truth', 23.

[230] Here is a very strong version of what I am denying: 'The idea of verification-transcendent truth is just the idea of truth that the [?] correspondence theory makes use of' (Walker, *The Coherence Theory of Truth*, 35). (The question mark is mine.)

[231] Many authors have made this point (but it still bears repeating): Vision, *Modern Anti-Realism*, 35; Kirkham, *ThT*, 133–4 (curiously mistaking Vision for an opponent); David, *C&D*, 18; Alston, *RCT*, 83; and, most recently, D. Lewis, 'Correspondence', 277.

His ally John Dewey, too, is 'not concerned with denying, but with understanding' the characterization of truth in terms of agreement or correspondence.[232] Substituting 'fact' for 'reality', he proudly proclaims:

[Pragmatists] supplied (and I should venture to say for the first time) an explanation ... of the nature of fact and idea, and of the kind of agreement or correspondence between them which constitutes the truth of the idea. (*Essays in Experimental Logic*, 24, 231)[233]

The explanation supplied by James is clearly anti-realist, and in this respect it is congenial to Dewey:[234]

What does agreement with reality mean? It means verifiability. Verifiability means ability to guide us prosperously through experience. (*Pragmatism*, 8)

I am not sure I understand the last statement,[235] and as you know from my programmatic pronouncements in Chapter 1, I am not willing to accept this kind of position. By presenting it at this juncture I only want to corroborate my tenet that a philosopher who accepts a definition of truth in terms of correspondence can consistently *reject* alethic realism.

Is there a commitment in the other direction? Davidson thinks there is: 'The realist view of truth, if it has any content, must be based on the idea of correspondence.'[236] But if Dummett is right about Frege, he has managed to refute

---

[232] Dewey, *Essays in Experimental Logic*, 236 (= *MW*, 4: 82). Davidson rightly emphasizes (against Rorty) that Dewey 'saw no harm in the idea of correspondence as long as it was properly understood' ('Structure', 280). For some pedantic complaints against his presentation of Dewey, see n. 234.

[233] In Dewey, *MW*, 10: 334; *MW*, 4: 78. (In the critical edition of Dewey's Works the book has been torn apart: see my bibliography.)

[234] See, for example, Dewey, *Reconstruction in Philosophy*, 169–71, and *Essays in Experimental Logic*, ch. XII (*MW*, 4: 98–115). When Davidson, in his Dewey Lectures, tries to pay homage to the patron, he refers to the introduction of that chapter, but he seems not to have noticed that it is just a quick rehearsal of some leitmotifs of James's recently published book, which is then followed by a rather careful examination of what Dewey takes to be the book's (many) strengths and (few) weaknesses. First Davidson mistakes what is (almost) a quotation from James, page number given by Dewey, for Dewey's own statement. Then he claims that Dewey 'quotes with approval', on p. 304, a certain passage from James, which (understandably enough) does not find Davidson's approval: 'Probably [only] few philosophers', he says, 'are now tempted by these swinging, sweeping formulations' (Davidson, 'Structure', 280). But Dewey was not tempted either. He returns to this very passage a few pages later and points out that it suffers from a fatal ambiguity (323 (*MW*, 4: 111)).

[235] I shall make an attempt at explication and evaluation in the postscript to Ch. 7.3.1. The two excerpts from James above suffice to show that Rorty is as wrong about James as he is about Dewey: 'James', he tells us, 'thought the claim that truth is correspondence to reality unintelligible' ('Universality and Truth', 25).

[236] Davidson, 'Structure', 304; cf. also 'Epistemology and Truth', 185. Since Davidson takes correspondence theories to be hopeless (for the reasons explained and discussed in sect. 3.3.3 above), one can understand why he sees 'no point in declaring oneself a realist, or, for that matter, an anti-realist' ('Is Truth a Goal of Inquiry?', 17).

this claim long before it was made: 'Frege, although a realist, did not believe in the [?] correspondence theory of truth.'[237] If Frege was an alethic realist, it is plain which content his view has: the concept of truth is not definable in terms of correspondence or of whatever,[238] and truth is not epistemically constrained.

Was Frege an alethic realist? In the course of his attack on psychologism (and the idealism which is consequent upon it), he declares:

Wahrsein ist etwas anderes als Fürwahrgehaltenwerden, sei es von Einem, sei es von Vielen, sei es von Allen, und ist in keiner Weise darauf zurückzuführen.... Das Wahrsein [ist] unabhängig davon, dass es von irgendeinem anerkannt wird. [Being true is something different from being taken to be true, whether by one, by many or by all, and is in no way reducible to it.... Being true does not depend on being recognized by anyone.] (*Grundgesetze der Arithmetik*, Preface to vol. I, xv–xvi)

Gedanken ... können wahr sein, ohne von einem Denkenden gefaßt zu werden. [Thoughts ... can be true without being grasped by a thinker.] ('*Der Gedanke*', 77)[239]

I hesitate to join Dummett in calling this declaration 'a classic pronouncement of the realist faith',[240] for wouldn't every sane alethic *anti*-realist admit that, as a matter of contingent fact, many a true proposition which we are able to comprehend will never become the content of a non-committal thought, let alone of a judgement? There are ever so many comprehensible and decidable yes/no questions which nobody ever bothers to ask, let alone to answer. (The question whether the letter A occurs more than 12,345 times in *La Divina Commedia* would have been such a question, I guess, had I not wasted a bit of this paper by posing it.) The sanity of sane alethic anti-realists consists in their refusal to embrace what Dummett describes as extremist constructivism:

[To deny] that there are true statements whose truth we do not at present recognize and *shall not in fact ever* recognize ... would appear to espouse a constructivism altogether too

---

[237] Dummett, *FPL*, 442. (The reader will understand why I have inserted a question mark.) Cf. ibid., 464; *LBM*, 331.   [238] See the Frege extracts cited in Ch. 1 (p. 16) and sect. 3.3.2 above.

[239] Frege, *NS*, 133 (144, trans. corrected) combines both claims: 'In order to be true, thoughts ... not only do not need to be recognized by us as true: they do not even have to be thought by us at all'. Cf. also *NS*, 206 (223).

[240] Dummett, *LBM*, 325 (on the slightly weaker claim in *Grundgesetze*). 'The crux of the dispute concerning realism is precisely where Frege locates it ... namely in the relation between truth and our recognition of truth ... / ... In drawing his distinction between being true and being taken to be true, Frege hits the very centre of the issue concerning realism' (*IFP*, 433, 511). Unfortunately the Preface to *Grundgesetze* does not contain a convincing argument for alethic realism; Frege seems to think that alethic realism follows immediately from the premiss that a (non-indexical and non-ambiguous) sentence expresses the same proposition to all who understand the language. Dummett takes him to task for this (*IFP*, 65).

extreme. One surely cannot crudely equate truth with being recognized...as true. ('Wittgenstein on Necessity', 446)[241]

But alethic anti-realists do maintain that every true proposition we can grasp is such that in principle we can recognize its truth. Frege's declaration allows for rejecting this tenet without implying its rejection.

One can rebut the contention 'No Alethic Realism Without Correspondence' also by referring to the view of truth-theoretical nihilists which we scrutinized in Chapter 2. They can capture the spirit of alethic realism by saying: it is *not* the case that for all p, if we can comprehend the thought that p, and (indeed) p, then we can come to be justified in believing that p. And by deleting the prefixed negation operator we obtain the nihilists' rendering of alethic anti-realism. Actually, all conceptions of truth which are discussed in Chapters 2–6 of this book are neutral with respect to the issue of alethic realism. So this matter will now be put aside for quite a while.

---

[241] On pp. 458–60 of the same paper Dummett unambiguously declares extremist constructivism to be 'totally implausible'.

4

In and Out of Quotation Marks

The conceptions of truth to be discussed in this chapter assume that truth is a property of sentences (see QUESTION 8 on the flow chart[1]), of utterances or tokens of declarative sentences, or of types of such tokens. As announced in Chapter 1, I shall leave Davidson's Sentential Primitivism aside, i.e. the view that the concept of (sentential) truth is bound to resist any attempt at an explanation (QUESTION 9). Can one finitely state what sentential truth is (QUESTION 10)? Alfred Tarski's work on the Semantic Conception of Truth appears to give an affirmative answer to this question, and because of this appearance, it is (tentatively) registered under the right branch of QUESTION 10. Tarski offered a Criterion of Material Adequacy for any account of sentential truth, and this criterion has been a, if not the, source of inspiration for disquotationalism, the entry under the left branch of QUESTION 10.

4.1 The Semantic Conception

> Many claims and counter-claims have been made on behalf of Tarskian truth-definitions that have little to do with Tarski's original intentions. Indeed, it is unclear whether his own later estimation of the significance of such a truth-definition did not diverge considerably from his original intentions.
>
> (Michael Dummett, 'The Source of the Concept of Truth', 197)

In the philosophical, as distinct from the mathematical, community reactions to Tarski's work on truth differ wildly. Carnap hailed it as a liberating step forward in philosophy and gratefully acknowledged that his own approach to semantics 'owes very much to Tarski, more indeed than to any other single influence'.[2] But not all Logical Empiricists shared Carnap's enthusiasm. When

---

[1] See Ch. 1, Fig. 1.2.   [2] Carnap, *IS*, x.

Tarski presented his ideas at a congress in Paris in 1935, Carnap was taken by surprise that 'there was vehement opposition even on the side of our philosophical friends.... Neurath believed that the semantical concept of truth could not be reconciled with a strictly empiricist and anti-metaphysical point of view.'[3] Popper repeatedly expressed his great admiration for Tarski's 'rehabilitation' of the 'correspondence theory of absolute or objective truth', adding somewhat maliciously that this theory is 'accepted today with confidence by all who understand it'.[4] But one is not really encouraged to rely on Popper's understanding of Tarski's theory when one reads Putnam's harsh verdict: 'When Popper says that this view [a correspondence view] of truth has been rehabilitated by Tarski, he simply doesn't know what he is talking about.'[5] Worse than that, Putnam maintains that 'as a philosophical account of truth, Tarski's theory fails as badly as it is possible for an account to fail'.[6] Several decades earlier Black and Strawson had come to much the same conclusion.[7] In the 1970s Davidson convinced many philosophers of language that Tarski's work on truth opens the royal road to meaning-theories for natural languages.[8] But Dummett had argued earlier that if Tarski had really given a satisfactory account of our concept of truth, then the prospects for meaning-theories of the Davidsonian type would be very bleak.[9] All in all, Etchemendy cannot be accused of exaggerating when he says that 'opinions have not exactly converged'.[10] Let us try to form a balanced opinion—with deference to Tarski's own intentions.

4.1.1 *Preliminaries on 'semantic'*

One of the main problems of what Tarski called the 'methodology of the deductive sciences' was that of giving an account of such notions as validity, consequence, consistency, and completeness. In the systematic study of these notions an appeal to the concept of truth could hardly be avoided. But this very concept was known to allow the derivation of a flat contradiction from what seem obvious principles. So an account of the concept of truth was desirable that satisfied

---

[3] Carnap, 'Intellectual Autobiography', 61. Neurath's conception of truth will demand our attention in Ch. 7.1.2.

[4] Popper, 'Truth, Rationality, and the Growth of Scientific Knowledge', 223–5; cf. also his 'Philosophical Comments on Tarski's Theory of Truth', 323–9.

[5] Putnam, 'A Comparison of Something with Something Else', 342.   [6] Ibid., 333.

[7] Black, 'The Semantic Definition of Truth'; Strawson, 'Truth' (1949).

[8] Davidson, 'Truth and Meaning'.   [9] Dummett, 'Truth'.

[10] John Etchemendy, 'Tarski on Truth and Logical Consequence' (henceforth 'Tarski'), 51. Among German philosophers you will find equally divergent assessments of the philosophical importance of Tarski's work on truth: a very high estimation in Wolfgang Stegmüller, and a very low one, for a while, in Tugendhat (see Bibliography).

the needs of the methodology of the deductive sciences and did not give rise to paradox. Providing us with such an account was the foremost goal of what Tarski called the 'semantic conception of truth'. Now what does 'semantic' mean here? How does a predicate such as 'true' earn itself the sobriquet 'semantic'? Tarski's own answers to this question are not very helpful.[11] Semantic predicates signify, we are told,

[A] certain relations [of dependence] between the expressions of a language and the objects [']about which these expressions speak['] [*gewisse Abhängigkeiten zwischen den Ausdrücken der Sprache und den Gegenständen, 'von denen in diesen Ausdrücken die Rede ist'*]. (*WB*, 116 (252))

[B] certain connexions between the expressions of a language and the objects and states of affairs referred to by these expressions [*gewisse Zusammenhänge zwischen den Ausdrücken einer Sprache und den durch sie angegebenen Gegenständen und Sachverhalten*]. ('*Grundlegung*', 261 (401), cf. 263 (403))

[C] certain relations between expressions of a language and the objects (or 'states of affairs') 'referred to' by those expressions. ('Semantic', §5, cf. §20)

[D] relations between linguistic objects, e.g. sentences, and what is expressed by these objects. ('Proof', 403, cf. 411) [T.1]

Each of these formulations is hedged by a parenthetical 'loosely speaking' or interspersed with scare quotes, and rightly so. Talk of 'dependence' and 'connection', as in [A] and [B], is rather unhappy, so let us stick to the colourless word 'relation' of [C] and [D].[12] Other infelicities remain. A name like 'Warsaw' may be said to 'refer to' a town, but it certainly cannot be said to 'speak about', let alone 'express', that town. By contrast, a sentence as a whole does not seem to 'refer to' anything. But of a sentence like 'Warsaw was completely destroyed', one can say (if only metaphorically) that it speaks about a certain object, though in cases like 'Nobody is perfect' and 'It is snowing' it is none too easy to specify the objects they speak about. (In Chapter 3 (p. 111) we saw that this was Tarski's objection against Aristotle.) A sentence may also be said to express something, but (as we shall see) Tarski does not dream of characterizing truth

---

[11] '*WB*' abbreviates the title of Tarski's monograph *Der Wahrheitsbegriff in den formalisierten Sprachen*. The revised and enlarged German translation was published in 1935 and reprinted in the same year. In my quotations from *WB*, the first page number refers to the 1935 reprint, the number in brackets to the English translation which is based on the German text. '*Grundlegung*' is short for '*Grundlegung der wissenschaftlichen Semantik*' (numbers in brackets refer to the English translation), 'Semantic' for 'The Semantic Conception of Truth...', quoted by section number, and 'Proof' for 'Truth and Proof'. The paper '*Der Wahrheitsbegriff in den Sprachen der deduktiven Disziplinen*' (which has not been translated into English) will be referred to as '*Wahrheit*'. Finally, '*Briefe*' abbreviates '*Alfred Tarski: Drei Briefe an Otto Neurath*'. This cluster of quotations will be referred to henceforth in the text as [T.1]. Subsequent Tarski quotations in this chapter will be labelled, and referred to, as [T.2], [T.3], etc.

[12] Cf. Marja Kokoszyńska, '*Über den absoluten Wahrheitsbegriff*', 143.

as a relation between sentences and anything that could sensibly be said to be expressed by them. So we do not get much illumination from any of the formulations in [T.1].

'Semantics', Quine once said, 'would be a good name for the theory of meaning, were it not for the fact that some of the best work in so-called semantics, notably Tarski's, belongs to the theory of reference.'[13] Tarski's paradigmatic semantic predicates

- 'designates', 'denotes' ['*bezeichnet*']
- 'applies to', 'is satisfied by' ['*wird erfüllt durch*']
- 'determines uniquely', 'defines' ['*bestimmt eindeutig*']
- 'is true'

squarely belong to the latter province of 'what is loosely called semantics'.[14] Perhaps this is what Tarski means when he starts his paper 'The Establishment of Scientific Semantics' by saying, 'The word "semantics" is used here in a narrower sense than usual.' In Quine's sketch of the landscape the predicates 'is synonymous with (has the same meaning as)' and 'is analytic (is true by virtue of meaning alone)' belong to the other province of semantics in the broad sense. (Interestingly, Quine's bracketed paraphrases of the key terms of the 'theory of meaning' use the term 'meaning', whereas he does not try to paraphrase the key predicates of the 'theory of reference' in terms of 'reference'.) If one wants to know when a predicate is semantic in the broad sense, then Quine is no more helpful than Tarski.[15]

---

[13] Quine, 'Notes on the Theory of Reference' (henceforth 'Notes'), 130. According to Carnap, *IS*, 238, the French counterpart of the term 'semantics' was put into general currency by the historical linguist Michel Bréal, whose *Essai de sémantique: Science des significations* (Paris, 1897) was translated into English as *Semantics: Studies in the Science of Meaning* (London, 1900). In the late 1920s, Tarski's teachers Kotarbiński and Leśniewski had begun to use the term '*semantyka*', but the terminology in the theory of language was still rather unsettled. When announcing his forthcoming Polish monograph in a Viennese journal in 1932, Tarski used the term '*Semasiologie*' in the same sense in which he soon afterwards came to use '*Semantik*' ('*Wahrheit*', *passim*). Heinrich Gomperz, Schlick's colleague in Vienna and in close contact with several members of the Circle, had used the former term as title for a volume of his *Weltanschauungslehre* (1908), and in Prague it served the Brentanist Anton Marty as a key term in his *Untersuchungen zur Grundlegung der allgemeinen Grammatik und Sprachphilosophie* (1908), where it is used interchangeably with '*Bedeutungslehre* [theory of meaning]'. Marty's work is known to have influenced Leśniewski (see Pearce and Woleński (eds.), *Logischer Rationalismus*, 23). When Kazimierz Ajdukiewicz expounded his theory of meaning in the journal of the Vienna Circle in 1934, he still called 'meaning [*Sinn*]' a concept of *Semasiologie* (see Pearce and Woleński (eds.), 147).   [14] Quine, 'Notes', 130.

[15] In *IS*, §§7 and 12, Carnap seems to give us one relational concept covering names, predicates, and sentences when he says about (sentences like) '*Socrates is wise*': (1) the name designates Socrates, (2) the predicate designates the property of being wise, and (3) the sentence designates the proposition that Socrates is wise. But this serves only to muddy the water. The term 'designates' cannot mean in (2) and (3) what it means in (1), for in *that* sense the property mentioned in (2) is designated rather by singular

The following explanation conforms, I think, with a rather firmly established usage: a predicate ϕ is *semantic in the broad sense* if and only if (1) ϕ signifies either a property which only a (linguistic) expression can have or a relation in which only an expression can stand to something, and (2) whether ϕ holds of an expression E of a language L always depends at least in part on the meaning of E in L. (If we follow Strawson rather than Quine in our usage of 'x refers to y',[16] then this predicate is excluded by condition (1), because speakers, not expressions, are the elements of the left field of the relation it signifies. Condition (2) excludes 'x has five letters.') Some semantic predicates are, as Tarski puts it, 'directly' relational, some are 'indirectly' relational.[17] The former are two-place predicates, the latter are one-place predicates which can be correctly explained in terms of two-place predicates.[18] The first three items in Quine's list of key terms in the 'theory of reference' are directly relational semantic predicates. As used by Tarski, they signify relations in which some expressions stand to non-linguistic objects. Thus designation is a relation in which the name 'Warsaw' stands to the capital of Poland, application is a relation in which the predicate 'is a capital' stands to all capitals, and unique determination is a relation in which the 'equation' 'Warsaw is the capital of x' stands to Poland. (The entities in the right field of these relations are, of course, not always non-linguistic: what 'Alpha' designates, what 'is a letter' applies to, and what 'the Greek alphabet is what x is the first letter of' uniquely determines, are linguistic objects.) A two-place predicate may signify a relation which obtains between expressions and non-linguistic objects, although it is not a semantic predicate. The word 'table' has more letters than the table I am working at has legs; but 'x has more letters than y has legs' is not a semantic predicate,[19] since the relation signified obtains quite independently of the meaning of the word 'table'. Some two-place semantic

terms like 'wisdom', 'the property of being wise', and 'the property for which Solomon and Solon were famous', and in *that* sense the proposition mentioned in (3) is designated rather by the sentence-nominalization 'that Socrates is wise' and by singular terms like 'Plato's favourite proposition'. So what is the common meaning of 'designates' in (1), (2), and (3)? By the time he wrote *Meaning and Necessity*, Carnap had become aware of this obscurity (166–7 n.). (I follow Tarski in my use of 'designate'. Under this reading only (1) is correct.)

[16] Strawson, 'On Referring'. (I follow Strawson in my use of 'refer'.)   [17] 'Proof' 411.

[18] Compare the definability of monadic predicates like 'is a natural satellite' and 'is a spouse' in terms of dyadic predicates.

[19] It would have to be one if the following argument were any good: 'Since satisfaction is a relation between expressions and parts of the world, it counts as a semantic concept' (Kirkham, *ThT*, 153). Even Prior is a bit careless here when he implicitly takes 'all terms which concern the relations between the expressions of a language and the objects which this language is used to describe or talk about' to be semantic terms ('Correspondence Theory of Truth', 230).

predicates signify relations which only obtain between expressions, for example 'is co-designative with' (the relation in which 'a' and 'b' stand to each other iff 'a is identical with b' holds) and 'is synonymous with', or 'materially implies' (the relation in which 'p' stands to 'q' iff 'p → q' holds) and 'entails' (when used for the relation in which 'p' stands to 'q' iff 'p → q' is analytic).

This attempt at specifying features common to all semantic predicates calls upon our pre-theoretical grasp of the notion of (conventional linguistic) meaning. This notion is to be clarified in the theory which bears its name—in that province of semantics about whose 'sorry state' Quine never tired of complaining.[20] He has weighty reasons for his complaints, but one starts wondering whether he doesn't overstate his case when he declares the two provinces 'not to deserve a joint appellation at all'.[21] It is noteworthy that on one occasion at least Quine himself marks out the 'semantic properties' of an expression as those 'properties which arise from the meaning of the expression'.[22] Now a predicate ϕ is semantic in the *narrow* sense which I take Tarski to be aiming at in [T.1] just in case ϕ is a semantic predicate and either (i) ϕ itself or (ii) a predicate needed for defining ϕ signifies a relation in which expressions of a certain kind typically stand to non-linguistic objects. Henceforth I shall call such predicates *narrowly semantic*.

Now what about 'true'? By Tarski's lights, it is (at least for some languages) a narrowly semantic predicate of kind (ii). But this is to anticipate.

4.1.2   *Formal correctness and material adequacy*

In his famous monograph *Der Wahrheitsbegriff in den formalisierten Sprachen* (1933/35)[23] Tarski poses his problem in the following way:

The present article is almost wholly devoted to a single problem—the definition of truth. Its task is to construct—with reference to a given language—a materially

---

[20] Quine, 'Notes', 132. As far as I can see, in his published work Tarski only once, in an aside, refers to predicates of this province of semantics: 'Within theoretical semantics, we can define and study some further notions, whose intuitive content is more involved and whose semantic origin is less obvious; we have in mind, for instance, the important notions of ... synonymity and meaning' ('Semantic', §13). (Nothing could be more obvious than that synonymy is a semantic notion if one takes 'semantic' in the *broad* sense I tried to elucidate above.) In n. 20 of 'Semantic' he declares, 'All notions mentioned in this section can be defined in terms of satisfaction', and he refers his readers for a definition of synonymy to Carnap's *IS*. This is confusing, for in *IS* 'synonymy' is defined in terms of designation. (In n. 15 above we found reasons for dissatisfaction with Carnap's use of this term.) Carnap's definition has the consequence that 'the Morning Star' and 'the Evening Star' are synonymous; which can hardly be said to capture the 'intuitive content' of the notion of synonymy.   [21] Quine, 'Notes', 130.

[22] Quine, *Mathematical Logic*, 24.

[23] The Polish original was published two years before the (enlarged and revised) German version.

adequate and formally correct definition of the term 'true sentence' [*eine sachlich zutreffende und formal korrekte Definition des Terminus 'wahre Aussage'*]. This problem, which belongs to the classical questions of philosophy, raises considerable difficulties . . . / . . .

The extension of the concept to be defined depends in an essential way on the particular language under consideration. The same expression can, in one language, be a true sentence, in another a false one or a meaningless expression. There will be no question at all here of giving a single general definition of the term. The problem which interests us will be split into a series of separate problems each relating to a single language. (*WB*, 4, 5 (152, 153); [T.2])

Taking 'true' to be a semantic predicate implies, of course, treating linguistic entities, (declarative) sentences, as truth vehicles. By 'sentence [*Aussage*]' Tarski means an orthographically individuated declarative type-sentence: if spelling includes mention of blanks between words and of punctuation marks, we can say that several sentential inscriptions are tokens of the same sentence just in case they spell the same.[24] As to the language-relativity incurred by taking sentences to be truth-value bearers, consider the sentence

(S)   One billion is one thousand million.

It is true in American English (in other words, what is literally said when it is used as a sentence of AE is true), it is false in British English, and it is meaningless in Polish (it simply has no use as a sentence of Polish). Hence what Tarski wants to define are predicates of the type 's is a true sentence of language L' ('s is true in L', for short).[25] So far there is not much reason for those who take propositions to be the primary truth-value bearers to demur from the exposition of the problem: they can translate the Tarskian definiendum 's is a true sentence in L' into their own idiom (as I did a moment ago): 'what is literally said when s is used as a sentence of L is true'. (If s contains elements that are ambiguous or context-sensitive, then both formulations are equally inadequate.) What is *literally* said when the sentence 'War is war' is used as a sentence of English is certainly as true as can be, but unfortunately it is very often used to convey something that is not true.[26]

---

[24] *WB*, 9 n. (156 n.); 'Semantic', §2 n. The above formulation is meant to improve a bit on Tarski's own. He demands of the inscriptions that they be 'of like shape [*gleichgestaltet*]'. But one may very well wonder whether the next two numbered inscriptions and a transcription of either in Gothic letters are 'of like shape': (1) She is blond. (2) **She is blond.** And doesn't the shape of (2) resemble that of (3) at least as much as that of (1) (or that of its Gothic transcription)? (3) **She is bland.**

[25] Cf. *WB*, 128 (263); 'Semantic', §2; cf. Quine, 'Notes', 135.

[26] For the time being I shall follow the (dubious) advice, 'When in Rome do as the Romans', and say of sentences that they are true (rather than that they express truths). In the next chapter I shall dissociate myself from this practice.

The languages to which sentential truth is relativized are not individuated by their syntactical properties alone: since 'billion' in American English does not mean what it means in British English, AE has a property that BE lacks; hence (by the Leibnizian Principle of the Indiscernibility of Identicals) AE and BE are not identical, whether or not they are syntactically indistinguishable. Tarski hesitated to acknowledge that the identity of a language is not simply a matter of syntax, as can be seen from his comments on a paper by Marja Kokoszyńska. At a congress in Cracow in 1936 she had argued that sentential truth is to be relativized to meaning.[27] Tarski asked, 'Would it not be simpler to relativize the concept of truth to the concept of language which seems to be clearer and logically less complicated than the concept of meaning?'[28] Kokoszyńska answered that the concept of meaning is assumed when one speaks of the translation of sentences of an object-language into its metalanguage. This is correct, but it appeals to a component of Tarski's theory which we have yet to introduce. But her point can be made already on the basis of the argument for relativization to a language which Tarski himself gives in our extract [T.2]. If languages were individuated purely syntactically and if AE and BE were syntactically indistinguishable, then they would be strictly one and the same language—call it (as you may be prone to do in any case) 'English'. Now we would have to describe (S) as both true in E and not true in E. Of course, we could dispel the impression of self-contradiction by taking a deeper breath and saying that (S) is true in E under one reading and not true in E under another reading, but then the concept of meaning, only thinly disguised, would turn up. (We have to face this situation also *within* a language if it contains lexically or syntactically ambiguous sentences like 'Our mothers bore us' or 'Visiting relatives can be boring'. But, as we shall see, Tarski defines 'true' only for languages that are purged of ambiguity.)

The first part of [T.2] is still awaiting comment. It lays down two requirements that any definition of a truth-predicate for a given language L must satisfy. Which constraints are imposed on a definition of a truth-predicate for a language L by Tarski's insistence on *formal correctness* or, as he sometimes puts it, *methodological correctness*? This requirement concerns the form of the definition and the vocabulary in which it is framed. Two of the vices it is meant to ban are giving a circular definition and using in the definiens vocabulary that is less clear than the definiendum. As to formal correctness, the definition 'For all s, s is a true sentence of English iff s is identical with s' is immaculate, but of course, since it

---

[27]   Kokoszyńska, 'On the Relativity and Non-Relativity of Truth'.

[28]   Tarski, 'Remarks on Kokoszyńska', 401 (trans. by Woleński); cf. Peter Simons and Jan Woleński, '*De Veritate*', 416.

implies that all English sentences are true, it jars with our pre-theoretical understanding of 'true': it is not adequate to its subject-matter; it is not, as Tarski puts it, *materially adequate*. How can we recognize whether a definition of a truth-predicate for a given language is not only formally correct but also in harmony with our workaday concept of truth? Tarski's answer is his famous 'Convention T [*Konvention W*]',[29] which I prefer to call, as he himself sometimes does, a criterion:[30]

> Criterion T   A formally correct definition of 'true' for a given object-language L in the metalanguage English is materially adequate if and only if it implies all sentences which can be obtained from the schema
>
> (T)   s is true in L if and only if p
>
> by substituting for the place-holder 's' a revealing designator of a declarative sentence of L and for the place-holder 'p' the English translation of that sentence.

Several comments are in order. A language *for which* a truth-predicate is defined is called object-language (with respect to this definitional endeavour),[31] and a language *in which* a truth-predicate is defined is called metalanguage (of the language under consideration). In Criterion T, as formulated above, English is the metalanguage. If German, L_G for short, is our object-language, then the biconditional

(T^a)   '*Warschau ist in Polen*' is true in L_G iff Warsaw is in Poland

---

[29] *WB*, 45–6 (187–8). (Following Tarski's own expositions elsewhere and the standard practice in the literature, I have quietly dropped a clause of which Tarski himself says on p. 188 that it is 'not essential': A materially adequate definition of 'true in L' is to imply that only the sentences of L are true in L.)

[30] 'Semantic', title of §4. Calling it a convention, or, as in 'Proof', 405, a stipulation, is somewhat misleading. The specification of a condition whose fulfillment ensures that a definition of 'true' is, as Tarski puts it in '*Grundlegung*', 264 (404), 'in accordance with common usage [*Sprachgebrauch*]', can hardly be a matter of convention or stipulation. I share Putnam's terminological preference here, but unfortunately he also brought a plain error into circulation: Tarski called this "[K]riterium W" in his *Wahrheitsbegriff*—and this somehow got translated into English as "Convention T" ' (*Meaning and the Moral Sciences*, 28). The English translation is fine: in *WB* Tarski, or rather his translator Blaustein, did not use '*Kriterium*'. McDowell was perhaps one of Putnam's first 'victims': see 'Physicalism and Primitive Denotation' (henceforth 'Physicalism', 132 n., 142. Samuel Guttenplan followed suit, invoking the authority of the German text (of Putnam's imagination): *The Languages of Logic*, 314. Putnam is not responsible, of course, for the German contribution to this little comedy. Thus Karl-Otto Apel refers to Tarski's criterion as '*Konvention T*': see '*Fallibilismus, Konsenstheorie der Wahrheit und Letztbegründung*', 30 *et passim*. (What is less funny is that he identifies Criterion T with schema (T). As we shall soon see, this confusion is endemic in Frankfurt.)

[31] In *WB* the object-language is referred to as '*betrachtete Sprache* [language under consideration]' (*WB*, 46 (188)). The former term seems to have been coined by Carnap (see *Die Logische Syntax der Sprache*, 4. Cf. Tarski, '*Briefe*', 17 (26–7)).

is an instance of schema (T). Tarski demands that the definition of a truth-predicate for a language L is framed in a metalanguage ML which is not identical with L.[32] Non-identity does not imply separation. The restriction is already heeded when L is a proper part of ML—in other words, when ML is an expansion of L. In the latter case we can take the translation of a sentence S to be S itself. If a fragment of English, L_E, in which one can say, 'Warsaw is in Poland', is our object-language, then the disquotational biconditional

(T^h) 'Warsaw is in Poland' is true in L_E iff Warsaw is in Poland

is an instance of schema (T). Obviously, Criterion T can only be complied with if the metalanguage has the resources for designating sentences of the object-language and for translating them. A designator of an expression is (what I have called) revealing if and only if somebody who understands it can read off from it which (orthographically individuated) expression it designates. Thus the quotational designator ' "*Das Ewigweibliche zieht uns hinan*" ' is revealing, whereas the (co-designative) definite description 'the last sentence in Goethe's *Faust*' is not.[33] In the formulation of Criterion T in his monograph *WB* Tarski requires that the instances of schema (T) contain in the 's'-position so-called 'structural-descriptive names', such as 'the sentence which begins with a capital Dee, followed by... and ends with a small En'. To be sure, such designators are also revealing in my acceptation of this term, but since they are rather cumbersome, I shall go on using quotational designators (as Tarski himself also does most of the time).[34]

I have slightly altered the standard formulations of the criterion, including Tarski's own, by inserting a name of the metalanguage. This is meant to draw attention to

[32] *WB*, 21–2 (167); '*Grundlegung*', 263 (403); 'Semantic' §9; 'Proof', 413.

[33] If you can confirm now from your own experience that one can know which expression is designated by a revealing designator without knowing what the designated expression means, you will not mind if I tell you: the quoted sentence means that the eternally female draws us upwards. (Whatever that may mean.)

[34] In 'Proof', 405, Tarski claims that the quotational and the structural-descriptive designator of the same sentence do 'not differ in meaning', since the former 'can simply be regarded as an abbreviated form of' the latter. But compare the quotational designator of a Greek sentence with its structural-descriptive name: somebody who does not know the Greek alphabet can understand the former, but not the latter, so they are not 'conceptually balanced'. For further criticism, see Davidson, 'Quotation', 86–9. In *WB*, 9–10 (156–7), Tarski makes no such claim. Commenting on Davidson's programme for semantics, Neale classifies quotational designators as 'structural descriptions' (*FF*, 21–5): this is faithful neither to Tarski's nor to Davidson's usage, and it isn't a good idea anyway. For support of his classification, Neale refers his readers to ch. 4 of his book, but there one looks in vain for a word about designators of expressions. Gupta says of revealing designators of expressions that their 'sense can be identified with their reference' ('An Argument Against Tarski's Convention T', henceforth 'Convention T', 227). This characterization fits the occurrence of 'wisdom' in 'The meaning of "*Weisheit*" is WISDOM', but *not* the quotational designator therein.

something that seems seldom to be noticed: with or without that name, Criterion T is, strictly speaking, just the English member of a 'multilinguistic' family. As it stands, it cannot be applied to definitions of 'foreign' truth-predicates like '*prawdziwy*' or '*wahr*' for any object-language; but certainly for such definitions, too, the question of material adequacy arises. If we translate 'true' and schema (*T*) into Polish or German, as the case may be, and replace 'English' by the name of that language, we obtain the criterion we need.

Following Carnap's footsteps,[35] I have taken the liberty of modifying Tarski's formulation (in the monograph and elsewhere) in a further respect. Tarski formulates Criterion T as if it were only a *sufficient* condition of material adequacy: the definition of a truth predicate is materially adequate, he says, '*if* it implies . . .'.[36] But I take it that he wants to specify a condition which is sufficient *and necessary*. A few lines before presenting the criterion he writes that it is '*to be demanded*' of a definition of 'true' for a given language that it should 'comprise' all pertinent instances of schema (*T*),[37] and elsewhere he says that such a definition '*has to be*, in a certain sense, a logical conjunction of all [pertinent sentences of form (*T*)].'[38] Furthermore, Tarski's monograph culminates in a proof that under certain conditions it is not possible to give a materially adequate definition of a truth-predicate, and for this demonstration he needs a necessary condition of material adequacy.[39]

As for the notion of implication (*als Folgerung nach sich ziehen*) deployed in Criterion T, we shall soon see that Tarski allows for the use of some non-logical resources in deriving instances of schema (*T*).[40] But of course, whatever a definition logically implies, it implies. In classical logic a contradiction logically implies anything, so the perverse definition 'For all s, s is a true sentence of German iff s isn't a true sentence of German', which is tantamount to a contradiction, does imply all substitution-instances of schema (*T*) in which 's' is replaced by a German sentence and 'p' by its translation into English. It is banned because Criterion T specifies the condition under which a *formally correct* definition of a

---

[35] Carnap, *IS*, 26–8.

[36] *WB*, 45 (188): '*eine zutreffende Definition der Wahrheit . . . wenn sie folgende Folgerungen nach sich zieht*'.

[37] The passage will be quoted in full below, as [T.14].   [38] 'Semantic', §4, penultimate paragraph.

[39] In sect. 5 of *WB* Tarski shows that a materially adequate and formally correct definition of a truth-predicate is only possible if the metalanguage is 'essentially richer' in its logical part than the object-language. Many authors present Criterion T as a necessary condition of material adequacy (thus McDowell, 'Physicalism', 142; Etchemendy, 'Tarski', 54; Simons and Woleński, '*De Veritate*', 409; Gupta and Belnap, *RTT*, 2–3), without even mentioning that Tarski declares it to be a sufficient condition. (In the next section we will see the criterion at work in the latter role.) Wiggins, 'Meaning and Truth Conditions' (henceforth 'Meaning'), 16, explicitly gives a biconditional. Only Gupta acknowledges that there is a textual problem here, and I have drawn on his treatment of the problem: 'Convention T', 227.

[40] See sect. 4.1.3, *sub* (Df. 1).

truth-predicate is materially adequate: obviously, our perverse definition is circular.[41]

The 'if and only if' in schema (*T*) is to be understood as synonymous with the truth-functional connective '$\leftrightarrow$', hence as definable in terms of '&' and '$\neg$'. Following Tarski, I shall use the term 'T-equivalence' for all and only those substitution-instances of schema (*T*) which mention on their left-hand side a sentence of the object-language for which 'true' is to be defined and use on their right-hand side a translation of that sentence (into our metalanguage).[42] Hence an instance of schema (*T*), 'S_1 is true iff p_1', is a T-equivalence only if what is literally said when S_1 is used as a sentence of the object-language under consideration is that p_1. (So the true biconditional ' "*Warschau ist in Polen*" is true iff Oxford is in England' does not deserve this title.[43]) T-equivalences like (T^h) are nowadays often called *homophonic*, because the sentence used echoes the sentence mentioned. Those like (T^a) go by the name *allophonic*, since the sentence used and the sentence mentioned don't sound alike.[44]

There are counterparts to homophonic T-equivalences for the other key terms of the 'theory of reference':[45]

(D^h) 'Warsaw' designates a certain object
      iff that object is identical with Warsaw

(A^h) Take any object you like, 'is a capital' applies to it iff it is a capital

(U^h) 'Warsaw is the capital of x' determines uniquely a certain object
      iff that object is what Warsaw is the capital of.

---

[41] Of all the authors mentioned n. 39 above, only Wiggins preserves this feature of Tarski's own formulation of Criterion T; which makes it immune against the putative counter-example (due to Gupta, 'Convention T').

[42] 'Semantic', §4 (for those cases in which the metalanguage is an expansion of the object-language).

[43] Notice that the demands for a biconditional's being a Davidsonian 'T-sentence' are lower than those for its being a Tarskian T-equivalence. A biconditional cannot be a T-equivalence if the sentence used in its right branch doesn't translate the sentence mentioned in its left branch. But according to Davidson, one may very well wonder with respect to a certain T-sentence whether 'the right branch of the biconditional really does translate the sentence whose truth value [*sic*] it is giving' ('Reply to Foster', 173). ('Truth value' seems to be a slip of the pen, surely it should read 'truth-condition'.)

[44] It should go without saying that Criterion T is not identical with schema (*T*), but, alas, it doesn't. When Jürgen Habermas takes issue with what he calls 'a deflationism that relies on the semantic conception of truth' ('*Wahrheit und Rechtfertigung*', 231 (trans. 32)), he sets the stage as follows: 'Tarski's Convention T—" 'p' is true if and only if p"—relies on a disquotational use of the truth-predicate that can be illustrated by the example of confirming another person's statements: "Everything that the witness said yesterday is true" ' (251 (42)). This is trebly confused. Habermas mistakes something like schema (*T*) for Convention T; he mistakes the real schema (*T*) for the schema of *homophonic* T-equivalences; and he 'illustrates' the disquotational use of the truth-predicate by an example in which nothing is quoted. (No disquotation without quotation, one would have thought.) This infelicitous start makes one fear that the ensuing critique of 'a deflationism that relies on the semantic conception of truth' might be less than convincing. [45] I surpress relativization to English and neglect tenses.

Here again an expression that is quoted on the left-hand side of the biconditional gets disquoted on the right-hand side.[46] Quine ascribes the 'peculiar clarity' for which he celebrates this province of semantics to the availability of such disquotational paradigms.[47] But this does not seem to be quite right. After all, sentences like

> 'Warsaw is in Poland' expresses the proposition that Warsaw is in Poland
> 'Trilateral' means TRILATERAL

are also disquotational, although they belong to the 'theory of meaning'. But there remains a vast difference. As Quine himself pointed out more than once,[48] whenever the disquotation is done across a key term of the 'theory of reference', one can replace the item between the quotation marks *salva veritate* by another expression that has the same truth-value (*designatum*, extension, as the case may be). The last-displayed sentences lack this feature: here, a substitution for the expression between quotation marks has to have the same *sense* as the original if the truth-value is to remain undisturbed. Even substitution of the intensionally equivalent term 'triangular' for the first occurrence of 'trilateral' would turn a truth into a falsehood.

Unfortunately, acceptance of homophonic T-equivalences and of some seemingly unassailable inference rules and semantical principles of classical logic leads to antinomies such as the (notoriously mislabelled) Paradox of the Liar.[49] Tarski's example is a sentence like the one in line (*), i.e. in that line on this page which is marked by an asterisk on its left:

(*)   The sentence in line (*) is not true.

(Take 'true' in (*) as abbreviating 'a true sentence of English'.) The first premiss of the derivation is this:

(P1)   'The sentence in line (*) is not true' is true iff
          the sentence in line (*) is not true.

In the first branch of this biconditional the predicate 'is true' is attached to the quotational designator of a sentence which is then disquoted in the second branch. So (P1) is a substitution-instance of the Disquotation Schema; in other words, it is a homophonic T-equivalence. Now a biconditional

---

[46] For (D^h) and (U^h), cf. *WB*, 52 n. (194 n.); '*Grundlegung*', 261 (401); 'Semantic', §13 n. 20. We shall soon come across something very much like (A^h) in *WB*.   [47] Quine, 'Notes', 134.

[48] See, for example, Quine, *W&O*, §30.

[49] It was discovered by the Megarian logician Eubulides in the fourth century BC (and it is about utterances that apparently declare themselves to be lacking truth rather than about lack of sincerity in utterers).

(as understood in classical logic) is false only if one of its branches is true and the other false. But in a homophonic T-equivalence such a divergence in truth-value cannot arise. Hence (P1) cannot be false, and so we seem to be obliged to accept it as true. By inspecting line (*) we learn:

(P2)   The sentence in line (*) = 'The sentence in line (*) is not true.'

From (P1) and (P2) we reach, by Identity Elimination, the conclusion

(C)   'The sentence in line (*) is not true' is true iff
      'The sentence in line (*) is not true' is not true.

This is tantamount to a contradiction.[50]

The lesson of the 'Liar' is that we cannot avoid a contradiction unless we revise some intuitively plausible assumption or restrict some apparently reliable inference rules or modify some of the semantical principles underlying classical logic. In Tarski's eyes, the culprit is the assumption that there could be a truth-predicate which was legitimately applicable to a sentence involving that very predicate. (This assumption is intuitively very plausible. If Ann spoke the truth when she said, 'Ben was with me at the time of the murder,' it seems to be perfectly legitimate to apply the English truth-predicate to the English sentence 'What Ann said is true.') As we already know, Tarski demands that the definition of a truth-predicate for an object-language L is framed in a metalanguage ML which is not identical with L. By itself this does not exclude that the truth-predicate which is applied to a quoted sentence of L is also a part of L. In order to prevent applications of a truth-predicate to sentences that involve that very predicate, Tarski lays down a further *formal* requirement: he insists that languages be arranged in a hierarchy. A basic object-language, say L_x, would not contain any truth-predicate. If L_x satisfies certain further conditions (which will occupy us later), then a truth-predicate, say 'true in L_x', can be defined in a metalanguage ML_x that contains every sentence of L_x together with that truth-predicate. The predicate 'true in L_x' does not apply to any sentences containing it, so it can apply only to those sentences of ML_x which it shares with L_x. We can also ascribe (un)truth to the (un)truth-ascriptions formulated in our metalanguage ML_x, but only by using a predicate 'true in ML_x' that belongs to a meta-metalanguage MML_x, etc. So for any language L, the predicate 'true in L' is

---

[50] In this context Tarski acknowledges his indebtedness to his logic teachers at Warsaw University: Stanisław Leśniewski, the supervisor of his doctoral dissertation, had already pointed out the role of substitution-instances of (Dis) as premisses in 'Liar'-type antinomies ('Semantic', §4 n. 7; cf. *WB*, 7 n. 3 (155)), and the special formulation of the antinomy given above is due to Jan Łukasiewicz (*WB*, 10 (157), 'Semantic', §7 n.).

banished from L itself. This restriction blocks the paradox.[51] Properly expanded, our ill-starred sentence would look like this:

(*)   The sentence in line (*) is not true in L_E.

If Tarski's restriction is obeyed, this is not a true sentence of L_E *under any conditions whatever*, since it is not even a *sentence* of L_E.

Tarski frequently calls T-equivalences 'partial definitions [*Teildefinitionen*]' of the truth-predicate as regards the sentences mentioned on their left-hand sides.[52] (We may presume that he would be ready to call the biconditionals (D^h), (A^h), and (U^h) partial definitions of 'designates', 'applies to', and 'determines uniquely' with respect to the expressions mentioned in their first branches.) In section 4.2.1 I shall question this characterization of T-equivalences. But let us right now consider a certain tension between this characterization and one aspect of Tarski's insistence on formal correctness, his prohibition of circular definitions. This apparent conflict was first noted by Gupta and Belnap. They applaud Tarski's describing T-equivalences as partial definitions, but, they protest:

> one cannot say what Tarski says and also accept his requirement that definitions be for-mally correct. Formal correctness rules out circular definitions, yet the partial defini-tions we obtain from the biconditionals may be circular. There is thus a conflict between the two requirements Tarski accepts on a definition of truth, the requirement of formal correctness and that of material adequacy (Convention T). . . . It is a common strategy to resolve this conflict in favor of the formal correctness requirement. (*RTT*, 132)

(The authors then go on to explore, and to recommend, the other altern-ative.[53]) As an example of a biconditional that has the blessing of Criterion T but offends against the ban on circular definitions if read as a 'partial definition', Gupta and Belnap present

(GB)   'Everything Jones says is true' is true iff everything Jones says is true.[54]

As a definition, we are told, this is circular, since the definiens ineliminably contains the word 'true'.

As it stands, this does not yet drive the point home, for in the unlikely case that Jones of all people says whatever he says in Polish, the appearance of circu-larity vanishes as soon as we make the language parameters in (GB) explicit. But the circularity is real if the language of Jones's sayings is the same as that in

---

[51] *WB*, 10–11 (157–8), 19 n. (165 n.); '*Grundlegung*', 262 (402); 'Semantic', §§5 and 7; 'Proof', 407–11.
[52] *WB*, 8–10 (155–7) on schema (2) and sentences (3) and (4); 98 (236), 116 (253), 129 (264); '*Grundlegung*', 264 (404); 'Semantic', §4, 'Proof', 413.   [53] See esp. ibid., ch. 5.   [54] Gupta and Belnap, *RTT*, 132.

which (GB) is formulated. In (GB) the quoted sentence happens itself to contain a truth-predicate, and since (GB) can only be formulated if the metalanguage is an expansion of the object-language, that truth-predicate is also available in the metalanguage. The distinctness of object-language and metalanguage that is appealed to in Criterion T does not exclude that the truth-predicate which is applied to the quoted sentence in (GB) is also a common part of both languages. This is only prevented by the hierarchical approach which answers a *formal* requirement. So Gupta and Belnap seem to be right in saying that there is a conflict between Tarski's criterion of material adequacy and his strictures against circularity. But perhaps appearances are deceptive. Gupta and Belnap are working with a formulation of Criterion T which is common in the literature. But as soon as one pays heed to a certain feature of Tarski's *own* formulation of Criterion T in his monograph (which I took pains to preserve above), the alleged conflict disappears, I think. Tarski assumes that what is tested for material adequacy is formally correct. If materially adequate definitions are a proper subset of formally correct definitions, then a so-called partial definition of a truth-predicate cannot be a materially adequate *definition* unless it is formally correct and hence free of circularity.

Our 'partial definitions'

(T^h) 'Warsaw is in Poland' is true in L_E iff Warsaw is in Poland
(T^a) '*Warschau ist in Polen*' is true in L_G iff Warsaw is in Poland

'define' the truth-predicate as applied to certain sentences in a way that cannot give rise to semantic antinomies, since those sentences contain no semantic vocabulary whatsoever. Such attributions of truth are every bit as clear and unequivocal as the sentences to which truth is attributed. This sets a shining standard for definitions of 'true' for all sentences of a given object-language:[55]

[I]n constructing the definition of truth … I shall not make use of any semantic concept if I am not able previously to reduce it to other concepts. (*WB*, 5 (153))

[I]f this postulate is satisfied, the definition of truth, or of any other semantic concept, will fulfil what we intuitively expect from every definition; that is, it will explain the meaning of the term being defined in terms whose meaning appears completely clear and unequivocal. And moreover, we have then a kind of guarantee that the use of semantic concepts will not involve us in any contradictions. ('Semantic', §9; [T.3])

---

[55] Cf. also '*Wahrheit*', 615. The definition of 'true in a model', developed in the 1950s by Tarski and his collaborators in Berkeley, does not meet, and is not meant to meet, the constraint formulated in [T.3], since it uses the notion of the interpretation of an expression as an undefined semantic primitive. Such a definition does not comply with Criterion T either (see Gupta and Belnap, *RTT*, 23).

We only have 'a kind of guarantee', because the object-language for which the semantic concepts are defined might still involve us in contradictions.

At one point, and only at one point, Tarski hints at an additional motivation for his reductive endeavour. It has an unmistakably Viennese ring:

> [If we were to treat semantic concepts as primitive our procedure would not be in] harmony with the postulates of the unity of science [*Einheitswissenschaft*] and of physicalism (since the concepts of semantics would be neither logical nor physical concepts). ('*Grundlegung*', 265–6 (406) [T.4])[56]

Even if conformity with the postulate of reducibility as set up in [T.3] is a necessary condition for physicalistic acceptability as characterized in [T.4], the former is certainly not sufficient for securing the latter. (Nor does Tarski claim that it is.) Consider again so-called 'partial definitions' of truth: the clarity of a 'definition' of truth as attributed to a certain sentence cannot be inferior to that of the sentence it is attributed to, but of course it can't be superior either: if S is a dark saying, then so is 'S is true.' (As we shall soon see, the same holds if truth is defined for all sentences of the language to which S belongs.) Presumably, St Paul's 'Charity rejoiceth not in iniquity' invokes concepts that are neither logical nor physical. Hence a Tarskian truth definition for (a carefully regimented part of the language of) this sentence will invoke such concepts as well. It is hard to see why this should be held against it. Hence, in what follows I shall put Tarski's somewhat incidental remark on physicalism in [T.4] aside.[57]

---

[56] In the Polish version of '*Grundlegung*', Tarski was quite explicit: '... the postulates of the unity of science and of physicalism, which are propagated by a great number of philosophers from the so called Vienna Circle' (as trans. in Rojszczak, '... Truth-Bearer', 123). Tarski visited the Vienna Circle in the spring of 1930 and again in 1935; Carnap visited Warsaw University in the winter of 1930, as did Neurath in 1934 (cf. Tarski, '*Briefe*'; Carnap, 'Intellectual Biography', 60–1; and Woleński, *Essays*, 46). The Circle organized the International Congress of Scientific Philosophy held in Paris in 1935. Ayer reports: 'It was a big affair, with all the affiliates of the Circle strongly represented.... Philosophically, the highlight of the congress was the presentation by Tarski of a paper which summarized his semantic theory of truth' (*Part of My Life*, 164). Passage [T.4] is taken from this very paper.

[57] For a stark contrast, compare Field's influential 1972 article 'Tarski's Theory of Truth' (henceforth 'Tarski'). Field declared (T.4) to be 'of utmost importance in evaluating the philosophical importance of Tarski's work' (ibid., 91). For illuminating discussion of Field's arguments, cf. Putnam, *Meaning and the Moral Sciences*, Lects I & II; Leeds, 'Theories of Reference and Truth'; Grover, 'Prosentential', §4.6; McDowell, 'Physicalism'; Soames, *UT*. 107–16; and the partial retractation in Field, *Truth and the Absence of Fact*, 'Postscript' to 'Tarski', §§4 and 6. In view of this protracted debate, it is worth reading Kokoszyńskas's apparently forgotten paper '*Bemerkungen über die Einheitswissenschaft*'. (She had been sent to Vienna by her mentor Twardowski and from November 1934 she regularly attended the meetings of the Circle (Rojszczak, '... Truth-Bearer', 117).) Kokoszyńska argued that the doctrine of the unity of science, as understood by Carnap, implies that 'all scientific statements can be expressed in one and the same language', and that the latter contention can be *refuted* along Tarskian lines. She did not mention passage [T.4], and one can be sure that she was not fond of it: under her reading of 'the postulate of unity of science', no harmony with this postulate is desirable. Judging from various references to Kokoszyńska's

As Marja Kokoszyńska observed, Criterion T appeals, under the guise of translation, to a concept clearly belonging to the 'theory of meaning'. But the concept of translation will not appear within the definition of a truth-predicate for a given language (unless that language happens to contain translation vocabulary). So

[it is] not being used here in a manner that offends against Tarski's professed attitude to semantic notions. It occurs only...(as one might fancifully say) in...Tarski's philosophy of truth, [where] it presupposes only this: that a logician [or for that matter, anybody assessing a proposed definition of a truth-predicate] can recognize when the sentence given on the right-hand side of a T-equivalence is faithful to the meaning of the sentence mentioned on the left. (Wiggins, 'Meaning', 16)[58]

Max Black and Wilfrid Sellars once suggested that Criterion T has no real philosophical bite for the reason that biconditionals such as (T^h) and (T^a) will be 'indifferently accepted',[59] or 'viewed with the greatest equanimity',[60] by advocates of correspondence, coherence, or pragmatist conceptions of truth alike. This reasoning betrays a fundamental misunderstanding. From the alleged fact that proponents of those conceptions have this attitude towards T-equivalences, it does not at all follow that their accounts of truth *imply* T-equivalences.[61] It certainly takes more to show that one's conception of truth implies a given T-equivalence than simply to maintain the truth of the latter.[62]

4.1.3 *Three Tarskian truth-definitions*

I shall now give an exposition of the first steps in Tarski's execution of his programme. Tarski himself defined a truth-predicate for the language of a fragment of set theory known as Boole's calculus, or algebra, of classes. But he took pains to avert a possible misunderstanding of the point of this illustration as well as of the very title of his monograph:

[W]hen using the term 'formalized languages', I do not refer exclusively to linguistic systems that are formulated entirely in symbols, and I do not have in mind anything

---

work it seems that Tarski thought highly of her, and it is very probable that he read this paper, too. One can speculate that it prevented him from ever repeating the claim he had made in [T.4].

[58] Cf. Wiggins, 'Moral', 144n.; 'Postscript 3', 338. ('T-equivalence' in the above quotation only means: instance of schema (*T*), because Wiggins says 'when', not 'that'.) Field, 'Tarski', 10, makes the same point.

[59] Black, 'The Semantic Definition of Truth', 258.

[60] Sellars, 'Truth and "Correspondence"', 197.   [61] This is rightly stressed in Kirkham, *ThT*, 184.

[62] For example, the version of a Correspondence Theory which Field upheld in 'Tarski', does *not* meet Criterion T (as was shown by McDowell, 'Physicalism', sect. 4, and by Gupta and Belnap, *RTT*, 26).

essentially opposed to natural languages. On the contrary, the only formalized languages which seem to be of real interest are those which are fragments of natural languages (fragments provided with complete vocabularies and precise syntactical rule), or those which can be adequately translated into natural languages. ('Proof', 412–13; [T.5])

Encouraged by this emphatic declaration, I shall exemplify Tarski's method by defining truth-predicates for three more or less minute fragments of a natural language.[63] Like the algebra of classes, each of these mini-languages will be basic in the sense of Tarski's hierarchy: none of them will contain a truth-predicate (nor any other semantic term). Tarski contends:

If the language investigated only contained a finite number of sentences fixed from the beginning, and if we could enumerate all these sentences, then the problem of the construction of a correct definition of truth would present no difficulties. (*WB*, 46 (188); [T.6])

Let the finite number be very small. My first sample language, L_1, consists of just two German sentences: '*Die Erde bewegt sich*' and '*Der Mond ist rund*.' (The point to be made would be exactly the same, only more tedious to formulate, if we were to consider a portion of German comprising, say, 20,000 sentences.) The following definition of 'true' for L_1 meets Tarski's demands perfectly:

(Df. 1) $\forall s$ (s is a true sentence in $L_1 \leftrightarrow$
      ((s = '*Die Erde bewegt sich*',   and the earth moves)   or
      (s = '*Der Mond ist rund*',   and the moon is round))).

In the definiens of (Df. 1) the logical and syntactic resources of the metalanguage are employed, but, as in the 'partial definition' (T^a), no descriptive vocabulary is used except translations from the object-language. Obviously (Df. 1) is not a sentence of L_1, since the sentences of L_1 form a proper part of it.[64] Hence it meets Tarski's formal requirements.

One can easily check that (Df. 1) also complies with Criterion T. Let us abbreviate the sentences of L_1 by 'E' and 'M' respectively. If we replace the variable in the matrix of (Df. 1) by 'E' we obtain:

(1)   'E' is a true sentence in L_1 $\leftrightarrow$ (('E' = 'E', and the earth moves) or
                                                     ('E' = 'M', and the moon is round)).

---

[63] I shall not bother to specify the vocabulary and the syntactical rules for those mini-languages. In each case the vocabulary can be taken in at a glance, and the syntax is crystal-clear.

[64] Tarski, 'Proof', 406.

The second conjunction is obviously false, so (1) implies

(2)   'E' is a true sentence in L_1 $\leftrightarrow$ ('E' = 'E', and the earth moves).

Now the first conjunct in the consequent of (2) is a logical triviality. Hence (2) implies one of the required T-equivalences:

(3)   'E' is a true sentence in L_1 $\leftrightarrow$ the earth moves.

The same works, of course, for 'M'. In moving from (1) to (2) I have appealed to obviousness. What is obvious is the truth of an additional premiss, namely 'E' $\neq$ 'M'. So, strictly speaking, (3) does not follow just from (Df. 1), but from (Df. 1) plus a trivial truth of syntax. (A certain lack of clarity about the intended sense of 'implies' in Criterion T becomes manifest here. As far as I know, Tarski does not say explicitly *which* non-logical resources can legitimately be appealed to. In practice, he permits invoking trivial syntactic truths as well as some principles of set theory.[65])

Let us call languages such as L_1 for which we can give a complete sentence-by-sentence list of truth-conditions *codes*.[66] (One's resistance to calling them 'languages' may be softened when one remembers the expressive paucity of Wittgenstein's simple *language*-games.) If the language for which a truth-predicate is defined is a code, the definition treats sentences as seamless wholes, and yet, as the case of (Df. 1) shows, it may satisfy Tarski's demands on a truth-definition perfectly.

There is a further fact about (Df. 1) that should not be overlooked. The construction of this definition was guided by an antecedent grasp of meaning, by linguistic knowledge with the following content: what is literally said when 'E' ('M') is used as a sentence of (the L_1-fragment of) German is that the earth moves (that the moon is round). If one were to switch 'E' and 'M' in (Df. 1), the result would not be acceptable: it would yield instances of schema (T) that are not T-equivalences. Recall our reflections on language-identity. L_1 is not individuated by its syntax alone (according to which S is a sentence of L_1 iff S is either identical with 'E' or with 'M'). Suppose a language L consists of the same two sentences but what is literally said when 'E' is used as a sentence of L is *not* that the earth moves: then L is not a tiny fragment of German, hence L is not identical with L_1.

Let us enrich the meagre resources of L_1 by adding two sentential operators: the prefix '*Es ist nicht der Fall, dass*' and the connective '*und*'.[67] This gives us L_2. Since

---

[65] See Gupta, 'Convention T', 228.   [66] Cf. Carnap, *IS*, 23.

[67] Strictly speaking, the syntax of L_2 (and L_3) will differ from that of the corresponding portions of German, since L_2 (and L_3) don't comply with the rule of 'real' German that the application of our one-place sentential operator on a sentence enforces a change of word order in the sentence to which it is applied. Good riddance, you may say: it is because of this tedious feature that the German translation

these operators are capable of iterated application, L_2 contains infinitely many sentences. Now this makes for a problem:

> Whenever a language contains infinitely many sentences, the definition constructed automatically according to the above scheme [i.e. in the style used for L_1] would have to consist of infinitely many words, and such sentences cannot be formulated either in the metalanguage or in any other language. Our task is thus greatly complicated.

> The idea of using the recursive method suggests itself. Among the sentences of a language [like L_2] we find expressions of rather varied kinds from the point of view of logical structure, some quite elementary, others more or less complicated. It would thus be a question of first giving all the operations by which simple sentences are combined into composite ones and then determining the way in which the truth or falsity of composite sentences depends on the truth or falsity of the simpler ones contained in them. Moreover, certain elementary sentences could be selected, from which, with the help of the operations mentioned, all the sentences of the language could be constructed.... In attempting to realize this idea we are however confronted with a serious obstacle. (*WB*, 46–7 (188–9) ; [T.7])

Let me break off at this point, since as far as L_2 is concerned we are not yet confronted by such an obstacle. L_2 isn't a code. How can we define a truth-predicate for such a language? From the two elementary sentences of L_2 all sentences of L_2 can be constructed by applying the sentential operators. So we start by providing 'direct' truth-conditions for the elementary sentences; that is to say, we specify their truth-conditions without referring to other sentences. Then we provide 'indirect' truth-conditions for the compound sentences by referring to other sentences they are made up of. This indirect specification of truth-conditions will finally bring us back to the elementary sentences. In other words, we give a *recursive* (or inductive) definition[68] of 'true' for L_2:

(Df. 2)　$\forall s$ (s is a true sentence in L_2　$\leftrightarrow$

[a]　((s = '*Die Erde bewegt sich*', and the earth moves)　　　　or

[b]　(s = '*Der Mond ist rund*', and the moon is round)　　　　or

[c]　(s is formed by placing '*und*' between two sentences, and both sentences are true in L_2)　　　　or

[d]　(s is formed by prefixing '*Es ist nicht der Fall, dass*' to a sentence, and it is not the case that the embedded sentence is true in L_2)))

In constructing (Df. 2) we do not only rely, in clauses [a] and [b], on an antecedent understanding of the elementary sentences 'E' and 'M'. Using

---

of schema (Dis) has no grammatically correct substitution-instance. (Perhaps it serves as an apology that similar grammatical adjustments are required in many other languages as well.)

[68] For homely applications of the recursive method, cf. Kirkham, *ThT*, 147–9.

clauses [c] and [d] we also take for granted (i) that the connective and the prefix in the L_2-fragment of German express conjunction and negation respectively (as my compatriots will be ready to confirm), (ii) that a conjunction is true iff the one constituent *and* the other are true, and (iii) that a negation is true iff the embedded sentence is *not* true. The italics in (ii) and (iii) may serve as reminders that these biconditionals should not be seen as explanations of the concepts of conjunction and negation: if we are to understand the second halves of (ii) and (iii), we must have those concepts already at our disposal. Tarski sees these biconditionals not as explaining conjunction and negation, which would involve a vicious circle, but as contributing to the definition of truth-predicates. He quite explicitly denies that the meanings of the sentential operators are given by the truth-tables (which were partially spelt out in (ii) and (iii) above); instead, they are determined by an axiomatic, or natural deduction, system for sentential logic.[69]

(Df. 2) fulfils the formal conditions. In order to test it for material adequacy, we try to find out whether each in a reasonable sample of T-equivalences is derivable. If a sentence is complex, we start with applying clause [c] or clause [d] of our definition, apply them repeatedly if necessary, and then remove in a last step the truth-predicate by applying clause [a] or [b]. (So our definition, being recursive, makes use of the predicate 'true in L_2', but it is not circular, since this predicate drops out as the application of the definition proceeds.[70]) Now the sample will always be finite, of course, whereas the definition has to yield a T-equivalence for each of the infinitely many sentences of our language.[71] Hence, unsurprisingly, this kind of test cannot be conclusive here.

In virtue of its recursive character (Df. 2), as opposed to its predecessor, does throw light on the logico-grammatical structure of the object-language. But notice for future reference that the truth-predicates for L_1 and L_2 are not *narrowly semantic* (in the sense explained in section 4.1.1), for in constructing their definitions there was no need to make use of any auxiliary two-place semantic predicate. Tarski himself defined for a far more powerful language a truth-predicate which is not narrowly semantic either. He described (what is in effect) a Turing machine M which is such that for all s, s is a true sentence in the language of elementary geometry iff s is accepted by M.[72] The definition entails all pertinent

---

[69] 'Semantic', §15.

[70] By using a technique (due to Frege and Dedekind) that mobilizes set-theoretic resources, such a recursive definitions can be converted into a direct, eliminative definition. As to the conceptual disadvantages of such conversions, see *WB*, 32 n. (175 n.).   [71] Cf. *WB*, 54 (195).

[72] I owe the reference to, and the illuminating characterization of, Tarski's *Decision Method for Elementary Algebra and Geometry* (1948) to Vann McGee, 'A Semantic Conception of Truth?', 86.

T-equivalences, but it does not mobilize any ancillary two-place predicate signifying a relation in which the atomic non-logical expressions of the language stand to points, lines, and planes.

Natural languages pleasantly differ in many respects from L_2, and one of these respects is the source of the 'serious obstacle' alluded to at the end of quotation [T.7]. Quantified sentences like

(S1)   No number is odd and even

cannot be paraphrased as conjunctions of closed sentences, for

(S2)   No number is odd, and no number is even

is obviously false, whereas (S1) is true. Hence the complex sentence (S1) does not owe its complexity to its being a concatenation of simpler sentences. We can rephrase (S1) in such a way that we have the operator 'and' between open sentences[73] or 'sentential functions [*Aussagefunktionen*]', as Tarski calls them:

(S3)   It is not the case that there is at least one number x such that x is odd and x is even.

The truth-value of a complex sentence which contains open sentences cannot depend on the truth-values of these parts, since open sentences are not truth-evaluable. For a language with complex sentences of this type, 'true' cannot be defined in the same style as for L_2. How does Tarski surmount this obstacle?

In view of this fact, no method can be given which would enable us to define the required concept directly by recursive means. The possibility suggests itself, however, of introducing a more general concept which is applicable to any sentential function, can be recursively defined, and, when applied to sentences, leads us directly to the concept of truth. These requirements are met by the notion of the satisfaction [*Erfüllung*] of a given sentential function by given objects. (*WB*, 47 (189); [T.8])

Roughly, satisfaction is the converse of the relation signified by 'applies to': a number satisfies the open sentence 'x is odd' just in case the predicate 'is odd' applies to it. Sometimes Tarski refers to sentential functions (open sentences) as 'conditions [*Bedingungen*]':[74] this explains, I think, why he finds it so natural to talk of their being, or not being, satisfied (fulfilled, *erfüllt*). The definition of this notion for given languages is subjected to a counterpart to Criterion T which Tarski might have called Criterion S.[75] For simplicity's sake, let us assume that

---

[73] Open sentences aren't really *sentences*, of course, just as toy ducks aren't ducks.

[74] Cf. '*Grundlegung*', 261 (401); 'Semantic', §5.

[75] Putnam actually did call it thus: see *Meaning and the Moral Sciences*, 31. Cf. Field, 'Tarski', 18 and n., on Convention D.

the open sentences in our object-languages never contain more than one free variable. Then the criterion of material adequacy runs like this:

<u>Criterion S</u>   A definition of 'satisfies' for a given object-language L in the metalanguage English is materially adequate if and only if it implies all sentences which one can obtain from the schema

(S)   *For any object y, y satisfies φ (in L) iff p*

if one replaces 'φ' by a revealing designator of an open sentence of L and 'p' by the English translation of that open sentence (after having systematically substituted 'y' for all occurrences of the free variable).

Criterion S imposes a further constraint, over and above those already enforced by Criterion T, on the metalanguage in which 'satisfies' is to be defined for L: the metalanguage must provide us with the resources needed to quantify over the objects which are talked about in L.

Depending on whether the metalanguage is an expansion of the object-language or not, we get homophonic or allophonic S-equivalences:[76]

(S^h)   For any object y, y satisfies 'x is round' iff y is round.
(S^a)   For any object y, y satisfies '*x ist rund*' iff y is round.

Tarski calls S-equivalences 'partial definitions' of 'satisfies' with respect to the open sentences mentioned on their left-hand sides.[77] One might try to define satisfaction for all open sentences φ that contain only one free variable by saying that an object satisfies φ iff φ becomes a true sentence when the free variable is replaced by a name of that object. But this can work only if the object-language has a name for each and every satisfier of its open sentences, and even if this precondition is fulfilled, the strategy is not available for us: since we want to creep up on truth by first defining satisfaction, we cannot explain satisfaction in terms of truth. So we should rather look, just as Tarski suggests, for a *recursive* definition of 'satisfies' for a given language L. This would have to specify first 'direct' satisfaction-conditions for the elementary open sentences of L and then 'indirect' satisfaction-conditions for the compound open sentences of L by referring to open sentences they are composed of. The latter part of the definition would finally bring us back to the elementary open sentences of L.

Let me again exemplify Tarski's procedure by applying it to a (slightly stylized) fragment of German. L_3 extends L_2 by allowing the construction of sentences that are built up from open sentences. In addition to the operators of

---

[76] The first one is the Tarskian counterpart to (A^h) on p. 186 above.
[77] '*Grundlegung*', 264–5 (405).

L_2 its base vocabulary contains two singular terms, '*die Erde*' and '*der Mond*', two open sentences, '*x bewegt sich*' and '*x ist rund*', and an existential quantifier, '*Es gibt mindestens ein Objekt x, das die folgende Bedingung erfüllt:*', which transforms open sentences into sentences.[78] Since L_3 (unlike Tarski's set-theoretical sample language) contains singular terms, we must first define 'designates'.[79] We can easily do this in the case-by-case manner of (Df. 1). Then we give a recursive definition of 'satisfies', and finally a recursive definition of 'true'. (I reserve the variable 'x' for the object-language.)

(Df. 3a) $\forall \alpha \, \forall y \, (\alpha$ in L_3 designates y $\leftrightarrow$

[a1] $((\alpha = $ '*die Erde*',   and y = the earth)   or

[a2] $(\alpha = $ '*der Mond*',   and y = the moon$)))$

(Df. 3b) $(\forall \varphi \forall y \, (\varphi$ is an open sentence in L_3 which is satisfied by y $\leftrightarrow$

[b1] $((\varphi = $ '*x bewegt sich*',   and y moves)   or

[b2] $(\varphi = $ '*x ist rund*',   and y is round)   or

[b3] $(\varphi$ is formed by placing '*und*' between two open sentences, and y satisfies both open sentences in L_3)   or

[b4] $(\varphi$ is formed by prefixing '*Es ist nicht der Fall, dass*' to an open sentence, and it is not the case that y satisfies φ in $L_3)))$

(Df. 3c) $\forall s \, (s$ is a true sentence in $L_3 \leftrightarrow$

[c1] $((s$ is formed by substituting a singular term α for the variable in an open sentence φ, and the object designated by α satisfies $\varphi)$ or

[c2] $(s$ is formed by prefixing '*Es gibt mindestens ein Objekt x, das die folgende Bedingung erfüllt:*' to an open sentence φ, and there is at least one object which satisfies $\varphi)$ or

[c3] $(s$ is formed by placing '*und*' between two sentences, and both sentences are true in $L_3)$ or

[c4] $(s$ is formed by prefixing '*Es ist nicht der Fall, dass*' to a sentence, and it is not the case that the embedded sentence is true in $L_3)))$

So 'true' as defined for L_3 *is* a narrowly semantic predicate.

---

[78] L_3 is a kind of logicians' German: the variable 'x' has taken over the role of the pronoun '*es*'. Similarly, the metalanguage used in (Df. 3) is Loglish rather than ordinary English.

[79] For the sake of this move I have replaced Tarski's notorious 'Snow is white' by logico-grammatically more perspicuous examples: since 'snow' is a mass-term, it is unclear what the logical form of Tarski's own example is. When Tarski talks in 'Semantic', §5 of 'using other semantic notions, e.g. [!] the notion of satisfaction' in order to define truth, I take him (*pace* García-Carpintero, '[T]he Frege-Gödel-Church Argument', 78–9) to allude to the role of the concept of *designation* in defining truth for languages like our L_3. The fact that designation can in turn be defined in terms of satisfaction—cf. n. 80—does not refute this reading.

The construction of the definition of 'satisfies' for L_3 was guided by an antecedent grasp of meaning. This antecedent linguistic knowledge has the following content: take any object you like, what is literally said of it when the L_3-predicate '*bewegt sich*' ('*ist rund*') is applied to it is that it moves (that it is round). If one were to switch the two open sentences in (Df. 3b), the result would not be acceptable: it would yield instances of schema (T) that are not T-equivalences. No language, in which '*bewegt sich*' does not mean MOVES, is identical with L_3. (The same holds, *mutatis mutandis*, for our definition of 'designates'.)

In relying on clause [c2] we assume (i) that the quantifier in the L_3-fragment of German expresses existential quantification (for which you may take my word), and (ii) that an existential quantification, with one variable, is true iff *there is* at least one object that fulfils the condition specified by the matrix. The italicization in (ii) may again serve to stress that (ii) cannot sensibly be considered as an explanation of the concept of existential quantification: we would not be able to understand the second branch of (ii) if we did not yet have this concept in our repertoire. Tarski sees such biconditionals not as explaining existential quantification, which would involve a vicious circle, but as paving the way for the definition of truth-predicates.

Like its predecessors, (Df. 3) meets Tarski's formal and material requirements. In order to check for material adequacy, we proceed like this: if a sentence contains a sentence we start by applying clause [c3] or clause [c4] of our definition. We then remove the predicate 'true' with the help of [c1] or [c2]. Then we apply [b3] or [b4], if necessary. Finally we use the remaining clauses in order to remove the two-place semantic predicates 'designates' and 'satisfies'.[80]

Incidentally, if we assume that in every language each sentence is built up from an open sentence by inserting a singular term, then we can transform the first part of (Df. 3b) into the following (very un-Tarskian) definition of 'true in L' for *variable* L:

$\forall s \, \forall L$ (s is a true sentence in L. $\leftrightarrow$.

$\exists a \, \exists \varphi$ (a is a singular term of L   &

φ is an open sentence of L with one free variable   &

s is formed by substituting a for the variable in φ &

the object designated by a satisfies φ)).

---

[80] Tarski actually defines both designation and unique determination in terms of satisfaction (*WB*, 52 n. (194 n.); 'Semantic', §13 n. 20). A singular term a *designates* a given object a iff a satisfies the open sentence which is obtained by inserting a in the schema 'x is identical with___'. An open sentence *determines uniquely (defines)* a given object a iff a is the only object which satisfies it.

I mention this only because it gives us a kind of semantic counterpart to Bolzano's conception of truth as object-based correspondence.[81] The 'semanticized' Bolzanian definition is un-Tarskian because the definiens contains unreduced semantic terms, hence it does not comply with the constraint formulated in [T.3].

Before entering the philosophical discussion, let me finish my survey by indicating the next steps in Tarski's monograph.[82] The open sentences in our sample language L₃ contain only one free variable. Open sentences with more than one free variable are said to be satisfied by sequences [*Folgen*] of objects. Thus 'x revolves around y' is satisfied by ordered pairs such as {the moon; the earth}. Notice that at this point Tarski's procedure becomes ontologically more demanding. He takes ordered pairs to be classes (in which the order of the elements matters), and classes are *abstract objects*. Both in 'The moon is round' and in 'The moon revolves around the earth' only particulars are designated, and the specification of the satisfaction-conditions of 'x is round' also assumes no more than the existence of particulars. But the specification of the satisfaction-conditions of 'x revolves around y' assumes the existence of classes. Now the number of variables in an open sentence could be any finite number. In order to cover all conceivable cases in one stroke, Tarski finally redefines the concept of satisfaction in such a way that open sentences are satisfied by infinite sequences of objects. This step increases the risk that the ontological commitment incurred by applying the alleged definiens of a truth-predicate go well beyond those we incur when we apply the definiendum: as long as S in L does not itself imply the existence of infinite sets, a strict finitist (who believes that there are no such things) may be ready to accept that S is true in L.[83] (The point at issue is not that of nominalism vs. platonism: in taking type-sentences to be the entities to which truth is ascribed, we have already brushed the nominalist's scruples aside.)

At this point Tarski suggests[84] that we treat sentences as degenerate cases (as mathematicians say) of n-place predicates, where n = 0. This move was already foreshadowed in [T.8] when Tarski called the ancillary concept of satisfaction 'more general' than that of truth. Now we know why: Tarski takes the former to apply to open *and* closed sentences. (One may very well wonder whether this

---

[81] See Ch. 3.1.3 above. [82] *WB*, 49–53 (191–5).

[83] The satisfaction of an open sentence φ depends only on a finite sub-sequence whose members are correlated with the free variables in φ. Modern versions of Tarski's theory often employ only finite sequences. This possibility, mentioned in passing in *WB*, 49 n. 40 (191 n. 1), 53 n. 43 (195 n. 1), 108 n. 87 (245 n. 2) and in 'Semantic' §11 n. 15, was formally developed by Popper (in the 'Addendum' [1955] to his 'Philosophical Comments on Tarski's Theory of Truth', 335–40).

[84] *WB*, 33–5 (176–8), 53 (195); 'Semantic' §11.

is not philosophically as dubious as Frege's treatment of sentences as a kind of complex singular terms, but let that pass.[85]) Applying this strategy to the sentences of the set-theoretical language he has chosen as object-language (call it L*), Tarski shows that a sentence is a *true* sentence of L* iff it is a sentence of L* which is *satisfied by all sequences*.[86]

Soon after the establishment of this definition Tarski reaches the point where his logico-mathematical high-altitude flight takes its departure. But worries about the philosophical relevance of his work on truth always began in those down-to-earth parts of the project which I have tried to explain in detail. One can distinguish two types of philosophical question which have been provoked by Tarski's work: questions concerning its scope, and questions concerning its explanatory claims. I shall explore them in this order.

4.1.4 *Recalcitrant features of natural languages*

Let us first consider some of the questions that arise if one tries to apply Tarski's techniques to a natural language in its entirety (and not just to a stunted portion of it, like our sample languages L_1, L_2 and L_3). Tarski himself did not believe that they are applicable here, and he had (at least) three weighty reasons for his pessimism.

[1] His primary reason is a certain feature of natural languages which he thought responsible for the semantic antinomies. Natural languages are 'semantically closed':[87] they contain for every (declarative) sentence S another sentence ascribing (un)truth to S (and similarly for all other semantic predicates). As we saw, Tarski's remedy against the antinomies was to allow ascriptions of (un)truth only to sentences not belonging to the language in which the ascriptions are formulated. (Among the many problems that arise when one tries to apply Tarski's hierarchical approach to perfectly comprehensible truth-talk in natural languages, only one can be mentioned here. What if on a certain day Jim says of Jules, and Jules says of Jim, that everything he says that day is true? Each of these two statements would have to rank higher in the Tarskian hierarchy than the other.[88]) Tarski himself suggested that there are other ways

---

[85] The question was posed by Evans: see his 'Pronouns, Quantifiers, and Relative Clauses (I)', 86. The Fregean assimilation was criticized by Dummett in *FPL*; see esp. 3–7, 180–6, 192–6 (and partly rehabilitated by Burge in 'Frege on Truth').

[86] For more detailed expositions, see Quine, *PL*, ch. 3, and Soames, *UT*, ch. 3.

[87] 'Semantic', §8. In his monograph Tarski calls this feature of natural languages their 'universality': *WB*, 18–9 (164–5), 132–3 (267). As to his perplexing contention that natural languages like English are 'inconsistent' (ibid.), cf. the critical discussion in Soames, *UT*, 51–6, 62–4 n. 53, 151.

[88] This is one of the problems Saul Kripke pointed out: see his 'Outline of a Theory of Truth', 696.

out: one could restrict the inference rules of classical logic, or modify the semantical assumptions underlying classical logic. He himself rejected such escape routes out of hand.[89] But in the last quarter of the twentieth century alternatives to his approach have been seriously tried. In different ways C. Parsons, Burge, and Barwise and Etchemendy take the extension of the natural language predicate 'true' to be context-dependent like that of an indexical predicate ('loves me', 'is a foreigner'). Martin and Woodruff, and Kripke construct 'fixed-point theories' which exploit the idea that some sentences fall into a truth-value gap, the 'Liar' being one of them. Herzberger and Gupta develop the 'revision theory', extended by Gupta and Belnap to a general theory of circular definitions.[90] As I had to confess already in the preface to this book, I have nothing enlightening to say about, let alone to contribute to, this debate. So I quickly, and somewhat shamefacedly, move on to Tarski's second reason for pessimism.

[2] Will a natural language yield to Tarski's techniques if it is curtailed of its semantic vocabulary? If a declarative sentence s of such natural language L is void of truth-value, then the ascription of truth to s is false. Consequently, some T-equivalences for L-sentences will not be correct, provided that truth in a biconditional requires that both sides either receive the same truth-value or none. So let us assume a natural language that is also purged of truth-candidates which fall into a truth-value gap. Even then it will not yield to Tarski's techniques, for it will not comply with his constraint that

the meaning of an expression should depend exclusively on its form.... It should never happen ... that a sentence can be asserted in one context while a sentence of the same form can be denied in another. (Hence it follows, in particular, that demonstrative pronouns and adverbs such as 'this' and 'here' should not occur in the vocabulary of the language.) ('Proof', 412; [T.9])

If a type-sentence of L contains such *context-sensitive* elements, it can be used to make many different claims, some of which may be true and others false, depending on various features of the context of its use, in particular on when and by whom it is used. If our object-language is (a fragment of) German and the sentence is '*Es schneit hier*', then 'It is snowing here' has a very good claim to be

[89] 'Semantic', §8.
[90] See McGee, 'Semantic Paradoxes and Theories of Truth' (with a bibliography that identifies all the contributions referred to above), Martin (ed.), *Recent Essays on Truth and the Liar Paradox* (which contains several of these contributions), and the extended discussion of Kripke's 'Outline of a Theory of Truth' in Soames, *UT*, chs. 5–6.

a fine translation into our metalanguage. But we do not want our T-equivalence to look like this:

(?*) '*Es schneit hier*' is a true sentence in German iff it is snowing here,

because this tells us only under which condition contemporary utterances of the German sentence in our vicinity would express a truth. We can see to it that other times and other places are also covered if we follow Davidson and opt for relativization to utterers and times:[91]

(Rel) $\forall$u $\forall$t ('*Es schneit hier*' is a true sentence in German with respect to an utterer u and a time t iff there is a snowfall in the vicinity of u at t).

(Read the quantifier phrase 'there is' as tenseless, like its counterpart in the predicate calculus,[92] and suppress the entirely reasonable question, which structure (if any) Tarski would assign to feature-placing sentences with dummy 'it'.[93]) In pleading for the strategy exemplified by (Rel) we give up Criterion T in its original Tarskian format, for the open sentence after the 'iff' certainly does not translate the German sentence. Nevertheless, (Rel) goes at least some way to explain to a monolingual Englishman what '*Es schneit hier*' means in German. So, in a modified form, Tarski's translation requirement survives.

Occasionally, Tarski himself neglects the requirement stated in [T.9]. At two places he offers *The sentence 'it is snowing' is true iff it is snowing* as a homophonic T-equivalence.[94] This sounds right—and the German translation even more so, for the connective '*wenn*' is often used in the sense of 'when(ever)': we hear it as a universally quantified biconditional.[95]

According to [T.9] languages for which a strictly Tarskian truth-definition can be given are such that 'the sense of every expression is uniquely determined by its form'.[96] Obviously, natural languages do not meet this requirement. We cannot correctly specify the satisfaction-condition of the German open sentence '*x ist eine Bank*', which is *lexically ambiguous*, by saying

(??*) $\forall$y (y satisfies '*x ist eine Bank*' $\leftrightarrow$ y is a bank),

since no sloping side of a river satisfies the German open sentence. If we replace the ambiguous metalanguage predicate by (a hopefully unambiguous expression such as) 'is a monetary institution', we again obtain a false biconditional: benches satisfy the German open sentence, but no bench is a monetary

---

[91] Davidson, 'Truth and Meaning', 34; 'True to the Facts', 45.   [92] Cf. Ch. 5.2.
[93] Cf. above, p. 111–12.   [94] *WB*, 9 (156); '*Grundlegung*', 264 (404).
[95] Cf. Frege, '*Über Sinn und Bedeutung*', 43–4.   [96] *WB*, 20 (166).

institution. We could mark the 'monetary' reading of the German word by adding a subscript:

(Sub) $\forall$y (y satisfies 'x *ist eine Bank$_M$*' $\leftrightarrow$ y is a monetary institution).

But now we have a different object-language: so far, we have taken portions of German to be our object-languages, but '*Bank$_M$*' isn't a German word. Is there no way to specify the satisfaction-conditions of an ambiguous object-language predicate φ unless there happens to be a predicate in the metalanguage whose ambiguity exactly matches that of φ?[97] There might seem to be an easy way out. Why not give the satisfaction-conditions by using a disjunctive predicate? To be sure, if we offer something like

(Disj) $\forall$y (y satisfies 'x *ist eine Bank*' $\leftrightarrow$ y is a monetary institution, or
                      y is a bench),

we do not comply with Criterion S, since the predicate on the right-hand side of (Disj) certainly does not translate the German predicate, but (Disj) goes at least some way to explain to a monolingual Englishman what 'x *ist eine Bank*' means in German. So again, in a watered-down form, Tarski's translation requirement seems to be respected. But systematically (Disj) is fatally flawed, for it delivers incorrect truth-conditions for many '*Bank*' sentences. The German sentence '*Jede Bank ist ein Geldinstitut*', for example, can be used to express a truth, but 'Everything that is a monetary institution or a bench is a monetary institution' expresses a falsehood.

[3] Natural languages do not seem to fulfil Tarski's demand, raised in [T.7] above, that '[for the sake of a recursive definition we must be able to specify] the way in which the truth or falsity of composite sentences depends on the truth or falsity of the simpler ones contained in them'. There is, for example, what Davidson calls 'the whole unholy array of attitude-attributing locutions'.[98] Thus

(P)   Ben believes that George Eliot was a man

seems to be a paradigm case of a composite sentence whose truth-value does not depend on that of the simpler sentence (the content clause) contained in it. But perhaps we suffer from a kind of optical illusion when we see an embedded

---

[97] Davidson accepts such dependence on sheer luck with equanimity in 'Truth and Meaning', 30. Ambiguity troubles with *homophonic* T-equivalences are discussed in Kathryn Pyne Parsons, 'Ambiguity and the Truth Definition'.   [98] Davidson, 'Moods and Performances', 118.

sentence in (P). This was suggested in 1935 by Tadeusz Kotarbiński (with whom Tarski had studied philosophy at Warsaw University). Kotarbiński claimed that all singular 'psychological enunciations', as he calls them, have the logical form 'A Vs thus: p', where the colon after the prologue isn't a complementizer, but an inscriptional surrogate for a pointing gesture. Kotarbiński argues:

> [The] two sentence-components of a psychological enunciation do not form a sentence, just as . . . any enunciation of the form: 'p, hence q' is not a sentence, though it is a whole consisting of sentences. . . . And if singular psychological enunciations are all of this kind the conclusion follows that they are wholes which are not sentences and which hence are not subject to the classification into true or false enunciations. But, nevertheless, there are psychological truths! And there are errors in psychology! Of course. Essentially, however, what is subjected in these cases to logical evaluation is the pre-colon part of the psychological enunciation: 'John sees thus' . . . and the like. This is in full harmony with the fact that the truth of a psychological enunciation (strictly speaking, of its pre-colon part) does not depend on the truth or falsity of the post-colon part. Whether indeed it is light or not is irrelevant for the truth . . . or for the falsity of the sentence that John sees thus. ('The Fundamental Ideas of Pansomatism', 498.)[99]

(I quote from Tarski's translation of his teacher's article.) The example is rather infelicitous: 'sees that' is factive, so the truth-value of 'it is light' is by no means irrelevant for the truth-value of 'John sees that it is light.' The context of our quotation shows that Kotarbiński treats this sentence as if it meant the same as 'It looks to John as if it is light,' paratactically construed as 'It looks to John thus: it is light.'

Some decades later, Davidson's treatment of *oratio obliqua* and attitude reports follows the same lines.[100] He, too, suggests that the logical form of sentences like (P) is to be represented as a parataxis:

(Par)   Ben believes that (☞). George Eliot was a man.

The prologue of (Par), we are told, expresses a truth in the mouth of utterer u at time t if and only if the utterance designated by the demonstrative as used by u at t has the same content as one of Ben's beliefs. By (somewhat playfully) describing the switch from (P) to (Par) as no more than a change in punctuation, Davidson gave to many readers the false impression that the paratactic strategy depends on a rather parochial feature of English, i.e. on the fact that in English the complementizer 'that' happens to be spelt the same as the demonstrative 'that'.[101] If you hear the German translations of (P) and (Par), you may

---

[99] Cf. Kotarbiński, '*Grundgedanken des Pansomatismus*', 249–50.

[100] Davidson, 'On Saying That', 104–8, 'Thought and Talk', 165–7, 'Reply to Foster', 176–8.

[101] Rumfitt has shown that the impression of dependence is false: 'Content and Context', 433–8.

think that in German there is a similar coincidence, but you will recognize your mistake as soon as you look at the written versions.[102] Anyway, translations of (P) and (Par) into Polish, French, or Latin will not contain the same orthographic word first as complementizer and then as demonstrative. Hence Kotarbiński's 'thus' is philosophically less misleading than Davidson's 'that': the fate of the paratactic strategy does not hang by the thread of English spelling.[103]

What matters is that in (Par) there is no composite sentence which offends against the Tarskian demand of extensionality. The demonstrative in an utterance of the prologue designates a further sentential utterance the speaker is just about to produce. If this further utterance had been of a different sentence, the prologue might not have been true. But a replacement of 'George Eliot' in (Par) by 'Mary Ann Evans' would be misdescribed as an exchange of co-designative singular terms *within one composite sentence*. It is more like the truth-value affecting operation that goes on when somebody says, 'This is my favourite colour', and the sample pointed to is either exchanged by one of a different colour or changes in colour.

Many objections have been raised against this ingenious proposal, and obviously this is not the place to weigh up all the pros and cons. Let me just present what I take to be the strongest objection. Consider the following argument:

(A1)   Many believe that the earth moves.
        Therefore, many believe that the earth moves.

(A1) exemplifies the schema of arguments by repetition, 'A ∴ A', hence it is formally valid. So a fortiori it is valid; that is, it is impossible for the premiss to be true when the conclusion is not true. Now compare the paratactic counterpart of (A1),

(A2)   Many believe that (☞). The earth moves.
        Therefore, many believe that (☞). The earth moves.

If (A2) is understood as Davidson wants it to be understood, the objects designated by the two demonstratives are two different utterances (inscriptions). Let

---

[102] Of course there may very well be an *etymological* connection between the complementizer '*dass*' and the demonstrative '*das (dies)*' in German, as Meinong and many linguists (not only of his time) conjecture for: cf. *Über Annahmen*, 48. The same holds, *mutatis mutandis*, for English—according to the *Oxford English Dictionary*, to whose authority Davidson needlessly appeals in support of his paratactics. The pertinent *OED* entry is quoted and criticized in Rundle, *GP*, 283–5.

[103] It has to be admitted, though, that a Kontarbińskian use of 'thus' in English would be rather strained. 'A Vs thus' is more naturally instantiated by sentences like 'Alec sings (speaks, walks) thus' where the utterance may be an overture to an imitation of Alec's *manner* of singing etc. which the utterer is on the verge of producing.

us call them 'Supra' and 'Infra'. If the demonstratives designate Supra and Infra respectively, then the truth of the premiss depends on the existence of Supra, and the truth of the conclusion depends on the existence of Infra. Since there is no necessity that Supra and Infra co-exist, we can conceive of circumstances in which Supra exists without Infra. But under such circumstances the premiss would be true, while the conclusion would not be true. So (A2) is not valid, let alone formally valid.[104] Now even if the Kotarbiński–Davidson treatment of attitude reports and indirect speech could be defended against these, and many other, objections, much labour would be still left for those who want to show that *all* features of natural languages, which at least prima facie resist the application of Tarski's recursive machinery, can be tamed.[105]

4.1.5 *Explanatory ambitions*

Even if all obstacles which stand in the way of providing, say, in English a Tarski-style definition of 'true' for German (purged of its semantic vocabulary) were overcome, the question would remain how much light this would shed on the Socratic question we are concerned with in this book, 'What is truth?'

[1] We are often told that Tarski defends, or at least tries to defend, a correspondence conception of truth.[106] Tarski himself seems to share this view of his work. But perhaps appearances are deceptive. So let us carefully weigh the evidence. In 1932, announcing his forthcoming Polish monograph in the journal of the Viennese Academy of Sciences, Tarski appeals to a correspondence formula and mentions his philosophical source of inspiration:

The basic problem is the construction of a methodologically correct and materially adequate [*meritorisch*[107] *adäquat*] definition of 'true sentence'. This definition should preserve

---

[104] This objection is due to Burge ('On Davidson's "Saying That"', 200–5). I have tried to strengthen Burge's case by removing the name 'Galileo' from the two sample arguments, since it is context-sensitive. I take the objection to be lethal *for Davidson's own interpretation* of the paratactic formulations. In his 'Reply to WK', 22–3, Davidson concedes Burge's diagnosis of (A2) without confessing defeat. So he must bite the bullet and maintain that (A1) is not formally valid. Like Burge, I cannot help wondering whether *any* argument in natural language is formally valid if (A1) isn't. (Needless to say, I no longer think that my attempt, in 'Truth, Meaning and Logical Form', 13–5, to defuse his objection really works.) In Ch. 6.1.2 I shall revisit the paratactic account, and then I shall propose a 'propositionalist' reading of Davidson's paratactic formulations which, though hardly to his liking, would no longer fall victim to Burge's objection.   [105] Cf. p. 125 above for a list of troublemakers.

[106] See the list of defendants and opponents of these claims in Kirkham, *ThT*, 170. On the pro side of that list Simons and Woleński should be entered, and Wiggins on the contra side.

[107] According to my dictionary, this old-fashioned word means MERITORIOUS (*verdienstlich*), hence it is not easy to make sense of it here—apart from the fact, duly registered by the translator, that it occupies the position of '*sachlich*' ('materially') in Tarski's other writings.

the intuitions which are contained in the so-called classical conception of the concept of truth [*Auffassung des Wahrheitsbegriffs*], i.e. in the conception according to which 'true' means the same as 'agreeing with reality [*mit der Wirklichkeit übereinstimmend*]'.

More precisely, I consider a definition of truth to be adequate with respect to a given language if it implies all statements [*Thesen*] of the type: 'x is true if and only if p', where 'p' is to be replaced by any sentence of the language under investigation and 'x' by any individual name of that sentence. ('*Wahrheit*', 615; [T.10])

Thus Tarski elucidates the 'intuitions which are contained in the so-called classical conception' with the help of Criterion T.[108] In a footnote to the first paragraph of [T.10], he recommends the analysis of various conceptions of truth in Kotarbiński's book *Elements of the Theory of Knowledge, Formal Logic, and the Methodology of the Sciences*. In his monograph he declares:

[T]hroughout this work I shall be concerned exclusively with grasping the intentions which are contained in the so-called classical conception of truth ('true—agreeing with reality [*mit der Wirklichkeit übereinstimmend*]'. (*WB*, 5 (153); [T.11])

To this he adds a footnote: 'Cf. Kotarbiński, *Elements*, p. 126 (in writing the present article I have repeatedly consulted this book and in many points adhered to the terminology there suggested).' He will keep on referring to this book for many years. In the chapter which is pertinent here, Kotarbiński argues that truth talk is at bottom talk about persons thinking truly, and he pleads for what he calls the *classical* understanding of this adverb:

In the classical interpretation, 'truly' [in 'Jan thinks truly'] means the same as 'in agreement with reality' ... Jan thinks truly if and only if Jan thinks that things are thus and so, and things are indeed thus and so. (*Elements*, 106–7.)

When is Jan thinking truly (that is, in agreement with reality) that there are bears in the Carpathians? Just in case Jan is thinking that there are bears in the Carpathians, *and* there really are bears in the Carpathians. Thus Kotarbiński elucidates the correspondence formula by means of a *conjunction*. In Chapter 6.2.2, I shall have ample reason to return to Kotarbiński's reflections on the classical doctrine (and to quote them at greater length), since they point in the direction of the 'modest account of truth' which I shall explain and try to defend in that chapter. For the time being, let us just register that the author who inspired Tarski's appeal to a correspondence formula explains this formula not only without any appeal to the notion of facts, but in thoroughly non-relational terms.

---

[108] Here and in [T.12] (as well as in the expositions of his theory in 'Semantic', and 'Proof') Tarski assumes for simplicity's sake that the metalanguage is an expansion of the object-language.

Let us turn to the next piece of evidence. In a paper read in Paris in 1935 Tarski says:

We regard the truth of a sentence as its 'agreement with reality [*Übereinstimmung mit der Wirklichkeit*]'. This rather vague phrase, which can certainly lead to various misunderstandings and has done so repeatedly in the past, is interpreted as follows.... We shall accept as valid [*gültig*] every statement of the form: 'x is true if and only if p', where 'p' is to be replaced by any sentence of the language under investigation and 'x' by any individual name of that sentence. (*'Grundlegung'*, 264 (404); [T.12])

As in [T.10] the correspondence formula is elucidated with the help of T-equivalences.[109]

Tarski's most extensive remarks on the so-called classical conception are to be found in his 1944 paper. This is not surprising, because this time, writing for *Philosophy and Phenomenological Research*, he is primarily addressing a philosophical audience. He says:

We should like our definition to do justice to the intuitions which adhere to the *classical Aristotelian conception of truth*—intuitions which find their expression in the well-known words of Aristotle's Metaphysics... [110]

If we wished to adapt ourselves to modern philosophical terminology, we could perhaps [!] express this conception by means of the familiar formula: *The truth of a sentence consists in its agreement with (or correspondence to) reality.* (For a theory of truth which is to be based upon the latter formulation the term 'correspondence theory' has been suggested.)

If, on the other hand, we should decide to extend the popular usage of the term 'designate' by applying it not only to names, but also to sentences, and if we agreed to speak of the designata of sentences as 'states of affairs', we could possibly [!] use for the same purpose the following phrase: *A sentence is true if it designates an existing state of affairs.*

However, all these formulations can lead to various misunderstandings, for none of them is sufficiently precise and clear (though this applies much less to the original Aristotelian formulation than to either of the others); at any rate, none of them can be considered a satisfactory definition of truth. It is up to us to look for a more precise expression of our intuitions. (*'Semantic'* §3; bracketed insertions are mine; [T.13])

And then he gives 'A Criterion for the Material Adequacy of the Definition', Criterion T. In a footnote the reader is again referred to Kotarbiński's *Elements*, 'so far available only in Polish'.

---

[109] Kokoszyńska follows Tarski in taking compliance with Criterion T to be a sufficient condition for conformity with the spirit of the correspondence formula: '*Über den absoluten Wahrheitsbegriff*...', 151, cf. 143.

[110] Tarski then goes on to quote the monosyllabic pronouncement from the beginning of *Met.* IV 7 which we sounded out on pp. 95–102. Aristotle's dictum is also quoted by Kokoszyńska, ibid., and in the English translation of *WB*, at 155 n. 2. On p. 111 we discussed a passage from Tarski's 'Proof' which echoes [T.13]. Only in that passage does Tarski come round to saying *why* he thinks that even the Aristotelian explanation 'leaves much to be desired'.

Let me briefly comment on the somewhat irritating third paragraph of |T.13|. When reading the first if-clause, one might get the impression that Tarski is alluding to Frege's use of '*bedeuten*' or to Carnap's use of 'designate',[111] but this does not fit the second if-clause, for in Frege the *Bedeutungen* of sentences are truth-values, and in Carnap sentences are said to designate propositions. As to the formula then non-committally presented, neither here nor anywhere else does Tarski talk of existing states of affairs as something true sentences *correspond* with.[112] (Some friends of the category of states of affairs will find Tarski's qualifier 'existing' less than happy: they tend to say rather that 'there are' states of affairs, roughly half of them 'obtain', and those that do obtain are 'facts'.[113])

In taking stock let us put to use some observations and distinctions made in Chapter 3. First, Tarski likes Aristotle's way of expressing the so-called classical conception of truth best, but we found Aristotle silent on 'obtaining states of affairs' (or 'facts'). So Tarski's very few uses of the locution 'states of affairs' hardly make him an ally of (either sort of) Cambridge Correspondence.[114] Secondly, the correspondence formula Tarski uses most of the time is firmly rooted in the tradition of object-based correspondence. But Tarski takes himself to be at one with Kotarbiński's reading of this formula, and Kotarbiński explains it in non-relational terms. This suggests that Tarski isn't a friend of Object- or Event-based Correspondence either. Thirdly, Tarski is convinced that the semantic conception of truth is 'but a modernized form' of the classical conception,[115] and he keeps on declaring Criterion T to be the clearest articulation of the intuitions which underlie the correspondence formula.[116] But Criterion T does not mention any relation between words and something else. Fourthly Tarski believes that *a definition's conformity with the classical conception can be ensured wholly by its compliance with Criterion T*. But we saw in the first section of this chapter that a definition of 'true' for a given language can comply with Criterion T without

[111] Frege, '*Über Sinn und Bedeutung*'; Carnap, *IS*, §12.

[112] Cf. 'Semantic', §5, where 'designates' is replaced by 'describes' and the non-committal 'possibly' is repeated, and §17.

[113] Such metaphysicians distinguish between the existence of a state of affairs and its obtaining just as Plato and Platonists distinguish between the existence of a universal and its being instantiated. Cf. my *Abstrakte Gegenstände*, 96–101, and the remarks on Meinong above on p. 7.

[114] They are to be found in our extracts [T.1[b]] and [T.13], in 'Proof' 402 and in the mistranslation of a passage in *WB*, which I shall point out in Ch. 6.2.2. In ontology Kotarbiński pleaded for a materialist variety of Reism ('Thingism'): cf. his paper 'The Fundamental Ideas of Pansomatism', 488–93, and below Ch. 6.2.2. For a Reist non-things like obtaining states of affairs *alias* facts look very suspicious. This attitude may have influenced Tarski (as Woleński, *Essays*, 174, suggests), but then, from the Reist point of view, sets are also creatures of darkness, and yet Tarski takes them to be indispensable.

[115] That's the way he puts it in 'Semantic', §14.

[116] As we saw in Ch. 3.5.1, this is an error (which Quine and Davidson have perpetuated).

specifying any relation between words and something else. This is entirely consistent: after all, *conformity with the classical conception* does not entail relationality if that conception is spelled out along Kotarbińskian lines.

Popper triumphantly presents quotations [T.11] and [T.12] as clearly confirming his claim that Tarski intended to rehabilitate the 'intuitive idea of truth as correspondence to the facts'.[117] Now this formula, which occurs in neither of these passages, speaks collectively of 'the facts', and can be read as not seriously dyadic. But this is not Popper's reading. He maintains that in T-equivalences we 'speak about two things: statements; and the facts to which they refer'.[118] This could be correct at best for those T-equivalences that mention *true* sentences. But actually it isn't correct at all: 'facts' as something 'referred to' by whole sentences (if true) do not appear in Criterion T at all, nor do they turn up in the Tarskian definitions of truth-predicates for our three sample languages.

For some time, Davidson, too, maintained that 'by appealing to Tarski's semantic conception of truth we can defend a ... purified version of the correspondence theory of truth'.[119] But he praised Tarski's theory precisely for *not* making any use of the category of facts. In 1969 Davidson was convinced that

the semantic conception of truth as developed by Tarski deserves to be called a correspondence theory because of the part played by the concept of satisfaction; for clearly what has been done is that the property of being true has been explained, and non-trivially, in terms of a relation between language and something else. ('True to the Facts', 48)

What figures as 'something else' are not facts, but objects (or sequences of objects, if the language for which 'true' is defined via 'satisfies' contains many-place predicates). So this would make Tarski a partisan of what I have called Object-based Correspondence (with rather peculiar objects when the language contains polyadic predicates). But as we saw when defining 'true' for our sample languages L_1 and L_2, the auxiliary concept of satisfaction is not always needed when one wants to give a definition of a truth-predicate along Tarski's lines. Whether it does enter the definition depends on the complexity of the language for which 'true' is to be defined. So, with respect to some languages 'true' is not a narrowly semantic predicate: it is not always defined in terms of a relation

---

[117] Popper's reading of Tarski was criticized by Susan Haack in 1976; the quotation is from his 1979 reply (if I can call it that): see Bibliography.

[118] Popper, 'Truth, Rationality, and the Growth of Scientific Knowledge', 224.

[119] Davidson, 'True to the Facts', 54.

between language and something else.[120] Davidson himself has come to emphasize another problem for the assimilation of satisfaction to correspondence. He asks us to consider Tarski's own definition of 'true' for a complex quantificational language:

Truth is defined on the basis of satisfaction: a sentence of the object language is true if and only if it is satisfied by every sequence of the objects over which the variables of quantification of the object language range. Take 'corresponds to' as 'satisfies' and you have defined truth as correspondence. The oddity of the idea is evident from the counterintuitive and contrived nature of the entities to which sentences 'correspond' and from the fact that *all true sentences would correspond to the same entities*. ('Structure', 302 n.; my italics)[121]

Thus what truths are satisfied by is more like The Universe or The Great Fact than like the discriminating facts of Cambridge Correspondence.[122] So once again the case for Tarski's alleged rehabilitation of a correspondence theory of truth is not very strong.

[2] Up to now we have taken it for granted that Tarski, even if not an adherent of a correspondence theory of truth in any of the senses explored in Chapter 3, is at least in the same line of business as the proponents of such a theory. That is to say, we have assumed that Tarski really went in for explaining or analysing the concept of truth. Davidson, for one, clearly took this to be Tarski's project when he said:

Tarski intended to analyse the concept of truth ... (*ITI*, xiv)

This raises at least *two questions*: first, did Tarski really *intend* to do that? Secondly, did he actually *do* it?

In the late 1980s Davidson arrived at an unequivocally negative answer to the second question, thereby denying a basic assumption of his early paper 'True to the Facts':

Correspondence theories have always been conceived as providing an explanation or analysis of truth, and this a Tarski-style theory of truth certainly does not do. ('Afterthoughts', 155)

---

[120] Davidson concedes this in his 'In Defence of Convention T', 67, and in the Introduction to his *ITI*. xv. Cf. also 'Epistemology and Truth', 180; 'Structure', 296. As to the question whether the detour through the subsidiary concept of satisfaction is required for a Tarski-style truth-definition if the expressive power of the language under consideration approximates that of a natural language, cf. the reflections on [T.7] on p. 219 below.

[121] Cf. Davidson, 'Folly', 268; 'Reply to Neale', 669; 'The Centrality of Truth', 110 (= 'Truth Rehabilitated', 69).

[122] For The Universe, cf. Ch. 3.5.3, p. 160; for The Great Fact, cf. Ch. 3.3.3 on Davidson's Slingshot.

Now he feels obliged to play down Tarski's repeated invocations of the 'classical conception' as rather unfortunate 'nods in the direction of a correspondence theory'.[123] Perhaps Davidson's statements about Tarski are both correct: perhaps Tarski had the intention ascribed to him, but unfortunately he failed to achieve his goal. Let us start with the first question posed above.

It is beyond reasonable doubt that Tarski really did want to catch hold of the meaning of 'true' as it is used in ordinary truth-ascriptions.[124] If he had been intending to *stipulate* a new sense for the old term, he would be a bit of an impostor when in [T.2], at the beginning of his monograph, he presents himself as concerned with one of the 'classical questions of philosophy'.[125] Throughout [T.10–13], Tarski keeps on averring that he wants to remain faithful to (what Kotarbiński called) the 'classical conception of truth', and he states repeatedly that T-equivalences enshrine what is right in this conception. When he classifies T-equivalences as 'partial definitions', he certainly does not take them to be stipulative, nor does he assign such a status to non-partial definitions of 'true' for languages with infinitely many sentences:

[T-equivalences] explain in a precise way, in accordance with linguistic usage [*Sprachgebrauch*], the meaning [*Bedeutung*] of the phrases 'x is a true sentence' which occur in them. Not much more in principle is to be demanded of a general definition of true sentence [sc. for the language under investigation] than that it should satisfy the usual conditions of methodological correctness and include all partial definitions of this type as special cases; that it should be, so to speak, their logical product. (*WB*, 45 (187); [T.14])

Admittedly, there is some lack of clarity about the claim that a 'general definition' of a truth-predicate for a language with infinitely many sentences 'is' a conjunction of infinitely many 'partial definitions',[126] but surely it leaves no room for maintaining that such a 'general definition' is just a stipulation, and hence no longer obliged to capture, as far as possible, the meaning of 'true' in ordinary truth-ascriptions. Requiring 'material adequacy' of a definition just is putting it under such an obligation. (It makes no sense to demand of a stipulative definition that it be materially adequate.) Tarski made this unambiguously

---

[123] Davidson, 'Folly', 268; cf. 'Epistemology and Truth', 182 n. Wiggins concurs: see his 'Meaning', 24 n. 29; 'Postscript 3', 333, 338.

[124] The observations in the next few paragraphs are meant to refute Etchemendy's claim that a Tarski-style truth-definition 'is intended as a stipulative definition' ('Tarski', 58). In this respect I side with Davidson: see his 'Structure', esp. 291.

[125] He repeats this claim at the very end of his monograph: *WB*, 132 (266–7).

[126] Cf. *WB*, 100 n. (238 n.), 116–17 (253), 'Semantic', §4.

clear when he wrote in a mathematical paper:

Now the question arises whether the definitions just constructed (the formal rigour of which raises no objection) are also adequate materially; that is, do they in fact grasp the current meaning of the notion as it is known intuitively [*le sens courant et intuitivement connu de la notion*]? Properly understood, this question contains no problem of a purely mathematical nature, but it is nevertheless of capital importance for our considerations. ('*Sur les ensembles définissables de nombres réels*', 538 (128–9); [T.15])

It has been said that Tarski 'grew bolder later in life'.[127] This may very well be so, but the following assertion he made in his 1944 paper[128] provides no evidence for it:

The desired definition does not aim to specify the meaning of a familiar word used to denote a novel notion; on the contrary, it aims to catch hold of the actual meaning of an old notion. ('Semantic' §1; [T.16])

This had been his intention all along.

Passages like [T.14–16)] do not only refute the contention that a Tarskian definition of a truth-predicate is a stipulation; they also provide evidence against the claim, made by Quine and Wiggins,[129] that such a definition is only meant to determine the *extension* of the definiendum.

'Being a mathematician (as well as a logician, and perhaps a philosopher of a sort)',[130] Tarski sometimes shows symptoms of fatigue caused by philosophical discussions of the concept of truth (as continued in this book). As to 'non-classical conceptions of truth', he complains that so far none of them has ever been put forward 'in an intelligible and unequivocal form', but he wants them to be submitted to systematic study, too, and occasionally he seems to think that the 'classical conception' and its 'non-classical' rivals (if they were ever clearly articulated) might turn out to be equally legitimate.[131] One may wonder[132] whether this can really be his considered position.

Orthogonal to the somewhat nebulous pluralism just mentioned there is a clear-cut pluralism which is essential to the semantic conception. This pluralism is already enforced by Tarski's taking type-sentences to be the primary truth-value bearers: 'There will be no question at all here of giving a single general definition of the term ['true sentence'].'[133] Thus the problem of defining 'true' is immediately

---

[127] Kirkham, *ThT*, 144.   [128] Cf. also the quotation from 'Semantic', §9 in [T.3] above.

[129] Quine, 'Notes', 132, 137; Wiggins, 'Replies', sect. 59.   [130] Tarski about Tarski: 'Semantic', §23.

[131] 'Semantic', §14, cf. §18.

[132] As does Manuel García-Carpintero, 'What is a Tarskian Definition of Truth?', §1.

[133] From [T.2] above.

transformed into the problem of developing a general strategy for defining different truth-predicates for different languages.

Tarski does not deny that there are other entities that truth can sensibly be ascribed to, but he assigns priority to sentences:

Of course, the fact that we are interested here primarily in the notion of truth for sentences does not exclude the possibility of a subsequent extension of this notion to other kinds of objects. ('Semantic', §2; [T.17])

If our workaday truth-predicate is primarily applied to *propositions* rather than sentences (as I shall argue in the next chapter), it does not have the *same* sense as any of the predicates Tarski tries to explain. Of course, there is a connection between sentential truth and propositional truth: provided that S in L is free of ambiguity and of context-sensitivity, S is a true sentence in L if and only if what is literally said when S is used as a sentence of L is true. Hence one can respect the priority of propositions and yet provide predicates with the same extension as Tarskian truth-predicates, namely 'is a sentence in L that can be used to say literally something true', or less laboriously, 'is a sentence in L that expresses a truth'.

The need for a plurality of truth-predicates does not yet prevent us from hoping for a definition of the form 'For all sentences x, for all languages y, x is a true sentence in y iff...x...y...' (such as '...iff x expresses in y a proposition that corresponds to a fact'). But this hope is dashed by Tarski's diagnosis of the semantic antinomies. The ordinary English predicate 'true' (or 'expresses a truth') can be applied to Polish sentences as well as to English sentences which themselves contain the word 'true', and it can be used in wild speculations about the first sentence to be uttered, in a language none of us understands, on the top of Mount Everest in the year 4000. Tarski holds this unrestricted use of 'true' responsible for the semantic antinomies, and it is because of this diagnostic conviction that he does not aim at an explanation of 'true' that is completely faithful to its ordinary usage. Therefore we are not to expect an explanation of an unrestricted predicate, 'true in L' (or 'expresses a truth in L'), for *variable* L.

So, on the one hand, Tarski does not want to graft a new meaning upon an old term, and on the other hand, the explanation he intends to give is decidedly revisionary. He is acutely aware that this makes his explanatory target Janus-faced:

The explanation which we wish to give...is, to an extent, of mixed character. What will be offered here should be treated in principle as a suggestion of a definite way of using the term 'true', but the offering will be accompanied by the belief that it is in agreement with the prevailing usage of this term in everyday language. ('Proof' 402; [T.18])

Now there is a way of explaining a predicate which combines revisionism and conservatism. Carnap called it *explication*. Putting 'true' aside for a moment, let 'free action' be our *explicandum*. Arguably, the meaning of this predicate in the mouth of ordinary folk is such that no action can correctly be called free if determinism is true. Compatibilists can be seen as offering an *explicatum*, which has the following features: whether an action can rightly be said to be free in the sense of the explicatum is independent of the truth or otherwise of determinism, but the meaning of the explicatum is near enough to that of the explicandum so that it can play the role we ordinarily give the predicate 'free action' when we adjudicate questions of moral responsibility and punishment.[134] The kind of explanation of truth-predicates Tarski is aiming at is also best characterized as explication in Carnap's sense, and Carnap himself actually did characterize it thus.[135] For each language L, the Tarskian explicatum, the definiens of 'is a true sentence in L', does not give rise to paradox, it applies to all non-pathological instances of the explicandum and to nothing else, but (if Tarski is right) its meaning is so close to the meaning of the pre-theoretical explicandum that the explicatum may replace the explicandum in all theoretical contexts where truth-talk is legitimately required.

So much for Tarski's intentions. Let us now take up the second question posed above.

4.1.6 *Explanatory success?*

Did Tarski actually do what he set out to do? Did he achieve his goal of explicating various substitution-instances of 'is a true sentence in L (an L-sentence that expresses a truth)'? I shall now rehearse four arguments for a negative answer to this question.

(I) *The Argument from Truth-conditional Semantics*

In the late 1960s Davidson's illuminating use of the Tarskian machinery in the philosophy of language began to engender bright expectations for the theory of meaning even among those who had always despaired of its future:

What goes by the name of semantics falls into two domains, the theory of reference and the theory of meaning. Truth is on one side of the boundary, meaning on the other. The

---

[134] Cf. Frank Jackson, *From Metaphysics to Ethics*, 44–5.
[135] Carnap, *Meaning and Necessity*, 7–8, and *Logical Foundations of Probability*, 1–8. Cf. Soames, *UT*, 98–9, 238.

two domains are conspicuously distinct, but still there is this fundamental connection between them: you have given all the meanings when you have given the truth-conditions of all the sentences. Davidson took the connection to heart and drew this conclusion: the way to develop a systematic account of meanings for a language is to develop Tarski's recursive definition of truth for that language. To the notoriously flimsy theory of meaning, this idea offers new hope: the discipline of Tarski's theory of truth. (Quine, 'Reply to Davidson', 333)[136]

Dummett was the first to notice a tension between the project of giving a truth-conditional account of meanings for a language and the project of giving a Tarskian truth-definition for that language. He argues that such a definition can only serve to interpret the sentences of a language if it fails as a *definition*:

[A Tarski-style] truth-definition, which lays down the conditions under which an arbitrary sentence of the object-language is true, cannot simultaneously provide us with a grasp of the meaning of each sentence, unless, indeed, we already know in advance what the point of the predicate so defined is supposed to be. But, if we do know in advance the point of introducing the predicate 'true', then we know something about the concept of truth expressed by that predicate which is not embodied in that, or any other, truth-definition. (*TOE*, xxi)[137]

The question is: can the Tarskian definition of a truth-predicate for a given language L simultaneously supply (i) a complete explication of this predicate and (ii) an interpretation of the sentences of L? And the answer is, No. If it is to play role (i), for which Tarski intended it and for which the title 'definition' is suitable, it relies on an antecedent understanding of L. On the other hand, if the Tarskian definition is to play role (ii), for which Davidson appropriates it and for which the title 'theory' would be far more suitable, it relies on an antecedent understanding of 'true'. (Davidson has long since conceded Dummett's point: 'My mistake [in "Truth and Meaning"] was to think that we could both take a Tarski truth definition as telling us all we need to know about truth *and* use the definition to describe [to give a meaning-theory for] an actual language.'[138] This is like having an equation with two unknowns and trying to solve both simultaneously: it is only by fixing one unknown that we can solve the other.[139])

---

[136] Cf. Quine, 'On the Very Idea of a Third Dogma', 38.

[137] Cf. Dummett, *FPL*, 459–62, *LBM*, 68–72, *OAP*, 16–18; 'Is the Concept of Truth Needed for Semantics?', 5, 11. The germs of this argument are already to be found in his 1959 paper 'Truth', 7. Variants of the Dummettian argument from truth-conditional semantics have been endorsed by Strawson, 'Meaning and Truth', 180; Etchemendy, 'Tarski' §1.2, and Soames, *UT*, 102–7.

[138] Davidson, 'Structure' 286. He makes the same criticism of his paper 'Truth and Meaning' already in *ITI*, xiv, 134, 150, 173, 204.   [139] The comparison is due to Horwich, *Truth*, 68.

Look again at Quine's praise of the Davidsonian programme. It is certainly no accident that he speaks of 'Tarski's *recursive* definition of truth for the language' for which we would like to have a 'systematic account of meanings': it is due to its recursive character that Davidson's account of meanings for a language L (at least apparently) explains how mastery of a finite set of linguistic elements and constructions can generate a limitless grasp of conditions of truth for the sentences of L. But a Tarski-style truth-definition is not necessarily recursive: if the language under study is a code, for example L_1, then the truth-definition, e.g. our (Df. 1), is non-recursive, and, measured by Tarski's standards, it is none the worse for that. If the language contains infinitely many sentences, then he does indeed offer a recursive definition. But remember the reason he gave in [T.7]: 'Whenever a language contains infinitely many sentences, the definition constructed [in the style of (Df. 1)] would have to consist of infinitely many words, and such sentences cannot be formulated either in the metalanguage or in any other language.' When he wrote his monograph, Tarski did not seriously entertain the possibility of infinite disjunctions in the metalanguage.[140] If he had allowed for this possibility, then he would have accepted definitions in the style of (Df. 1) even for languages with infinitely many sentences, and then neither the recursive technique nor the detour through satisfaction would have been needed. Etchemendy rightly takes this to show how far the project of truth-conditional semantics was from Tarski's mind:[141] a list-like definition of 'true in L', whatever the length of the list, does not highlight the compositional features of L, hence it does not even seem to illuminate our mastery of L.

The Argument from Truth-conditional Semantics is only a *conditional* refutation of the claim that Tarski's alleged explicatum can replace the explicandum in all theoretical contexts where truth-talk is legitimately required:[142] *if* our understanding of the (declarative) sentences of a language L consists in our knowledge of their truth-conditions, *then* what these conditions are conditions *of* is not identical with what Tarski calls 'truth in L'. One could defend the claim by denying the consequent of this conditional (rather than affirming the antecedent). After all, there are quite a few philosophers who think that the programme of truth-conditional semantics is doomed to failure. But perhaps the claim of explicatory success is forced into unconditional surrender under the pressure of the second objection.

---

[140] In the late 1950s Tarski did enquire into the syntax and semantics of infinitary languages, but he did not connect these investigations with his work on truth. References are given in Etchemendy, 'Tarski', 56 n.   [141] Ibid., 56, 58.   [142] This point is emphasized in Soames, *UT*, 106–7.

(II) *The Argument from Modal Difference*

In order to set the stage for this argument (and those that are to follow) let us repeat the Tarskian definition of 'true' for our code:

(Df. 1)　$\forall$s (s is a true sentence in L_1 $\leftrightarrow$

　　　　((s = '*Die Erde bewegt sich*',　and the earth moves) or

　　　　(s = '*Der Mond ist rund*',　　and the moon is round))).

If we replace the predicate in

(Q^1)　'*Der Mond ist rund*' is true in L_1

by its Tarskian definiens, we obtain (using the same abbreviations as above)

(Q^2)　('*M*' = '*E*', and the earth moves) or ('*M*' = '*M*', and the moon is round).

At this point Hilary Putnam, who first formulated the modal objection, raises his finger:[143]

Now, pay close attention, please! This is just where, it seems to me, philosophers have been asleep at the opera for a long time!... The property to which Tarski gives the name 'true-in-$L_{[1]}$' is a property which the sentence '*Der Mond ist rund*' has in every possible world in which the moon is round, *including worlds in which what it means is that the moon is cubical*.... A property that the sentence '*Der Mond ist rund*' would have (as long as the moon is round) no matter how we might use or understand that sentence isn't even doubtfully or dubiously 'close' to the property of truth. It just isn't truth at all. ('A Comparison of Something With Something Else', 333)

As Etchemendy in his version of the Modal Objection puts it,[144] the modal status of (Q^1) differs sharply from that of (Q^2). If the sentence '*M*' had meant that the moon is *cubical*, then it might have been the case that (Q^1) even if the moon had not been round, and if the sentence '*M*' had meant that *the sun* is round, then it might not have been the case that (Q^1) even though the moon is round. None of this holds of (Q^2), which is provably equivalent to 'The moon is round'.

The proper reply to this objection[145] is based on our earlier observation that the languages for which Tarski-style truth-definitions are given are not individuated by their syntactical properties alone. The name 'L_1' fixes the semantic properties for the sentences of L_1 for all possible worlds. No language in which

---

[143] First in Putnam, 'On Truth', 316–18. I quote a rhetorically more effective formulation from a later paper. I have taken the liberty of replacing Putnam's snowbound example by my own.

[144] Etchemendy, 'Tarski', 61.

[145] Cf. the references to Wallace, Baldwin, Lewis, and Peacocke in Martin Davies, *Meaning, Quantification, Necessity*, 6, 28.

the orthographically individuated sentence 'M' does not mean that the moon is round is identical with L^1. (It is a necessary truth that 'M' means in L_1 that the moon is round, whereas it is a contingent truth that it means that among those who nowadays happen to use 'M'.) A sentence does not fall under the truth-predicate which is defined by (Df. 1) if it is understood otherwise than it has to be understood as a sentence of L_1. So, contrary to what Putnam says, the property to which Tarski gives the name 'truth in L_1' is *not* a property that the sentence 'M' would have (as long as the moon is round) no matter how we understand 'M'. Since there is no possible world in which 'M' is both a sentence that belongs to L_1 and a sentence that does not mean that the moon is round, the modal properties of (Q^1) are the same as those of (Q^2): in every possible world in which the moon is round it is the case not only that Q^2, but also that Q^1. So the modal objection does not show that Tarski failed to reach his explicatory goal. More powerful, I think, is the challenge provided by the third objection.

(III) *The Argument from Non-projectibility*

Let me introduce this objection by comparing (Df. 1) with the following universally quantified biconditional which exactly determines the extension of the predicate 'is a daughter of Laban':

(D) $\forall x\,(x$ is a daughter of Laban $\leftrightarrow (x = $ Rachel $\vee\, x = $ Leah$))$.

If you want to know under what conditions the predicate 'is a daughter of King Lear' applies to someone, (D) provides no help. The predicate on the left-hand side of (D) is a relational predicate that contains a name. A statement fixing the extension of such a predicate explains its meaning only if it can be projected to variants of the predicate where the embedded name has been replaced by a name of a different individual. This demand can easily be satisfied for the predicate in (D):

(D*) $\forall x\,(x$ is a daughter of Laban $\leftrightarrow (x$ is female $\&\, x$ was begotten by Laban$))$.

The universally quantified biconditional (D*) makes us see what Rachel and Cordelia have in common:

(D**) $\forall x \forall y\,(x$ is a daughter of $y \leftrightarrow (x$ is female $\&\, x$ was begotten by $y))$.

Now these complaints about (D) apply to our Tarskian definition of 'true in L_1' as well. This was first pointed out by Black.[146] (Df. 1) does not give us any hint as

---

[146] Black, 'The Semantic Definition of Truth', 256–7; cf. also Davidson, 'Structure', sect. I.

to when predicates like 'true in L_2', 'true in L_3', 'true in the language of the calculus of classes', etc. etc. hold of sentences. What we are told in (Df. 1) cannot be projected to variants of the predicate 'true in L_1' where the embedded name has been replaced by the name of another language. Tarski made it clear at the outset that, and why, we should not hope for a definition like (D**) for 'x is a true sentence in language y'. Nevertheless, we may reasonably want the contribution of 'true' to the meaning of, say, 'true in L_1' to be somehow displayed and illuminated by the definition of this predicate, and expect that having grasped that meaning should be helpful when it comes to understanding, e.g., 'true in L_3'.

The Non-projectibility Objection does not lose its force when the language for which a Tarski-style truth-definition is given isn't a code. If the definition is recursive without appealing to the auxiliary concept of satisfaction, it will always start with clauses that explain enumeratively what it is for a sentence to be (as one might say) *directly true* in the language under investigation. Thus a sentence is directly true in L_2 iff it is true in L_1:

(Df. 2*) $\forall s$ (s is a directly true sentence in $L_2 \leftrightarrow$
            $((s = \text{'}E\text{'}, \text{ and the earth moves) or}$
            $(s = \text{'}M\text{'}, \text{ and the moon is round}))$.

If the recursive definition makes a detour through satisfaction, the definition of the latter concept will always start with clauses that explain enumeratively what it is for an open sentence to be (as one might say) *directly satisfied* in the language under consideration. Thus in the case of our L_3:

(Df. 3b*) $\forall \varphi \, \forall y$ (φ is an open sentence in L_3 which is directly satisfied by $y \leftrightarrow$
            $((\varphi = \text{'}x \text{ } bewegt \text{ } sich\text{'}, \quad \text{and y moves) or}$
            $(\varphi = \text{'}x \text{ } ist \text{ } rund\text{'}, \qquad \text{and y is round}))$.

Furthermore, the definition of 'designates' for the names in L_3 was wholly enumerative. So again the Non-projectibility Objection applies: as Davidson puts it, 'by employing a finite and exhaustive list of basic cases in the course of defining satisfaction [or designation] (in terms of which truth is defined), [Tarski] necessarily failed to specify how to go on to further cases'.[147]

It might be suggested that Criterion T provides an adequate answer to the question of what Tarski's various truth-predicates have in common. It does indeed answer this question, but the answer is not adequate to our problem. Criterion T requires that the right-hand side of an instance of schema (T) translates the sentence mentioned on its left-hand side. But translation succeeds only

---

[147] Davidson, 'Structure', 287.

if it preserves truth-value: if a definition were to pair the German sentence '*Der Mond ist rund*' with the English sentence 'The moon is cubical', it would not be a definition of *truth* for (a fragment of) German.[148] So Criterion T implicitly appeals to an interlinguistic, pre-theoretical notion of truth, but it does nothing to elucidate this sense of 'true' in which both a German and an English sentence may be said to be true. We rely on this notion when we make an intuitively compelling claim such as:

(C)   If ('*Der Mond ist rund*' is true in L_G iff the moon is round), then for any sentence s in whatever language L, if s in L is a good translation of '*Der Mond ist rund*', then (s is true in L iff the moon is round).

It is an unpleasant feature of 'intuitively compelling claims' that their negations are sometimes declared to be intuitively compelling, too: '[Church] assumes that a sentence and its translation can't diverge in truth-value, but surely this is false. "He thinks that Phil's a groundhog" and "He thinks that Phil's a woodchuck" may diverge in truth-value; but they are both translated by the same sentence in French, which has but a single word for the woodchuck.'[149] Surely? Wouldn't a French (or German) translator, were she to realize that with respect to a certain context those belief-ascriptions diverge in truth-value, rather give up in despair than translate both by '*Il croit que Phil est une marmotte*' (or by '*Er glaubt, dass Phil ein Murmeltier ist*')? Here is the German revenge: '*Hänschen glaubt, dass sie bis Samstag bleibt, aber er glaubt nicht, dass sie bis Sonnabend bleibt*' (the boy thinks, reasonably enough, that '*Sonnabend*' means SUNDAY EVENING). Surely 'Little Hans believes that she will stay till Saturday but he doesn't believe that she will stay till Saturday' wouldn't do as a translation. The desperate translator could add a footnote, or she could enlarge the vocabulary of English by '*Sonnabend*'.[150]

So, back to (C). Note that the phrase 'true in L' in (C) contains 'L' as an (objectually) quantified variable one of whose values is named by 'L_G'. By contrast, Tarskian truth-predicates do not have 'L_G' in a position which can be (objectually) quantified into. In order to mark this difference notationally one could hyphenate the latter predicates (as many authors do): 'true-in-L_G', etc. The legitimate desire to have the sense of 'true' in the second pair of brackets in (C) displayed and illuminated is neither satisfied by any particular Tarskian

---

[148] See Peacocke, 'Truth Definitions and Actual Languages', 163; Davidson, 'The Centrality of Truth', 110 (= 'Truth Rehabilitated', 70).   [149] Mark Richard, 'Propositional Attitudes', 207.

[150] Cf. Burge, 'Belief and Synonymy', 122. More on this topic in Ch. 6.2.3.

truth-definition nor by the criterion of material adequacy they all meet.[151] The force of this objection is strengthened by the fourth argument.

(IV)   *The Argument from Epistemic Difference*

Let me again introduce the objection with the help of my philosophically unencumbered example from the Hebrew Bible. Since

(D) $\forall x \, (x \text{ is a daughter of Laban} \leftrightarrow (x = \text{Rachel} \lor x = \text{Leah}))$.

is true, the following sentences have the same truth-value:

(R^1)   Rachel is a daughter of Laban
(R^2) $(\text{Rachel} = \text{Rachel}) \lor (\text{Rachel} = \text{Leah})$.

If you know that R^1 you are justified in believing that Rachel is a close relative of Laban. But it is by no means the case that if you know that R^2 you are justified in believing that Rachel is a close relative of Laban. Knowing that R^2 does not entitle you to *any* belief about Rachel's family relations. But if (D) were an explanation of the meaning of 'is a daughter of Laban', then there could not be such an epistemic difference between (R^1) and (R^2). Hence (D) cannot lay claim to explaining what 'is a daughter of Laban' means. Again, (D*) contrasts starkly with (D): knowledge that Rachel is female and was begotten by Laban legitimizes the same beliefs as does knowledge that Rachel is a daughter of Laban.

Soames has given an argument to the effect that Tarski-style truth-definitions are in the same boat as (D).[152] According to our (Df. 1),

(S^1)   'M' is true in $L_1 \leftrightarrow$ the moon is round

has the same truth-value as

(S^2) $(('M' = 'E', \text{ \& the earth moves}) \text{ or } ('M' = 'M', \text{ \& the moon is round}))$
           $\leftrightarrow$ the moon is round.

---

[151] The Non-projectibility Objection is analogous to the objection Quine raised (in section 4 of his classical paper 'Two Dogmas of Empiricism') against Carnap's definition of 'analytic in L_n'. It is hard to understand why Quine thinks, or thought, that Tarski's definition of 'true in L_n' does not fall victim to the same kind of objection. His argument to this effect in 'Notes', 138 does not carry much conviction: see Marian David, 'Analyticity, Carnap, Quine, and Truth'. But critics should also take into account a concession Quine made many years later: 'Peacocke [in 'Truth Definitions and Actual Languages'] wants truth explicated in general, for arbitrary languages. He cites Dummett's analogy [cf. 'Truth', 2, 8, 19–20; *FPL*, 413]: to define winning for this and that kind of game is pointless except as we know what winning in general is. My complaint to Carnap on analyticity long ago was parallel, so I can sympathize' ('Review of Evans and Mc Dowell (eds.)', 229, references added).

[152] Soames, 'T-Sentences', 252–5, and *UT*, 105, 243–4. The same kind of argument is hinted at in Etchemendy, 'Tarski,' 57.

Perhaps knowledge that ('*M*' is true in L_1 iff the moon is round) is not *sufficient* for understanding the German sentence '*M*', but surely such knowledge of truth-conditions provides some 'negative' information about the sense of a sentence: if you know that S^1, you are justified in believing that '*M*' does *not* mean that the moon is not round, that nothing is round, that the moon is cubical, etc. (Take anything that is self-evidently incompatible with the moon's being round.) But it is certainly not the case that if you know that S^2, you are justified in believing that '*M*' does not mean that the moon is cubical. Knowing that S^2 does not entitle you to *any* belief about the sense of '*M*'. But if (Df. 1) were an explanation of the meaning of 'is true in L_1', then there could not be such an epistemic difference between (S^1) and (S^2). Hence (Df. 1) cannot lay claim to explaining what 'is true in L_1' means. Since the Tarskian definitions of predicates like 'directly true in L_2' or 'directly satisfied in L_3' are just as enumerative as (Df. 1), the same kind of argument applies to Tarskian truth-definitions for more complex languages. Thus, such a definition does not even provide us with an explanation of the concept of truth as applied to a particular language.

4.2 Disquotationalist Conceptions

'Truth is disquotation', Quine says,[153] and this slogan, like all the others he has coined, bears spelling out:

To say that the statement 'Brutus killed Caesar' is true ... is in effect simply to say that Brutus killed Caesar. (Quine, *W&O*, 24)

The truth predicate is a reminder that, despite a technical ascent to talk of sentences, our eye is on the world. This cancellatory force of the truth predicate is explicit in Tarski's paradigm: 'Snow is white' is true if and only if snow is white. Quotation marks make all the difference between talking about words and talking about snow. The quotation is a name of a sentence that contains a name, namely 'snow', of snow. By calling the sentence true, we call snow white. The truth predicate is a device of disquotation ... / ... So long as we are speaking only of the truth of singly given sentences, the perfect theory of truth is ... the disappearance theory of truth. (Quine, *PL*, 12,11)

To ascribe truth to the sentence ['Snow is white'] is to ascribe whiteness to snow.... So the truth predicate is superfluous when ascribed to a given sentence; you could just utter the sentence. (Quine, *PT*, 80)

Attaching the predicate 'is true' to the quotational designator of a (declarative) sentence has the same effect, or so we are told, as would be obtained by simply

---

[153] Quine, *Pursuit of Truth* (henceforth *PT*), 80.

erasing the quotation marks: what is said by such a truth ascription could just as well be said by uttering the quoted sentence itself. This redundancy claim is the first tenet of disquotationalism. The 'So long as' clause at the end of the second extract and the 'when' clause in the third extract hint at the limitations of this claim. As it stands, it can at best hold of *revealing* truth-ascriptions, i.e. of those that display a truth-candidate between quotation marks: no disquotation without quotation (if I may venture to offer a slogan myself). Since ever so many truth-ascriptions are unrevealing, it is to be hoped that the redundancy thesis isn't the whole message of disquotationalism, and indeed it isn't. In *unrevealing* truth-ascriptions—this will be the second part of the message—'true' helps us to save breath. In putting forward these two tenets, disquotationlists take themselves to have told us 'all, or just about all, we need to know about truth'.[154]

4.2.1 *Redundancy again*

The *disquotationalist* redundancy claim should be strictly distinguished from another one, which was the topic of Chapter 2.1. Frege and Ramsey focus on instances of the Denominalization Schema

(Den)   It is true that p, iff p.

They maintain that what is said remains unaffected whether we attach '(it) is true' to a that-clause or whether we simply erase the complementizer 'that':

(Den =)   To say that *it is true that p* is to say that *p*.

As we saw in Chapter 2.1, the Denominalization Schema is weaker than this identity schema. By contrast, disquotationalists take homophonic T-equivalences, i.e. instances of the Disquotation Schema

(Dis)   'p' is true iff p

---

[154] Michael Williams, 'Do We (Epistemologists) Need a Theory of Truth?', 223. In a paper attacking what he takes to be Williams's and Horwich's 'disquotational theory of truth', Putnam attributes to both philosophers the tenet that 'to say that a statement is true is not to ascribe *any* property to it' (264). But for Williams, as for any other disquotationalist, truth *is* a property, sc. of sentences; and for Horwich who isn't a disquotationalist anyway, it *is* a property, namely of propositions. The title of Putnam's paper is, 'Does the Disquotational Theory of Truth Really Solve All Philosophical Problems?' Of course, the answer to this question has got to be, No. But did any disquotationalist ever plead for the opposite answer? In his reply to Putnam's paper ('On Some Critics of Deflationism'), Williams charitably ignores its title.

as their starting-point and contend that what is said remains unaffected whether we append the truth-predicate to the quotational designator of a (declarative) sentence or whether we simply delete the quotation marks:

(Dis =)   To say that '*p*' *is true* is to say that *p*.

The Disquotation Schema, too, is weaker than the corresponding identity schema: if you accept an instance of (Dis =), you are committed to endorsing the corresponding instance of (Dis), but there is no such obligation in the other direction. In Chapter 2.1, I spent quite some time in disputing the Fregean Identity Thesis; now I shall try to refute its disquotationalist counterpart. Most of the arguments that can be used here would have been entirely inappropriate there.

Not every philosopher who seems to endorse (Dis =) is a disquotationalist. He might use this schema but really have (Den =) in mind. He might deny that the first and the second tenet of disquotationalism give us almost the whole truth about the concept of truth. Wittgenstein, Carnap, and McDowell, for example, all declare their allegiance to (Dis =), as you can see from the following extracts:

'*p*' *ist wahr, sagt nichts Anderes aus als p!* ['p' is true, says nothing else but p!] (Wittgenstein, *Notebooks*, 6.10.1914)[155]

Was heißt denn, ein Satz 'ist wahr'? 'p' ist wahr =p. (Dies ist die Antwort.) [What does it mean, a sentence 'is true'? 'p' is true = p. (This is the answer.)] (Wittgenstein, *Bemerkungen über die Grundlagen der Mathematik*, 117)[156]

To assert that a sentence is true means the same as to assert the sentence itself; e.g. . . . ' "The moon is round" is true' and 'The moon is round' are merely two different formulations of the same assertion. (Carnap, *IS*, 26)[157]

Appending a truth predicate to a designation of a sentence produces a sentence apt . . . for saying . . . the very thing . . . that could have been said by using the original sentence. (McDowell, 'Truth-Conditions, Bivalence and Verificationism', 7)

---

[155] Cf. 'Notes Dictated to G. E. Moore in Norway', 113.

[156] Wittgenstein's use of '=' here is ungrammatical, and his use of quotation marks tends to be sloppy. In spite of the two passages from his early and late work (to which *Philosophische Grammatik*, 123 and *Philosophische Untersuchungen*, §136 could be added), it is by no means clear that he really favours (Dis =) rather than (Den =). In one of his unpublished manuscripts and in his *Phil. Gramm.*, he seems to find fault with (Dis =): 'The proposition [*Satz*] "It is raining" surely says something about the weather but nothing about the words I am speaking. But how can "It is raining" say the same as: "The proposition [*Satz*] 'It is raining' is true", since *it* does say something about the words?' (ms., quoted after Garth Hallett, *Companion*, 237). Cf. *Phil. Gramm.*, 123–4.

[157] Carnap's first remark is confusing. First he takes what is asserted to be a proposition (albeit one about a sentence), then he takes it to be a sentence. But the second claim makes only dubious sense (as was pointed out by Moore in 1942: see his *Common Place Book*, 229): by uttering certain words one can assert something, but in so doing one does not assert *those words*.

But arguably, none of these philosophers is a partisan of disquotationalism, and, as we shall soon see, there is reason to suspect that even Quine does not belong to this camp, although disquotationalism owes more than its name to him.

For the remainder of this chapter let us assume that no truth-candidate is void of truth-value, for we have already seen that gappiness does not just cause problems for disquotationalists. To facilitate the present discussion, let us also pretend that all truth-candidates are free of ambiguous and context-sensitive elements.[158] Even if the Disquotationalist Identity Thesis, the *Identity Thesis* for short, is able to cope with these phenomena, it is fraught with difficulties. I shall now present six objections against the Identity Thesis. We will see that it can be defended against the first ones, but that in the end it will be defeated. Or so I think.

(I)   *The Argument from Explanatory Loss*

If Ann understands 'Snow is white' and 'iff' but not yet 'is true', Ben can begin to explain to her what that predicate means by telling her that

(A)   'Snow is white' is true iff snow is white.

But, so the objection runs, the Identity Thesis, if true, nips all such explanatory aspirations in the bud. For if the Identity Thesis is true, then the left branch of (A) has the same (conventional linguistic) meaning as the right branch, hence (A) has the same meaning as the tautology

(B)   Snow is white iff snow is white.

(Within an environment like (A), supplanting an embedded sentence by another sentence with the same meaning leaves the meaning of the whole intact.) But then telling somebody that A can no more help explaining 'true' (or anything else) than would telling her that B.

This worry is just another illustration of a general problem that has surfaced in the debate about the Paradox of Analysis.[159] Compare the following pair of sentences:

(a)   Donald is a drake iff Donald is a male duck
(b)   Donald is a male duck iff Donald is a male duck.

---

[158] See pp. 203–5 above. Disquotationalist strategies for handling ambiguity and indexicality are sketched in Field, 'Deflationist Views of Meaning and Content' (henceforth 'Deflationist'), 134–7, 'Disquotational Truth and Factually Defective Discourse' (hereinafter 'Disquotational'), 222 n., 239–40.

[159] Cf. Carnap, *Meaning and Necessity*, 63.

Since 'drake' and 'male duck' have the same meaning, (b) has the same meaning as (a). Nevertheless, (a) can, whereas (b) cannot, be used to explain the meaning of 'drake'. The fact that the predicates in (a) are related as *analysandum* and *analysans* is quite accidental to the problem. What really matters is that only one of the biconditionals can play an explanatory role, as the next example shows:

(a*)   Kaa is a serpent iff Kaa is a snake
(b*)   Kaa is a snake iff Kaa is a snake.

As the two predicates have the same meaning, so do (b*) and (a*). But once again, (a*) can, whereas (b*) cannot, be used to explain the meaning of 'serpent'.[160] So the disquotationalist can disarm the objection along the same lines: why should (A) not be used to explain the meaning of 'true' as applied to the quoted sentence even though (B) is entirely useless for this explanatory purpose?

In Chapter 3.5, brooding upon 'Aristotle's basic insight', we tried to determine the explanatory point of statements like

(C$_p$)   It is true that snow is white, because snow is white.

In order to obtain the counterparts to such statements for *sentential* truth, we have to expand the explanatory clause:

(C$_s$)   'Snow is white' is true because (*'Snow is white' means that snow is white, and* snow is white).

In both versions the 'because' seems to pose a strong challenge to an Identity Thesis. The objections run on parallel lines. If the advocates of the Fregean Identity Thesis were right about the sentences flanking 'because', then (C$_p$) would have the same content as

(D$_p$)   Snow is white because snow is white.

If the advocates of the Disquotationalist Identity Thesis were right about the sentences flanking 'because', then (C$_s$) would have the same content as

(D$_s$)   Snow is white because (*'Snow is white' means that snow is white, and* snow is white).

But (D$_p$) is clearly a pseudo-explanation, and so is (D$_s$): neither snow's being white nor the quoted sentence's meaning what it does are parts of an explanation of

---

[160] Pairs like (a*/b*) show that Carnap's attempt to solve the problem with the help of his notion of intensional isomorphism doesn't work (see ibid.). Cf. my *Abstrakte Gegenstände*, 219–20.

snow's being white. The Identity Theses, so the objector concludes, drag (C_p) and (C_s) down with (D_p) and (D_s): reasonable conceptual explanations would be certain to evaporate if either Identity Thesis were correct.

It can easily be seen that this objection is just a variant of the Argument from Explanatory Loss, and a look at the 'because' variants of (a) or (a*) shows that it can be defused in a similar way. (In one respect, the present objection may seem to be stronger than its predecessor: sentences of the form 'p iff p' are at least true, though trivial, whereas sentences of the form 'p because p' or 'p, because q and p' are always false.) The fact that the conceptual explanations given in our (C) sentences evaporate as soon as they are replaced by their (D) counterparts shows that these explanations do not only depend on the meaning of their respective *explananda* but also on the way they are formulated. (In virtue of the latter feature the 'because' of conceptual explanation creates a context which is hyper-intensional to the same degree as that which is formed by quotation marks.) That two sentences have the same meaning does not exclude the possibility that only one of them has an explanatory potential.

The next objection against the Disquotationalist Identity Thesis comes from Dummett. It is an argument from explanatory loss in the opposite direction (and you know its essentials from our discussion of Tarski).

(II)   *The Argument from Truth-conditional Semantics*

Here are two presentations of the argument:

[I]n order that someone should gain from the explanation that P is true in such-and-such circumstances an understanding of the sense of P, he must already know what it means to say of P that it is true. If when he enquires into this he is told that the only explanation is that to say that P is true is the same as to assert that P, it will follow that in order to understand what is meant by saying that P is true, he must already know the sense of asserting that P, which was precisely what was supposed to be being explained to him. (Dummett, 'Truth', 7) [161]

[I]f the *whole* explanation of the sense of the word 'true', as applied, e.g., to the sentence 'Frege died in 1925', consisted in saying that ' "Frege died in 1925" is true' is equivalent to 'Frege died in 1925', then my understanding of the sentence 'Frege died in 1925' could not in turn consist in my knowing what has to be the case for the sentence to be true. Given that I knew what it meant to apply the predicate 'true' to that sentence, such knowledge would reduce to knowledge of a mere tautology in the most literal sense: if *all* that it means to say that 'Frege died in 1925' is true is that Frege died in 1925, then

---

[161] When Dummett speaks of the sense of P, he takes the schematic letter to be a place-holder for quotational designators of sentences. When he speaks of asserting that P, grammar demands that the schematic letter is a place-holder for sentences.

the knowledge that 'Frege died in 1925' is true just in case Frege died in 1925 is simply the 'knowledge' that Frege died in 1925 just in case Frege died in 1925. (Dummett, *FPL*, 458)[162]

The Argument from Truth-conditional Semantics is a *conditional* refutation of the Identity Thesis: *if* our understanding of the (declarative) sentences of a language consists in our knowledge of their truth-conditions, *then* what these conditions are conditions *of* is not the same as disquotational truth. Dummett affirms the antecedent and applies *modus ponens*. Disquotationalists deny the consequent and apply *modus tollens*. Field, who has become the most resourceful advocate of disquotationalism,[163] writes:

Accepting [disquotationalism] requires dethroning truth conditions from the central place in the theory of meaning... that Frege... and many others have given to them. My current view is that this is probably a good thing. ('Disquotational', 224–5)

It is noteworthy that Quine does not share this view: 'First and last, in learning language, we are learning how to distribute truth values. I am with Davidson here; we are learning truth conditions.' So in spite of Quine's midwifery at the birth of disquotationalism, charity forbids to count him among its supporters.[164] But perhaps the Identity Thesis is unconditionally refuted by the notorious

(III) *Argument from Modal Difference*

Let us embed the sentences

(S)   Snow is white
(T)   'Snow is white' is true

in a modal context, as consequents in a subjunctive conditional:

(MS)   If we all came to use the sentence 'snow is white' for saying that snow is black, it would not be the case that *snow is white*.

(MT)   If we all came to use the sentence 'snow is white' for saying that snow is black, it would not be the case that '*snow is white*' *is true*.

Obviously (MT) is true, whereas (MS) isn't. The colour of snow does not depend on the way the word 'white' is used. After all, one cannot change the

---

[162] Cf. p. 218 and n. 137 above.

[163] Field's earlier highly influential plea for a *correspondence* theory was mentioned in n. 57 above.

[164] The quotation is from Quine, *The Roots of Reference*, 65, see also 'On the Very Idea of a Third Dogma', 38; and the 'Reply to Davidson', 333, quoted on pp. 217–18 above. (Davidson has repeatedly drawn attention to the first two passages: 'What is Quine's View of Truth?'; 'Pursuit of the Concept of Truth', 7–9; 'Folly', 270–1.)

colour of snow simply by using the word 'white' for the colour of coal. Now the application of the modal operator 'it would not be the case that' to (S) and (T) could not enforce the assignment of different truth-values to (MS) and (MT), if an ascription of truth to 'Snow is white' were really nothing but an ascription of whiteness to snow. Hence, the objector concludes, the Identity Thesis is false.

Disquotationalists can shield off this attack if they take to heart the following point (made by a philosopher who does not at all intend to help them):

The instances of the disquotational schema are guaranteed to be true, in fact, only in the very special case where the quoted sentences are guaranteed to have the same truth-values as those same sentences shorn of quotation marks on the right of the biconditional. This guarantee is lacking, for example, when I surmise that *your* sentence 'Snow is white' is true if and only if snow is white. (Davidson, 'What is Quine's View of Truth?', 439)[165]

Disquotationalists can claim that the Identity Thesis is based on a reading of substitution-instances of (Dis) under which they *are* guaranteed to be true. Thus understood, a speaker risks no more in stating that

(A)   'Snow is white' is true iff snow is white

than if he had asserted that

(A*)   'Snow is white' *as used by me now* is true iff snow is white.

Now if we apply (A*) to the consequent of (MT) we obtain a plain falsehood:

(X)   If we all came to use the sentence 'snow is white' for saying that snow
       is black, it would not be the case that 'snow is white' is true
       as used by me now.

So the intended reading of (MT) must be rather something like this:

(Y)   If we all came to use the sentence 'snow is white' for saying that snow
       is black, it would not be the case that 'snow is white' is true
       as used by me then.

Why shouldn't disquotationalists assent to (Y), and hence to (MT), without any reservation? Now consider (MS). According to circumspect advocates of the Identity Thesis, this amounts to the same as the falsehood (X). Hence

---

[165] Cf. Davidson, 'Epistemology and Truth', 181; 'Reply to W. V. Quine', 85.

disquotationalists can deny (MS) as firmly as anyone else.[166] So let us consider a more powerful objection against the Identity Thesis.

(IV) *The Argument from Entailment*

It is a conceptual truth that a meaningless sentence cannot have a truth-value. So there is a reading of 'entails' under which

(T)   'Snow is white' is true

entails, whereas

(S)   Snow is white

does not entail,

(M)   'Snow is white' is meaningful.

Therefore (S) does not have the same content as (T).[167]

In our reply to the Argument from Modal Difference we have assumed an interpretation of the biconditional connecting (T) and (S) on which it is necessarily true. So we must take the conception of entailment appealed to in objection (IV) to be such that two sentences which are necessarily equivalent (have the same truth-value in all possible worlds) may nevertheless differ as to what they entail. Certainly we have an intuitive conception of entailment which allows us to say, for example, that although '2 is prime' and 'All drakes are ducks' are necessarily equivalent, only the latter sentence entails 'If Donald is a drake then Donald is a duck', and Relevance Logics respect this feature of our pre-formal conception of entailment by precluding theorems of the form $A \rightarrow B$ where A and B do not share a parameter.

But we need not rest our criticism of the Identity Thesis on forsaking both classical and intuitionistic logic. Here is the most powerful, indeed lethal challenge to that claim.

(V) *The Argument from Doxastic Difference*

In spite of its somewhat pompous name, the objection is exceedingly simple. If (S) and (T) were to express the same proposition, then nobody could believe what either of these sentences expresses without *eo ipso* believing what the other

---

[166] This attempt at answering the Modal Objection is essentially due to McGee, 'A Semantic Conception of Truth?', 92–3. Cf. also David, *C&D*, 130–5; Field, 'Deflationist', 133; 'Disquotational', 224.

[167] This argument is sketched in passing, and with very little sympathy, in Quine, 'Meaning and Existential Inference', 163–4.

expresses. But a monoglot German who believes that snow is white may not believe that the English sentence 'Snow is white' is true, and if a monoglot German with defective eyesight believes that snow is bluish but takes my word for it that the sentence 'Snow is white' is true, then he believes the sentence to be true without believing snow to be white. Hence (S) and (T) do not express the same proposition.[168] We can drive home the same point with our next argument.

(VI)   *The Argument from Conceptual Overloading*

Consider the Identity Thesis in the light of our Conceptual Balance Requirement: two utterances express the same proposition only if there is no concept whose mastery has to be exercised only in understanding *one* of them.[169] Surely one cannot understand an utterance of the English sentence (S) without exercising one's mastery of the concept of snow. But imagine a Bedouin whose rudimentary English comprises only vocabulary that is useful in the desert: he might very well understand the truth ascription (T) without even having the concept of snow. In order to understand a quotational designator, one does not have to understand the quoted expression. Otherwise the following verdict would be comprehensible only if it is false: ' "*Asa nisi masa*" is incomprehensible.' So (S) and (T) do not express the same proposition. Arguments (V) and (VI) show that the Disquotationalist Identity Thesis cannot be upheld.

Let me briefly go into the question whether *Tarski* takes a T-equivalence like

(A)   'Snow is white' is true iff snow is white

to be, as Dummett puts it, 'the whole explanation' of the sense of the word 'true' as applied to the quoted sentence. According to Quine and Dummett, the answer is No. 'It is sometimes overlooked', Quine says, 'that there is no need to claim, and that Tarski has not claimed, that [homophonic T-equivalences] are analytic.'[170] Dummett concurs, 'Tarski was concerned to claim no more than material equivalence, i.e. identity of truth-value' for the two sides of a T-equivalence.[171] Criterion T lends no support to the Disquotationalist Identity

---

[168] Notice that this kind of argument would not be convincing if we were to replace (T) by (T*) 'It is true that snow is white'. Claiming that somebody might believe that S without believing that T* would be a *petitio* against advocates of the Fregean Identity Thesis, and the claim that somebody might believe that T* without believing that S would be plainly wrong.

[169] See p. 47 above on (B-Nec).

[170] Quine, 'Notes', 137 n. 9 (cf. also 'Meaning and Existential Inference', 164).

[171] Dummett, *Truth and Other Enigmas*, xx.

Thesis, for it demands only that in a T-equivalence 'p' translates S, not that it translates 'S is true'. But at other places Tarski is concerned to claim far more than material equivalence. He calls T-equivalences 'partial definitions [*Teildefinitionen*]':[172] they are only partial because they do not tell us what being true comes to in all cases (i.e. for all sentences of the given language), and they are definitions because they tell us completely what being true comes to in the case at hand (i.e. for the quoted sentence). Recall the beginning of [T.14], where Tarski explicitly declares the right branch of a T-equivalence to be an explanation of the meaning of its left branch: '[T-equivalences] explain in a precise way, in accordance with linguistic usage [*Sprachgebrauch*], the meaning [*Bedeutung*] of the phrases "x is a true sentence" which occur in them.'[173] So even if there were no *need* for Tarski to claim more than identity of truth-value for the two branches of a T-equivalence, as a matter of fact he *does* claim more than that, and what he claims at this point is refuted by the Arguments from Doxastic Difference[174] and from Conceptual Overloading. Calling (A) a partial definition of 'true' is open to a further objection raised by Quine:[175] if (A) were such a definition, then it should allow us to eliminate 'is true' from all contexts in which it is applied to the sentence 'Snow is white'. Now in 'Tarski's favourite English sentence is true' we do apply this predicate to the sentence 'Snow is white', because Tarski's favourite English sentence is 'Snow is white'. But of course, we cannot remove 'is true' from this context. Since the alleged definition allows us to eliminate 'is true' only from positions in which it is preceded by the quotation of that sentence, it scarcely deserves to be called a definition.

But is there really no need for Tarski to require anything stronger than material equivalence? As we saw, Quine absolves him from any obligation to maintain even the necessitation of (A),

(NecA)   Necessarily, 'snow is white' is true iff snow is white.

In 'Two Dogmas of Empiricism',[176] Quine took 'Necessarily, p' to come to the same (obscure) thing as ' "p" is analytic'.[177] Now the truth of (NecA) is

---

[172] Tarski, *WB*, 8–10 (155–7) on schema (2) and sentences (3) and (4); 98 (236), 116 (253), 129 (264), '*Grundlegung*', 264 (404); 'Semantic', §4, 'Proof', 413.

[173] See p. 214 above. The claim is repeated almost verbatim in Tarski, '*Grundlegung*', 264 (404).

[174] This was pointed out by Soames, *UT*, 240.

[175] Quine, 'Notes', 136.

[176] Written at about the same time as the two papers referred to above.

[177] Maybe equally obscure, but certainly not the same thing (as David Kaplan has taught us): every utterance of 'I am here now' is true solely in virtue of the meaning of this sentence (as friends of analyticity would put it), but no utterance of 'Necessarily, I am here now' is true. Cf. Ch. 5.2.2 below.

a necessary (but not a sufficient) condition for the truth of the corresponding identity claim. (Although necessarily, ABC is an equilateral Euclidean triangle iff ABC is an equiangular Euclidean triangle, it is not the case that anyone who was to say the former / the latter would thereby be saying the latter / the former.) So, when speaking on Tarski's behalf, Quine denies any need to embrace (NecA), but, when speaking *in propria persona*, as documented in the passages cited above on p. 225, he upholds a thesis that is stronger than (NecA). (There is nothing contradictory about this in a philosopher who declares talk of analyticity/necessity to be at bottom incomprehensible.) But let us return to our question: is Tarski really not committed to accept (NecA)? I think he *is*. Recall, for example, the definition of 'true' for the code L_1, given in section 4.1.3 above. As demanded by Criterion T, the two pertinent T-equivalences follow from the definition (plus some non-contingent syntactical truths such as ' "Snow is white" is not identical with "Blood is red" '). The definition itself is not a contingent truth, for it is constitutive of L_1 that its sentences mean what they do mean. Now a (conceptually) necessary truth N cannot entail a contingent truth C; for otherwise, by contraposition, the negation of C, which is as contingent as C, would entail the negation of N, which is necessarily false. And this is absurd, since whatever entails a necessary falsehood is itself necessarily false.[178] Hence Tarski ought to be ready to accept (NecA).

Disquotationalists should weaken their first tenet, but they can make a stronger claim than that of necessary equivalence.[179] They can plausibly maintain that an ascription of truth to a sentence in a certain context is *cognitively equivalent* with the sentence itself as used in that context. Nobody who understands both (T) and (S) can take one of them to express a truth without immediately being ready to take the other to express a truth as well.[180] That's why for most, if not all, communicative purposes of those who *understand* the sentence to which truth is ascribed, the plain sentence itself will do just as well as the truth ascription. But of course, what remains of the first tenet of disquotationalism after this weakening is, or should be, conceded on all sides. So the specific profile of a disquotationalist conception of truth now depends entirely on what I announced as its second tenet.

---

[178] This argument is used, in a different context, by Casimir Lewy in *Meaning and Modality*, 49. Since Polish contributions to our topic play a fairly large role on these pages, it is worth mentioning that Lewy (who spent his academic life in Cambridge) was born in Warsaw and drawn into philosophy by Kotarbiński.

[179] As we shall soon see, Field is a disquotationalist who does weaken it in a similar way.

[180] See pp. 42–3 above, on (CognE).

4.2.2 *Truth for the sake of brevity*

When it comes to stressing the *importance* of the truth-predicate, advocates of disquotationalism again take a leaf out of Quine's book:

The truth predicate proves invaluable when we want to generalize along a dimension that cannot be swept out by a general term. The easy sort of generalization is illustrated by generalization on the term 'Socrates' in 'Socrates is mortal'; the sentence generalizes to 'All men are mortal.' The general term 'man' has served to sweep out the desired dimension of generality. The harder sort of generalization is illustrated by generalization on the clause 'time flies' in 'If time flies then time flies.' We want to say that this compound continues true when the clause is supplanted by any other; and we can do no better than to say just that in so many words, including the word 'true'. We say 'All sentences of the form "If p then p" are true.' We could not generalize as in 'All men are mortal', because 'time flies' is not, like 'Socrates', a name of one of a range of objects (men) over which to generalize. We cleared this obstacle by semantic ascent: by ascending to a level where there were indeed objects over which to generalize, namely linguistic objects, sentences. (*PT*, 80–1)

Disquotationalists are prone to add here a further observation. Sometimes we want to voice our acceptance or rejection of what somebody said when the speaker's words are unavailable for quotation. In such situations, too, the truth predicate proves invaluable. Here are two examples: 'We shall never know how she answered his question, but her answer was certainly true, for she knew the answer, and she would never have lied to him,' or 'What he said to our pursuers cannot have been true, for otherwise they would have found us.' (One may have doubts whether such statements are really about the speaker's *words*, but let us postpone the examination of this issue till the next chapter.)

Disquotationalists like to say that the *raison d'être* of a truth-predicate resides entirely in its utility for the kinds of generalization and of 'blind' acceptance or rejection just described.[181] This is an exaggeration even if they are right in pushing truth-conditions from their throne in the theory of meaning. In his description of the performative potential of 'true', Strawson pointed out various other purposes that are served by this word: it allows us, for example, to endorse somebody's statement without parroting.[182]

How do disquotationalists account for *unrevealing* truth ascriptions of the compendious, and the indirect, kind whose availability they esteem so highly? They maintain that an unrevealing *general* truth ascription like

Every English sentence of the form 'If p then p' is true

---

[181] Cf., e.g., Field, 'Postscript' to 'Tarski', 28.   [182] See Ch. 2.2.1 above.

abbreviates (or 'encodes') an infinite *conjunction*

If time flies then time flies,   and
if duty calls then duty calls,   and
if lions roar then lions roar,   and ...,

which contains all English sentences of the form 'if p, then p' as its conjuncts. (As Quine said, 'if we want to affirm some infinite lot of sentences ... then the truth predicate has its use'.[183] Thus, in asserting that every English sentence of that form is true, you perform the remarkable feat of affirming, in one fell swoop, each and every instance of that form.) Similarly, disquotationalists contend, an unrevealing *singular* truth ascription like 'The last sentence of Goethe's *Faust* is true' or

(U)   Alfred's favourite English sentence is true

abbreviates an infinite *disjunction*. Here is a tiny fragment of this disjunction, using 'a' as short for 'Alfred's favourite English sentence':

(V)   (a is 'blood is red',   and blood is red),   or
        (a is 'coal is black',   and coal is black),   or
        (a is 'snow is white',   and snow is white),   or ...

From here it is only a short step to the second tenet of disquotationalism: 's is true in L' abbreviates an infinite disjunction of conjunctions.[184] Let us try to capture this by

(Df. DisT) $\forall s$ [s is true in L if and only if (s is 'p_1', and p_1), or (s is 'p_2', and p_2), or (s is 'p_3', and p_3), or ...],

where 'p_1', 'p_2', 'p_3', etc. are (almost[185]) all and only declarative sentences of English if L is English. (The dots explain why disquotationalism was entered as the negative answer to QUESTION 10 on our flow chart—see Figure 1.2.) As a

---

[183] Quine, *PL*, 12.

[184] The idea, hinted at by Quine, was first put into relief in Leeds, 'Theories of Reference and Truth', 121, and a few years later it was developed in Soames, 'What Is a Theory of Truth?', 412–14.

[185] Because of the 'Liar', exceptions must be made for certain sentences (or utterances) containing 'true' (if classical logic and its semantical principles are to remain unmodified). Hence, like all other conceptions of truth, disquotationalism must be supplemented by an answer to the question how the exceptions are to be circumscribed (or how classical logic is to be modified). The question which reaction to the semantic paradoxes is most attractive to disquotationalism is canvassed in Field, 'Postscript' to 'Deflationist', 143–6.

handy notational variant of (DisT), we could use

(Df. *DisT*)   ∀s [s is true in L iff {∃p}(s is 'p', and p)],

where the substitution-class of 'p' is taken to comprise (almost) all and only declarative sentences of L, and the 'existential' substitutional quantification '{∃p}(...p...)' is understood as tantamount to the disjunction of all the substitution-instances of the open sentence after the quantifier.[186]

As we saw above, Tarski endorses something like (DisT) for *codes*, i.e. for languages that contain only a *finite* number of sentences that can be enumerated: truth in a code is defined by means of a disjunction of conjunctions.[187] For languages that are not codes Tarski mobilizes the technique of recursion (and in this respect Quine always remained faithful to him).[188] When the language for which a truth-predicate is to be defined is sufficiently complex to demand the detour through satisfaction, Tarski's method still turns on disquotation (provided that the object-language is part of the metalanguage), but what gets disquoted are singular terms, open sentences, and logical operators, which, though finite in number, suffice to form all sentences of the language.[189] But the recursive machinery works only if the language obeys certain tight syntactical and semantical constraints. Unlike Tarski, disquotationalists do not presuppose that the language for which 'true' is to be defined has a specific kind of syntactic structure, and they do not have to worry about the apparent non-extensionality of many constructions in natural languages.[190]

When it comes to determining their relation to Tarski's work, disquotationalists are likely to remind us that Tarski says even of a definition of a truth-predicate for a language with infinitely many sentences that it is, in a sense, tantamount to a conjunction of infinitely many T-equivalences. The second statement in [T.14] is pertinent here (see above, p. 214):

Not much more in principle is to be demanded of a general definition of true sentence [sc. for the language under investigation] than that it should satisfy the usual conditions of methodological correctness and include all partial definitions of this type [sc. T-equivalences] as special cases; that it should be, so to speak, their logical product.

---

[186] Field, 'The Deflationary Conception of Truth' (henceforth 'Truth'), 58–9; David, *C&D*, 98–100. Assuming that for every sentence there is exactly one quotational designator, the right-hand side of *(DisT)* is logically equivalent with '{∀p} ((s = 'p') → p)'. Following Horwich (*Truth*, 25), I enclose substitutional quantifiers in curly brackets. The peculiarities of substitutional quantification will occupy us in Ch. 6.2.3.   [187] Cf. L₁ in sect. 4.1.3 above.

[188] It is significant that in a footnote to the statement in *W&O* that was cited on p. 225 above, Quine asks his readers to see Tarski for the 'classic development' of the disquotation theme.

[189] See pp. 198–200 above, on L₃.   [190] Cf. Field, 'Deflationist', 125.

Given a suitable infinitary logic allowing conjunctions and disjunctions to be of infinite length,[191] we can derive T-equivalences from (DisT): if we replace 's' by 'Snow is white', there will be just one true disjunct on the right-hand side. After eliminating '("snow is white" is "blood is red", and blood is red)' and all the other false disjuncts, we are left with this:

> 'Snow is white' is true in English iff
> ('snow is white' is 'snow is white', and snow is white).

We then drop the 'tautologous' conjunct and obtain our snow-bound triviality. So (DisT) complies with Criterion T.

If L is not English, friends of (DisT) must be ready to put up with such language-mixtures as 's is "*Schnee ist weiß*", and *Schnee ist weiß*.'[192] And there will be much more of this they have to face. Suppose we replace (U) by 'Alfred's favourite sentence is true' (i.e. 'There is a language L such that Alfred's favourite sentence is a true sentence of L'). Then the disjunction has to contain odd-looking, and odd-sounding, clauses such as 'Alfred's favourite sentence is "*Śnieg jest biały*", and *śnieg jest biały*, or it is "*Schnee ist weiß*", and *Schnee ist weiß*, or it is "*La neve è bianca*", and *la neve è bianca*, or . . .'. Such motley sentences would have to be taken as true in a hybrid language which results from pooling English, Polish, German, Italian, . . .[193] and which is spoken at best by a very few polyglots. But I cannot see that registering this linguistic oddity by itself amounts to making a principled objection against (DisT).[194]

But as it stands, (DisT) falls victim to another Argument from Conceptual Overloading. Consider (U) again. If (U) *abbreviates* something that contains (V), then the sense of (V) is a component of the sense of (U), and necessary conditions for understanding (V) are also necessary conditions for understanding (U). In order to understand the disjunction (V), you must understand 'Blood is red', 'Coal is black', and 'Snow is white', for in (V) these sentences do not only appear between quotation marks. So you cannot understand (V) without exercising your mastery of the concepts of blood, of coal, etc. But you do not have to understand any of the sentences mentioned and used in (V) in order to understand the truth-ascription (U), hence grasping the concepts of blood etc. is not involved in

---

[191] As was mentioned in p. 219 n. 140 above, in the late 1950s Tarski himself published pioneering work in this field. For a more precise rendering of the derivation of T-equivalences from (DisT) with the help of an infinitary logic, cf. David, *C&D* 100–4.

[192] In presentations of disquotationalism this need to mix languages is often swept under the carpet: thus Blackburn and Simmons (eds.), *Truth*, 12–13, assume as a matter of course that their speaker Claire speaks English.   [193] Cf. Quine, 'Notes', 135.

[194] As to the actual use of hybrid languages in certain circles, let me mention in passing that in Germany you will nowadays occasionally hear sentences that can be assigned a truth-value only in the hybrid language German-English (often referred to as '*Denglisch*').

grasping the content of (U). And this is just a tiny portion of the conceptual load which is to be carried when it comes to understanding the whole disjunction which (U) is supposed to abbreviate. Surely, understanding that is no small feat. Is there anyone who understands all English sentences? And even if there were such a person, her spectacular conceptual competence is certainly not required for understanding such a humble truth-ascription as (U). So application of our Conceptual Balance Requirement shows that 'true' is *not* a device for abbreviating infinite disjunctions in the sense of (DisT).[195]

Truth-ascriptions would not only be *conceptually* beyond our reach if (Df. DisT) were correct. A conceptually very undemanding finite part of (V) is the disjunction whose components are the first thousand instantiations of the schema 'Alfred's favourite English sentence is "n is odd", and n is odd' (where 'n' is replaced successively by '1', by '2',... and finally by '1,000'). Virtually each speaker of English understands each of these disjuncts, but no speaker of English understands the conjunction of all these disjuncts. Of course, we all understand the fairly brief description of that very long sentence which I just gave. But we can no more think the thought that is expressed by the perfectly meaningful sentence I described than we can visualize a chiliagon.[196] This is one more reason for denying that 'true' is a device for abbreviating infinite disjunctions in the sense of (DisT).

Once again, a weakening of the disquotationalists' claim may seem commendable: instead of maintaining that (U) abbreviates an infinite disjunction of which (V) is a fragment, they should contend at most that (U) and its infinitely long disjunctive counterpart are *cognitively equivalent*. But is this weaker contention really correct? Consider the following existential quantification and (what could with some patience be turned into) the alphabetically ordered disjunction of all its instances:

(P)   At least one Oxford college is a graduate institution
(Q)   Either All Souls is an Oxford college that is a graduate institution, or Balliol is,..., or Wolfson is, or Worcester is.

Somebody who understands both sentences might take (P) to express a truth without being ready to take (Q) to express a truth as well: he might suspect that (P) is true because an Oxford college which is *not* mentioned in (Q) is a graduate institution. Now the same applies, *mutatis mutandis*, to (U) and its infinitely long disjunctive counterpart: even if there were somebody who understood that

---

[195] The final move in this application of the Argument from Conceptual Overloading is identical with Gupta's 'objection from ideology': see his 'A Critique of Deflationism' (henceforth 'Critique'), 69–71.

[196] The comparison as well as the argument is van Inwagen's: see his 'Truth-Sentences', 216.

disjunction, she might not realize that it comprises all English sentences, and then she might very well suspect that (U) owes its truth to a sentence omitted in the disjunction.[197]

4.2.3 *Truth in my present idiolect*

Let us now scrutinize the version of disquotationalism which is favoured by Hartry Field. (It was foreshadowed in the reply to the Argument from Modal Difference given above.) Field replaces (DisT) by two concepts of disquotational truth, a primary notion and a derivative one, both relativized to a speaker and a time. (The relativization to time is not officially taken into account, but it is clearly implied.) Here is his exposition of what he takes to be the primary notion of truth:[198]

[I]n its primary ('purely disquotational') use,

(1) 'true' as understood by a given person applies only to utterances that that person understands, and
(2) for any utterance u that a person X understands, the claim that u is true is cognitively equivalent for X to u itself.

... The intelligibility of such a disquotational notion of truth should not be in doubt: you could think of it as an indexical concept, meaning in effect 'true on my understanding of the terms involved' ... [T]he deflationist allows that there may be certain extensions of the purely disquotational truth predicate that don't have features (1) and (2); but he requires that any other truth predicate be explainable in terms of the purely disquotational one, using fairly limited additional resources. ('Disquotational', 222–3)

By clause (2) Field does not commit himself to identity claims like 'What (S), "Snow is white", expresses in X's present idiolect is the same as what is expressed by " 'Snow is white' is true" in X's present idiolect.' He takes 'cognitive equivalence' to be a matter of inferential role: 'for one sentence to be cognitively equivalent to another for a given person is for that person's inferential rules to license ... fairly directly the inference from either one to the other.'[199] Presumably my inferential rules license a very direct inference from 'Snow is white, and two is larger than one' to (S), and vice versa, but since the conjunction is conceptually more

---

[197] Cf. the analogous reflections on infinite conjunctions and universal generalizations in Gupta, 'Critique', 63, 77, and 80 nn. 21 and 31.

[198] See also Field, 'Truth', 58; 'Deflationist', 105–6, 119–23; and David, *C&D*, 135–48. Michael Resnik calls this 'the immanent approach to truth': cf. his 'Immanent Truth', 414.

[199] Field, n. 1 to the passage cited. Cf. 'Deflationist', 106 n.

demanding than either of its conjuncts, it is reasonable to deny that they have the same propositional content either in English or in my present idiolect. So cognitive equivalence à la Field no more guarantees identity of content than does our (Fregean) condition of the same name. In any case, the Arguments from Doxastic Difference and from Conceptual Overloading do not apply to Field's view, for a thinker who does not know what (S) means (e.g. because she has not mastered the concept of snow) cannot believe that (S) is true, if the only notion of truth currently available to her is the one she could now express by 'true on my understanding of that sentence'.

I shall call this notion of truth, which Field takes to be primary, *Idiolectic Disquotational Truth*. Using the substitutional quantification format, we can codify it as follows:

(Df. *IdDisT*) $\forall$s [s is true in my present idiolect iff
$\{\exists p\}_{m.p.i.}$ (s is identical with 'p', and p)].

If this is said by myself, the substitution-class of 'p' is to comprise (almost) all and only those declarative sentences which belong to m(y) p(resent) i(diolect). (As before, the substitutional quantification '$\{\exists p\}(\ldots p \ldots)$' is supposed to abbreviate the disjunction of all substitution-instances of '$\ldots p \ldots$'.) The right-hand side of the biconditional is guaranteed to mention only sentences I now understand. This multitude happens to contain elements from various 'national' languages, most of them from German, many of them from English, and a few from some other languages: so there will again be plenty of motley clauses in the disjunction. Never mind!

What we should mind is something else. The concept of idiolectic disquotational truth, or rather each of the numerous concepts of idiolectic disquotational truth, differs widely from our everyday concept of truth. Here are two respects in which they are unlike.

1. It is extremely improbable that any of my readers would express by 'true in my present idiolect' a concept that has the same extension as the concept I now express by this locution. Furthermore, the latter concept also differs from the one I expressed by it, say, three years ago (when I had no idea what 'Śnieg jest biały' means). Such concepts are not expressed in ordinary truth talk. Here are three pieces of evidence. First, suppose Ann comments on a newspaper report by saying, 'That's true', and Ben retorts, 'No, it isn't true, I am afraid.' Obviously Ben takes himself to be contradicting Ann, but then the concept that he refuses to apply to the report in question must be the *same* as the one Ann applied to it. (The information that she speaks English and German fluently whereas he is a monoglot Englishman doesn't disconfirm this sameness claim in the least.)

Secondly, suppose he says, 'If that report is true, the government is in trouble', then she hastens to assure him, 'It *is* true', and finally he concludes: 'So the government is in trouble.' This distributed reasoning very much looks like a *modus ponens* argument, but it is formally valid only if the truth-predicate in his utterance of the first premiss expresses the *same* concept as the truth-predicate in her utterance of the second premiss. (The above information about the difference between our speakers' linguistic abilities does not provide us with a reason for condemning the argument as exemplifying the fallacy of equivocation.) Thirdly, suppose several years later she confesses, 'At that time I thought that the report was true, but now I no longer think so.' According to her confession, *the very concept* she once took to apply to that report does not really apply to it. (This identity claim is not refuted by the information that she has learnt a third language in the meantime.)

2. In the following episode from Alessandro Manzoni's novel *I promessi sposi*, another important aspect of our everyday use of 'true' becomes conspicuous. The simple-minded old sacristan was shocked to see Father Cristoforo late at night with two women in the church, but a few words set his mind at rest: although he did not understand a word of Latin, he took Father Cristoforo to have spoken the truth when he said to him, '*Omnia munda mundis*', since he had uttered these 'solemn, mysterious words with great determination'.[200] (By taking these words to express a truth, the old sacristan did not acquire the belief that to the pure all things are pure, although this is what those words mean.) It is a constitutive feature of our concept of truth that we can suppose, and even believe, that something true is being said in an utterance that we do *not* understand. As long as children can think of what is said as true only when they understand the utterance, they have not yet fully grasped our concept of truth.

Field tries to accommodate this feature of our concept by extending the notion of disquotational truth:

[W]hat we are doing when we conjecture whether some utterance we don't understand is true is conjecturing whether a good translation of the utterance will map it into a disquotationally true sentence we do understand. ('Deflationist', 129)[201]

Whether this explanation of a non-idiolectic truth-predicate in terms of the idiolectic one uses only 'fairly limited additional resources', as was required in the passage cited at the start of this section, depends on what is meant by 'good translation'. So Field adds that this 'should be taken to be a highly

---

[200] Manzoni, *The Betrothed*, ch. 8 (quoting from St Paul, Titus 1: 15).
[201] Cf. Field, 'Truth', 61; 'Disquotational', 224; David, *C&D*, 177–86; McGee, 'A Semantic Conception of Truth?', 99.

context-sensitive and interest-relative notion' (ibid.). One may wonder whether it is possible to explain without recourse to the notion of truth-value preservation what the goodness of a good translation consists in. But let us subdue all nagging doubts.

Field's derivative concept of disquotational truth—I shall call it *Translational Disquotational Truth*—can be captured by the following universally quantified biconditional:

(*TrDisT*) $\forall L \forall s [s$ is true in L iff

$\exists x$ (x is a good translation of s into my present idiolect) &

$\forall x$ (x is a good translation of s into m.p.i $\rightarrow$ x is true in m.p.i.)].

As this is conceptually dependent on the notion of idiolectic disquotational truth, it does not reduce the distance between disquotational truth and truth in the first respect that I described above (and it is not meant to do so). Let us return briefly into the Lombardian church. Suppose the old sacristan's anti-clerically minded wife, who doesn't understand a word of Latin either, was also witness to the midnight event, but she took the priest to have lied. When the trustful sacristan comments on Father Cristofero's utterance, 'That's true', his distrustful wife retorts, 'No, it is not true'. Now this very much looks as if she has contradicted her husband, but Translational Disquotational Truth does not save the appearance, for the matrix on the right-hand side of (*TrDisT*) expresses different concepts in our quarrelling speakers' mouths.

There is a further respect in which the derivative notion of disquotational truth fails to match the real thing. You could very well speculate that the hypothesis for which a scientist will receive the first Nobel Prize for physics in the twenty-second century is true, even if you are convinced that this hypothesis cannot be translated from that physicist's language into any sentence you now understand. Our everyday concept of truth allows you to reckon with the possibility that there are true sentences which cannot be translated into any sentences you now understand.[202] Let us consider the following remarks by Field in the light of this Argument from Untranslatability Into My Present Idiolect:

Doesn't this show that the average person is clearly not using the word 'true' in its . . . disquotational sense? And doesn't that in turn show that a version of deflationism that puts . . . disquotational truth at the centre of things . . . is gratuitously departing from common sense? I don't think so. . . . [Perhaps] ordinary speakers are committed to

---

[202] Once again I wholeheartedly agree with Gupta: 'The problem of explaining how one goes from "true-in-my-present-idiolect" to "true" seems to me much harder than that of explaining "true" using a limited ideology [i.e. limited conceptual resources]' ('Critique', 81 n. 48).

a notion of truth that goes beyond the...disquotational. But if we can lessen those commitments in a way that is adequate to all practical and theoretical purposes...then the charge that we are 'gratuitously departing from common sense' is quite unfounded. ('Deflationist', 133)

This reply will not satisfy philosophers like the author of this book who aim at elucidating our workaday concept of truth. They do not want to lessen the commitments of those who use this concept, since their theoretical purpose is to get clear about these very commitments, and they will take the Argument from Untranslatability to show that the derived notion of disquotational truth, or rather each of the numerous concepts of translational disquotational truth, is by no means 'adequate to all practical and theoretical purposes'. It is only a poor surrogate for the concept of truth that we all have.

Adherents of idiolectic disquotationalism could deflect the objection from untranslatability, as presented above, if they were to replace 'translation into my present idiolect' in (*TrDisT*) by 'translation into a *potential expansion* of m.p.i.'.[203] But this proposal falls victim to a variant of the original objection (which I promise to refer to only once as the Argument from Untranslatability Into Any Potential Expansion of My Present Idiolect). Not *every* possible language which contains my present idiolect, I take it, is a potential expansion of this idiolect, but only a language that humans can come to be able to understand. Now there could be intelligent beings, Alpha-Centaurians, say, endowed with modes of sensory awareness and conceptual abilities that we and our descendants constitutionally lack. We may have the resources to understand the linguistic expression of *some* of their thoughts and thus have very good reasons for taking certain other noises they produce to be assertoric utterances in 'Alpha-Centaurian' as well, although they are such that humans are constitutionally incapable of ever understanding them. Why should the fact that some of their utterances are forever incomprehensible to members of our species prevent them from being true? Mimicking Peter Singer, one might dub the position under attack 'alethic speciesism'. Non-human animals, Wittgenstein avers, 'do not use language—if we except the most primitive forms of language'.[204] Assuming that he is right, let us call the primitive form of language in which certain West African apes communicate 'Chimpanzee'. Now many of our sentences, such as 'This is a worthless nineteenth-century copy of a painting most art-historians nowadays attribute to Giorgione', cannot be translated into a possible expansion of

---

[203] As recently suggested in Field, 'Postscript' to 'Deflationist', 148.
[204] Wittgenstein, *Philosophische Untersuchungen*, §25.

Chimpanzee, i.e. into a language that chimps could come to be able to understand. But we do not take this to prevent those sentences from being true. So why should it be legitimate to conclude from the untranslatability of some sentences used by Alpha-Centaurians into a possible expansion of my idiolect that they cannot be true?

Here is another comparison which is closer home. Imagine a community of humans who are all red/green colour-blind. Let us call the language in which they communicate 'Daltonian'. The word 'gred', we have found out, is a Daltonian predicate which is correctly applied to an object iff it is grey, green, or red. Samples which we (the normal-sighted) would use severally and non-interchangeably to explain what 'grey', 'green', or 'red' mean, are used interchangeably by them when they ostensively explain 'gred'. Whenever coloured objects that are neither grey nor green nor red are concerned, the hypothesis that one of their predicates means the same as our 'x and y differ in colour' works perfectly. But when they talk about objects which they call 'gred', that hypothesis lets us down. If we were to stick to it, we would have to say that those people seriously maintain that rain clouds, emeralds, and poppies do *not* differ in colour. Since 'there can be . . . no stronger evidence of bad translation than that it translates earnest affirmations into obvious falsehoods',[205] we give up that hypothesis. It seems that our sentence 'Rain clouds, emeralds, and poppies differ in colour' can be translated neither into Daltonian nor into a possible extension of Daltonian, i.e. into a language which the red/green colour-blind could ever come to be able to understand. Being endowed with discriminatory capacities which they lack, we do not take the untranslatability of our sentence into a language that would be fully comprehensible to them to foreclose the truth of that sentence. So, once again, why should it be legitimate to conclude from the untranslatability of some sentences used by Alpha-Centaurians into a possible expansion of my idiolect that they cannot be true?

Our concept of truth allows us to reckon with the possibility that there are true sentences which cannot be translated into any sentences humans could ever learn to comprehend.[206] Though richer than its predecessors, the *extended*

---

[205] Quine, *The Ways of Paradox*, 113.

[206] See Thomas Nagel, *A View From Nowhere*, 90–9; Timothy Williamson, 'Anthropocentrism and Truth', 35–7; and Peter Hacker, 'On Davidson's Idea of a Conceptual Scheme', 304–7. (The Daltonism example is Hacker's. The phenomenon was initially named after the chemist John Dalton who registered it in 1798.) Both Williamson and Hacker extricate the assumption that there could be a language, segments of which are irremediably incomprehensible to us, from the objections Davidson posed in his paper 'On the Very Idea of a Conceptual Scheme'. Of course, we could not give a Tarski-style definition of 'true in Alpha-Centaurian' (Williamson, 'Anthropocentrism', 39–42); which is one more reason for maintaining that the semantic conception of truth does not fully capture our concept of truth.

derivative notion of disquotational truth, or rather each of the numerous notions of this type, is again only a substitute of the concept we esteem, chicory rather than coffee.

Notice that the last argument, even if successful, does not save us from the labours to be undertaken in the final chapter of this book. A rebuttal of alethic speciecism is not a refutation of alethic anti-realism.[207] We took the latter to be a thesis about truths which are comprehensible to human beings, and by showing that there may be truths which are too discriminating for our sensorium or too recondite for human wit, one has not shown, of course, that there are humanly comprehensible truths which cannot be rationally accepted.

---

[207] As characterized in Ch. 1, pp. 20–32.

5

Propositions, Time, and Eternity

Is truth a property of *propositions*? (This was QUESTION 11 on our flow chart.[1]) In section 5.1. I shall argue that propositions are the primary truth-value bearers. Is truth a *stable* property of propositions, a property that cannot be lost? (This was QUESTION 12.) In sections 5.2 and 5.3 I shall map the options and plead for a kind of eternalist (as opposed to temporalist) position. In the final section I shall make a concession to temporalism.

5.1 What Is It that Is True or False?

> Some philosophers [sc. the Stoics] placed the true and the false...in the incorporeal sayable [ἐν τῷ ἀσωμάτῳ λεκτῷ], others in the utterance [ἐν τῇ φωνῇ], others in the process of thought [ἐν τῷ κινήματι τῆς διανοίας].
>
> (Sextus Empiricus, *Adversus Mathematicos*, VIII. 69 (cf. 11))

> I see no reason now to think that we ever do call sentences or forms of words 'true', except in such an archaic-sounding expression as 'A true word is often spoken in jest.'
>
> (Moore, *SMPP*, 262, note added in 1952)

> There was no hope for him this time: it was the third stroke....He had often said to me: 'I am not long for this world,' and I had thought his words idle. Now I knew they were true.
>
> (James Joyce, 'The Sisters')

5.1.1 *Introducing 'proposition'*

At least prima facie we ascribe truth and falsity to a motley multitude of entities such as allegations, beliefs, conjectures, contentions, judgements, reports,

---

[1] See Ch. 1, Fig. 1.3.

statements, suppositions, thoughts, and so on. But perhaps this appearance of multiplicity is deceptive.

Consider beliefs and statements. If we say 'Ben's belief that one day all the dead will rise is due to childhood indoctrination, whereas Ann's belief that one day all the dead will rise is the result of adult conversion', we do not ascribe two different origins to one and the same item. Similarly, if his belief that p is firm whereas her belief that p is easily shaken, there is no one thing that is both firm and easily shaken. In both cases we take beliefs to be identity-dependent on believers. Let us call beliefs, thus understood, 'believings'. When Ann changes her mind (with respect to the question whether p) whereas Ben remains obstinate, then only one of the two believings is left. But of course, in another sense of 'belief' Ben and Ann *share* the belief that p, for a while: his long-standing and firm belief (believing) and her more recent, easily shaken and finally lost belief (believing) have the same *content*.[2] The same holds, *mutatis mutandis*, for statements.[3] When we say 'Ben's statement that p was followed by a startled silence, but only two days later Ann's statement that p was received with thunderous applause', we treat statements as identity-dependent on speakers, i.e. as datable illocutionary acts. But in another sense of 'statement' both speakers made the *same* statement: his ill-received, and her well-received, speech-act have the same *content*. When we ascribe truth (or falsity) to beliefs and statements we do not ascribe it to believings or statings, but rather to *what is believed* and *what is stated*, and that may be something that various believings and statings have in common. What A believes, namely that p, is true iff A is right in believing that p. What B believes, namely that q, is false (a falsehood) iff B's believing that q is erroneous (an error). In saying that somebody's belief or statement is true (false) we characterize in one breath, as it were, a believing or stating and its content.

Of course, not all truths are contents of statings and believings. You might entertain a true thought without belief, and you might formulate a truth in the antecedent of a conditional although you don't assert the antecedent.[4] Furthermore, there are ever so many truths which will never actually become the contents of any thought or speech-act, whatever its psychological or illocutionary mode. (There is a true answer to the question 'How many commas occur in the first edn. of the *Encyclopaedia Britannica*?', but presumably nobody will ever answer it, whether in speech or in thought.) Finally, not all sayings and thinkings have a truth-evaluable content: when you ask yourself or others how

---

[2] For further reflections on Sextus Empiricus' third option, see Ch. 6.2.2.
[3] Strawson, 'Truth' (1950), 190.   [4] Strawson, 'A Problem about Truth', 216–20.

often the letter A occurs on this page, the content of your mental or illocutionary act is not a truth-candidate.

At this point the term '*proposition*' as used in many philosophical writings (including this book) promises help. We can introduce this term in the following way. Starting from a thought-ascription or a speech-report of the form

(I)   A Vs that p

we first bring it into the format

(II)   That p is the content of A's V_n,

where 'V_n' is a verbal noun (such as 'belief' or 'statement') corresponding to the verb (e.g. 'believes', 'states') in (I). Then we adorn the clause in (II) with a prefix:

(III)   The proposition that p is the content of A's V_n.

And finally we add the caveat that something which could be thought or said in some mode or other may never in fact be thought or said in any mode, in which case some proposition would never actually be the content of anyone's Ving. You come to understand the word 'proposition' by learning to accept, as a conceptual matter of course, any inference from (a substitution-instance of) schema (I) via (II) to the corresponding instance of (III), and vice versa, and to acknowledge the possibility mentioned in the caveat.

Understanding 'proposition' in this way, we only need the Leibnizian Principle of the Indiscernibility of Identicals in order to show that the following holds: if A Vs that p but does not V that q, then the proposition that p differs from the proposition that q. For according to the transformation of (I) into (III), A Vs that p without Ving that q just in case the proposition that p has a property which the proposition that q lacks, namely the property of being the content of A's V_n at the pertinent time.[5] (Under the title 'Argument from Doxastic Difference' this very reasoning was turned against the disquotationalist identity thesis in Chapter 4.2.1.) Again and again I have appealed to the Cognitive Equivalence Criterion and the Conceptual Balance Requirement.[6] The rationale

---

[5] Distinctness can also obtain when one and the same sentence occurs in the content clause. Kripke's famous example of the Polish musician-statesman can be used to show this ('A Puzzle About Belief', 265–6). Suppose that Ben does not know that the Paderewski whom he knows to have been a great pianist is identical with the Paderewski whom he knows to have been Prime Minister of the Polish Republic in 1915. Then it is very well possible that both (S1) 'Ben believes that Paderewski was a great pianist' and (S2) 'Ben does *not* believe that Paderewski was a great pianist' serve to make true statements about Ben. But then the that-clause in the utterance of (S1) does not single out the same proposition as the that-clause in the utterance of (S2).

[6] Introduced in Ch. 2.1.3.

for accepting these constraints on propositional identity is, at bottom, that the results of their application agree with our intuitive verdicts of propositional difference which are based on thought-ascriptions and indirect speech-reports. Admittedly, those constraints provide us only with *necessary* conditions of propositional identity, hence with criteria that can be appealed to in justifying affirmations of propositional *difference*. But the lack of a criterion which could be used for justifying affirmations of propositional *identity* doesn't seem to matter. In our practice we get along perfectly well without it.[7]

In view of my misgivings concerning the extended notion of disquotational truth[8] it should be emphasized that, by conceiving propositions in the manner just explained, one does not foreclose the possibility that there might be propositions which cannot be expressed in any language that humans could ever come to be able to understand (and which cannot become the contents of human thinking). What *is* excluded as inconsistent, however, is the idea that there might be propositions which cannot become the contents of *anyone's* saying or thinking (in whatever mode),[9] but who will bemoan this as a loss?

The list of truth-candidates with which I began this section consisted of verbal nouns. We saw that all of them have readings under which they are used to refer to propositions. Unlike 'proposition', those words for partly overlapping sets of propositions (for things believed, things stated, etc.) have no technical philosophical flavour whatsoever. Plenty of non-verbal nouns, such as 'axiom', 'dogma', 'tenet', 'theorem', and 'thesis', which also determine partly overlapping sets of propositions, are certainly not kept for the special use of philosophers either. Those who are keen to ban talk of propositions often seem not to realize how many general terms which are common coin in non-philosophical discourse do 'specialized' duty for 'proposition'.

In claims of the sort '*What A thought (said) was that p*' both clauses specify a proposition (the same proposition, if the claim is correct). But notice that neither kind of phrase always serves to single out a proposition. What-clauses do so only when they are what grammarians call free relatives. By contrast, the clause in 'She asked what A said' is the *oratio obliqua* counterpart of the search interrogative 'What did A say?', and it does not specify a proposition. And even if a what-clause is a free relative, it may single out a *state of affairs* rather than a proposition: 'What A thought was the case.' That-clauses do not always specify propositions either. Sometimes they are relative clauses, as in 'The proposition

---

[7] As was emphasized by Strawson in his 'Reply to John Searle', 403.

[8] On the final pages of Ch. 4.

[9] Cf. Hofweber, 'Inexpressible Properties and Propositions', §5, on 'completely alien propositions'.

that Ben wrote on the blackboard yesterday was the Pythagorean Theorem'. In the Christmassy message 'It came to pass in those days that there went out a decree from Caesar Augustus', the that-clause does not specify a proposition, but an *event*, for only events come to pass (happen, occur).[10] A that-clause may single out a *property* rather than a proposition, as is unmistakable in 'It is one of the properties of a triangle that its internal angles add up to 180°'. And we should also recall that sometimes a that-clause does not specify a proposition but a *state of affairs* (something that may obtain or be the case and, if so, is a *fact*): 'It is a disgrace that she gets so little acknowledgement'.[11] But in the context of 'What is said in Luke 2: 1 is that there went out a decree from Augustus', both clauses do single out a proposition. Obviously, the event-reading of the that-clause is now precluded. The state-of-affairs reading is also foreclosed, since in this context replacement of 'Augustus' by the co-designative name 'Octavianus' might affect the truth-value. (Generally, taking 'a' and 'b' to be place-holders for atomic singular terms, if a is identical with b then the state of affairs that Fa is the same as the state of affairs that Fb.[12])

Often propositions are singled out by nominal phrases or by accusative-cum-infinitive constructions from which a that-clause can easily be recovered: 'A suspects foul play (that there is foul play)', 'A doubts B's sanity (that B is sane)', 'A fears the loss of her reputation (that she might lose her reputation)', 'A advises a return to work (that there be a return to work)', 'A expects B to come tomorrow (that B will come tomorrow)', etc. As Frege pointed out, a yes/no interrogative expresses the same proposition as the corresponding declarative sentence. So propositions can also be specified by whether-clauses, the *oratio obliqua* counterparts of such interrogatives. Thus in '*What A asked (herself, or B) was whether p*', both clauses single out a proposition.[13]

It is high time to disclose a contentious claim that I have tried to veil for a while: the expressions of which I said that they 'single out', or 'specify', an event, a state of affairs or a proposition are *singular terms* which *designate* such

---

[10] Here is another example: 'And it came to pass, as they journeyed from the east, that they found a plain in the land of Shi-nar; and they dwelt there' (Genesis 11: 2).

[11] See Edmund Husserl, *Logische Untersuchungen* (hereinafter *LU*), vol. II/1: V. §33. This point is denied, of course, by all those who identify true propositions with facts (cf. pp. 7–12 above). The systematic ambiguity of that-clauses is often overlooked: see, for example, Alston, *RCT*, 17; Schiffer, 'A Paradox of Meaning', esp. 279, 304–8, and *TWM*, ch. 2.4 ('the concept of a proposition—that is to say, of a that-clause referent').   [12] See pp. 11–12, 116, 139 above.

[13] Frege, '*Der Gedanke*', 62, '*Die Verneinung*', 143–7; Horwich, *Truth*, 130 n. Often we ask yes/no questions by uttering declarative sentences with a certain intonation contour, and we could always do it this way. So the illocutionary potential of our language would not shrink if it did not contain any yes/no interrogatives. If somebody asks a yes/no question in that way, it is quite natural to comment on her utterance: 'What she said is true (false), but her saying it was a request to tell her whether it is true.'

entities. Recall that in Chapter 2, in the course of our reflections on names like 'Pythagoras' Theorem' and 'logicism', it has emerged that an argument of the type

(A1)   a is true

a is the proposition that p

Therefore, the proposition that p is true

is valid in the predicate calculus: 'Fa, a = b ∴ Fb'. The predicate 'is true' is preceded in both of its occurrences in (A1) by a singular term, and (provided that the second premiss is true) that singular term designates the same entity as does the name 'a'. Now if unadorned that-clauses can also be construed as singular terms which designate propositions, then, for one thing, arguments such as

(A2)   Annabella believes that Vesuvius is still active, and so does Barbarella.

Therefore, there is something they both believe (namely, that Vesuvius is still active)

also turn out to be valid in the predicate calculus: 'aRc & bRc ∴ ∃x(aRx & bRx)'. (In examples of type (A1) that-clauses interact with names like 'Pythagoras' Theorem'. Since this makes them clearly resistent against Prior's strategy of dissolving that-clauses, I used them rather than something like (A2) in Chapter 2. For in the case of (A2), Prior's parsing might look attractive at first sight: 'aΠq & bΠq ∴ ∃p(aΠp & bΠp)', where 'Π' is a place-holder for prenectives such as '[ ] believes-that ( )', which have a gap for singular terms at the front and a gap for *sentences* at the rear.[14] But notice that the 'namely'-rider which accompanies the conclusion of (A2) already provides us with counterevidence: Prior's parsing is not faithful to English, which treats that-clauses as syntactical units.[15]) Furthermore, if the that-clause in (A2) is a singular term, then there is also no good reason to shy away from talk of designation.

Now all this was rather iffy. Is it correct to construe not only (substitution-instances of) 'the proposition that p' in (A1), but also the unadorned that-clause in (A2) as singular terms? Consider

(a)   That Vesuvius is still active is true

(a+)   The proposition that Vesuvius is still active is true.

---

[14] Cf. Prior, 'Berkeley in Logical Form', 'Oratio Obliqua', and *OT*, 16–21.

[15] Horwich also argues that we should account in first-order logic for the validity of inferences like (A2): see *Truth*, 86–90; and so does Schiffer: 'A Paradox of Meaning', 280; 'Pleonastic Fregeanism', 2; and, esp., *TWM*, ch. 1.2. Dialectically, I think, they commit a mistake in hushing up Prior's view. But in the end I believe they are in the right as against Prior: for the reason I just gave and because of further observations which were presented on p. 69 above.

How is a sentence like (a) related to its expanded counterpart (a+)? Similarly, I think, as (b) is related to (b+):

(b)   Seven is prime
(b+)   The number seven is prime.

First, in both pairs there is something pleonastic about the longer sentence, because the prefixed noun explicitly introduces a concept for which the place is ready, as it were, when one understands the shorter sentence.[16] Secondly, in both pairs the sentences are cognitively equivalent. (These observations should not be taken to imply that that-clauses can always be replaced *salva veritate* by their more verbose counterparts. I shall return to this point in the next subsection.) Thirdly, in neither pair is the enlarged term a definite description (of the standard kind).

The last remark bears spelling out. A definite description of the standard kind, 'the Φ-er', contains a part, '(is a) Φ-er', which signifies a condition that could be met by exactly one object (provided 'Φ' is consistent). Now compare the subject-phrase in (b+). Here a singular term is prefixed by an *appositive* which specifies the kind of things to which the entity designated by that term belongs. As it stands, no part of the subject-phrase of (b+) signifies a condition that could be met by exactly one number.[17] The same kind of structure can be recognized in the complex subject-term of (a+): a that-clause is preceded by an appositive which specifies the kind of thing to which the designatum of the clause belongs. As it stands, no part of the subject-phrase of (a+) signifies a condition that could be met by exactly one proposition.

Of course, a standard definite description may also contain a singular term whose designatum is identical with that of the whole, as witness 'the person whom Narcissus loves most'. But note the following contrast with the complex singular terms in (a+) and (b+). No garbage results when you replace the name in 'the person whom Narcissus loves most', by any co-designative singular term, even if it is the definite description it is embedded in. But in our pleonastic sentences the singular term embedded in the subject-phrase cannot be exchanged *salva congruitate* (that is, without destroying syntactical coherence), let alone *salva veritate*, by a co-designative term. Seven is the successor of six, but the result of substituting 'the successor of six' in (b+) is grammatically garbled. The subject-terms in (b) and (b+) are co-designative, but when you exchange

---

[16] Cf. my 'Constituents of Concepts', 282–3, on the philosophical bite Bolzano gave to the notion of pleonastic concepts.

[17] Contrast 'the successor of six', 'the natural number between six and eight'.

'seven' in (b+) for its pleonastic counterpart, you produce a stutter. Similarly, that Vesuvius is still active may be a geologist's most cherished belief, but substituting 'B's most cherished belief' for the that-clause in (a+) produces nonsense. The subject-terms in (a) and (a+) are co-designative, but replacing the that-clause in (a+) by its pleonastic counterpart results in a stammer.

The phrase 'the proposition which Ben wrote on the blackboard yesterday' *is* a (standard) definite description. It contains a part, namely '(is a) proposition which Ben wrote on the blackboard yesterday', signifying a condition that could be met by exactly one proposition. Now whenever terms of the form 'the proposition that...' function as stylistic variants of 'the proposition which...', they, too, are (standard) definite descriptions. Thus the phrase

(a)   The proposition that Ben wrote on the blackboard yesterday

is clearly a definite description when it saturates '... was the Pythagorean Theorem', for within this sentence (as was pointed out above) the that-clause functions as a relative clause. The sentence which results from inserting (a) into '... is true' is ambiguous, however: what it is used to say in a given context can be unambiguously expressed either by 'The proposition *which* Ben wrote on the blackboard yesterday is true' or by 'That Ben wrote on the blackboard yesterday is a true proposition'.[18] Under the second reading, (a) designates the proposition expressed (with respect to a given context) by the sentence embedded in (a). Normally, terms of the form 'the proposition that...' have only this reading. So I take it that terms like the subject-phrase in (a+) are not definite descriptions (of the standard kind).

In saying that a+, one does certainly not say that *the proposition which is expressed by 'Vesuvius is still active'* is true, for a monoglot German can believe the latter (perhaps because he takes my word for it) without believing that a+. Nor does one say anything to the effect that *the proposition whose subject-constituent is such-and-such and whose predicate-constituent is so-and-so* is true, for surely one can believe that a+ without conceiving the pertinent proposition as having this, or any other, make up. Quine has suggested that in a regimented language 'the proposition that p' may be rephrased as 'the unique x such that x *is-the-proposition-that* p'.[19] English as it is does not contain the atomic operator 'is-the proposition-that' which is applied to ordered pairs of names and sentences. But it does contain the predicate 'is a proposition', an identity operator, and that-clauses, and if the latter are, as I have

---

[18] This point is due to Cartwright, 'A Neglected Theory of Truth', 89–90.

[19] Quine, *W&O*, 185. Maybe this was the second of the two points in the philosophy of logic in which Prior thought Quine to be dead right? See above, p. 68 n. 106.

argued, singular terms, then one can try to defend the claim that phrases of the form 'the proposition that p' are a special kind of definite description by ascribing more structure to them than meets the eye: 'the unique x such that x is a proposition & x = that p'.[20] It was because of the possibility of this move that I kept on using the hedging adjective 'standard'.

There is, as we saw, an urgent need to distinguish the proposition that there went out a decree from Caesar Augustus (which may be true) both from the state of affairs of the same appellation (which may obtain) and from the homonymous event (which may have come to pass at a certain time). In such cases the appositives play a similar role as those in 'the poet Brentano' and 'the philosopher Brentano', which serve to distinguish the uncle from his nephew. The distinction between propositions and states of affairs is easily blurred. After all, substitution-instances of 'It is true that p' are cognitively equivalent with their counterparts of the form 'It is the case that p' or 'It is a fact that p'. But to conclude from this observation that 'is true' and 'is the case (is a fact)' are co-extensive would be an example of the cancelling-out fallacy exposed by Geach.[21] You might as well argue: 'Socrates defends Socrates' and 'Socrates defends himself' are cognitively equivalent, hence (?) the predicates 'defends Socrates' and 'defends himself' are co-extensive. Some axioms, beliefs, dogmas, and statements are true, but no axiom, belief, dogma, or statement is the case. The things that are true are propositions, and they cannot sensibly be said to be the case. The things that are the case (or that obtain) are states of affairs, and they cannot sensibly be said to be true. So the predicates 'is the case' and 'is true' have not even overlapping extensions.[22] (Here is a comparison. The extension of the set-theoretical predicate 'has members' does not overlap with that of the predicate 'is exemplified' as used of properties. Now imagine a variant of English in which for any univocal predicate 'F' the sentences 'F-hood has members' and 'F-hood is exemplified' are equally well formed: then singular terms of the type 'F-hood' would be systematically ambiguous, designating in the former use the

---

[20] In *Descriptions*, 116 n. 55, Neale suggests applying this strategy to terms like 'the sculptor John Smith', which have the same structure as my (b+): 'the unique x such that x is a sculptor & x = John Smith'. I have tentatively applied the strategy to 'the fact that p' on p. 10 n. 23 above .

[21] Geach, *Reference and Generality*, 61.

[22] Lewis comes at least dangerously close to committing the cancelling-out fallacy when he writes, 'More often than not, saying it's true that cats purr is synonymous with calling it a truth that cats purr, and that in turn is synonymous with calling it a fact that cats purr, or with saying that there is such a fact as the fact that cats purr. In short: a fact on this usage is nothing other than a true proposition, whatever that is' ('Correspondence', 276–7). Incidentally, characterizing acts (of saying or calling) as synonymous is hardly felicitous, and the point of the first four words eludes me.

set of all F's and in the latter use the property of being F, and prefixing the appositive 'the set' or 'the property' to 'F-hood' would serve to disambiguate.)

In taking the term 'proposition' to be introduced by means of the transformation of (I), 'A Vs that p', into (III), 'The proposition that p is the content of A's V_n', I come fairly close to the view of propositions to which Stephen Schiffer has forced his way in recent years.[23] Apart from the caveat concerning that-clauses which I entered above, I agree with some of his central contentions: (i) 'What is required for our knowledge of propositions, and all that is required, is that we be party to our that-clause involving linguistic and conceptual practices', that is, our practice of ascribing 'propositional attitudes' and reporting speech by means of that-clauses. (ii) 'There's nothing more to the nature of propositions than can be read off [from] our that-clause involving practices', and, consequently, (iii) propositions are individuated by antecedently available criteria for evaluating attitude reports and *oratio obliqua*. As for (iii), notice the following contrast emphasized by Schiffer: it would be absurd to attempt to establish that Annabella is not identical with Barbarella by showing that somebody might (dis)like the former without (dis)liking the latter. But we do establish that the proposition that p differs from the proposition that q by showing that somebody might (dis)believe that p without (dis)believing that q. If talk of 'attitude towards' weren't so infelicitous with respect to propositions (as we shall see in the next subsection), we could epitomize this contrast by saying: persons are not, whereas propositions are, distinguished by the possibility of taking conflicting attitudes towards them.

5.1.2 *Contents and (intentional) objects*

Following Bolzano, Husserl, and Searle I have called propositions (possible) *contents*, rather than *objects*, of certain speech acts and of certain mental acts and states.[24] Of course, in one sense of the term 'object' everything that can be referred to is an object (an entity), hence propositions, too, are objects on this acceptation of the term. In another sense objects are things, more or less bulky

---

[23] The quotations that follow come from Schiffer, 'Pleonastic Fregeanism', 8–10; cf. also his 'A Paradox of Meaning', 311–13. Schiffer's present position, as developed in *TWM*, can no longer be characterized as pleonastic *Fregeanism*, but the tenets I am about to endorse are also cornerstones of his present views: see *TWM*, ch. 2.4.

[24] On Bolzano's notion of the 'matter [*Stoff*]', and Husserl's concept of the 'intentional matter [*Materie*]', of acts of judgement, see my 'Propositions in Bolzano and Frege' and 'The Nature of Acts'. See also Searle, *Intentionality*, ch. 1, esp. 17. Frege is rather fond of the metaphor that one and the same proposition can 'stand vis-à-vis [*gegenüberstehen*]' various thinkers (*NS*, 138 (127), 145 (133), 160 (148), 214 (198); 'Der Gedanke', 66, cf. 75; 'Die Verneinung', 147). But the act-object model is hardly essential to his theory. In '*Über Sinn und Bedeutung*' (32 n. 5), he uses the term 'content [*Inhalt*]' in order to make the point which that metaphor is meant to convey.

particulars, and under this reading propositions are not objects, of course, anymore than events, properties, or numbers are. But there is a third use of 'object' which contrasts with both: when we talk about the object of her admiration, of his hatred, of their quarrel, the term 'object' could not be replaced by either 'entity' or 'thing'. It is this use which is pertinent here.[25] The issue is whether the proposition that p is the (intentional) object *of* saying or thinking, in whatever illocutionary or psychological mode, that p.

'What is gained by calling [the proposition that p] the content rather than the object of my thinking [that p]?'[26] For one thing, the terminological policy I suggest can help us to distinguish several possibilities which ought to be kept apart. First, if Ben judges that

(P)   the square on the hypotenuse is equal to the sum of the squares on the other two sides,

then the Pythagorean Theorem is not an object to which he adverts, or which he thinks about, but the content of his thinking. Secondly, if Ann judges that

(Q)   the Pythagorean Theorem is still unknown to many people,

then this theorem is not the content of her thinking but an object to which she adverts. She might judge that Q even if she is not able to entertain the thought that P. Thirdly, sometimes a proposition is both an object to which a thinker adverts and *part of* the content of his or her judgement.[27] If Ann judges that

(R)   the theorem that P is still unknown to many people,

then she adverts to the Pythagorean Theorem by entertaining the thought that P. Nevertheless, in this mixed case as in its predecessors, the proposition which is the content of her judgement is different from the object she adverts to.

The following observations point to a further gain I expect from studiously observing the content-object distinction.[28] Suppose

(A)   Annabella asserts
(B)   Barbarella believes   } that Vesuvius is still active.
(C)   Cinderella knows
(D)   Dorabella fears

---

[25] Cf. Wittgenstein, *Philosophische Bemerkungen*, §§93, 115; my comments on these passages in *Abstrakte Gegenstände*, 41; and Hanjo Glock's comments on my comments in 'Does Ontology Exist?', 251–2.

[26] Dummett, 'Comments on WK's Paper', 242.

[27] Cf. my criticism of Soames on p. 73 above.

[28] My comments on (A–E) draw on White, 'What We Believe'; Rundle, *GP*, 293–8; Hugly and Sayward, *I&T*, 28, 132–3; Friederike Moltmann, 'Nominalizing Quantifiers' (Ms.); and Hacker, *Wittgenstein: Mind and Will*. Pt. I, 28–35.

Pre-theoretically at least, we would not call anything the object of A.'s assertion. (Of course, we would be ready to say that her assertion is *about* an object, namely a volcano.) If the proposition that p were the object of C.'s knowledge, (C) would tell us that C. knows this proposition. Now this proposition is something B. knows as well, for one cannot believe a proposition without knowing it. But of course, B. may not know *that p* in spite of knowing *the proposition that p*.[29] (In German '*A weiß die Proposition, dass p*' is not even grammatically acceptable: one has to replace the verb '*wissen*' by '*kennen* [be acquainted with]'. In French it would have to be '*connaître*' rather than '*savoir*'.) Finally, if the proposition that p were the object of D.'s fear, one might wonder whether she is a neurotic nominalist who is generally afraid of propositions.[30] So the claim that the proposition that p is the object of the acts or states ascribed to our four graces either makes no pre-theoretical sense at all, as in case (A), or it does not preserve the sense of the original ascription, as in cases (C) and (D), or it may not even preserve its truth-value, as in case (D). In our sample sentences grammar allows us to slip the noun phrase 'the proposition' between verb and that-clause, but at least in cases (C) and (D) the sense changes drastically. It is noteworthy that sometimes such an insertion is not even grammatically admissible, as in the next example:[31]

(E)   Emanuela hopes that Vesuvius is still active.

None of these observations is embarrassing if we say that in cases (A–E) one and the same proposition is the *content*, rather than the object, of various acts and states. By contrast, if in a sentence of the type 'A Vs the proposition that p' the noun-phrase 'the proposition' (or one of its specialized variants) is *not* eliminable *salva congruitate*, as in

They debated (attacked, defended) the proposition that power corrupts,

then the proposition that p is the *(intentional) object*, rather than the content, of the Ving. Generally, if the gap in 'A Vs . . .' is filled by 'the proposition that p' or by a more specific appositive description ('the theorem that p'), a standard definite description ('the proposition which is F') or a name ('logicism') of a

---

[29] Dummett stipulates: 'here *Galileo knew the proposition expressed by "The Earth moves"* is used simply to mean *Galileo knew that the Earth moves*' ('Is the Concept of Truth Needed for Semantics?', 6). This stipulation jars with our ordinary understanding of the first italicized sentence. Galileo also knew the proposition expressed by 'The Earth does not move', but he did *not* know that the Earth doesn't move.

[30] Surely one should not shrug this off as Russell did: 'It seems natural to say one believes a proposition and unnatural to say one desires a proposition, but as a matter of fact that is only a prejudice' ('*PLA*', 218).

[31] There are plenty of such cases: 'A is afraid (boasts, is certain, complains, is convinced, gathers, objects, protests, replies, is sorry, is sure, is worried) that p.'

proposition, then we are told which proposition is the intentional object of A's Ving. By contrast, 'A Vs that p' tells us that the content of A's Ving is the proposition that p.[32]

Using Fregean language to make a Husserlian point, we can say: propositions are 'modes of presentation [*Arten des Gegebenseins*]' of states of affairs; the former are the contents of certain mental acts and states, whereas the latter are their (primary) intentional objects.[33] Thus the state of affairs of Vesuvius still being active is what the mental acts and states ascribed to our graces are (primarily) 'directed at'. (What their acts and states are *about* is not that state of affairs, but rather the volcano or, depending on the conversational context in which the ascriptions are made, the property of still being active.[34] So we have actually three claimants for the title 'intentional object' of their 'propositional attitudes',—two *Sachen* and one *Sachverhalt*. Husserl argues that states of affairs, *Sachverhalte*, are what such acts and states are 'primarily' directed at.[35]) Knowing that the proposition that a is F is the content of a state or act, we know which state of affairs is its intentional object. The reverse claim, though, is not correct. If a is identical with b and if being F is nothing but being G, then the state of affairs that a is F is the same as the state of affairs that b is G, but even then the proposition that a is F is different from the proposition that b is G if somebody might V that a is F without Ving that b is G.

Sometimes states of affairs appear in philosophical discussions under a different (and very misleading) title. I am alluding here to the debate between advocates of so-called 'Russellian propositions' and friends of 'Fregean propositions'. Both camps promote a structuralist view of propositions according to which they have constituents that are ordered in a certain way. Thus the proposition that the sun is larger than the moon is said to contain the same constituents as the proposition that the moon is larger than the sun, but in a different order. The two views differ as to what sorts of things the constituents of structured propositions are supposed to be.[36] What Russellians take to be the proposition expressed by 'Hesperus lacks water' is ontologically hybrid: it consists of a particular, namely Hesperus (*in propria persona*, as it were), and a universal, namely the property of lacking water. By contrast, the Fregean proposition expressed by that sentence is ontologically homogeneous: it consists of the sense

---

[32] Compare (i) 'She explained the proposition that space is non-Euclidean' and (ii) 'She explained that she could not stay': in (i) the object of her act is specified, in (ii) its content.

[33] Husserl, *LU*, vol. II/1: V. §§20, 28.

[34] See Strawson, *Individuals*, 144 (with a bow to Cook Wilson), on conversationally induced shifts in aboutness. [35] Husserl, *LU*, II/1: I. §12, V. §17. Cf. Searle, *Intentionality*, ch. 1.

[36] For references, see Ch. 1 above, p. 8 and n. 16.

(*Sinn*) of 'Hesperus' and the sense of 'lacks water'. The former constituent is supposed to be (something like) the way one has to think of the planet in order to understand the name, and the latter constituent is said to be (something like) the way one has to think of the property of lacking water in order to understand the predicate. I dub advocates of the Russellian view 'hybridizers', as opposed to the 'purists' who favour the Fregean view. As will emerge in section 5.2.3 of this chapter, the debate between hybridizers and purists is largely orthogonal to the controversy over truth-value stability. This controversy would even arise if propositions were not composed of anything. And this neutrality may be all to the good, since *both* structuralist positions are plagued by formidable difficult- ies.[37] In any case, the entities hybridizers call propositions do not comply with the Cognitive Equivalence Criterion. 'Hesperus lacks water' and 'Phosphorus lacks H_2O' express one and the same 'Russellian proposition', but somebody who understands both sentences might very well take only one of them to express a truth. (Perhaps he doesn't know that the two names designate the same planet, or that the two predicates signify the same property.) By taking our astronomical propositions to be as fine-grained as Frege would have taken them to be (after all, we applied *his* criterion), we are not committed to accept his structuralism. The verdict that 'Russellian propositions' are definitely not propositions in our acceptation of the term[38] does not imply that there are no such things: epilepsy isn't what it used to be called, a Sacred Disease, but unfor- tunately it exists all the same. Reinach's complaint about the 'Austrian confu- sion' (which I quoted in Chapter 1) applies equally well to the hybridizers. What they misclassify as 'Russellian propositions' are rather *Sachverhalte*, Reinach would have maintained, and, indeed, *states of affairs* have at least the same 'grain' as these so-called 'propositions'. (The same holds for facts and 'true Russellian proposi- tions'.) Interestingly Reinach's 'canonical name' for the state of affairs which one takes to obtain when one judges that a is F was not 'that a is F' but rather '*das F-sein*

---

[37] As is shown (for all latter day variants of these two positions as well) in Schiffer, *TWM*, ch. 1.

[38] Biting the bullet, hybridizers contend that whoever believes that Hesperus lacks water *does* believe that Phosphorus lacks H_2O, and they have worked hard to make this contention seem less unpalatable, most notably Salmon in *Frege's Puzzle*. I agree with Schiffer (and Dodd, *ITT*, 57–60), that the results of their labour are not convincing. What holds for 'Russellian propositions' applies a fortiori to the far more coarse-grained 'propositions' of some possible world semanticists. They maintain that the 'proposi- tion' that Hesperus lacks water, say, is identical with the set of possible worlds at which the sentence 'Hesperus lacks water' (as used by us) is true. If 'propositions', thus individuated, are the contents of our beliefs, then nobody believes that all drakes are male without believing that 5^7 isn't 75,125 (because both content-sentences are true at *each* possible world), and whoever believes that 5^7 equals 75,125, believes that triangles have four angles (because the set of worlds at which the content-sentences are true is the same, i.e. the null-set). Robert Stalnaker's valiant attempt, in ch. 1 of *Inquiry*, to make this view of belief reports appear less outrageous has met with less than universal assent.

des a [the being F of a]'. Actually, 'a's being F' would have been more appropriate, I think, but in any case, one strategic advantage of employing gerunds is clear: unlike that-clauses, they do not fit into the slot of '... is true', so the danger of confusing states of affairs and propositions is warded off.[39] Hesperus's lacking water (the state of affairs that Hesperus lacks water) is the same as Phosphorus's lacking H_2O (the state of affairs that Phosphorus lacks H_2O), and if this state of affairs obtains, it is a fact. But, *pace* Reinach, there is no need to conceive of this state of affairs as somehow containing a planet and a property.[40]

5.1.3 More on truth-value bearers

In our everyday employment of 'true', we normally, if not exclusively, take propositions to be the things that are susceptible of truth. This practice, be it noted, allows us to take claims of the form 'What A believes (what B denies) is true' at face value.[41]

[W]e talk ordinarily and readily enough of, e.g., *What John said*; of *its* being believed or doubted by Peter; of Paul denying *it*; of William saying *the same thing*, though in different words; of *its* being more elegantly expressed in French by Yvette; of *its* being true (or false); and so on. On the face of it, the noun-phrases and attendant pronouns here do not refer to the token words, the token sentence, which John uttered; or, indeed, to the type-sentence of which he uttered a token; or even to the meaning of that sentence, since the same type-sentence, with constant and unambiguous meaning, can be used to say different things with different truth-values (as is the case with any sentence containing deictic or indexical elements).... Philosophers have a word for it—or several words: they may speak, with Frege, of the *thought* expressed by the utterance; or of the *proposition* or *propositional content* asserted, denied, believed, surmised, true or false. (Strawson, *Scepticism and Naturalism*, 69–70)

An account that aims to be faithful to our workaday concept of truth cannot afford to turn its back on propositions: they are the *primary truth-value bearers*.[42] Following Tarski's lead, many philosophers, logicians, and mathematicians prefer to take declarative (type-)*sentences*, orthographically individuated, as truth-value

---

[39] All this (as well as the claim that it is states of affairs that are bearers of modal properties like necessity and possibility) is to be found in Reinach, 'Zur Theorie des negativen Urteils'. For exegesis and references see my 'The Intentionality of Thinking', §§7–8.

[40] In *LU*, II/2: VI. §47 (beginning), Husserl also seems to endorse such a conception of states of affairs. On pp. 121–2 above, I have intimated my reservations.   [41] See pp. 39–40 above.

[42] Lest it be thought that in a post-Tarskian age this is a minority view, let me register here that the primacy tenet is upheld, among others, by Cartwright, 'Propositions'; Horwich, *Truth*, chs. 2.1, 6 and pp. 129–35; Alston, *RCT*, 9–22; Soames, *UT*, ch. 1; Dodd, *ITT*, ch. 2; Lewis, 'Correspondence', 276; and Schiffer, *TWM*. As for Strawson, see also his 'Reply to John Searle'.

bearers (or rather as bearers of the relational property ascribable by something like 's in L is true with respect to context c'). But the technical advantages this strategy may have for the purposes of mathematico-logical theory construction[43] should not make us forget that before we took our first course in philosophical logic, we hardly if ever encountered applications of a relativized truth-predicate to sentences, and when we learned to use it, our teachers had to rely on our grasp of the everyday concept of truth by using a fairly complex Bridge-Principle:

(BP)   s in L is true with respect to c iff *what is literally said when s is used as a sentence of L in c* is true.

Hence I wonder whether the Disquotation Schema, '*p*' *is true iff p*, really 'embodies our best intuition as to how the concept of truth is *used*', as Davidson says.[44] The use of 'true' as an instrument of everyday discourse is quite different from the metalinguistic use exemplified in the Disquotation Schema.

But don't we ascribe truth (without relativization) to *utterances* in our daily transactions? I don't think we do. Suppose somebody makes an assertion by uttering sentence *S*, and you concede, 'That's true, but...' Some time later you are annoyed by another assertoric utterance of *S*, and you reply wearily, 'As I said half an hour ago, that's true, but...' This rejoinder is absolutely correct: you did twice ascribe truth to one and the same 'thing'. But surely in your earlier (later) comment you did not ascribe truth to the later (earlier) utterance of *S*. So what is called 'true' in your comments is not a datable speech episode. Pointing to an utterance, you refer to something else—i.e. to what is said in this utterance. Here are two structurally similar cases of ostension. Pointing at a picture on the wall, you might truly say, 'That's a former president of the college', although fortunately the honourable gentleman is not himself hanging on the wall. The pertinent satisfier of the predicate 'is a former president of the college' is picked out here by an act of (what Quine calls[45]) deferred ostension, demonstration by proxy. My second example is closer still to the case at hand. Listening to Classic FM at 11 p.m., you must prepare for the worst. You might hear an assertive utterance of 'Mozart's greatest tune is this', followed by some humming. Here the alleged satisfier of the predicate 'is Mozart's greatest tune' is identified by means of deferred ostension, the proxy being a particular series

---

[43] Kripke says, 'The main reason I apply the truth predicate directly to linguistic objects is that for such objects a mathematical theory of self-reference has been developed.' But he also emphasizes that he does *not* think 'that the objection that truth is primarily a property of propositions is irrelevant to serious work on truth...on the contrary' ('Outline of a Theory of Truth', 691).

[44] Davidson, 'On the Very Idea of a Conceptual Scheme', 195 (my italics).

[45] See the title essay of *Ontological Relativity and Other Essays*, 40.

of sounds that you never wanted to hear (even if you love the 'tune'). Similarly, in your comments on the two utterances of *S* you single out the relevant satis-fier of 'is true' by deferred ostension.[46]

Mutatis mutandis the reflections of the last paragraph also apply to audible *token-sentences*, i.e. certain series of sounds which are the products of particular acts of uttering. I take it that in the oral case this distinction is no less real, though certainly less obvious, than that between visible token-sentences, i.e. inscriptions, and the acts of writing from which they result.[47]

For Davidson and Quine, arguments such as the one I gave in the penultim-ate paragraph seem not to carry much weight:

> It has been argued, and convincingly, that we do not generally, or perhaps ever, say of a speech act, utterance, or token, that it is true. This hardly shows why we ought not to call these entities ... true. No confusion would result if we said that the particular speaking of a sentence was true just in case it was used on that occasion to make a true statement; and similarly for tokens and utterances. (Davidson, 'True to the Facts', 44)

> What are best seen as primarily true or false are ... events of utterance. (Quine, *PL*, 13)

Would really no confusion result if we were to follow Davidson's and Quine's advice? For one thing, what becomes of logical laws such as the principle of non-contradiction or the principle of self-implication, and what becomes of logical rules such as *modus ponens*, if we take truth and falsity to be properties of utterances (or of their products)? Suppose Socrates utters, with Theaetetus before him,

(1)   Theaetetus is sitting, and it is not the case that Theaetetus is sitting.

(2)   If Theaetetus is sitting, then Theaetetus is sitting.

Each time Theaetetus is and remains seated when Socrates starts speaking, but he stands up as soon as Socrates says 'and' or 'then'. So, due to Theaetetus' somewhat malevolent behaviour, Socrates' utterance of the contradiction (1) consists of true conjuncts,[48] and his utterance of the tautological conditional (2) consists of a true antecedent and a false consequent.[49] Or suppose Socrates runs through the following argument aloud, again with Theaetetus before him:

(P1)   If Theaetetus is sitting, then Theaetetus is not standing.

(P2)   Theaetetus is sitting. Therefore,

(C)   Theaetetus is not standing.

---

[46] There is an important restriction to our use of 'That's true (false)': it is never used to comment on utterances of non-declarative sentences. This restriction is observed even if an utterance of a non-declarative sentence does express a proposition ('Did Frege die in 1925?').

[47] Cf. Twardowski, 'Actions and Products', esp. §§23–7, 35.

[48] Buridanus, *Sophismata*, ch. VII, 4th Soph.; Wittgenstein, *Bemerkungen über die Philosophie der Psychologie*, I, §37.

[49] Kaplan, 'Afterthoughts', 585 n.

His utterances of (P1) and (P2) are true, and yet his utterance of (C) is false because cheeky Theaetetus stands up when Socrates says 'therefore'.[50] Our vocal organs being what they are, a single speaker will find it hard to follow Jean Buridan's advice to utter the component sentences simultaneously.[51]

Kaplan playfully suggests that one might write down the complex sentence or the argument ahead of time and then hold up the inscription at the moment when one wants to be understood as making a logically false, or logically true, assertion or as presenting a formally valid argument.[52] But if inscriptions were taken to be primary truth-value bearers, we would again run into trouble with some of our most cherished logical principles. For example with this one: an argument is valid only if it is impossible for the premiss(es) to be true without the conclusion's also being true. The following argument is valid,

(P)   Every word contains several letters. Therefore,
(C*)   no word contains only a single letter.

But if we take premiss and conclusion to be the sentence-inscriptions to the right of (P) and (C*), this is not so. We can conceive of a possible circumstance in which the premiss is true while the conclusion is not. After all, the conclusion(-inscription) is under *no* circumstances true, since it contains an inscription of a one-lettered word.[53] None of these problems arises if we take propositions that are expressed by (type-)sentences in a context to be bearers of truth and falsity and evaluate different indexical (type-)sentences, whenever they are parts of a complex sentence or of an argument, with respect to the *same* context and, in particular, to the same time.[54]

But let us put problems connected with logical truth and validity aside. Suppose a speaker is talking on the phone to his worst enemy while looking at his best friend: in a single utterance of 'You are my best friend' he might address both persons simultaneously and thus express two propositions (make two statements) with different truth-values.[55] Surely confusion would result if we were to call the utterance (or the token[56]) true and not true. Or suppose you utter a grammatically and/or lexically ambiguous sentence, intending your

---

[50] Prior, 'Fugitive Truth', 6.   [51] Buridanus, *Sophismata*, ch. VIII, 1st Soph., line 83.

[52] Kaplan, 'Afterthoughts', 585 n., 587.

[53] Example borrowed, with a minor change, from Buridanus, *Sophismata*, ch. VIII, 1st Soph., l. 66–7.

[54] Kaplan, 'Demonstratives', 522, 546.

[55] Cf. Bolzano, *WL*, III. 550–1, 553; Barry Taylor, 'Truth-Theory for Indexical Languages', 185.

[56] I have explained above my understanding of 'utterance' and 'token (sentence)'. I cannot figure out how Davidson thinks of the relation between what he calls a particular speaking of a sentence, an utterance and a token.

utterance to be understood both ways.[57] (Perhaps you are making a joke, and the point of the joke depends on the sentence being given both readings by the person you are addressing.) Then it may very well be the case that you express a truth and a falsehood at one stroke. Again, confusion would result if we were to call the utterance (or the token-sentence) true and not true.

Davidson's alternative strategy of treating truth as a property of ordered triples of (type-)sentences, persons, and times would lead here to the same confusion.[58] A further consequence of the triple strategy is worth noticing. Barring resurrection (and mesmerizing *in articulo mortis*, as described in Poe's horrific story 'The Facts in the Case of M. Valdemar'), nobody can ever truthfully say,

(S)   I have been dead now for more than 150 years,

but the triple strategy does allow us to assign truth to {(S); Bolzano; first midnight in 2002}. Dummett, who approves of the strategy, asks potential critics to keep cool: 'There is no reason to be disconcerted by [this fact].'[59] I shall follow his advice. After all, a propositionalist should be ready to admit that (S) expresses a truth with respect to that person and that time. The *post mortem* example only dramatizes a point which can be made with 'I am not uttering anything now'. Nobody can ever truthfully say this, and yet the sentence expresses a truth with respect to every person at any time at which she or he does not utter anything.

Brian Ellis has nicely combined both confusion-engendering features, which were mentioned in the penultimate paragraph, in one and the same example:

My friend, Mr Alfred Duplex, has two telephones on his desk. Two women he knows, both called 'Mary', rang him simultaneously wanting to know where their respective husbands were. Alfred picked up both receivers and said, 'Hello, Mary, I think he has gone to the bank. Sorry I cannot stop and talk to you now. I hope you find him.' And then he hung up. Alfred intended one Mary to understand that her husband had gone fishing, and the other to understand that her husband was at the trading bank. In this case, there was only one utterance, or sequence of utterances, but there are at least two, and possibly as many as four different truth bearers. There are the two things Alfred intended the women to believe, and there are the two things the women understood Alfred to be saying—and conceivably they are all different. Therefore, if utterances are the bearers of truth, a bearer could be both true and false.[60]

Furthermore, there is only one ordered triple of a sentence, a person, and a time involved. Hence, if such triples are the bearers of truth-values, one and the same entity could be both true and not true.

---

[57] Cf. Bolzano, *WL*, III. 549–50, 553.

[59] Dummett, 'Sentences and Propositions', 9.

[58] Davidson, 'In Defence of Convention T', 74.

[60] Ellis, *Truth and Objectivity*, 172.

Let me round this off by adding an interlingual example which has served us before. Annabella, a business woman in Milan, has two telephones on her desk (as you may have anticipated). An American colleague and a British friend rang her simultaneously wanting to know how much profit her firm made last year. She wanted only her friend to know the truth. So picking up both receivers she said, 'One billion lira. But excuse me, I have a visitor in my office. Let's talk tomorrow.' And then she hung up. Annabella intended her American colleague to understand that the profit amounted to 10^9 lira, and her British friend to understand that it amounted to 10^{12} lira. A falsehood as well as a truth were conveyed by just one utterance, or by just one ordered triple of a sentence, a person, and a time. Therefore, if utterances, or such triples, were themselves truth-value bearers, some bearers would be both true and not true. All this is certainly unbearable.[61]

By taking what is, or could be, said (rather than the vehicle used for saying it or the act of saying it or the product of this act) to be the primary truth-value bearer, the issue which will occupy us in the remainder of this chapter is not prejudged. This issue concerns the question whether one and the same thing was said in several utterances. Such a question will often receive conflicting answers, and neither side in the ensuing debate can lay claim to the one and only correct understanding of the phrase 'what is said'. There are various reasons for this, and one of them should at least be registered in passing. Let us suppose that the following encounter occurs in the unabridged version of Fellini's *Otto e mezzo*. (The protagonists speak English for our convenience.) At 11 a.m. Guido's over-protective mother turns up at his flat. Carla, Luisa, and Claudia rush to open the door. His mother would like to take him out for lunch, so she asks whether he is hungry. Guido's room-mates answer simultaneously on his behalf,

C. No.
L. Guido isn't hungry.
Cl. Guido has just had breakfast.

[61] Dummett adopts Davidson's triple strategy, but he adds: 'I shall presume that the identification of a type sentence depends on identifying the language to which it belongs' ('Sentences and Propositions', 9). This helps with my interlingual case, but all cases of *intra*lingual ambiguity are as recalcitrant as ever. As to my indexical examples, Dummett would perhaps take them to be covered by his remark: 'Demonstrative expressions like "that house", "this country", etc., are less easily dealt with. Many should be regarded as devoid of reference unless, [at time] t, [the speaker] i actually makes a pointing gesture or the equivalent' (ibid.). It is none too easy to say what 'the equivalent' of a pointing gesture is in the phone examples given above (for 'you' and 'he'). But even if there occurs such an equivalent (as Kaplan argues in 'Afterthoughts', 582–90), I cannot see that it extricates the triple strategy from the objection that was put forward above. After all, the alleged truth-value bearer is constituted by a (type-)sentence, a person and a time: the identity of the triple is entirely independent of what the person does at the time in question. (It is even independent of whether the person actually utters, or can utter, the sentence at that time.)

Did they all say one and the same thing? Of course, they uttered different *words*, but this is not to the point. We could correctly report their utterances by saying, 'They all told Guido's mother that he wasn't hungry.' (Our standards for judging the correctness of *oratio obliqua* reports are very flexible, and under normal circumstances they are far less strict than, say, for statements of witnesses reporting under oath, 'The accused said to me that one day she would stab her husband.') So in a sense, yes, they did all say the same thing. But in another sense, they didn't. Luisa *said* that Guido wasn't hungry, and so did Carla, though in a more economical manner. But Claudia only *indirectly conveyed* this by saying something else.[62]

In what follows we will be interested in quite a different reason for conceding that the question whether one thing was said in different utterances may receive conflicting but equally reasonable answers. For many centuries philosophers have been divided over the question whether the truth-values of sayables are stable. *Eternalists* contend that truth is a property which cannot be lost: if something is true at all, then it is true once and for all. *Temporalists* deny this. If one maintains that propositions have truth-values 'absolutely (i.e. without relativization to anything)', hence a fortiori without relativization to time, one takes the side of eternalism.[63] In the end, this may very well be the right decision, but it needs argument. We shall also see that the locution 'not relative to time' permits, and has actually received, two rather different readings.

5.2 Eternalism

Jede Wahrheit ist ewig. [Every truth is eternal.]
(Gottlob Frege, '*Kernsätze zur Logik*' [c. 1876], *NS*, 190 (175))

The occurrence of tense in verbs is an exceedingly annoying vulgarity due to our preoccupation with practical affairs. It would be much more agreeable if they had no tense, as I believe is the case in Chinese, but I do not know Chinese.

(Bertrand Russell, *PLA*, 248)

---

[62] See Grice, 'Logic and Conversation', esp. 24–5. For serious enquiries into the problems lightly touched in the text above, cf. Andreas Kemmerling, '*Die Objektivität von Glaubenssätzen*', Kent Bach, 'You Don't Say?', and François Recanati, 'What Is Said'.

[63] The quotation is from Schiffer, 'A Paradox of Meaning', 281; 'Pleonastic Fregeanism', 3; *TWM*, ch. 1.2.

Among the most important eternalists of the last two centuries are Bolzano, Frege, Twardowski, Husserl, Moore, and Russell. Eternalism itself is not, as is often assumed, a monolithic position. I shall point out several respects in which eternalists are at variance.

5.2.1 *A first division in the eternalist camp*

Russell's 1906 criticism of the conception of 'variable' statements (as proposed by the Scottish logician Hugh MacColl) has been called a *locus classicus* of eternalism:

> As an instance [for a statement which is 'variable' insofar as it 'sometimes represents a truth and sometimes an untruth'] he [MacColl] gives '*Mrs. Brown is not at home*' .... What is expressed by the form of words at any given instance is not itself variable; but at another instant something else, itself quite invariable, is expressed by the same form of words.... Ordinary language employs, for the sake of convenience, many words whose meaning varies ... with the time when they are employed; thus statements using such words must be supplemented by further data before they become unambiguous.... When we are told '*Mrs. Brown is not at home*', we know the time at which this is said, and therefore we know what is meant. But in order to express explicitly the whole of what is meant, it is necessary to add the date, and then the statement is no longer 'variable' but always true or always false. ('Review', 256–7)

When we look closely at this passage, we can actually discern two claims. Let me illustrate them by a different example, which will accompany us through to the end of this chapter. Suppose that at 10 a.m. Greenwich Mean Time, 18 May, *Anno Domini* 1906, somebody utters the sentence

(1)   It is raining in London,

referring to the capital of the United Kingdom. Russell's first contention is that 'what is expressed' by this utterance never changes its truth-value. Generally, any utterance of a sentence that 'sometimes represents a truth and sometimes an untruth' (as MacColl put it) expresses something that has a stable truth-value. This claim makes Russell an *eternalist*. Notice that the 'variation of meaning with the time of utterance' which Russell would ascribe to (1) cannot be a change of conventional linguistic meaning:[64] when words undergo that kind of

---

[64] Cf. Cartwright, 'Propositions', 42–3.

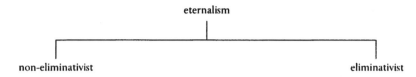

Figure 5.1. Eternalism (1)

change ('He speaks with the vulgar'), they do not do so from one moment to the next. What varies with the time of uttering (1) is the proposition expressed.

Russell's second contention is that 'the whole of what is meant' in that 1906 utterance of (1) is completely expressed by

(2)   There is rain in London (England) at 10 a.m. (GMT), 18 May, (AD) 1906.

(From now on I shall omit the bracketed embellishments as understood.) The quantifier phrase 'there is' in (2) is not time-specific ('there is *now*'), anymore than its counterpart in the predicate calculus signifies present, as opposed to past and future, existence. Generally, 'the whole of what is meant' by an utterance of a sentence that sometimes represents a truth and sometimes an untruth can be completely expressed by a sentence which, as used in present-day English, is not subject to this fluctuation. This claim makes Russell a spokesman of *eliminativist eternalism*: like Husserl (at least in one mood) and Twardowski before him, Russell maintains that tenses can be eliminated *salva propositione*.[65] Bolzano and Frege do not belong to this camp, I think. Our first division can be seen in Figure 5.1.

Sentence (2) is what Quine would call an *eternal sentence*:[66]

An eternal sentence is a sentence whose tokens all have the same truth value.... When we call a sentence eternal ... we are calling it eternal relative only to a particular language at a particular time. (*PL*, 14)[67]

---

[65] On Husserl's brief flirtation with eliminativism (*LU*, II/1: 1. §28), cf. my '*Indexikalität. Sinn und propositionaler Gehalt*', 53–7. A kind of eliminativist position was also upheld by another pupil of Brentano: according to Twardowski, the founder of analytical philosophy in Poland, the sentence 'On 1 March 1900, in accordance with the Gregorian calendar, at noon, Central European Time, it is raining in Lwów, on the High Castle Hill and in its vicinity' is the 'full-fledged expression' of the judgement voiced by an utterance of 'It is raining' at the indicated time by a speaker at the indicated place ('On So-Called Relative Truths', 43 (152), 46 (156)). (I call this 'a kind of' eliminativism, because Twardowski's truth-value bearers are mental acts and states.) Eliminativism in the strict sense of my definition is propounded by Carl Ducasse in his 'Propositions, Truth, and the Ultimate Criterion of Truth', 169.

[66] Notice that there is a certain tension as to truth-value bearers between this quotation, and the passages cited on pp. 265 and 273, if one accepts the distinction between tokens and utterances that I suggested on p. 265 above. As the difference is irrelevant for the discussion that is to follow, I shall conduct the discussion only in terms of utterances.

[67] Cf. Quine, *W&O*, 193, 227; *Theories and Things*, 26.

The relativization is meant to take care of the possibility that a type-sentence (individuated by spelling) might be eternal in one (stage of a) language and non-eternal in another.[68] Quine represents the view held by propositionalists in the following way:

[O]ne and the same sentence can be...true or false depending on who says it and when.... Propositions, thought of as sentence meanings, were the meanings exclusively of sentences of a firmer sort, not subject to such vacillations; what we may call eternal sentences. (*PT*, 78)[69]

Obviously, advocates of this view follow Russell's footsteps in opting for the eliminativist variety of eternalism. Needless to say, in the remark just quoted Quine is 'in the position of a Jewish chef preparing ham for a gentile clientèle': propositions are not his meat,[70] they are 'creatures of darkness', *entia non grata*. It is not so much the eliminativist eternalism described here which he disapproves of. Quine himself thinks that eternal sentences are all we need in order to say whatever is scientifically worth saying.[71] But even if the *results* of scientific research are, and ought to be, formulated only by means of such sentences, non-eternal sentences are indispensable in the laboratory when we *do* science collaboratively and even more so outside the laboratory when we converse as agents, victims, and spectators.[72]

5.2.2 *A critique of eliminativist eternalism*

Let us start with a preparatory question: *what is an eternal sentence?* In order to serve the eliminativist's needs, Quine's answer in *PL* (cited above) covers too many sentences containing temporal (or other) indexicals. (I use 'indexical' to cover not only words and phrases such as 'this', 'I', 'here', 'now', 'present', 'last year', etc., but all elements or features of a sentence, the semantical values of which vary systematically, in accordance with a rule of language, from one context of use

---

[68] Quine asks his readers for a convincing example (*Ontological Relativity and Other Essays*, 141). Perhaps one can construct a moderately convincing case from certain proverbs in which indexicals are, as it were, de-indexicalized. In somebody's idiolect the sentence 'You shouldn't put off until tomorrow what you can do today' might start its career as a non-eternal sentence (whose truth-value depends on who is addressed and when) and end up as an eternal sentence, as a stylistically superior variant of 'For all persons x, for all days d, x should not put off until the day after d what x can do on d.'

[69] Cf. Quine, *W&O*, 200–1.   [70] Quine, *Theories and Things*, 116.

[71] Cf. *W&O*, 227. In the same spirit Russell contends in ch. 7 of *An Inquiry into Meaning and Truth* that 'egocentric words...are not needed in any part of the description of the world, whether physical or psychological' (102, 108). In Ch. 6.2.3 I shall argue that, contrary to what is suggested in the Quine extract above, one should *not* think of *any* proposition as the meaning of an eternal sentence.

[72] In *W&O*, 228 Quine acknowledges this need.

to another. Thus the Latin sentence '*ambulo*' contains just as many indexicals as its translation, 'I am taking a stroll', namely a personal indexical and a temporal indexical, the latter being in this case a tense.) Quine assumes that we can obtain eternal sentences only by eliminating what he calls 'indicator words' and tenses (which he mentions on the next page):

It is only thus [i.e. by banishing indexicals] that we come to be able to speak of sentences, i.e., certain linguistic forms, as true and false. As long as the indicator words [and other indexicals] are retained, it is not the sentence but only the several events of its utterance that can be said to be true or false. ('The Scope and Language of Science', §III)

This is mistaken. Although the next sentence is by no means free of indexicals:

(3)   If yesterday a drake was run over on Trafalgar Square then at least once a duck was run over on Trafalgar Square,

it is an eternal sentence in the sense of *PL*, since every utterance of (3) in present-day English is true (or rather expresses a truth), regardless of speaker and occasion. So if truth-values can be ascribed to repeatable 'linguistic forms' at all, then (3) as currently used in English can certainly be called true. But do any two utterances of (3) in present-day English express the same proposition? An utterance of (3) on 18 May 1906 is about another day than an utterance of (3) today.[73] This is a feature (3) shares with an example made famous by Kaplan:[74]

(K)   I am here now.

(K) is also an eternal sentence by Quine's standards, and, like (3), utterances of (K) at different moments or places, or by different speakers are about different moments, places, or speakers. But notice the vast modal difference between (K) and (3): every utterance of (3) expresses a necessary truth, whereas each utterance of (K) expresses a contingent truth.[75] What matters in the context of our reflections, though, is not this difference in modal status but rather the feature that indexical eternal sentences such as (3) and (K) have in common, i.e. the 'referential' difference between some utterances of the same sentence. Eternalists take this feature to preclude their expressing the same proposition, for according to them two utterances that have the same propositional content cannot but be about the same things. Let us call this the *Aboutness Principle*. (By contrast, in two

---

[73] Similarly, different utterances of 'I was born some time ago' and 'If this is a piece of copper then it expands when heated' may be about different items, yet (by conceptual or natural necessity) they all have the same truth-value. Cf. my *Abstrakte Gegenstände*, 279–80.

[74] Kaplan, 'Demonstratives', 508–9 *et passim*.

[75] In this respect '*cogito*' and '*sum*' are in the same boat as (K).

utterances of the same sentence which are about different people or different times the sentence may very well have the same meaning.) Thus Frege says in his *Basic Laws of Arithmetic*:

[D]er Satz 'Ich bin hungrig' [kann] für den Einen wahr und für den Andern falsch sein ... aber der Gedanke nicht; denn das Wort 'ich' bedeutet in dem Munde des Andern einen andern Menschen, und daher *drückt auch der Satz, von dem Andern ausgesprochen, einen andern Gedanken aus.* [[T]he sentence 'I am hungry' can be true for one person and false for another ... but not the thought (proposition); for the word 'I' in the mouth of the other person denotes a different man, and *hence* the sentence uttered by the other person expresses a different thought.] (*Grundgesetze* I. xvi–xvii; my emphasis)

Applying this reasoning to the sentence 'Today is a religious holiday', we obtain: the denotation of 'today' shifts with the day of utterance, *hence* the sentence expresses different propositions on different days (even if it happens to be uttered on different religious holidays). Moore invokes the Aboutness Principle in his 1927 symposium with Ramsey:

As a general rule, whenever we use a past tense to express a proposition, the fact that we use it is a sign that the proposition expressed is *about* the time at which we use it; *so that* if I say twice over 'Caesar was murdered', the proposition which I express on each occasion is a different one—the first being a proposition with regard to the earlier of the two times at which I use the words, to the effect that Caesar was murdered before *that* time, and the second a proposition with regard to the later of the two, to the effect that he was murdered before *that* time. So much seems to me hardly open to question. ('Facts and Propositions', 71; second italics added)[76]

Of course, an eliminativist can respect the Aboutness Principle which underlies Frege's 'hence' and Moore's 'so that' by modifying Quine's explanation of the technical term 'eternal sentence'. Expanding the relative clause in that explanation (see above p. 271) she could say something like this: an eternal sentence is a sentence, all tokens of which are alike both in truth-value *and* in reference of their corresponding parts.

For three reasons this emendation is not yet sufficient. We know one of them already from section 5.1.3 above. Some sentences of present-day English are ambiguous. As a result, some utterances of the sentence 'Every bank is a monetary institution' are true, some false. Still, we may want to say that *under one reading* of this sentence it *is* an eternal sentence. (But we can be sure that Quine's eyebrows would lift at this talk of readings. Instead, he asks us to 'think of ambiguities ... as resolved by paraphrase—not absolutely, but enough to immobilize

---

[76] If you feel inclined to question what Moore takes to be hardly open to question, I assure you of my sympathy. At the end of this subsection we will have another look at this extract.

the truth value of the particular sentence'.[77] But if we paraphrase my last sample sentence as 'Every monetary institution is a monetary institution', we transform it into a logical truth, whereas the original was under no reading *logically* true.) The second reason is this. By an extraordinary coincidence, the definiens might cover sentences which Quine certainly does not want to classify as eternal. All actual utterances of the sentence that consists of the words 'It', 'is', 'raining', 'in', and 'London', in this order, may by chance be made simultaneously by speakers of present-day English referring to the capital of the United Kingdom, or there may happen to be only one such utterance.[78] This suggests that in explaining 'eternal sentence', we must talk about *possible* utterances. (Judging by Quine's mockery about possible fat men in a certain doorway,[79] he can be expected to frown upon this revision of his definition.) Here is the third reason. If it were always (never) raining in London (GB), then each and every utterance of

(1)   It is raining in London

in which London (GB) is referred to would yield a truth (falsehood). (Again, revising Quine's explanation by having recourse to possible worlds would hardly be to his liking.) Of course, one could bite the bullet and say that under the counterfactual circumstances described in my second and third objection, sentence (1) would indeed be an eternal sentence. But do we want the eternality, or otherwise, of a sentence to be at the mercy of the weather in London or of human talkativeness concerning this topic?

Let us suppose that the eliminativist has solved these problems somehow (and perhaps even to Quine's satisfaction). Then he must cope with a certain *embarras de richesse*: which eternal sentence expresses what is expressed by (1) at the time in question? Why (2) rather than, say, (2*)?

(2)   There is rain in London at 10 a.m., 18 May 1906
(2*)   There is rain in London at 10 a.m. on the 34th birthday of the author of 'On Denoting'.

Sentences (2) and (2*) express different propositions. This can be shown, first, by an Argument from Doxastic Difference. Ben is convinced that it is always raining in London anyway, and he has never heard of Russell's paper. He believes

---

[77] Quine, *PT*, 78.

[78] Quine secures the distinctness of *unuttered* sentences by taking sentences not to be classes of their tokens, but sequences, in the mathematical sense, of their successive characters or phonemes whose actual existence can be taken for granted (*W&O*, 194–5; *PL*, 56). This will not help with the present problem.

[79] See the first essay in Quine's collection *From a Logical Point of View*.

that 2 without believing that 2*, so the proposition that 2 has a property which the proposition that 2* lacks, and hence (by Leibniz's Law) they are two propositions. Secondly, it is possible for somebody who understands (grasps the conventional linguistic meaning of) both (2) and (2*) to take one of them to express a truth without immediately being ready to take the other to express a truth as well. Thus they do not meet the Cognitive Equivalence Criterion. Thirdly, one can understand (2), but one cannot understand (2*), without having mastered the concept of authorship. Thus they do not fill the Conceptual Balance Requirement either. Nothing can be identical with two different things. So *which* of these two propositions is the proposition expressed by an utterance of (1) at the time in question?

If we insist on eternalization by dates, as in (2), we run into the Trivialization Objection. Consider an utterance of

(4)   Today is 18 May 1906,

made on 18 May 1906. This certainly does not express the same proposition as the eternal sentence

(5)   18 May 1906 is 18 May 1906,

for the former provides information which may be urgently needed, whereas the latter is a boring triviality. (If we have recourse to a different dating system on the left, the result will no longer be 'tautologous', but still it will convey a conceptual truth, in marked contrast to (4).) To be sure, the eliminativist eternalist does not have to follow Russell and Quine by insisting on eternalization by date. The replacement of (5) by 'The day on which the author of OD has his 34th birthday is 18 May 1906' does not fall victim to the Trivialization Objection. But then, of course, the *embarras de richesse* reappears.

Let us return to the question we asked a moment ago: *which* eternalization of (1) as uttered at a certain time expresses the proposition that is expressed by (1) at that time? Applications of the Argument from Doxastic Difference, of the Cognitive Equivalence Criterion and of the Conceptual Balance Requirement show that the answer must be, None. We often do not know what time it is, but that doesn't prevent us from having beliefs about the then current state of the weather. A speaker who lost track of time may believe that it is raining in London without believing anything to the effect that it is raining in London at time t. So the content of the former belief is not a proposition of the latter type. Furthermore, somebody who lost track of time may understand the sentence 'It is raining in London' and take it to express a truth (falsehood) now, without immediately being ready to take any of its eternalized variants to express a truth (falsehood) as well. Hence no proposition expressed by a sentence of the latter type is identical with the propositional content of her belief.[80] (We should not claim that by uttering (2) one gives 'more information' to the addressee than by uttering (1) at the time specified in (2). In a certain respect it's just the other way round: an utterance of (1) does, whereas an utterance of (2) does not, indicate whether the reported event is, at the time of utterance, past, present, or future.) And finally, there will always be a concept whose mastery has to be exercised in understanding an eternalization of (1), but not in understanding (1). One cannot understand (2), for example, without having mastered a system of chronological representations. So once again we reach the conclusion that the propositions expressed are different.

In sum, eternalists should not go in for eliminativism. They should acknowledge the fact that an utterance of an indexical (non-eternal) sentence never expresses the same proposition as an utterance of a non-indexical (eternal) sentence. That is, they should opt for non-eliminitavist eternalism. I take it that this was both Bolzano's and Frege's considered view.

As to Frege, let us look at a passage in his paper 'The Thought' which might easily give one the impression that he was an eliminativist, contrary to what I am saying:

[A] [G]*ibt es nicht auch Gedanken, die heute wahr sind, nach einem halben Jahr aber falsch? Der Gedanke z. B., daß der Baum dort grün belaubt ist, ist doch wohl nach einem halben Jahre falsch? Nein; denn es ist gar nicht derselbe Gedanke.* [B] *Der Wortlaut 'dieser Baum ist grün belaubt' allein genügt ja nicht zum Ausdrucke, denn die Zeit des Sprechens gehört dazu.* [C] *Ohne die Zeitbestimmung, die dadurch gegeben ist, haben wir keinen vollständigen Gedanken, d.h. überhaupt keinen Gedanken.* [D] *Erst der durch die Zeitbestimmung ergänzte und in jeder Hinsicht vollständige Satz drückt einen Gedanken aus.* [E] *Dieser ist aber, wenn er wahr ist, nicht nur heute oder morgen . . . wahr.*

[[A] Are there not thoughts (propositions) which are true today but false in six months' time? The thought, for example, that the tree there is covered with green leaves, will surely be false in six months' time? No, for it is not the same thought at all. [B] The words 'This tree is covered with green leaves' are not sufficient by themselves to constitute the expression [of thought], for the time of utterance belongs to it as well. [C] Without the time-determination thus given we have no complete thought, i.e. we have no thought at all. [D] Only a sentence supplemented by a time-determination and complete in every respect expresses a thought. [E] But this thought, if it is true, is true not only today or tomorrow.] ('*Der Gedanke*', 76; bracketed letters added)

On my literalist reading of passages like [B], Frege regards as 'part of the thought-expression [*Teil des Gedankenausdrucks*]' whatever has to be identified if one

---

[80] Cf. Hector-Neri Castañeda, 'Indicators and Quasi-Indicators'; Perry, 'The Problem of the Essential Indexical'; Evans, 'Understanding Demonstratives'.

wants to know which proposition is expressed in a given situation.[81] Hence in the case of an utterance of a sentence such as (1), 'It is raining in London', the time of the utterance is part of the thought-expression. So with regard to such cases Frege has a rather non-standard view of the make-up of the complete expression of a proposition: it consists of a token of the sentence (1) *and* the time at which it is produced. In earlier work I have called such thought-expressions 'hybrid'.[82]

What is misleading in our extract is the way Frege talks in [D] about time-determinations [*Zeitbestimmungen*].[83] Suppose (1) is uttered at time t_0. Then three items should be carefully distinguished:

(i)   the time t_0 of the utterance of (1) (t_0 being part of the hybrid thought-expression),

(ii)   the part of the thought expressed which determines the time t_0, and

(iii) the component of an eternalized variant of (1) which designates t_0.

The difference between (i) and (iii) is obvious. Entry (ii) is required by Frege's structuralist conception of propositions. Both (ii) and (iii) can be called 'time-determinations', which makes this term dangerously ambiguous.[84] In [D] it seems to stand for (iii), but it is not easy to see how (iii)—or (ii), for that matter—can be 'given' by (i), as we are told in [C].

---

[81] Cf. also *Der Gedanke*, 64: '*Wenn mit dem Praesens eine Zeitangabe gemacht werden soll* , . . . *ist die Zeit des Sprechens Teil des Gedankenausdrucks* [If a time-indication is to be conveyed by the present tense . . . the time of utterance is part of the expression of the thought.]'

[82] Cf. my 'Hybrid Proper Names'; Edward Harcourt, 'Reply to WK', and my 'First Person Propositions', esp. §1. Salmon reads Frege as claiming that in such cases the time of the utterance 'serv[es] as a specification or indication of itself' or 'act[s] as a self-referential singular term': see his 'Tense and Singular Propositions' (henceforth 'Tense'), 349, 359. I cannot find any basis for this reading in Frege's text. To shield off a possible misunderstanding which might be encouraged by my terminology, let me remark that Frege's hybrid *expressions* of 'pure' propositions are of course to be distinguished from Russell's hybrid '*propositions*'.

[83] As to the locution 'complete sentence' in [D], compare Cartwright's terminological proposal: 'If the meaning of a sentence is such as to permit utterances of the sentence to vary as to statement made, let us call the sentence *incomplete*' ('Propositions', 46).

[84] Certainly its use for (i) is a misuse. This misuse is unmistakable in Frege's 'Logic' manuscript of 1897 (*NS*, 147). The English translation (*Posthumous Writings*, 135) makes this invisible by 'correcting' the text in the direction of (iii). In a letter to Jourdain, presumably of 1910 (*WB*, 120–1 (191)), Frege writes: 'A complete sentence (thought-expression) must also contain the time-determination [*Ein vollstaendiger Satz (Gedankenausdruck) muss auch die Zeitangabe enthalten*].' And he continues: if somebody correctly reports on an event by using a tensed sentence, then 'the time' of the reported event 'belongs to the thought-content of the sentence [*gehoert die Zeit . . . zum Gedankeninhalt des Satzes*].' Cf. '*Anmerkungen zu Jourdain . . .*', in *Kleine Schriften*, 338. This is doubly confusing: the first statement embraces eliminativist eternalism, which is inimical to Frege's conception of propositional identity. The second statement contains a glaring category mistake: it declares a time to be a component of something which Frege takes to consist exclusively of senses (*NS*, 203–4 (187), 243 (225), 250 (232), 275 (255); *WB*, 127 (79), 245(163)).

Sometimes Frege uses 'time-determination' in the sense of (ii). Talking about temporally indexical sentences, he takes time-determinations to be components of the *propositions* expressed, when he writes in *Basic Laws*:

> Bestimmungen der Zeit ... gehören zu dem Gedanken, um dessen Wahrheit es sich handelt. [Determinations of ... time belong to the thought whose truth is in point.] (*Grundgesetze*, 1. xvii)

One of the senses which, according to Frege's structuralist view, jointly make up the thought expressed by a temporally indexical sentence like (1) with respect to a certain context c must determine the time of c, otherwise the thought would not be true or false *simpliciter*, without relativization to time, and the Aboutness Principle would be violated. So the proposition expressed by (1) at c is as time-specific or *temporally determinate* as the propositions expressed by appropriately eternalized variants of (1). But since Frege regards cognitive equivalence as a necessary condition of propositional identity, his considered view cannot be that the component to which the indexically expressed proposition owes its time-specificity is identical with the sense of a non-indexical designator of the time of c.[85] The trouble with this view is, of course, that we only know what that component is supposed to achieve: we know how it does *not* achieve it (i.e. not in the way the sense of a definite description does), but not how it does.

Let us not close this subsection before we have had another look at Moore's contention about past-tense sentences (cited on p. 274 above). At time t_0 an utterance of Moore's sample sentence

(P)   Caesar was murdered

expresses a truth if and only if at t_0 an utterance of any of the following three sentences would also express a truth:

(P1) $\exists t$ (Caesar's murder takes place at t & t is earlier than the time of this very utterance)
(P2) $\exists t$ (Caesar's murder takes place at t & t is earlier than now)
(P3)   Caesar was murdered before now.

In an earlier paper Moore himself specified the truth-conditions of propositions expressed by past-tense sentences like (P) along the lines of (P1), thereby anticipating the key idea of Reichenbachs's theory of token-reflexivity by four decades.[86] But let us focus rather on (P3), for here Moore's additional claim is

---

[85] *Pace* Carruthers, 'Eternal Thoughts', §1.

[86] Moore, 'William James' *Pragmatism*', 135–6. Cf. Hans Reichenbach, *Elements of Symbolic Logic*, sect. 50. Martha Kneale and William Kneale, 'Propositions and Time', provide a lucid commentary on Moore's position. Austin Duncan-Jones's earlier 'Fugitive Propositions', which surprisingly fails to mention Moore, is also still worth reading.

most plausible. The additional claim is that with respect to t_0 (P) and (P3) express one and the same proposition. (In the case of (P1) and (P2) one can rebut the identity claim by appealing to the Conceptual Balance Requirement, but in the case of (P3) this does not seem possible.) If Moore is right, each utterance of (P) is partly about the time of the utterance, and consequently, the proposition which (P) expresses at t_0 is not expressed by it at any other time. Now this alleged difference between what is said in consecutive utterances of (P) doesn't make any difference to our practice of reporting such utterances. (If Ann utters (P) assertively on Tuesday, and Ben does so on the next day, then 'Ann said that Caesar was murdered, and so did Ben' would be a perfectly correct report, provided they were both talking about the same man. If Ann utters (P) with assertoric force and Ben retorts, naturally a bit later, 'No, he wasn't', we take him to have asserted the contradictory of what she said.) By appealing to the Aboutness Principle, one can justify the claim that the propositions expressed by (P3)—or by (P2) or (P1), for that matter—at different times after the stabbing in the Senate House, although never differing in truth-value, really are distinct, but that principle cannot be used to justify Moore's contention about (P) without assuming what stands in need of justification. Since we explained the notion of a proposition via thought-ascriptions and indirect speech-reports, we have to acknowledge that there can be nothing more to the identity of propositions than can be read off from our practice of making such ascriptions and reports, and so we should be very hesitant about accepting Moore's claim concerning (P).[87]

By contrast, the claim that, with respect to the same time t, present-tense sentences such as

(1)   It is raining in London
(1*)   It is *now* raining in London

express the same proposition (provided they are unembedded) does not conflict with our ordinary use of 'what is said'. Why the proviso? Consider

(E1)   Tomorrow Ben will believe that it is raining in London
(E1*)   Tomorrow Ben will believe that it is *now* raining in London.

The first sentence may now express a truth, while the second yields a falsehood. Since the temporal adverb 'now' has wide scope, a present assertoric utterance of (E1*) is a prediction of a future belief (believing) about the *present* weather. ('You will always regret what you are *now* doing' is not something one likes to be told, but 'You will always regret what you are doing' is even worse.)

---

[87] For an alternative treatment of (P), see Salmon, 'Tense', 378–87.

But doesn't the point about embeddings amount to an Argument from Doxastic Difference against the contention that (1) and (1*) express the same proposition with respect to the same time? Not really. The possible truth-value divergence between (E1) and (E1*) does not show that the proposition now expressed by (1*) is distinct from the proposition *now* expressed by (1). The content of the believing we now predict in uttering (E1) is the proposition that will *tomorrow* be expressed by (1). After all, we can rephrase (E1) as 'Tomorrow Ben will believe that it is *then* raining in London', where the added adverb anaphorically harks back to 'tomorrow'.[88]

5.2.3 *An alleged metaphysical vindication of eternalism*

In his crusade against the loose talk of variables, which was all too common among his mathematical contemporaries, Frege presents a kind of metaphysical argument against the contention that *numbers* are changeable. If his reasoning is successful, a strictly parallel argument will vindicate the claim that *propositions* cannot change either. Suppose an iron rod, which was 999 millimetres long half an hour ago, has been heated, and now it is 1,000 millimetres long: there is no need to say that the number which gives the length of the rod in millimetres is now greater than it was half an hour ago. And it is all to the good, Frege argues, that such a representation can be avoided, since variable numbers of this kind cannot be identified with the numbers that belong to our mathematical number-system. The change in question can far more aptly be described by saying: 'The length (in millimetres) the rod *then had* = 999, and the length (in millimetres) the rod *now has* = 1,000.' In this perspicuous representation we use two definite descriptions designating two different numbers. (Frege offers an illuminating comparison. Suppose ten years ago the King of Norway, say, was an old man, whereas now the King of Norway is a young man: there is no one King who has miraculously become younger. Rather, the *former* King was an old man, whereas the *present* King is a young man.) So far Frege's argument carries conviction.[89] But Frege thinks he can show that numbers are not only barred

---

[88] In 'Demonstratives', 503 n., Kaplan says that (1) and (1*) are 'synonymous'. Since he also advocates the thesis that 'if two compound well-formed expressions differ only with respect to components which have the same Character [= conventional linguistic meaning], then the Character of the compounds is the same' (507), he is committed to declaring (E1) and (E1*) to be synonymous, too. I do not take this to be a *reductio ad absurdum*, but I wonder whether the synonymy contention was plausible in the first place.

[89] Frege, *Die Grundlagen der Arithmetik*, §46; '*Logik*' (1897), in *NS*, 147 (135); '*Logische Mängel in der Mathematik*' (1898?), in *NS*, 173–4 (159–60); '*Was ist eine Funktion?*' (1904), 657–8 (286–7); '*Logik in der Mathematik*' (1914), in *NS*, 254 (237–8). So 'the Fregean solution' to the problem sketched in Salmon, 'Tense', 249 n., is *Frege's* solution. Cf. Dummett, *FPL*, 491–3; my *Abstrakte Gegenstände*, 45–57.

from growing and shrinking but from *any* kind of change:

Wenn sich etwas verändert, so haben wir nacheinander verschiedene Eigenschaften, Zustände an demselben Gegenstande. Wäre es nicht derselbe, so hätten wir gar kein Subjekt, von dem wir die Veränderung aussagen könnten. Ein Stab dehnt sich durch Erwärmung aus. Während dies vorgeht, bleibt er derselbe. Wenn er statt dessen weggenommen und durch einen längeren ersetzt würde, so könnte man nicht sagen, daß er sich ausgedehnt habe. Ein Mensch wird älter; aber wenn wir ihn nicht trotzdem als denselben anerkennen könnten, hätten wir nichts, von dem wir das Altern aussagen könnten. Wenden wir das auf die Zahl an! Was bleibt dasselbe, wenn eine Zahl sich verändert? Nichts! Folglich verändert sich die Zahl gar nicht; denn wir haben nichts, von dem wir die Veränderung aussagen könnten. Eine Kubikzahl wird nie zu einer Primzahl, und eine Irrationalzahl wird nie rational. [If anything varies, we have in succession different properties, states, in the same object. If the object were not the same one, we should have no subject of which we could predicate variation. A rod grows longer through being heated; while this is going on, it remains the same one. If instead it were taken away and replaced by a longer one, we could not say it had grown longer. A man grows older; if we could not nevertheless recognize him as the same man, we should have nothing of which we could predicate growing older. Let us apply this to number. What remains the same when a number varies? Nothing! Hence a number does not vary at all; for we have nothing of which we could predicate variation. A cube never turns into a prime number; an irrational number never becomes rational.] (*'Was ist eine Funktion?'*, 658)

In this style one could also argue: if a *proposition* were to vary we would have nothing of which we could predicate variation. A general proposition never turns into a singular proposition; a consistent proposition never becomes inconsistent.

Something has gone wrong here. According to the 'Cambridge Criterion of Change', as Geach has called it,[90]

(C)   x *changes* iff there is a property which x first has and then hasn't.

This legitimizes the contention that a certain number *did* change in the case under discussion. To be sure, 1,000 did not lose any of its *mathematical* properties, but half an hour ago the number 1,000 had a property which it now no longer has: the property of being larger than (the number which is) the length of our rod in millimetres. In the passage just cited Frege equivocates on the notion of change.[91] If the number 1,000 had to be classified as invariant because it never becomes *another* number, then the heated rod and the ageing man would also have to be described as invariant: after all, the former will never become a numerically different rod, nor will the latter ever become a numerically different

---

[90] Geach, 'What Actually Exists', 71–2. The nickname of (C) alludes to the fact that this criterion was espoused by two great Cambridge philosophers, by Russell (in *The Principles of Mathematics*, §442), and by McTaggart (in *The Nature of Existence*, vol. II, sect. 313–14).

[91] This was pointed out by Tichý, *The Foundations of Frege's Logic*, 192.

man. No proposition will ever become another proposition, but that is not yet a good reason for contending that propositions cannot cast off old properties for new.

Whatever object x may be and whatever property 'is F' may signify, being F is an *essential* property of x if and only if x is F and it is not possible that x exists and is not F. Hence an object cannot as long as it exists acquire or lose any of its essential properties. (Being F is an inessential or *accidental* property of x just in case x is F and it is possible that x exists and is not F.) Being self-identical is an essential property of our iron rod and of our man, since it is an essential property of every object. Being made of iron is (arguably) an essential property of our rod, and being a human being is (arguably, *pace* Kafka's 'Metamorphosis') an essential property of our man. On the other hand, being less than 1,000 millimetres long is an accidental property of our rod, and being sad is an accidental property of our man, for they can survive the loss of these properties. Similarly, the mathematical property of being even is an essential property of the number 1,000, but being larger than the length of our rod in millimetres and being larger than the number of Garibaldi's soldiers are accidental properties of this number, since it can acquire and lose the latter properties (although it exists in every possible world). Similarly with propositions. The logical property of being consistent is an essential property of the proposition that the moon is round, and so is the property of entailing that something is round. But being a content of my thinking is a property of that proposition which it has only occasionally, hence it is one of its inessential properties. As Frege himself came to concede:

Unwesentlich wird man eine Eigenschaft eines Gedankens nennen, die darin besteht oder daraus folgt, daß er von einem Denkenden erfaßt wird. [A property of a thought will be called inessential which consists in, or follows from the fact that, it is grasped by a thinker.] ('*Der Gedanke*', 76)

Consider the following consequence of this. Suppose at t_0 Ann grasps *the proposition that she can then express by saying, 'I am now thinking.'* Call it '*P*'. According to Frege, being grasped by a thinker is an inessential property of *P*. Now from the fact that *P* is grasped by Ann at t_0, it follows that *P* is true. Hence being true is one of *P*'s inessential properties. So eternalists must maintain that a property can be stable and yet accidental. And they are right in maintaining this. The property of being 1,000 millimetres long on the first day of 2000 at high noon (as distinct from the property of being 1,000 millimetres long) is not a property which an object can either acquire or lose, and yet it is obviously an inessential property of our rod. Temporalists and eternalists are agreed that the propositions expressed by 'No human being *ever* swims the Pacific within an hour' and 'It *sometimes* rains in London' can neither acquire nor lose the property of being true. Nevertheless this property is not one of their essential properties, for there are possible worlds in which they are false. Truth is an essential property only of those propositions that are necessarily true. So the fact that it is contingent that Ann is thinking anything at t_0 already ensures that truth is not an essential property of P.

In spite of the undeniable weakness of Frege's argument in '*Was ist eine Funktion?*' (cited above) one cannot help feeling that he is getting at something which is worth preserving. After all, the changes of numbers and propositions we mentioned are rather peculiar: numbers and propositions do not seem to *alter* when undergoing these changes. (Notice that many authors call what I refer to as alteration 'real or genuine change'.[92]) Let us try to consolidate this impression. Ann alters, we are inclined to say, when she becomes sad, or when she gets a headache, but she does not alter when Ben catches sight of her, or when it becomes true of her, perhaps only some months after her death, that she is sadly missed. But of course, in the sense of the Cambridge Criterion (C) she undergoes a change in all four cases. Purely spatial, and purely temporal, changes of an object do not seem to be alterations either. We hardly want to say that Ann alters just because her spatial distance from Ben increases or decreases.[93] Simply by staying alive long enough, Ben acquires and loses the property of being 55 years old, but we would not want to say that an object alters just by persisting. (In Ben's case, as we all know, becoming older is unfortunately combined with various kinds of decay. But this is no conceptual implication: there could be persistence without decline.) Socrates did not alter when you started admiring him. It was you who altered: he only underwent a change in the sense of (C). In that sense the number 1,000 changed when it became the number of Garibaldi's soldiers: what underwent an alteration was not this number but Garibaldi's army. Similarly, when Ann first grasped the proposition that hemlock is poisonous, this proposition only underwent a change whereas she also altered. Such changes of numbers and of propositions are just 'phoney changes' or 'mere "Cambridge" changes'.[94]

---

[92] Cf. Lawrence Lombard, *Events*, ch. IV; David-Hillel Ruben, 'A Puzzle about Posthumous Predication'.

[93] I agree here with Lombard, *Events*, 99–102 (as against Dummett, *FPL*, 492).

[94] Cf. Plato, *Theaetetus* 155 b–c; Aristotle, *Metaphysics* xiv, 1: 1088 a 34–5; and Bolzano, *WL*, I. 389. There is a temptation to think that if we had a definition of relational change we could simply define alteration as non-relational change. Lombard (*Events*, 94 and 252–3 n. 26) yields to this temptation. But the change which occurs when Ben makes love to Ann is presumably a relational change of Ben and of Ann, and yet both alter when undergoing this change. Hence some relational changes seem to be alterations. (Dummett had cautioned already in *FPL*, 492 against the mistake of declaring all relational changes to be phoney or bogus.) In any case, it is none too easy to define relational change in such a way that not *every* change turns out to be relational. According to Lombard's proposal in *Events*, 97, a change of an object x is a relational change just in case it could not take place if there were no object which is distinct from x and any of x's parts and which changes in the sense of (C). But this doesn't work. For all F, if Ben

Does this reflection finally vindicate eternalism? Surely not. Temporalists take truth to be a stable property of the proposition that $2 + 2 = 4$ and an unstable property of (what they would call) *the* proposition that Socrates is pale. They would argue: when the latter proposition acquires or loses the property of being true, what alters is not the proposition but the man. For this reply to the Fregean argument temporalists could invoke Aristotle's authority:

[A predication] is said to be able to receive contraries... because of what has happened to something else. For it is because of the thing's being, or not being, thus-and-so [τῷ ... τὸ πρᾶγμα εἶναι ἢ μὴ εἶναι] that the predication is said to be true or false. (*Cat.* 5: 4b 6–10)

What Aristotle means by '*ἀλλοίωσις*'[95] is not change in the sense of the Cambridge Criterion (C), but rather alteration. Eternalism may be right, but it cannot be vindicated along the lines of Frege's metaphysical argument.

5.2.4 Further divisions in the eternalist camp

A while ago I promised to point out *several* respects in which eternalists are at variance. In the continuation of our Frege extracts on pp. 277 and 279 above, the second issue on which eternalists are divided comes to the surface:

[D]*as Wahrsein selbst ist ... zeitlos.* [Truth itself is ... timeless.] (*Grundgesetze*, 1. xvii)

[*Ein Gedanke*] *ist, wenn er wahr ist, nicht nur heute oder morgen, sondern zeitlos wahr. Das Praesens in 'ist wahr' deutet also nicht auf die Gegenwart des Sprechenden, sondern ist, wenn der Ausdruck erlaubt ist, ein Tempus der Unzeitlichkeit.* [(A thought), if it is true, is true not only today or tomorrow but timelessly. Thus the present tense of 'is true' does not point at the speaker's present but is, if the expression be permitted, a tense of timelessness.] ('*Der Gedanke*', 76)

Notice that Frege does not continue: 'true not only today and tomorrow, but *always*'. By his lights, 'always' has no real traffic with 'true'.[96] Again, Frege is at

---

becomes F then the property of being F (which is certainly neither identical with him nor with any of his parts) changes from not being a property of Ben to being a property of him, but, of course, Lombard doesn't want to classify *each* case of somebody's becoming such-and-such to be a relational change.

[95] Cf. *Cat.* 5: 4 a 31. For further comments on the passage quoted above, see Ch. 3, p. 150 ff.

[96] Cf. Frege, '*Logik*' (1897), in *NS*, 147 (135). Husserl concurs: *LU*, I: *Prolegomena*, §39. Writing in 1913, Leśniewski puts the point Frege makes in the second quotation above in very similar terms: in such cases 'the present tense of the verb... is only used in lieu of a non-existing verbal expression of a "timeless" import' ('Is a Truth Only True Forever...?', 101). Carnap says in 'Truth and Confirmation', 122: '[T]he term "invariable truth"... is not quite appropriate; it would be more correct to say instead that truth is a "time-independent" or "non-temporal" concept.'

odds with Russell,[97] but this time he apparently stands also in opposition to Bolzano:[98]

Unläugbar aber ist jeder gegebene Satz nur Eines von jenen Beiden allein [i.e. *wahr oder falsch*] *und solches fortwährend; entweder wahr und dieses dann für immer, oder falsch und dieses abermals für immer.* [Undeniably every proposition has only one of these properties (i.e. truth or falsity), and it has it permanently; either it is true and then it is so forever, or it is false and then again forever.] (*WL*, II. 77)

So let us distinguish two varieties of eternalism: *atemporalism* and *sempiternalism*.[99] Atemporalists contend that the copula in 'is true' (or in 'is false') contains no time-indication at all. Due to the (next-to-)ubiquity of tense in ordinary language[100] truth-ascriptions, too, are grammatically tensed but logically, it is claimed, they are tenseless. Atemporalists like to compare the predicate 'is true' to that in an equation such as

$$(=) \quad 2 + 2 = 4.$$

There just isn't any expression in $(=)$ which could be tensed. Admittedly, the English counterpart of $(=)$ contains a verb like 'is', 'equals', or 'makes', which is grammatically tensed. But surely one could learn arithmetic without ever using such ordinary language counterparts of equations. (In German there is a way of reading $(=)$ aloud which simply omits the verb: '*Zwei plus Zwei gleich Vier.*')

Sempiternalists, on the other hand, claim that a true (false) proposition is *always* true (false): truth (falsity), they contend, is a property of a proposition that is forever retained by its owner. According to sempiternalism it is not false (let alone senseless) to say of a true proposition that it is *now* true: it is only misleading, since it suggests that it may not remain true. It is alleged to be misleading in the same way in which the statement 'Ben is sober today' is only misleading, but not false, if Ben is a determined anti-alcoholic.

C. Wright's use of 'timeless' is hardly felicitous when he writes:

The thesis of the timelessness of truth is here to be understood as the quite ordinary-seeming idea that [1] what is ever true is always true. More specifically: [2] whatever

---

[97]   See the last statement in our extract on pp. 270 above.

[98]   For reasons I cannot go into here I doubt whether this passage or its parallels in *WL*, II. 7, 129, articulate Bolzano's considered view. There can be no such doubt in the case of Twardowski: his paper 'On So-Called Relative Truths' is an attempt to prove that what is true never ceases to be true but always remains so. Moore pleads for this view in §III of 'William James' *Pragmatism*'.

[99]   The Latin abstract noun '*sempiternitas*' is derived from the adverb '*semper* [always]': the translation 'alwaysness' would mimick this.

[100]   Is it ubiquitous in English? Apparently, the embedded sentence in (S) 'It was important that *Ann see her doctor regularly*' is not tensed, and this grammatical appearance seems to be semantically relevant: unlike its (clearly) tensed counterpart which has 'saw' instead of 'see', (S) does not imply that Ann did see her doctor regularly.

someone can truly state at a particular time can be truly stated by anyone, no matter when, where, and who; though to effect the same statement on a different occasion will frequently involve changes in mood, tense, pronoun and adverb. ('Anti-Realism, Timeless Truth and *1984*', 177; numerals added)[101]

Wright's [1] is rather the thesis of the sempiternality of truth, but this is just a terminological complaint. Actually, Wright's mislabelled Timelessness Platitude combines two theses, and we would do well to reject the second at the outset. I shall first argue that [1] is logically independent of [2] and then pour some cold water on [2]. According to Frege, truth is (*sensu proprio*) timeless, but only the notorious Dr Lauben can express, and grasp, the (atemporally true) proposition he would express by saying 'I am Dr Lauben'.[102] So Wright's 'no matter who' requirement is not met. Fregean propositions are structured and pure, and if expressed by first-person sentences they contain rather special modes of presentation (ways of thinking of an object). For each thinker there is an *ego*-mode of presentation, where a is an *ego*-mode of presentation iff a is simple & $\exists x$ (a is a mode of presentation of x) & Nec $\forall x$, y (x is presented to y by $a \rightarrow x = y$). According to Bolzano, truth is everlasting, but the (sempiternally true) proposition expressed in an utterance of 'It is exactly 12 p.m.' at the turn of the last millennium could only be expressed, and grasped, at that time.[103] So Wright's 'no matter when' requirement is not met. Bolzanian propositions, too, are structured and pure, and if expressed by present-tense sentences they contain rather special modes of presentation. For each instant there is a *nunc*-mode of presentation, where a is a *nunc*-mode of presentation iff a is simple & $\exists t$ (a is a mode of presentation of t) & Nec $\forall t$, t^* (t is presented at t^* by $a \rightarrow t = t^*$). (Recall our discussion of Moore at the end of section 5.2.2.) Such propositions, in spite of their severely limited expressibility and graspability, can be *identified* by various people at various times: I have just identified them for you.[104]

I have mentioned Frege's and Bolzano's views here only as evidence for my claim that one can consistently accept Wright's [1] and deny his [2], provided that their views are consistent. I do not want to suggest that their contentions are unproblematic. The Fregean view of 'I' comes to grief over *shared* propositional attitudes. When I confess, 'I am German', you may be absolutely right in replying, 'I know', and I could in turn correctly register this by saying, 'So we

[101] Henceforth 'Timeless'. In 'Assertibility', 407, Wright calls statement [2] 'more accurate' than [1]. In 'Debate', 227 (= 'Minimalism', 760), he connects both statements by saying: [1] so that [2], and he dignifies the combination with the epithet of a 'basic a priori principle' ('Debate', 226).

[102] Frege, *'Der Gedanke'*, 65–6.   [103] Bolzano, *WL*, IV. 48.

[104] For more leisurely explanations (marred by a regrettably confused version of the second definition), see my 'First Person Propositions'. Cf. Peacocke, *Being Known*, 249.

both know that I am German.' This very much looks as if one and the same proposition were said to be the content of your and of my thinking, and what could this proposition be if not the one I express by the embedded clause? If you were to say what knowlege you claimed to have in your reply, you would not use my sentence, but, rather, 'You are German.' The Bolzanian view of the present tense comes to grief over *retained* propositional attitudes. Yesterday, at noon, I said, 'It is raining.' Today, you remind me of that utterance and ask, 'Do you still believe what you said yesterday?' I reply, 'Yes, I do. I see no reason for suspecting that I was under a delusion when I said that.' If I were to voice my continuing belief today, I'd better not employ the sentence I used yesterday. I'd rather say, 'It was raining then.'[105]

Now even if we do not accept Frege's and Bolzano's contentions, we should not endorse Wright's thesis [2], let alone subscribe to it as to a 'basic a priori principle' about the concept of truth. Suppose I say, pointing at the object you are currently looking at, 'I wrote this book' (and then quickly run away for fear of abuse). How could the temporally (and agentially) determinate proposition expressed by those words in that context have been asserted by Cicero in Rome in 44 BC? After all, I wasn't around then, not to mention the product of my labour.

The sempiternalist contention that truth (falsity) is a property which is never lost is compatible with the assumption that truth (falsity) is a property which can be *acquired*. The tenet, '*Quod est semel verum, semper est verum* [once true, always true]',[106] does not exclude the possibility that what never ceases to be true may once have *begun* to be so.[107] Ever since Aristotle's thought-provoking chapter on tomorrow's sea fight,[108] predictions have provided philosophers with the main motive for reckoning with this possibility. According to them, the proposition that on 1 October 480 BC, there is a naval battle in the Gulf of Salamis may on 30 September of that year not yet be either true or false, but it becomes true or false on 1 October, at the latest, and then remains so forever. I shall call this view '*unilateral sempiternalism*'. But perhaps truth and falsity are rather properties which a proposition can neither lose nor acquire but has throughout *all* of time: this position I propose to call '*bilateral sempiternalism*' or '*omnitemporalism*'.[109] The divisions in the eternalist camp can be seen in Figure 5.2.

---

[105] Frege acknowledged this for 'today'/'yesterday' (but did not make a similar move for 'I'/'you'): see '*Der Gedanke*', 64. Cf. Strawson, 'Truth' (1950), 192; Cartwright, 'Propositions', 44; Kaplan, 'Demonstratives', 501, 507, 521 and pp. 88–9 above.

[106] Aquinas reports (and rejects) this contention in *Summa theol*. Ia, q. 14, a. 15, ad 3.

[107] Compare '*Once* more than 55 years old, *always* more than 55 years old', '*Once* circumcised, *always* circumcised' and '*Once* deflowered, *always* deflowered', which are all about properties that can be acquired but not lost.   [108] *De Interpretatione*, 9.

[109] In a memorable controversy in 1913, Kotarbiński argued for the former view, till Leśniewski converted him to the latter. See Kotarbiński, 'The Problem of the Existence of the Future'; Leśniewski, 'Is a Truth Only True Forever . . . ?' The debate is summarized in Simons and Woleński, '*De Veritate*', §6.

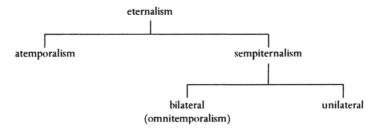

Figure 5.2. Eternalism (2)

Atemporalists claim that

(A)   if something is true, then there is neither a time at which it is true nor a time at which it is not true.

By contrast, all sempiternalists are agreed, not only that for each truth there is a time at which it is true, but also that

(S)   if something is true at time t, then it is also true at any time *later* than t.

But whereas bilateral sempiternalists (omnitemporalists) accept that

(bS)   if something is true at t, then it is also true at any other time,

unilateral sempiternalists maintain:

(uS)   it is not the case that if something is true at t, then it is also true at every time *earlier* than t.

There is a respect in which advocates of (A) and (bS) are agreed against unilateral sempiternalists. Atemporalists and omnitemporalists alike maintain that if P is a true proposition then there has never been any time at which it would have been right to say, 'P is not (yet) true.' However, this negative agreement should not make us play down the difference between (A) and (bS). Atemporalists can concede that there is a weak sense in which it may be said of any true proposition, 'P has always been true', namely that there has never been any time at which it would have been correct to say, 'P is not true.' But they will rightly emphasize that this is an etiolated sense.[110] If the age of the universe is finite, then there has never been any time at which it would have been right to say, 'The universe does not exist.' So in the weak sense it may be said, 'The universe has always existed.'

---

[110] The following observation is due to Dummett, 'Reply to McGuinness', 356.

But notice that it is this very sentence which would naturally be used to express the thought that the universe is of an *infinite* age.[111]

Atemporalists and omnitemporalists are also agreed that true propositions are true 'without relativization to time', but their reasons are very different. The latter say so because by their lights 'P is true' can always be safely converted into '∀t (P is true at t)', whereas the former say so because they take 'true at t' to make as little sense as 'true on High Street'.[112]

Let us now have a closer look at unilateral sempiternalism. Suppose we say of the proposition expressed by the eternal sentence

(2)   There is rain in London at 10 a.m., 18 May 1906

that it is true. Advocates of omnitemporalism contend that 'is true' here abbreviates a conjunctive tensed predicate: 'is, always has been, and always will be true'. Partisans of unilateral sempiternalism are not committed to the claim that the proposition expressed by (2) has always been true. They are even ready to maintain that there has been a time at which it would have been right to call that proposition 'not true'. They may declare that it did not have either truth or falsity before (or much earlier than) 10 a.m., 18 May 1906. Now consider a tensed sentence:

(6)   It will be raining in London in 7 days' time.

According to both atemporalism and omnitemporalism, the proposition expressed today by (6) is true if and only if the sentence 'It is raining in London' expresses a truth in a week's time. Adopting the symbolism of Prior's metric tense logic, let 'Fn' abbreviate 'It will be the case n time-units hence that', and let 'Fn A' be the result of prefixing 'Fn' to a present-tense (declarative) sentence 'A'. Then we can generalize the point just made: atemporalists and omnitemporalists are agreed that, whatever substitution-instance you take, 'Fn A' expresses a truth at time t if and only if 'A' expresses a truth at time t + n.

---

[111] Another omnitemporalism/atemporalism issue is debated in systematic theology and the philosophy of religion. Western theists agree that (E) '*God is eternal*' expresses a truth, but they disagree over which truth (E) expresses. In the Bible (e.g. Ps. 102: 12–13, 28), its counterpart [olâm, αἰώνιος, aeternus] is used to say that *God exists everlastingly, throughout all of time*. In Proclus' *The Elements of Theology*, the *Summa* of Neoplatonic metaphysics, a distinction is drawn between ἀϊδιότης κατὰ χρόνον, temporal eternity, and ἀϊδιότης αἰώνιος, non-temporal eternity (52: 30–1). Influenced by such sources, Jewish and Christian theologians and philosophers came to use (E) to say that *God's existence does not endure through, and has no location in, time*. Clearly the conception of God associated with the omnitemporalist reading of (E) is profoundly different from the one which is associated with the atemporalist reading.

[112] See p. 269 and n. 63 above.

Champions of unilateral sempiternalism deny the right-to-left half of this claim. Dummett describes their position sympathetically when he writes about utterances of a sentence of the form 'Fn A' at different times:

> The only natural way to take the notion of a thought here appears to be to allow that each specific utterance expresses a unique thought ... but to deny that a thought always has a truth-value: the thought expressed by 'Fn A', uttered at t, first acquires a truth-value at the time t + n. The grounds which philosophers have had for believing in variable truth-value, or what is the same thing, for believing in the indeterminacy of the future ... may be sound or they may be confused ... [but they] cannot be dismissed in advance. (*FPL*, 400)

Actually, this description will not quite do as it stands.[113] First, unilateral sempiternalists may be ready to admit that the prediction that a certain man would be dead at time t_0 may have been true already when he fell over the barrier at the top of the Tour Eiffel. (After having fallen over the barrier he was 'doomed'.) Secondly, unilateral sempiternalists may be prepared to concede that a prediction, made in 1899, of an eclipse of the sun for a certain day in 1999 already had a truth-value at the time when it was made. (Perhaps it was settled 'from the dawn of creation' that this eclipse would occur.) So let us describe their position rather thus: depending on the kind of event which 'A' can be used to report, the proposition expressed by a substitution-instance of 'Fn A', uttered at t, may first acquire a truth-value at the time t + n or at some intervening time.[114]

One should not dismiss this position in advance by declaring sentences like 'Proposition P began to be true at time t' to be as nonsensical as '7 began to equal 4 + 3 some centuries ago' or 'Ben began to be identical with Ben at his fifth birthday.' But one may very well wonder whether the grounds philosophers have offered for believing in the indeterminacy of the future provide us with good reasons for unilateral sempiternalism. The impression that they do give us such reasons rests, I suspect, on assuming too close a connection between being *true* and being *definitely settled (fixed, ineluctable, inevitable, unavoidable, unpreventable, necessary).*[115] Suppose an event of kind X occurs in location L at time t_0: if the future is (for some time) open with respect to X-events, then at many times before t_0 one would have expressed a falsehood by saying 'It is now definitely settled that there will be an X-event in L at t_0', or 'There is no longer any chance

---

[113] The claim that the grounds for believing in variable truth-value are the same as the grounds for believing in the indeterminacy of the future is indefensible. In 'Realism' (1982), 256–7, Dummett himself spells out the reasons for rejecting it.

[114] Dummett himself adds the second disjunct in 'Realism' (1982), 255.

[115] Here I am following Georg Henrik von Wright, 'Determinism and Future Truth'.

now that there will not be an X-event in L at t_0.' But this is entirely compatible with the claim, made by atemporalists and omnitemporalists alike, that at any time before t_0 one would have expressed a truth by saying '(It is true that) there will be an X-event in L at t_0' (and one would have made a true statement, no matter how ill-founded and capricious, by asserting this). The suspicion of incompatibility seems to rest on a metaphysical assumption which may be only a deep prejudice: if something is now rightly called 'true', then it must be true in virtue of something that exists or occurs *now*. Notice that this assumption goes beyond the ontic conception of making true pondered in Chapter 3.5.3 above, by requiring the truth-donor to exist or occur at the time when the true statement is made. (We shall soon re-encounter this requirement, on the other side of the eternalism/temporalism divide.)

Talk of something's being *true (already) now* only tends to muddy the water in this area. Compare the logical behaviour of the time-indication apparently qualifying 'true' in 'It soon will be true that department stores in Germany are open on Sundays.' This can be paraphrased in such a way that the time-indication qualifies the verb in the subordinate clause: 'It is true that department stores in Germany soon will be open on Sundays', hence it doesn't cause any headache for atemporalists. (I shall return to this paraphrastic strategy in section 5.3.2 below.) But if you try to move the '(already) now' from its position in 'It is true (already) now that it will be raining tomorrow' into the that-clause, you slide down into palpable nonsense: (?*) 'It is true that it will be raining (already) now tomorrow', or some such.[116]

Some eternalists shy away from sempiternalism although they pay lip service to it and do not endorse atemporalism either. Their reason for taking this uncomfortable stand comes close to the surface in Nathan Salmon's comments on Frege's tree example:[117]

Consider... Frege's 'thought' that a particular tree is covered with green leaves. Six months from now, when the tree in question is no longer covered with green leaves, the sentence

(S)   This tree is covered with green leaves

uttered with reference to the tree in question, will express the information that the tree is *then* covered with green leaves. This will be misinformation; it will be false. But that information is false even now. What is true now is the information that the tree ... is *now* covered with green leaves.... This is the information that one would currently express

---

[116] This point was first made by Friedrich Waismann in 'How I See Philosophy', 10, and subsequently spelt out by White in *Truth*, 43.   [117] Quoted on p. 277 above.

by uttering sentence (S). It is eternally true, or least true throughout the entire lifetime of the tree and never false. ('Tense', 344; example relabelled)

Let us use 'P' to stand for the proposition which (S) expressed in Frege's mouth in summer 1918 when he pointed at a certain tree that was covered with green leaves. How did things stand with P when that tree did not yet exist? How do things stand with P now when that tree has long ago fallen victim to pollution? To be sure, P isn't *false* before or after the lifetime of that tree, but was P true already before that time, and will P still be true afterwards? Salmon seems to find these questions awkward, and consequently he makes eternity shrink rather drastically: P is true, we are told, throughout the entire lifetime of the tree and never false outside its lifetime, and 'in this sense' it is eternally true.[118] I dare say that there is no such sense of 'eternal': surely Socrates is not eternally famous if his fame came to an end with his life.

Putting truth aside for a moment, does P *exist* outside the lifetime of the tree Frege pointed at? Did it survive the death of the demonstrated tree? The Stoics (who were temporalists, as we shall soon see) maintained that in some cases what is said is 'perishable (φθαρτόν)',[119] and our P is a case in point. By now, so Chrysippus would claim, it 'has perished, since the object of the demonstration (δεῖξις) no longer exists'.[120] Did P exist before the tree came into being? It is more than likely that the Stoics would have said No,[121] but our meagre sources contain no explicit statement to this effect. We do know Whitehead's answer. He would have classified P as a 'hybrid proposition' which contains an 'actual entity' (the tree demonstrated by Frege) and an 'eternal object' (the property ascribed to it), and he was the first to call such propositions 'singular propositions'.[122] Of hybrid, or singular, propositions, Whitehead said that they both come into being and perish together with the actual entities they contain.[123] Now even if, endorsing this view, we were to maintain that the proposition P which (S) expressed in Frege's mouth passed away with the tree he pointed at, why should this prevent P from staying true? After all, Socrates is still very famous. There are properties[124] which can be correctly ascribed to an object at time t even though the object no longer exists at t. Truth may very well be one of them.

---

[118] Salmon, 'Tense', 342.

[119] Karlheinz Hülser, *Die Fragmente zur Dialektik der Stoiker*, fr. 695 (Philo Judaeus).

[120] Ibid., fr. 993 (Alexander Aphrodisiensis). Cf. Gabriel Nuchelmans, *Theories of the Proposition*, 82; Susanne Bobzien, 'Logic: The Stoics', 100, 116.   [121] Cf. Michael Frede, *Die stoische Logik*, 49.

[122] Alfred N. Whitehead, *The Concept of Nature*, ch. 1; *Process and Reality*, 257, 185–6.

[123] *Process and Reality*, 22, 188.   [124] In the broad sense elucidated on pp. 53–6, 89–91 ff. above.

But should we endorse Whitehead's view? Since he individuates 'hybrid propositions' as all hybridizers do, his view was already rejected in principle on the last pages of section 5.1.2 above. But at this point we come across an additional difficulty for the *mereological* conception of hybrid 'propositions' (which is equally pressing when we take hybrid 'propositions' to be states of affairs miscategorized). Hybridizers often maintain that sentences that are built up from n proper names and an n-place predicate express 'propositions' which contain as parts (an ordered n-tuple of) the objects designated by those names and the n-adic properties signified by the predicates. Now if those objects are located in time, then such a 'proposition' is also time-bound: it can exist at a time t only if all its constituent objects exist at t. But then hybridizers have to face an embarrassing question which we had occasion to ask before:[125] when does the 'proposition' expressed by 'Socrates lived long before Wittgenstein' exist? Since there is no time at which both Socrates and Wittgenstein exist, the hybrid 'proposition' never exists. And yet, what is now said by 'Socrates lived long before Wittgenstein' is as true as can be. The minimal moral we should draw from this is, I think, that 'propositions' as individuated by hybridizers—that is to say, states of affairs—should not be conceived of in mereological terms.[126]

Back to Salmon's, as it were, compressive treatment of eternal truth. Oddly enough, he quotes Frege's tree passage in its entirety and comments on it fairly extensively, but he does not seem to register at all Frege's positive contention: a proposition, if true, is *timelessly* true. As an atemporalist, Frege does not have to worry whether P is already, or still, true at such-and-such a time: such questions simply do not arise for him.[127] Similarly, an atemporalist can and should say that

---

[125] It was posed by Almog, and presumably the reader will experience a certain déja vu here: see p. 122 above.

[126] It is noteworthy that Kaplan introduces the idea of hybrid propositions into his theory of 'direct reference' by saying, 'if I may way wax metaphysical in order to fix an image' ('Demonstratives', 494). What matters for Kaplan's theory is not the image, but the contention that the identity of a proposition expressed in a certain context by a sentence containing proper names or indexicals is determined, as far as their contribution is concerned, by the identity of the items designated by those terms—and not by the modes in which those items are presented to the speaker. The same point was independently made by Strawson in 'Direct Singular Reference', 93.

[127] Salmon himself occasionally invokes a 'tenseless use' of the present tense: 'Tense', 385 n. 30. Carruthers contends, 'Frege is correct: one cannot believe in the omnitemporality of truth without being committed to the omnitemporal existence of Thoughts' ('Eternal Thoughts', §IV). This is historically incorrect and philosophically very doubtful. First, Frege was not an omnitemporalist, but an atemporalist. Secondly, why should the assumption that truth is a property of P which P neither gains nor loses entail that P exists throughout all of time? You might just as well argue that the assumption that self-identity (and identity with Tully) is a property which Cicero never gains nor loses entails that Cicero always exists.

P also *exists* timelessly, and Frege does say it.[128] Atemporalists should not let themselves be bullied by questions such as 'Do you *really* think that P existed already in the first glacial epoch and that it will still exist when all life has vanished from the earth?' They should cooly reply that the questioner's use of 'already' and 'still' betokens a category confusion. There is something which is expressed by (S) in Frege's mouth at some moment in 1918, namely P, so P exists. But there is neither a time at which P exists, nor a time at which P does not exist. In view of our discussion of Wright's so-called Timelessness Platitude, let us add: P is one of those ever so many truths that cannot be expressed (or thought) at *every* time.

Prima facie, at least, propositions might exist timelessly and yet have shifting truth-values. Of course, these truth-value shifts cannot be alterations (real or genuine changes) of propositions if the latter exist timelessly, any more than the vicissitudes which the number 1,000 gets involved in when Frege's rod is heated and then cools down again can be alterations of that number if numbers exist timelessly.[129] So let us now consider the alternative to eternalism.

5.3 Temporalism

According to temporalism, truth (falsity) is a property of sayables and think-ables which they can lose. This view has been upheld by many distinguished philosophers since antiquity, and like eternalism it isn't a monolithic position.

5.3.1 *Who is afraid of temporally indeterminate propositions?*

Here are three key passages in which Aristotle declares that truth-value bearers may undergo a truth-value shift:

Suppose that the predication [λόγος (ἀποφαντικός)] that so-and-so is sitting is true: after he has got up this predication will be false.... Suppose you believe truly that so-and-so is sitting: after he has got up you will believe falsely if you hold the same belief [δόξα] about him. (*Cat.* 5: 4 a 23–8; [A. I])[130]

[A belief] becomes false when a change in the thing occurs without being noticed [(δόξα) ψευδὴς ἐγένετο, ὅτε λάθοι μεταπεσὸν τὸ πρᾶγμα]. (*De anima* Γ 3: 428 b 9–10; [A. II])

---

[128] Frege, '*Der Gedanke*', 76. Unfortunately he slides when he says that a proposition which is grasped at t by A 'already existed beforehand [*schon vorher bestand*]' (69 n.).   [129] See sect. 5.2.3 above.
[130] Cf. Plato, *Sophistes*, 264 b.

Whereas some things are always combined and cannot be separated, and some things are always separated and cannot be combined, others again admit the opposite [i.e. they can be combined as well as separated].... Therefore as regards those things which admit both combination and separation, it happens that one and the same belief and one and the same predication comes to be false and comes to be true, and it is possible at one time to be right with it and at another wrong. But as regards things which cannot be otherwise it never happens that the same [belief or predication] is sometimes true and sometimes false—it is always true or always false. (*Met.* Θ 10: 1051b 9–17; [A. III])

The chapter from which passage [A. III] is extracted contains Aristotle's explanation of truth and falsity in terms of combination [σύνθεσις] and separation [διαίρεσις].[131] The number two, for example, is always combined with evenness, and it is always separated from oddness,[132] whereas Socrates and the property of being pale are sometimes combined and sometimes separated. In the latter type of case, Aristotle claims, the same belief and the same predication is true at one time and false at another. Thus the truth-value of an Aristotelian truth-value bearer can change.

Nevertheless, Aristotle is a dubious witness for temporalism as defined above. It can hardly be doubted that by (what I have translated as) 'predication' he means a declarative (type-) sentence, and it cannot be excluded that by (what is translated above as) 'belief' he means a mental state or act, an 'affection in the soul [πάθημα ἐν τῇ ψυχῇ]'.[133] Brentano certainly thinks of judgements or beliefs (which he never clearly distinguishes) as mental items, as judgings or believings, and he takes himself to endorse Aristotle's view on vacillating truth-values when he says about judgements (or rather beliefs) concerning things that come into being and pass away:

Ohne daß das Urteil selbst sich geändert hätte—wenn draußen die betreffende Realität erzeugt oder zerstört wird, gewinnt oder verliert ein solches Urteil oft seine Wahrheit. [Without itself undergoing any change, the judgement will gain or lose its truth if the external reality in question is created or destroyed.] ('*Über den Begriff der Wahrheit*', §55)[134]

---

[131] Quoted as [A.6] on p. 99 above.

[132] If Aristotle were to accept the prodigal sense of 'property' appealed to in Ch. 2 above, then [A. III] would be open to the following objection: Socrates is a thing that 'can be otherwise', and yet, if he is pale at t_0, he will never lose the property of being pale at t_0, and since he is the son of Sophroniscus, being identical with the son of Sophroniscus is also a stable property of Socrates.

[133] *De Interpretatione* 1: 16 a 3–4. A few lines later (a 9–11) some 'affections' are characterized as true or false 'thoughts [νοήματα]' which are in the soul.

[134] Cf. Brentano, *Von der mannigfachen Bedeutung des Seienden nach Aristoteles*, 26 on [A. III]. On this point Meinong, Twardowski, and Husserl came to disagree with their teacher.

But then, Aristotle does not ascribe a truth-value shift to what is expressed by a sentence or to what a believer believes.

Aquinas moves towards the latter conception, and he motivates this move by an appeal to (what we have called) the Correspondence Formula. Here is the passage from which I extracted the Aquinas quotation on p. 103 above:

Cum . . . veritas intellectus sit adaequatio intellectus et rei . . . , ad illud in intellectu veritas pertinet quod intellectus dicit, non ad operationem qua illud dicit. Non enim ad veritatem intellectus exigitur ut ipsum intelligere rei aequetur, cum res interdum sit materialis, intelligere vero immateriale: sed illud quod intellectus intelligendo dicit et cognoscit, oportet esse rei aequatum, ut scilicet ita sit in re sicut intellectus dicit. [Since the truth of the intellect is the agreement between intellect and thing . . . truth pertains here to what the intellect says, and not to the operation by means of which it says it. For the truth of the intellect does not require that the (act of) thinking itself agrees with the thing: after all, the thing is sometimes material whereas the (act of) thinking is immaterial. Rather, what the intellect in the (act of) thinking says and grasps must agree with the thing—in the sense that the thing is just as the intellect says.] (*Summa contra gentiles*, I, c. 59)

Talk of what the intellect 'says' is metaphorical, and while the phrase 'operation of the intellect' may be appropriate for acts of judging (and of merely entertaining a thought), it is certainly not appropriate for beliefs. Still, the distinctions between what is thought in episodic thinking that p and this act, between what is thought (believed) in believing that p and this state, and between what is said in saying that p and the act of saying it, can all be understood as distinctions between a proposition and what it is the content of. So Aquinas may well be talking of a variation of truth-value in a proposition (held true by a thinker) when he takes up the point Aristotle made in [A. II]:

Si, opinione eadem manente, res mutatur . . . fit mutatio de vero in falsum. [If the thing changes while the belief remains constant . . . a change from truth to falsity occurs.] (*Summa theol. Ia*, q.16, a. 8, resp)

Be that as it may, the Stoics are unambiguous witnesses for the position to be examined in this section. Reviewing Benson Mates's pioneering book on Stoic logic, Geach asks:

May not the Stoics well have thought that, though the truth-value of 'Dion is alive' changes at Dion's death, the sentence still expresses the same complete meaning (λεκτόν)?[135]

The answer is that this does indeed come fairly close to what they thought. The misleading term 'meaning' should be replaced by 'sayable', and actually it

---

[135] Quoted in Evans, 'Does Tense Logic Rest upon a Mistake?' (henceforth 'Tense Logic'), 348–9.

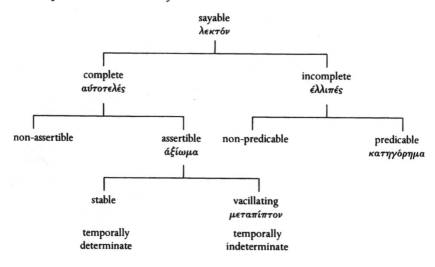

Figure 5.3. The Stoic classification of sayables

was the 'complete sayable [λεκτὸν αὐτοτελές]' itself, or more precisely, the 'assertible [ἀξίωμα]', to which the Stoics assigned a truth-value—and not the sentence used for saying it.[136] What is said in an utterance of 'Be careful, Dion!' or 'Who murdered Dion?' is 'complete', but not truth-evaluable. What is said *of* Dion in an utterance of 'Dion is alive'—i.e. *that he is alive*—is neither complete nor truth-evaluable, though it is true-or-false-*of* Dion. It is an '*incomplete* sayable [λεκτὸν ἐλλιπές]'; more precisely, it is a 'predicable [κατηγόρημα]'.[137] In one sense of the slippery phrase 'what is said', what is said in an utterance of 'Dion is alive' before Dion's death is the same as what is said when he is again referred to in an utterance of '*Dion ist am Leben*' after his death.[138] The Stoics called assertibles which are sometimes true and sometimes false 'vacillating [μεταπίπτοντα]'. I shall call them *temporally indeterminate propositions*. Like (most) tensed type-sentences, temporally indeterminate propositions are not true *simpliciter*, but rather true with respect to a time, but, like temporally determinate propositions that are true *simpliciter*, they do not consist of words. The Stoic distinctions are summarized in Figure 5.3.

---

[136] Recall the first epigraph to sect. 5.1 above. Cf. M. Frede, *Die stoische Logik*, 44–9; Bobzien, 'Logic: The Stoics', 92–6.   [137] Cf. Nuchelmans, *Theories of the Proposition*, 57–8.

[138] Since this is a venerable and still very common use of this locution, one registers with surprise that Salmon (in his criticism of Kaplan) almost sweats with conviction that only eternalists properly understand the phrase: 'it is known in advance that what is asserted is not the sort of thing that can switch in truth-value from one moment to the next' ('Tense', 375). Cf. the almost hymnal passage on the eternality of What-is-said on p. 372 of the same paper.

A bit more recently, the temporalist conception was endorsed by Arthur Prior, the founder of Tense Logic, and by David Kaplan who created the Logic of Indexicals. Suppose 'p' is a temporally indexical sentence, can God know that p? He could not, Prior suspects, if some philosophers of religion were right about Him:

> Many very reputable philosophers, e.g. St. Thomas Aquinas, have held that God's knowledge is in some way right outside of time. . . . I want to argue against this view, on the ground that its final effect is to restrict *what God knows* to those truths, if any, which are themselves timeless. For example, God could not, on the view I am considering, know that the 1960 final examinations at Manchester are now over; for this isn't something that He or anyone could know timelessly, because it just isn't true timelessly. It's true now, but it wasn't true a year ago (I write this on 29th August 1960). ('The Formalities of Omniscience', 29)

What is the *it* that is here alleged to change its truth-value? The answer is obviously given by the clause, 'that the 1960 final examinations at Manchester are now over'. So Prior takes what is singled out by this clause to be a temporally indeterminate proposition.[139] (To be sure, he would also say that the (type-) *sentence* 'The 1960 final examinations at Manchester are now over' fluctuates between truth and falsity, but that is not the issue in our quotation.)

When Kaplan talks about what is expressed in context c by a tensed sentence S like our

(1) It is raining in London,

he puts the term 'proposition' between scare quotes:

> The 'proposition' [expressed by S in c] (the scare quotes reflect my feeling that this is not the traditional notion of a proposition) is neutral with respect to time. . . . We can ask whether it would be true at times other than the time of c. Thus we think of the temporally neutral 'proposition' as changing its truth-value over time. Note that it is not just the noneternal sentence S that changes its truth-value over time but the 'proposition' itself. ('Demonstratives', 503)

Kaplan's temporally neutral 'propositions' vacillate between truth and falsity,[140] so they are what I have called temporally indeterminate propositions. Kaplan

---

[139] As to the challenge Prior poses for Aquinas' God, several questions arise. Presumably 'God knows timelessly that . . .' means something like 'God knows that . . ., but there is no time t such that God knows at t that . . .' Prior takes it for granted that a sentence 'p' which expresses a temporally indeterminate proposition cannot make that schema true, but is this really a matter of course? Furthermore, would the problem not arise if the tensed sentence 'p' expresses a timelessly true proposition that can only be expressed by a tensed sentence? Finally, as we shall see in sect. 5.3.3 below, it is deeply problematical to take temporally indeterminate propositions to be contents of knowledge, no matter whether of our knowledge or of God's.

[140] Shortly before introducing the notion of temporally indeterminate propositions, Kaplan argues: suppose you and I were to utter now the same first-person sentence, then 'if what we say differs in

argues convincingly that temporal operators would be otiose if what is said were always temporally determinate.[141] As to calling what is said when it is temporally indeterminate a proposition, the passage does not give us much reason to be scared: after all, there is no such thing as *the* traditional notion of a proposition.

What is the relation between temporally indeterminate propositions and the (conventional linguistic) meanings of the sentences used to express them? Temporally *determinate* propositions that are expressed by tensed sentences in certain contexts are to be distinguished from the meanings of those sentences: the meaning of 'Today . . .' does not change every day at midnight, but each day the sentence expresses a different temporally determinate proposition. But perhaps identity of meaning *is* sufficient for the same temporally *indeterminate* proposition's being expressed. So our question is whether the temporally indeterminate proposition that is expressed in a certain context by (1), say, can be identified with the meaning of (1).

Let us first reflect on the example used by the Stoics.

(Δ)   Dion is alive.

Suppose in 354 BC, shortly before the murder of the Sicilian politician Dion, Plato assertorically and sincerely uttered (Δ), or rather its Greek counterpart, referring to a young Athenian potter of the same name who had just survived an accident and was to carry on his life for many more years. Then, shortly after the political murder in Syracuse, of which he has not yet heard anything, Plato assertorically and sincerely uttered (Δ) again, but this time referring to the Sicilian politician. In this case one cannot sensibly maintain that, because of the event in Syracuse, what Plato said and thought has become false. But if the first utterance, too, had been about his Sicilian admirer, then it would not be unreasonable at all to make this claim (and temporalists subscribe to it). So the Stoics

---

truth-value, that is enough to show that we say different things' (500; cf. 530). This suggests that a simple appeal to Leibniz's Law suffices to justify the contention that what is said by S in c is different from what is said by S in c*. But when it comes to tensed sentences, Kaplan is ready to allow for the possibility that the same thing is said twice although truth-values differ: what is said may be true at t and false at t*. But then, why couldn't one argue similarly in the first-person case: 'What is said by "I am WK" is true with respect to me and false with respect to you'? See below, n. 171.

[141] 'Demonstratives', 502–4. Both Richard, 'Tense, Propositions, and Meanings', and Salmon, 'Tense', agree with Kaplan that eternally (omnitemporally or atemporally) true (false) propositions cannot be the operands of temporal operators. I wonder, though, whether Kaplan is *quite* right in saying that '[t]emporal operators applied to eternal sentences . . . are redundant' (503). Couldn't we convey that the reported event is past by applying 'It was the case that' to 'There is rain in London at 10 a.m., 18 May 1906'? After all, in idiomatic English one would say 'There *was* (*will be*) rain in London at t' whenever one knows t to be earlier (later) than the time of utterance.

were wise to keep the reference of 'Dion' constant when they assigned the same sayable to successive utterances of (*Δ*).[142] We should follow them and keep the reference of 'London' fixed when assigning the same temporally indeterminate proposition to non-simultaneous utterances of (1). Two utterances of a tensed sentence containing a name express the same temporally indeterminate proposition only if the name designates the same object in both utterances.

My answer to the question posed at the end of the paragraph before last consists of a reminder of a well-known fact about the vocable 'London', a conditional assertion—and an autobiographical remark. In some utterances of (1) the capital of the United Kingdom is designated, in others a city in Ontario, Canada. If this fact does not indicate *ambiguity* (namely that in those utterances we use one name, or two names which spell the same, with different conventional linguistic meanings), then the temporally indeterminate proposition expressed in an utterance of (1) is not identical with the meaning of (1). I think that we should affirm the antecedent.[143]

Luckily we don't have to base the distinction on a controversial claim about proper names. Consider the following example. Addressing Ann, I assert sincerely

(7)   You are angry,

and I am right. Shortly afterwards, now talking to Ben, I again utter (7) sincerely and with assertoric force, but this time I am wrong. Nobody would be inclined to describe my error by saying that what I thought and said has become false. One would be tempted to say this only if in my second utterance Ann had been referred to again after her anger had died away. (Temporalists yield to this temptation.) Now what may be controversial as regards (1) cannot seriously be

---

[142] Nuchelmans conjectures that this was indeed the Stoics' view (*Theories of the Proposition*, 83). Cf. M. Frede, *Die stoische Logik*, 46, and Bobzien, 'Logic: The Stoics', 99. The assertible *that it is day*, which is another favourite example of the Stoics, should be treated along similar lines, for it contains a hidden (indexical) reference to a place: the point they want to make with this example is not that the sentence 'It is day' now expresses a truth in Greece, say, and at the same time a falsehood somewhere beyond the Columns of Hercules, but rather that what it expresses with respect to one and the same place shifts in truth-value over time.

[143] It seems to me that the ambiguity view distorts the very concept of ambiguity. Consider two standard cases of lexical ambiguity (exemplifying what linguists tend to classify as polysemy and homonymy respectively): one's knowledge of English is imperfect if one does not know that 'chip' is not only used for potato chips and 'bank' not only for river banks. Since such manifolds of meaning associated with one (orthographic) word are surveyable, it makes sense to aspire to remedy this kind of defect in one's knowledge of a language. But if 'John Smith' has as many meanings as there are (living, dead, or still unborn) John Smiths, then nobody knows more than a minute part of this unsurveyable crowd, and nobody will sensibly try to make good this lack of knowledge. This lack seems to be misdescribed as an indication of a deficiency in one's knowledge of a language. Cf. the criticism of the ambiguity view in Jonathan Cohen, 'The Individuation of Proper Names', but also its defence in Kaplan, 'Demonstratives', 558–63, and 'Words'.

doubted in the case of (7): whether 'you' designates different persons in my two utterances or not, it has the same (conventional linguistic) meaning on both occasions. So the temporally indeterminate proposition expressed in an utterance of (7) is not identical with the meaning of (7). It is *not* the case that if a tensed sentence s in context c has the same meaning as s* in c*, then the same temporally indeterminate proposition is expressed in c and c*.[144]

In spite of the caveat entered above, it is instructive to recall under which circumstances Aristotle and Aquinas, in the passages I quoted, are ready to say that somebody's belief 'has become false': they presume that a belief which is first true and then false preserves its subject-matter, that it is at both times about the same 'thing'.

It is noteworthy that sometimes the meaning of a tensed sentence determines the number of truth-value shifts that the temporally indeterminate proposition it expresses may undergo. Consider, for example, the temporally indeterminate proposition expressed by 'Ben was born exactly 55 years ago': it can shift only once from being false to being true and only once from being true to being false.

Temporalism is not a monolithic position any more than eternalism is. Thus, within the camp of temporalists, we find a division which echoes that between bilateral and unilateral sempiternalists. Let us focus on an example. The temporally indeterminate proposition expressed by the present-tense sentence

(P)   A man is setting foot on the moon,

after having been *false* for ages, was true when Neil Armstrong was setting foot on the moon, and by the time I am writing this it has again been false for quite a while. Now a temporalist who believes in the indeterminacy of the future might make two additional claims. First, the temporally determinate proposition expressed by an utterance of the eternal sentence

(E)   At 3:56 a.m. (GMT), 21 July 1969, a man sets foot on the moon

acquires the property of being true at (a certain time before) the time specified in (E), after having been *neither true nor false* for aeons. Secondly, the temporally indeterminate proposition expressed by the future-tense variant of (P),

(F)   A man will be setting foot on the moon,

---

[144] In Kaplan's work on indexicals, the meaning of an indexical sentence, insofar as it is determined by the rules of the language, is called its *character*, and 'what is said' by such a sentence in a certain context c is called its *content* at c ('Demonstratives', 500–7, 523–4). Hence, when Kaplan suggests that we take the temporally indeterminate proposition expressed by an utterance of (1) or (7), when London (GB) is referred to or Ann is addressed, to be the *content* of that utterance, he discriminates between that proposition and the meaning of the sentence used for expressing it. So in this respect there is no difference between Kaplan's view and the position outlined above.

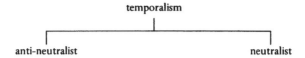

Figure 5.4. Two varieties of temporalism

was also *neither true nor false* for ages, it became true at a certain time before the 'historical moment' in 1969, and from that moment onwards it would have been false forever, if the moon had been spared further human visitors.

Let us label the view that some propositions are for some time *neither true nor false* and then become either true or false, *'neutralism* (about the future)'. Of course, a temporalist may perfectly well oppose neutralism. (Figure 5.4 registers this division in the temporalist camp.) Unilateral sempiternalists are also neutralists about the future. Many, if not all, combatants in the philosophical battle about tomorrow's sea-battle were temporalists.

A philosopher can deserve the title 'temporalist' (as used in this chapter) not only by maintaining that some propositions expressed by present-tense sentences are first true and then *false*. One can meet the condition required for being a temporalist also by maintaining that some propositions are first true and then *neither true nor false*. But is that a sensible option? As we shall see now, some bold philosophers took it by endorsing *neutralism about the past*.

It is well known that Jan Łukasiewicz was a neutralist about the future, since this neutralism was the very starting point for his conception of many-valued logic. Near the beginning of his famous paper on determinism he says:

We believe that what has been done cannot be undone: *facta infecta fieri non possunt*.[145] What was once true remains true for ever. All truth is eternal. These statements seem to be intuitively certain. We believe, therefore, that if an object A has the property b at time t, it is true at any instant later than t that A has b at t …

Intuition fails us … and the problem becomes controversial [as soon as we ask whether] if A has the property b at time t, it is true at any instant earlier than t that A has b at t. ('On Determinism', §2; [Ł.1])

Łukasiewicz then goes on to show that the strongest argument for determinism is based on the latter contention, and he aims at defusing that argument by

---

[145] Cf. Aristotle, *Nicomachean Ethics*, vi. 2: 1139b10–11, quoting Agathon. Cf. Aquinas, *Summa theol Ia*, q. 25, a. 4, resp.: if Rachel has already lost her virginity there is nothing that even the Almighty can do about it. (The example is Aquinas' own, more or less.) As to the use of '*factum*' in the Latin saying and a similar use of 'fact' in 16–17th-century English, see the extract from Austin on p. 11 above.

refuting this contention. Since it seems that one can consistently pursue this critical goal while taking the 'intuitive certainty' described in the first paragraph of [Ł.1] at its face value, the reader easily gets the impression that Łukasiewicz is a unilateral sempiternalist.[146] But he is not. In that paragraph the author is not speaking *in propria persona*. This becomes clear at the very end of his paper:

We should not treat the past differently from the future. If, of the future, only that part is now real which is causally determined at the present time... then also, of the past, only that part is now real which is now still active in its effects. Events whose effects are wholly exhausted by now, so that even an omniscient mind could not infer them from what is happening now, belong to the realm of possibility. We cannot say of them that they *took place* but only that they were *possible*. And this is as well. In the life of each of us there are grievous times of suffering and even more grievous times of guilt. We should be glad to wipe out these times not only from our memories but from reality. We may now believe that when all the effects of those fatal times are exhausted, even if this happened only *after* our death, then their causes too will be erased from the world of reality and pass over to the realm of possibility. Time is a great healer, and it grants us forgiveness. ('On Determinism', §12; [Ł.2])

This is not compatible with unilateral sempiternalism. According to [Ł.2], Ben may have committed a misdeed at time t_0 although it is *not* true at every instant later than t_0 that he did. There might come a time when his wrongful act is no longer remembered by anyone and when no non-mental traces of that event are left either,[147] and from that moment onwards, or so we are told, the proposition that Ben did something wrong at t_0 is no longer true. (Łukasiewicz's claim that Ben's guilt will by then be *forgiven* is of dubious coherence: can somebody be forgiven for having done such-and-such when the proposition that he actually did it is not true?) We can read [Ł.2] as a plea for neutralism about the past: some propositions are for some time true (false) and then become neither true nor false.

Dummett seems to have [Ł.2] in mind when he says:

[A bold anti-realist thesis] has been advanced by some philosophers (Łukasiewicz, C. I. Lewis, and, at one time, A. J. Ayer) concerning statements in the past tense, to the effect that such a statement cannot be true unless some statement about the existence of present... evidence and memories is also true; if every trace of the occurrence of

---

[146] This is how he is understood by von Wright, 'Determinism and Future Truth', 9 n. 10, and by Simons and Woleński, '*De Veritate*', 400.

[147] Nowadays, physicists (or popularizers of physics?) seem to take the second part of this condition to be unfulfilled. ('Shake your fist and you shake the Universe', we are assured in *New Scientist* (Dec. 2001), 27.) I'm grateful to Galen Strawson for pointing this out to me—and for not trying to seduce me into taking a stand on this issue.

the alleged past event has disappeared, the statement that it occurred is devoid of truth ... / ... For an anti-realist about the past, a past-tense statement can be true only if there is present evidence for its truth. ('Realism' (1982), 244, 249)

Now the thesis that truth (about the past, or whatever) does not outrun rational acceptability, that it is not evidence-transcendent, has certainly been upheld by the pragmatist Lewis and by Ayer in his Logical Positivist beginnings.[148] But I very much doubt that Łukasiewicz would have accepted it. His claim in [Ł.2] seems to be based on a metaphysical postulate, which may be dubbed the *Requirement of Compresence*: if a proposition is true at a certain time, then it must have (what Łukasiewicz calls) a 'real (actual) correlate', i.e. its truth must be guaranteed by something that exists or occurs *at that very time*, and if a proposition is false at a certain time, then its negation must fulfil this condition.[149] If at t we correctly report an event that occurs at t, then the 'real correlate' is the reported event itself. But if at t we predict an event, the Requirement of Compresence can only be met by a *cause* of the alleged future event, and if at t we 'retrodict' a certain event, only an *effect* (a trace) of the alleged past event can fill that requirement. Nothing Łukasiewicz says excludes the possibility that we might be unable to recognize the presence of the cause, or of the effect. In such a case our prediction or retrodiction would be true (false) although its truth (falsity) would be evidence-transcendent.[150] Pending a powerful (non-verificationist) argument for Łukasiewicz's Requirement of Compresence, I shall put aside metaphysically motivated 'irrealism' about the past and about the future for the rest of this chapter—and of this book.[151] (The claim that truth is evidentially constrained, which is common to C. I. Lewis, the young Ayer, and the anti-realist as described by Dummett above,

---

[148] Since Dummett does not give any reference, let me here make good for the omission: Clarence Irving Lewis, *Mind and the World Order*, 150–3; Ayer, *Language, Truth and Logic*, 1st edn., 134–5 (where the view is derived from Lewis). Incidentally, the problem was not overlooked by the Viennese positivists (as Ayer sometimes suggests): see Hans Hahn, 'Logik, Mathematik und Naturerkennen', §VI; and it was already faced by the founder of American pragmatism: Peirce, *CP*, 5.565 (1901), 5.543 (1902), 5.461 (1905). Nowadays Dummett's own paper 'The Reality of the Past' (repr. in his *TOE*) is generally considered to be the classical exposition of anti-realism about the past. For further elaboration, cf. Wright, *Realism, Meaning and Truth*, chs. 3 and 5. The most powerful attack on this local anti-realism I know is ch. 3 of Peacocke's *Being Known*.

[149] Łukasiewicz, 'On Determinism', §§8–9, 11. Recall our first encounter with this principle on p. 202 above.

[150] The position Dummett characterizes at the top of p. 258 of 'Realism' (1982) seems to coincide with the view I ascribe to Łukasiewicz.

[151] As we saw, Łukasiewicz combines neutralism about the past with neutralism about the future. Thus he takes truth to be both losable and gainable. As far as I can see, no philosopher held or holds the view that truth is a property which can be lost, but not acquired. Somebody who accepts neutralism about the past but rejects neutralism about the future would be a temporalist of this stripe.

will come in for a good deal of discussion in the last chapter.) Our concern in the remainder of the present chapter is the temporalist claim that what is said in various utterances of, e.g., 'Ben is committing a misdeed' (if one and the same person is referred to) may vacillate between truth and *falsity*.

5.3.2 Over-hasty arguments for temporalism

Certain rather plain linguistic data may seem to speak clearly in favour of temporalism, and at least one logician, Pavel Tichý took this evidence to be unequivocal. What is the alleged evidence?

Suppose at time t_0 it is very sultry in London, and Ben wishes it were raining. Then a false proposition, Tichý maintains, is the content of Ben's wish. Now Ben 'may be lucky and his wish may, as we say, *come true*. But if so, the proposition [which is the content of Ben's wish] must be susceptible to changes in truth-value.'[152]

This argument will leave the atemporalist thoroughly unimpressed. Is it really so clear that the content of Ben's wish is a false proposition? Ben's wish at t_0 may be an 'idle' present-directed wish: as regards t_0, he may wish that it were raining *then*. In that case the content of his wish, the atemporalist will concede, is a false proposition, but *this* wish cannot come true, any more than my idle past-directed wish concerning one of my earlier misdeeds, that I had not done it, can come true. So Ben's wish has only a chance of coming true when it is a future-directed wish, but then the atemporalist can easily deflect Tichý's attack. He can say: what Ben wished at t_0 was that it soon start raining, the earlier the better. Ben was lucky, it did soon start raining. So the content of his wish was a *true* proposition after all. A wish comes true as soon as the content of the wish turns out to *be* true. To be sure, the proposition which is the content of Ben's future-directed wish is not true *unless* it starts raining, but that does not entail that it is not true *until* it starts raining.[153]

The other piece of linguistic evidence Tichý presents is more impressive.[154] We often hear exchanges like the following. Entering the room Ben says, 'It is raining.' Ann who is looking out of the window corrects him:

(P1)   That was true a moment ago, but it isn't true now
(F1)   That will soon be true, but it isn't true now.

---

[152] Tichý, 'The Transiency of Truth', 168. I shall only discuss Tichý's 'linguistic evidence' against atemporalism. His 'epistemological evidence' (168–9) can only be used against *eliminativist* eternalism.

[153] White, *Truth*, 44–6. For more on ascriptions of wishes, see p. 312 below.

[154] Tichý, 'The Transiency of Truth', 168.

Ben remarks, 'The Polish Pope is abroad,' and again Ann contradicts him:

(∃1)   That is sometimes true, but today it isn't.

We cannot take the second speaker in these little dialogues to ascribe shifting truth-values to *utterances* (or audible tokens). Gareth Evans spells out the reason:

One who utters the sentence type 'It is raining' rules out dry weather only at the time of utterance; he does not rule out later dryness, and hence there can be no argument from the later state of the weather to a re-appraisal of his utterance. ('Tense Logic', 350)[155]

In section 5.1.3 I suggested that we describe the use of the demonstrative 'that' in utterances of sentences like (P1–∃1) as a case of deferred ostension: pointing to an utterance, the second speaker refers to something else—i.e. to the proposition expressed in the utterance pointed to. But if the second speaker refers to a proposition, isn't it obvious that she ascribes shifting truth-values to it? Doesn't such talk clearly confirm temporalism?

Not at all, the atemporalist will reply,[156] for instead of (∃1) our speaker might just as well have taken a deeper breath and said:

(∃2)   It *is* true that the Polish Pope is sometimes abroad, but it *is* not true that he is abroad today.

The copula in '*is* true', the atemporalist will insist, is to be thought of as tenseless. (I use italics to suggest this intended reading.) Since the speaker of (∃1) wanted to save breath, she had to move the quantificational temporal modifier 'sometimes' into the truth predication. And as to (P1) and (F1), the atemporalist will continue, our speaker might as well have used more verbose formulations for making her points:

(P2)   It *is* true that it was raining a moment ago, but it *is* not true that it is now raining.

(F2)   It *is* true that it will soon be raining, but it *is* not true that it is now raining.

As the speaker of (P1) or (F1) wanted to be brief, she had to shift the temporal modifications from the that-clauses into the truth predication. So in all three cases the atemporalist can retort that the time-indication which seems to qualify 'true' really qualifies the verb in the that-clause which can be recovered from the context.

---

[155] This argument does not establish that we can apply to utterances a truth-predicate which is not relativized to *anything*. Certain telephone stories in sect. 5.1.3 were meant to show that the stronger claim is false.   [156] Cf. White, *Truth*, 25–6, 43–4; von Wright, 'Determinism and Future Truth', §7.

Some symbols may help to give a general characterization of the atemporalist's strategy. Let A be any atomic present-tense sentence which is indexical just with respect to the tense of its verb, and let $A_{[past]}$ and $A_{[fut]}$ be sentences one obtains by putting the main verb of A in the simple past tense and the simple future tense respectively. The sign '——' is to mark the (possibly empty) position of all sorts of temporal operators: these operators may serve to indicate a specific time (like 'on 18 May 1906, at 10 a.m.', 'when Russell was in prison', 'a moment ago', 'yesterday', 'soon', 'tomorrow', etc.), or they may be quantificational (like 'sometimes' or 'often', etc.). Tarski's symbol '⌒' is to be read as 'followed by'. Atemporalists contend:

(P)   'That was true ——',
(F)   'That will be true ——',

where 'that' harks back to A, can be used to express the same proposition as

(P⁺)   'It *is* true that' ⌒ '——' ⌒ $A_{[past]}$,
(F⁺)   'It *is* true that' ⌒ '——' ⌒ $A_{[fut]}$,

and in all such cases formulations of the second type are less misleading. Iterations of tensed truth-ascriptions, such as 'Soon it will be true that it was true that Ann finishes her thesis', likewise yield to the atemporalist's paraphrastic endeavour. Here the availability of complex tenses like the future perfect proves to be a blessing: 'It *is* true that soon Ann will have finished her thesis.' So the mere fact that we sometimes use tensed truth-ascriptions does not vindicate temporalism, since the atemporalist can offer reformulations which no longer suggest that a proposition can have different truth-values at different times.

All in all, it seems that the chances for vindicating temporalism by appealing to ordinary usage are dim. But, of course, the paraphrase relation is symmetrical, so the defence of eternalism in this subsection certainly did not show that temporalism is wrong. In any case, what I plan to do now is not to rebut temporalism, but rather to show that it would be unwise to eschew the eternalist (atemporalist) notion of a proposition for the sake of the temporalist notion.

5.3.3 *Limits of temporalism*

Let us start with what is perhaps only a minor difficulty. Like advocates of omnitemporalism, partisans of temporalism sometimes contend that their atemporalist opponents misdescribe eternal sentences. Such sentences, they claim, are by no means (logically) tenseless. Rather, they are conjunctively (or disjunctively) tensed:

[A]llegedly tenseless statements . . . are statements which happen to be either always false or always true, and the 'is' that occurs in them is not really a tenseless 'is' but is just short for 'is, always has been, and always will be'. (Prior, 'Two Essays on Temporal Realism', 48)

Prior seems to be thinking here of sentences like '2 is prime', but his idea can be easily applied, *mutatis mutandis*, to a copula-free sentence like '7 divides 49' as well. The propositions expressed by such sentences, he maintains, are so obviously always true (if true at all) that to ask *when* they are true is pragmatically (though not logically) inept. But if we were to apply his suggested paraphrastic strategy mechanically to apparently tenseless existential generalizations like

(8)   There is such a thing as a dinosaur (Dinosaurs exist),

we would obtain a sentence that is all too obviously not equivalent, since dinosaurs are extinct. In cases such as (8) the temporalist's contention can only be that what looks untensed is in effect *disjunctively* tensed:

(8*)   There was, is (now), or will be a dinosaur.

(A sentence like our (2) would have to be construed in the same way.) A disjunctive expansion of an apparently tenseless sentence, so the temporalist will say, is a multiply tensed molecular sentence which, though composed of sentences that express propositions with variable truth-values, itself expresses a proposition with invariant truth-value.[157]

But does this strategy really work for arithmetical equations? The temporalist will try to cover

(=) $2 + 2 = 4$

by restating his position: to every eternal sentence, he claims, a conjunctively tensed *operator* can be applied. So the equation gets tensed from the outside, so to speak:

(=*)   It is, always has been, and always will be the case that $2 + 2 = 4$.

---

[157] Notice that (8*) expresses *different* temporally *determinate* propositions at different times, since the present tense (+ 'now') indicates different times in successive utterances of (8*). And so do the other tenses if Moore and Reichenbach are right (cf. my reflections on (P1–3) on pp. 279–80 above). (8*) is an eternal sentence in Quine's sense (cf. p. 291 above), but not in the modified sense (suggested on p. 274 above) that respects the Aboutness Principle.

But does the second (or third) conjunct really make sense? Surely 'It has always been the case that' followed by a sentence A is necessarily equivalent with 'It has always been true that' followed by A. In the previous subsection we saw that the latter formulation comes to the same thing as 'It is true that' followed by the past-tense variant of A. But ($=$) simply has no past-tense variant. Hence it is hard to see (to put it mildly) what significance 'It has always been the case that $2 + 2 = 4$' could have.

Now this is a problem (if it is a problem) for *all* opponents of atemporalism alike. But there is a major difficulty in which temporalists are bound to be entangled if they eschew the concept of indexically expressed propositions with stable truth-values entirely. This difficulty, which was pointed out by Mark Richard,[158] can be called the *Problem of Belief Retention*. Consider the following argument:

(B1)   Yesterday Ben believed that it was (then) raining in London.
(B2)   Today Ben still believes everything he believed yesterday.
(B3)   Therefore (?), today Ben believes that it is raining in London.

Richard's objection to temporalism is, roughly, this. The displayed argument is intuitively *in*valid. But the temporalist is driven to acclaim it as valid. So much the worse for his position: 'The temporalist is unable to give an adequate treatment of attributions of belief.'[159] In order to bring this into line with the terminology adopted in this chapter, we must read 'temporalist' as 'temporalist who shuns the concept of indexically expressed propositions with stable truth-values', or 'bold temporalist' for short.

Why is the bold temporalist driven to acclaim the fallacious argument as valid? If premiss (B1) is true, yesterday the sentence

(1)   It is raining in London

expressed something Ben believed then. Call it 'Proposition X'. From (B1) and (B2) it follows that Ben today still believes X. (So far, no disagreement between temporalists and their opponents.) Now for temporalists, (1) is, of course, a paradigm case of a sentence which expresses a temporally indeterminate proposition. Hence they will affirm: at any time at which (1) is understood as in present-day English and 'London' is used to refer to the same city, (1) expresses the same (temporally indeterminate) proposition. So today, (1) still expresses the same (temporally indeterminate) proposition it expressed yesterday. But if this temporally indeterminate proposition is taken to be identical with

---

[158] 'Temporalism and Eternalism'.   [159] Ibid., 3.

Proposition X, then the temporalist is in trouble. For then (B3) has got to be true if (B1) and (B2) are true.

One can easily construct an analogue of Richard's problem for indirect speech reports, the *Problem of Re-affirmation*:

(S1) Yesterday Ben said that it was (then) raining in London.
(S2) Today Ben re-affirms everything he said yesterday.
(S3) Therefore (?), today Ben says that it is raining in London.

This argument is intuitively invalid. But the bold temporalist is driven to acclaim it as valid. So he is unable to give an adequate treatment of *oratio obliqua*.

We can reinforce Richard's argument if we focus on ascriptions of knowledge (rather than of belief or of saying) and reflect on the *Problem of Diachronic Knowledge-Identity*. (Remember that Prior quite explicitly takes temporally indeterminate propositions to be contents of knowledge.) Suppose an utterance of

(K1) Bertie knows that it is raining in London

on 18 May 1906, yields a truth, and so does an utterance of

(K2) Ann knows that it is raining in London

on 18 May 2000. Certainly we do *not* want to conclude from this that the knowledge fairly recently attributed to Ann is the *same* as the knowledge that was attributed to Bertie some decades earlier. But this is exactly what would follow from (K1) and (K2) if one were to take the temporally indeterminate proposition, which is expressed on both occasions by the embedded sentence (1), to be the content of the knowledge ascribed.[160]

Consider the reverse side of the same coin. Suppose that an assertive utterance of (K3) on the evening of day D yields a truth:

(K3) That today a bomb exploded in Belfast will not be known in Moscow before tomorrow morning.

In this utterance the speaker clearly claims that her 'explosive' knowledge has the *same* content as the knowledge which, according to her prediction, will be acquired in Moscow some hours later. But this content cannot be the temporally *in*determinate proposition expressed by the embedded sentence, for that proposition is expressed in reports about various explosions in Belfast on different days. Rather, it must be the temporally determinate proposition which is expressed, on day D, by the sentence embedded in (K3) and, on the day after D, by 'Yesterday a bomb exploded in Belfast.'

Let me clinch my critique of bold temporalism by presenting the *Problem of Wish Fulfilment*.[161] Consider the following argument:

(W1)   What Bertie wished at 10 a.m., 18 May 1906, was that it would soon stop raining in London.

(W2)   What Ann wished at 10 a.m., 18 May 2000, was that it would soon stop raining in London, and what she wished came true 5 minutes later.

(W3)   Therefore (?), at 10:05 a.m., 18 May 2000, what Bertie wished came true.

This argument is obviously invalid: surely Bertie's wish can only be satisfied by a termination of rain soon after the time indicated in (W1). But, again, bold temporalists are driven to acclaim a fallacious argument as valid. If the content of Bertie's wish is the temporally indeterminate proposition designated by the that-clause in (W1), then that proposition is also the content of Ann's wish (provided that the same London is referred to),[162] and the conclusion (W3) follows via transitivity of identity and Leibniz's Laws. (Arguments of the form 'a = b, c = b & Fc ∴ Fa' are formally valid.)

None of these four arguments shows that we should abandon the concept of temporally indeterminate propositions. They do not even show that this notion is irrelevant for an account of our practice of reporting propositional attitudes or of *oratio obliqua*. But those arguments do show that the concept of temporally indeterminate propositions does *not suffice* for an adequate treatment of attributions of propositional attitudes or of indirect speech. They convict bold temporalism of rashness.

It has turned out that the contents of sayings-that and thinkings-that, in whatever mode, are not temporally indeterminate propositions. But at the beginning of this chapter we introduced 'proposition' in such a way that 'A Vs that p' trivially entails 'The proposition that p is the content of A's V_n.' Hence, strictly speaking, temporally indeterminate propositions are not *propositions*. (So Kaplan's scare quotes were not misplaced, after all.) But let us not overlook the similarities between them. Strictly speaking, toy ducks aren't ducks, but there are various salient respects in which toy ducks resemble real ducks. (Real) proposition and temporally indeterminate proposition are similar in that both can be singled out by that-clauses and both can be taken to be what is said in an

---

[161] Cf. pp. 259–60 and 306 f above.

[162] At this point it should be conceded on all sides that there is a level of description at which it is correct to say that Bertie and Ann had the same wish. I shall soon come back to this observation.

utterance of a sentence. Suppose that Ben assertively utters on Monday, 'It is raining in London (GB)', and he is wrong, and that Ann does the same on the following day, but she is right. Did they both say the same thing? Well, yes and no. If your answer is Yes, then what is said is false on Monday and true on Tuesday: it is a temporally indeterminate proposition, and it does not coincide with the content of either utterance. If your answer is No, then what is said on Monday is false *simpliciter* and what is said on Tuesday is true *simpliciter*: in both cases what is said is a (real) proposition, and in both cases it coincides with the content of the utterance. (So in the end, Schiffer is vindicated: propositions, real propositions, that is, are not true relative to a time.[163])

Is truth a property that can be lost? Well, yes and no. Under one perfectly legitimate reading of 'what is said', what is said can undeniably lose as well as acquire the property of being true. But if we take what is said to be a (real) proposition, then truth is both unlosable and ungainable (unless neutralism about the future or neutralism about the past is correct). The things of which temporalists affirm that they can lose truth are not the things of which (anti-neutralist) eternalists deny it. So the two camps do not flatly contradict each other, and there is occasion for

5.4 An Irenic Epilogue

The Arguments from Belief Retention, Re-affirmation, Diachronic Knowledge-Identity, and Wish Fulfilment supply grist to Evans's mill:

There is no objection to introducing an equivalence relation, 'says the same thing as', according to which all utterances of the same [sc. unambiguous] tensed sentence type say the same thing, nor to introducing an abstract object—a 'Stoic-proposition'—on the back of this relation. What we cannot do is to regard a Stoic-proposition as a complete proposition, in the sense that describing an utterance in terms of the Stoic-proposition it puts forward is a complete semantic description of the utterance. On this point, therefore, we must agree with Frege: 'A thought is not true at one time and false at another . . .'. ('Tense Logic', 350)[164]

Evans's verdict leaves the question open whether there is ever any *point* in introducing what he calls a 'Stoic-proposition', and this question comes close to the

---

[163] See above, p. 269 n. 63.
[164] I have taken the liberty of inserting 'unambiguous'. There seems to be no sense of 'says the same thing as' which would allow us to maintain that all utterances of a lexically or syntactically ambiguous sentence 'say the same thing'.

one I want to answer in this section: is there ever any point in introducing a temporally indeterminate proposition? The questions don't coincide because Evans's Stoic-propositions are not identical with what I have called temporally indeterminate propositions. I see no good reason to discriminate between his Stoic-propositions and the (conventional linguistic) meanings of unambiguous tensed sentences,[165] but in section 5.3.1 I argued that we should distinguish temporally indeterminate propositions from meanings. As to the appropriateness of the nickname 'Stoic-proposition', it is perhaps not worth quibbling over. It is somewhat ironical, though, that it is from Evans's paper that I picked up Geach's characterization of the position of the Stoics, which provided us with a motive for drawing that distinction.

The concept of temporally indeterminate propositions may be useful for an account of our practice of reporting beliefs, even if they do not *suffice* for an adequate treatment of attributions of belief, and the same may hold, *mutatis mutandis*, for an adequate treatment of indirect speech.[166] Actually I think that some linguistic data in this area can be accounted for by invoking *both* temporally determinate propositions *and* temporally indeterminate ones.

Here is an *oratio obliqua* example. Suppose in 1998 somebody reports:

(S4)   Last Monday Ben said that the 1998 Tour de France would begin in a week's time, and last Tuesday Ann said the same thing.

This report is ambiguous. Under one reading of (S4) both speakers were agreed as to the day on which the Tour was to begin. On this interpretation the truth of the report (if it is true) may be due to the fact that the utterances of the two speakers expressed one and the same *temporally determinate* proposition. Perhaps both said, referring to the same Monday, 'The 1998 Tour de France will begin next Monday.' Under the other (perhaps less strained) reading of (S4) the two speakers referred to different days, so it cannot be the case that both were right in saying what they said. On this interpretation the two utterances reported by (S4) may have expressed one and the same *temporally indeterminate* proposition, which can be expressed on many different days by saying, 'The 1998 Tour de France will begin in a week's time.'

My second example is a belief report.[167] Suppose in 1998 I said to you, 'Cecilia Bartoli is the greatest of all mezzo-sopranos', and, alluding to that utterance,

---

[165] They seem to be identical with what Perry calls 'relativized propositions': cf. 'The Problem of the Essential Indexical', 12–13.

[166] *Pace* Evans, I think that Kaplan has shown that *temporal operators* would be otiose if what is said were always temporally determinate: cf. p. 300 and n. 141 above.

[167] A similar case is discussed in Gregory Fitch, 'Tense and Contents', 153–4.

you ask me now, 'Did you believe what you said then?' I reply:

(B4)   Yes, I did, and I still believe what I said then.

Clearly my reply can be understood in two ways. Under one reading I still think about 1998 that she was the greatest then, but I do not commit myself as to her present rank. On this interpretation my utterance of (B4) relates both my current and my former believing to one and the same *temporally determinate* proposition, and I claim belief retention (in the sense appealed to in my rendering of Richard's argument above). Under the other reading my reply is riskier: it declares La Bartoli to be currently the greatest, too. Understood this way, my utterance of (B4) relates both my current and my former believing to one and the same *temporally indeterminate* proposition, and I claim more than belief retention.

So our practice of ascribing sayings and beliefs to others and to ourselves can sometimes be illuminatingly described by invoking propositions and 'propositions'.

The relation between temporally indeterminate propositions and (real) propositions is one—many. This relation is best conceived of, I think, on the analogy of the relation between an open sentence with one free variable and the many sentences which result from saturating it. A temporally indeterminate proposition, we can say, is an 'open proposition' (or an 'unsaturated proposition' or a 'proposition matrix') of a special kind.[168] In specifying an open proposition of this kind, we specify something which can be said *of*, or thought *about*, a time (an interval or a moment) and which is true, or false, *of* the time it is said of or thought about.[169] The copula in '*is* true of' is best construed as logically *tenseless*.

Consider (S4) and (B4) again. Under the second reading of (S4), the day, of which Ben says that the Tour begins on it, is different from the day, of which Ann says the same thing, and this 'thing' can be true only of one of these days.

---

[168] The first title, which echoes Quine's talk of open sentences, is used by Perry (see his 'The Problem of the Essential Indexical', 10, 19–20); the second title, which alludes to Frege's characterization of concept-words as having unsaturated senses, is due to von Wright (see his 'Demystifying Propositions', 24–5), and the third title is Salmon's (see his 'Tense', 342–6). Ducasse uses 'propositional function' with the same intent ('Propositions, Truth, and the Ultimate Criterion of Truth', 170), which would be fine, too, were it not for the fact that Russell (mis)used this term to refer to open sentences.

[169] Cf. von Wright, 'Demystifying Propositions'; White, *Truth*, 23–4; and, for a similar idea, Salmon, 'Tense', 346. Since Salmon advocates hybrid propositions, his proposition matrices are *properties* of times (rather than senses of concept-expressions that apply to times). The difference becomes manifest as soon as you ask, for example: do 'Ben is taking a bit of salt' and 'Ben is taking a bit of sodium chloride', provided that the same Ben is referred to, express the same open proposition? Hybridizers will nod, purists will shake their heads. In the latter spirit Peacocke distinguishes between 'thoughts which are truth-evaluable outright, and those entities in the third realm [sc. of Fregean senses] which have a truth value only relative to a time' (*Being Known*, 57), or, as I would prefer to put it, 'entities in the third realm which are true or false of times'.

Under the second reading of (B4), I think about the present time what I thought about the earlier time, too, namely that it is a time at which La Bartoli *is* the greatest, and what *is* true of one of these times may not be true of the other. Or recall one of the examples used in section 5.3.2: 'It is sometimes true that the Pope is abroad.' Applying the strategy of embrace, we can take this to be tantamount to 'It *is* true of some times that the Pope *is* abroad at them.'

Thus the relativized truth predicate 'true at a certain time' of temporalism can be mimicked by 'true of' as applied to ordered pairs of open propositions and times. Adapting the terminology of the Stoics[170] and changing their doctrine, we can say: the one thing that is expressed by a temporally indexical sentence like 'It is raining in London (GB)' at various times is an *in*complete sayable, a κατηγόρημα [predicable], rather than an ἀξίωμα [assertible].[171]

---

[170]   See Figure 5.2 above.

[171]   What is said by an indexical sentence in a certain context may be indeterminate also with respect to other features of the context. Let me briefly illustrate this for what Kaplan calls the agent of the context. For the semantics of the following excerpt from a script for a soap-opera, the notion of an *agentially indeterminate* proposition is highly pertinent: 'Good Lord,' Ben exclaims, recognizing the noises on the upper floor for what they are, 'my wife and my mistress are shouting at each other.' 'Damn,' grumbles Ben's best friend who stands behind him on the staircase, 'I was about to say the same thing.' With this remark their friendship comes to a sudden end. As can be seen from the deplorable consequence of this exchange, both speakers take the thing that had almost been said by Ben's (former) friend to be the agentially indeterminate proposition expressed by Ben (and not the agentially determinate proposition which only Ben can express by the sentence he used): each of the two men thinks about himself that his wife and his mistress are currently shouting at each other up there. Here is an analogue of the ambiguity of (B4). The belief ascription 'On that evening Tony thought he would win the 1997 general election in Britain, and John thought so, too' has a 'one pessimist' reading and a 'two optimists' reading, and the latter relates both thinkers to the same agentially indeterminate proposition which both believers could have expressed by saying, 'I shall win the 1997 general election in Britain.'

6

Two Pleas for Modesty

In Chapter 3.1.3, I pointed out a difficulty that all theories of Object-based Correspondence from Aristotle to Bolzano share. This difficulty arises from a Procrustean structural presumption concerning truth-value bearers, the presumption that all truth-candidates ascribe a property to one or several objects. One can try to avoid this difficulty by applying the Tarskian strategy of recursion. But this strategy applies only to those complex truth-candidates whose truth-values are determined by the truth-values of their constituents, and there are long-standing questions as to whether every truth-candidate has such a structure. So one should rather try to avoid the difficulty by explaining the concept of truth in such a way that the internal structure of the truth-value bearers is left entirely open. This is the way the difficulty *is* avoided by nihilists, since they try to explain this concept without assuming that there are *any* truth-value bearers at all (Ch. 2.2), and, less ironically, by theorists of Fact-based Correspondence of the prodigal variety (Ch. 3.2.1) and by disquotationalists (Ch. 4.2). The two views of truth which form the topic of the present chapter both take truth to be a property of propositions (see QUESTION 11[1]). Like the theories just mentioned, they put no constraints on the internal structure of truth-candidates, but arguably they do not run foul of the problems that plague those theories. By taking the concept of truth not to be explanation-resistant, they oppose Propositional Primitivism, the position of Frege, on the one hand, and early Moore and Russell on the other, which I sketched out in my first chapter only to set it aside (see QUESTION 13). I shall start with an exposition and discussion of Paul Horwich's *Minimalism*, registered under the left branch of QUESTION 14. Most of the time, however, I shall be occupied with propounding and defending its opposite number, the conception of truth that I call the *Modest Account*. Note that the notion of a *property* which is used in both accounts is the liberal one I explained in Chapter 2.2: properties are ascribables, which can be

---

[1] See Ch. 1, Fig. 1.3, for QUESTIONS 11–14.

singled out by nominalizations of genuine predicates, just as propositions are (according to the account in Chapter 5.1) sayables and thinkables, which can be singled out by nominalizations of declarative sentences.

6.1 Minimalism

Minimalist, n. (1) Orig., a Menshevik. Later also, any person advocating small or moderate reforms or policies. (2) An advocate or practitioner of minimal art; a composer of minimal music.

The New Shorter Oxford English Dictionary, 1993

6.1.1 *Clinging to the Denominalization Schema*

What is it to go in for the very small with respect to truth? The first of the above dictionary entries is not very helpful, I am afraid. Horwich does indeed advocate a kind of moderation, but I presume that his opponents, most of them anyway, would not like to be thought of as truth-theoretical Bolsheviks (Maximalists). As we shall soon see, the second dictionary entry does point in the right direction.

Horwich's 'minimalist conception' of truth is a thesis about what he calls 'the minimal theory' of truth. According to that thesis, the minimal theory (virtually) exhausts the theory of truth.[2] Let us begin with a provisional description of the *minimal theory*, or MT for short. MT is a collection of infinitely many propositions ('axioms'), comprising the propositions expressed by the biconditionals

> The proposition that snow is white is true, iff snow is white
> The proposition that lions roar is true, iff lions roar

and (almost) all other propositions of that ilk. A proposition is of that ilk if it is expressed by a substitution-instance of the Denominalization Schema

(Den)   The proposition that p is true, iff p,

to which Horwich refers as 'the Equivalence Schema'. The connective 'iff' is no stronger than the material equivalences ('$\leftrightarrow$') of classical logic.[3] The bracketed 'almost' alludes to the exclusion of those propositions that are expressed by paradox-engendering instances (of translations) of (Den).[4] Since the collection

---

[2] Horwich, *Truth*, 6–7, 43, 65. (In this chapter, '*Truth*', followed by page number, is always used to refer to the second edition of Horwich's work.) It is a rather unfortunate coincidence that Wright uses the title 'minimalism' for a view that rejects this very thesis: see his *T&O*, 12 ff., and 'Minimalism', sect. 1.

[3] *Truth*, 77, 124; *Meaning* 104 n. 2, 'Defense', 559, 573 n. 2.   [4] *Truth*, 40–2, 136.

of axioms that make up MT is uncountable (and too large even to constitute a set[5]), I have placed minimalism under the left branch of QUESTION 14. Notice that the axioms of MT are not sentences, but propositions.[6]

MT accords perfectly with what Horwich takes to be 'the *raison d'être* of the concept of truth'.[7] His account of the needs which the notion of truth satisfies transposes a Quinean melody we have heard before into a propositionalist key.[8] Suppose you wish to state a logical law, e.g. the principle of self-implication whose instances include

(a) If time flies then time flies
(b) If duty calls then duty calls
(c) If lions roar then lions roar.

It would be a blessing if you could compress this tedious litany of conditional propositions into a single proposition. Or suppose you have great confidence in the last statements people make on their deathbeds, and you are told that just before he died Alfred made an assertion, but, alas, nobody tells you what he said. Because of your general confidence concerning last statements, you do acquire a belief about Alfred's statement. But you would be bound to run out of mental breath if you were to say to yourself (with 'a' as short for 'the last thing Alfred asserted') that

(d) if a is the proposition that blood is red then blood is red, and
     if a is the proposition that coal is black then coal is black, and
     if a is the proposition that snow is white then snow is white, and . . .

Is there a way of supplanting the infinite conjunction of which (d) is a tiny fragment by one laconic proposition that could form the content of your belief about Alfred's last statement?

It is merely in order to solve this kind of problem, Horwich maintains, that we have the concept of truth, and in the light which the minimal theory throws upon this concept we can see how it solves those problems. MT allows us to convert (a), (b), and (c) into

(a*) The proposition that if time flies then time flies is true
(b*) The proposition that if duty calls then duty calls is true
(c*) The proposition that if lions roar then lions roar is true,

---

[5] As can be shown by Cantor's diagonal argument: see *Truth*, 20–1, n. 4.

[6] In this respect, Horwich's use of 'axiom' is the same as Frege's: see *NS*, 221–2 (205–6). In sect. 6.2.3, (p. 354 and n. 112 below), we will have occasion to remark on a difference.

[7] *Truth*, 3, 118, 123. As I said on p. 237 above, I do not believe that 'true' (or any other predicate) has just *one* function, but let that pass.   [8] Cf. Ch. 4.2.2 on the second tenet of disquotationalism.

in which the same property is attributed to objects of a certain kind, namely to propositions (which can be expressed by sentences) of the form 'if p then p',[9] and now we can concisely formulate the principle of self-implication by quantifying over these objects:

(T1)   For all propositions x, if x is of the form 'if p then p' then x is true.

Similarly, MT allows us to convert (d) first into

(d*)   If the last thing Alfred asserted is the proposition that blood is red then the proposition that blood is red is true, and . . .

This can now be quantificationally summarized as

(T2)   For all propositions x, if the last thing Alfred asserted is x then x is true,

and finally we can put it into a nutshell:

The last thing Alfred asserted is true.

Notice that the quantifications in (T1) and (T2) use only pro*nominal* variables. Wherever we employ a truth-predicate in propositionally unrevealing truth-ascriptions—whether it be in logic, as in (T1), or in everyday life, as in (T2), or in philosophy ('A proposition x is true just in case it would be rational to accept x if epistemic conditions for assessing x were good enough')—it functions as a 'device of generalization' which facilitates expression.[10]

According to the *minimalist conception*, a theory of truth should comprise no more than is contained in the minimal theory, since MT is explanatorily adequate: 'All of the facts whose expression involves the truth predicate may be explained . . . by assuming no more about truth than instances of the equivalence [i.e. denominalization] schema.'[11] As it stands, this requires two corrections. First, since the minimal theory consists of propositions, whereas instances of (Den) are sentences, the formulation should be amended: '. . . assuming no more about truth than *what is expressed by* instances of the schema'. Secondly, as Gupta pointed out in a critical review of the first edition of Horwich's book, a theory that contains only axioms expressed by instances of (Den) is unable to explain why, for example, the moon is not true.[12] In response to this, Horwich has slightly (minimally) lifted the ban on further axioms in the second edition of the book: a complete theory of truth, he now says, requires the additional axiom *that only propositions are true*.[13] As to any further contentions philosophers

[9] *Truth*, 123 n.   [10] See, e.g., the very last sentence of *Truth*.   [11] Ibid., 23.
[12] Gupta, 'Minimalism', 363–4.   [13] *Truth*, 23 n., 43; 'Defense', 576 n. 20.

took to be integral to their accounts of truth, the minimalist declares: *Si tacuisses, philosophus mansisses*, or in terms more easily comprehensible to non-classicists, silence is golden.

Here is a successful minimalist explanation of a fact whose expression involves the truth predicate.[14] The fact to be explained is that from (1) 'Pythagoras' Theorem is true' and (2) 'Pythagoras' Theorem is the proposition that the square on the hypotenuse is equal to the sum of the squares on the other two sides', one can conclude 'The square on the hypotenuse is equal etc.' Minimalism can account for this fact by invoking the following inference rule:

Min   You may introduce into a proof at any stage a sentence which expresses (one direction of) an axiom of MT, resting on no assumptions.

('a' is short for the name of Pythagoras' Theorem, and 'S' abbreviates the sentence expressing it.[15])

1	(1)	a is true		Assumption
2	(2)	a = the proposition that S		Assumption
1, 2	(3)	The proposition that S is true	1, 2	= Elimination
	(4)	The proposition that S is true → S		*Min*
1, 2	(5)	S	3, 4	Modus Ponens

The reader will have noticed that I have reactivated here an earlier example: in Chapter 2 the observation that the intuitively valid argument from (1) and (2) to (3) is best construed as formally valid in classical logic played an important dialectical role. Horwich shows that the intuitively valid argument from (1) and (2) to (5) can also be construed as valid in classical logic provided we allow ourselves to invoke *Min* as an additional rule in line (4).[16]

---

[14] Cf. *Truth*, 21, 125, 141; 'Defense', 559–60.

[15] I adopt Lemmon's 'natural deduction' style of setting out formal arguments. Since more of this is to follow, let me briefly and roughly explain the notation just in case it is unfamiliar to you. The lines of a derivation are numbered consecutively, '(1)', '(2)', etc. If the formula on a certain line depends on one or more assumptions, they are registered to the left of that line. Assumptions are premisses that do not depend on any *other* premisses in the derivation. To the right of each line the rule is mentioned which justifies the appearance of a formula at that stage and (where necessary) the line(s) that contain the premiss(es) to which the rule has been applied. Some rules permit the introduction of a formula as not dependent on *any* assumptions. (For more details and explanations of the inference rules of classical first-order logic with identity see E. J. Lemmon, *Beginning Logic*.) Names of *additional* rules are italicized and explained in the text.

[16] The explanandum of the above explanation was not a generalization about truth, and the explanation had to appeal only to logic and *Min*: this makes it untypically straightforward. Several critics have argued that MT is too weak to explain any *general* truths about truth, such as the truth (C) that for all x, for all y, the conjunction of x and y is true iff x is true and y is true. MT, together with a proposition that tells us what counts as a conjunction, logically implies each instance of (C), but not (C) itself (see Gupta,

Let us now scrutinize 'The Proper Formulation' of MT, which is meant to replace the preliminary characterization with which we started. Horwich employs angled brackets, '<...>', to abbreviate the noun phrase 'the proposition that...', where the gap can be filled with a declarative sentence of English or with a sentence letter,[17] and in this section I will adopt his notation.

The axioms of the theory are propositions like

(1) ≪Snow is white> is true iff snow is white>

...; that is to say, all the propositions whose structure is

(E*) ≪p> is true iff p>.[18]

...[T]he axiom (1) is the result of applying the propositional structure (E*) to the proposition

(3*) <snow is white>.

...Indeed, when applied to any proposition, y, this structure (or function) yields a corresponding axiom of the minimal theory, MT. In other words, the axioms of MT are given by the principle

(5) For any object x: x is an axiom of the minimal theory if and only if, for some y, when the function E* is applied to y, its value is x. (*Truth*, 17–19)

If you spell out the singular term in line (E*) in accordance with Horwich's explanation of his angled brackets, then the first statement in this extract tells us: the proposition which is designated in line (1) has a structure which it shares with many other propositions, and this *structure* is—the proposition that the proposition that p is true iff p. Does this make sense at all? Then we are told that what is designated in line (E*) is a *function* from propositions to propositions. A function which really deserves this name specifies a value for every entity in the domain independently of the way the argument is given. Suppose y is the

---

'Minimalism', 361, 363–5; 'Critique', 65–7; Soames, *UT*, 247–8, 259–60 n. 33). The objection echoes, as the reader may recall, Russell's insight that universal generalizations are not logical consequences of the set of all their instances (see p. 121 above). Horwich tries to defuse the objection in *Truth*, 137 and in 'Defense', 567–9. Vulnerable points in his reply are identified by David in 'Minimalism and the Facts About Truth', 169–75. In Ch. 3, I criticized the minimalist attempt to account for the so-called Correspondence Intuition (see pp. 156–7).

[17] *Truth*, 10 n. Sometimes Horwich seems to forget how he introduced his notation. Thus his formulation of (Den) on p. 13, 'The proposition <p> is true iff p', begins with a stutter. Because of the ambiguity of 'The proposition that...' (which was commented upon in Ch. 5.1.1), we should add: Horwich's notation abbreviates that locution only if the latter designates the proposition expressed by '...'.

[18] Save for those, Horwich intimates in a footnote, that induce 'Liar' paradoxes.

proposition that snow is white: then the alleged function E* assigns a value to y if y is given as the proposition that snow is white. But what if y is given in some other way, e.g. as the proposition which is designated in line (3*) above, or as the last thing Alfred asserted? 'On the face of it,' it has been objected, 'E* only assigns a value to a proposition when the proposition is given by a sentence that expresses it, not when it is named in any other way.'[19] So it seems that E* only purports to be a function. But perhaps appearances are deceptive. Consider $2x^2 + x$, surely as decent a specimen of a function as can be. For 1 as argument it specifies 3 as value. Now if 1 is non-canonically given, e.g. as the number of natural satellites of the earth, does the function not assign a value to it? Of course it does. The problem is only that we first have to find out what the number of natural satellites of the earth is before we can determine the value of the function. Similarly in the case of the last thing Alfred asserted and Horwich's function E*: we must first figure out which proposition was the last one Alfred asserted. So the objection crumbles.

The alternative to the Proper Formulation, which Horwich presents in a long footnote to the passage cited above, characterizes the axioms of MT indirectly by characterizing the sentences that express them. Even if everything that can be expressed in some actual foreign language were also expressible in current English, we could scarcely hope to cover all axioms by saying that they are what is expressed by substitution-instances of the English Denominalization Schema, for there may very well be propositions which are not expressible in any language as it is actually spoken at some time or other at some place or other. But, Horwich argues, this unwanted restriction can be removed:

[W]e can make do with our own language supplemented with possible extensions of it. ... Thus we may specify the axioms of the theory of truth as what are expressed when the schema

(E) '$<$p$>$ is true iff p'

is instantiated by sentences in any possible extension of English. (*Truth*, 19 n.)

Possible expansions of English are presumably within our cognitive reach: humans could learn to comprehend them (and the anglophone among them would be in a privileged initial position). But then the proposal is open to the charge of alethic speciecism, which we had occasion to raise in the final stage of our discussion of disquotationalism:[20] is there any good reason to assume that every truth-candidate is expressible in a language which humans could come to

---

[19] García-Carpintero, 'A Paradox of Truth Minimalism', 60.   [20] See pp. 246–8 above.

be able to understand? Hence I prefer the formulation which Horwich airs on his way to that proposal, namely:

> [W]e might suppose that every proposition, though perhaps not expressed by any actual sentence, is at least expressed by a sentence in some possible language. And we can then regard the [minimal] theory of truth as whatever would be expressed by instances of translations of the equivalence schema into possible languages. (*Truth*, 19 n.)

(I take it that by 'actual sentence' Horwich means a sentence of a language actually used somewhere somewhen.) This passage allows us to reckon with the possibility that there are propositions which can only be expressed in languages that are irremediably incomprehensible to us. For all we know, perhaps such a language is not a bare possibility: maybe one of them is actually spoken by Alpha-Centaurians.

For all its informational poverty and formal monotony, MT is *conceptually* as rich and variegated as can be. As it contains, *inter alia*, all propositions which can be expressed by non-pathological instances of (Den), it comprises, *inter alia*, each and every concept expressible in English (including concepts such as Correspondence, Coherence, Idealized Rational Acceptability, etc.).[21] That makes the minimal theory conceptually maximal.

According to Horwich, a speaker of English has the concept of truth (or understands the truth predicate) iff she has the 'inclination to accept' as a matter of course, without supporting argument, any substitution-instance of (Den).[22] What does he mean by 'accepting a sentence'?[23] This is less clear than one would like it to be. A sentence's being 'privately accepted', Horwich says, comes to the same thing as its being 'uttered assertively to oneself'.[24] So, presumably, accepting a sentence (whether privately or in public) is uttering it assertively. But then he also says that accepting a sentence is 'what Davidson calls "holding [a sentence] true" '. For two reasons I find this confusing. First, the former kind of acceptance is a speech-act, whereas the latter is a psychological state or attitude, so they cannot be identical.[25] Secondly, Horwich wants to explain 'person x accepts sentence s' in non-semantic terms. But 'holding s true' all too obviously involves a semantic term. So the invocation of the Davidsonian

---

[21] Gupta, 'Minimalism', 365.

[22] *Truth*, 35; *Meaning*, 45, 104; 'Davidson on Deflationism', 20; 'Defense', 559, 567.

[23] Because of the context-sensitivity of most sentences, we would do well to hear this either as 'x accepts sentence s in context c' or as 'x accepts utterance u of s'.

[24] *Meaning*, 94–5, where he comes closest to explaining his use of this locution. The next quotation is from the same passage.

[25] Only under the former reading is the inclination an inclination to *do* something. In the passage I quote below, Gupta adopts the 'act' reading, for he identifies accepting with affirming.

notion can at best be a provisional expository device.[26] At any rate, the assimilation suggests that an assertive utterance betokens acceptance only if it is sincere. (There can be insincerity even in silent soliloquies.[27]) A further question obtrudes itself. Suppose Ann picks up from an English translation of Heidegger a sentence that she does not understand. Assuming that there is something to be understood, she now holds true, and assertively utters, the following biconditional which contains that sentence: 'The proposition that every open relatedness is a comportment is true iff every open relatedness is a comportment.'[28] Ann believes that this biconditional expresses a truth, but she has no idea which truth it expresses. Does she accept the biconditional? Under a rather natural reading of the verb, this certainly is a case of accepting, but at one point Horwich describes the inclination which he takes to be constitutive of our comprehension of the truth-predicate as 'our inclination to accept any instance of the schema that we understand'.[29] So Ann's performance with, and attitude towards, the Heideggerese biconditional does not really count.

For our purposes, this may have thrown enough light on Horwich's answer to the question what understanding 'true' consists in. Now the combination of this answer with the conceptual opulence of MT seems to fall victim to Gupta's objections:

> None of us has more than a minute fraction of the concepts employed in the biconditionals, yet we have a good understanding of the concept of truth. Similarly, we lack a disposition to accept the vast majority of the biconditionals, but this casts not the slightest doubt on our understanding of truth. In fact, dispositions to affirm the biconditionals exist in different people to different degrees; some are disposed to affirm more, some less. But this variation does not correspond to a variation in our grasp of truth. Finally, perfect possession of the disposition requires possession of all the concepts. But this is not a requirement for a perfect understanding of the meaning of 'true'. ('Minimalism', 366)

This criticism is barking up the wrong tree, I think. It would be pertinent if Horwich had offered a definition of 'true' along the following lines:[30]

(Df. MinT?) $\forall x$ [x is true iff (x is <blood is red>, and blood is red), or (x is <coal is black>, and coal is black), or ..., and so on].

---

[26] Horwich goes on to sketch an (admittedly) over-simple account of acceptance in terms of 'a functional theory that simultaneously characterizes "acceptance", "desire", "observation", and "action" by means of ... principles that relate these notions to one another, to behaviour, and to environmental conditions' ('Meaning', 95–6).

[27] As has been observed by novelists. In *The Metaphysics of Mind* (26–7, 126) Anthony Kenny illuminatingly comments on a striking passage from Trollope which illustrates the point.

[28] The sentence is from Heidegger, *On the Essence of Truth*, 124.   [29] 'Defense', 567.

[30] Lewis presents (MinT) as 'the truth about truth': see his 'Truthmaking and Difference-Making', 602.

This is the propositionalist counterpart of (Df. DisT) that was discussed in Chapter 4.2.2, and like its predecessor it falls victim to the Argument from Conceptual Overloading, concisely presented by Gupta at the beginning of our extract. But Horwich emphasizes that MT 'does not say explicitly what truth is; it contains no principle of the form, "$\forall$x (x is true iff...x...)" '.[31] He does not try to say what all true propositions have in common. (In the second half of this chapter I shall try to do so, in my own 'minimalist' way.) As to Horwich's conception of understanding 'true' or of having the concept of truth, Gupta takes the 'reach' of the relevant inclination to depend on the vocabulary of the speaker. If that is correct, then the inclination does indeed vary between different speakers as well as change with the expansion of a speaker's vocabulary, and for no speaker does it cover all instances of (Den). But one can describe the relevant inclination in such a way that these variations and limitations become irrelevant: one understands 'true', Horwich maintains, if and only if one has the inclination to accept without any further ado any instance of (Den) in which a sentence one understands occupies the 'p'-position.[32]

As the reader will have noticed, Gupta uses the term 'disposition' rather than 'inclination'. Sometimes, in the very same context, Horwich himself employs the former term.[33] But this is rather unfortunate, for the following passage shows that by his own lights only the latter term is appropriate. His talk of an inclination to accept instances of (Den), as distinct from a disposition to do so, is motivated by the stance he takes towards the 'Liar':[34]

I would argue that the moral of the 'liar' paradoxes is that not *all* instances of the equivalence schema [i.e. (Den)] are correct. But I don't believe that those who come to accept [*sic*] this moral, and who come to balk at certain instances, are thereby altering what they mean by the truth predicate. This is my motivation for supposing that the meaning-constituting fact about 'true' is a mere *inclination* to accept any instance of the schema, rather than a *disposition* to accept any instance. In problematic cases the inclination will be overridden. But its continued existence is what sustains the sense of paradox. ('Defense', 576 n. 22)

Certainly Ann's inclination to punch Ben's nose may persist even when she has an opportunity for attack but does not seize it. Horwich's argument presupposes that

---

[31] *Truth*, 20, cf. 23, 33, 111; 'Defense', 560. Sometimes Horwich describes the minimal theory as an implicit definition of 'true' (with the peculiar feature that it cannot be written down *in toto*): see *Truth*, 1st edn, 52. (In *Truth*, 121 and *Meaning*, 107, he says that the Denominalization *Schema* implicitly defines 'true'. This seems to me to be a rather idiosyncratic use of the phrase 'implicit definition', but I must confess that I am none too clear about the sense of this phrase.)

[32] This paragraph has echoed Horwich's own reply to Gupta in 'Defense', 567.

[33] Not only on p. 36 of the first edn. of *Truth* (on which Gupta's discussion is based), but also in the 2nd edn., 35, 128–9, 135, and in *Meaning*, 107 n., 140.   [34] Cf. also *Truth*, 136.

a similar story could not be told about a disposition, properly so called. This is debatable, I think, but I shall not debate it here.

6.1.2 *A denial of intelligibility*

Let us now consider Davidson's main objection against truth-theoretical minimalism. (It can be directed against the modest account as well, so I have to be keen to defuse it.) Davidson bluntly declares: 'I do not understand the basic [denominalization] schema or its instances.'[35] The second half of this confession, one feels inclined to say, is quite unbelievable. Certainly Davidson does not fail to understand the canine triviality

(T)   The proposition that dogs bark is true iff dogs bark

which *is* an instance of (Den). So let's apply the Principle of Charity and look for another reading of Davidson's confession. We don't have to look very far. After putting aside 'the doubts many of us have about the existence of propositions, or at least [about] the principles for individuating them', he argues:

> [T]he same sentence appears twice in instances of Horwich's schema [i.e. (Den)], once after 'the proposition that', in a context that requires the result to be a singular term, the subject of a predicate, and once as an ordinary sentence. We cannot eliminate this iteration of the same sentence without destroying all appearance of a theory. But we cannot *understand* the result of the iteration unless we can see how to make use of the same semantic features of the repeated sentence in both of its appearances—make use of them in giving the semantics of the schema instances. I do not see how this can be done. ('Folly', 274)[36]

So the self-confessed lack of understanding is a lack of *theoretical* understanding: how can we make use of the same semantic features of the sentence which occurs on both sides of the 'iff' in giving the semantics of (T)? Davidson is surely right in saying that singular terms like 'that dogs bark' must not be treated as structureless names. After all, we recognize what such a singular term designates in and through understanding the embedded sentence. Horwich's rejoinder is a rather effective *argumentum ad hominem*:

> One might suspect that Davidson's attitude derives from scepticism about propositions; however he is quite explicit that this is not the objection. But in that case—if there really *are* such things—how can the expressions specifically designed to refer to them be

---

[35] Davidson, 'Folly', 273. Readers who have superiority feelings here should be warned: according to 'The Centrality of Truth', 108 (= 'Truth Rehabilitated', 68), *we* do not understand the schema or its instances either.

[36] Geach had mounted essentially the same objection against Ramsey and Prior: 'Truth and God', 85–6.

unintelligible? And if, for example, 'The proposition that dogs bark' is not unintelligible, how can there be a problem about using it to say that its referent, in certain specified conditions, is true?

Davidson's answer is that it is obscure how the referents of such alleged singular terms could be determined by the referents of their constituent words. Now, insofar as this is so, it will be obscure how to develop a Davidsonian truth-conditional meaning-theory for such expressions. But are we really entitled to conclude that they are unintelligible? Why not instead suppose—as Davidson himself has done in certain other cases[37]—that they are amongst the various recalcitrant constructions that, though perfectly meaningful, have so far resisted assimilation to the truth-conditional paradigm? After all, especially if we are waiving any objection to propositions as such, the expressions in question would appear to be on a par with 'The hypothesis that dogs bark', 'The supposition that dogs bark', etc.—which have no technical flavour and which are even more obviously meaningful singular terms.

Moreover, if there really is an overwhelming reason to conclude that the referents of such expressions could *never* be shown to derive from the reference of their parts, then – instead of questioning the intelligibility of what would seem to be perfectly comprehensible ways of speaking – should we not be induced to look with an even more sceptical eye at the Davidsonian truth-conditional approach to compositionality? ('Davidson on Deflationism', 23–4)

This shows that minimalism is not rebutted by the observation that it does not (yet) comply with Davidson's strictures on semantics, but it does not take up the challenge posed by Davidson: what is the logical form of instantiations of (Den)? So let us try to go a step further. Davidson's 1967 list of difficulties for his programme includes belief ascriptions, and as we saw in Chapter 4.1.4, this is a worry he did try to lay to rest. Now, prima facie at least, sentences like (T) share the very feature Davidson is complaining of with equally comprehensible sentences like

(B)   Ann believes that dogs bark, and dogs (do) bark.

Davidson maintains, as Kotarbiński did before him, that the belief ascription in (B) is at bottom not a sentence containing another sentence in a non-transparent position, but rather a sequence of sentences. But this contention has met with less than universal assent.[38] If Davidson's paratactic analysis of indirect speech

---

[37] This is an allusion to Davidson's own 'staggering list of difficulties and conundrums' in 'Truth and Meaning', 35–6. Even enthusiasts of the Davidsonian programme would not claim that in the meantime those problems have *all* been solved.

[38] For some critics it is in the same boat as John Stuart Mill's claim about the conjunction 'Caesar is dead and Brutus is alive': 'we might as well call a street a complex house, as these two propositions a complex proposition' (*System of Logic.* bk. I, iv. 3). Actually, if it were not for embeddings of conjunctions, e.g. 'If Caesar is dead and Brutus is alive, then Antony has a topic for a demagogic speech', Mill's claim would not be bizarre at all: there is not much of a difference between a free-standing utterance of that conjunction and an utterance of 'Caesar is dead. Brutus is alive.'

reports and propositional attitude ascriptions is *not* acceptable (as Burge's objection from arguments by repetition seems to show[39]), then his complaint against minimalism also applies to sentences like (B) and should be registered as a reminder of unfinished work in the semantics of natural languages. But let us not leave it at that. Suppose that Davidson's paratactic analysis of sentences like (B), which represents its logical form as that of

(B-Par)   Dogs bark.   ☞That (is what) Ann believes, and dogs bark,

is on the right track. Then it is hard to see why one shouldn't treat (T) in the same way. Davidson seems to have completely forgotten that he himself suggested this strategy three decades earlier:[40]

(T-Par)   Dogs bark.   ☞That proposition is true iff dogs bark.

But isn't this again open to Burge's objection? The argument

(A1)   The proposition that dogs bark is true. Therefore,
       The proposition that dogs bark is true

is formally valid, but isn't its paratactic counterpart

(A2)   Dogs bark.   ☞That proposition is true. Therefore,
       Dogs bark.   ☞That proposition is true

again invalid because the first occurrence of the demonstrative does not designate the same object as its second occurrence? This question obviously fails to pay attention to the noun accompanying the demonstrative. Moreover, even if we delete the word 'proposition' in the displayed arguments, we should not follow Davidson in taking the demonstratives in the shortened version of (A2) to designate the utterances (inscriptions) that precede them.[41] As we saw in Chapter 5.1.3, utterances of 'That's true' are best construed as involving demonstration by proxy, deferred ostension: pointing at an utterance, one refers to something else, namely to the proposition expressed by what is pointed at. The same applies even more clearly, of course, to the locution 'That proposition is true.' But then (A2) is as valid as (A1): both demonstratives designate one and the same object. To be sure, this presupposes that the sentence 'Dogs bark' expresses the same

---

[39] See pp. 207–8 above.

[40] Davidson, 'True to the Facts', 51–2 (minus 'proposition'). Recently, this suggestion was reactivated and carefully modified in Dodd, *ITT*, 44–5, 146–8.

[41] Cf. Rumfitt, 'Content and Context', and Dodd, *ITT*, 28–34. Dodd seems to think that we have to eliminate the word 'proposition' from (Den) and its instances before we can apply the emended paratactic strategy (148). If so, he is mistaken, as can be seen from (A2).

proposition in both occurrences, but that presupposition is also in play when we declare (A1), or 'Dogs bark, so dogs bark', to be formally valid.[42] Now what is designated by the demonstrative in (B-Par) is what is designated by the demonstrative description in (T-Par). So the Davidsonian logical form proposal for attitude reports and *oratio obliqua* should be emended in the same way.

Let us register in passing that the problem Davidson articulates in his objection against minimalism (cited above, p. 327) does not only arise with respect to that-clauses. Consider

(M) If the meaning of 'redundant' is SUPERFLUOUS, then whatever is redundant is superfluous.

This is certainly true, and all speakers of English understand it (even if one of them should *say* he doesn't). Mimicking Davidson's objection against Horwich, one might argue: 'The expresssion "superfluous" appears twice in (M), once in a context that requires the occurrence to be a singular term, and once as a general term. We cannot eliminate this iteration of the same expression without destroying all appearance of a theory. But we cannot *understand* the result of the iteration unless we can see how to make use of the same semantic features of the repeated expression in both of its appearances, make use of them in giving the semantics of (M). Does anyone see how this can be done?' Clearly the role of 'superfluous' in the antecedent of (M) is not its ordinary role. (I have tried to suggest this optically by the capitalization.) The change of role of the capitalized word is even more obvious in the case of

The German word '*nichts*' means NOTHING.

This is true, but if 'nothing' had its standard role here, then it would falsely declare '*nichts*' to be meaningless. (If I tell you that the meaning of '*unbekannt*' is UNKNOWN, I do not want to convey a sense of philological mystery. Quite the contrary.) To say (1) that 'redundant' means SUPERFLUOUS is not to say (2) that 'redundant' means the same as 'superfluous', for one can know (2), but one cannot know (1), without knowing what 'redundant' means.[43] If you exchange the first occurrence of 'superfluous' in (M) by a coextensive term, such as 'superfluous and not both odd and even', you turn a truth into a falsehood. So what is that familiar word doing in the antecedent of (M)? So far, the paratactic

---

[42] See Strawson, 'Propositions, Concepts, and Logical Truths'; Burge, 'On Davidson's "Saying That"', 201.

[43] Nor is the antecedent of (M) tantamount to ' "Redundant" means "superfluous" ', for that is plain nonsense: words don't mean *words*. Moore dwells upon '*means*'-statements in his *Commonplace Book*, 303–11.

account has been explained to us only for cases where two sentences are placed side by side, but it seems we can apply it to (M) as well:

(M-Par) Superfluous. If (☞)that is the meaning of 'redundant', then whatever is redundant is superfluous.

Again the proposal falls victim to Burge's objection from arguments by repetition unless we assume that in an utterance of (M-Par) the speaker points at a token, or an utterance, of the word 'superfluous' in order to refer to something else. To what? The only reasonable answer seems to be: to the meaning of this word.

From all this we can safely draw two conclusions. First, if Davidson's paratactic account of belief ascriptions and indirect speech does *not* work even when modified along the lines sketched above, then his complaint against Horwich should be read as a call for increasing our efforts to give a theoretical account of our undeniable (pre-theoretical) understanding of all sorts of that-clauses. Secondly, if the emended paratactic account *does* work, then it works for the that-clause in (T), and, by a small extension, for the meaning-specification in (M), just as well as for the that-clause in (B). So much for 'that'.

6.1.3 *Modest enough?*

Minimalists take MT to be a true theory, hence they must claim that all substitution-instances of (Den) which do not engender paradox express truths. Whoever makes this claim, no matter whether friend or foe of minimalism, seems to be committed to endorse the principle of *tertium non datur*, i.e. the principle that no proposition is neither true nor false.[44] The argument for this was given by Dummett in his 1959 paper 'Truth'.[45] If the right branch of a non-paradoxical instance of (Den) expresses a proposition that falls into a truth-value gap, then the left branch yields a proposition that is *false*, since it attributes truth to a proposition that is not true, and it seems that such biconditionals cannot count as true. After all, the assumption looks plausible that a biconditional expresses a truth only if both sides receive either the same truth-value or none. Frege, Geach, and Strawson maintain that what is said by utterances of sentences like 'Immanuel Kant's wife was Protestant' or 'Vulcan moves' (when the speaker

---

[44] As to the name of the principle, I follow Dummett's regimentation of the received terminology (see his *TOE*, xix).

[45] The pertinent passage was cited and discussed in, Ch. 2.1.2. Cf. also McGinn, *Logical Properties* 94–5. Unlike Frege, Horwich clearly takes instances of the left-hand side of (Den) to be ascriptions of the property of being true to propositions, so the way out to which I pointed in Ch. 2 is not open to him.

tries to refer to a planet in Mercury's orbit) is void of truth-value because the subject-terms are non-designating.[46] If they are right, there are counter-examples to the claim that all non-paradoxical instances of (Den) express truths, provided that truth in a biconditional requires that both sides receive the same valuation.

Horwich explicitly subscribes to the principle of *tertium non datur*, but his own argument for it depends on an account of falsity: he defines 'x is false' as 'x is a proposition which lacks truth', and then he goes on to argue that declaring a proposition to be not true and not false amounts to saying that it fails to be true and that it does not fail to be true, which is a contradiction.[47] Horwich avers that his account of falsity 'reflects our pre-theoretical intuition that if a proposition is not true then it is false'.[48] But this is just to appeal to an 'intuition' that there are no truth-value gaps, and one may very well wonder whether there is any such intuition and, if so, whether it is 'pre-theoretical'. In any case, if one defines 'x is false' rather as 'the negation of x is true', there *is* room for opposite intuitions. Certainly, there is a reading of 'negation' under which the negation of the proposition that Vulcan moves is the proposition that Vulcan does not move (but rests), and under this reading it is not counter-intuitive at all to say of both members of the pair that they fail to be true.[49]

Is your understanding of 'true' somewhat deficient if you have no inclination to accept as a matter of course instances of (Den) in which non-designating singular terms occur? Does your local disinclination betoken an insufficient mastery of the concept of truth? Are those whose inclination to accept non-paradoxical instances is unrestricted the real masters? This is indeed Horwich's way of dealing with the disinclined:[50]

[A] good case can be made that it is indeed those who restrict the schema, rather than those of us who do not, who are confused and mistaken. For they tend to be in the grip of the idea that truth is a substantive property, analysable in terms of 'correspondence with facts'.... Thus one can say that the meaning-constituting fact about the truth predicate is the fact that explains the overall use of it by those who are not under the spell of a misbegotten philosophical theory. And this fact is our allegiance to the fully general equivalence schema. ('Defense', 569–70)

Frege, Geach, and Strawson are certainly above any suspicion of being in the grip of the idea that the concept of truth is analysable in terms of 'correspondence with the facts'. So if they were to restrict (Den) on the assumption that a biconditional cannot be true unless both branches receive the same valuation,

---

[46] For references, see above, p. 37 n. 20.   [47] I take this to be the gist of *Truth*, 71–2, 76–7.
[48] *Truth*, 77.   [49] I shall enlarge upon the topics of this and the last paragraph in sect. 6.2.3.
[50] Cf. also *Truth*, 128–9. Soames concurs: *UT*, 259 n. 29.

the diagnosis Horwich suggests would not apply to them. If minimalism underwrites the principle of *tertium non datur*, it is by no means minimally contentious.[51] It has been a matter of fierce philosophical dispute for more than two millennia whether that principle is correct. I am not saying that Horwich is clearly wrong in embracing that principle.[52] All I am saying is that a truly modest account of truth and falsity will make no pretensions to terminate the debate about that principle. In the course of presenting such an account, I shall also highlight (what I take to be) some additional advantages of the latter over Horwich's minimalism.

6.2 A Modest Account of Truth

> Truth . . . means, in Mr Pratt's words, merely 'this simple thing, that the object of which one is thinking is as one thinks it.' . . . I now formally ask of Professor Pratt to tell what this 'as'-ness in itself *consists* in—for it seems to me that it ought . . . not remain a pure mystery. . . . I myself agree most cordially that for an idea to be true the object must be 'as' the idea declares it, but I explicate the 'as'-ness as meaning the idea's verifiability.
>
> (William James, 'Professor Pratt on Truth', 92–4)

6.2.1 *Exposition*

'Things are as they are said to be': this is a phrase that was common coinage in Greece long before philosophical reflection on the concept of truth set in. When Hermes, in juvenile disguise, told Priam that he was in great danger, the king admitted, 'Things are, dear child, just as you tell me [οὕτω πῃ τάδε γ' ἐστί, φίλον τέκος, ὡς ἀγορεύεις].'[53] Some centuries later we find the same kind of locution[54] in tragedies and philosophical dialogues. Lichas is driven to confirm the messenger's fatal report: 'It is just as he says [ἔστιν γὰρ οὕτως ὥσπερ οὗτος ἐννέπει].'[55] The Sophist Hippias concedes to his interlocutor, 'These things are just as you say, Socrates [ἔστι μὲν ταῦτα ὦ Σώκρατες, οὕτως ὡς σὺ λέγεις].'[56] Now clearly, things are as they are said to be just in case what is

---

[51] See John Burgess, 'What Is Minimalism about Truth?'.

[52] Dummett defends it in 'Truth', 8–14; cf. also *TOE*, xiv–xviii, 27–8. Dummett then goes on to attack the principle of bivalence according to which every proposition is either true or false (14–19). By contrast, Horwich endorses bivalence (*Truth*, 77, 80), thereby precluding one way of avoiding the semantical antinomies.

[53] Homer, *Iliad*, 24: 373.

[54] That is to say, an absolute use of 'εἶναι [to be]' accompanied (sometimes by a dummy subject and) by an adverb of comparison that governs a clause with a verb of saying.

[55] Sophocles, *Trachiniae*, 474.   [56] Plato [?], *Hippias Major*, 282 a 4.

said is true.[57] All philosophers, I dare say, would most cordially agree that what you say or think is true if and only if *things are as you say or think they are*. Aquinas, for example, appeals to this common understanding of 'true' when he maintains: if what the intellect says is true then 'things are as the intellect says [*ita (est) in re sicut intellectus dicit*]'.[58] Bolzano articulates the same pre-theoretical understanding when he remarks, 'In our ordinary transactions it is very common indeed to use the phrases "That is true" and "Things are as they are said to be [*es ist so, wie es ausgesagt wird*]" as interchangeable.'[59] Wittgenstein writes in the same vein:

[W]ahr ist ein Satz, wenn es sich so verhält, wie wir es durch ihn sagen. [A sentence is true if things are as we, by using it, say they are.] (*Tractatus*, 4.062.)[60]

Was er sagt, ist wahr = Es verhält sich so, wie er sagt. [What he says is true = Things are as he says.] (*Philosophische Grammatik*, 123)

Presumably we may add, imitating Wittgenstein's (mis)use of '=': 'What she thinks is true = Things are as she thinks they are'. My last witness is Strawson:

A statement is true if and only if things are as one who makes that statement thereby states them to be. A belief is true if and only if things are as one who holds that belief thereby holds them to be. ('Knowledge and Truth', 273)[61]

I must confess that I like the German way of putting it better, for '*es ist so*' and '*es verhält sich so*' do not contain a noun like 'things', which might be taken to impose a certain predicative structure on the truth-candidate. But I hasten to add that the English way of putting it is really equivalent, for if you correctly state that it is snowing, you can be said to have stated 'how things are', even though no *thing* is having anything predicated of it.

For most philosophers, such truisms about truth are only a preparatory step on their way towards more demanding accounts of truth. I propose to take the alleged stepping-stone as a firm resting place. (I think this was Wittgenstein's position, too, and I am certain that it actually is Strawson's view.)

Now, as it stands, the quotation from Strawson gives us two accounts, one for statements and one for beliefs. This duality should be avoided if possible, since a

---

[57] It is time to acknowledge my indebtedness to the erudition of Charles Kahn. He comments upon these passages (and many similar ones) as examples of the *veridical* use of '*εἶναι*': see his monumental study *The Verb 'be' in Ancient Greek*, 334–6.   [58] From the passage quoted on p. 297 above.

[59] Bolzano, *WL*, I, 124.

[60] As I shall explain in n. 64 below, the Pears-McGuinness translation is not quite accurate at this point. Cf. also Wittgenstein, 'Notes on Logic', 97: '[A] proposition is then true when it is as we assert in this proposition.'

[61] Cf. also Strawson, 'A Problem about Truth', 226–7; 'Reply to Grover', 325–6; and *Analysis and Metaphysics*, 51, 85–91, as well as Mackie, *Truth, Probability, and Paradox*, 22, 50, 53, 57; Rundle, *GP*, 363–4, 375; and Sainsbury, 'Philosophical Logic', 105.

pair of explanations seems to offer both too little and too much. It seems to offer too much because 'true' as applied to statements and 'true' as applied to beliefs appears to be univocal. (The sentence 'His opinion was as true as her assertion' isn't a zeugma: it does not force one word into two conflicting services, as is done with the verb in Alexander Pope's 'She sometimes counsel took and sometimes tea'.) In another respect a pair certainly does not offer enough, because not all truths are contents of statings or believings. Taking the variable 'x' to range over propositions (in the sense elucidated in Chapter 5.1.1), we can condense Strawson's dual characterization into something like this:

(Mod$_1$) $\forall$x (x is true $\leftrightarrow$ Things are as x has it)

or, as a stylistic variant,

(Mod$_2$) $\forall$x (x is true $\leftrightarrow$ Things are as they are according to x).

Thus, for example, Ann's favourite theory is true iff things (really) are as her theory has it,[62] or iff things (really) are as they are according to that theory. (As you may have guessed, 'Mod$_n$' is to abbreviate 'the modest conception of truth, formulation n'.)

One senses a certain air of correspondence when one stares at the little word 'as' in those formulations (or at 'οὕτως—ὡς', 'ita—sicut' and 'so—wie' in the corresponding Greek, Latin, and German locutions).[63] In order to see what this trace of correspondence amounts to (how little it amounts to), let us focus on that two-letter word for a moment. Suppose

(1) Ann's belief that it's almost dawn is true.

Applying the modest account we get

(1Mod) Things are *as* Ann's belief that it's almost dawn has it.
  Things are *as* they are according to Ann's belief that it's almost dawn.

The correspondence hinted at by the word 'as' can be made more perspicuous by a sentence which is cognitively equivalent with (1) and (1Mod):

(2) Ann believes that it's almost dawn, *and* it is almost dawn.

---

[62] Some of my anglophone friends have voiced doubts about the linguistic propriety of the right-hand side of (M$_1$), where 'x' ranges over *truth-candidates*, not over persons. So let me quote, somewhat defiantly, a sentence from ch. 6 of Paul Auster's novel *City of Glass*: 'As for the Tower [of Babel], legend had it that one third of the structure sank into the ground, one third was destroyed by fire, and one third was left standing.' Exploiting this way of talking, I say: If legend x had been true, then things would have been as x had it. What's wrong with that?

[63] Kahn has the same impression: *The Verb 'be' in Ancient Greek*, 336.

In (2) the point of the word 'as' is shown by a conjunction; more exactly, by the interplay between the second conjunct and the specification of the content of Ann's belief in the first conjunct by means of the same sentence taken in the same sense. My formulation of the modest conception of truth draws upon this observation. Let me apologize in advance for its clumsiness, but I trust that you understand it.

(Mod₃) $\forall$x (x is true $\leftrightarrow$ For some way things may be said to be, x is the proposition that things are that way, *and* things are that way).[64]

At this point we can benefit from our reflections on proforms in Chapter 2.2.2. Just as the word 'them' in 'Ann admires Bacon's paintings, whereas Ben detests them' is a pro*noun* of laziness (which can be replaced by its nominal antecedent 'Bacon's paintings'), so the sentence 'things are that way' in a context like

(S)   Most students make fun of Professor X and some even hate him, but the dean doesn't know that things are that way

is a pro*sentence* of laziness (which can be replaced by its sentential antecedent, i.e. the conjunction which precedes 'but'). Let me emphasize that it is not the phrase 'that way' which functions anaphorically in (S), but *the sentence* 'things are that way' *as a whole*. The phrase by itself functions anaphorically in a context like

(S*)   Ann moves gracefully, but Ben does not move that way.

Here it is a pro-*adverb* of laziness, which can be replaced by its adverbial antecedent, whereas in (S) the phrase 'that way' is only a syncategorematic part of a prosentence. Now proforms of laziness are to be distinguished from quantificational proforms. In 'Ann is fond of something, and Ben is also fond of it' the word 'it' is a quantificational pronoun, and, similarly, in a context like (Mod₃) the sentence 'things are that way' is a quantificational prosentence. As you see, I concur with Grover in thinking that there is a generally available prosentence in English,[65] but, unlike her candidate, the locutions 'Things are that way' or 'This is how things are' (or more clearly, perhaps, '*Es ist so*' and '*Es verhält sich so*') really don't have a subject-predicate structure.

In his *Philosophical Investigations* Wittgenstein points out that '*Es verhält sich so*' can be regarded as the colloquial counterpart to a sentential variable in a formal

---

[64] The Pears-McGuinness translation of *Tractatus*, 4.062 (see p. 334 above) is misleading, since it wrongly suggests that Wittgenstein's text explicitly anticipates this move: 'A proposition is true if we use it to say that things stand in a certain way, *and* they do.' A quantifier phrase which is similar to (Mod₃) is used in Hugly and Sayward, *I&T*, 59, 165, and in Wright, 'Debate', 218–19.   [65] See Ch. 2.2.3.

language.[66] Using a few symbols from the (Polish) logicians' toolbox we obtain a semiformal rendering of the modest conception which is less cumbersome than (Mod₃):

(MOD) $\forall x \, (x \text{ is true} \leftrightarrow \exists p \, (x = [p] \, \& \, p))$.

This may be called the *minimal definition* of (propositional) truth. The pair of square-brackets in (MOD) is borrowed from Quine[67] (and it is of course just a notational variant of Horwich's '< ... >'). Syntactically, it functions as a singular-term-forming operator on sentences, and it can be read as 'the proposition that'. The square-brackets operator makes scope explicit: 'the proposition that p & q' goes either into '[p] & q' or into '[p & q]'. Semantically, the square brackets form, from a sentence which expresses a particular proposition, a singular term which designates that proposition. Remember that the English phrase 'the proposition that' does not always play this role.[68] If the 'that' in the syntactically ambiguous sentence 'The proposition that Ben wrote on the blackboard yesterday is true' is understood as a relative pronoun (=: 'which') then the embedded sentence does not express the proposition to which truth is ascribed, so under this reading the whole sentence cannot be rendered by '[Ben wrote on the blackboard yesterday] is true'. A substitution-instance of the open sentence '(x = [p] & p)' would be 'The Pythagorean Theorem = the proposition that the square on the hypotenuse is equal to the sum of the squares on the other two sides, & the square on the hypotenuse *is* equal etc.' An identity claim of the form 'x = [p]' holds just in case the following condition is fulfilled: anyone whose utterance was to express x would thereby be saying that p, and anyone who was to say that p would thereby make an utterance which expresses x.

Unlike Correspondence conceptions of truth, the modest account makes no use of a two-place predicate signifying a relation between a truth-value bearer, or a part of it, and something else (whether an object, a fact, or an event). After all, in (Mod₃) and (MOD) the point of the 'as' of (Mod₁) and (Mod₂) is captured by a *connective* rather than a two-place predicate. On the other hand, there is a similarity with (Moorean) Correspondence in that the modest account also tries to tell us what all true propositions have in common. So here is one respect in which it differs markedly from Horwich's minimalism, for the latter refrains from offering any principle of the form, '$\forall x \, (x \text{ is true iff} \ldots x \ldots)$'.[69] Moreover, whereas Horwich's 'minimal theory' is conceptually extremely corpulent, the

---

[66] Wittgenstein, *Philosophische Untersuchungen*, §134. Prior emphasized the philosophical fecundity of this passage in 'Correspondence Theory of Truth', 229, and *OT*, 38.   [67] Quine, *W&O*, 165.
[68] See Ch. 5.1.1.   [69] See sect. 6.1.1 on Horwich, *Truth*, 20, 33, 111 and 'Defense', 560.

modest account is conceptually very slim. Seen in the light of (MOD) the modest account explains 'true' in terms of a few logical operators (and the concept of a proposition). Thus it appears reasonable to call truth a broadly logical property.[70] (Only '*broadly* logical', because the concept of a proposition is not a logical concept.[71]) Furthermore, Horwich's 'minimal theory' had to be supplemented by the axiom that only propositions are true. By contrast, (MOD) ensures this by itself, in virtue of the component '$\exists p \, (x = [p])$'.[72]

Considered in the light of (Mod$_3$) and (MOD), the minimalist contention about the *raison d'être* of the truth-predicate turns out to be doubtful. Is deployment of the truth-predicate really the *only* way to generalize 'If time flies then time flies' and to state the principle of self-implication compendiously? There is no need to put it in terms of truth, as in

(T) $\forall x$ (If x is of the form 'if p then p' then x is true),

if we can allow ourselves the use of sentential quantification:

(SQ)   However things may be said to be, if things are that way then things are that way

(SQ′) $\forall p$ (If p then p).

As regards terseness, (SQ′) does not look at all inferior to (T). The expressive facilities provided by sentential quantification are considerable. If we invoke the rule

Tautology   You may introduce into a proof at any stage the universal closure of a tautology of the sentential calculus, resting on no assumptions,

---

[70] *If* the modest account is taken as a reductive (dismantling) analysis rather than as a 'connecting analysis' or elucidation which explains a concept by showing its connections with other concepts (see p. 13 above), one has to face the charge of vicious circularity here. The charge could be deflected by assuming that the meaning of '&', for example, is not given by truth-tables, but rather by a natural deduction system, or by an axiomatic system, which codifies the role this connective plays in the context of inference. When Tarski heard rumours about his theory being circular, he gave a reply along the same lines: see above, p. 196 with n. 69.

[71] According to the title of McGinn's book (*Logical Properties: Identity, Existence. . . . , Truth*), truth is a logical property *sans phrase*. The only passage in the book, registered in the index, where he comes close to explaining what he means by 'logical property' runs as follows: 'logical properties (such as the property of not being both red and not red at the same time) . . . apply to all conceivable objects' (31). Surely McGinn cannot mean to say that the property of being true applies to the Tour Eiffel, the proposition that Paris is in Scotland, and all other conceivable objects. What, then, does he mean by calling truth a logical property?

[72] As was pointed out above (pp. 321–2 n. 16), the explanation of universal generalizations about truth causes grave problems for minimalism. Since (MOD), unlike MT, is itself a universal generalization, the *generality* of general facts about truth causes no problems for the modest account.

we can derive theorems in the resulting system of sentential quantification by appealing to (counterparts of) the standard quantifier rules. For example, we can derive '$\forall p\, \exists q\, (q \to p)$' as theorem:

(1)	$\forall p\, (p \to p)$		*Tautology*
(2)	$p_1 \to p_1$	1,	$\forall$ Elimination
(3)	$\exists q\, (q \to p_1)$	2,	$\exists$ Introduction
(4)	$\forall p\, \exists q\, (q \to p)$	3,	$\forall$ Introduction

In the meantime Horwich has come round to concede that (SQ') is a serious competitor of (T), but he has some reservations about this rival:

> It was perhaps an exaggeration to have suggested that the concept of truth is needed for this generalizing purpose. An alternative strategy would be to introduce some form of non-standard ... quantification. ... But in that case there would be required a battery of extra syntactic and semantic rules to govern the new type of quantifier. Therefore, we might consider the value of our concept of truth to be that it provides, not the only way, but a relatively 'cheap' way of obtaining the problematic generalizations—the way actually chosen in natural language. (*Truth*, 124–5)

In due course we will have to consider this reservation and others that are far more hostile, for of course, I cannot expect you to accept the quantificational rendering of the modest conception without further ado. But before we directly face these problems, let me present some anticipations of (MOD) or structural analogues thereof. This will shed some new light on Ramsey and Tarski, it will prepare us for some of the work to be done in the final section of this chapter, and perhaps it will make even the sceptics among my readers concede that investing more labour in (MOD) might be worthwhile.

6.2.2 A new theory?

> A propos of [a short article of mine in *Analysis* 1949] I remember fatuously announcing to George Paul that I had a new theory of truth; to which he sensibly and characteristically replied: 'Come on now, which of the old ones is it?'
>
> (P. F. Strawson, 'Intellectual Autobiography', 8)

The earliest proponent of an account of truth that comes very close to (MOD) is Frank Ramsey, who is better known as a proponent of a redundancy theory of truth. In his famous paper of 1927 Ramsey pointed at the main obstacle to a redundancy theory:

> [I]f I say 'He is always right', I mean that the propositions he asserts are always true, and there does not seem to be any way of expressing this without using the word 'true'. But

suppose... for a moment that only one form of proposition is in question, say the relational form aRb; then 'He is always right' could be expressed by 'For all a, R, b, if he asserts aRb, then aRb'.... When all forms of proposition are included the analysis is more complicated but not essentially different. ('Facts and Propositions', 39)

The tentative rephrasal of 'He is always right' is not without its own logico-grammatical problems. First, since 'He asserts the moon is smaller than the sun' is not well formed, we should insert a 'that' before the first occurrence of 'aRb'. Secondly, it is worth noting that the sequence of quantifiers in 'For all a, R, b,... aRb...' is heterogeneous: the second quantifier binds a predicate variable. There is nothing intrinsically objectionable about this. If you want the quantification in this schema to be first-order throughout, you should replace 'aRb' by 'a stands in R to b' so that 'R' is also a place-holder for singular terms. But we will soon see that the quantification cannot remain first-order anyway.

Now if the inclusion of 'all forms of proposition' is to complicate the analysis, then, as Davidson in his comments on this passage observed, the analysis must be recursive in character, for the forms of proposition are infinite in number. So there would be a close kinship between the project Ramsey hints at and the project carried out by Tarski.[73] But actually, in an unfinished manuscript written a year or so after his paper, Ramsey pursues an entirely different strategy: one of simplification rather than of complication, one of including all forms of proposition at one fell swoop, rather than of recursively taking their differences into account. Of course, Ramsey argues, 'we cannot... assign any limit to the number of forms which may occur', so it seems that 'if we try to make a definition to cover them all it will have to go on forever'. Obviously, at this point the idea of a recursive strategy did *not* occur to Ramsey. He goes on to say:

In order to avoid this infinity we must consider the general form... of which all these forms are species; any belief whatever we may symbolise as a belief that p, where 'p' is a variable *sentence*.... We can then say that *a belief is true if it is a belief that p, and p* .../... In Mr. Russell's symbolism

B is true :=:   (∃p). B is a belief that p & p. Df.

(*On Truth*, 9, 15 n.; second italics mine.)

The indefinite article in '*a* belief that p' suggests that Ramsey is here taking believings, rather than what is believed (or more generally, propositions), as truth-value bearers.[74] Earlier he had maintained: 'Truth and falsity are primarily

---

[73] Davidson, 'True to the Facts', 40, 'Structure', 282, 'The Centrality of Truth', 108 (= 'Truth Rehabilitated', 68). In his 'Introduction' to Ramsey's *Philosophical Papers* (at p. xix), Mellor concurs.

[74] He had announced this a few pages earlier: see *On Truth*, 7.

ascribed to propositions',[75] and if we bring his account into a propositional format we obtain (MOD).

The second time close analogues of (MOD) make their appearance in the literature is in section 1 of Tarski's *Wahrheitsbegriff*.[76] As an example of the kind of data a definition of 'true' has to respect, he presents a (slightly infelicitous[77]) homophonic T-equivalence,

T(3) 'It is snowing' is a true sentence ↔ it is snowing.

He then asks whether we cannot obtain a definition of 'true' simply by generalizing T(3), that is to say, by replacing the two occurrences of 'It is snowing' with a sentential variable and binding it by a universal quantifier:

T(5) ∀p ('p' is a true sentence ↔ p).

One objection against T(5), Tarski argues, is that it deals only with those truth ascriptions in which the truth-candidate is singled out by a quotational designator: a proper definition of 'true' should specify the conditions under which the definiendum applies to a sentence regardless of how the sentence is designated. Tarski notes that there is hope for a solution if for each sentence there is a quotational designator, and the formula he then offers for consideration has the same structure as (MOD):

T(6) For all sentences x, x is a true sentence ↔ ∃p (x = 'p' & p).

Tarski's objection against T(6) also applies to T(5). It is an objection, *not* against sentential quantification, but against quantification into quotational designators, or quotation-mark names (*Anführungsnamen*) as he calls them:

Every quotation-mark name [may be treated as] a constant individual name of a given expression (the expression enclosed by the quotation marks) and in fact a name of the same nature as the proper name of a man. For example, the name 'p' designates one of the letters of the alphabet. With this interpretation, which seems to be the most natural one and completely in accordance with the customary way of using quotation marks, partial definitions of the type (3) cannot be used for any reasonable generalizations. The sentences (5) or (6) cannot at all be accepted as such generalizations. (*WB*, 159–60 (12–13); trans. slightly changed)[78]

---

[75] Ramsey, 'Facts and Propositions', 142. Actually there is some tension, to put it mildly, between this statement and the refusal to countenance propositions on p. 138. The same sort of tension is to be found in Russell's writings in those years (see p. 118 n. 93 above).

[76] Tarski, *WB* 8–15 (155–62). To facilitate comparison with Tarski's text, I preserve in brackets Tarski's own numbering of the indented formulae. Like Tarski, I suppress parenthetical relativization to a language.

[77] On p. 204 I commented briefly on the infelicity of using a context-sensitive sentence.

[78] The tenet about quotation is repeated in 'Proof', 404.

Not all is well with this argument. Taking quotation marks and what they surround to form a semantically unbreakable unit is far from 'natural', for it neglects a fundamental difference between, e.g., the quotational designator of the first letter of the Greek alphabet and its name, 'Alpha': the latter really is a semantically indivisible name of a certain letter, and consequently understanding it is no help when it comes to understanding, say, 'Lambda'. But the quotational designator of the first letter of the Greek alphabet contains a device the mastery of which suffices for understanding all other designators of its ilk. (Similarly, the schematic singular term 'the proposition that p' or '[p]' in (MOD) cannot be treated as semantically unstructured either, for otherwise the reappearance of the embedded sentence letter 'p' as a free-standing second conjunct would be of no help in understanding the explanans, and the same would hold, *mutatis mutandis*, for all substitution-instances of the matrix.) Even so, Tarski's objection stands. T(6) has the 'obviously absurd consequence', as he points out, that all true sentences are identical with the sixteenth letter of the Roman alphabet.

Tarski then considers as a possible escape route replacing the quotation-marks in T(6) by a 'quotation functor [*Anführungsfunktor*]', which takes expressions as input and delivers singular terms designating those expressions as output. Using a bold-face 'Q' for this functor we can rewrite T(6) in the following way:

T(6*)   For all sentences x, x is true $\leftrightarrow \exists p\, (x = Q(p)\, \&\, p)$.

Tarski's main objection against this move is that it leads to a 'Liar' paradox. Ruth Barcan-Marcus and others have shown that this worry is baseless: under a substitutional interpretation of the sentential quantifier no inconsistency is lurking in T(6*).[79] Of course, one may wonder whether an appeal to substitutional quantification is legitimate when one attempts to define 'true'. Since a similar question will arise with respect to (MOD), I postpone this issue and turn instead to the very beginning of section 1 of Tarski's *Wahrheitsbegriff*, for it contains another highly interesting sentential analogue to our (MOD).

Let me set the stage for the relevant passage by reminding you of some points made in Chapter 4.1. In the Introduction to his monograph Tarski says: '[T]hroughout this work I shall be concerned exclusively with grasping the intentions which are contained in the so-called classical conception of truth ('true— agreeing with reality [*mit der Wirklichkeit übereinstimmend*]').[80] Popper took this passage to confirm his claim that Tarski intended to rehabilitate the 'intuitive idea of truth as correspondence to the facts'. But facts do not appear in Tarski's

---

[79] For a lucid reconstruction of the argument and references to the literature, see Soames, *UT*, 88–90, 96 n. 30. A reference to Grover, *PrTh*, 234–75, should be added. One may very well wonder whether the original T(6) isn't also beyond reproach if one adopts substitutional quantification. Field, for one, takes T(6) to define 'true': cf. his 'Deflationist', 120 n. 17.   [80] Quoted as [T.11] on p. 209 above.

Criterion T, nor do they turn up in his actual definition of a truth-predicate for a particular formal language. Hence Davidson feels obliged to play down Tarski's repeated invocations of the 'classical conception' as rather unfortunate 'nods in the direction of a correspondence theory'.[81] Both Popper and Davidson assume that by 'agreement with reality' Tarski must mean correspondence with facts. I have argued that this assumption is false. Part of my evidence was Tarski's reference to Kotarbiński's *Elements* in his footnote to the passage quoted above. (Tarski had studied philosophy with Kotarbiński, and he always thought very highly of him: some decades later he dedicated his collection *Logic, Semantics, Metamathematics* 'To His Teacher Tadeusz Kotarbiński', and he translated his teacher's article on 'Pansomatism' into English.[82]) In the third chapter of his *Elements*, entitled 'Thought', Kotarbiński reviews conceptions of truth. After a brief and dismissive account of two varieties of (what he calls) the 'utilitarian' view of truth,[83] he turns to (what he calls) the 'classical' conception. Here is the passage Tarski has in mind (we have already had occasion to quote part of it):

In the classical interpretation, 'truly' [in 'Jan thinks truly'] means the same as 'in agreement with reality'.... Let us... ask what is understood by 'agreement with reality'. The point is not that a true thought should be a good copy or likeness of the thing of which we are thinking, as a painting or a photograph is. Brief reflection suffices to recognize the metaphorical nature of such comparison. A different interpretation of 'agreement with reality' is required. We shall confine ourselves to the following:

> *Jan thinks truly if and only if*
> *Jan thinks that things are thus and so,*
> *and things are indeed thus and so.*

... For instance, the central idea of the Copernican theory is... that the earth revolves around the sun; now Copernicus thought truly, for he thought that the earth revolves around the sun, and the earth does revolve around the sun. (*Elements*, 106–7; my italics)[84]

---

[81] See p. 212 n. 117 and p. 214 n. 123 above.

[82] See pp. 206–7 above. Jan Tarski reports that his father 'kept a photo-portrait of Kotarbiński hanging in his study to the end and carefully kept on saving the latter's booklet of poems' ('Philosophy in the Creativity of Alfred Tarski', 158).

[83] One variety is William James's pragmatism, the other variety is (presumably Georg Simmel's) biologism. According to Kotarbiński's reading, both contend that 'It is true that p' means: in the long run it is advantageous to believe that p. They differ as to who is to profit: the person who has the belief, or the species to which the believer belongs (*Elements*, 106). For James, see also Twardowski's lecture course 'Theory of Knowledge', 222–39; for Simmel see the reference to works by Ajdukiewicz (like Kotarbiński, a pupil of Twardowski) in *Elements*, 129. For a different reading of James, cf. Ch. 7.1.3, Postscript.

[84] The indented biconditional translates the following Polish sentence (*Elementy*, 112):

> Jan myśli prawdziwie zawsze i tylko, jeżeli
> Jan myśli, *że tak a tak rzeczy się mają*,
> i jeżeli przy tym *rzeczy się mają tak właśnie*.

(My italics may ease the comparison with Tarski for those who find Polish as difficult as I do.) In 1966

In the indented biconditional there is no appeal to facts or states of affairs as 'correspondents'. (The adverbial phrase 'indeed [*właśnie*]' in the second part of the consequent is logically redundant: it serves the same purpose as the move from 'revolves' to 'does revolve'.[85]) Kotarbiński tries to capture the point of 'agreement' or 'correspondence' by means of the connective 'and':[86]

(K)   x thinks truly ↔ (x thinks that . . . , and . . .)

where, for any given episode or state of thinking truly, the two blanks are to be filled by occurrences of the same declarative sentence.

Let us first consider the left-hand side of (K). Kotarbiński's ontology was a materialist variety of the Reism ('Thingism', if you insist on a translation) that had been adopted by Brentano in his later years.[87] According to Reism, there are no true or false propositions, nor even mental states or acts, or illocutionary acts, of which propositions could be the contents. There are only 'things [*res*]', and as regards truth talk Kotarbiński contends that the pertinent things are either persons who think *truly* or *falsely*, or utterances, which are *true* or *false*. (The second kind of truth talk is secondary, or so we are told: utterances are true or false in virtue of being vehicles of communication of those who think truly or falsely.)

As for mental and linguistic acts, this is an interesting inversion of Davidson's position: metaphysical illumination is to be sought in the adverbial construction rather than in its adjectival counterpart. According to Davidson's theory of (some) adverbs, it is the right-hand side of the biconditional 'Jan Vs F-ly iff there is an event which is both a Ving by Jan and F' that wears the ontological trousers, as it were: it shows that something different from Jan must exist if the left-hand side is to yield a truth.[88] For Kotarbiński, it is the other way round: the left-hand side of that biconditional shows that only Jan has to exist if the right-hand side

---

the book Tarski refers to was translated under the unappealing title *Gnosiology*. I quote, with minor changes which have received the blessing of my Polish friends, from this translation. Incidentally, when Wiggins quotes the above passage, he omits the words 'Jan thinks that' in the indented biconditional; unsurprisingly, this oversight makes for some major interpretative contortions (Wiggins, 'Meaning', 15; 'Postscript 3', 334–5).

[85]   The logical redundancy of 'indeed' or 'in fact' was pointed out in Bolzano, *WL*, I, 123–4, and Ramsey explained it thus: 'In a sentence like this [i.e. "The things he believed to be connected by a certain relation were, in fact, connected by that relation"] "in fact" serves simply to show that the *oratio obliqua* introduced by "he believed" has now come to an end. It does not mean a new notion to be analyzed, but is simpl[y] a connecting particle' (*On Truth*, 15 n. 8).

[86]   Alluding to the passage I quoted, Wiggins says: 'Let me take the opportunity to stress that Kotarbiński's discussion of truth is professedly anti-correspondentist' ('Replies', 283). I seize the opportunity to emphasize that Kotarbiński's discussion is by no means anti-correspondentist, but professedly anti-*pictorialist*.

[87]   Cf. Kotarbiński, 'Franz Brentano as Reist' (and the comments in Barry Smith, *Austrian Philosophy*, 193–242; Woleński, *Essays*, 179–90).   [88]   See Davidson, *Essays on Actions and Events*, ch. 6.

is to yield a truth. However *this* stalemate is to be overcome, Kotarbiński's assimilation of 'truly' and 'falsely' to 'manner' adverbs is misguided. Admittedly, 'we say about a given person that he thinks truly or falsely, as we say about him that he walks well or lamely',[89] but apart from surface-grammar the similarity is not very close. When he thinks truly (falsely), then it is at any rate correct to say, 'What he thinks is true (false).' But 'What he walks is good (lame)' is nonsense, and although 'What she plays is good (lame)' does make sense, it is certainly not equivalent with 'She plays well (lamely)': as we all know, rubbish can be played well, and some instrumentalists manage to play even a tarantella lamely. The peculiarity of the adverbs 'truly' and 'falsely' can be clearly marked by saying: in characterizing a person as thinking truly (falsely), we characterize what she thinks as true (false).[90] So even if Kotarbiński were right in claiming that the adjectives 'true' and 'false' apply *simpliciter* to utterances,[91] he would still be wrong in contending that they *only* apply to utterances.

Now consider (K) as a whole. It is open to a logico-grammatical objection. The left-hand side is a predicate: if you substitute 'Jan' for the variable, you obtain a complete sentence. But the right-hand side is only a predicate-schema. A proposal made by Prior can be read as an improvement on this (the fact that he does not defer to Kotarbiński makes the near-coincidence all the more remarkable):

The truth and falsehood with which Tarski is concerned are genuine properties of genuine objects, namely sentences. The truth and falsehood with which we [are] concerned here might be described as properties not of sentences but of propositions; but this means that they are only quasi-properties of quasi-objects, and it might be less misleading to say that we have not been concerned with the adjectives 'true' and 'false' at all but rather with the adverbs 'truly' and 'falsely'. The basic form which Tarski defines is 'The sentence S is a true one'; the form which we define is not this, but rather 'x says truly (thinks correctly,...) that p'. And we define this quite simply as... 'x says (thinks,...) that p; and p'. (*OT*, 98)[92]

---

[89] Kotarbiński, *Elements*, 105.

[90] My argument is an adaptation of White's objection (in ' "True" and "Truly" ') against a philosopher who based large claims on the grammatical similarity between 'She smiled enchantingly' and 'She spoke truly'. With respect to Kotarbiński's adverbialism, the (authorized) German summary of his book (written by Rose Rand, a Polish member of the Vienna Circle and published in the 1937 issue of *Erkenntnis*) is interesting. The following passage is (apart from replacing 'Jan' by 'somebody') a literal translation of the indented biconditional in our extract: '*jemand denkt "wahr" dann und nur dann, wenn er denkt, daß die Dinge sich so und so verhalten[,] und wenn die Dinge sich geradeso verhalten*' (Rand, 'Kotarbiński "Elemente" ', 102). The fact that the German word for 'true' cannot be used as an adverb modifying a verb of thinking or saying causes an embarrassment for the translator, so she uses scare-quotes. The appropriate word would have been '*wahrheitsgemäß*' (literally: 'in-conformity-with-truth') or '*richtig* [correctly]'.

[91] On pp. 264–8, I argued against this claim.

[92] In Prior's text there is a third verbal phrase besides 'says truly' and 'thinks correctly', which I have omitted above, namely 'fears with justification'. I fear that this is an intruder here. Can one not fear with justification that p, even though not-p?

So Prior's counterpart to Kotarbiński's (K) is

(P) x thinks truly that p ↔ (x thinks that p, and p)

This is immune against the above objection, for it has predicate-schemata on *both* sides. The disadvantage is, of course, that Prior's formula allows us to characterize Jan as thinking truly only if we know what he thinks. *This* problem could be solved by a further modification:

(KP*) x thinks truly ↔ ∃p (x thinks that p, and p)

But in each of its guises 'adverbialism' fails to throw any light on truth talk like 'Logicism is true'.

Although Tarski departs from Kotarbiński in taking type-sentences to be truth-value bearers, he obviously defers to his teacher when he gives his first tentative formulation of an explanation of the notion of sentential truth (for a given language). But unfortunately the English translation makes this echo of (K) inaudible. In Woodger's translation we read: '(1) a true sentence is one which says that the state of affairs is so and so, and the state of affairs is so and so.'[93] Actually there is not the slightest trace of 'states of affairs' in Leopold Blaustein's German translation or in the Polish text.[94] The former, on which the English translation is based, reads as follows:

(1) eine wahre Aussage ist eine Aussage, welche besagt,
      dass die Sachen sich so und so verhalten,
      und die Sachen verhalten sich eben so und so. (*W B* 8)

This tells us that a true sentence is one which means *that things are thus and so, and things are (indeed) thus and so*, and it is an impeccable rendering of the Polish original:

(1) zdanie prawdziwe jest to zdanie, które wyraża,
      że tak a tak rzeczy się mają,
      i rzeczy mają się tak właśnie.

The italicized bit is lifted *verbatim* from Kotarbiński.[95] Hence Tarski's commentary on *his* (1) in the accompanying footnote is amply justified: 'Similar formulations can be found in Kotarbiński . . . , where they are treated as commentaries which explain the essence of the "classical" conception of truth.' Dropping the logically

---

[93] Tarski, *WB*, trans. 155.

[94] There is a chilling fact about the translator which should not sink into oblivion: Blaustein, a Husserl expert at the university of Lwów, was murdered by the Germans in 1942.

[95] Quoted above on p. 343 n. 84.

superfluous adverb 'indeed'[96] (and bearing the implicit relativity to a given language in mind), we can render (1) thus:

T(1)   For all sentences x, x is true ↔ x means that things are thus and so, and
things are thus and so.

The locution 'x means that' in T(1) can be taken as an abbreviation for something like 'anyone who were to use x (as a sentence of the language under consideration) would thereby literally say that'. As T(1) shows, there is no need to play down Tarski's appeal to the formula 'true—agreeing with reality', since the Kotarbińskian way he spells it out does not make him an adherent of Fact-based Correspondence. Tarski takes the 'general intention' of T(1) to be 'quite clear and intelligible'. One reason why he continues after T(1) for some 140-odd pages is his self-imposed restriction not to use undefined semantic predicates in the definition of a truth-predicate.[97] Tarski also indicates that T(1) does not have a 'correct form', without spelling this worry out. Whatever he may have in mind—apart from vulnerability to semantic antinomies, T(1) suffers from a defect which it shares with (K), its model in Kotarbiński: the right-hand side contains an unbound prosentence, hence unlike the explanandum it is not a predicate, but only a predicate-schema. When we treat the prosentence as a sentential variable and bind this variable by a quantifier, we arrive at a sentential counterpart to (MOD):[98]

T(1*)   For all sentences x, x is true ↔ ∃ p (what x means = [p] & p).

T(1*) presupposes that the sentences of the language for which truth is to be explained are free from context-sensitivity and ambiguity, for if they are not, there is no such thing as *the* proposition expressed by a sentence.

Without realizing that the 'simple definition' T(1*) is more or less Tarski's own point of departure, Prior gets things exactly right when he says:

This is much simpler than any of Tarski's definitions of truth for the various languages he considers. It ought in fairness to be added that part of Tarski's aim was to avoid the use

---

[96] Tarski himself stressed its redundancy in 'Semantic', §18.

[97] See extract [T.3] on p. 190. When Tarski takes it to be a matter of course that his readers will understand why he calls T(1) an attempt at a '*semantic* definition' (WB, 8 (155)), he appeals to the concept that I tried to convey in Ch. 4.1.1 by the phrase 'semantic in the broad sense'.

[98] I switch from 'x means that p' which can be given an operator reading ('means-that'), to 'what x means = [p]' in order to hammer out the structural similarity to (MOD) and as a reminder of the similar move from 'A Vs that p' to 'The proposition that p is the content of A's V$_n$', which played an important role in my explanation of 'proposition' in Ch. 5.1.1.

of 'intensional' conceptions like that of 'meaning'; but it is certainly worth noting that if we do not restrict ourselves this way, and get our grammar straight, it *is* possible to define 'true' very straightforwardly. ('Some Problems of Self-Reference in John Buridan', 138)[99]

Of course, Prior is aware that T(1*) needs to be protected against the menace of the 'Liar'. But he points out that it is hard to see why this protection could not be provided, e.g., by Tarski's own hierarchical approach: add 'in L' on the left-hand side of T(1*), insert it after 'means' on the right-hand side, and insist that no sentence of L can be used to say that a sentence means in L that p. Prior does not inquire whether T(1*) complies with Criterion T. So let us do it ourselves. It will be a good training for a similar exercise soon to be undertaken with respect to (Mod).

Using 'S' as short for 'Snow is white', the task is to derive

(Dis$_1$)   'S' is true $\leftrightarrow$ S.

Let us start with the left-to-right half. For this derivation we need an inference rule which is a higher-order counterpart to Identity Elimination in the predicate calculus:

$$(= Elim.) \quad \Gamma: \quad \text{What 'A' means} = [B] \quad \Gamma: \quad \text{What 'A' means} = [B]$$

Δ:	B	,
Γ, Δ:	A	

Δ:	A	,
Γ, Δ:	B	

where A and B are any two declarative sentences, and the Greek letters register the assumptions on which the premises (above the line) and the conclusion (below the line) rest. This rule strikes me as compelling. After all, we readily grant the validity of

(P1)   What 'Catchup is sweet' means is that ketchup is sweet.
(P2)   Ketchup is sweet.
(C)   Therefore, catchup is sweet.

and of all other arguments of its ilk. Once ($= Elimination$) is available, we can prove in the following way that *'S' is true* $\to S$.[100]

1	(1)	'S' is true	Assumption
1	(2)	$\exists p$ (what 'S' means $= [p]$ & p)	1, *Df. T(1*)*
3	(3)	What 'S' means $= [T]$ & T	Assumption (for $\exists E$)

---

[99] Some decades later Beckermann, '*Wittgenstein, Neurath and Tarski über Wahrheit*', 547, independently made the same point (without registering the deficiency of T(1) as it stands).

[100] The $\exists$-rules I invoke are higher-order counterparts of the corresponding first-order $\exists$-rules.

3	(4)	What 'S' means = [T]	3,	& Elimination
3	(5)	T	3,	& Elimination
3	(6)	S	4, 5,	(= *Elimination*)
1	(7)	S	2, 3, 6	∃ Elimination
	(8)	'S' is true → S	1, 7	→ Introduction

In order to derive the right-to-left half of (Dis₁) we need the following inference rule which may be called Disquotational Meaning Specification, or *M-Disquotation* for short:[101]

M-Disquotation   You may introduce into a proof at any stage an expression of the form *What '...' means = [...]* in which the gaps are filled by the same (English) declarative sentence, resting on no assumptions.

If we take this to be tacitly restricted to sentences free of ambiguous and context-sensitive elements, it is intuitively compelling. We are ready to accept sentences such as 'What "Snow is white" means is that snow is white' (or ' "Snow is white" means that snow is white') without supporting argument. A proof of $S →$ 'S' is *true* can be set out as follows:

1	(1)	S		Assumption
	(2)	What 'S' means = [S]		*M-Disquotation*
1	(3)	What 'S' means = [S] & S	1, 2,	& Introduction
1	(4)	∃p (what 'S' means = [p] & p)	3,	∃ Introduction
1	(5)	'S' is true	4,	*Df.* T(1*)
	(6)	S → 'S' is true	1, 5	→ Introduction

So T(1*) is a materially adequate definition of sentential truth. All things considered, Tarski's reservations boil down to his methodological decision not to use expressions such as 'means that' in a definition of a truth-predicate.

The remainder of the history of (Mod) is quickly told. In his book *Introduction to Semantics*, Rudolf Carnap endorsed in 1942 something like T(1*) as 'a general explicit definition for truth'.[102] In 1972 William Kneale adopted (Mod) itself in his unjustly neglected article 'Propositions and Truth in Natural Languages',[103] and so did John Mackie in his 1973 book *Truth, Probability, and Paradox*.[104] Since then

---

[101] See p. 187 above on disquotational paradigms in the 'theory of meaning'. The idea of invoking this rule in the course of the next derivation is borrowed from Peter van Inwagen, 'Truth-Sentences', 211. The derivation I give may be the one he has in mind.

[102] Carnap, *IS*, §12: '(D 1)'. I say 'something like' because (for the reasons given on p. 178 n. 15 above) I find the use of 'designates' in Carnap's definitions confusing.

[103] In §4. (All differences are just notational.)   [104] In ch. 2: 'Simple Truth', esp. 52, 59.

(MOD) has been the Sleeping Beauty of the philosophy of truth. At present, you are witnessing my unprincely attempt to kiss her.[105]

6.2.3 *Questions, objections, and rejoinders*

But is the Sleeping Beauty really that beautiful? In the final part of this chapter I want to present and to answer (what I take to be) the main questions and objections that an adherent of the modest conception, and in particular of its symbolic rendering, must come to terms with.

[A] The *semantic antinomies* are a menace to all formulations of the modest account as well as to any other attempt at explaining the notion of truth: if you substitute a 'Liar' sentence, you can quickly derive a contradiction. Hence a restriction seems to be needed. But whatever may be the best way, or ways, of stating such a restriction,[106] one may wonder whether we really need a strategy for shielding off the semantic paradoxes *in order to defend the modest account of truth*. Perhaps one should rather turn the tables. If truth-ascriptions sometimes risk being paradoxical, then no account of the workaday concept expressed by the truth-predicate would be faithful that did not share this feature: it would be objectionable if the explanans of 'true' were protected against the risk of occasionally exhibiting paradoxical features. After all, the aim was not that of finding a better-behaved substitute for the natural language predicate 'is true'. (It is similar with vagueness. The predicate 'is a foal' is vague, hence it counts in *favour* of the explanation in my dictionary, 'A foal is a very young horse', that 'very young horse' is vague, too, and in the same way.) It hardly needs saying, I hope, that these remarks are not meant to disparage the vast amount of ingenious work on conceptual revision which was, and still is, triggered by the antinomies.

[B] Doesn't the modest account only elucidate the predicate '... is true', which can be transformed into a sentence by inserting singular terms such as 'Goldbach's Conjecture', 'what Ann told me last Tuesday', 'Ben's most astonishing contention', or '(the proposition) that snow is white'? But what about the *unary*

---

[105] I first endorsed (MOD) in *Abstrakte Gegenstände*, 126.

[106] You have heard me confess before that I have nothing useful to say about how such a restriction should be stated (and neither does Horwich in his book, if that's an excuse). Kneale maintained that 'the paradox of the Liar holds no terror for those who realize how the notion of truth is related to that of a proposition', since 'Liar' sentences fail to express propositions (Kneale, 'Russell's Paradox and Some Others', 321). Sobel defends the same idea in 'Lies, Lies, and More Lies'. For a useful survey of the literature and a very clear summary of the main objections against this strategy, cf. Gupta and Belnap, *RTT*, 7–12.

connective 'It is true that . . .', which transforms sentences into sentences? Isn't the modest account inapplicable to the truth *operator*?

Bolzano and Horwich have pointed towards a solution to this problem.[107] Sometimes pronouns are used *cataphorically*. Consider the role of 'he' and 'it' in 'He was wise, the man who drank the hemlock' or 'It is true what Ann told me': these sentences are just stylistic variants of 'The man who drank the hemlock was wise' and 'What Ann told me is true'. Similarly, we can treat the pronoun in 'It is true that p' as cataphoric. So far, this argument cuts both ways, since the relation signified by 'is a stylistic variant of' is symmetrical. But there is some grammatical evidence, I think, which points in the direction favoured by Bolzano and Horwich. Consider

(1)   It is true that his paper is clever, but her objection is *also* true.

We can make literal sense of the 'also' if it is preceded by another application of the predicate 'is true' in the first half of the sentence. But on the operator reading we can find no predication of 'is true' there. In any case, we should not think of the sentence fragment 'It is true that' as semantically unbreakable like the negation operator in the calculus, for then the presence of 'true' in 'It is true that' would be just as much an orthographic accident as its presence in 'obstruent', and sentences like (1) would make no sense.

[C] Falsity implies absence of truth, but absence of truth does not imply falsity, for otherwise we would have to call friends and teeth false even if they are neither false friends nor false teeth. But does a proposition's failing to be true imply that it is *false*? By itself, the modest account does not enforce any particular answer. But we can allow for *truth-value gaps* if we explain falsity (for propositions) as follows:

(Falsity) $\forall x$ (x is false $\leftrightarrow$ the negation of x is true).

Applying the modest account to the definiens, we obtain the result that x is false iff things are as the negation of x has it, or, using the machinery of (Mod), x is false iff for some p, the negation of x is the proposition that p, and indeed p. What are we to say now about the proposition that Vulcan moves? Is it neither true nor false? This depends on what we take to be its negation. As such, our accounts of propositional truth and falsity are silent on this matter.

But let me not remain entirely silent on this issue. We are familar with the operation that transforms, say, 'Vulcan moves' into 'Vulcan does not move'

---

[107] Bolzano, *WL*, ii, 216; Horwich, *Truth*, 16 n.

Table 6.1. (1) *Internal negation,*
(2) *truth ascription, and* (3) *external negation*

	A	t	f	n
(1)	$\neg_I A$	f	t	n
(2)	$\top A$	t	f	f
(3)	$\neg_E A$	f	t	t

where the latter sentence expresses a truth if and only if Vulcan rests. We know that it cannot be true that Vulcan moves when it is true that Vulcan does not move, and vice versa. We are agreed that due to Vulcan's non-existence it is neither true that Vulcan moves nor true that Vulcan does not move. And so on, for ever so many similar examples. So we have a working grasp of negation as a contrary-forming operation. Let us call it *internal negation,* and let us write the internal negation of a statement A thus: $\neg_I$ A. (The idiosyncratic symbolism is meant to ease comprehension.) Relying on this understanding of A's internal negation, we can now explain falsity by saying: *falsity of A is truth of A's internal negation.* Line (1) in the truth-table shown in Table 6.1 is faithful to this account. I am invoking here Dmitri Bochvar's so-called 3-valued system, and Timothy Smiley's adaptation thereof.[108] I use 'n' as short for 'neutral (= neither true nor false)', which no more signifies a third truth-value, I think, than 'either true or false' does.[109] The system caters for the possibility that some propositions which are not true are not false either, and it regards falling into a truth-value gap as an infectious disease (just as lack of *Bedeutung* in Frege's semantics is): if a component of a molecular proposition suffers from it, then so does the whole proposition. Bochvar actually calls $\neg_I$ A the internal negation of A; Smiley names it primary negation. A and $\neg_I$ A are contraries, in that they cannot simultaneously take the value *true.*

Bochvar adds to his system the operator ⊢, which he somewhat misleadingly calls assertion operator.[110] It has the same effect as inserting sentences that can take *true, false,* and *neutral* in the frame 'The proposition that ... is true.' So I prefer to set Bochvar's operator upright, $\top$, and call the operation 'truth ascription'. (This is the key idea in Smiley's adaptation of Bochvar's system.) The table

---

[108] Bochvar, 'On a Three-valued Logical Calculus', and Smiley, 'Sense without Denotation'.

[109] Bochvar renders 'n' as 'nonsensical' or 'meaningless'. He develops his system primarily as an instrument for tackling antinomies. This motivation is alien to Smiley's development of a logic with 'n'.

[110] It is vastly different from Frege's sign with the same name and a similar look. To mention just one difference: unlike Bochvar's operator, Frege's assertion sign can only stand at the outermost left of a formula.

for $\top$ in line (2) of Table 6.1 takes account of the fact that an attribution of truth to a proposition which lacks truth-value yields a proposition that is *false*—and not a proposition that is itself void of truth-value. The *external*, or secondary, *negation* of A is then defined as follows:

(Df. 1) $\neg_E A = $ Df. $\neg_I \top A$.

Its table is given in line (3) of Table 6.1. It captures a, if not the, natural understanding of a sentence mainly used in logic lectures, 'It is not the case that Vulcan moves'. A and $\neg_E A$ are contradictories, for always one and only one of them has the value *true*. Advocates of truth-value gaps can distinguish untruth from falsity by saying: *untruth* of A is truth of A's *external* negation.

[D]   Which status is to be assigned to (non-pathological) *instances of the Denominalization Schema* if we adopt (Mod)? Answer: they are derivable (more or less along the same lines as the corresponding instantiations of the Disquotation Schema).[111] Abbreviating 'Snow is white' as before, this time our task is to derive

(Den$_1$)   [S] is true $\leftrightarrow$ S.

In order to derive the left-to-right half, we need the following inference rule:

$$(= Elim.)^* \quad \begin{array}{ll} \Gamma: & [A] = [B] \\ \Delta: & A \\ \hline \Gamma, \Delta: & B \end{array} \quad , \quad \begin{array}{ll} \Gamma: & [A] = [B] \\ \Delta: & B \\ \hline \Gamma, \Delta: & A \end{array}$$

This rule is, I think, as compelling as its sibling ($=$ *Elimination*) which was invoked in the last subsection. We are ready to accept arguments such as

(P1)   The proposition that Prague and Cracow are similar $=$ the proposition that Cracow and Prague are similar.
(P2)   Prague and Cracow are similar.
(C)   So, Cracow and Prague are similar.

as intuitively valid. Unsurprisingly, my proof of *[S] is true* $\to S$ echoes that of its disquotational counterpart:

1	(1)	[S] is true		Assumption
1	(2)	$\exists p\,([S] = [p]\ \&\ p)$	1,	Df. (Mod)
3	(3)	$[S] = [T]\ \&\ T$		Assumption (for $\exists$ Elim.)

---

[111] I repeat here the derivations I gave in 'Truth and a Kind of Realism', 31. The proof of (*Den*) which van Inwagen recently outlined in 'Truth-Sentences', 208, is a notational variant.

3	(4)	[S] = [T]	3,	& Elimination
3	(5)	T	3,	& Elimination
3	(6)	S	4, 5,	(= *Elimination*)*
1	(7)	S	2, 3, 6	∃ Elimination
	(8)	[S] is true → S	1, 7	→ Introduction

The derivation of the right-to-left half of (Den₁) is even more straightforward than in the case of (Dis₁), for in the second line we can invoke a rule of first-order logic:

1	(1)	S		Assumption
	(2)	[S] = [S]		= Introduction
1	(3)	[S] = [S] & S	1, 2,	& Introduction
1	(4)	∃p ([S] = [p] & p)	3,	∃ Introduction
1	(5)	[S] is true	4,	*Df.* (Mod)
	(6)	S → [S] is true	1, 5	→ Introduction

By presenting these proofs, I do not want to contradict Horwich's claim that (Den₁) does not stand in *need* of a proof. He is right: it doesn't. (This is not to deny that (Den₁) is derivable from true premisses. Every truth is; e.g. from itself, or from its conjunction with another truth.) But the fact that not only (Den₁) but, along the very same lines, all the other 'axioms' of the 'minimal theory' can be proved by appealing to (Mod) and some logical rules of inference shows, I think, that (Mod) is more fundamental than those 'axioms'. At this point one might even wonder whether the propositions that make up MT really are axioms. 'Traditionally,' Frege rightly says, 'what is called an axiom is a thought whose truth is certain without, however, being provable by a chain of logical inference.'[112] Here is a comparison (drawn from Leibniz): we are ready to accept '2 + 2 = 4' as a matter of course, without supporting argument—failure to accept this equation would count as manifestation of deficient understanding. But for all that, '2 + 2 = 4' is provable.[113]

---

[112] Frege, '*Über die Grundlagen der Geometrie*, 319. An axiom, Leibniz says, is 'neither capable of being proved nor in need of it [*n'est point capable d'estre prouvée et n'en a point besoin*]' (*Nouveaux Essais*, bk. IV, ch. 9, sect. 2, 434). In §3 of *Die Grundlagen der Arithmetik* Frege echoes this when he characterizes axioms as truths which are 'neither capable, nor in need of, being proved [*eines Beweises weder fähig noch bedürftig*]'. For a thorough discussion of Frege's indebtedness to, and development of, the Euclidean rationalist tradition, see Burge, 'Frege on Knowing the Foundations'. In Ch. 7.1.1 we will hear Brentano's echo of Leibniz.

[113] Contrast Horwich, *Truth*, 50. Horwich himself compares the axioms of MT rather with the Peano axioms for elementary number theory (ibid. 138). But of course, which comparison is more apt is part of the issue. (On proving '2 + 2 = 4', see Leibniz, *Nouveaux Essais*, IV, 7, §10, 413–14, and the emendation of his proof in Bolzano, *Beyträge zu einer begründeteren Darstellung der Mathematik*, Appendix §8, and in Frege, *Die Grundlagen der Arithmetik*, §6.)

Table 6.2. (1) *Internal biconditional and* (2) *external biconditional*

	A	t	t	f	f	t	n	f	n	n
	B	t	f	t	f	n	t	n	f	n
(1)	$A \leftrightarrow_I B$	t	f	f	t	n	n	n	n	n
(2)	$A \leftrightarrow_E B$	t	f	f	t	f	f	t	t	t

The provability of instances of (Den) with the help of (Mod) may seem to be an embarrassment for those who want to allow for truth-value gaps. Doesn't it show that by accepting the modest account one incurs an obligation to subscribe to the principle of *tertium non datur*? I do not think so. The critical instantiations of (Den) are those where, according to the advocates of truth-value gaps, the left-hand side expresses a *false* proposition because it ascribes truth to a neutral proposition that is expressed on the right-hand side. None of the critical instantiations is such that one of its branches receives the value *true* while the other does not. So if we opt for a reading of the biconditional according to which it fails to yield truth only if one component expresses a truth whereas the other does not, (Mod) has no false (non-paradoxical) consequences. This means, of course, to give up the constraint, provisionally accepted in section 6.1.3 above, that a biconditional expresses a truth only if both sides receive either the same truth-value or none. Once again, Bochvar and Smiley can help us to fix this idea. Since being void of truth-value is infectious, the *internal*, or primary, *biconditional*, $A \leftrightarrow_I B$, takes *neutral* iff at least one component takes *neutral*. This is registered in line (1) of Table 6.2. So the internal biconditional still complies with the constraint of section 6.1.3. But with the help of the truth-ascription operator one can define the *external*, or secondary, *biconditional* as follows:

(Df. 2) $A \leftrightarrow_E B = Df. \ \top A \leftrightarrow_I \top B$.

As you can see in line (2) of Table 6.2, an external biconditional receives the value *true* if A takes *false* and B *neutral*.[114] So one can consistently endorse (Mod) and reject the principle *tertium non datur*, if one reads the substitution-instances of (Den) as external biconditionals.[115]

---

[114] Wright's 'weakly valid' biconditional and his 'polar negation operator' seem to be Bochvar's external biconditional and his external negation operator by other names: *T&O*, 63–4. Cf. also Sainsbury, *Philosophical Logic*, 106. Actually, for Horwich, too, it is the 'weak' or 'external' reading of the biconditional that matters: '[T]he explanatorily basic fact about our use of the truth predicate is our tendency to infer instances of "The proposition that p is true" from corresponding instances of "p", and vice versa' (*Truth*, 126; cf. 121).

[115] If we were to assume that a conditional is true in all cases except when its antecedent is true and its consequent is false, we would get the same irenic result. But this assumption does not respect (what

[E] Let us now turn to some pressing questions which concern the *quantificational structure* of

(MOD) $\forall x\,(x \text{ is true} \leftrightarrow \exists p\,(x = [p] \,\&\, p))$.

They foster the suspicion that (MOD) is either incomprehensible or circular. I will do my best to dispel this suspicion. Here, I shall focus on the right branch of (MOD). The question is: how are we to understand the non-standard quantifier '$\exists p$'?

The quantifiers of first-order logic are *objectual*. Whether or not a quantification is true depends on how matters stand with certain *objects*. Whether '$\exists x\,(x \text{ is a river})$', for example, or '$\exists x\,(x \text{ is a theorem})$', express truths depends on whether or not there is an *object* (within the range of the variable) which satisfies the condition signified by the open sentence 'x is a river' or 'x is a theorem'. Since the Danube satisfies the former condition and the Pythagorean Theorem the latter, our quantifications are true. In first-order logic variables bound by objectual quantifiers are place-holders for singular terms, such as 'the Danube', 'the Pythagorean Theorem', or 'that snow is white', which designate values of those variables. In other words, objectual (first-order) quantification is always *nominal* quantification, i.e. quantification into singular-term positions. Consequently, the quantifier on the right-hand side of (MOD) cannot be the objectual quantifier of first-order logic, for the sentential operator '&' cannot be followed by a place-holder for a singular term. (Obviously, expressions like 'the Danube', 'the Pythagorean Theorem', or 'that snow is white' cannot appear as conjuncts in a conjunction.) So on this understanding of quantification, the right branch of (MOD) simply makes no sense.

But this observation is not yet a reason for despair. The variable which is bound by the quantifier in the right half of (MOD) is a place-holder for sentences, so what we have here is *sentential* quantification, i.e. quantification into sentence position.[116] Now if one construes the quantifiers *substitutionally*, quantification into positions of any grammatical category is permitted.[117] So there is reason for

I take to be) an essential feature of conditionals: that they are not true if the antecedent is true while the consequent isn't. As the columns for the combinations t/n and n/t in Table 6.2 show, Bochvar's conditionals both comply with this constraint.

[116] Do not be misled by the title. 'Sentential quantification' no more means quantification *over* sentences than 'nominal quantification' means quantification over names. Note also that some authors call sentential quantification 'propositional quantification': see, for example, Richard's paper of this name or Grover, *PrTh*, ch. 1. This cannot mean quantification into 'proposition position', since propositions do not have a position in a sentence. So it strongly suggests quantification over propositions. But in setting up the issues in this area it is worth trying to be neutral for a while as to whether that is the right idea.

[117] The terminological distinction between 'substitutional' and 'objectual' (alias 'referential') quantification is due to Quine. As champions of substitutional quantification, he has Leśniewski and Ruth Barcan Marcus in mind: see 'Ontological Relativity', 63–5; 'Existence and Quantification'; *PL*, 91–4. As regards Leśniewski, this attribution seems to me mistaken.

hope that armed with this construal one can quite easily make sense of the right-hand side of (Mod). Substitutionally conceived, whether or not a quantification is true depends on whether or not some or all sentences that are obtained by deleting the quantifier and *substituting* expressions of the appropriate kind for the variables yield truths. Variables bound by a substitutional quantifier do not have values at all: they are not associated with domains of objects over which they range, but with substitution-classes, i.e. with sets of expressions appropriate for substitution. Let us mark the 'existential' substitutional quantifiers by placing the '∃' and the adjoining variable between curly brackets.[118] There are many contexts in which an objectual quantification makes no sense while the corresponding substitutional quantification is true. Take the set of singular terms to be our substitution-class and consider

(O1) ∃x (x was so-called because of his bravery)
(S1) {∃x} (x was so-called because of his bravery).

Since the proforms 'so' and 'his' are left dangling, 'x was so-called because of his bravery' does not signify a condition which an object could satisfy or fail to satisfy,[119] hence (O1) is nonsense. But since the name 'Richard the Lion-Hearted' belongs to the class of permissible substituends, and the sentence 'Richard the Lion-Hearted was so-called because of his bravery' expresses a truth, (S1) does so as well. If declarative sentences of English make up our substitution-class,

(S2) {∃p} (The Pythagorean Theorem = [p] & p)

clearly also makes sense. When the two occurrences of 'p' in the open sentence which remains after deletion of the quantifier are replaced by 'The square on the hypotenuse is equal to the sum of the squares on the other two sides', a sentence results which expresses a truth.

So far, so good. But one may very well wonder whether

{Mod*} ∀x (x is true ↔ {∃p} (x = [p] & p))

gives us what we want. {Mod*} seems to tell us that x is *true* if and only if there is a substitution-instance of '(x = [p] & p)' which expresses a *true* proposition. But

---

[118] The convenient notation is adopted from Horwich, *Truth*, 25. In 'Is There a Problem About Substitutional Quantification?' (hereinafter 'Substitutional'), Kripke uses 'Σ' for the substitutional existential quantifier and 'Π' for the substitutional universal quantifier. (A minor disadvantage of this symbolism is that it looks 'Polish' without being so.)

[119] Or, as the same point was put in Ch. 2.3 above, the predicate 'was so-called because of his bravery' is not a genuine predicate. If it were, it would have to apply to King Richard regardless of how he is designated—whether by 'Cœur de Lion' or by 'Richard I'.

this is circular in a way that makes it explanatorily useless, since the diameter of the circle is so small.[120]

Perhaps this is too quick. The argument assumes that the above specification of the truth-conditions of substitutionally quantified sentences gives us their meaning, and to make this assumption may be to confuse substitutional quantification with objectual quantification over expressions. After all, 'Snow is white, and blood is red' expresses a truth iff both 'Snow is white' and 'Blood is red' express truths, but that does not imply that conjunctive statements are about their conjuncts and ascribe truth to them.[121] 'Like these logical operators,' Soames says, 'substitutional quantification is primitive, if it is legitimate at all.'[122] But then, how *are* we to understand the substitutional quantifiers? One can sympathize here with van Inwagen's complaint.[123] Suppose I tell you about the sentence 'Sometimes somebody is cissed' (C, for short) no more than this: 'What is said by C is true iff sometimes somebody is kissed, but C does not mean that sometimes somebody is kissed.' Do you now know what C means? You do not. I have excluded some meanings, to be sure: if I am right, then C does not mean that everybody always remains unkissed, nor does it mean that nobody ever kisses anyone.[124] But still, for all you know, C may mean the same as 'Sometimes somebody is kissed, and a rose is a rose', or the same as 'Sometimes somebody is kissed, and either Mozart was married or he wasn't', etc. Are we not in a similar predicament with respect to substitutional quantifications? Let us consider the following example taken from Kripke.[125] Suppose that the class of permissible substituends for the variable 'ξ' comprises all and only those strings of English expressions that consist of a binary connective followed by a declarative sentence. Then, however odd we might find the look of

(S3)   {$\exists \xi$} (Snow is white ξ),

it expresses a truth, since 'Snow is white, and blood is red' does so. But if (S3) does *not* mean that at least one continuation of 'Snow is white' by such-and-such a string results in a sentence which expresses a *truth*, what on earth does it mean?[126]

In Chapter 4.2.2 we encountered Field's proposal for interpreting substitutional quantifiers. He does not define them in terms of truth, nor does he

---

[120] Thus Horwich, *Truth*, 25; 'Defense', 573 n. 1. Davidson, 'Folly', 273, concurs.

[121] See Dunn and Belnap, 'The Substitution Interpretation of the Quantifiers', 184–5.

[122] Soames, *UT*, 92; cf. 60 n. 35.

[123] van Inwagen, 'Why I Don't Understand Substitutional Quantification'.

[124] Cf. p. 225 above.   [125] Kripke, 'Substitutional', 334.

[126] Forbes, 'Truth, Correspondence and Redundancy', 35.

declare them to be primitive. The existential substitutional quantifier is explained as abbreviating (possibly) infinite disjunctions: '$\{\exists n\}$ (n is odd)', for example, is said to be tantamount to '0 is odd, or 1 is odd, or 2 is odd, or ...'. But do we really understand the alleged explanans? Or (since infinite length is not the real issue) at least that very long fragment of it which begins with '0 is odd' and ends with, say, 'or '999,999 is odd'? I think van Inwagen speaks for all of us when he says about a similar sentence: 'I recognize ... that [it] is a perfectly meaningful English sentence and that it is true. But to say that is not to say that I understand it.'[127] Now in the arithmetical example we have mastered the concepts needed to understand each of the disjuncts. In this respect things get even worse when we consider the alleged explanans in the right branch of $\{\text{Mod}^*\}$. It is tantamount to an infinite disjunction of conjunctions:

$$(x = [p_1] \,\&\, p_1) \lor (x = [p_2] \,\&\, p_2) \lor \ldots,$$

where the 'p_1', 'p_2', etc. include, to begin with, all declarative sentences of present-day English. Does this give us an interpretation of (Mod) which renders it plausible as an account of the meaning of 'is true'? From our discussion of disquotationalism we know why it does not: the proposal invites another application of the Argument from Conceptual Overloading. If 'is true' abbreviates that infinite disjunction, then you cannot have the concept of truth without having, *inter alia*, all concepts expressible in English. Nobody has all these concepts, but every competent speaker of English understands 'is true'.

Let us register in passing two problems for substitutional sentential quantification which arise for those who have somehow overcome worries about the very intelligibility of this kind of quantification. First, if you think (unlike myself) that the logical form of a sentence such as

(4)   Yesterday Ann suspected something which she knows today

can only be captured by means of sentential quantification, you would be ill-advised to construe this quantification substitutionally:[128]

(S4) $\{\exists p\}$ (yesterday Ann suspected that p & today Ann knows that p).

Suppose yesterday Ann suspected that today it would be raining in London, and now she knows that today it is raining in London: then (4) expresses a truth.

[127] So two decades after the publication of his aforementioned paper he confesses that he still doesn't understand substitutional quantification: 'Truth-Sentences', 216. (As you can see above, I take this not to be a sign of extraordinary woodenness on the part of the confessor, but as a symptom of a very real problem.)

[128] For a detailed discussion of this problem (which was first pointed out by Richard), see Soames, *UT*, 43–5, 233. The issues raised on pp. 288, 310–12 above are also pertinent here.

In formulating this supposition I have used different sentences after the occurrences of 'that', hence I did not present a truth-yielding substitution-instance of the open sentence to which the quantifier in (S4) is prefixed. It seems that there would be such an instance only if eliminativist eternalism were correct, for then the proposition yesterday expressed by 'Tomorrow it will be raining in London' and today by 'Today it is raining in London' would also be expressed by an eternal sentence. But we saw in Chapter 5.2.2 that eliminativist eternalism is to be rejected. So (S4) does not seem to preserve what is said by (4).[129]

Secondly, it may very well be the case (or so I argued in Chapter 4.2.3) that

(5) Some truths can only be expressed in a language which humans are constitutionally unable to master.

Suppose you wanted to interpret (5) as a substitutional sentential quantification:

(S5) $\{\exists p\}$ (It is true that p, and that p can only be expressed in a language which humans are constitutionally unable to master).

Obviously (S5) cannot yield a truth unless you include in the class of permissible substituends sentences of humanly incomprehensible languages. (The substitution-instances to which (S5) owes its truth would be sentences of a hybrid language which results from pooling English with Alpha-Centaurian, say, and only those Alpha-Centaurians who know English would understand them.) I have never seen friends of substitutional quantification cast their nets that wide.

So, where are we now? We got out of the frying-pan of objectual (and first-order) quantification which makes nonsense of (Mod), into the fire of substitutional quantification which makes (Mod) either circular or cognitively inaccessible (and which is in itself hard to understand). In order to get out of this impasse we must construe '$\exists p$ $(\ldots p \ldots)$' as non-substitutional quantification into sentence positions.

The following construal, I think, gives us what we need. Put in a nutshell, it is this: the sentential quantifier on the right-hand side of (Mod) subserves *higher-order quantification over propositions*. So it is objectual quantification, after all: the bound variable 'p' is associated with a range of objects, viz. propositions, which are its values. But since it is quantification into sentence position, it is not nominal (or first-order) quantification: permissible substituends for 'p' do not designate, but rather *express* the values of this variable. Both nominal and sentential

---

[129] For further criticism of substitutional accounts of attitude reports and *oratio obliqua*, see Richard, 'Propositional Quantification', 442–50. All this confirms Kripke's attitude: 'I am sceptical about the role of the substitutional quantifier for interpreting natural language' ('Substitutional', 380).

variables, if objectually understood, have values, but 'having a value is not the same for both'.[130]

If we are to believe Davidson, there cannot be a quantification of this kind. In his attack on Horwich's minimalism he first puts substitutional quantification aside and then goes on to say:

[Why should one not generalize the Denominalization Schema] by quantifying over propositions? The answer should be: because then we would have to view ordinary sentences as singular terms *referring* to propositions, not as *expressing* propositions. ('Folly', 273)[131]

If this is correct then it would equally apply to (MOD). Davidson takes it to be a matter of course that non-substitutional variables are always place-holders for *singular terms*, that non-substitutional quantification is always *nominal* quantification. But perhaps this assumption is a matter of deeply entrenched Quineanism rather than a matter of course. In one of his earliest papers, Quine had already maintained:

Variables are pronouns, and make sense only in positions which are available to names. ('A Logistical Approach to the Ontological Problem', 198)

When he repeated this contention some decades later, focusing on quantification into predicate position, he offered a remarkably feeble argument:

Consider first some ordinary quantifications: '∃x (x walks)', ..., '∃x (x is prime)'. The open sentence after the quantifier shows the 'x' in a position where a name could stand: a name of a walker, for instance, or of a prime number. ... What are said to walk or to be prime are things that could be named by names in those positions. To put the

---

[130] Hugly and Sayward, *I&T*, 174. Cf. also Grover, *PrTh*, 143. (Hugly and Sayward do not pursue this line, though, but appeal to a very dubious distinction: 'Do variables for sentences have *values*? Of course. Their values are what can be said. Is what can be said an *entity*? Of course not' (ibid.). As we will see below, *sub* [F], they are biting Prior's bullet.) Like Prior, I take non-substitutional quantification into sentence position to be intelligible. Contrary to what is often said in the literature, Prior did not plead for substitutional quantification. According to *OT*, 35–6, 68, an existential quantification, whether it be into the position of names, of predicates, or of sentences, can yield truth even if the open sentence to which the quantifier is prefixed has no truth-yielding substitution-instance. But Prior takes sentential quantification not to be over propositions (or anything else). Richard has shown that Prior's view makes sentential quantification 'unduly mysterious' (see his 'Propositional Quantification', 438–42). Please remember also that I do *not* propose to dissolve that-clauses, as Prior and his followers C. J. F. Williams, Hugly, and Sayward do. They take 'that' to fuse with verbs or adjectives to form prenectives (e.g. 'believes-that'), or unary connectives (e.g. 'It-is-true-that'). But according to the view I defended on pp. 68–9 above, 'that' combines with sentences to form singular terms. Hence the quantificational structure of 'Ben does not believe everything Ann believes' is exactly what it seems to be: it is the same as that of 'Ben does not touch everything Ann touches', that is, ¬ (∀x) (aRx → bRx). It may also bear repeating that one can consistently take 'that p' to be a genuine singular term and allow quantification into the position of the embedded sentence. By taking 'the capital of Sweden' to be a genuine singular term, Frege was not prevented from allowing quantification into the position of the embedded name: '∃x (Ingmar lives in the capital of x)'. [131] Cf. Davidson, 'Truth Rehabilitated', 68.

predicate letter 'F' in a quantifier, *then*, is to treat predicate positions suddenly as name positions, and hence to treat predicates as names of entities of some sort. . . . Predicates have attributes as their 'intensions' . . . and they have sets as their extensions; but they are names of neither. Variables eligible for quantification *therefore* do not belong in predicate positions. They belong in name positions. (*PL*, 66–7; my italics)

The core of the argument is this: (P1) If one quantifies into a position which is not that of a name (singular term), then one treats the expression in that position as if it were a name. (P2) But one should not treat non-names as names. (C) Therefore, such quantifications are illegitimate.

Now (P2) looks reasonable enough, but why should we accept (P1)? As we saw in our discussion of truth-nihilism, non-nominal quantification is very common in natural languages.[132] From 'Ann and Ben are both courageous', we can infer 'There is something Ann and Ben both are'. This is quantification into general term position, but it does not treat this position suddenly as a name position, as the appropriate expansion by a 'namely'-rider shows: 'namely courageous'. The rider could not be 'namely courage', or 'namely {x: x is courageous}'. Quine's argument does nothing to show that we cannot construe a sentence like '∃F (Ann is F & Ben is F)' as involving *higher-order quantification over properties*. Thus understood, the quantification is not substitutional, but objectual: the bound variable 'F' is associated with a range of objects, viz. properties, which are its values. But it is quantification into general term position, hence it is not nominal (or first-order) quantification. Permissible substituends for 'F' do not designate the values of this variable. (That would be done by singular terms such as 'courage'.) Rather, combined with the copula, they *signify* those values.[133] Both nominal and 'predicational' variables, if objectually understood, have values, but having a value is not the same for both.

---

[132] Quine has heard this objection very often: Geach, 'On What There Is', 132–3; Strawson, 'Singular Terms and Predication', 65; 'Positions for Quantifiers'; *Subject and Predicate in Logic and Grammar*, 32–4; Prior, *OT*, 35–7; Dummett, *FPL*, 61, 214 ff.; Davies, *Meaning, Quantification, Necessity*, 136–42. For a discussion of Quine's animadversions upon standard second-order logic, see George Boolos, 'On Second-Order Logic'.

[133] If one were to take non-substitutional quantification into general term position to be quantification over *concepts* (rather than properties), the substituends for 'is F' would *express* (rather than signify) the values of this variable. For present purposes, I see no need to decide this issue. (In *standard* semantics for second-order logic the variables range over sets, their substituends are predicates in the Fregean sense, and yet they are allowed to flank the identity operator. I think that there is no quantification into *predicate* position in a natural language like English, and I agree with Frege that only singular terms and variables reserved for them can sensibly flank ' = '.) Here is a further observation that should be budgeted for when the aim is a general theory of quantifications in natural languages. From 'A and B met in the garden [at midnight]', we can infer, 'A and B met somewhere [somewhen]'. This is quantification into adverbial positions, as the appropriate 'namely'-rider shows: 'namely, in the garden [at midnight]'. Surely this does not force us to view adverbials as singular terms. So what kind of quantification is it? We can construe it as higher-order quantification over places [times].

What if a predication has the form 'A Vs'? From 'The owl complains to the moon', we can infer 'There is something she does (viz. complain to the moon)'. The line in Thomas Gray's 'Elegy' which is echoed in the premiss, 'The moping owl does to the moon complain', makes it easier to recognize that in the conclusion we quantify into the position of an infinitive or verb-stem. In making that inference we do not treat this position suddenly as a name position. The corresponding proform of laziness is 'so', as witness 'The owl complains to the moon, and so does the wolf'.[134] Note that neither in 'There is something Ann is (viz. courageous)' nor in 'There is something the owl does (viz. complain)' do we quantify into the position of a predicate in the Fregean sense of a sentence-forming operator on singular terms: the *predicates* are 'is courageous', 'complains', and 'does complain'.[135]

If we understand such non-nominal quantifications as higher-order quantifications over properties, they are objectual. So whether '∃F (Ann is F & Ben is F)' expresses a truth depends on whether there is an object within the range of the variable—that is to say, a property (of being somehow)—which satisfies the condition signified by the open sentence 'Ann is F & Ben is F'. A property (of being somehow) meets this condition if and only if it is exemplified by Ann and by Ben. Similarly, whether '∃V (The owl Vs & the wolf Vs)' expresses a truth depends on whether there is an object within the range of the variable—i.e. a property (of doing something) which satisfies the condition signified by 'The owl Vs & the wolf Vs.' A property (of doing something) meets this condition if and only if the owl and the wolf exemplify it.

If the sentential quantifier subserves higher-order quantification over propositions, it is objectual. Hence whether '∃p (The Pythagorean Theorem = [p] & p)' expresses a truth depends on whether there is an object within the range of the variable, a proposition, that is, which satisfies the condition signified by the open sentence 'The Pythagorean Theorem = [p] & p'. A proposition meets this condition if and only if it is identical with the Pythagorean Theorem and true. Unsurprisingly, at this point we cannot avoid employing the concept of truth.

Can the notation of higher-order quantification over propositions be explained as the codification of some antecedently available common idiom that is 'truth-free'? Can it be 'convincingly read in English'?[136] Compare the language of objectual *first-order* quantification. Obviously, we did not learn it as our first

---

[134] Things are very similar in German: see my *Abstrakte Gegenstände*, 107.

[135] Most critics of Quine seem to have overlooked this, but Wiggins, 'The Sense and Reference of Predicates', 317, 326, and Strawson, *Entity and Identity*, 'Introduction', 5, did not.

[136] Davidson, 'True to the Facts', 40.

language, but the weird notation 'ョx' was explained to us with the help of our mother tongue. As Quine rightly says about this notation,

The meaning of so-called existential quantification is... that which ordinary usage accords to the idioms 'there is an entity such that', 'an entity exists such that', etc. Such conformity was the logistician's [*sic*] objective when he codified quantification; existential quantification was designed for the role of those common idioms. ('A Logistical Approach', 198)

'ョx' [is] explained by the words 'there is an object such that'. (*PL*, 89)[137]

We saw that, *pace* Quine, the notation of higher-order quantification over properties can also be explained by a common idiom: our prior grasp of sentences like 'There is something Ann and Ben both are' enables us to understand 'ョF (a is F & b is F)'. Is there also a foothold for higher-order quantification over propositions in some common idiom or other? Yes, there is, and I actually used it when introducing (Mod) in section 6.2.1. Everyday language provides us with prosentences such as 'Things are thus', 'This is how things are', 'Things are that way' ('*Es verhält sich so*'). So we can explain 'ョp (... p ...)' by 'For some way things may be said to be ... things are that way ...'. Van Inwagen finds Grover's attempt to explain sentential quantification by means of the alleged prosentence 'it is true' wanting.[138] In the course of his criticism he formulates two very reasonable constraints.[139] First, an explanation of sentential quantification by means of prosentences should enable us to 'understand sentences that contain arbitrarily many sentential quantifiers and arbitrarily many sentential-position variables'. Secondly, the explanation should formulate the prefixed quantifier-phrase in such a way that it 'interacts in the appropriate way' with what it is prefixed to.[140] Van Inwagen concedes at the outset that in English, say, we cannot even paraphrase complex *first-order* objectual quantifications unless we attach (numerical) subscripts to the pronoun 'it'. So, paraphrase in a variant of English with denumerably many distinct proforms and quantifiers is accepted as explanation. When this concession is

---

[137] Basically, this is why van Inwagen *does* understand objectual (first-order) quantification: 'Why I Don't Understand Substitutional Quantification', 285 n. 4. Cf. Kripke, 'Substitutional', 379–80. As to the second, historical, statement in the first quotation from Quine, let me add a historical footnote: At least one outstanding philosopher of logic disagreed with the 'logisticians': '*Nicht vergessen, daß (ョx)fx nicht heißt: es gibt ein x so daß fx, sondern: es gibt einen wahren Satz "fx"* [Do not forget that (ョx)fx does not mean: There is an x such that fx, but: There is a true sentence "fx"]' (Wittgenstein, *Notebooks* (9.7.1916)). Not that this is a very attractive proposal: it would make all existential quantifications metalinguistic existence statements. Interesting reflections on this topic are also to be found in Wittgenstein, *Philosophische Grammatik*, 203–4.   [138] In Ch. 2.2.3 we reached the same conclusion.

[139] Cf. van Inwagen, 'Truth-Sentences', 217 and 221 respectively.

[140] It was one of my complaints against Grover's theory that her quantifier-phrase 'there is a proposition such that' does not meet this requirement.

made, we see that neither of the two constraints is an embarrassment to my proposal. Each prosentence as a whole gets its own numerical subscript, and the same subscript is attached to the quantifier-phrase which governs it. So, for example, '$\forall p \, \exists q \, (q \rightarrow p)$', the theorem we derived in section 6.2.1 above, is rendered as '(For all ways things may be said to be)$_1$ (there is a way things may be said to be)$_2$ such that [if (things are that way)$_2$ then (things are that way)$_1$]'. To be sure, this is not exactly a jewel of English prose, but in that respect renderings of mildly complex first-order objectual quantifications by means of sentences with numerically decorated occurrences of 'it' are also not above reproach.

Disappointed by the performance of the alleged prosentence 'it is true', van Inwagen gives up with a sigh:

> Maybe there are prosentences hiding somewhere in the jungle of natural language, and perhaps they can be used to make sense of sentential quantification. But if there are natural-language prosentences, I have no idea what they might be. ('Truth-Sentences', 222)

What he has been looking for in vain was actually found in the jungle a long time ago: Wittgenstein's prosentence '*Es verhält sich so*' does the job of which van Inwagen despairs. In view of our quotidian use of locutions such as 'However she says things are, thus they are', it is misleading to call the language of the modest account a 'new form of quantification' or a 'new linguistic apparatus', as Horwich does.[141] What is comparatively new is its notation in Loglish. But the logicians' notation for first-order objectual quantification isn't so very ancient either, so this kind of age comparison is hardly to the point.

[F] If we now look at both branches of (MoD) we see that it contains quantification into singular-term position *and* quantification into sentence position, but both the singular term variable 'x' and the sentence variable 'p' have the same range. Thus in one breath we quantify in two *different* styles, in the nominal mode and in the sentential mode, over the *same* range of objects. Isn't that bizarre?

Before I try to alleviate this worry, let me report in passing that the characterization of (MoD) I just gave[142] makes a meteoric appearance early on in Soames's *Understanding Truth*:

> [H]igher-order objectual quantification over propositions can be used to define the property of being a true proposition: For all propositions x [x is true iff $(\exists P)$ (x = the proposition that P & P)]. Here we set the range of the ordinary first-order variable x to be the same as the higher-order existential quantifier over propositions.... [S]ome may question this definition because they question the legitimacy of higher-order propositional quantification.... However, once the quantification is allowed, the property of being

---

[141] Horwich, *Truth*, 37, 4 n.   [142] Echoing my 'Truth and a Kind of Realism', 29–30.

true is definable in terms of it. . . . An objectual interpretation in which the higher-order quantifiers range over propositions provides the means for defining a truth predicate after all. (*UT*, 48)[143]

But alas, this conception then disappears from the stage almost without trace: it is only briefly referred to in a footnote towards the end of the book, where the reader is told that lack of space prevented a discussion.[144]

The following comparison (which is largely inspired by Strawson) may help us to get used to the idea that the same objects can be values of both first-order and higher-order variables. There are two modes of introducing a *property* into an atomic statement: by an expression that signifies it ('is wise') or by an expression that designates it ('wisdom'). In the former case we ascribe that property, in the latter case we may, or may not, do so ('Socrates has wisdom', 'Wisdom is a virtue').[145] The first mode is exclusively used for introducing *properties* into discourse. Our grasp of the second mode is based on our comprehension of the first mode. It is noteworthy that sometimes we employ both modes almost in one breath. In

Ben is impatient, and that is a bad quality in a teacher

one and the same property is first signified by a predicate and then designated by a singular term. If we acknowledge that there are *two* modes of introducing properties, we do not have to bite *Frege's bullet*, i.e. we are not driven to say: (*?) *The property courage is not a property.*[146]

If there are two modes of introducing properties *individually* into discourse, then it should not come as a big surprise that we can also *quantify* over properties in two different styles, predicatively and nominally. And so we actually do in a natural language like English:

(1)p   There is something Ann and Ben both are—*to wit, courageous.*

(1)n   There is something Ann and Ben have in common—*viz. courage.*

---

[143] The very same conception was sketched (under the odd title 'the correspondence theory') by Mark Kalderon in his paper 'The Transparency of Truth', 490–2. He repeatedly refers to ch. 2 of Soames's (at that time still forthcoming) book from which my extract is taken (see Kalderon, nn. 3, 4, 15).

[144] Soames, *UT*, 256 n. 8. (Needless to say, the value of this book, at the heart of which lies the discussion of Tarski's and Kripke's responses to the 'Liar', is not diminished by the fact that it did not help me in spelling out the modest account.) With utmost discretion, the construal of (MOD) I am pleading for is alluded to in Horwich's remark: 'An alternative strategy would be to introduce some form of nonstandard (*e.g.* substitutional) quantification' (*Truth*, 124; my italics, of course). The only alternative that gets discussed in *Truth* relies on substitutional quantification.

[145] See Strawson, *Individuals*, 146 ff. and pt. II *passim*. In *Subject and Predicate in Logic and Grammar*, chs. 1 and 5, §2, Strawson uses 'specifying' rather than 'introducing', but the underlying idea is the same. Cf. also his 'Reply to Geach', 293.

[146] I am alluding to Frege's notorious claim that 'the concept *horse* is not a concept' (see '*Über Begriff und Gegenstand* [On Concept and Object]', 196).

Semiformal renderings that respect the structural difference between these sentences would look like this:

(1)p*   ∃F (Ann is F & Ben is F)

(1)n*   ∃x (Ann has [exemplifies, instantiates] x & Ben has x).

We have no trouble in understanding the argument

> Ann is lazy, so she has at least one vice,

even though the existential generalization is a nominal quantification into a position in the premiss which is not occupied by a singular term. The validity of the displayed argument depends only on whether the property introduced in the premiss is a vice: the style in which it is introduced is irrelevant. We can even use both modes of quantification over properties within one and the same sentence, as in

> Ann has many qualities Ben would also like to have—*courage, for example*—, but there is one thing Ann is which Ben does not want to be—*namely, lazy*,

without thereby becoming incomprehensible.[147]

Now, quite similarly, there are two modes of introducing *propositions* into discourse: the sentential mode (which is primary) and the nominal mode. Propositions can be expressed—by sentences—and they can be referred to, e.g. by sentence nominalizations. The sentential style is exclusively used for introducing *propositions* into discourse. Our grasp of the second mode is based on our comprehension of the first mode. If we acknowledge that there are *two* modes of introducing propositions into discourse, we do not have to bite what might be called *Prior's bullet*. Prior maintained that 'what a sentence says cannot be named'.[148] This implies that what is said in an utterance of 'Snow is white' is not what the singular term 'The proposition that snow is white' designates. But then we have a paradox that is as intolerable as the Fregean one: (?*) *The proposition that snow is white is not a proposition.*

If there are two modes of introducing propositions *individually* into discourse, it is not too surprising that one can also *quantify* over them in two different styles. We quantify in the sentential style when we assert, for example, that

(2)s   For all ways things may be said to be, if the oracle says that things are that way, then things are that way,

---

[147] There are also two modes of quantification over places and times in a natural language like English. Sometimes we quantify into a singular-term position: 'There is a place, namely, the garden, in which A and B met. There is a time, namely, midnight, at which A and B met.' But, as was registered in n. 133 above, we also quantify into an adverbial position: 'A and B met somewhere, namely, in the garden. A and B met somewhen, namely, at midnight.'

[148] Prior, 'Correspondence Theory of Truth', 228; cf. *OT*, 20. Hugly and Sayward call this 'Prior's Basic Principle' (*I&T*, 22, 238, 262, 345–6).

or more colloquially

(2)s′   However the oracle says things are, thus they are,

or in Loglish

(2)s* $\forall p$ (the oracle says that $p \rightarrow p$).

And we quantify in the nominal style when we assert:

(2)n   Whatever the oracle says is true
(2)n* $\forall x$ (the oracle says $x \rightarrow x$ is true).

Or, to take the limiting case, in

(3)s   For some way things may be said to be, things are that way
(3)s′   Things are somehow
(3)s* $\exists p.\, p$

we quantify sententially over propositions, and we do so nominally in

(3)n   There is at least one truth
(3)n* $\exists x$ (x is true).

In (Mod) you have both modes of quantification over propositions within the confines of one and the same sentence. Why not? At any rate, it is the only faithful semiformal rendering of the modest conception of truth I can think of.

[G] Let me bring this chapter to an end by facing an objection against the modest account which is quite independent of its Loglish formulation. In discussion, Dummett has accused it of *subverting any systematic philosophy of language*. Dummett's argument, as it struck me, runs like this:

(P1)   The modest account presupposes a grasp of the concept of a proposition.
(P2)   Propositions are sentence-meanings.
(P3)   The notion of sentence-meaning cannot be explained independently of the notion of truth.
(C)   Hence the modest account is circular.

You can take the term 'modest account' here to cover Horwich's minimalism as well. Actually, Dummett uses this type of argument as a multi-purpose weapon: replacing 'modest' by 'correspondence' and 'coherence', he employs it to demolish what he calls 'the classical "theories of truth", developed contemporaneously with Frege's work'.[149] But this is to overestimate the force of the

---

[149] Dummett, *OAP*, 15; cf. *The Seas of Language*, 118, 178–9; *LBM*, 158.

argument. The conception of truth as object-based correspondence, which ante-dates Frege's work by a couple of centuries, was inspired by Aristotle, who took sentences and believings, not propositions, to be truth-value bearers. Frege him-self criticized this variety of a correspondence view for regarding mental entities ('ideas'), not propositions, as truth-value bearers. For Frege's contemporary Russell, the left field of the correspondence relation was occupied by sentences, not by propositions. So presupposing a grasp of the concept of a proposition can hardly be the cardinal error of all correspondence theorists: Dummett's argu-ment hits at best the Moorean variety of Cambridge Correspondence. (The claim that it rebuts coherentism is equally dubious.) But all this is only an aside here. Even if an analogous argument is toothless against various correspondence and coherence theories, the argument as presented above is certainly a powerful challenge to the modest account.[150]

(P1) is obviously correct (and was conceded at the outset). So let us focus on (P2). I shall argue that this premiss is false. One thing should be uncontroversial: to be plausible at all, (P2) must be restricted to a subset of declarative sentences. If a sentence contains context-sensitive elements (e.g. indexicals) but is free from lexical and grammatical ambiguity, we have *one* sentential meaning but many *different* propositions. This objection cannot be circumvented by retreating to utterances of sentences. Remember the speaker in the phone-booth, who is talking to his worst enemy while looking at his best friend: in a single utterance of the unambiguous sentence 'You are my best friend', he might address both persons simultaneously and thus express two propositions with different truth-values.[151] But suppose that a sentence is lexically and syntactically univocal and contains no elements with contextually shifting designation. (Let us call such sentences 'stable' and abbreviate 'conventional linguistic meaning' as 'mean-ing'.) Can it be upheld that what a thinker or speaker says or thinks in saying or thinking that p really is *the meaning of the sentence 'p'*, provided that 'p' is stable?

For three reasons I do not think so. The first two arguments are meant to show that such an identification is at least sometimes inacceptable. They rely on two assumptions: (*A1*) Some expressions which belong to the same language, 'serpent' and 'snake', for example, and 'drake' and 'male duck', are strictly syn-onymous—in other words, their meaning is the same. (*A2*) Replacement of an expression with a synonym from the same language does not affect the mean-ing of the sentence in which the substitution takes place, unless the expression is mentioned rather than used.

---

[150] If my attempt at defusing the argument works, the analogous objection against Moorean Correspondence is also blocked. [151] See p. 266 above.

Substitute two stable sentences with the same meaning for 'p' and 'p*' in

(M)   Whoever believes that p, believes that p.
(M*)   Whoever believes that p, believes that p*.

Benson Mates pointed out that, for all such substitutions, nobody doubts that M, but somebody may very well doubt that M*.[152] Suppose Ann now believes that whoever believes that some snakes are dangerous believes that some snakes are dangerous, but she does not believe that whoever believes that some snakes are dangerous believes that some serpents are dangerous. Then the proposition which is designated by the nominalized (M)-sentence has the property of now being the content of one of Ann's beliefs, whereas the proposition which is designated by the nominalized (M*)-sentence lacks that property, and hence, by the Leibnizian Principle of the Indiscernibility of Identicals, they are different propositions. But according to our assumptions *(A1)* and *(A2)*, these sentences have the same meaning. Therefore the propositions expressed by the members of (M-M*) pairs are not identical with the meanings of the paired sentences.

Essentially the same point can be made, I think, for propositions which are (unlike the standard examples in the debate instigated by Mates) not 'about believing', and the verdict of propositional difference need not appeal to *belief* reports. Take the following two sentences:

(P)   Snakes are snakes
(P*)   Serpents are snakes.

Reading the Bible in the classroom, a child *wonders whether* serpents are snakes, without wondering in the least whether snakes are snakes. Whereupon the teacher *explains that* P*, but wisely refrains from explaining that P. At this point another child *shows astonishment that* P* but, of course, no astonishment that P. Friends of a metalinguistic 'solution' of Mates-type puzzles would take the propositional acts ascribed in my story to demand possession of the concept of being called 'serpent'. (Thus what the first child *really* wonders, they would say, is whether the creatures called 'serpents' are snakes.) This offends against the Conceptual Balance Requirement. Of course, in the classroom talk about words has become

---

[152] Mates, 'Synonymy', 215 (where the observation is turned against Carnap's joint analysis of synonymy and indirect discourse in *Meaning and Necessity*). Jerry Fodor uses Mates's point to throw doubt on the claim that failure of substitution *salva veritate* in belief contexts entails non-synonymy ('Substitution Arguments and Individuation of Beliefs', 164–6), and so did Israel Scheffler long before him ('On Synonymy and Indirect Discourse'). For a very thorough discussion of the issues raised by Mates, see Burge, 'Belief and Synonymy'. He argues convincingly (I now think) that we should take the relevant ascriptions of propositional attitudes and acts at face-value rather than reconstrue them metalinguistically (as I did in *Abstrakte Gegenstände*, 270–1).

routine, but somebody who has learnt to use words might not have learnt to make semantic statements, or to ask semantic questions, about them. A speaker may not have acquired the metalinguistic concept of being called 'serpent' and yet be correctly described as Ving that / whether P*. Hence I take it that my story provides us with three reasons for saying that sentences (P*) and (P) do not express the same proposition.[153] But according to *(A1)* and *(A2)*, they do have the same meaning.

Here is my second argument for distinguishing the meaning of a stable sentence from the proposition it expresses.[154] Consider the sentence

(S)   13 is greater than 1, and for all n, if n divides 13, then n = 13 or n = 1.

By removing all occurrences of the numeral '13' from (S), you obtain the complex predicate

(F)   ... is greater than 1, and for all n, if n divides ..., then n = ... or n = 1.

Now the meaning of (F) is the same as that of

(F*)   ... is prime.

Hence, again relying on assumption *(A2)* above, (S) has the same meaning as

(S*)   13 is prime.

But (S) and (S*) do not satisfy our Conceptual Balance Requirement.[155] Nobody can understand (S*) without having the concept of primality. By contrast, in order to understand (S) one needs the concepts expressed by the simple components of (S)—that is, the concepts expressed by the two numerals, the three two-place predicates, the three connectives, and the universal quantifier contained therein, but one can very well understand (S) without having the concept expressed by the predicate (F). You cannot entertain the thought expressed by (S) without, *inter*

---

[153] Notwithstanding the fact that (P) and (P*) are cognitively equivalent: see pp. 42–3 above. Of course, somebody who is not ready to assent to (P*) does not fully understand that sentence. (Recall the example used on p. 223 above: someone might believe that Woody is a groundhog, yet not believe that Woody is a woodchuck.) Cognitive equivalence is only a necessary condition of propositional identity.

[154] In what follows, I use a splendid Dummettian example as grist to my own mill: *Frege and Other Philosophers*, 26–7, 194–5, 297–8.

[155] See pp. 47–50 above. Conceptual balance by itself is also only a necessary condition of propositional identity, as witness [Cain slew Abel] and [Abel slew Cain]. Conceptual balance and identity of truth-value together do not guarantee propositional identity either, as you can see from pairs like $[\exists x \neg(x$ travels faster than light)] and $[\neg \exists x(x$ travels faster than light)]: for a while, most of us believed the former without believing the latter. And if the point I tried to make with (P/P*) or with the woodchuck/groundhog example holds good, even joint fulfilment of the Conceptual Balance Requirement and the Cognitive Equivalence Criterion does not ensure propositional identity.

alia, being able to think of one number as greater than another, but you need not be able to think of a number as prime. You are no more required to see (F) in (S) than you are required to see (S) as built up from the numeral '1' and the complex predicate that results from deleting both of *its* occurrences. (Compare camouflage cases in perception: you may very well see the trunk with four butterflies sitting on the side facing you without seeing the four butterflies.) We can, as Frege and Dummett would say,[156] *acquire* the concept of primality by 'dissecting' (S) in the way we did, taking it as the result of saturating the open sentence (F) by the numeral '13'. So (S) and (S*), though having the same meaning, do not express the same proposition.

My third argument is meant to show that we should *never* identify the proposition expressed by a stable sentence with the meaning of that sentence. What Ann said or thought may be plausible or implausible, remarkable or trivial, well supported or completely unsubstantiated, but a sentential meaning does not have any of these virtues or vices. What Ben thought or said may be confirmed or repudiated, endorsed or challenged, it may be universally acknowledged or contradicted in some quarters, but no sentence-meaning ever undergoes any of these vicissitudes. What is said in an utterance of a sentence has ever so many properties that are not shared by the meaning of the sentence uttered even if the sentence is stable. Hence, by Leibniz's Law, propositions are not sentential meanings.[157]

If I am right in rejecting (P2), Dummett's objection is blocked. But even then it is worth asking which attitude towards (P3) a friend of the modest account should adopt. (P3) is one of the central claims in Dummett's philosophy of language, and it is one that he shares with Davidson.[158] It is by no means uncontroversial. The late Wittgenstein was far from accepting it. It was denied by Sellars and Harman. Philosophers as diverse as Brandom and Soames oppose it,[159] and it is also controverted by Field and Horwich.[160] Of course, presenting a list of dissidents is no substitute for offering a fully worked-out alternative to truth-conditional semantics.

---

[156] Frege, *Die Grundlagen der Arithmetik*, §64.

[157] Cartwright made this point forcefully many years ago, in sect. 12 of his classic paper 'Propositions', and Austin had insisted on it before him: 'Truth', sect. 2. (b). In the meantime, it seems to have been thoroughly forgotten.

[158] See the passages referred to in n. 149 above. As these passages and many others show, Dummett takes the explanations of the two notions to be interdependent. So he would add to (P3): *nor can the notion of truth be explained independently of the notion of sentence-meaning.* (In 'Afterthoughts', 156, Davidson, too, subscribes to this explanatory interdependence claim; which makes for a certain tension with his primitivism as regards the notion of truth.) As far as I can see, the explanation of the notion of truth I have offered does not invoke the notion of sentence-meaning.

[159] Brandom, *MIE*; Soames, 'Semantics and Semantic Competence', and *UT*, 37, 58 n. 15.

[160] Field, esp. 'Deflationist'; Horwich, *Truth*, sects. 32–3, and *Meaning*.

But actually I do not see any need to place the stakes of the modest account on the success of that project.

Knowing what proposition a sentence expresses with respect to a given context depends on knowing what that sentence means, but that does not imply that knowing what a proposition is depends on knowing what meaning is. Propositions are essentially truth-evaluable, but that does not imply that the concept of a proposition is to be explained in terms of truth. (Triangles are essentially figures whose internal angles add up to 180°, but we can say what a triangle is without invoking the notion of a sum of angles.) If the concept of a proposition is explained in the way I suggested in Chapter 5.1.1, without invoking either the notion of meaning or the notion of truth, then there is room for combining a modest account of truth with a potentially illuminating theory of *expressing a truth*. The latter would try to answer questions such as these: what do the components of a sentence and the mode of their composition contribute to enabling the sentence to serve as a vehicle for saying something true? Which relation obtains between knowledge of those contributions and comprehension of the meaning of those sentences? By advocating the modest account of truth, one does not incur an obligation to reject such questions as not worth asking or as being incapable of having substantial answers. One is only committed to the refusal to regard those answers as contributing to an explanation of the concept of truth. The modest account can consistently be combined with the truth-conditionalist tenet that knowing the meaning of a declarative sentence depends on knowing under what conditions this sentence expresses, with respect to a given context, a true proposition. If this tenet is correct, knowing which proposition is expressed by a sentence and knowing the meaning of that sentence are distinct but interdependent achievements.

A proposition X is true, according to the modest account, if and only if things really are *as* they are according to X. In this section I have tried to do what William James formally asked of his critic James B. Pratt to do, namely 'to tell what this "as"-ness consists in', for I share James's conviction that 'it ought not remain a pure mystery'[161] I hope I have succeeded in dispelling the mystery. I take the modest account to offer *common ground* to all parties in the realism/anti-realism controversy.[162] So I see no reason for surprise when James goes on to say: 'I myself

---

[161] See epigraph on p. 333 above.

[162] In 'Debate', 218–19 Wright *blames* a formula very close to (Mod$_3$) for not engaging in 'the metaphysically substantial matters'. From my point of view, this abstention is *praiseworthy*, since the modest account is meant to provide neutral common ground for those who engage in such matters. I think that (Mod) is better suited for this job than Wright's open-ended list of so-called platitudes, some of which are at least controversial and at least one of which is downright false (or so I have argued on pp. 286–8 above).

agree most cordially that for an idea to be true the object must be "as" the idea declares it.' (In their phrasing of the 'as'-formula, both Pratt and James presuppose that truth-candidates always have a subject-predicate structure. Shades of Aristotle! The modest account is careful to avoid this presupposition.) James takes sides in the realism/anti-realism controversy when he adds, 'I explicate the "as"-ness as meaning the idea's verifiability.' The question how wise this kind of addition is will occupy us in the last chapter of this book.

7

Truth and Justifiability

In the final chapter of this book we shall ponder over QUESTIONS 15 and 16 on the flow chart.[1] According to alethic anti-realism (as defined in Chapter 1), truth is epistemically constrained: it does not outrun rational acceptability. In the first section I shall sketch three classical versions of alethic anti-realism and point at (some of) the problems that are peculiar to them. In the second section I shall scrutinize Putnam's very liberal variety, and, after comparing and contrasting it with its source of inspiration, Dummett's characterization of 'global anti-realism', and with kindred proposals made by Goodman and by Wright, I shall present various reasons for dissatisfaction, among them the reason why Putnam himself later recanted. In the third and last section of this chapter I shall try to support this recantation by offering an argument against all versions of alethic anti-realism: the argument from blind spots in the field of justification.

7.1 Classical Versions of Alethic Anti-Realism

> I cannot see how to defend truth which is external to knowledge.
>
> (F. H. Bradley, 'On Truth and Copying', 111)

7.1.1 *Foundationalism*

According to Franz Brentano, truth stands and falls with the possibility of *Evidenz*:

Wahrheit [kommt] dem Urteile dessen [zu], der urteilt, wie derjenige darüber urteilen würde, der mit Evidenz sein Urteil fällt; also der das behauptet, was auch der evident Urteilende behaupten würde. [Truth belongs to the judgement of a thinker who judges about the issue as someone would judge who made an evident judgement about it; i.e. who asserts what someone who made an evident judgement about the issue would also assert.] (*Wahrheit und Evidenz* (5.3.1915), 139 (122))

---

[1] See Ch. 1, Fig. 1.4.

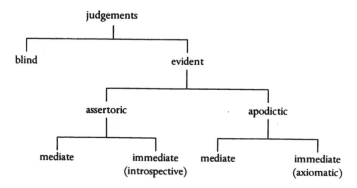

Figure 7.1. Brentano's Table of Judgements

At first sight it is unclear how the phrase 'about the issue [*darüber*]' is to be understood. (The context of our quotation is of no help.) But we can make sense of it if we think of a judgement as an answer to a question. Suppose the question is whether $100 = 1^3 + 2^3 + 3^3 + 4^3$. A schoolchild confidently copying the affirmative answer from her neighbour judges without *Evidenz*, or 'blindly', as Brentano would say.[2] Nevertheless her judgement is true, since one can judge with *Evidenz* that $100 = 1^3 + 2^3 + 3^3 + 4^3$. Or suppose the question is whether Ben is in pain now. According to Brentano, Ann can only judge blindly that he is, but if her judgement agrees with Ben's, who alone can pronounce on this issue with *Evidenz*, then her judgement is true. So Brentano's tenet is that a judgement is true if and only if it is, or has the same content as,[3] an 'evident' judgement. In order to spell this out, we need at least a rough idea of the basic distinctions in his theory of judgement (see Figure 7.1).

A judgement, Brentano maintains, is either 'blind' or 'evident', and it is either 'assertoric' or 'apodictic'. *Evidenz* is a property which a judgement 'either possesses immediately, or which it acquires via a proof by its connection with other judgements which are immediately evident'.[4] Since *Evidenz* can be mediated, 'self-evidence' would be a mistranslation. 'Immediately evident' judgements, Brentano says (closely following Leibniz's footsteps), 'are neither capable of proof nor in need of one [*keines Beweises fähig und keines Beweises bedürftig*]. The axioms

---

[2] Perhaps the terminology is meant to remind us of Plato's characterization of 'judgements without knowledge' in the *Republic*: of such judgements [δόξαι] 'even the best are blind [τυφλαί], or do you think that those who judge without insight are better than blind people who find the right way?' (*Resp.* VI, 506 c).

[3] I use this relational predicate in such a way that it is correct to say: 'His judgement that he himself is in pain *has the same content as* her simultaneous judgement about him that he is in pain.' Within the framework of Brentano's Reism, it is not to be taken as relating two acts to a third entity (a content); rather, it is used to say that two thinkers judge alike. Or so Brentano would maintain: cf. *Die Lehre vom richtigen Urteil* (henceforth *LRU*), 195.   [4] Brentano, *Wahrheit und Evidenz* (5.3.1915), 137 (120).

and the judgements of inner perception belong in this category.'[5] Axiomatic judgements are 'apodictic': what you take to be the case in such judgements is necessarily the case. You make an axiomatic judgement when you judge, for example, that there is no property an object simultaneously has and lacks, or that 2 is the successor of 1. What is accepted in an axiomatic judgement defies disbelief. You make an apodictic judgement that is 'mediately evident' if axiomatic judgements provide deductively conclusive reasons for it. (Our arithmetical example from the classroom was of this type.) Introspective judgements are 'assertoric': what you take to be the case in such judgements is only contingently the case. You make an introspective judgement, for example, when you judge that it now looks to you as if the light were fading. (Self-ascriptions of current pain also fall under this category.) What you accept in an introspective judgement is undisbelievable for you. You make an assertoric judgement that is 'mediately evident' if introspective judgements provide deductively conclusive reasons for it, e.g. when you judge that sometimes it looks to someone as if the light were fading. Using these distinctions, we can capture Brentano's *foundationalist* conception of truth by the following universally quantified biconditional:[6]

(Found) $\forall x$ (x is true $\leftrightarrow$

    (a) x is an immediately evident judgement, or

    (b) x is a judgement for which immediately evident judgements of the thinker provide deductively conclusive reasons, or

    (c) x has the same content as a judgement that fulfils clause (a) or clause (b)).

Brentano seems to regard truth as a property of mental acts.[7] As to QUESTION 16 on our flow chart, he makes it unambiguously clear that he is not a definitional alethic anti-realist:

Es läßt sich von Wahrheit überhaupt keine zerlegende Definition geben, weil es sich beim Unterschied von wahren und falschen Urteilen um etwas Elementares handelt . . . [It is impossible to give an analytic

---

[5] Brentano, *LRU*, 111. Leibniz also takes the formula Brentano is echoing here to apply to some necessary *and* to some contingent truths: see *Nouveaux Essais*, bk. IV, ch. 7, sect. 7, 411; ch. 9, sect. 2, 434. As was mentioned on p. 354 n. 112, Frege uses the same formula to characterize axioms; and so does Hermann Lotze: *Metaphysik*, bk. I, ch. 1, sect. 1; *Logik*, bk. II, ch. 4, §200.

[6] Cf. Brentano, *Versuch über die Erkenntnis*, 150; or the echoes in the work of his former students: Husserl, *LU*, vol. I, *Prolegomena*, §50; Stumpf, *Erkenntnislehre*, 63. In claiming that something is true (false) iff it is ultimately undisbelievable (unbelievable), Ducasse advocates a very similar position: 'Propositions, Truth, and the Ultimate Criterion of Truth', 172–8.

[7] Bolzano and Husserl call judgings correct (*richtig*) rather than true. Actually Brentano's Reism obliges him to take ontologically perspicuous truth talk to be irreducibly adverbial: 'The thinker X judges truly.' See pp. 344–6 above on Brentano's philosophical 'grandson' Kotarbiński.

definition of truth, since the difference between true and false judgements is something elementary ...] (*Versuch über die Erkenntnis*, 149)

The foundationalist conception gives rise to several questions. Brentano takes for granted that 'immediately evident' judgements are *infallible*,[8] for if they were not immune against the risk of error, then something might satisfy the right-hand side of the matrix in (Found) without satisfying the left-hand side. But, (1), are there any infallible judgements at all?

If there are not any infallible judgements, then the charge against Brentano would have to be that his constraint condemns the concept of truth to emptiness. But even with respect to 'assertoric' judgements, Brentano is right in answering question (1) affirmatively: whenever one makes a judgement that could be voiced by an utterance of 'I am now thinking' or 'I exist', one cannot be mistaken. What is thought in such a judgement cannot even be *entertained* without being true. Let us call all and only those judgements that fulfil this condition 'Cartesian'.[9] Certainly, judgements about one's current sensations ('I am in pain') or sensory experiences ('It looks to me as if the light were fading') are *not* Cartesian, whatever Descartes may have thought about them. Brentano makes a substantial (and notoriously controversial) claim when he contends that they are as infallible as Cartesian judgements.

But let us concede to Brentano that such non-Cartesian introspective judgements are also immune against the risk of error, and ask, (2), can introspective judgements really play the role they are supposed to play? Can such judgements provide what Brentano calls 'the solid foundation [*das tragfähige Fundament*]'[10] for all non-introspective 'assertoric' judgements which we deem to be candidates for truth?

Disjunctive judgements that contain an introspective judgement as a disjunct, or existential generalizations entailed by introspective judgements, are covered by (Found). But no unrestrictedly general 'assertoric' judgement (that all storks are red-legged, for example, or that nothing travels faster than light) is entailed by any finite set of judgements about a thinker's current mental acts or states. Even a judgement of external perception (that the light is fading, say) does not meet Brentano's constraint. (If it is false that p, then it is true that not-p; so (Found) does not legitimize calling such 'assertoric' judgements false either.) Sometimes Brentano seems to rest content with saying that they are at best *probable*.[11] But that does not really keep them out of the domain of truth-candidates, for if it is probable that p, then

---

[8] As for introspective judgements, see Brentano, *LRU*, 154: '*Was uns im inneren Bewußtsein erscheint, ist wirklich so, wie es erscheint* [what appears to us in inner consciousness actually is, as it appears].' As for axiomatic judgements, see *LRU*, 162–7.

[9] 'This proposition [*pronuntiatum*]: I am, I exist, whenever it is pronounced by me, or mentally conceived [*mente concipitur*], necessarily is true' (Descartes, *Second Meditation*, 25 (tr. 17)).

[10] Brentano, *Versuch über die Erkenntnis*, 169.   [11] Ibid., 158–70, 237–58.

it is probably true that p, and hence it could be true that p. Thus the judgement that p must be a truth-candidate if it is probable that p. But its candidacy for the title 'true' cannot be explained in terms of (Found): the proffered basis is just too meagre.

Some decades later this problem reappeared in the Vienna Circle when Moritz Schlick characterized (the introspective judgements voiced by) *Konstatierungen* as the ultimate arbiters for all non-introspective assertoric judgements: 'Science makes prophecies. . . . It says, for example, "If, at such and such a time, you look through a telescope focused in such and such a manner, you will see a speck of light (star) coinciding with a black line (cross-wires)." . . . Have our predictions in fact come true? In every single case . . . a *Konstatierung* answers unambiguously with yes or no.'[12] But how can this be? Suppose I exclaim, under the conditions described in the prediction, 'I now see a speck of light coinciding with a black line.' This is a *Konstatierung* only if it is taken to amount to no more than 'It looks to me now as if there were a speck, etc.' But the experience I thus ascribe to myself might be hallucinatory, and then it gives no clearly affirmative answer to the question whether the prediction (of an astronomical observation) is true. And it is of course a fallible hypothesis, not a *Konstatierung*, that my experience is not delusive. Furthermore, my judgement is only relevant for the confirmation of the hypothesis if it is really made at the critical time with a telescope focused in such and such a manner. And it is of course a fallible hypothesis, not a *Konstatierung*, that these conditions are really satisfied.

Immediately evident 'assertoric' judgements just cannot play the role Brentano—and Schlick—assigned to them. Hence, the foundationalist version of an epistemic conception of truth is hopeless, even if there are infallible 'assertoric' judgements. By accepting Brentano's conception of truth, we would confine the realm of empirical truths to judgements about a thinker's current mental acts and states and to judgements that can be proved from such premisses.

This brings me to a final and even more elementary question concerning (Found). According to Brentano's constraint, truths are a proper subset of judgements. But, (3), are only judgements true?

Let us broaden this question by taking (Found) to cover beliefs as well.[13] (Judgements, conceived of as mental items, are *acts* of judging, whereas beliefs are certainly not acts or any other kind of events. But there are close connections between both notions: in many cases of judging that p one comes to believe that p, and one believes that p only if one is ready to judge that p whenever one considers the question whether p.[14]) Sometimes, as in our quotation at

---

[12] Schlick, '*Über das Fundament der Erkenntnis*', (henceforth '*Fundament*'), 304–5 (2: 382–3).
[13] Brentano did not make a clear distinction between mental acts and mental states.
[14] For more on this topic, see my paper 'Some Varieties of Thinking', and below, pp. 420.

the start of this section, Brentano speaks in one breath of judgements and of assertions or statements, so let us take utterances with assertoric force also to be covered by (Found). Now isn't it more than likely that many a truth will never even be non-committally entertained or formulated, let alone accepted or asserted? There is a true answer to the question how many times the numeral '1' occurs in the London telephone directory of 1955, but presumably nobody will ever entertain or formulate an answer, much less acquire or voice an opinion about this non-issue.

Before we move on, let me stress that a repudiation of the foundationalist conception of *truth* does not prejudge the outcome of a discussion of foundationalist theories of *justification*. These theories contend that

(FoundJust) $\forall x, y$ (x is a justified belief of y $\leftrightarrow$
          (A) x is a basic belief of y, or
          (B) x is a belief of y that rests on y's basic beliefs).

As to clause (A), not every adherent of (FoundJust) takes empirically basic beliefs to be about mental states or acts, as Brentano did,[15] nor do all proponents of (FoundJust) think of empirically basic beliefs as infallible, as he did.[16] As to clause (B), not every partisan of (FoundJust) regards the support, which empirically basic beliefs are alleged to give to non-basic beliefs, as that of a deductively conclusive reason, as Brentano did.[17] But none of these options is inviting for an anti-realist theory of *truth,* for they allow that an empirical belief might be basic but false, and that a belief might rest on empirically basic beliefs and yet be false. So foundationalists concerning truth just have to take the hard line: they must specify the epistemic constraint in terms of deductively conclusive justification.

Just as beliefs that comply with clause (A) of (FoundJust) are not justified by virtue of their relation to other beliefs, so judgements that meet condition (a) of the foundationalist conception of truth do not owe their truth to a relation towards other judgements. This is one of several respects in which the conception of truth that we shall consider next differs sharply from foundationalism. According to this view, the truth of a belief (judgement, statement) is always due to its relation to other beliefs: truth is declared to be a relational property: namely, coherence with a certain set of beliefs. Since the implied relation, coherence, obtains between truth-candidates, proponents of this conception accept the affirmative answer to QUESTION 3 on our flow chart.[18]

---

[15] Anthony Quinton doesn't: cf. his *The Nature of Things*, pt. II. He would classify your current belief that there is a book in front of you as basic.

[16] Quinton doesn't.   [17] Chisholm doesn't: cf. his *Theory of Knowledge*, 3rd edn.

[18] See Ch. 1, Fig. 1.1.

7.1.2 *Coherentism*

Let us see whether alethic anti-realism fares better in its coherentist version, which also had some partisans in Vienna. In his paper 'On the Foundation of Knowledge' Schlick vigorously attacked a conception of truth that was maintained by some of his friends: 'This doctrine (expressly stated and defended... by Otto Neurath, for example [19]) is well known in the history of philosophy. In England it is commonly referred to as the "coherence theory of truth" and contrasted with the older "correspondence theory".'[20] In 1931 Neurath had argued:

Aussagen werden mit Aussagen verglichen, nicht mit 'Erlebnissen', nicht mit einer 'Welt', noch mit sonst etwas.... Jede neue Aussage wird mit der Gesamtheit der vorhandenen, bereits miteinander in Einklang gebrachten, Aussagen konfrontiert. Richtig heißt eine Aussage dann, wenn man sie eingliedern kann. Was man nicht eingliedern kann, wird als unrichtig abgelehnt. Statt die neue Aussage abzulehnen, kann man auch, wozu man sich im allgemeinen schwer entschließt, das ganze bisherige Aussagensystem abändern, bis sich die neue Aussage eingliedern läßt.../... Einen anderen 'Wahrheitsbegriff' kann es für die Wissenschaft nicht geben.
[Statements are compared with statements, not with 'experiences', not with a 'world' nor with anything else.... Each new statement is confronted with the totality of existing statements that have already been harmonized with each other. A statement is called correct if it can be incorporated in this totality. What cannot be incorporated is rejected as incorrect. Instead of rejecting the new statement, one can alter the whole existing system of statements until the new statement can be incorporated; in general, however, this decision is taken with hesitation.../... There can be no other 'concept of truth' for science.] (*'Soziologie im Physikalismus'*, 541 (66); *'Physikalismus'*, 419 (53))[21]

What is it for a body of statements to be coherent? Neurath's answer to this question is far clearer than the pronouncements of most of his fellow-coherentists, but it is clearly unsatisfactory. A new statement, he contends, can be 'incorporated' into a set of statements if and only if the set 'remains *consistent* [widerspruchslos] if the statement is added'.[22] The obvious objection is that a body of statements might be consistent and yet contain some, or even only, false statements.

We must be careful not to overstate the case against Neurath here. Schlick is unfair to him (as was Russell, three decades earlier, to the Oxford neo-Hegelians[23]) when he claims that a partisan of the coherence theory 'must consider any arbitrary fairy tale to be no less true than a historical report or the propositions in a chemistry-book, so long as the tale is well enough fashioned to harbour no

---

[19] Within the Vienna Circle it was also maintained by Carnap (before he had read Tarski) and by Carl Gustav Hempel (who answered Schlick in his paper 'On the Logical Positivists' Theory of Truth').

[20] Schlick, *'Fundament'*, 295 (374).

[21] The tendency towards doxastic conservatism was already registered by William James: see *Pragmatism*, 34–5, 104.   [22] Neurath, *'Protokollsätze'*, 581 (95).

[23] Russell, 'The Monistic Theory of Truth', 136; *The Problems of Philosophy*, 71.

contradiction anywhere'.[24] When Neurath spoke of statements [*Aussagen*] he meant truth-claims. A fabricated tale might be a consistent body of sentences (or of thoughts), but that does not make it a consistent body of truth-claims (or of beliefs or judgements). If we have excogitated something, we cannot simply decide to believe it. So Davidson is wrong when he maintains that truth is 'wholly severed from belief...by coherence theories'.[25] The set intended by coherence theorists is a set of truth-claims, or a set of beliefs or judgements.[26] (For the topic of this section, differences between assertions or statements on the one hand and beliefs or judgements on the other are irrelevant. What matters is that they all involve a commitment to truth.)

Even so, the obvious objection stands. Suppose the 'new' statement that Q is confronted with the 'old' set

(Old) $\{[P], [P \rightarrow \neg Q], \ldots\}$.

We cannot simply add [Q] to (Old), for, as an application of *modus ponens* quickly reveals, the set $\{[P], [P \rightarrow \neg Q], [Q], \ldots\}$ is inconsistent. In order to prevent this calamity, we can either reject [Q] and stick to (Old), or we can revise (Old) so that the newcomer can be incorporated. But there are of course two ways of doing the latter,

(New 1) $\{[P], [Q], \ldots\}$
(New 2) $\{[P \rightarrow \neg Q], [Q], \ldots\}$,

and at least one of these two sets must contain a *false* statement. This observation is the firm basis for Schlick's attack on Neurath's coherentist conception of truth: not every consistent body of statements contains only true statements.[27] And if Davidson is right in claiming that 'coherence is nothing but consistency', this is the death-blow to any coherentist conception of truth.[28] But perhaps this death notice is premature. Judging from his references, Davidson seems to have only the Viennese version of coherentism in mind. Yet a brief look into the works of the Oxford Idealists suffices for recognizing that these coherentists emphatically denied that coherence is nothing but consistency. Schlick should have been aware of this: in his *Habilitationsschrift* of 1910, 'The Nature of Truth in

[24] Schlick, '*Fundament*', 297 (376).   [25] Davidson, 'Afterthoughts', 155.

[26] This is rightly stressed in Blackburn's sympathetic and illuminating discussion of coherentism in *Spreading the Word*, 235–48.   [27] Schlick, '*Fundament*', 297–8 (376–7).

[28] Davidson, 'Afterthoughts', 155. In 'Epistemology and Truth', 184–5 (= 'Structure', 305) and 'The Centrality of Truth', 107–8 (= 'Truth Rehabilitated', 67), he still takes a coherence account of truth to be refuted by the observation that 'there is no reason to suppose every consistent set of beliefs contains only truths'. Popper's one-line rebuttal of coherentism is based on the same contention: see his 'Truth, Rationality, and the Growth of Scientific Knowledge', 225, and so is Tugendhat's swift critique of this view in his *Logisch-semantische Propädeutik*, 239–40.

Modern Logic', he had discussed Harold H. Joachim's book on truth. Here is what Joachim said in 1906:

> The 'systematic coherence'... in which we are looking for the nature of truth, must not be confused with the 'consistency' of formal logic. A piece of thinking might be free from self-contradiction, might be 'consistent'... and yet it might fail to exhibit that systematic coherence which is truth. (*The Nature of Truth*, 76)[29]

Presumably Neurath would have ruled out as inconsistent not only *formally* inconsistent sets of statements but *any* set which includes a statement that p and a statement that q such that it is conceptually impossible that both p and q. (This rules out sets containing both the statement that Kant was a bachelor and the statement that he was married, or both the statement that Abraham was the father of Isaac and the statement that Isaac was the father of Abraham.) If so, Neurath's conception of inconsistency is broader than Joachim's reference to formal logic suggests. But this is only an aside. The decisive point is that coherence, according to the Oxford Idealists, requires more than consistency.[30] Francis H. Bradley, the most important and influential of all British neo-Hegelians, maintained that comprehensiveness is another essential aspect of coherence:

> In speaking of system I mean always the union of these two aspects [i.e. consistency and comprehensiveness], and this is the sense and the only sense in which I am defending coherence.... [N]either of these aspects of system will work by itself. ('On Truth and Coherence' 202–3)

Comprehensiveness is, at least partly, a matter of (descriptive and explanatory) scope: a set of beliefs α is *more comprehensive*, and to that extent more coherent, than a set β if α answers not only all questions answered in β but also at least one further question which remains unanswered in β.

Now the very word 'coherence' carries the suggestion that coherence is a matter of how well the parts of a manifold 'hang together'. (Neurath's, Bradley's, and Joachim's talk of 'system' points in the same direction.) Consider the following consistent subset of the set of my beliefs: {[Oxford has many spires], [Caesar was assassinated], [My name is 'WK']}. It is more comprehensive than any of *its* subsets, to be sure, but one is inclined to say that the elements of this helter-skelter collection do not 'hang together'. What is the cash-value of

---

[29] Henceforth *NT*. Cf. *NT*, 170.

[30] In 1939 Brand Blanshard, the American advocate of coherentism, concurred: coherence 'goes far beyond consistency' (*The Nature of Thought* (henceforth *NTh*), vol. 2, 284; cf. 292). To my mind, exposition and defence of coherentism in chs. 25–7 of this book by far surpass its Oxford sources of inspiration as regards conceptual clarity and argumentative force.

this metaphor? Replacing the metaphor by a simile, we can say that a set of beliefs is coherent only if its members mutually support each other like the poles in a tepee. This support can only be due to justificatory connections within the set. Some coherentists have suggested that a maximally coherent set would be one 'in which every judgement entailed, and was entailed by... the others jointly and even singly'.[31] But this is absurd if 'entailment' is taken in any of the senses logicians have tried to clarify: it would condemn even the best chemistry-book for lack of coherence. But of course, co-entailment is not the only way in which beliefs can support each other. Thus the inferential connections that obtain within the following set exemplify a weaker kind of mutual support:[32] {[Most of the people here are happy, and Ben is here iff Ann is here], [Ben is here and is happy], [Ann is here and is happy]}. The conjunction of any two elements of this set confirms the third in the sense that the probability of any one element will be increased if the remainder is assumed. A set of beliefs may be tightly unified by deductive, probability-conferring, and explanatory relations obtaining between its members. Let us assume that there is a way of determining when a set of beliefs α is *more tightly unified* by such relations, and to that extent more coherent, than another set β.

Even so, our problem remains: couldn't a consistent, comprehensive, and tightly unified set of beliefs comprise many errors? After all, 'the most hopeless form of insanity is that in which the various factors of the delusion are most systematically rationalized with reference to one another.'[33] Adherents of coherentism try to dispel this suspicion of Systematic Delusion by pointing out that the stock of previously acquired beliefs must come to terms with new perceptual judgements which may put it to a strain. These judgements are not the thinker's judgements on his current sensations, sensory experiences, or thoughts, but rather his judgements on what he currently perceives in his environment—'The light is fading' rather than 'It now looks to me as if the light were fading.' Without taking such statements or judgements to be infallible, coherentists tend to assign to them a critical role:

[As to perceptual judgements] we cannot anticipate them or ever become independent of that which they give us.../...[W]ith regard to the world as perceived...my power is very limited. I cannot add to this world at discretion and at my pleasure create new and opposite material. Hence, to speak broadly, the material here is given and compulsory, and the production of what is contrary is out of my power.../...[But] it is one thing... to allow the existence of a fundamental element, and it is another thing to admit this in

---

[31] Blanshard, *NTh*, 264–5 (following Joachim).
[32] Borrowed from Chisholm, *Theory of Knowledge*, 3rd edn., 70–1, 87.
[33] Dewey, 'The Problem of Truth', 34.

the form of an infallible judgement.... [A]ll sense-judgements are fallible. ('On Truth and Coherence', 203, 215, 216–17)

Gewiß haben auch wir eine Instanz, das sind die von uns anerkannten Protokollsätze; aber sie sind nicht endgültig fixiert. Wir verzichten nicht auf den Richter, aber er ist absetzbar.... So reduziert sich für uns das Streben nach Wirklichkeitserkenntnis auf das Streben, die Sätze der Wissenschaft in Übereinstimmung zu bringen mit möglichst vielen Protokollaussagen. [Certainly we too have a court to appeal to, one that is formed by the protocol statements accepted by us; but it is not finally fixed. We do not renounce the judge, but he is replaceable.... Thus for us striving after knowledge of reality is reduced to striving to establish agreement between the statements of science and as many protocol statements as possible.] ('*Radikaler Physikalismus und "Wirkliche Welt"*', 618–19 (107, 109))

Since protocol statements intimate perceptual judgements, both passages suggest the same reply to the Systematic Delusion objection: if α accommodates more perceptual judgements than β, then α is *better controlled*, and to that extent more coherent, than β—even though it is sometimes rational not to yield to the pressure of perceptual judgements.

In various dimensions coherence has turned out to be a matter of degree. This by itself does not make truth, as conceived by coherentists, a matter of degree. Let us say, tentatively pulling the above threads together, that a set of beliefs is *maximally coherent* only if it is consistent and second to none as regards comprehensiveness, perceptual control, and tight justificatory unification. This makes no pretension of fully clarifying the notion of coherence. Obviously, the features of coherence we registered would bear more explanation, and the question is left open whether a set of beliefs must be endowed with additional virtues if it is to count as maximally coherent. Still, our sketch may suffice to give us some hold on the *coherentist* conception of truth:

(Coh) $\forall x$ (x is true $\leftrightarrow$ x belongs to a maximally coherent set of beliefs).

According to (Coh), the predicate 'coherent' applies to sets of beliefs, not to members of such sets, and only the members are claimants for the title 'true'. As it stands, (Coh) gives no sense to an ascription of truth to a set of beliefs, for no set of beliefs is a belief.

Let me postpone discussion of (Coh) for a moment, in order to add one or two more brush-strokes to the picture of the Oxford neo-Hegelians. Bradley, if Ralph Walker gets him right, accepts (Coh), but 'he accepts it not because of something about the nature of truth. He accepts it because of something about the nature of reality. Reality is the one fully coherent and comprehensive whole. Our judgements are true just to the extent that they correspond to this reality.'[34] The trouble with this is, of course, that a notion of coherence which applies to a set of beliefs (or to a whole consisting of beliefs) cannot apply to reality unless reality is a set of, or consists of, entities that are, or have, propositional contents, for consistency and inferential relations can only obtain between such entities. This variety of idealism, I dare say, is wildly implausible.

Walker's 'true to the extent that' alludes to the fact that British Idealists often talk as if they took a certain set of beliefs, or presumably, rather, a certain whole consisting of beliefs, to be the only thing that deserves to be called 'true' and not just 'true to some extent'. They make the truly astounding claim that, strictly speaking, no single belief is *wholly* true. (You may find some consolation in their supplementary contention that, strictly speaking, no belief is entirely *false* either.) But why, you may well ask, has the uncontroversial judgement that Caesar crossed the Rubicon in 49 BC no chance of being wholly true, of being true without any reservations? Here is Joachim's answer:[35]

The 'brute' fact that Caesar crossed the Rubicon in 49 BC is pregnant with significance, owing to the concrete political situation within which it took place.... It was Caesar, at the head of his army and animated by conflicting motives of patriotism and ambition, who crossed. And he crossed the Rubicon at this determinate political juncture, with a full consciousness of the effect of his action on the political crisis at Rome. This—and more—is the meaning of the historical judgement in its proper context, its *definite* meaning. This concrete happening is 'the fact' affirmed in the judgement, if indeed you can arrest the expansion of its meaning even here. We can be sure, at any rate, that the actual happening contains *no bare crossing of a stream by a man in the abstract* as a solid grain of fact, separable from the complicated setting which particularizes it....

'Well,' I shall be told, 'the brute fact still remains, Caesar *did* cross the Rubicon. You cannot get over that.' But I am not maintaining that the judgement ... is wholly false. I am only denying that it is ... wholly or absolutely true.... Such truth as the 'isolated' judgement involves—and every judgement involves *some* truth—'persists' in the fuller truth ... not as a pebble persists in a heap of pebbles, but as the first rough hypothesis survives in the established scientific theory. (*NT*, 107–8)

It is good now to have Ramsey's sober comment on this flamboyant speech:

[I]t is obvious that 'Caesar crossed the Rubicon' is not the whole truth about that event, but I cannot see that Prof. Joachim's arguments have any tendency to show that it is not part of the whole truth. Because he was at the head of the Army, was he not still Caesar? Because he was led to cross by motives of ambition and patriotism, did he any the less cross? When we say simply that he crossed, we do not particularise where, when and

---

[34] Walker, 'Bradley's Theory of Truth', 99; cf. 106.
[35] Cf. Blanshard, *NTh*, ch. 27. For exposition and criticism of Bradley's 'degrees of truth' doctrine, see Dodd, *ITT*, 166–74.

from what motives, but we are not denying that he must have crossed at some definite place and time for definite reasons. Because we call him simply a man and say no more about him, we do not mean he was a 'man in the abstract' without body parts or passions. If I asked someone whether there was a dog in the house, would it be reasonable for him to reply 'No; there isn't an abstract dog, but only a poodle'?

Nor do I see how a complete life of Caesar could be written which did not say either that he crossed the Rubicon, or something else from which that fact could at once be extracted.... Prof. Joachim is, indeed, prepared to allow that 'Caesar crossed the Rubicon' is not wholly false, but since he thinks that every judgement, e.g. 'Caesar did not cross the Rubicon,' involves some truth, this concession seems hardly to do justice to the facts. (*On Truth*, 30–1)

Joachim has still another argument for the claim that no particular statement is 'wholly or absolutely true'. It does not prove his point either, but it contains an important insight. A chronicle of a series of events may be accurate in every detail, yet 'it may entirely miss the "significance" of the piece of history, and so convey a thoroughly false impression'.[36] This is correct, as far as it goes, but it would better be taken to show that a true statement may make the interpreter believe a falsehood. Josiah Royce, the American neo-Hegelian, is reported often to have told the following story which makes this point vivid:[37] 'The Captain recorded in the log, "Mate drunk today," and refused to cancel it, because it was true. Then came the Mate's turn to keep the log. "Captain sober today." The Captain stormed, but the Mate answered blandly, "It is true, isn't it?".' Why did the captain get angry? Because the mate's true statement is relevant only if the captain's sobriety on the day in question was remarkable. So the reader of the log will be led to believe of the captain (who was always sober, of course) that he was drunk most of the time. In such cases, it is wrong to make the statement even though what is stated is nothing but the truth, since making the statement is bound to produce all the effect of the grossest falsehood. A statement can be criticized in many dimensions, and by calling its content (wholly, entirely, perfectly), true we do not approve of it in all respects. (Something may have the truth-value T without having much value.) So there is again no convincing argument for Joachim's refusal to apply the predicate 'true' (without a 'partly' rider) to single statements.

If no belief is entirely false, what then is *error*? A belief is erroneous, Joachim contends, in so far as the believer is under the illusion that what is at best 'partial knowledge' on his or her part is 'complete'.[38] If this were correct, then a pupil's belief that Caesar crossed the Rubicon in 39 BC would not be an error as

---

[36] Joachim, *NT*, 16.   [37] Quoted in T. H. Costello, 'Royce's Encyclopaedia Articles'.
[38] Joachim, *NT*, 143–4, 161–2.

long as the pupil does not take himself to be in possession of complete knowledge (about Caesar, let us say). This theory is too good to be true, for it makes getting rid of one's errors far easier than it actually is: humbly acknowledging that one isn't omniscient would do the trick.[39] Fortunately the contention that no single belief is either wholly true or wholly false is not part of (Coh). An advocate of (Coh) can say that the belief that p is false iff the belief that not-p belongs to a maximally coherent set of beliefs.

Our attempt at partially spelling out the doctrine which is summarized in (Coh) made consistency a necessary condition of maximal coherence. This requirement is indispensable if a belief's or statement's belonging to a maximally coherent system is to be a sufficient condition for its *truth*. For coherence theories of *justification*, the requirement of consistency is too demanding.[40] Such theories claim something like this:

(CohJust) $\forall x, y$ (x is a justified belief of y $\leftrightarrow$
x is a belief of y that coheres with the rest of y's beliefs).

Presumably we all harbour some inconsistency or other in the set of our beliefs. Ben, for example, is justified in his belief that

(Q) $\neg \, (6{,}561 > 6{,}562)$,

and he is also justified in his belief that

(R) $3^8 > 6{,}562$,

because his normally reliable pocket calculator twice computed that 3^8 equals 6,567 and his trustworthy mathematician friend confirmed this result for him. But, alas, man and machine are equally wrong: 3^8 equals 6,561, so (R) entails that

---

[39] Hegel makes a similar claim about the history of (pre-Hegelian) philosophy: earlier philosophical positions were erroneous, he maintains, just in so far as they did not acknowledge their own one-sidedness. (For references and criticism, see my '*Hegel als Leser Platos*', 142.) 'Error is truth when it is supplemented', Bradley contends (*Appearance and Reality*, 173). This makes some sense for statements that we tend to call 'not quite true'. Take White's example: 'the report that Negroes in Alabama have been deprived of their right to vote might be said to be not quite true, either on the ground that they have been denied the opportunity to exercise their right rather than been deprived of their right, or on the ground that, although there has been a deprivation of the right, it extends only to [black] women' (*Truth*, 117). But when it comes to errors that are not 'near misses' (like 'Socrates wrote several books' or '143 is prime'), one wonders what supplementation Bradley would propose. The only safe way of turning falsehood into truth is, of course, prefacing it by (something to the effect of) 'It is not the case that', but one would hardly want to describe this as a supplementation. In any case, as White emphasizes, we should carefully distinguish between being *not quite true* (which excludes being [wholly] true) and being *only part of the whole truth* (which does not exclude being [wholly] true). It is the second property that Joachim and Ramsey were concerned with.

[40] *Pace* Lawrence BonJour, *The Structure of Empirical Knowledge*, 95; Keith Lehrer, *Theory of Knowledge*, 94.

6,561 > 6,562. Hence Ben's system of beliefs is inconsistent. But this fact does not prevent his two conflicting arithmetical beliefs from being justified, not to mention his opinions about today's weather.[41]

Or take Ann. She did a thoroughly good job: after many months of careful research for her historical dissertation, she is justified in all claims p_1, p_2, p_3, ... p_n she put forward in her thesis. She is rightly pleased with the marks she gets, but she does not suffer from epistemic *hubris*: she knows only too well that even the most circumspect historians have made mistakes and that there is no reason to think that she of all people is an exception. In addition, one of the renowned authorities in her field of research told her that he had discovered a minor mistake in her thesis. (Unfortunately, before having identified the alleged error for her, he died in a car accident.) So Ann is justified in her self-critical conviction, compactly expressed in the preface to the published version of her thesis, that $\neg$ (p_1 & p_2 & p_3 ... & p_n). Consequently, she has an inconsistent system of beliefs, for she believes that

(S) p_1, p_2, p_3, ... p_n, and $\neg$ (p_1 & p_2 & p_3 ... & p_n).

But surely this fact does not imply that *none* of her beliefs is justified. The inconsistency does not even detract from the justification of the beliefs voiced in the preface and in the body of her thesis, let alone from the justification of her present meteorological convictions.[42] Ann's case is more remarkable than Ben's because her being justified in her self-critical judgement as well as in her historical claims survives even her discovery that (S) is inconsistent. Actually, every reasonable person shares Ann's predicament, since every reasonable person should be ready to confess,

(T)   At least one of my (first-order) beliefs is false,

where a person's belief is first-order when it is not about the beliefs of that person. (The restriction is needed to avoid paradox.[43]) But, alas, believing what she could express by (T) saddles our reasonable person with an inconsistent set of beliefs. One can sympathize with Quine's melancholy comment, 'I, for one, had expected better of reasonable persons.'[44] (Epistemologists who accept the possibility of inconsistent sets of justified beliefs have to face the delicate task of both properly acknowledging and carefully limiting the role of *deduction* in the justification of beliefs.)

---

[41] The example is borrowed from Richard Foley, 'Justified Inconsistent Beliefs', 249.

[42] Surprisingly, BonJour himself mentions this problem (first posed in D. C. Makinson, 'The Paradox of the Preface'), but only in one line in a footnote, where it is simply set aside (BonJour, *The Structure of Empirical Knowledge*, 240).   [43] Roy Sorensen, *Blindspots*, 23–4.

[44] Quine, *Quiddities*, 21.

Back to the coherentist conception of *truth*:[45]

(Coh) $\forall x$ (x is true $\leftrightarrow$ x belongs to a maximally coherent set of beliefs).

Let us pretend that my above attempt to spell this out left nothing to be desired. Even then, this conception of truth invites many questions. Let us briefly consider some of them.

(1) Which beliefs aspire for membership in the set? Since advocates of a coherentist conception of truth are rather reticent at this point,[46] let me give a provisional answer on their behalf: each belief held now or in the future by at least one human being is a candidate for membership in the set, and nothing else is. (Notice that question (1) does not arise for the coherentist conception of *justification* as characterized above.)

(2) Why do coherentists regard consistency as a virtue of a body of statements or beliefs? If their aim is to define the concept of truth, they'd better not answer, 'Because an inconsistent system contains at least one element which is not *true*.' The diameter of this circle would be too small. It might be thought that coherentists could easily give an alternative answer which avoids recourse to truth: 'From an inconsistent set of statements one can (classically) derive any statement, but we do not want to be committed to accepting just any statement.' So far, so good, but why do they want to avoid such a commitment? Presumably because among those statements there are many (roughly half of them) that are not *true*. Short of yet another plausible answer, coherentists should not be *definitional* alethic anti-realists.[47]

(3) Does the right-hand branch of (Coh) really tell us, as coherentists claim, what being true consists in?[48] From the shipwreck of foundationalism, at least

---

[45] What Nicholas Rescher elaborates in his book *The Coherence Theory of Truth* seems to be, rather, a coherence theory of justification, for a 'criterial' theory of truth in his sense can hardly be distinguished from a 'definitional' theory of justification.

[46] Hempel is an exception, but his answer is hardly satisfactory. He maintains that the perceptual beliefs of 'the scientists of our culture circle' actually *are* members of the set. Admittedly, some of these beliefs might contradict each other, but 'fortunately', Hempel avers, 'this possibility is not realized' ('On the Logical Positivists' Theory of Truth', 57). Scientists of other cultural circles might find this a bit chauvinistic, but let that pass. Even if Hempel's consistency assumption were (historically) correct, it would make the acceptability of coherentism dependent upon a stroke of epistemic luck.

[47] Recall QUESTION 16 in Ch. 1, Fig. 1.4.

[48] 'Truth', Blanshard maintains, '*consists* in coherence' (*NTh*, 269). There is no tension between this claim and the rejection of (Coh) as definition. Not only is an empirical claim like 'Being a lump of salt is being a lump of sodium chloride' compatible with the denial that 'sodium chloride' expresses the same concept as 'salt'; one can also consistently embrace a conceptual claim like 'Being a triangle is being a closed plane rectilinear figure whose internal angles add up to 180°', without taking 'closed plane rectilinear figure etc.' to spell out the sense of 'triangle'. See pp. 25–7 above. Blanshard, *NTh*, 272–4, ascribes the constitutive claim to Bradley. (For different readings of Bradley, cf. Baldwin, 'The Identity Theory of Truth', and Walker, 'Bradley's Theory of Truth', who also disagree with each other as to the proper interpretation.) There can be no doubt that Joachim endorsed the constitutive claim: see, for example, the passage cited on p. 383 above.

one plank ought to be saved: namely, Descartes' insight that some judgements have contents that cannot even be entertained without being true. Such Cartesian judgements (as I called them in the last subsection) falsify the general constitutive claim, since they at any rate do not owe their truth to their coherence with other beliefs. Admittedly, I could not judge that I exist, or that I am now thinking, if I were not able to make many other judgements which involve the concepts of existence or thinking or my ability to think first-person thoughts. But this only shows that the *existence* of Cartesian judgements is dependent on other judgements. The objection is that their *truth* is not due to their relation to other judgements. The same point can be made, *mutatis mutandis*, with reference to self-evident beliefs (Brentano's 'axioms'): neither the belief that a year has twelve months, nor the belief that a rose is a rose, owes its *truth* to its relations to other beliefs.[49] (This also sets limits, I think, to a coherentist theory of justification; as Frege emphasized: 'it is part of the concept of an axiom that it can be recognized as true independently of other truths.'[50])

(4) Can it be a priori excluded that the set of truth-candidates specified in (1) contains *two* maximally coherent subsets α and β such that α and β, though compatible, involve different sets of theoretical concepts which are not reducible in either direction? Suppose this possibility is actual: then there are beliefs whose truth consists in their belonging to one system and other beliefs whose truth consists in their belonging to a different system, and thus we will have two different kinds of truth, truth in α and truth in β. This diversification smacks of relativism about truth. But the situation may be even grimmer:

(5) Can it be a priori excluded that the set of truth-candidates specified in (1) contains *two* maximally coherent subsets α and β such that the belief that p is an element of α while the belief that not-p belongs to β? If this possibility cannot be excluded, then coherentism is unable to sustain the principle that contradictory beliefs cannot both be true, and this would be a sufficient ground for declaring it to be a total failure. Surely the principle, 'If it is true that p, then it is not true

---

[49] Blanshard faces only the second kind of apparent counter-examples, but I cannot see that his attempt at defusing them succeeds (*NTh*, 244, 274). In his book *The Coherence Theory of Truth*, Walker raises a purely structural objection against coherentism, which also seeks to show that the theory does not live up to its aspiration of being a general constitutive account of truth. According to Walker, the specification of the set, to which a belief allegedly must belong in order to be true, is itself a truth-candidate, but *its* truth cannot be accounted for along coherentist lines (esp. 178, 199, 210). For discussion and refinement of this objection, see C. Wright's 'Critical Study'; Walker, 'Theories of Truth', §§5–6; Wright, 'Truth: A Traditional Debate Reviewed' (henceforth 'Debate'), §5.

[50] '[*Es gehört*] *zum Begriff des Axioms, dass man zur Anerkennung seines Wahrseins nicht anderer Wahrheiten bedarf*' (Frege, *NS*, 183 (168)). Burge argues plausibly that the tension between this claim and the way Frege introduces his axioms in *Grundgesetze* is only apparent: 'Frege on Knowing the Foundations', esp. sect. II.

that not-p,' is not negotiable.[51] Instead of speculating how coherentists might protect the right-to-left half of (Coh) against this menace, let us move on and scrutinize the left-to-right half.

(6) Can something be true only if it is part of a maximally coherent set of beliefs? Two varieties of coherentism have to be considered here. Are we to regard the elements of a maximally coherent set as parts of an ideal theory which is endorsed at some time or other? If the answer is Yes, then the following objection against the left-to-right half of (Coh) obtrudes itself. There is no good reason to believe that at some time or other every discoverable truth about Shakespeare's plays or Kafka's novels, Bach's fugues or Beethoven's string quartets, Giorgione's paintings or Donatello's sculptures will have been discovered. There will always be truths about such objects that do not follow from the truths that have already been hit upon. So an ideal theory that covers all such truths is a chimera.[52] Suppose the answer is No: the elements of a maximally coherent set are *not* to be regarded as parts of an ideal theory endorsed at some time or other. Then another problem remains. Perhaps Caesar scratched his head while crossing the Rubicon, perhaps he didn't. Suppose (what is very likely in any case) that by now any information that might provide us with a reason for believing either hypothesis is irretrievably lost. This does not entail that from now on nobody will ever believe either of these hypotheses: after all, tomorrow a hypnotist might see to it that somebody acquires such a belief. It does entail, however, that no maximally coherent set of beliefs held now or in the future includes the belief that Caesar scratched his head while crossing the Rubicon or the belief that he did not do so. But is this a sufficient reason for the verdict that neither hypothesis is true?

(7a) Can something be true only if it is part of a set of *human* beliefs? There might be extraterrestrials, endowed with conceptual abilities and modes of sensory awareness that we lack, who are able to answer questions which we and our descendants are constitutionally unable even to pose.[53] Why shouldn't their answers be true?

(7b) Can something be true only if it is part of a set of *beliefs*? This question echoes one of those that arose with respect to the foundationalist conception of

---

[51] Questions (4) and (5) are prompted by Quine's famous underdetermination thesis: even all possible observations together with the best scientific methodology do not determine one particular empirical theory as uniquely best. See his *PT*, 95–101.

[52] This objection is raised in Mark Johnston, 'Objectivity Refigured: Pragmatism Without Verificationism', 90; 'Verificationism as Philosophical Narcissism', 322. In an aside, Austin anticipates the objection when he debunks 'the whole truth' about Botticelli's *La Primavera* as an 'illusory ideal' ('Truth', 130).

[53] The Alpha-Centaurians have already been put into argumentative service in earlier chapters (and they will soon have to serve us again).

truth. (Coh) restricts the realm of truths to beliefs (judgements, statements). But are only beliefs true? Isn't it extremely likely that many a truth will never even be entertained or formulated, let alone accepted or asserted? There is a true answer to the question how many commas occur in this book, but presumably nobody will ever entertain or formulate an answer to this tedious question, much less acquire or voice an opinion about it. If so, then the true answer to that question does not belong to any system of beliefs, hence a fortiori it is not a member of a set of beliefs which comply with the right-hand side of (Coh).

Coherentists can try to counter the objections under (7a) and (7b), without conjuring up Schlick's and Russell's fairy-tale objection, by rejecting the proposal made in (1). Not only human beliefs, and not only beliefs that either are or will be held, are elements of the set, a coherentist might say, but all beliefs that *would* be held if such-and-such conditions *were* fulfilled.[54] Which conditions? We will now scrutinize some answers to this question.

7.1.3 *Consensualism*

'The best definition of truth from the logical standpoint which is known to me', John Dewey once declared, 'is that of Peirce.'[55] In this subsection I shall canvass Charles Sanders Peirce's attempt to delineate the bounds of truth by what he calls 'general agreement' or 'catholic [all-embracing] consent'.[56] (In a postscript I shall comment briefly on a rather different pragmatist conception of truth and on two developments of the Peircean motif in twentieth-century philosophy.) The formula applauded by Dewey strongly suggests that the founder of American pragmatism does indeed aspire to be a *definitional* alethic anti-realist.[57]

---

[54] Cf. Joachim, 'Ideal Experience', in *NT*, 78–84; and, esp., Blackburn, *Spreading the Word*, 246 n. 12.

[55] Dewey, *Logic: The Theory of Inquiry*, 343 n. (Prima facie, at least, there is a certain tension between this declaration and the affinities between Dewey and James, which were registered in Ch. 3.5.3 above.)

[56] Peirce, 'Critical Review' (1871; of a new edition of Berkeley's works), in *CP*, vol. 8, sect. 12. Henceforth, references will be by volume number and section number: '*CP*, 8.12'.

[57] Cf. also the passage quoted on p. 25 above. If Peirce *is* a definitional alethic anti-realist, then he has to face the forceful part of Alston's objection against alethic anti-realism (which was discussed in Ch. 1). Wiggins maintains that it is 'strictly unnecessary for [Peirce] to give a strict analytical definition of truth' ('Postscript 3', 341 n.); his pupil Cheryl Misak, makes this one of the central contentions in her book *Truth and the End of Inquiry*. (It is noteworthy that her evidence is culled from texts that Peirce wrote *after* the revision of his view, which I shall describe below.) Commenting on a passage in which Peirce declares that 'truth is nothing more nor less than ...', Wiggins poses a rhetorical question: 'If I say that the character of being red is nothing more nor less than the character of being the colour thought by blind people to be well grasped by a comparison with the sound of a trumpet, do I have to be interpreted as offering a definition?' ('C. S. Peirce: Belief, Truth, and Going from the Known to the Unknown', 15). Surely not, but still, if you are right in what you are saying, then nothing can have the 'former' character without having the 'latter', and vice versa, for they are supposed to be the same. Similarly, if Peirce is, as Wiggins says, 'equating truth ... with a certain character' (ibid., 16), then he is committed to the

It occurs at the end of the following passage from his 1878 paper, 'How to Make Our Ideas Clear':

[T]he followers of science [. . .][58] may at first obtain different results, but, as each perfects his method and his processes, the results are found to move steadily together toward a destined center. . . . Different minds may set out with the most antagonistic views, but the progress of investigation carries them by a force outside of themselves to one and the same conclusion. . . . The opinion which is fated* to be ultimately agreed to by all who investigate, is what we mean by the truth.

* Fate means merely that which is sure to come true, and can nohow be avoided. . . . We are all fated to die. (*CP*, 5.407)

This sounds like a plea for an alethic fatalism of the cheerful kind. Presumably it 'can nohow be avoided' that one day all human life will be extinct. Does Peirce really want to suggest (a) that *all* beliefs which the last human investigators actually share are true and (b) that *only* those beliefs are true?[59] As to contention (a), why shouldn't the last researchers pass away with a shared prejudice that they might have overcome if only they had been given a chance? As to contention (b), isn't it more than likely that by that time ever so many truths will have fallen into oblivion? (At the 'Omega Point', so we are told by the cosmologists John Barrow and Frank Tipler, life 'will have stored an infinite amount of information, including all bits of information which it is logically possible to know'; and they add: 'A modern-day theologian might wish to say that the totality of life at the Omega Point is . . . omniscient.'[60] Although there is no restriction to *human* life, one cannot but wonder whether scientific cosmology should persuade anyone to say this.) Furthermore, (b) implies that only beliefs actually held at some time or another are true, and we have seen reason to deny this. As we read on, we soon begin to suspect that we may not yet have grasped what Peirce is getting at:

Our perversity and that of others may indefinitely postpone the settlement of opinion; it might even conceivably cause an arbitrary proposition to be universally accepted as

---

claims that nothing can be true without having that character and that nothing can have that character without being true. I have been careful to make my objections against the view Peirce held in 1878 largely independent of whether his biconditional is meant to be a 'strict analytical definition' of the concept of truth or rather, as Wiggins puts it, a 'fix upon the character of truth' (ibid., 17).

[58] I skip here an example from the history of science, which illustrates how a sequence of measurements can settle down to one basic value. Peirce was a distinguished experimenter. He published many papers and a book (*Photometric Researches*, 1878) on topics in astronomy and the theory of measurement.

[59] Cf. Russell's astonishment at this suggestion: 'Dewey's New *Logic*', 145 (and Dewey's 'Rejoinder', 571–4).

[60] Barrow and Tipler, *The Anthropic Cosmological Principle* (Oxford, 1986), as quoted in Kvanvig, 'The Knowability Paradox', 499 n.

long as the human race should last. Yet even that would not change the nature of the belief, which alone could be the result of investigation carried sufficiently far; and if, after the extinction of our race, another should arise with faculties and disposition for investigation, that true opinion must be the one which they would ultimately come to. '*Truth crushed to earth shall rise again*,' and the opinion which would finally result from investigation does not depend on how anybody may actually think. (*CP*, 5.408)[61]

This suggests that the right-hand side of Peirce's *consensus* conception of truth is to be formulated as a subjunctive conditional:[62]

(Cons)   ∀x (x is true ↔

x is a belief that all who investigate *would* finally share

if their investigations *were* pursued long enough and well enough).

This answers the first as well as the last objection posed above. ('Her belief that p is never held by anyone' has no chance of yielding a truth, but 'The belief that p is never held by anyone' may very well express a truth, for it means only that nobody ever believes that p.) The question about oblivion, however, will soon have to occupy us again. It is one of several challenges that (Cons) has to face. Let us start with the right-to-left half of the biconditional.

(1) Does satisfaction of the Peircean condition really guarantee truth? Suppose a minute error (concerning the date of the publication of a certain book, say) occurs in a bibliography, it is overlooked by those who know better, and then the same mistake is repeated again and again whenever that book is referred to. Why should we assume that this trifle of a mistake would be detected if enquiry were pursued long and well enough, whether by humans, extraterrestrials, or robots? If Peirce were to reply, 'Because investigation would not have been carried sufficiently far before this error was detected', then circularity threatens. When has investigation been 'carried sufficiently far'? Only if no error remains undetected, i.e. only if solely *truths* are held to be true. If Peirce is a definitional alethic anti-realist, he cannot make light of this circularity. And then, why should indefinitely prolonged and maximally careful bibliographical research have a chance to set the matter straight? Perhaps Peirce would say of the early stage of that tiny error's proliferation that it was due to a 'perversity'

---

[61] As to non-human enquirers, compare the earlier statement in Peirce's Berkeley review: 'the catholic consent which constitutes the truth is by no means to be limited to men in this earthly life or to the human race, but extends to the whole communion of minds to which we belong, including some probably whose senses are very different from ours' (*CP*, 8.18 [1871]).

[62] This 'subjunctivization' became a constant feature of Peirce's reflections on truth. 'I hold that truth's independence of individual opinions is due (so far as there is any "truth") to its being the pre-destined result to which sufficient inquiry *would* ultimately lead' (*CP*, 5.494 [1907]; his italics). See also *CP*, 6.485 [1908].

of the investigators. (Whatever that may exactly mean,[63] it does seem to imply
a fault on their part.) But after that early stage, a discovery of the mistake may
be prevented, once and for all, by bad luck: all evidence to the contrary may
have been obliterated for ever. Let us now ponder the left-to-right half of (Cons)
and ask:

(2) Does truth really demand satisfaction of the Peircean condition? In the
case of Cartesian and self-evident beliefs, being true can scarcely consist in meeting this condition, for they simply do not call for any future agreement: you
hold the belief that you are sometimes conscious, or that a month is longer than
a week, come what may, and reasonably so. Furthermore, some questions may
be such that they can be enquired into only by beings with a certain cognitive
equipment. All extraterrestrials and robots may be wired up in such a way that
they will never ever recognize the parody of a literary style or the variation of a
certain musical theme for what they are. But then no truly catholic consent is
to be expected in this area. Finally, consider the following plain fact of which
Moore reminds us:

There seems to be an immense number of true ideas [thoughts], which occur but once
and to one person.... I may, for instance, idly count the dots on the back of a card, and
arrive at a true idea of their number; and yet, perhaps, I may never think of their number again, nor anybody else ever know it. We are all, it seems to me, constantly noticing
trivial details, and getting true thoughts about them, of which we never think again,
and which nobody else ever gets. ('William James' *Pragmatism*', 111)[64]

Is it reasonable to believe that scientists would unanimously answer the question how many dots were on the back of that card, if only research were pursued
long and well enough? (Perhaps, sitting by the firseside, Moore threw the card
into the fire after his idle count.) Let me call this the *Minima Trivialia* Objection.[65]
Actually, Peirce anticipated this challenge:

But I may be asked what I have to say to all the minute facts of history, forgotten never
to be recovered, to the lost books of the ancients, to the buried secrets....[66] To this I
reply that...[A] *it is unphilosophical to suppose that, with regard to any given question (which has any
clear meaning), investigation would not bring forth a solution of it, if it were carried far enough.* Who would
have said, a few years ago, that we could ever know of what substances stars are made

[63] The point of the opening statement of the Peirce quotation above is repeated in *CP*, 5.430 [1905], but
again Peirce does not pause to explain what he means by 'perversity'.
[64] Russell makes essentially the same point when he says: 'During breakfast, I may have a well-
grounded conviction that I am eating eggs and bacon. I doubt whether scientists 2,000 years hence will
investigate whether this was the case, and if they did their opinions would be worth less than mine'
('Dewey's New *Logic*', 146; cf. 154). In his 'Rejoinder' Dewey does not reply to this Objection.
[65] It might as well be called the British Objection: Ayer repeats it in *The Origins of Pragmatism*, 37.
[66] At this point Peirce quotes Thomas Gray; I cite the same stanza below as an epigraph to sect. 7.3.

whose light may have been longer in reaching us than the human race has existed? Who can be sure of what we shall know in a few hundred years? Who can guess what would be the result of continuing the pursuit of science for ten thousand years, with the activity of the last hundred? And if it were to go on for a million, or a billion, or any number of years you please, [B] *how is it possible to say that there is any question which might not ultimately be solved?* (*CP*, 5.409; bracketed letters and italics added)

Unfortunately, in this reply Peirce only mentions problems that tend to excite scientists—and not humdrum questions concerning 'minute facts of history' such as this one: how many dots were on the back of the card Moore looked at on a certain winter evening in 1908? So the *Minima Trivialia* Objection is not really faced. It is very improbable indeed that future researchers will ever ask, let alone bother to answer that question, and even if they were to, why should their answer not conflict with the answer Moore could have given in his epistemically far more favourable position? Many a truth isn't worth a candle, and the correct answer to our dull question is such a truth if anything is. But a conception of truth must cover trifling observations as well as bold scientific hypotheses. Plato knew that. His deepest reflections on truth, in the *Sophist*, are focused on the example 'Theaetetus is sitting.'

In any case, the conclusion suggested by the rhetorical question in the sentence I marked as [B] does not follow from the premiss given in [A]: from the observation that it would be unphilosophical to suppose, with regard to a given question, that *it* would never be answered in a sufficiently prolonged enquiry, it does not follow that it would be unphilosophical to suppose that *there are* questions that have this property. (I could not justifiably assert of anyone that *he or she* is a spy, but that does not imply that I could not justifiably assert that *there are* spies.)

It is of more than historical interest that, and how, Peirce's account of truth altered after the publication of 'How to Make Our Ideas Clear'. In the original text of that paper the followers of science were said to be 'fully persuaded' that, with respect to each significant question, one day a stable catholic consent will be reached, and the content of this alleged persuasion was called 'a great law'. But when Peirce thought of republishing the paper in 1903 he changed both passages: now researchers were said to be 'animated by the cheerful hope' for a final consensus, and 'great law' was replaced by 'great hope'. Already a decade earlier Peirce had cleared his conception of truth from all prognostic pretensions:

We cannot be quite sure that the community ever will settle down to an unalterable conclusion upon any given question. Even if they do so for the most part, we have no reason to think the unanimity will be quite complete, nor can we rationally presume any overwhelming *consensus* of opinion will be reached upon every question. All that we are entitled to assume is in the form of a *hope* that such conclusion may be substantially reached concerning *the particular questions with which our inquiries are busied*. ('Rejoinder to Carus' (1893), *CP*, 6.610; last italics mine)

If one *hopes* that p, then one is uncertain whether p, but one believes that it is possible that p, and one desires that p. Without the belief in the possibility of a final catholic consent with regard to the question we set out to enquire about and without the desire for such a consent, Peirce plausibly contends, 'we should not trouble ourselves to make the inquiry'.[67] An enquirer must have such a hope, Peirce says, 'for the same reason that a general who has to capture a position or see his country ruined, must go on the hypothesis that there is some way in which he can and shall capture it'.[68] Now in my formulation of (Cons) I have already defused the alethic fatalism, apparently endorsed in our first quotation from 'How to Make Our Ideas Clear', by 'subjunctivizing' it along the lines suggested in our second quotation from that paper. But with respect to the subjunctive conditional that under certain circumstances such-and-such would happen, it also makes a difference whether one uses it to make an assertion or to voice a hope. In his work after 1880, Peirce seems to subscribe to the following (one way) conditionals:

(C_1) $\forall x$ ((x is a belief such that all who enquired into the question to which x is an answer would finally share x, if their investigations were pursued long and well enough) $\rightarrow$ x is true),

(C_2) $\forall x$ (x is true $\rightarrow$ (x is a belief such that *it is reasonable to hope that* all who enquired into the question to which x is an answer would finally share x, if their investigations were pursued long and well enough)).

Conditional (C_1) is open to the objection posed above under (1) on p. 395. Is (C_2) plausible? In the case of Cartesian judgements and of self-evident beliefs this requirement seems to be as pointless as its predecessor. Moreover, the *Minima Trivialia* Objection shows, I think, that (C_2) is too restrictive anyway. Suppose, once again, that on a winter evening in 1908, in the solitude of his study, Moore scribbled a few dots on the back of a card, idly counted them, threw the card into the fire, and then forgot the result of his count without having told the result to anyone else. Now what about the proposition that there were eight scribbled dots on that card? Under the circumstances I just described, it would be unreasonable to assert this proposition (or its negation) either now or in the future, and surely we would not trouble ourselves to enquire into the question how many scribbled dots were on that card. After all, we have no reason to hope that all investigators who looked long enough and well enough into this question would end up with

---

[67] Peirce, *CP*, 3.432 [1896].   [68] Ibid., 7.219 [1901].

the same answer, because we know only too well that no enquiry would yield *any* answer. But does that deprive our proposition of a truth-value? A long time ago Moore *knew*, if only for a short time, which truth-value that proposition has. So it looks as if (C_2) should be replaced by a claim about the rationality of a certain kind of truth-related project:

$(C_2{}^*)$ $\forall x$ (*it is reasonable to inquire whether* x is true $\rightarrow$ it is reasonable to hope that (all who enquired into this question would finally assign the same truth-value to x if their investigation were pursued long and well enough)).

This is very plausible, but it is no longer a constraint on *truth*.[69]

****

Let me finish this subsection with a comparative postscript, including (1) a critique of (what seems to me to be) James's conception of truth, (2) some comments on a Peircean motif in Wiggins's writings on truth, and (3) a laconic remark on a variant of Peirce's view once advocated by Habermas.

[1] William James's theses about truth have 'evoked howls of indignation as well as exaggerated praise' among 'careless readers', as Putnam somewhat indignantly puts it.[70] (One may wonder whether Putnam would count Peirce also among the careless readers: after all, Peirce so much disliked James's popularization of pragmatism in general and his conception of truth in particular that he invented a new name for his own philosophy: 'pragmaticism', ugly enough, he hoped, 'to be safe from kidnappers'.[71]) Here is a mosaic of quotations from James's most controversial book:[72]

Truth, as any dictionary will tell you, is a property of certain of our ideas. It means their 'agreement', as falsity means their disagreement, with 'reality'. (*Pragmatism* [1907], 96)

What does agreement with reality mean? It means verifiability. Verifiability means ability to guide us prosperously through experience. (ibid., 8)

[T]ruth is one species of good. . . . The true is the name of whatever proves itself to be good in the way of belief, and good, too, for definite, assignable reasons. (ibid., 42)

---

[69] Christopher Hookway argues in *Truth, Rationality, and Pragmatism* that a contention like $(C_2{}^*)$ is at the centre of Peirce's mature reflections on truth, or rather on the search for truth. If Hookway gets him right, then Peirce does not really aim at a constitutive account of truth and hence can afford to disregard the truth, or otherwise, of propositions that are not matters of any serious enquiry.

[70] Putnam, 'James's Theory of Truth', 166 (alluding to Russell as one of the indignant critics and to Rorty as one of the misguided enthusiasts). As was mentioned on p. 32 n. 81, Putnam himself is far from accepting James's theory: he just wants it to be given a fair hearing.

[71] Peirce, *CP*, 5.414 [1905].   [72] The first two were cited above on pp. 171–2.

'The true,' to put it very briefly, is only the expedient in the way of our thinking.... Expedient in almost any fashion; and expedient in the long run and on the whole of course; for what meets expediently all the experience in sight won't necessarily meet all farther experiences equally satisfactorily. Experience, as we know, has ways of boiling over, and making us correct our present formulas. (ibid., 106)

[U]ntrue beliefs work as perniciously in the long run as true beliefs work beneficially. (ibid., 110)

James confesses to be a *definitional* alethic anti-realist:

I say 'working' is what the 'truth' of our ideas means, and call it a definition.... I call a belief true, and define its truth to mean its working. ('Two English Critics' [1909], 148–9)[73]

One would like to know how this (gesture at a) definition and the definition in the dictionaries that is appealed to in the first quotation are related. Perhaps James would call the definition reported there a 'nominal' definition, as Kant famously did,[74] and the one hinted at here a 'real' definition of the concept of truth. In our context, I think, the second kind of 'definition' is best seen as an attempt at specifying a different concept which can be known a priori to be co-extensive with the concept of truth, and clarity would be served by refusing to call it a definition.[75]

From the bewildering multiplicity of formulations in *Pragmatism*[76] a charitable reader can distil what might be called the *satisfaction* theory of truth:

(Sat)　$\forall x$ (x is true $\leftrightarrow$ $\exists t$ (x is a belief acquired at time t &
　　　　　x meets satisfactorily all experiences at t and after t)).

Here is a first problem with (Sat). For James, truth-value bearers are believings, beliefs taken as identity-dependent on believers.[77] Now unlike Peirce, and

---

[73] Cf. also James, *The Meaning of Truth*, 120.　　[74] Kant, *Kritik der reinen Vernunft*, B 82.

[75] See pp. 25–7 above, on strength (III).

[76] As McTaggart said in his 'Critical Notice' of *Pragmatism*, 'Dr James, though always picturesque, is very far from lucid' (104). Several passages in that book, and especially the argument for the truth of theism, seem to confirm McTaggart's, Moore's, and Russell's suspicion that, according to James, it is true that p iff it makes for happiness to believe that p. (Even Dewey, surely as fair a critic of James as one could wish for, got nervous at this point: see his *Essays in Experimental Logic*, 319–20.) McTaggart has no difficulty in making fun of this biconditional: 'Suppose that X sees a lion on the point of devouring, as he supposes, a stranger. X is about to shoot the lion, when he recognises that the victim is not a stranger, but his dearest friend. In his increased agitation his hand trembles, and his bullet kills his friend, instead of the lion' ('Critical Notice', 107). That X recognizes that the victim is his friend entails that he acquires a true belief. But X's belief seems not to contribute to anyone's happiness, with the possible exception of the lion. (Neither in the short nor in the long run, if we assume that the victim was a universally loved benefactor of mankind.)

[77] See Chisholm, 'William James's Theory of Truth', and Putnam's homonymous paper, 182.

deliberately so, James does not formulate his constraint in terms of a subjunctive conditional.[78] So the same objection obtrudes itself which I first raised with respect to Brentano's (Found): the domain of truths is implausibly restricted to beliefs actually held at some time or other.

In James's usage, the term 'satisfaction' is meant to cover emotional as well as intellectual satisfaction, and it is notoriously hard to figure out what relations he takes to obtain between these kinds of satisfaction. (When one's belief that something terrible is about to happen is confirmed, or disconfirmed, the two kinds of satisfaction seem to come drastically apart.) But we do not have to dwell on this question,[79] for the second problem with (Sat) arises anyway. It is due to the fact, much emphasized by Moore, that some beliefs simply '*have no run at all.*'[80] That is to say, some beliefs are such that they are held only by one person and only for a very short time (in the most dramatic case: because of the sudden death of that single believer just after he has acquired the belief). Let us call such belief-states 'ephemeral', and let us focus on the intellectual side of satisfaction. If 'x meets satisfactorily all future experiences' means that x is not unsettled by any future experiences, then *every* ephemeral belief-state somebody is currently in will trivially satisfy the condition specified on the right-hand side of (Sat), for a state that no longer obtains cannot be undermined by subsequent experiences. If 'x meets satisfactorily all future experiences' means, rather, that x is corroborated by all future experiences, then *no* ephemeral belief-state somebody is currently in complies with this constraint, for a state that no longer obtains cannot be confirmed by subsequent experiences. Thus, under the first reading all ephemeral beliefs are true, whereas under the second none is true. I venture to say that from this theory one can get no satisfaction.

Notoriously, critics of James risk being accused of caricaturing his conception of truth. Nobody phrased this reproach as wittily as James himself did: 'Whether such a pragmatist as [described by my critic] exists, I know not, never having met with the beast.... But, in setting up the weird type, he quotes words from me; so, in order not to be classed by some reader along with so asinine a being, I will

---

[78] Putnam, 'James's Theory of Truth', 170, 178–9, explains why James would not accept (Cons). In this respect, Putnam's reading of James differs sharply from Chisholm's.

[79] It is here that Dewey asked James for clarification: *Essays in Experimental Logic*, 316–24. Invoking the emotional sense of 'satisfaction', James cheerfully embraces the most astounding and disturbing consequences of his view of truth. Consider this one: if men were to believe that women are female zombies or 'automatic sweethearts', to use his own phrase for this sexist idea, 'performing all feminine offices as tactfully and sweetly as if a soul were in [them]', then men's craving for 'inward' recognition and admiration of women would not be satisfied. So 'belief in an automatic sweetheart would not *work*', and, consequently, it is not true that women are 'soulless bodies' (*The Meaning of Truth*, 103). That's reassuring, isn't it?

[80] Moore, 'William James' *Pragmatism*', 122.

reassert my view of truth once more.'[81] Let me somewhat defiantly rejoin (on behalf of Professor Pratt, who was the addressee of this remark,[82] and myself): if among James's ever so many reaffirmations of his view, there is one that does not have weird consequences, I have not yet seen it.

[2] David Wiggins maintains a thesis about truth which, admittedly, has a certain Peircean flavour. Wiggins unequivocally denies (C_1),[83] but he takes the following conditional to reveal what he calls a Mark of Truth, i.e. a condition of which one can know a priori that any truth-candidate x has to satisfy it if x is to be true:[84]

If x is true, then x will under favourable circumstances command a convergence of opinion among those properly placed to judge the matter in question, and the best explanation of the existence of this convergence will require the actual truth of x. ('Indefinibilist', 329)[85]

Wiggins's convergence constraint states a necessary condition of truth. What if the convergence of opinion as regards a certain question were universal (among humans)? Kant has argued that this would give us a good, though not a conclusive, reason for ascribing truth to that opinion,[86] and his argument also relies on an inference to the best explanation: if the statement that the object A is F were to win acceptance among all human beings, then this would be a prima facie good reason for assuming that it is true, for a satisfactory explanation of this convergence may have to advert to A's really being F. In the passage I am about to quote, Kant's controlled play on the word 'agreement' is noteworthy: almost in one breath it is used to refer to object-based correspondence and to a consensus between thinkers.

Wahrheit . . . beruht auf der Übereinstimmung mit dem Objecte, in Ansehung dessen folglich die Urtheile eines jeden Verstandes einstimmig sein müssen. . . . Der Probirstein des Fürwahrhaltens . . . ist also . . . die Möglichkeit, dasselbe mitzutheilen, und das Fürwahrhalten für jedes Menschen Vernunft gültig zu befinden; denn alsdann ist wenigstens eine Vermuthung, der Grund der Einstimmung aller Urtheile ungeachtet der

---

[81] James, 'Professor Pratt on Truth', 90–1.

[82] As the reader may have already noticed in the previous chapter, I have a soft spot for Professor Pratt.

[83] Wiggins, 'Postscript 3', 340.

[84] In 'Replies', Wiggins explicitly distances himself from what I call definitional alethic anti-realism (sect. 67), and he emphasizes that he has no definitional aspirations whatsoever as regards the concept of truth (sect. 59). So he takes the 'marks' he enumerates not to be constituents of the concept of truth. (For this very reason, I have criticized Wiggins's claim that his 'marks' are what Frege calls *Merkmale*: see my 'Constituents of Concepts' and pp. 132–3 above.)

[85] For earlier attempts to formulate this constraint see Wiggins, 'Substantial', 206–8, and 'Moral', 147.

[86] For a strangely unguarded remark to the effect that acceptance by all human beings *guarantees* truth, see Aristotle, *Nicomachean Ethics*, x. 2: 1172^b36–1173^a1.

Verschiedenheit der Subjecte unter einander werde auf ... dem Objecte beruhen. ... [Manchmal aber kann man ein] Fürwahrhalten als eine Begebenheit in unserem Gemüthe erklären, ohne dazu die Beschaffenheit des Objects nöthig zu haben. [Truth depends on agreement with the object concerning which the judgements of all intellects have to be in agreement with each other. ... The touchstone of belief ... is the possibility of communicating it and of finding it to be valid for all human reason. For there is then at least a presumption that the ground of the agreement of all judgements with each other, notwithstanding the difference between the thinkers, rests ... upon the object. ... [By contrast, sometimes] one can explain the occurrence of a belief in our mind without any recourse to the properties of the object.] (*Kritik der reinen Vernunft*, B 848–9)

Sometimes even a convergence of opinion concerning the F-ness of A can be explained 'without any recourse to the properties of the object': the consensus may owe its existence, for example, to the gullibility, or to the propensity to follow the dictates of fashion, of most of those who take A to be F.

Wiggins's proviso 'under favourable circumstances [i.e. of appraisal]' in his convergence constraint on truth is of utmost importance. One reason, which he does not consider, is that it protects his constraint against the *Minima Trivialia* Objection. Ever since Moore threw the notorious card into the fire, the conditions for an enquiry into the 'how many dots' question are as unfavourable as can be, but Wiggins's constraint allows for truths that by now have irrevocably lost rational acceptability. The second reason is this:

Some truths may be unknowable. In that case there are no sufficiently favourable conditions of investigation. The claim that [the convergence constraint] is a mark of truth leaves it open whether such favourable conditions always exist. ('Moral', 149)

Wiggins's constraint seems not to exclude that some truths (which we can comprehend) may always be beyond rational acceptability. But then, unlike Peirce, he is *not* an alethic anti-realist.[87]

[3] In his paper '*Wahrheitstheorien*', Jürgen Habermas championed a variant of Peirce's conception, which he called 'the consensus theory of truth'. Its central tenet was

---

[87] Here is a way of making this more clearly visible. The schemata 'P → (Q → R)' und '(P & Q) → R' are interderivable; the Wiggins passage cited at the start of subsection [2] above is a stylistic variant of a sentence which instantiates the first schema; hence the following statement is logically equivalent with the convergence constraint as formulated in that quotation: *If x is true and conditions for inquiry into the question to which x is an answer are favourable, then x will command convergence and....* Wright claims that 'each [of Wiggins's Marks of Truth] is a feature of superassertibility' (cf. 'Introduction' to his *Realism. Meaning and Truth*, 40, and 'Assertibility', 424). Now Wiggins allows for the possibility that something is true although conditions that are sufficiently favourable for its appraisal never obtain. Can something be 'superassertible' (hence a fortiori assertible) although etc.? The notion of superassertibility will be explained and briefly discussed in sect. 7.2.2.

something like this: a claim x is true iff x would finally be accepted by all parties if an exchange of arguments concerning the question to which x is an answer were to take place in an 'ideal speech-situation'. Consequently, Habermas's reflections culminated in an attempt to determine what the ideality of an ideal speech-situation consists in. In my opinion, this theory is open to the same objections, or variants thereof, which I raised against Peirce's consensus conception of truth. In any case, Habermas himself has recanted, and in '*Wahrheit und Rechtfertigung*' he has usefully summarized his reasons.[88] Apparently following Rorty's footsteps, he sees not only Apel,[89] but also Putnam (more precisely, the Putnam of the 1980s, whose more recent anti-anti-realist turn seems to have escaped his attention) in the same boat as his earlier self. As for Putnam, I disagree. In the next section we will see that his (interim) position was less Peircean than Rorty and Habermas think. It is fraught with its own difficulties, but it does not come to grief over the objections that were lethal to the consensus theories of truth once propagated in Frankfurt.

7.2 'A Long Journey from Realism back to Realism'

hilary, n. (*from* hilary term)   A very brief but significant period in the intellectual career of a distinguished philosopher. 'Oh, that's what I thought three or four hilaries ago.'

(D. Dennett (ed.), *The Philosophical Lexicon*, Newark: American Philos. Ass., 1987)

By the 1980s Hilary Putnam had moved from his earlier 'Realism' to a very different position, which he was drawn into calling '*Internal* Realism' (and which he would have liked to have called 'Pragmatic Realism'). This move caused consternation among many of his followers and made them write articles with titles such as 'Realism and the Renegade Putnam'. One strand in his new position was a certain account of truth. According to this account, truth is somehow epistemically constrained. Since I have subsumed such views under the label 'Alethic *Anti*-Realism', I'd better forestall terminological confusion: henceforth, I shall call the 'internal realist' account of truth 'Internalism' (as Putnam himself occasionally does), and I shall refer to its creator and leading advocate as 'Interim Putnam'. Internalism saw the light of the day in 1981, in chapter 3 of

---

[88] Habermas, '*Wahrheit und Rechtfertigung*', 256–7 (trans. 44–5).
[89] Cf. Apel, '*Fallibilismus, Konsenstheorie der Wahrheit und Letztbegründung*'.

Reason, Truth and History.[90] At that time Putnam seems to have thought that without imposing an epistemic constraint on truth one could not break the spell of that many-faceted doctrine he called 'Metaphysical Realism',[91] but this alleged connection is not our topic. What *is* highly pertinent to our topic is the way Interim Putnam tried for ten years to protect his account of truth against various misunderstandings (which were only partly due to certain features of his original exposition). Yet in spite of all his efforts at clarification, people kept on characterizing Internalism as follows: 'Putnam, in the tradition of C. S. Peirce, holds that [truth is] warranted assertibility in the limit of an ideal science' (thus Smart). Putnam's conception of truth, we were told, 'involves... the idea of completion of all empirical enquiry' (thus Wright). Internalism was then criticized on the basis of this reading: as to 'Putnam's neo-Peircean account of truth, I cannot imagine my descendants saying: "At last! Inquiry is finally over!" ' (thus Rorty).[92]

In section 7.2.1 I shall first try to reconstruct the view Putnam *really* held in the 1980s. Then I will point out that Internalism, though admittedly 'inspired by the position Dummett calls "global antirealism" ',[93] is in some respects more 'moderate' than the latter, and I will go on to compare Internalism with the kindred conceptions of truth that can be found in Goodman and Wright (section 7.2.2). Finally, I shall present reasons for dissatisfaction with Internalism and show that, and why, Putnam unambiguously recanted it in his 1992 papers (section 7.2.3).[94] (As far as I know, no article with the title 'Anti-Realism and the Renegade Putnam' has yet been published.[95]) Putnam came to use the label

---

[90] Further pertinent texts by '*Interim*' Putnam are 'A Defence of Internal Realism' (1982), *Realism and Reason*, 'Introduction' and ch. 4 (1983b), *Representation and Reality*, ch. 7 (1988), 'Why Is a Philosopher?' (1989), *Realism With a Human Face*, 'Preface' (1990), and, finally, 'Reply to Terry Horgan' (1991b). (In finding my way through Putnam's writings I have profited from the well-documented discussion in Richard Schantz, *Wahrheit, Referenz und Realismus*, chs. 11 and 12.) In this chapter I shall refer to Putnam's work simply as 'year: page number' (adding where necessary a letter to the first numeral). The corresponding titles can be found in this note and in n. 94 below. Full details are given in the Bibliography.

[91] 1981: 49; 1982: 30.

[92] Two of my quotations are taken from reviews of Putnam, *Realism and Reason*: Smart, 'Review', 534, Rorty, 'Life at the End of Inquiry', 7. The 'Introduction' of the book under review was designed, among other things, to prevent this very reading. Wright's remark in *T&O*, 68, is rather surprising, for a few pages earlier he had reported that 'Putnam himself has protested against a Peircean reading of his discussion' (45). In 'Truth as Sort of Epistemic: Putnam's Peregrinations' (henceforth 'Epistemic'), 336–9, and 'Minimalism', 761–3, he sets the matter straight.   [93] 1994c: 17.

[94] Pertinent texts by '*Realism Regained*' Putnam include 'Reply to Gary Ebbs' (1992a), 'Reply to David Anderson' (1992b), 'Reply to Richard Miller' (1992c), 'The Permanence of William James' (1992d), 'Blackburn on Internal Realism' (1994a), 'Michael Dummett on Realism and Idealism' (1994b), 'Sense, Nonsense, and the Senses' (1994c), 'Pragmatism' (1995), 'Comment on WK's Paper' (2002). I have drawn the title of sect. 7.2 from Putnam's self-description in 1994c: 49.

[95] Though, apart from its more restrained title, Wright's 'Epistemic' fits this bill.

'common-sense realism' for the position he has occupied ever since. Since he is a very mobile target, I shall be at pains to document his movements (since 1981) carefully.

7.2.1 *'Idealized' rational acceptability*

According to Interim Putnam, *truth is a kind of rational acceptability*. Instead of 'rational acceptability' (or 'justifiability'[96]), he often uses the Deweyan phrase 'warranted assertibility',[97] and, if we are to believe Wright, it does not really matter which of these locutions we use:[98]

Naturally, there can be conversational or social reasons why a belief which one is warranted in holding had better not be expressed in a particular context. But if we are concerned only with *epistemic* justification, then each of one's warranted beliefs corresponds to a justified possible assertion and vice versa. ('Introduction', 37)

This 'correspondence', which is presumably to be taken as a matter of conceptual necessity, has to be characterized carefully. It is *not* true that necessarily, for any time t, if something can be justifiably believed or rationally accepted at t, then it can also be warrantedly asserted *at t*. One day there may be a prearranged intercontinental minute's silence. It is common knowledge, especially among obsessive non-stop talkers and writers, that one would risk one's life if one were to make any assertion once that minute has started. Now suppose the global minute's silence has begun ten seconds before t_0. Under these circumstances it is rational to accept at t_0 the proposition that is then expressed by the sentence 'Nobody is asserting anything now.' But this proposition is not warrantedly assertible at t_0, for if you were to assert it then, you would falsify the content of your linguistic act by performing it. Does this refute Wright's 'correspondence' claim? It does not if, as I have argued in an earlier chapter, the very same proposition can be expressed *at another time*, e.g. by 'Nobody was asserting anything then.'[99] In what follows I shall stick to the notion of rational acceptability.

Truth cannot be identified with rational acceptability *sans phrase*, 'for any number of reasons'.[100] Here is one of them. Yesterday we said, 'Ben is in pain', and in view of his behaviour, what we said was rationally acceptable. But by now we have come to suspect that he was shamming, hence we begin to doubt the truth of what we reasonably accepted. In so doing, we obviously reckon with

---

[96] e.g. 1983b: 85.   [97] e.g. 1983b: xviii, 167.

[98] Commenting on Putnam, he says, 'We may take it that this [i.e. *rational acceptability*] is the notion which is now standardly called *assertibility*' ('Epistemic', 337 n. (= 'Minimalism', 784 n. 17)).

[99] See above, p. 288 with n. 105, and pp. 311–12 on (K. 3).

[100] 1983b: 84. All these reasons count a fortiori against Habermas's erstwhile contention that 'truth *means* warranted assertibility' ('*Wahrheitstheorien*', 160; cf. also 135, 153).

the possibility that truth and rational acceptability may come apart. Putnam's most prominent argument to the same conclusion, his Argument from Stability (as I shall call it), proceeds as follows:[101]

[A] Truth is supposed to be a property of a statement that cannot be lost, whereas justification can be lost.

[B] The statement *The earth is flat* was, very likely, rationally acceptable 3,000 years ago; but it is not rationally acceptable today.

[C] Yet it would be wrong to say that *the earth is flat* was *true* 3,000 years ago; for that would mean that the earth has changed its shape.

[D] In fact, rational acceptability is ... tensed. (1981: 55; bracketed letters inserted. [P.1])[102]

There is a certain oscillation in this passage which threatens to spoil Putnam's point: if a 'statement' cannot lose the property of being true [A], how could one *ever* correctly maintain that a 'statement' was true many years ago but is not true now [C]? Let me try to rephrase the argument in such a way that it sidesteps the eternalism/temporalism issue we explored in Chapter 5. Suppose that our sentence 'The earth is flat' once expressed something true but does not do so now, although at both times its conventional linguistic meaning is the same and at both times the planet we live on is referred to. From this we could conclude that the earth has changed its shape in the meantime. But this conclusion does *not* follow from the assumption that our sentence (with meaning and reference kept constant) once expressed something rationally acceptable but does not do so now. So truth is not the same as rational acceptability *simpliciter*.

The Argument from Stability is meant to forestall a too simple-minded conception of an epistemic constraint on truth. Putnam goes on to make a more ambitious claim for his argument:

What this shows ... is ... that truth is an *idealization* of rational acceptability. We speak as if there were such things as epistemically ideal conditions, and we call a statement 'true' if it would be justified under such conditions. (1981: 55; [P.2])

Surely the first statement is an overstatement. The argument in [P.1] hardly *shows* that truth is idealized rational acceptability. At best, it shows that this identification

---

[101] In the remainder of this chapter quotations from Putnam will be labelled, and referred to, as [P.1], [P.2], etc.

[102] Just to set the record straight let me register here some anticipations of the Argument from Stability: Carnap, '*Wahrheit und Bewährung*' (presented at the International Congress of Scientific Philosophy held in Paris in 1935, which we had reason to mention on pp. 176, 191 n. 56), 119, 122–3; Ezorsky, 'Truth in Context', 133–4; and, finally, Goodman, *Ways of Worldmaking*, 123–5.

is not open to the same objection as the identification of truth with rational acceptability *sans phrase*.

Let us pause to consider two further arguments against this identification. The first one is Dummett's Argument from Embedding.[103] My dramatization of Dummett's point makes use of what I take to be his most convincing example, namely two kinds of future-directed assertions and beliefs. You would now be justified in believing and asserting that

(1)   Ben *will* get married next Monday at noon

if and only if you were also justified now in believing and asserting that

(2)   Ben *is going to* get married next Monday at noon.

The rational-acceptability (and warranted-assertibility) conditions of (1) and (2) are conditions that obtain *now*, and they coincide: the couple has put up the banns, many invitations have been sent, etc. Now embed both sentences in a conditional:

(C1)   If (1) then next Monday afternoon Ben will not be a bachelor
(C2)   If (2) then next Monday afternoon Ben will not be a bachelor.

Of these conditional predictions the latter is riskier than the former. Why? Quite generally, the rational acceptability of 'If A then B' goes with the conditional rational acceptability of B on the supposition that A is *true*—not on the supposition that A is rationally acceptable. Asserting (C1) you predict Ben's loss of bachelorhood on condition of the *truth* of the antecedent. What you now state by uttering (1) is true only if on Monday at noon one can truly say, 'Ben is currently getting married.' Hence the conditional prediction (C1) is not very risky: provided Ben survives the event, the truth of the antecedent guarantees that of the consequent. Asserting (C2), you again predict Ben's loss of bachelorhood on condition of the *truth* of its antecedent. But what you now state by uttering (2) might be true even if next Monday there will be occasion for reporting an embarrassing course of events: 'Ben was to get married today, but yesterday his fiancée eloped.' So the conditional prediction (C2) is far riskier than its predecessor. The embeddings of (1) and (2) force us to acknowledge that (1) and (2), though having the same rational acceptability conditions, have different truth-conditions.

---

[103] Cf. Dummett, 'Truth' ('Postscript (1972)'), 21–2; 'The Reality of the Past', 365; *FPL*, 350–1, 449–51; 'Meaning', 50–2; 'Source', 195–6. Putnam is clearly wrong when he says that 'Dummett identifies truth with justification' (1983b: 84). He corrects the mistaken attribution, although somewhat ambiguously, in the 'Introduction' to his 1983b, xvii, but he keeps on repeating it (1989: 114). Incidentally, as formulated by Putnam, the identification is not even *grammatically* acceptable.

Therefore, being true cannot be identical with being rationally acceptable. Quite generally,

[If] an operator is used in such a way that the condition for the justifiability of an utterance involving it could not be framed in terms only of the justifiability of certain of its subsentences, we are . . . compelled to form a pre-theoretical notion of what it is for such a sub-sentence to be objectively true or false, independently of whether an utterance of it on its own would be justifiable or not. ('Source', 192)

One of the conclusions Dummett draws from this is disjunctive: we must either accept the 'full-fledged realist notion of truth' or introduce a concept which, though 'more refined than the straightforward concept of justifiability', can be 'explained, even if in a complex and subtle way, in terms of justifiability'.[104] Interim Putnam opts for the second alternative, and I see no reason why he should not applaud the Argument from Embedding.[105]

Could he have the same attitude towards the ingenious argument to the effect that truth is different from rational acceptability, which Wright puts forward in the first chapter of his book *Truth and Objectivity*?[106] I shall alter it slightly so that it fits exactly into the present context. In this adaptation of Wright's Argument from Informational Neutrality (as I shall call it) the Denominalization Schema serves as the starting point ('T' abbreviates 'It is true that'):

(Den) $T p \leftrightarrow p$.

Replacing 'p' in (Den) by its negation we obtain

(i) $T \neg p \leftrightarrow \neg p$.

Relying on the rule that from a premiss of the form 'A $\leftrightarrow$ B' one may derive the conclusion '$\neg A \leftrightarrow \neg B$',[107] we can derive from (Den)

(ii) $\neg T p \leftrightarrow \neg p$.

Since '$\leftrightarrow$' is transitive we can derive from (i) and (ii) the 'Negation Equivalence'

(iii) $T \neg p \leftrightarrow \neg T p$.

---

[104] Dummett, 'Source', 201.

[105] However, in sect. 7.3.5 we will see that Dummett's argument undermines another thesis which Putnam did *not* give up after his recantation—the thesis that truth and justifiability are co-eval notions.

[106] Wright, *T&O*, 19–21, 32. (For Wright, this argument is part of an attempt at refuting 'deflationism'.) Unlike Alston, whose master argument against anti-realism also starts from (Den), as we saw in Ch. 1, Wright does *not* take his argument to refute *all* varieties of alethic anti-realism.

[107] The validity of this rule depends on two more basic rules, which are endorsed in both classical and intuitionistic logic, namely *Modus Tollendo Tollens* and Conditional Proof.

So negation commutes with truth. Now if truth were nothing but rational acceptability, negation should also commute with rational acceptability, and we ought to endorse ('R' abbreviates 'It is rationally acceptable that'):

(iii^R) $R \neg p \leftrightarrow \neg R p.$

But should we endorse (iii^R)? Consider the proposition that Socrates' paternal grandmother died before her fiftieth birthday. Our state of information is such that this proposition is not rationally acceptable, so in this case the right-hand side of (iii^R) yields a truth. But relative to our state of information, the negation of the proposition that Socrates' paternal grandmother died before her fiftieth birthday is not rationally acceptable either. So the left-hand side of (iii^R) yields a falsehood. Hence we should reject (iii^R). Consequently, if we subscribe to (iii), we must acknowledge that 'true' is not co-extensive with 'rationally acceptable' and, consequently, that truth is not the same as rational acceptability. Generally, in Wright's own words:

[iii^R] must fail for any discourse whose ingredient statements are such that a state of information may be *neutral*—may justify neither their assertion nor their denial. For with respect to such a state of information, and such a statement P, it will be correct to report that it is not the case that P is warrantedly assertible but incorrect to report that the negation of P is warrantedly assertible. Hence, since (iii) holds good for the truth-predicate, we have to acknowledge .../... that truth and warranted assertibility ... are potentially extensionally divergent. (*T&O*, 20, 22)

If one acknowledges the possibility of neutral states of information and accepts (Den) as conveying an essential truth about truth, one ought to resist the identification of truth with rational acceptability *sans phrase*.[108]

Can Putnam accept Wright's Argument from Informational Neutrality as further grist to his mill? We can see that the answer is No, as soon as we register another feature of his Internalism:

[I]f both a statement and its negation could be 'justified', even if conditions were as ideal as one could hope to make them, there is no sense in thinking of the statement as *having* a truth value. (1981: 56; [P.3])

This can be spelt out, I think, as follows: (1) A statement is true if and only if it is justifiable under epistemically ideal conditions, whereas its negation is not so justifiable. (2) A statement is false if and only if it is not justifiable under epistemically

---

[108] In *T&O* Wright runs the argument for the sibling of (Den), for the Disquotation Schema, '*p*' *is true iff p* (and the predicate 'warrantedly assertible'). But on pp. 22–3 he points out that the Argument from Informational Neutrality works just as well for (Den), and in 'Debate', 218–19, 233–4, and 'Minimalism', 756, he runs it for (Den).

ideal conditions, whereas its negation is so justifiable. (3) Otherwise, a statement is neither true nor false. Now, to take one of Putnam's favourite examples, consider the statements that are now expressed by 'The number of trees in Canada is odd' and (what is naturally taken to be its negation) 'The number of trees in Canada is not odd [is even].' Due to the vagueness of both 'tree' and 'in Canada', neither statement is justifiable under epistemically ideal conditions. So, according to [P.3], the former statement falls into a truth-value gap. But then the right-to-left half of Wright's Negation Equivalence

(iii) $T \neg p \leftrightarrow \neg T p$

is not universally valid.[109] A statement may lack truth without being false, and it is *falsity* that is truth of negation. So instead of (iii) we have, rather,

(F) $T \neg p \leftrightarrow$ It is false that p.

How are we to understand Putnam's talk of ideality when he identifies truth with idealized rational acceptability? Putnam's first attempt at an explanation of the ideality proviso was to become the main source of the most serious misrepresentations of his Internalism:

Epistemically ideal conditions, of course, are like frictionless planes: we cannot really attain epistemically ideal conditions. . . . But frictionless planes cannot really be attained either, and yet talk of frictionless planes has cash value because we can approximate them to a very high degree of approximation. (1981: 55; [P.4])

The contention of [P.4], foreshadowed in the 'as if'-clause in [P.2], that epistemically ideal conditions are not attainable for us, is hard to reconcile with other claims Putnam makes on behalf of his Internalism. Thus he claims for this position a close affinity to Kant:

Although Kant never quite says that this is what he is doing, Kant is best read as proposing for the first time what I have called the 'internalist' . . . view of truth, [i.e. the view that a true statement] is a statement that a rational being would accept on sufficient experience of the kind that it is actually possible for beings with our nature to have. (1981: 60, 64; [P.5])[110]

---

[109] Wright is fully aware of this problem (as well as of the trouble the admission of truth-value gaps makes for the right-to-left half of (Den)). In *T&O*, 63–4, he reinstalls the argument by means of a 'polar' negation operator and a 'weak' reading of the biconditional: the operator yields a false output if the input is true and a true output in *all* other cases (hence it is equivalent with 'It is not true that'); and under the 'weak' reading of the biconditional it fails to yield a truth only if one component expresses a truth whereas the other does not. On pp. 352 and 355 above, I have used the system of Bochvar and Smiley to spell this out.   [110] Cf. 1983b: 210.

If this is Interim Putnam's position, then his appeal to Kant is entirely appropriate. As far as the spatio-temporal world of 'appearances' is concerned, Kant takes truth to be epistemically constrained. Like Putnam's Internalism, Kant's so-called 'empirical realism' is a form of alethic anti-realism.[111] Putnam could have quoted, for example, the following passage from the first *Critique:*

Daß es Einwohner im Monde geben könne, ob sie gleich kein Mensch jemals wahrgenommen hat, muß allerdings eingeräumt werden, aber es bedeutet nur so viel: daß wir in dem möglichen Fortschritte der Erfahrung auf sie treffen könnten. [That there may be inhabitants in the moon, although no human being has ever perceived them, must certainly be admitted. But this only means that in the possible advance of experience we may encounter them.] (*Kritik der reinen Vernunft,* B 521)

Taking this to apply in general to statements about whatever 'inhabits' the spatio-temporal world and putting truth into the picture, Kant maintains this: admittedly it might be true that p, although no being with our nature is actually justified in believing that p, but if it is true that p, then it is at least possible that a being with our nature comes to be justified in believing that p. Obviously the Kantian position as characterized in [P.5] is incompatible with the view that beings with our ('rational and sensible') nature can never attain epistemically ideal conditions. Thus [P.2] is very misleading, and Putnam was ready to admit this:

To think of knowledge as something we never really possess but only 'approximate' is the first step on the slide to scepticism, and my talk of 'idealization' was unfortunate if it suggested such a view. (1991: 421; [P.6])

Perhaps it was not so much talk of ideal conditions in itself that suggested such a view (after all, weather that is ideal for a walk is sometimes real), but, rather, the comparison with frictionless planes.

Unfortunately, Putnam's talk of idealization has triggered false historical associations. To readers such as Smart, Rorty, and Habermas, it suggested a 'neo-Peircean' reading of Interim Putnam. According to this reading, there is such a thing as an epistemic situation which is ideal for giving a true answer to *any question whatsoever.* Putnam is vehemently opposed to such a view:

Many people have thought that my idealization was the same as Peirce's, that what the figure of a 'frictionless plane' corresponds to is a situation ('finished science') in which the community would be in a position to justify *every* true statement (and to disconfirm every false one). People have attributed to me the idea that we can sensibly imagine

---

[111] Whether the restriction to the world of appearances makes it illegitimate to call Kant an alethic anti-realist *tout court* depends on whether he takes propositions about '*Dinge an sich*' to be not only unjustifiable, but also unintelligible for us. In *Kritik der reinen Vernunft,* B 166 n., for example, Kant rejects the unintelligibility thesis. Cf. A. J. Clark, 'Why Kant Couldn't be an Anti-Realist'; Stevenson and Walker, Symposium on 'Empirical Realism and Transcendental Anti-Realism'.

conditions which are *simultaneously ideal* for the ascertainment of any truth whatsoever.... I do not by any means *ever* mean to use the notion of an 'ideal epistemic situation' in this fantastic (or Utopian) Peircean sense. (1990: viii; [P.7])

The order of quantifiers is all-important here. Interim Putnam *endorses* the following claim:

(IntPutnam) $\forall x \, \exists j$ (x is true $\rightarrow$ (j obtains $\Box \rightarrow$ it is rational to accept x)),

where the variable 'j' runs over ideal epistemic situations, and 'p $\Box \rightarrow$ q' is a subjunctive conditional. Interim Putnam *rejects* the 'Peircean' contention

('Peirce') $\exists j \, \forall x$ (x is true $\rightarrow$ (j obtains $\Box \rightarrow$ it is rational to accept x)).

I am not sure that Peirce really subscribed to ('Peirce'), but, be that as it may, Putnam's criticism of the 'neo-Peircean' view, which was falsely ascribed to him, is very convincing. What are better or worse epistemic conditions may vary from statement to statement, and they often do so: epistemic conditions that are optimal for somebody's being justified in believing that just now somebody is sneezing on the highest floor of the Empire State Building are rather bad for somebody's being justified in believing that just now somebody is bellowing out obscenities in a certain pub in Belfast. Furthermore, no progress that science may make in future millennia is likely to lead to an improvement of the epistemic situation in virtue of which you are now justified in the belief that there is currently a book in front of your nose.[112]

In the 1980s Interim Putnam came to prefer to put his position like this:

[T]o claim of any statement that it is true... is to claim that it could be justified were epistemic conditions good enough. (1990: vii; [P.8])

Now this formulation, like some of its predecessors, sounds very much as if Putnam wanted to identify the concept of being true with the concept of being rationally acceptable under sufficiently good epistemic conditions. It is very tempting to read [P.8] as giving a definition of the concept of truth. But this reading cannot be right, since Putnam quite explicitly rejects definitional alethic anti-realism:[113] 'I am not trying to give a formal *definition* of truth.'[114] The

---

[112] Recall the *Minima Trivialia* Objection raised against Peirce on pp. 396–9 above.

[113] See QUESTION 16 on the flow chart in Ch. 1 (Fig. 1.4).

[114] 1981: 56. In view of this remark (and its echoes in 1988: 115, and 1990: viii) I wonder whether Putnam was fair towards his earlier self when he wrote: 'It was the hope... that truth might be actually reduced to notions of "rational acceptability" and "better and worse epistemic situation" that did not themselves presuppose the notion of truth that was responsible for the residue of idealism in [1981]' (1992c: 373). (My question is meant to counteract the somewhat unkind suspicion expressed in Schantz, *Wahrheit, Referenz und Realismus*, 330–1.)

non-reductive character of Internalism becomes strikingly obvious as soon as we ask what a topic-specifically ideal (good enough) epistemic situation is. Interim Putnam answers that 'an ideal epistemic situation [for assessing the statement p] is one in which we are in a good position to *tell if p is true or false*.'[115] This reply would debunk [P.8] as unacceptably circular if an analysis of the concept of truth had been intended, since the diameter of the circle would be very small indeed.

Clearly, by accepting [P.8] one is committed to endorsing the following universally quantified biconditional, which gives us Putnam's conception of truth as *Topic-Specifically Idealized Rational Acceptability*:

(TIRA) $\forall x$ (x is true $\leftrightarrow$ (epistemic conditions are good enough
               for assessing x $\square\!\!\rightarrow$ it is rational to accept x)).

But [P.8] must come to more than this, since Putnam maintains that 'truth and rational acceptability are *interdependent* notions'.[116] Two concepts are interdependent, I take it, just in case one cannot possess either concept without possessing the other. Thus understood, two concepts can be interdependent without being co-extensive. Concepts expressed by lexical antonyms or by lexical complements make up such pairs: 'full' and 'empty', 'old' and 'young', 'virtue' and 'vice', for example; or the arithmetical concepts 'odd' and 'even'. Notions that are expressed by 'converse' relative terms such as 'someone's teacher' and 'someone's pupil' are also interdependent without being co-extensive. (All this is registered in Aristotle's slogans, 'Knowledge of opposites is the same,' and 'Knowledge of relative terms is the same.'[117]) Now (TIRA) does not convey any interdependence message, since it only requires that the concept 'true' has the same extension as the concept 'rationally acceptable under sufficiently good epistemic conditions'. Surely one might have the notion 'vertebrate with a heart' in one's conceptual repertoire without possessing the notion 'vertebrate with a liver', and yet both concepts are co-extensive.

One might hope that prefacing (TIRA) by the necessity operator '$\square$' would suffice to capture the point of [P.8]:

(TIRA*) $\square\forall x$ (x is true $\leftrightarrow$ (epistemic conditions are good enough
                 for assessing x $\square\!\!\rightarrow$ it is rational to accept x)).[118]

---

[115] 1991b: 421; cf. 1994a: 243. Incidentally, this answer shows that the objection against [P.8] in Schantz, *Wahrheit, Referenz und Realismus*, 329 misses its target.   [116] 1988: 115.

[117] Aristotle, *Topica* I, 14: 105ᵇ33–4.

[118] Interim Putnam explicitly endorses the left-to-right part of this biconditional: '[My] concession to moderate verificationism . . . was the idea that truth *could* never be totally recognition-transcendent' (1994a: 243; my italics). Cf. 1994b: 256; 1995: 299.

But (*TIRA**) only requires that *in every possible world* the two concepts have the same extension, and this condition, too, could be satisfied even if the two concepts were not dependent on each other. After all, somebody might have mastered the concept 'geometrical figure which is square' without yet having grasped the concept 'parallelogram which is square', nevertheless both notions have the same extension in every possible world.[119]

If Interim Putnam does not claim conceptual identity, *what* then does he identify with *what* when he contends that truth is (nothing but) rational acceptability under epistemically optimal circumstances? In a very different context, Putnam once proposed a distinction between concepts and properties, which may be helpful here.[120] When a scientist asserts that temperature is mean molecular kinetic energy, she asserts that temperature and mean molecular kinetic energy are *one and the same property* (physical magnitude), and her assertion is non-trivial, since she picks out this property by using *two different concepts*. (Similarly, being a lump of salt and being a lump of sodium chloride are one and the same property, and this identity statement is informative because that property is presented by two different concepts.) Thus understood, concepts are more finely individuated than, and they are modes of presentation of, properties. In this respect, the example is helpful indeed. But alas, in another respect there is a glaring disanalogy: the alleged identity between truth and a kind of rational acceptability is hardly to be discovered *empirically*.

Being a village with 100 inhabitants and being a village with $1^3 + 2^3 + 3^3 + 4^3$ inhabitants also seem to be one and the same (demographical) property picked out by two different concepts, and this is a case of a property identity that is *not* to be discovered empirically. Unfortunately, another disanalogy remains. As with the two geometrical notions mentioned above, the two notions representing that demographical property are not interdependent: after all, possessing the mathematical concept 'power' is surely no prerequisite for having the concept 'hundred'.

So a perfectly analogous case would have to be a non-empirical property identity statement in which one and the same property is specified by *two different but interdependent concepts*. It would be somewhat suspicious if adherents of Internalism could not offer any example that fits this bill except their own controversial identity statement. So let me offer on their behalf an example that, I think, can dispel this suspicion. (It comes from Bolzano.[121]) Arguably, the property of being smaller than 2^4 is the same as the property of being smaller than 4^2. But the predicates '$< 2^4$' and '$< 4^2$' express different yet interdependent

---

[119] See pp. 25–7 and 47–8 above on concept identity. [120] 1970: *passim*. [121] Bolzano, *WL*, i. 446.

concepts. (The sentences '$15 < 2^4$' and '$15 < 4^2$' are not cognitively equivalent, so those predicates express different concepts.[122] You cannot possess either of these concepts unless you have mastered the concepts expressed by the numerals and by '$<$' and learned to cope with calculations involving powers, but then you cannot have the concept expressed by '$< 2^4$' and lack the concept expressed by '$< 4^2$', or vice versa, hence they are interdependent concepts.) So even opponents of Interim Putnam should admit that the sub-class of true property identity statements to which the contention 'Truth is "idealized" rational acceptability', if true, belongs is in any case not empty.[123]

7.2.2 Kindred constraints

Putnam calls the verificationism of his interim position *moderate* (as compared, for example, with the verificationism that Dummett, at least for some time, took anti-realism to be committed to).[124] For several reasons this epithet seems quite appropriate:

For me, verification was (and is) a matter of degree. (1994c: 182 n.; [P.9a])

I have repeatedly argued that any theory that makes the truth or falsity of a historical claim depend on whether that claim can be decided in the future is radically misguided. (1992a: 357; [P.9b])[125]

[It] would be absurd to suppose that there *could not* be intelligent beings so much smarter than we that some of their thoughts could not even be understood by us; and surely ... some of those thoughts could be *true*. (They could also be warrantedly assertible by those beings, say Alpha Centaurians, even if not by us.) (1992b: 364; [P.9c])

According to Internalism, the truth of a proposition requires that evidence of its truth be available. *Does it have to be conclusive evidence?* In [P.9a] Putnam denies this: verification that indefeasibly establishes a proposition's truth is seldom attainable.[126] (As regards unrestrictedly general empirical statements, this was a matter of course for Kant,[127] and the Vienna Circle came round to acknowledging it in the early

---

[122] Cf. n. 119 above.

[123] Perhaps the following example would also do. The concepts of being half-full is different from the concept of being half-empty (optimists tend to apply the former whereas pessimists are prone to use the latter). These two concepts are interdependent, but they represent one and the same property. The question whether the interdependency thesis (which Putnam retained after his internalism period) is *correct* will be confronted in sect. 7.3.5 below.

[124] 1994a: 243, quoted above in n. 118.   [125] Cf. 1992b: 363; 1994b: 258–61; 1994c: 17.

[126] Dummett has long given up his earlier insistence on 'complete verification': 'As Putnam has recently pointed out ... it is misleading to concentrate too heavily, as I have usually done, on a form of anti-realist theory of meaning in which the meaning of a statement is given in terms of what conclusively verifies it; often such conclusive verification is not to be had' (*TOE*, xxxviii).

[127] Kant, *Kritik der reinen Vernunft*, B 3–4.

1930s.) *To whom must evidence be available?* To us, here and now? This issue is addressed in [P.9b] and [P.9c],[128] and again the answer is negative. It is only required that evidence be available at some time or other to some rational subject or other whose cognitive powers may (finitely) exceed ours. Putnam's Internalism agrees here with the liberal kind of anti-realism Wright calls 'In principle / Sometime' anti-realism.[129]

By maintaining [P.9b], Putnam denies that evidence must be available either now or in the future. It is sufficient if evidence is available to someone suitably placed in a spatio-temporal situation which may no longer be accessible to us or to our descendants. Thanks to [P.9b], Internalism is saved from an objection which is invited by the conception of truth that Nelson Goodman favoured (for a while). According to his version of alethic anti-realism, 'permanent credibility',[130] or 'acceptability that is not subsequently lost',[131] is a necessary and sufficient condition for truth. The following universally quantified biconditional captures Goodman's conception of truth as *permanent acceptability*:

(PermA) $\forall x \,[x$ is true $\leftrightarrow \exists t\, (x$ is credible at t &
$\forall t'\, (t'$ is later than t $\rightarrow x$ is credible at t'$))]$.

Like Interim Putnam, he did not plead for definitional anti-realism: 'I am not ... proposing to *define* truth as ultimate acceptability.'[132] With respect to the left-to-right part of (PermA), the following question suggests itself: can a statement not lose its credibility for ever and yet be true? Suppose at time t_1 the statement that event E happened at time t_0 is credible: at t_1 a hundred people who claim to have witnessed E are still alive, ninety-nine of them have an extremely good record as witnesses, and there is no reason whatsoever for suspecting that this time they are all in error. Only one person in this cloud of witnesses, a certain Mr X, is generally considered to be very unreliable indeed. At time t_2 all witnesses have been dead for a long time, almost all of them have fallen into complete oblivion, and almost no trace of their testimony concerning event E is left. Only one letter containing a report on E has survived, but unfortunately it was found in the estate of the notoriously unreliable Mr X, and he of all people *is* still remembered, namely as a proverbial paradigm of untrustworthiness. As a consequence, the

---

[128] Here is an early statement to the same effect as these two passages: '[My view] is not a "verificationism" which requires one to claim that statements about the past are to be understood by seeing how we would verify them in the future. All I ask is that what is supposed to be "true" be warrantable ... for creatures with "a rational and sensible nature". Talk of there being saber-toothed tigers here thirty thousand years ago, or beings who can verify mathematical and physical theories we cannot begin to understand (but who have brains and nervous systems) ... is not philosophically problematic for me' (1982: 41).

[129] Wright, 'Timeless', 180–1.   [130] Goodman, 'On Starmaking', 211; cf. *Ways of Worldmaking*, 123–4.

[131] Goodman, 'Notes on the Well-Made World', 35.   [132] Goodman, *Of Mind and Other Matters*, 38.

statement that E happened at time t_0 is no longer credible, and it might never recover from this misfortune. Does this prevent it from being true?[133] Perhaps as a reply to this Objection from Lost Information, Goodman would quote here the same line Peirce once took from the American poet and journalist William C. Bryant: 'Truth crushed to earth shall rise again.'[134] But is there any good reason for such cheerful optimism? Bolzano, for one, did not see any such reason: 'As far as I know the history of human opinions, it did not teach us at all that "truth once discovered will never perish".'[135]

Wright has outlined a conception of truth, which can be understood as a variant of (PermA), that does not fall victim to the Objection from Lost Information. He proposes to identify 'Dummettian semantic anti-realism' with the thesis that 'truth should be conceived globally as *superassertibility*':[136]

(SuperA) $\forall x$ (x is true $\leftrightarrow \exists y$ (y is an actually accessible state of information & x is warrantedly assertible in y & x remains warrantedly assertible no matter how y is enlarged upon or improved)).

The condition given on the right-hand-side is what Wright's somewhat ungraceful name for the constraint refers to. Now a state of information can hardly be enlarged upon or improved if the information gets lost. So a certain idealization is involved in (SuperA), an implicit counterfactual assumption that a state of information that is once 'actually accessible' remains so forever after.[137] (A while ago we saw which consequences Łukasiewicz drew from the factual falsity of this assumption.[138])

But not all is super about (SuperA), and the objection I have in mind has nothing whatsoever to do with what Wright himself takes to be the fundamental threat to this constraint, i.e. the possible recognition-transcendence of some

---

[133] In later writings, for reasons he does not spell out, Goodman has replaced (PermA) by a weaker tenet: permanent credibility is, 'within certain bounds', a 'sufficient condition for truth' (ibid., 38, 40). So only the (somehow weakened) right-to-left half of the universally quantified biconditional (PermA) survives. Cf. my 'Truth, Rightness, and Permanent Acceptability'.

[134] See the Peirce extract on p. 395 above.

[135] '*Übrigens hat die Geschichte der menschlichen Meinungen, soviel ich von ihr weiß, keineswegs gelehrt, daß 'die Wahrheit, einmal gefunden, nicht wieder untergehen könne*' (Bolzano, *Der Briefwechsel*, 297). The 'history of human opinions' teaches us rather that sometimes knowledge of a certain fact would have got lost, and irrevocably so, if it had not been for some fortuitous and fortunate circumstances that might all too easily not have obtained.

[136] Wright, *T&O*, 75; cf. 60–1. (SuperA) is culled from his 'Précis of *T&O*', 865, and 'Response to Commentators', 922; cf. 'Assertibility', 411–18; *T&O*, 47–8; 'Debate', 228–9, 236–8; and 'Minimalism', 771. (Wright himself does not introduce it as an improvement of Goodman's restriction. Goodman is hardly ever mentioned in recent debates about conceptions of truth.)   [137] Cf. Wright, *T&O*, 68.

[138] The pertinent passage was cited and discussed on pp. 304–5 above.

truth-candidates. (SuperA) falls victim, I believe, to John Skorupski's Argument from Defeated Warrant:

A true statement may not be superassertible. Suppose you are bored by my conversation. Suppose I see your eyes glazing, suppressed yawns, etc.—I am warranted in asserting that you are bored. But further information may defeat that warrant: I discover that you have been kept awake for the last forty-eight hours. (What I don't know is that you are taking pills to counteract the effects of lack of sleep—so *that's* not why you are suppressing yawns.) ('Critical Study', 522)[139]

A warrant, which is provided for an assertion by a certain state of information actually accessible at time t_1, is undermined by an enlargement of this information at t_2 (and then restored again at t_3). Due to the epistemic mishap at t_2, the statement is not superassertible, notwithstanding its truth.

Thanks to his contention in [P.9b], Interim Putnam is neither open to the Objection from Lost Information nor in need of Wright's counterfactual assumption of preserved information. He can readily admit that the misfortunes of the E-statement do not prevent it from being true. After all, there *was* a time at which sufficiently good epistemic conditions for reasonably accepting it *did* obtain.[140] Arguably, Interim Putnam can defuse the Argument from Defeated Warrant by declaring epistemic conditions to be good enough at a time t only if all relevant evidence that is actually accessible at t is actually registered at t. In [P.9c] Interim Putnam even concedes that there may be truths which our ancestors were, which we are, and which our descendants will be constitutionally incapable of grasping. This concession is in the very same spirit as my attack on alethic speciesism in an earlier chapter.[141] So, all in all, Interim Putnam's verificationism is very moderate indeed.

7.2.3 *Reasons for recantation*

For all its moderation, internalism does involve the following claim:

[E]very truth *that human beings can understand* is made true by conditions that are, in principle, accessible to some human beings at some time or other, if not necessarily at all times or to all human beings. (1992b: 364; [P.10])

---

[139] This is a study of the first edition of Wright's collection *Realism. Meaning and Truth* in which (SuperA) saw the light of the day. Unfortunately, the point is buried in a footnote. More than a decade later Jonathan Kvanvig repeats essentially the same point with much aplomb ('Truth and Superassertibility', 16–17). But he makes it unnecessarily dependent on intuitions about when we would be ready to ascribe *knowledge*, and, in his example, borrowed from the debate about (in)defeasibility theories of knowledge, the temporary defeat of the warrant depends essentially on the subject's being fooled by false testimony.

[140] This chimes with Wright's speculations as to Interim Putnam's views on statements about the past: 'Epistemic', 351–2.

[141] See the final pages of Ch. 4.2.3. [P.9c] is also conceded by Wright: see *T&O*, 159.

And it is this very claim which Putnam, after his anti-anti-realist turn, declares to be false. But before I present Putnam's most prominent argument for this turn, I want to consider three other serious challenges to his erstwhile Internalism.

[1] One cause of concern is that the right-hand side of

(TIRA) $\forall x$ (x is true $\leftrightarrow$ (epistemic conditions are good enough for assessing x
$\square\rightarrow$ it is rational to accept x))

specifies a necessary and sufficient condition of truth by means of a subjunctive conditional. Let me prepare the ground for the objection by recalling the way I tried to capture one of the connections that obtain between the notions Belief and Judgement:[142]

(B/J) $\forall x \, \forall t$ (x believes at t that p $\rightarrow$ (x considers at t the question whether p
$\square\rightarrow$ x judges at t that p)).

In (B/J) a subjunctive conditional is used to specify a necessary condition of belief. Why not take this condition to be sufficient as well?[143] Ann is always disposed to judge that she is awake whenever she considers the question. By rousing her from sleep at 4 a.m., Ben can easily, if somewhat brutally, check whether that disposition has survived her falling asleep. But we do not want to conclude from this that she always (even when sound asleep) believes herself to be awake. So here is the reason why we should not take the necessary condition for belief, which is specified in (B/J), to be sufficient as well: the implementation of the condition expressed in the antecedent of the subjunctive conditional may bring about a change in the actual truth-value of the categorical belief-ascription. In the case under consideration, a belief-ascription which is actually false ('She believes now that she is awake,' said while she is dreamlessly sleeping) would become true. This kind of danger is often imminent when the truth-conditions of a categorical statement are specified in terms of a subjunctive conditional. If you do not pay heed to this risk, you are liable to commit what has been called the 'Conditional Fallacy'.[144] Wright has shown that (TIRA) embodies this very fallacy.[145] Let me try to consolidate this critical insight by means of an example. Suppose Dr Crippen committed a murder. Call this proposition 'M'. If epistemic conditions for assessing M were good enough, it would be rational to accept M,

---

[142] Cf. p. 379 above.   [143] As is done, for example, by Evans in *Varieties of Reference*, 338.
[144] David Lewis ascribes the argument to C. B. Martin: cf. Lewis, 'Finkish Dispositions', 133, and the literature registered therein at n. 1. (Dispositions that would disappear if they were put to the test are 'finkish'.)   [145] See Wright, *T&O*, 117–19; 'Epistemic', 344–5 (= 'Minimalism', 769–70).

for then at least one of Dr Crippen's crimes would be detected. Now consider PM, the proposition that Dr Crippen committed a *perfect* murder. Implementation of conditions good enough for assessing PM would bring about a situation in which (the categorical ascription of truth to) PM turns out to be false. But it is to be feared that PM might be true. (Wright has advanced the same kind of objection against the '(neo-)Peircean' idea that x is true iff, were conditions which are epistemically ideal for appraising every truth-claim ever to obtain, it would be rational to accept x. The calamity strikes the eye when one substitutes 'the proposition that conditions which are epistemically ideal for appraising every truth-claim will never really obtain' for 'x'.[146]) So much for the first problem with Internalism.

[2] Truth is stable, whereas rational acceptability *simpliciter* is not: that was Putnam's point in [P.1]. In the continuation of that passage, he went on to mention a second respect in which these two properties differ. Rational acceptability comes in degrees, whereas truth does not (or not in the same sense):

In addition, rational acceptability is a matter of degree; truth is sometimes spoken of as a matter of degree (e.g., we sometimes say, '*the earth is a sphere*' *is approximately true*); but the 'degree' here is the *accuracy* of the statement. (1981: 55; [P.1+])

Our use of 'approximately true' does not refute Frege's contention that truth is an all-or-nothing matter,[147] for that locution can be eliminated along the following lines: 'The earth is a sphere' is approximately true iff 'the earth is approximately a sphere' is (plain) true.[148] By contrast, talk of degrees of rational acceptability is not just a *façon de parler*. Now Putnam obviously takes for granted that (topic-specifically) *idealized* rational acceptability is no longer a matter of degree, for otherwise it would not be a serious candidate for identification with truth. But this makes for a *second* problem with Internalism: is it really plausible to assume that any two statements justified under epistemically suitable conditions

---

[146] Wright, 'Epistemic', 344 (= 'Minimalism', 769), where the use of the schematic letter 'Q' is grammatically incoherent.

[147] '*Die Wahrheit verträgt kein Mehr oder Minder* [Truth does not tolerate a more or less]' (Frege, '*Der Gedanke*', 60). Wright calls Frege's principle the Absoluteness Platitude: see 'Debate', 227 (= 'Minimalism', 760). (In standard usage 'platitude' applies only to (tedious) truisms, so one may wonder whether it is a recommendable terminological policy to call something a platitude that has been strenuously denied, as we saw in sect. 7.1.2, by a whole philosophical movement. Whether the denial was reasonable is a different question, of course.)

[148] Compare Austin's example 'France is hexagonal' in *How To Do Things With Words*, 142. In his eagerness 'to play Old Harry with the true/false fetish' (150), Austin goes as far as to maintain that such a statement is neither true nor false. Surely, it is more plausible to call it 'roughly true' and then apply the strategy suggested above. See also Austin, 'Truth', 129–30, Strawson, 'Truth' (1950), 208–10, and, for the strategy, Peter Smith, 'Approximate Truth for Minimalists'.

are justified *to the same extent*?[149] Suppose that currently the conditions for verifying my statement that there are exactly eighty-three students in lecture-room D are good enough. Then surely the conditions are equally good for verifying the claim that there are more than three students in that lecture-room. But isn't the second statement justified to a greater extent than the first one? After all, the risk of counting wrong is far smaller in the latter case. Even under conditions that are optimal for assessing a statement, strength of warrant can be increased by decreasing the statement's exactitude or its concern with details.

[3] In the example just given, two statements are such that conditions which are sufficiently good for verifying one of them are equally good for verifying the other. But as Interim Putnam himself has emphasized, this is not always the case. The obtaining of epistemic conditions that are good enough for being justified in accepting one statement may actually *preclude* the obtaining of conditions that would be required if anyone is justifiably to accept another statement, even though they may both very well be true. I don't think we have to appeal to quantum mechanics, as Putnam does in the continuation of [P.7], in order to convince ourselves that such a situation may arise. Here is an example inspired by Fellini's *Roma*. In a newly discovered catacomb, workers are suddenly struck by the sight of a centuries-old fresco painting. But, alas, it is so sensitive to light that it is bound to disappear very soon. Let us suppose that it would disappear within seconds if enough light on it were thrown to recognize what it depicts, but that it would stay just long enough for its size to be carefully measured if the lighting were to remain as dim as it now is. Then one can either verify a statement to the effect that on that wall there is now a fresco painting which depicts such-and-such, or one can verify a statement to the effect that on that wall there is now a fresco painting which measures so-and-so many square centimetres, but one cannot verify their conjunction.

Such situations make for a *third* problem with Internalism, which was pointed out by Peacocke. Whenever we are in such a predicament with respect to two statements, no epistemic situation will be good enough for rationally accepting their conjunction, and yet that conjunction might be true.[150] The operator 'If epistemic conditions were topic-specifically ideal then it would be rational to accept that', '$\mathfrak{R}$' for short, does not collect across '&', i.e. from the premisses '$\mathfrak{R}p$' and '$\mathfrak{R}q$' we are not allowed to derive '$\mathfrak{R}$ (p & q)' as conclusion. But the operator 'It is true that' does collect across '&'. So Internalism has to be revised.

---

[149] The question is posed in Hugly and Sayward, *I&T*, 368.
[150] See Peacocke, 'Introduction' to *Understanding and Sense*, xxii, and *Being Known*, 30.

The most reasonable move may be to say that truth of a conjunction requires only that each of its conjuncts would be rationally acceptable if epistemic conditions were good enough: the revised account would claim that whatever is true either itself complies with the epistemic constraint or it follows from premises that comply with it.[151] But one may very well wonder why the truth of a conjunction (or of any other complex statement) can be absolved from an epistemic constraint to which its constituents are subject.

Putnam's most prominent argument against Internalism is what I shall call the Extraterrestrial Objection. Let me quote at length what I take to be his most perspicuous presentation of the argument:[152]

Consider the following pair of statements:

(1)   There is intelligent extraterrestrial life.
(2)   There is no intelligent extraterrestrial life.

(1) does not pose a problem for [Internalism], for if there *is* intelligent extraterrestrial life, then a properly placed human observer could be warranted in believing that there was. But (2) is more difficult. There might, of course, be some physical reason why

(3)   there *couldn't* be intelligent extraterrestrial life,

and in that case why should we not be able, in principle, to discover it? But that is not the only way (2) could be true. (2) could just *happen* to be true; that is, it could be the case that, although intelligent life might have evolved on some other solar system, this just never happened.... What makes us consider (2) a possible truth is not that we have any clear notion of what would make *it* warrantedly assertible [but rather] that *it is the negation of an empirical statement.* Our conception of what is a possible truth is not based *only* on what we could verify, even in the most generous and idealized sense of 'verify'; it is also based on our understanding of *logic.* (1992b: 364–5; [P.11])

Let me highlight two features of this argument.[153]

First, Putnam points out that comprehension of a possible truth like (2), which is beyond justification, is *based upon* comprehension of truths like (1),

---

[151] This revision differs from the one Peacocke envisages when he writes: '[I]t is not clear that this position should not also allow a universal quantification, itself undecidable, to be true, provided that each of its instances could be justified were epistemic conditions good enough' ('Introduction', xii). No matter how many of its instances you pile up, the universal quantification does not *follow* from them. So the second disjunct in my tentative revision would have to be watered down to something like 'or it is confirmed by premises that comply with it'.

[152] Cf. 1994a: n. 6; 1994b: 261; 1994c: 58; 1995: 293 ff. Wright's discussion of the Extraterrestrial Objection in 'Epistemic', 353–4, 364, is focussed on the rather sloppy formulation in 1994c.

[153] We know already from [P.3] that Putnam is not wedded to bivalence. In the present context he writes: '(2) is a claim that almost certainly has a truth value, and if it is true, it is very unlikely that this is

which can be the content of justified beliefs. This throws some light on (one half of) his contention that the concepts 'true' and 'rationally acceptable' are interdependent.[154] I shall return to this point in section 7.3.5.

Secondly, Putnam is careful to say that statement (2) is a *possible* truth. Now remember the difference, noted on p. 414, between *(TIRA)* and *(TIRA*)*. The Extraterrestrial Objection can only refute *(TIRA*)*, the stronger constraint on truth. It can only show that there is a proposition which we can grasp and which *could* be true although it would never be rational to accept it. (Actually, *this* can be shown by means of a very different kind of proposition, the recipe for which is due to Descartes: *the proposition that nobody ever accepts anything* is true in all possible worlds in which there are no believers, but it is not rational to accept that proposition.) A more radical attack on Internalism would aim at refuting even *(TIRA)*, the weaker constraint. It would try to show that (provided that no omniscient being exists) the concept 'x is true' and the concept 'x is rationally acceptable under sufficiently good epistemic conditions' are not even extensionally equivalent. It would attempt to demonstrate that there is a proposition which we can grasp and which *is* true although it would never be rational to accept it. In Chapter 1 this contention was called 'alethic realism'. In his less careful moments Putnam writes as if the Extraterrestrial Objection had already established alethic realism. Towards the end of his Dewey Lectures, for example, he claims to have shown that 'truth *is* sometimes recognition-transcendent'.[155] But can this be shown at all? My next section is an attempt to do just this.

7.3 Limits of Justifiability

> Full many a gem of purest ray serene
> > The dark unfathom'd caves of ocean bear:
> Full many a flower is born to blush unseen,
> > And waste its sweetness on the desert air.

> (Thomas Gray, 'An Elegy written
> in a Country Churchyard')[156]

because (3) is true...I say "almost certainly" because of the possibility that there might be *borderline* cases of extraterrestrial life. (2) could fail to have a truth-value because the state of things is such that it is indeterminate (just as "my watch is lying on the table" could fail to have a truth-value because the watch is standing on the end of the table, and we have not stipulated whether that counts as "lying" or not). Because of the possibility of *that* sort of truth-value gap, to say of an empirical statement S "S is either true or false" is to make a substantive claim' (1992b: 365 and n. 25). Cf. 1994a: 254; 1994c: 65; 1983b, Ch. 15.

[154] 1988: 115.
[155] 1994c: 69 (my italics); cf. 1994b: 261 and n. 31. Contrast 1994a: 243; 1994b: 256; 1995: 299.
[156] I am not the first philosopher to quote these verses, nor do I quote them here for the first time: Peirce, *CP*, 5.409; my *Abstrakte Gegenstände*, 117; and Timothy Williamson, *Knowledge and its Limits* (henceforth *KL*), 273.

Every sane opponent of alethic realism will be ready to admit that, as a matter of contingent fact, many a true proposition which we are able to comprehend will never be accepted by us, rationally or otherwise, for the simple reason that we do not bother to find out everything we could find out. Surely there is a true answer to the question how often the letter A occurs in *La Divina Commedia*, but presumably nobody will ever care even to guess the number, let alone to sit down and start counting. The sanity of sane alethic anti-realists consists in their refusal to embrace what Dummett describes as extremist constructivism:[157] '[To deny] that there are true statements whose truth we do not at present recognize and *shall not in fact ever* recognize... would appear to espouse a constructivism altogether too extreme. One surely cannot crudely equate truth with being recognized... as true.' But alethic anti-realists do maintain that every true proposition we can understand *could be* justifiably believed by us. Alethic anti-realism, I shall argue, is demonstrably incorrect.

I will now first present my source of inspiration and explain why I do not rest content with it. In section 7.3.2 I shall prepare the ground for my own attack, which I will eventually mount in section 7.3.3. Then I will try to defend it against those counter-attacks that can be anticipated in view of the criticisms that my source of inspiration has attracted over the years (section 7.3.4). In section 7.3.5, I shall argue that possession of the concept of truth is one-sidedly dependent on possession of the concept of justification. The book ends with a note of caution against the fragmentation of our workaday concept of truth.

7.3.1 *Anonym's argument*

My point of departure is an argument which was first published in 1963 by the American logician Frederic Fitch.[158] He attributes it to the anonymous referee of a paper he submitted to the 'Journal of Symbolic Logic', but did not publish, in 1945.[159] Hence my nickname for the argument. In my reconstruction I shall use

---

[157] In a passage we already had occasion to quote: see pp. 173–4 above.

[158] Fitch, 'A Logical Analysis of Some Value Concepts', 138, Theorem 1.

[159] Anonym's Argument (in the literature variously, and misleadingly, called 'The Fitch Argument' or 'The Paradox of Knowability') was effectively resurrected by William Hart in 1979. The first to study it in depth were Routley, Williamson, and Edgington (see Bibliography). Was the anonymous referee perhaps Gödel? As we shall see, for all its technical simplicity, Anonym's Argument is in one respect more ambitious than the argument for Gödel's Incompleteness Theorem, for the latter does not contend that any one truth of elementary number theory (i.e. in that modest part of mathematics which is concerned with the addition and multiplication of whole numbers) is in principle recognition-transcendent, but 'only' that each given axiom system, or any other sound proof procedure, will let some truths slip through its net: cf. Quine, 'The Limits of Knowledge', 65–6.

a format that will facilitate comparison with the anti-anti-realist argument I prefer. Anonym's Argument appeals to two rules governing truth-ascriptions. In my codification of the rules '[...]' is short for 'The proposition that...'[160] and 'T' abbreviates 'is true':[161]

T-Introduction	Γ:	A	*T-Elimination*	Γ:	T [A]
	Γ:	T [A]		Γ:	A

As regards the introduction rule, it is worth registering the following point: if we accept this rule *and* allow for truth-value gaps, then we must give up contraposition. Truth Introduction permits derivation of T[A] from A. If contraposition were to hold as well, it would follow that we can also derive ¬A from ¬T[A]. But if A falls into a truth-value gap, then the premiss ¬T[A] is true, while the conclusion ¬A is not true. (If A has no truth-value, then ¬A, understood as the internal negation of A, has no truth-value either.) So, assuming that in a correct derivation the truth of the premiss(es) necessitates that of the conclusion, ¬A is not derivable from ¬T[A]. Given Truth Introduction, one cannot allow for truth-value gaps unless one rejects contraposition. If one accommodates truth-value gaps, as was suggested in the last chapter, by adopting the system of Bochvar and Smiley, one does actually work with a logic in which contraposition fails (for internal negation).

Anonym's Argument invokes two further rules. They are concerned with ascriptions of propositional knowledge. The first one allows us to go from the premiss 'Someone knows that Romeo and Juliet are dead' to the conclusion 'Someone knows that Romeo is dead, and someone knows that Juliet is dead.' Reading 'K' as 'is at some time or other the content of some finite knower's knowledge', we can say that the rule permits distribution of the operator 'K [...]' across '&':

K-Distributivity	Γ:	K [A & B]
	Γ:	K [A] & K [B]

(I know of no persuasive objection against this rule, but I will mention a dissenter below.) The second K-rule registers an entirely uncontroversial feature of

---

[160] Keeping in mind the caveat on pp. 252–3 and 256 above.

[161] What follows is to be read thus: given an instance of the schema above the line as premiss, we may derive the corresponding instance of the schema below the line as conclusion; the latter depends on the same assumption(s), Γ, as the former.

our concept of propositional knowledge. It allows us to go from 'Someone knows that things are thus and so' to 'Things are (in fact) thus and so':

K-Factivity Γ: $\dfrac{\text{K}[\text{A}]}{\Gamma: \quad \text{A}}$

Anonym's Argument aims at showing this: the anti-realist principle that every truth *can in principle* be known, i.e. (using the diamond '✧' as short for 'It is in principle possible that')

(1) $\forall x\,(\text{T}x \to \diamond\,\text{K}x)$,

entails, on plausible assumptions, the insane conclusion that every truth *is in fact* known,

(C) $\forall x\,(\text{T}x \to \text{K}x)$.

(Or, as Fitch describes the argument, it is meant to show that a form of verificationism which is not obviously silly entails a 'very silly' form of verificationism.) If you suspect that no alethic anti-realist subscribes to (1), you must have forgotten the last pages of Chapter 1 (which is forgivable at this time of the day). As we saw there, Dummett finds (1) intuitively so compelling that he makes even realists somehow endorse it:[162]

[A] statement cannot be true unless it is in principle possible that it be known to be true. (*FPL*, 465)

[Even the realist] concedes the absurdity of supposing that a statement of any kind could be true if it was in principle impossible to know that it was true. (*LBM*, 345)

Anonym's Argument runs as follows. Let 'P' be a place-holder for the true answer to any decidable question which is so tedious that nobody ever cares to find out the answer:

(2) $\text{T}[\text{P}] \,\&\, \neg\,\text{K}[\text{P}]$.

Applying T-Elimination to the first conjunct in (2), we get

(3) $\text{P} \,\&\, \neg\,\text{K}[\text{P}]$.

From (3) we derive, in accordance with T-Introduction,

---

[162] Cf. pp. 23–4 above.

(4)   T [P & ¬ K [P]].

By applying universal instantiation and *modus ponens*, we obtain from (1) and (4):

(5)   ✦ K [P & ¬ K [P]].

Assuming that K-Distributivity can be applied within the scope of the modal operator, we move from (5) to

(6)   ✦ (K [P] & K [¬ K [P]]).

Assuming that K-Factivity can also be applied within the scope of the diamond, we apply it to the second conjunct of (6) and derive:

(7)   ✦ (K [P] & ¬ K [P]).

This tells us that a contradiction might be true, which is absurd. So from (1) and (2) we have derived an absurdity. If we keep premiss (1), the anti-realist principle of knowability, we must give up (2), *no matter which* decidable but actually never decided question is answered by 'P'. That is, we must deny the eminently reasonable assumption that at least one truth is in fact unknown:

(8)   ¬ ∃ x (Tx & ¬ Kx).

But (8) is (classically) equivalent to the preposterous contention that every truth *is* known:

(C)   ∀x (Tx → Kx).

So by accepting the apparently harmless principle of know*ability*, one incurs a commitment to collective omniscience (or to a 'very silly' form of verificationism). Hence we'd better give up that principle.

Since we have followed Putnam's long journey in search of the truth about truth rather closely, let me report here a finding that took me by surprise. Long before he adopted Internalism, Putnam used an abbreviated version of Anonym's Argument against Logical Empiricism:

[T]he claim . . . that having a truth value is the same as being verifiable is . . . untenable. The sentence

(3*)   There is a gold mountain one mile high and no one knows that there is a gold mountain one mile high

is, if true, unverifiable. No conceivable experience can show that both conjuncts in (3*) are simultaneously true; for any experience that verified the first conjunct would falsify the second, and thus the whole sentence. Yet no one has ever offered the slightest reason for one to think that (3*) could not be true in some possible world. ('Logical Positivism and the Philosophy of Mind', 443; [P.12]. Numbering of the indented sentence changed)[163]

Obviously Putnam's (3*) is a counterpart to line (3) in Anonym's Argument, and Putnam's argument is a reflection on line (5). If somebody were to know that P (that there is a gold mountain one mile high), he or she would be a living counter-example to the statement that ¬K[P] (that no one ever knows that there is a gold mountain one mile high). But a conjunction cannot be a content of knowledge if the first conjunct's being such a content entails the *falsity* of the second conjunct. So one can hear Putnam commenting on Anonym's Argument, 'Things are bad enough already at line (5).' Because of the peculiarity of the chosen example, [P.12], unlike Anonym's Argument, does not show that some proposition which is true *in our actual world* is knowledge-transcendent. And due to the fact that [P.12], like Anonym's Argument, uses the notion of knowledge, it is unclear whether it can also be used as a weapon for fighting Internalism.

If alethic anti-realists were to reject K-Distributivity they could escape Anonym's Argument. But would this be a reasonable strategy? K-Distributivity has been called 'an unimpeachable rule of epistemic logic',[164] and rightly so, I would have thought. It was impeached, though, by Robert Nozick: on his account, knowledge does *not* distribute over conjunction.[165] Since he does not support this denial by an independent argument, but only acknowledges it as an implication of his account of knowledge, 'it is hard not to regard [this implication] as a problem for his account'.[166] Moreover, just to be on the safe side, Williamson has constructed variants of Anonym's Argument which bring as much embarrassment to verificationists as the original, although they do not rely on K-Distributivity. One of them uses the predicate 'x is conjunctively unknown',[167] which applies to a proposition iff no conjunction is known of which it is a conjunct. Whatever proposition x may be, it cannot be known that (Tx & it is conjunctively unknown that Tx), for if that conjunction were known it would not be conjunctively unknown that Tx. Thus the principle of knowability entails that there are no conjunctively unknown truths. But this is preposterous: many a conjunction, one conjunct of which is the true answer to a

---

[163] Already in 1960 Popper had raised essentially the same objection against what he called 'subjective or epistemic theories of truth': see his 'Truth, Rationality, and the Growth of Scientific Knowledge', 225.

[164] Tennant, *Taming the True*, 260.   [165] Nozick, *Philosophical Explanations*, 228.

[166] As Peacocke very politely puts it: *Being Known*, 16. Williamson comes to the same result: *KL*, 278–9.

[167] Williamson's own locution, 'x is completely unknown', is somewhat misleading.

decidedly uninteresting decidable question that nobody ever cares to decide, will remain forever unknown. The formal version of this argument relies on K-Factivity but not on K-Distributivity.[168]

The argument I will offer in section 7.3.3 differs in several important respects from Anonym's Argument. First, in order to cover also Putnam's erstwhile Internalism, my argument does not centre around the notion of *knowledge* but around the non-factive notion of justified belief: it is an argument from blind spots in the field of justification (rather than in the field of knowledge). Secondly, my argument employs no distinctively *classical* rules of inference which are rejected by intuitionistic logicians. Thirdly, it abstains from substitution into *modal* contexts. The contrasting features of the original argument were seized upon by partisans of alethic anti-realism, for they seemed to provide them with various escape routes.[169]

7.3.2 *An example under hermeneutical presssure*

Since I want to ride my attack against alethic anti-realism on a concrete example, let us first have a close look at this example. According to the Gospel of St Matthew (10: 30), 'the very hairs of [my] head are all numbered', but let us suppose that the Gospel, taken literally, is wrong here. Although I am rather thin on top, I beg you to concede that I am definitely not bald (when writing this). Furthermore, let us make the (sadly counterfactual) assumption that whatever grows on my head is a paradigm case of a hair. Undisturbed by vagueness worries, we can now say: either it is true that the number of hairs now on my head is odd, or it is true that the number of hairs now on my head is even. (By maintaining this, one does *not* incur any obligation to subscribe to the general principle that

---

[168] Williamson, *KL*, 283–5, 318–9.

[169] For the 'knowledge reply', see Mackie, 'Truth and Knowability'. For the 'intuitionism reply', see the literature listed in Williamson, *KL*, 275 n. 3. Intuitionistically, the step from (8) to (C) is not valid, but isn't the result in (8) already bad enough? Moreover, suppose we have good reasons for believing that the end of the universe is imminent and let [Q] be a mathematical proposition which so far has neither been proved nor refuted. Our apocalyptic premiss supports the belief that not-K[Q]. From this and (8), assuming 'Q' for *reductio ad absurdum*, we can derive 'not-Q' (see Cesare Cozzo, '. . . Paradox of Knowability', 73). So we would be allowed to deny a mathematical proposition for a reason that has nothing to do with its content, and that is surely not acceptable. In 'The Knowability Paradox and the Prospects for Anti-Realism', 493–9, Kvanvig tries to block the argument by disallowing the step from (1) and (4) to (5), where application of universal instantiation requires substitution into the partially modal context of (1). I think Williamson has shown what is wrong with this strategy: *KL*, 285–9. However, in view of my reconstruction of Anonym's Argument in terms of *first-order* quantification (similar to Kvanvig's on pp. 481–2) it is somewhat misleading to describe Kvanvig's objection as directed against a certain 'use of universal instantiation into *sentence* position'.

of any two contradictory propositions one must be true.) Now *as a matter of contingent fact*, nobody ever bothers to count. But in the case at issue justification depends on someone's counting. Hence, nobody is in fact ever justified either in believing that the number in question is odd, or in believing that it is even. Therefore one of the following two sentences

(Σ_O)   The number of hairs now on my head is *odd*, but nobody is ever justified in believing that this is so

(Σ_E)   The number of hairs now on my head is *even*, but nobody is ever justified in believing that this is so

expresses a *truth* (with respect to me now),[170] and, as in the case of the A's in the *Divine Comedy*, every sane adherent of an epistemic view of truth is ready to concede this. We will see that this eminently reasonable concession will cause a lot of trouble for alethic anti-realism.[171]

But let us not be too quick here. In arguing that one of the two Σ-sentences expresses a truth, we took it for granted that these sentences make sense. But are our Σ-sentences comprehensible at all? (This is part of what I called Dummett's Hermeneutical Challenge. Wright explicitly raises it for Σ-like sentences.[172]) Nonsense is not always patent nonsense;[173] sometimes it masquerades as sense, so the impression of intelligibility can be deceptive. Of course, there is a meaning of 'meaning' according to which the type-sentence (Σ_O), for example, is clearly *not* meaningless. (I take type-sentences to be the things that have or lack significance.[174]) Sentence (Σ_O) does not contain any such non-word as Lewis Carroll's 'tove'. Unlike the result of reversing its word order, say, it is grammatically well-formed. And one can plausibly claim that its meaning is different from that of (Σ_E) and that substitution of 'no one' for 'nobody' would not affect its meaning. But these observations do not suffice to show that a declarative sentence is significant in a more demanding sense: they do not establish that

---

[170] Of course, this contention does not depend on acceptance of the general principle either: it is possible that our Σ-propositions are *both* false, so they don't make up a contradictory pair. Resistance motivated by the intuitionistic understanding of disjunction will be faced in sect. 7.3.4 below.

[171] Notice the decisive difference between Σ-like propositions and the macabre example used on pp. 420–1 above. That Dr Crippen committed a perfect murder does not imply that *nobody* is ever justified in believing that this is so. After all, the murderer may have good reasons for believing that his crime was perfect (and even his victim may have had time enough to acquire a well-grounded belief that nobody will ever find out that Dr Crippen killed him).

[172] See p. 24 above. We will shortly consider the 'argument from normativity', which Wright gives in 'Introduction', 23–6.

[173] Cf. Wittgenstein, *Philosophische Untersuchungen*, §464: '*Was ich lehren will, ist: von einem nicht offenkundigen Unsinn zu einem offenkundigen übergehen.* [My aim is to teach you to pass from a piece of disguised nonsense to something that is patent nonsense.]'   [174] Following Strawson, 'On Referring', sect. II.

it expresses a proposition which is apt for truth or falsity (T/F-apt, for short). After all, the next two sentences,

(A)   Seven is red
(B)   Friday is in the cave

are also neither (lexically) gibberish nor (grammatically) garbled. And the meaning of (A) differs from that of 'Seven is blue' but coincides with that of '*Sieben ist rot*', just as (B) has a different meaning from 'Friday is outside the cave' and the same meaning as '*Freitag ist in der Höhle.*' But for all that, philosophers like Carnap and Ryle would regard (A) and (B) as paradigm cases of a *Sphärenvermengung* (confounding of types), of a category mistake.[175] Let us assume they are right in denying that (A) and (B) express T/F-apt propositions and hence in setting them apart from self-evident falsehoods (like those that are expressed by 'Seven is smaller than six' and 'Friday is the day after Monday').[176] As a sufficient condition of being significant (expressive of a T/F-apt proposition), we can lay down this: if a type-sentence under standard readings of its constituents can be used to make a warranted assertion, then it *is* significant. Notice that if one were to drop the proviso 'under standard readings of its constituents', one would have to declare the type-sentences (A) and (B) to be significant: a speaker looking at the red-brick house at 7 Elm Street can make a true observation report by uttering (A), and the same holds *mutatis mutandis* for (B) in Robinson Crusoe's mouth.

Just in case you wonder why I take non-significant sentences to express propositions at all, let me remind you that I argued in Chapter 5.1.1 that the truth of a propositional attitude-ascription or of an indirect speech report, 'A Vs that p,' ensures that there is something that is Ved by A, namely the proposition that p. Now it would be perfectly correct to say, e.g., 'Prior denied that virtue is square.'[177] So I am obliged to concede that the embedded sentence expresses a proposition, no matter whether void of truth-value or glaringly false.

---

[175] For references, see p. 41 nn. 30–1. Ryle's approach to the idea of category mismatch was corrected and much refined in Strawson, 'Categories'. A very comprehensive and systematic account is to be found in Routley and Goddard, *The Logic of Significance and Context*.

[176] A proposition may be T/F-*apt* without *being* either true or false. According to Frege, Geach, and Strawson, 'The King of Switzerland in 2001 is rich' expresses such a proposition. Many philosophers would say the same about the proposition now expressed by 'The number of trees in Canada is odd.' Although it is very hard to imagine, Switzerland might have been a monarchy. There might have been no borderline case of 'tree' in Canada, and the Canadian trees might all have been situated at least 10 miles away from the Canadian border. So the propositions expressed by those sentences are T/F-apt even if they are neither T nor F.

[177] See Prior, 'Entities', 25 (and the well-taken criticism of Prior's argument against the doctrine of category mistakes in Routley and Goddard, *The Logic of Significance and Context*, 13).

Now the defence of our Σ-sentences against the imputation of non-significance seems to be very easy. Their *conjuncts* are *not* justification-transcendent. One gets into the position of verifying the first conjunct by making a careful count. As for the second conjunct, consider the following scenario: I am alone in the desert, and I am well aware of this fact. In a fit of desperation, I have just pulled out a handful of my hair. I am presently going to do the same again, and in the meantime I do not seize the opportunity to determine the number of hairs I have left. Then I can warrantedly assert that nobody is ever justified in believing that the number of hairs now on my head is odd [even]. Thus, the significance of the conjuncts is beyond doubt. From the fact that the conjuncts of a Σ-sentence are significant, it seems to follow that the conjunction is significant as well. How could the conjunction of two significant declarative sentences lack significance?

But this Internal Compositionality Argument may be less forceful than it looks. Consider the following conjunction:

(C*)   The last item mentioned on Ann's list weighs three tons, and the Pythagorean Theorem is the last item mentioned on Ann's list.

Both conjuncts of (C*) are significant: each could be used, under standard readings of its constituents, to make a warranted assertion. But isn't the conjunction as a whole in the same boat, as far as significance is concerned, as the next sentence?

(C)   The Pythagorean Theorem weighs three tons.

And, of course, (C) is bound to be abused, just like (A) and (B) above, as a category mistake. (We can derive (C) from (C*) if we allow for the application of elimination rules for 'and' and 'is (the same as)' to all conjunctions and identity sentences that are neither gibberish nor garbled. Such a derivation would literally be a reductio ad *absurdum*.) So it is not as plain as it first appeared that the Argument from Internal Compositionality succeeds in clearing Σ-sentences from the charge of being cases of disguised nonsense.

Can one secure the comprehensibility of Σ-sentences by an Argument from Analogy? I am not thinking here of the analogical extrapolation Dummett supposes the realist to rely upon, which was briefly discussed in Chapter 1.[178] That is to say, I am not appealing to an analogy in the mode of justification but, rather, to an analogy in truth-conditions.[179] (The beautiful comparison Lucretius used for explaining atomism might help to fix the distinction.[180] One states an analogy in truth-conditions when one says, along Lucretius' lines, 'The

[178] See above, pp. 23–4.   [179] Cf. Sklar, 'Semantic Analogy', esp. 227.
[180] Titus Lucretius Carus, *De Rerum Natura*, II. 312–22.

fact that macroscopic bodies are swarms of micro-particles is analogous to the fact that the herd on the slopes of a distant hill consists of sheep.' By contrast, one would state an analogy in the mode of justification if one were to say, 'As a shepherd on the hill is able to see each of his sheep individually, so a super-human verifier can perceive every single micro-particle.') The Argument from Analogy is meant to show that significance is projected out of sentences that express warrantedly assertible propositions to Σ-sentences by means of an analogy in truth-conditions. Suppose that at time t, shortly after I tore out some of my hairs and shortly before I did so again, only my barber and I were in a position to ascertain the number of hairs on my head, we *did* do so, the result of our count was an odd number, and each of us promised the other on oath to take this secret with him to the grave. Under these circumstances, I would have been justified in asserting at t that

(Σ_2) the number of hairs now on my head is odd, but *apart from me and my barber* nobody is ever justified in believing that this is so.

If you cut the barber out of the story, you have a situation in which I would be warranted in claiming at that

(Σ_1) the number of hairs now on my head is odd, but *apart from me* nobody is ever justified in believing that this is so.

At this point it seems that we can appeal to what the scholastics would have called an *analogia proportionalitatis*: keeping speaker and time constant, the truth-conditions of what is expressed by (Σ_2) are related to those of what is expressed by (Σ_1), as are the truth-conditions of what is expressed by (Σ_1) to those of what is expressed by

(Σ_0) The number of hairs now on my head is odd, but nobody is ever justified in believing that this is so.

So if this argument is to be trusted, significance accrues to (Σ_0) from analogy.

Unfortunately, analogical extrapolations of this type are not always legitimate, as Wittgenstein has pointed out.[181] We know, for example, the truth-conditions of what is said in an utterance of 'All five-pound notes now in my purse are counterfeit.' But from this we cannot conclude that 'All five-pound

---

[181] Wittgenstein, *Philosophische Untersuchungen*, §345; *Zettel*, §133. Remember also Alice's embarrassment after having recited a poem to the Caterpillar: ' "That is not said right," said the Caterpillar. "Not *quite* right, I'm afraid," said Alice, timidly; "some of the words have got altered." "It is wrong from beginning to end," said the Caterpillar decidedly, and there was silence for some minutes' (Lewis Carroll, *Alice's Adventures in Wonderland*, ch. 5).

notes are counterfeit' (taking the 'all' not to be contextually restricted) may also express a truth. This transition would be illegitimate because nothing can fall under the concept 'x is a counterfeit five-pound note' if the concept 'x is a (genuine) five-pound note' is empty.[182] So we need an additional argument which shows why, in the case of (Σ_0), projection of significance by analogy can be relied upon.

Here is another attempt to protect our Σ-sentences against accusations of non-significance. Sane alethic anti-realists admit that

(∃1)　∃p (p but nobody is ever justified in believing that p).

Hence, so the Global Argument from Existential Generalization runs, they must concede that some substitution-instance of the matrix expresses a truth— 'otherwise a general proposition would be true, when no instance of it was'.[183] But then the significance of substitution-instances such as our Σ-sentences cannot generally be in doubt, for only a significant sentence can express a truth. The weak link in this argument is the sweeping assumption that an existential quantification cannot yield a truth if none of its substitution-instances does so. The truth that there is an anonymous pebble in the dark unfathomed caves of the ocean rebuts this assumption.[184]

The next two arguments, I think, really do answer the Hermeneutical Challenge.[185] The first one might be called the Local Argument from Existential Generalization. The following sentence is significant:

(∃2)　∃n (The number of hairs now on my head is n, but nobody is ever justified in believing that n is the number of hairs now on my head),

since, in the scenario described above (alone in the desert and all that), I would be justified in uttering (∃2) with assertoric force. Now (∃2) cannot express a truth about me unless some number between 20 and 200,000 is such that *it* is the number of my hairs at the time in question. (Remember your kind concessions as to the state of my scalp.) So a sentence that is obtained from (∃2) by deleting the quantifier and substituting a designator of that number for the variable in the

---

[182] Some surprisingly ill-informed forgers in Britain might produce six-pound notes, but these odd items would not be counterfeit six-pound notes, and if we call them 'counterfeit banknotes', the argument can be repeated for this predicate.

[183] Skorupski, 'The Intelligibility of Scepticism' (henceforth 'Intelligibility'), 21; cf. his 'Critical Study', 524. (In n. 185 I will register that Skorupski has an argument for the conclusion we are aiming at, which is independent of this assumption.)　　　　　　　　　　[184] Cf. Prior, *OT*, 68.

[185] I have used variants of both arguments in '*Bolzano's blühender Baum*'. Skorupski employs versions of the second argument in 'Critical Study', 524, in 'Intelligibility', 20, and in 'Meaning, Use, Verification', 44, 47–8, to make the point that a sentential constituent of a meaningful sentence must itself be meaningful. (Surely he would agree to adding the proviso 'unless that constituent is flanked by quotation marks'.)

matrix expresses a truth about me. But that number is either even or odd. So one of our Σ-sentences follows from a truth, the other follows from many falsehoods, and, consequently, they must both be significant. Our understanding of ($\exists 2$) ensures, 'top-down' as it were, that our Σ-sentences do express T/F-apt propositions. Notice that in this argument no assumption about *all* existential generalizations was made.

The External Compositionality Argument gets us to the same destination. Surely the proposition that the number of hairs now on my head is odd does not logically imply that at some time somebody *is* justified in believing that this is so. So the following modalization of (Σ_0) is bound to be significant:

(M)   It is logically possible that (the number of hairs now on my head is odd although nobody is ever justified in believing that this is so).

But the modal operator in (M) cannot deliver a significant sentence as output when it receives a non-significant one as input. By contrast, the result of embedding (C) in 'It is logically possible that (...)' is no more significant than (C) itself. So (Σ_0) does express a T/F-apt proposition.[186]

The External Compositionality Argument can help us to alleviate Wright's worry about Σ-sentences. His 'argument from normativity' runs as follows:

'[Truth] is what our assertions are, other things being equal, aimed at, and its absence is a ground for their criticism. But how can undetectable truth discharge this role? What is it to *try* to record truth by use of [a Σ-sentence]?' ('Introduction', 24–5).

Answer: a sentence that is not assertible on its own may occur as a constituent in a complex sentence that can be used assertively, and when it is so used, it does serve an attempt to record truth (provided the speaker is sincere). This happens when I utter the modalization of (Σ_0) sincerely and with assertoric force.[187] Hence we do not suffer from an illusion when we take Σ-sentences to be significant. So let us put them to good use at last.

---

[186] Moore's objection against Russell's claim that 'This (sense-datum) exists' is 'meaningless' runs along similar lines: see 'Is Existence a Predicate?', 124–5.

[187] The fact that Σ-sentences are not assertible (which I took for granted in the above argument) can be explained on two assumptions: (i) you must not assert that p unless you know that p, and (ii) you cannot know that things are as a Σ-sentence says they are. Williamson, *KL*, 238–60, makes a very good case for (i), and on pp. 428–9 above we saw that (ii) is supported by Putnam's reflections on line (5) in Anonym's Argument. At this point it turns out that the negation of a Σ-sentence is assertible even on an intuitionistic account of '$\neg$' which permits us to assert '$\neg A$' iff we are warranted in asserting that there will never be a warrant for asserting 'A'. (For a critical discussion of this rule, see Edgington, 'Meaning, Bivalence and Realism', 166–8.)

7.3.3 *The argument from justification blindspots*

Alethic anti-realists maintain that every truth (which is comprehensible to human beings) can in principle become the content of a justified (human) belief. (In what follows I take the restrictions in parentheses as understood.) Anti-realists do not claim that a proposition's being true entails that it is rationally accepted at some time or other, but they are all agreed that the truth of a proposition does at least not *foreclose* its rational acceptance. This gives us a Common Denominator of all varieties of alethic anti-realism, including the most liberal one, Putnam's erstwhile Internalism:

(ComDen)   There is no true proposition such that the assumption that it is both *true* and the content of a *justified* belief implies a contradiction.

Notice that the first occurrence of 'true' in (ComDen) is not redundant.[188] Every logically inconsistent, hence necessarily *false*, proposition is such that the assumption that it is both true and the content of a justified belief implies a contradiction. Furthermore, the contingently *false* proposition that there are no believers is also such that the assumption that it is both true and the content of a justified belief implies a contradiction, because if a proposition is the content of a belief, then there is at least one believer. But the fact that some *false* propositions cannot consistently be assumed to be both true and justified cannot be held against alethic anti-realists. After all, their contention is that all *true* propositions can be justified.[189]

If (ComDen) can be shown to be incorrect, then alethic anti-realism is refuted. So let's see whether either of our Σ-sentences expresses a proposition that can consistently be assumed to be both true and justified. Apart from &-Elimination and &-Introduction, my argument for alethic realism uses two further rules. The first one does not stand in need of explanation, let alone defence. (It was also used in Anonym's Argument.)

T-Elimination $\dfrac{\Gamma\colon\ \mathrm{T}\,[\mathrm{A}]}{\Gamma\colon\ \mathrm{A}}$

The second rule permits us to move from a premiss in which justified belief in a conjunction is ascribed to a conclusion in which justified beliefs in each of the conjuncts is ascribed.[190] Using '$\mathfrak{J}$' as an abbreviation for 'is at some time or other

---

[188] In 'Truth and a Kind of Realism', 35, I still failed to notice it.

[189] To save breath, I sometimes use 'justified' as short for 'the content of a justified belief'.

[190] This principle is obviously the $\mathfrak{J}$-counterpart to K-Distributivity in Anonym's Argument as presented in sect. 7.3.1.

the content of a *justified* belief', we can say that the second rule permits distribution of the operator '𝔍 [...]' across '&':

𝔍-*Distributivity* $\dfrac{\Gamma:\ \ 𝔍[A\ \&\ B]}{\Gamma:\ \ 𝔍\,[A]\ \&\ 𝔍\,[B]}$

At this point I cannot do much more than try to evoke your consent by means of a rhetorical question. How on earth could somebody, who wasn't justified in believing a certain proposition, at the same time be justified in believing a conjunction containing this proposition? How could there fail to be evidence for either of the conjuncts if there *is* evidence for the conjunction as a whole?[191]

Often a conjunctive belief is inferentially due to prior beliefs in the conjuncts, and in such cases there is of course no justified belief in the conjunction without justified belief in the conjuncts. But there are also other ways of obtaining a justified conjunctive belief: it may owe its justification to testimony received for the conjunction as a whole, or its justification may be due to an inference from 'If C then (A and B)' and 'C', where these two premisses are reasonably believed.[192] Or perhaps a perceptual encounter provided the subject with an opportunity to realize at a glance that (A and B). So we cannot legitimize our acceptance of 𝔍-Distributivity by referring to something like a canonical way of obtaining a conjunctive belief. We should, rather, say that this rule is legitimate because one cannot be justified in believing a conjunction without *thereby* already being justified in believing the conjuncts.[193]

Obviously, for believing either of the conjuncts, one does not need any conceptual resources that were not already needed for believing the conjunction. It is instructive to compare &-Elimination with ∨-Introduction in this respect. In Fodor's 'Guide to Mental Representation' we read, 'To know that Sam thinks that it is raining is to know that it's highly probable that he thinks that either it is raining or John left.' Surely we should *not* follow our spirited guide at this point, for it is very improbable, to put it mildly, that Sam thinks the latter thought if he has neither ever heard about John nor ever come across him. That somebody believes that A, is never a good reason to ascribe to him the belief that (A or B), if grasping the proposition that B requires mastery of concepts

---

[191] No wonder, then, that the following dialogue ends in frustration: 'Why do you believe that (p & q)?' 'Because NN, a very reliable eye-witness, as you know, told me that (p & q).' 'I see, yes, that's a good reason. But I still do not understand why you believe that *p*? It's so very unlikely that p.' 'Good Lord, as I just said, I got my information from a trustworthy witness!'   [192] Cf. Williamson, *KL*, 282.

[193] Tennant, whom I have already reported as declaring K-Distributivity to be 'an unimpeachable rule of epistemic logic', continues: 'It holds good even for non-factive interpretations of "K" such as "There is good evidence for..."' (*Taming the True*, 260; cf. 265).

that are not available to him.[194] By contrast, there is no such risk if we ascribe belief in a conjunct on the basis of belief in the conjunction. Our readiness to take those who warrantedly believe that (A and B) to be *eo ipso* warranted in believing that A is based on more than just on the self-evidence of the conditional 'If A and B, then A', for the conditional 'If A, then A or B' is equally self-evident.

Let 'O' abbreviate the first conjunct of Σ_O, i.e. 'The number of hairs now on my head is *odd*.' Then the refutation of alethic anti-realism I promised can be set up like this:

1	(1)	T [O	&	¬ $\mathfrak{J}$ [O]]		Assumption
2	(2)	$\mathfrak{J}$ [O	&	¬ $\mathfrak{J}$ [O]]		Assumption
2	(3)	$\mathfrak{J}$ [O]	&	$\mathfrak{J}$ [¬ $\mathfrak{J}$ [O]]	2,	$\mathfrak{J}$-*Distributivity*
2	(4)	$\mathfrak{J}$ [O]			3,	&-Elimination
1	(5)	O	&	¬ $\mathfrak{J}$ [O]	1,	T-*Elimination*
1	(6)			¬ $\mathfrak{J}$ [O]	5,	&-Elimination
1, 2	(7)	$\mathfrak{J}$ [O]	&	¬ $\mathfrak{J}$ [O]	4, 6,	&-Introduction

From (1) and (2) we have derived a contradiction in (7); thus in the case of Σ_O, being true, line (1), and being justified, line (2), *do* exclude each other. As regards Σ_E, the argument runs on the very same lines, of course. Hence, each of these two propositions is such that the assumption that it is both true and (the content of a) justified (belief) implies a contradiction. But admittedly one of these propositions *is* true. (Don't ask me which one: how would I know?) Hence, either the above argument or its counterpart for Σ_E shows that there is a proposition that falsifies (ComDen) and thereby all versions of alethic anti-realism. One counter-example is enough, but of course, after the model of our two Σ-propositions, structurally similar examples could be multiplied *au plaisir*. Truth is not epistemically constrained. Some truths which we are able to comprehend are beyond justification, hence a fortiori beyond justifcation by a human being. Alethic realism is vindicated.

A super-human verifier, too, cannot verify Σ_O or Σ_E. But, of course, if there is a super-human verifier who literally knows *everything*, then 'the very hairs of our heads are all numbered' by Him, and both Σ_O and Σ_E are *false*. But that is another ball game.

This Argument from Justification Blindspots[195] aims at showing that in the case of propositions such as Σ_O, being true and being justified exclude each other,

---

[194] The quotation is from 'Fodor's Guide...', 15; cf. my 'Some Varieties of Thinking', 376–7. More recently, Williamson has raised exactly the same objection against Dretske: *KL*, 282–3.

[195] This appellation (deletion of space between 'blind' and 'spot' included) is borrowed from Sorensen's highly illuminating book of the same title. I do not use the term 'blindspot' *quite* in Sorensen's sense, however. In my usage, a truth P is a justification blindspot iff P cannot consistently be assumed to be both true and justified.

i.e. that

(1) $T[O \ \& \ \neg \ \Im \ [O]]$

(2) $\Im[O \ \& \ \neg \ \Im \ [O]]$

imply a contradiction. In order to reach this destination, the argument needed five more steps, but one may very well have the impression that, as Dorothy Edgington puts it, 'Things are bad enough at line (2)... . It is clear that no possible state of information could support the hypothesis "O, and no one at any time has any evidence that O".'[196] (This parallels Putnam's early reflections on line (5) of Anonym's Argument.) If (1) may be true whereas (2) cannot possibly be true, so much the worse for alethic anti-realism, of course. But are things already that bad at line (2)? Perhaps this is as clear as Edgington says it is, but I for one do not yet see it clearly.

Of course, if $\Im$ [O], then the Σ -proposition that (O & $\neg\Im$ [O]) is *false*. But that does not yet show that one could not, as assumed in (2), be *justified* in believing this conjunction.[197] Skorupski argues against this alleged possibility as follows: 'If we have grounds for asserting the first conjunct in Σ_O , we have grounds for denying the second.'[198] Yes, but couldn't we simultaneously also have grounds for *asserting* the second? Skorupski continues, 'And if we have grounds for asserting the second, we can have no grounds for asserting the first.' Why not? Imagine the following situation. For good reasons I believe that $\neg\Im$ [O]: after all, I do not care to find out whether O, and why should anyone else ever bother to go through such a wearisome procedure for obtaining such trivial information? But oddly enough, I also have testimonial evidence for the hypothesis that O. What has happened? One night, to my utmost surprise, I wake up in a hospital, with a dreadful pain in my chest. A nurse tries to cheer me up. She tells me that I have been through a dangerous operation, that ever since she has been sitting beside my bed while I was fast asleep, that she was all the time afraid of falling asleep herself, and that she kept herself awake by—counting the hairs on my head. With a faint sceptical smile I ask her for the result of the count, and when she gives her ('odd') answer she looks really quite sincere. In spite of my still having grounds for asserting the second conjunct of Σ_O , I now also have grounds for asserting the first.

But would the combination of these two bodies of evidence be evidence for the *conjunctive* belief that (O & $\neg\Im$ [O])? Would I, in such a state of information, be entitled to accept Σ_O , with a low degree of conviction perhaps? There seems to

---

[196] Edgington, 'The Paradox of Knowability', 558. (I have substituted my 'O'.) Wright, 'Assertibility', 427 and Williamson, 'Knowability and Constructivism', 423 (though not, or not explicitly, in his book) concur, and they also seem to think that the point does not stand in need of an argument. As we shall see in a second, Skorupski, who also accepts the point, does offer an argument.

[197] As against my '*Bolzanos blühender Baum*', 240.

[198] Skorupski, 'Intelligibility', 19–20 (example exchanged).

be a very strong argument for the answer *No* and hence in support of those who find the assumption in line (2) absurd. Either the testimony given by the nurse defeats my reasons for believing that $\neg\mathfrak{J}$ [O], or the latter reasons defeat the justificatory power of her testimony for [O], or both bodies of evidence keep each other in check. So either I have an all-things-considered justification only for the belief that O, or I have an all-things-considered justification only for the belief that $\neg\mathfrak{J}$ [O], or I have no all-things-considered justification for either belief.

But do bodies of evidence always interact in the way that is presupposed in this argument? Remember one of my examples (in sect. 7.1.2 above) for justified beliefs that form an inconsistent set. Let '$p_1, p_2, \ldots, p_n$' be all the statements in Ann's well-argued thesis. She is justified in believing that p_1, in believing that $p_2, \ldots$ and in believing that p_n. But she is also justified in her self-critical belief that $\neg(p_1 \ \& \ p_2 \ \& \ldots \& \ p_n)$. Her reasons for what she says in the preface do not overturn her reasons for what she says in the rest of the book, nor vice versa, and it is reasonable of her to keep all these beliefs even when she realizes what her predicament is. If this characterization of her cognitive state is correct, then bodies of evidence do not *always* interact in the way that was taken for granted in the previous paragraph.[199]

So far, our considerations have shown at best that I might be justified in believing that O and in believing (at the same time) that $\neg\mathfrak{J}$ [O]. But do the premisses 'At time t, person m is justified in believing that A' and 'At t, m is justified in believing that B' entail the conclusion 'At t, m is justified in believing that (A and B)'? Since our operator '$\mathfrak{J}$ [...]' contains no reference to a particular time or a particular believer, the inversion of $\mathfrak{J}$-Distributivity is all too clearly unacceptable: different people at different times may be justified in believing that A and that B, although nobody is ever justified in believing that (A and B).[200] But if we replace our operator by '$\mathfrak{J}_{t,m}$ [...]', to be read as 'At t, m is justified in believing that...', then the question does arise whether '$\mathfrak{J}_{t,m}$' *collects* across '&'. Now if we were to accept $\mathfrak{J}_{t,m}$-Collectivity, we would have to represent Ann as believing that $((p_1 \ \& \ p_2 \ \& \ldots \& \ p_n) \ \& \ \neg(p_1 \ \& \ p_2 \ \& \ldots \& \ p_n))$, hence as believing an explicit contradiction. I think this would be very unfair on her. The Paradox of the Preface, I take it, provides us with a good reason for rejecting $\mathfrak{J}_{t,m}$-Collectivity.[201] But then we cannot appeal to this discredited rule in support of the claim that I might be warranted in believing that (O & $\neg\mathfrak{J}$ [O]).

---

[199] Cf. Kvanvig, 'The Knowability Paradox', 485.

[200] Because of the 'existential' character of '$\mathfrak{J}$', line (3) in our Blindspot Argument is harmless: perhaps *I* secretly counted, while *you* still have the same excellent reasons for believing that nobody will ever bother, which I *had* before I engaged in that tedious activity.

[201] I agree here with Sorensen, *Blindspots*, 93, and Foley, *The Theory of Epistemic Rationality*, ch. 6. Of course, $\mathfrak{J}$-Distributivity shouldn't suffer from guilt by association. (On pp. 422 above, we saw reason to deny that '$\mathfrak{R}$' collects across '&', but that was a point about justifi*ability*, not about justification.)

So the question whether I might have such an entitlement is still open. The negative answer may very well be correct, but it cannot appeal to a generally valid principle concerning the interaction of bodies of evidence. The argument for the affirmative answer cannot appeal to a generally acceptable rule of inference. So I prefer not to base my case against alethic anti-realism on a verdict against assumption (2).

It is noteworthy that by thinning '$\Im$' out, so to speak, one gets counter-examples to common denominators of all positions opposed to alethic realism, which are yet smaller than (ComDen). If a truth can be the content of a justified belief, then a fortiori it can be the content of a belief—and of a (committal or non-committal) thought. These weaker predicates distribute over conjunction: one cannot believe or merely entertain a conjunctive proposition without thereby believing or entertaining its conjuncts.[202] Hence, if in the argument from (1) to (7) 'is at some time or other the content of a *justified belief*' is replaced by 'is at some time or other the content of a *belief*' or by 'is at some time or other the content of a *thought*', we can again derive a contradiction. You can move along the same path if you replace justified belief, belief, and thought by their counterparts in speech. Then you pass from 'is at some time or other *warrantedly asserted*' via 'is at some time or other *asserted*' to 'is at some time or other *expressed*', and in each case you can derive a contradiction, since these predicates, too, distribute over conjunction.[203]

Now let us look at the counterparts to line (2) in two of these 'thinner' cases. Surely it *is* possible to entertain the thought that (O, but nobody ever entertains the thought that O). Why? One can be justified in believing that it is *not* the case that (O, but nobody ever entertains the thought that O), and one cannot even grasp (let alone rationally accept) the negation of a proposition without grasping the proposition that is negated. Of course, since one cannot entertain a conjunction without

---

[202] Cf. my 'Some Varieties of Thinking', 372–6. As for belief, Brian Loar thinks that 'If at a time t somebody were to believe that (A & B), then he would believe that A at t and he would believe that B at t' is only an approximately true 'psychological assumption' concerning minimal rationality (*Mind and Meaning*, 71–3), but I could not figure out why he suspects there to be exceptions. Williamson's discussion of a prima facie exception culminates in the observation that 'the case is not terribly convincing' (*KL*, 280).

[203] As regards the indicator of assertoric force in his Concept Script, Frege would deny this, for '⊢ A and ⊢ B' is not a well-formed formula: cf. Stepanians, *Frege und Husserl*, 126–31, on 'judging that (A & B)'. But Frege does not claim that natural languages comply with the requirement that the indicator of assertoric force must never appear in an embedded position. In '*Der Gedanke*', 62 n., he writes 'that a subordinate clause can also contain an assertion (*daß auch ein Nebensatz eine Behauptung enthalten kann*)'. Presumably, he is thinking of examples such as 'B because A' or 'Gottlob knows (realizes, notices, sees, remembers) that A': in an assertoric utterance of such a sentence, you represent yourself as believing that A. It is noteworthy that a sentence can 'contain an assertion' even within a yes/no interrogative: asking 'Did Gottlob know (…) that A?', you also represent yourself as believing that A.

entertaining its conjuncts, assuming the 'entertainment' counterpart to (1) is bound to be making a false assumption. By contrast, assuming the 'belief' counterpart of (1) may be making a true assumption. But is it possible to *believe* that (O, but nobody ever believes that O)? Arguments to the effect that one cannot *assert* that (O, but nobody ever believes that O) abound in the literature on Moore's Paradox,[204] but they do not yet show that one cannot believe that things are that way.[205] But let us suppose this can be shown. Then it is a fortiori impossible to be justified in the belief that (O, but nobody ever believes that O). But this does not demonstrate the impossibility of being justified in believing that (O, but nobody is ever *justified* in believing that O). So again we are not provided with ammunition against the assumption in line (2).

7.3.4 *Attempts at answering the challenge*

Among the many attempts in the literature of the last two decades of the twentieth century to take the sting out of Anonym's Argument, there are some that might also be turned against my (purported) refutation of alethic anti-realism. I shall probe now three of these attempts and question their capacity to shield alethic anti-realism as it stands from the attack I mounted.[206]

---

[204] '[T]o say such a thing as "I went to the pictures last Tuesday, but I don't believe that I did" is a perfectly absurd thing to say, although . . . it is perfectly possible that you did go to the pictures and yet you do not believe that you did' (Moore, 'A Reply to My Critics', 543). Obviously, if (strictly) nobody ever believes that I went to the pictures last Tuesday then I don't believe it either. Hence, the 'nobody ever' variant of Moore's example suffers from the same kind of absurdity. (I have added 'strictly' for the sake of cases such as the following: worried by some noises after midnight, Ann has made Ben go into the cellar. 'Is anybody down there?', she asks. 'No, there is nobody here.' Let's hope that she won't infuriate him by becoming pedantic now.)   [205] This also applies to the argument in Williamson, *KL*, 254.

[206] Although Edgington's and Tennant's reactions to Anonym's Argument are also relevant for an appraisal of my argument, I shall confine my comments on their proposals to this footnote, since I think they have already been adequately dealt with in the literature. Neither author objects to any step in Anonym's Argument. Rather, they both plead for a modified principle of knowability, and it is more than likely that they would also argue for a corresponding modification of the principle of justifiability. Edgington's reformed anti-realist claims that if a proposition x is true *in this actual situation*, then there is a possible but non-actual situation in which it is known that x is true *in this actual situation* ('The Paradox of Knowability', esp. 566–7). This, she claims, leads to no trouble even if x is the proposition that (p & it is never known that p). One of the problems with this strategy is to explicate the notion 'knowing in a non-actual situation what is the case in the actual situation' in such a way that this kind of essentially modal knowledge is not obtained too easily. Cf. the discussion in Wright, 'Assertibility', 426–32; Percival, 'Knowability, Actuality, and the Metaphysics of Context-Dependence'; and Williamson, *KL*, 19, 290–301. Tennant's reformed anti-realist contends only that every true proposition *for which the assumption that it is at some time the content of someone's knowledge is consistent* is knowable (*Taming the True*, ch. VIII, esp. 273–4). But this is really an evasion. First we are told: 'Before he even considers what is peculiar to any discourse, the anti-realist will be committed to the tenet that truth is in principle knowable. That is, he will reject Knowledge-Transcendence across the board. . . . In every discourse the notion of truth will be epistemically

[1] In a discussion note on Anonym's Argument, Joseph Melia contends that it is quite harmless for alethic anti-realism.[207] If he were in the right as against that argument, he would also defuse my objection. Applying his reasoning to the latter, it runs like this: the argument is unproblematic for alethic anti-realists, since although Σ-propositions cannot be verified, they can be falsified. Melia's premiss is true. Consider Σ_O. One can have evidence against [O]'s being an undetected *truth* or against its being an *undetected* truth. Suppose I took the trouble of making a careful count. If the number I arrived at was even, my belief that the first conjunct of Σ_O is false warrants my assertion that not-Σ_O. If the number I arrived at was odd, my belief that I have verified the first conjunct justifies my belief that the second conjunct of Σ_O is false and thereby it warrants my assertion that not-Σ_O. *But* Melia's conclusion does not follow. The falsifiability of Σ-propositions does not help alethic anti-realists, for they maintain that all true propositions can be verified.

The point on which I am agreed with Melia is highly pertinent to the question whether there are unanswerable questions.[208] Peirce averred that 'there is to every question a true answer... to which the mind of man is, on the whole and in the long run, tending.'[209] As it stands, this is extremely implausible even with respect to the tiresome question whether the number of hairs now on my head is odd or even. One would hope that the mind of man will in the long run be occupied with more pressing problems than this one. More reasonably, Wittgenstein contended, '*Wenn sich eine Frage überhaupt stellen läßt, so* kann *sie auch beantwortet werden* [if a question can be put at all, then it *can* also be answered].'[210] The Logical Empiricists agreed: Carnap endorsed the principle of the '*Entscheidbarkeit aller Fragen* [decidability of all questions]',[211] and, according to Schlick, 'the impossibility of answering questions never belongs to the question *as such*, is never a matter of principle, but is always due to accidental empirical circumstances which may some day change'.[212] (Vagueness does not provide us with a good reason for contradicting these philosophers. A yes/no question such as 'Is he bald?' may have neither a 'definitely yes' nor a 'definitely no' answer, but it does not thereby become an unanswerable question.) Does inserting a Σ-sentence into

---

constrained' (ibid., 50). In the end we are given only a defence of the claim that all true propositions *that lack the property that was fatal for the original tenet* are knowable. It has also been argued that Tennant's restriction is in any case futile. The charges of ad hoc-ness and of futility were raised by Kvanvig and Hand and by Williamson respectively, and Tennant has tried to defuse them: see Bibliography.

[207] Melia, 'Anti-Realism Untouched'. Cf. Williamson, *KL*, 289–90, and Wright, 'Epistemic', 356–7.

[208] As the last paragraph of 'Truth and a Kind of Realism' shows, it took me a while to realize this.

[209] Peirce, *CP*, 8.12; cf. 7.319.   [210] Wittgenstein, *Tractatus Logico-Philosophicus*, 6.5 (my emphasis).

[211] Carnap, *Der Logische Aufbau der Welt*, §180.   [212] Schlick, 'Unanswerable Questions?', 373 (417).

the interrogative frame 'Is it the case that...?' yield an unanswerable question? It does not, since the answer '(Definitely) *no*' may be warranted. The peculiarity of Σ-questions consists in the fact that one cannot be warranted in answering 'Yes' even if things are as they are said to be by the Σ-sentence.

[2] In his reflections on Anonym's Argument, Wright replaces 'K', just as I did in the previous subsection, by '$\mathfrak{I}$', and he sees clearly that Σ-sentences can be used to refute Putnam's erstwhile Internalism.[213] (It is worth adding that they can also be employed to rebut the contention that truth is superassertibility.[214]) He goes on to recommend an 'adjustment': Interim Putnam's biconditional with a conditional consequent

(TIRA) $\forall$x (x is true $\leftrightarrow$ (epistemic conditions are good enough for assessing x
        $\Box\rightarrow$ it is rational to accept x))

should be replaced by a conditional with a biconditional consequent,[215]

(ProvE) $\forall$x (epistemic conditions are good enough for assessing x
        $\Box\rightarrow$ (x is true $\leftrightarrow$ it is rational to accept x)).

Wright points out that this Provisional Equivalence suffices to preclude undetectable error (which is allowed for by Metaphysical Realism as characterized by Interim Putnam), i.e. the possibility that even a 'theory that is "ideal" from the point of view of operational utility, inner beauty and elegance, "plausibility", simplicity, "conservatism", etc. might be false'.[216] (ProvE) excludes that something might be rationally accepted under epistemic conditions which are good enough for its appraisal although it is *not* true.[217] This is undoubtedly a very telling result. But alethic realism, as understood in this book, is not committed to allowing the possibility of undetectable error. Rather, it maintains a kind of *inevitable ignorance* on our part. Wright concludes his discussion of the challenge Σ-propositions provide for alethic anti-realism by saying:

It remains, to be sure, that such a proposition can be true only if an appraisal of it under sufficiently good circumstances never takes place, so that its truth is, in that sense,

---

[213] Wright, 'Epistemic', 356.   [214] See sect. 7.2.2.

[215] I assume that (ProvE) is what Wright intends. When he characterizes the form of Provisional Equivalences—see his schema (o*)—he keeps it free of subjunctives, and his allusion to Carnap's proposal to introduce disposition predicates by means of '(bilateral) reduction sentences' is to a proposal that was spelt out entirely without subjunctives. But when he 'instantiates' the schema, he switches to subjunctives: 'Epistemic', 347, 357; cf. also *T&O*, 119–20.

[216] See my references to Putnam (and Davidson) on p. 20 n. 54 above.

[217] Assuming that from 'P $\rightarrow$ (Q $\leftrightarrow$ R)' one can derive '(P & R) $\rightarrow$ Q', even if '$\rightarrow$' is read as '$\Box\rightarrow$'. See Wright, 'Epistemic', 349–50.

essentially recognition-transcendent. But that there are such recognition-transcendent truths...is...merely common sense. ('Epistemic', 357)

This sounds a bit like saying, 'Oh, such cases are just *recherché* counter-examples.' Well, they *are* counter-examples to the claim that no truth is recognition-transcendent, and if the alethic realist's denial of that claim agrees with common sense, is that supposed to be something he or she should be ashamed of?

[3] Recently, Dummett has surprised many of his readers (if I may extrapolate from my own experience) by dissociating himself from the principle of knowability which he had championed for some decades. In what is to the best of my knowledge the shortest paper he ever published, he tries to defuse Anonym's Argument by a draconian restriction on that principle.[218] 'A theorist with an epistemic notion of truth', we are told, will *not* endorse the 'blanket schema'

(1*)   If A, then $\diamond$ K (A),

unless he is 'careless'. 'K(...)' is to be read as 'Somebody at some time knows that'. Obviously (1*) is a schematic counterpart to assumption (1) in Anonym's Argument.[219] Dummett christens the theorist who heedlessly subscribes to (1*) 'Victor'. In view of the statements quoted on p. 427 and other passages to the same effect, I cannot help thinking that 'Michael' would have been at least as appropriate a name for that theorist. Dummett recommends Victor to give an inductive (recursive) characterization of truth, with

(Basic)   If A is a basic statement, then: it is true that A, iff $\diamond$ K (A)

as one of seven base clauses.[220] The other clauses specify truth-conditions for the results of applying the truth-operator to a conjunction, a disjunction, a conditional, a negation, or an existential or universal quantification, and in each case the logical operator on the right-hand side of the biconditional is to be understood as 'subject to the laws of intuitionistic logic'. Dummett concedes that now 'there is a good deal of work for Victor to do, particularly in specifying what is to count as a basic statement'. For the time being we are only given a necessary

---

[218] All Dummett quotations in this subsect. are from the two pages of 'Victor's Error'. I have taken the liberty of relabelling some of his inserted schemata (partly in order to call up the corresponding lines in Anonym's Argument as presented in sect. 7.3.1).

[219] Dummett's 'K(...)' is my 'K[...]', and by prefixing 'It is true that' to 'A' in the antecedent of (1*), one would only emphasize that this is meant to be a constraint on truth.

[220] Something like (Basic) was also proposed in Vincent Müller and Christian Stein, 'Epistemic Theories of Truth'.

condition for a statement's being basic: it has to be free of the logical connectives and quantifiers that are covered by the other six base clauses. Now suppose 'B' abbreviates a basic statement. If Victor subscribes to T-Introduction (which is not a matter of course, but we are authoritatively told that 'Victor is likely to accept it'), then he is committed by his inductive characterization of truth to infer from

(3*)   B, and it is not the case that K (B)

both that someone could know that B and that nobody ever does know that B. But 'there is now no contradiction in this; that was precisely the type of situation he wished to envisage.'

By laying down (Basic), the *provisoed* principle of knowability as one might call it, Dummett wants to avoid what 'led Victor into the trap posed by [Anonym's Argument]'. By his lights, just as for early Putnam, line (5) of Anonym's Argument is already disastrous: 'Substitute (3*) for "A" in (1*). It is obviously impossible that anyone should know both that B and that it will never be known that B.' (Perhaps he would deliver the same verdict upon assumption (2), $\mathfrak{I}$ [O & ¬$\mathfrak{I}$[O]], in the Argument from Justification Blindspots.) Extrapolating from the fact that Dummett replaces his erstwhile principle of knowability by its provisoed successor in order to evade Anonym's Argument, it is tempting to assume that he would be willing to make a similar move with the principle of justifiability in order to evade the Argument from Justification Blindspots. The provisoed principle of justifiability would look like this:

(Basic*)   If A is a basic statement, then: it is true that A, only if ◇ $\mathfrak{I}$ [A].

This is a principle an alethic *realist*, on my acceptation of this term, can endorse with equanimity, for it allows that truth outstrips justifiability.

So far this has a pleasingly pacificatory air about it, but I think the pleasure should not seduce us into embracing Dummett's inductive characterization of truth. First, there is the general worry (similar to one that surfaced in our discussion of Tarski) whether all operations used in natural languages to form complex sentences can be covered by the clauses of the inductive characterization and by 'supplementary clauses' of the same kind.[221] Dummett frankly acknowledges that 'there is a good deal of work for Victor to do, particularly in specifying what is to count as a basic statement'. Actually, this problem arises with respect to (Basic) itself: is 'x knows at t that p' supposed to receive a 'supplementary clause', or is it to be regarded as an open basic sentence?

---

[221] See Ch. 4.1.4.

Secondly, one may very well feel uneasy about the other six base clauses that we are offered. One reason for not endorsing the inductive characterization of truth as stated by Dummett concerns his clause for disjunctions:

(Disj)   It is true that (A or B) iff (it is true that A ∨ it is true that B).

Remember, the operator on the right-hand side is to be understood intuitionistically. Now the intuitionistic rule for '∨' is something like this:[222]

(Int-∨)   You may assert 'A ∨ B' iff you are warranted in asserting 'A', or you are warranted in asserting 'B' (or at least you know of a standard strategy which, if applied, is guaranteed to provide you with a warrant for asserting 'A' or with a warrant for asserting 'B').

Roughly put, the 'only if' part of (Int-∨) conveys the injunction not to assert 'A ∨ B' unless one can tell which. But in our empirical enquiries we often have good reasons for asserting a disjunction without any guarantee that we will ever be able to tell which disjunct is true. The following story illustrates this point nicely: 'A house has completely burnt down. The wiring was checked the day before, and two, independent, grave electrical faults [call them "X" and "Y"] were noted. Other possible explanations having been ruled out, we can (it seems) assert confidently "Either fault X caused the fire, or fault Y did". But this violates (Int-∨), as it is impossible to tell which fault caused the fire.'[223] So (Int-∨) jars with a cognitively essential feature of our use of disjunction. (Elsewhere, Dummett himself concedes this when he says that the 'ordinary use [of "or"] in natural language could not be captured by a straightforward intuitionistic explanation'.[224])

A closely related reason for resistance against the inductive characterization of truth as stated by Dummett concerns his clause for existential quantification:

(E.Q.)   It is true that something F iff ∃ x (it is true that Fx).

The intuitionistic rule for '∃' is something like this:[225]

(Int-∃)   You may assert '∃ x (Fx)' iff you are warranted in asserting a substitution-instance of the open sentence 'Fx' (or at least you know of a standard

[222] Cf. Dummett, 'Truth', 17; *Elements of Intuitionism*, 12–21.
[223] Edgington, 'Meaning, Bivalence and Realism', 157, with a bow to Ian Hacking. (I have relabelled the rule.) Actually, Dummett himself gives an example that serves the same dialectical purpose: 'Hardy may simply not have been able to hear whether [Admiral] Nelson said, "Kismet, Hardy" or "Kiss me, Hardy", though he heard him say one or the other' (*LBM*, 267).
[224] Dummett, 'Source', 194. (He goes on to suggest tentatively a 'more complicated explanation', which implies that one understands 'or' only if one has mastered *modus tollendo ponens*. Rumfitt has shown that this proposal fails to validate 'or'-elimination: see his 'Unilateralism Disarmed', 318–19.)
[225] See n. 222.

strategy which, if applied, is guaranteed to provide you with a warrant for asserting a substitution-instance).

The 'only if' part of (Int-∃) conveys the injunction not to assert '∃x(Fx)' unless one is entitled to assert some substitution instance 'Fa'. This does not capture our use of existential generalizations, any more than (Int-∨) captures our use of disjunctions, and, unsurprisingly, the incendiary story again serves to make the point. We can justifiably assert, 'Some electrical fault caused the fire', although we are not warranted to blame any particular electrical fault (and do not know of any strategy for removing this ignorance).[226] Furthermore, recall once again Thomas Gray: 'Some flower that is "born to blush unseen" is never referred to singly.' So even apart from the (admittedly) largely programmatic character of Victor's reformed position, there are reasons not to adopt it if we want to elucidate our workaday concept of truth, for this concept is expressed in the same language as (those) disjunctions and existential generalizations that do not comply with the intuitionistic rules.[227]

7.3.5 *The priority of justification*

According to a justificationist theory of *meaning* we do not understand a true declarative sentence unless we are able to recognize circumstances under which we would be justified in accepting it. If alethic realism is correct, this doctrine cannot be upheld. But not all is wrong with it. One of our two comprehensible Σ-sentences expresses a justification-transcendent truth, but its conjuncts are not justification-transcendent. Even if the Internal Compositionality Argument does not establish the significance of our Σ-sentences, it remains true that we could not understand such sentences if we did not understand their conjuncts and the connective 'and'. Our ability to understand sentences that express justification-transcendent truths is not a freely floating balloon: it rests firmly on our ability to understand certain other sentences which express recognizable truths. The very same contention is also supported by Putnam's 'extraterrestrial' counter-example to Internalism:[228]

[I]f we had no grasp of what made (1) *There is intelligent extraterrestrial life* warrantedly assertible, we would not be able even to understand (2) *There is no intelligent extraterrestrial life*. (1992b: 365)

Even if we take a statement we do not at all know how to confirm, [e.g. (2)], the fact is that the concepts which it employs are concepts which figure in other and simpler statements which we do know how to verify. (1992d: 12)

---

[226] Dummett himself points out that our use of existential generalizations as antecedents of conditionals is not captured by (Int-∃). This is another application of his Argument from Embedding: see pp. 408–9 above.   [227] Cf. also n. 230, on *conditionals*.

[228] Cf. Putnam 1994a: 242; 1995: 297. (Titles are spelt out above, on p. 405 n. 94.)

Our grasp of truths that are beyond justification depends upon our grasp of certain other propositions, whether atomic or not, which are justifiable.

We are now in a position to pick up a thread that was left dangling in section 7.2.1 when we tried to understand Putnam's tenet that the concepts of truth and of justifiability are interdependent, and to clinch the argument against Frege's Identity Thesis which was given on the last pages of Chapter 2.1.4. Putnam is surely right in saying that 'anyone who engages at times in debate about the credentials of a belief has an implicit notion of justification'. (He need not have a *word* for being justified in his repertoire, let alone be able to explain it.) Now somebody who does not know how to defend an assertoric utterance of a sentence like 'There is a pencil in this drawer' against dissenters does not know what it is for such an assertion to be *true*. So having at least an implicit conception of justification is a necessary condition for having the concept of truth. By conceding this, we subscribe to one half, as it were, of Putnam's interdependence thesis, and we *fully* endorse his weaker claim that 'truth . . . is connected with justification', for even if there is only a one-way dependency, there is a connection.[229] But should we also accept the other half of Putnam's interdependence thesis? Is having at least an implicit conception of truth a necessary condition for having the concept of justification?

In his paper, 'The Source of the Concept of Truth', Dummett emphatically denies this dependency, and I think he is right:

[T]he very concept of the truth of a statement, as distinct from the cruder concept of justifiability, is required only in virtue of the occurrence, as a constituent of more complex sentences, of the sentence by means of which the statement is made . . ./ . . . [T]he transition is a major conceptual leap . . ./ . . . [O]ur mastery of the most primitive aspects of the use of language to transmit information does not require even an implicit grasp of the concept of truth, but can be fully described in terms of the antecedent notion of justifiability. But comparatively more sophisticated linguistic operations, and above all, the use of . . . conditional sentences, demand, for a mastery of their use, a tacit appeal to the conception of objective truth; and so we have, in our conceptual furniture, a place exactly fitted for that concept as soon as it is explicitly introduced. ('Source', 193, 198, 199)

Surely you will have recognized here Dummett's Argument from Embedding, which I already employed in section 7.2.1 above. Suppose that somebody makes a conditional prediction by saying,

(S)   If Ben will get married next Monday, then we won't see much of him for the next three weeks.

---

[229] The last two quotations come from Putnam 2002: 166, which was his answer to my question, repeated above, concerning his interdependence claim. In his 1992d: 11–12, we read: 'I agree with the pragmatists that truth and verification are not simply independent and unrelated.' This is a weaker claim than the tenet, put forward a few lines later, that they are *inter*dependent.

Let 'A' stand for the proposition expressed by the antecedent of (S), and 'C' for what is expressed, in the same context, by the consequent of (S). The conditional prediction is justified if the speaker is in a position to offer a conditional justification of C, but the condition under which C has to be justified is the *truth* of A. This condition is not the same as the condition which has to obtain for A to be *justified*. (As we saw, A shares this justification condition with the proposition which is expressed in the same context by 'Ben is going to get married next Monday.') And what holds good for conditionals with an antecedent in the future tense, holds good for all conditionals: their use requires us to form an implicit conception of the truth of the statement that could be made by uttering the antecedent on its own, as distinct from the justifiability of that statement. (We need not yet have a *word* for this property in our repertoire, let alone be able to explain it.) As long as sentences that can be used as antecedents of conditionals are actually used only on their own, and for the purpose of transmitting information, knowing when it is reasonable to accept or reject what is said in their utterance, and hence an implicit conception of an assertion's being justified, is sufficient for employing them competently.[230]

I have inserted the proviso 'and for the purpose of transmitting information', because one performs what Dummett calls a 'more sophisticated operation' with a declarative sentence not only when one uses it within a conditional. Take future tense sentences again. More than knowledge of their justification conditions is required for competent use when they are employed in betting. If someone says today, 'Ben will get married next Monday', and he bets five pounds on it, then he knows that the taker will pay him only on condition of the *truth* of what he says. He knows that the fact that the prediction is justified because all evidence available today speaks in its favour does not suffice for urging the taker to pay. So in this use, an assertoric utterance of 'Ben will get married next Monday' does not come to the same thing as an assertoric utterance of 'Ben is going to get married next Monday,' for otherwise the bet could be settled already today.[231]

At any rate, the fact that for competence in 'less sophisticated' assertoric uses of declarative sentences only an implicit conception of *justification* is required shows that the notion of justification is not dependent on the notion of truth.

---

[230] Looking back, in the light of the Dummett passage cited above, at Dummett's recommendations to Victor, their revisionary character once again strikes the eye: if you take Victor's reformed stance, you must condemn our ordinary practice of using *conditionals* as ultimately unintelligible. I am inclined to contrapose here: this practice is intelligible, so we have one more reason not to take Victor's reformed stance.

[231] Even this minor modification of Dummett's argument is based on Dummett: in 'Meaning', 55; 'Realism' (1982), 255; and *LBM*, 172, he himself makes the point about betting, which is neglected in the first statement of our extract.

The same fact also refutes Frege's Identity Thesis, according to which one cannot assert *anything* without having mastered the concept of truth.

If you assert something, you represent yourself as believing what you say. So asserters, even if they are not yet as 'sophisticated' as we have managed to become in the fullness of time, are also believers. But then, shouldn't we refrain from claiming that 'to believe a proposition is to take it to be true'?[232] After all, taking a proposition to be true is believing that it is true,[233] and that's something you cannot 'do' unless you have acquired the concept of truth.

7.3.6 *Against alethic pluralism*

Let me end this chapter and this book with a note of caution. Nothing prevents alethic realists from accepting that for some region D of discourse there is an epistemic virtue E such that truth is subject to the following Local Constraint:

(*LocCon*)   For all propositions x, if x belongs to discourse D then:
x is true iff x has E.

Take an extreme case. Let D consist of all and only those propositions that a person m could express at time t by a present tense self-ascription of a sensation ('I am in pain now'). Perhaps person m has at t privileged access to those propositions: m cannot accept them at t without being right, and they cannot be true without m's accepting them at t (provided m has mastered the concepts necessary for grasping them). Now if these 'privileged access' claims are correct,[234] then for such propositions the predicate 'x is accepted by m at t (provided m is able to grasp x at t)' signifies a property that is both necessary and sufficient for truth. Of course, whether anyone ever really enjoys infallibility (immunity against error) and self-intimation (immunity against ignorance) with respect to certain propositions about her or his current sensations is a question to be discussed in epistemology and the philosophy of mind. My point here is only that alethic realism is silent on such questions. *Locally*, there may be an extensional equivalence of truth and a certain epistemic property. What alethic realists deny is a *global* claim; namely, the tenet that *no* proposition humans can comprehend is true unless it could be the content of a justified human belief.

Or consider a philosophically less encumbered kind of case—a region of discourse that comprises all and only those atomic statements in which something or somebody is said to have, or to lack, any of the following properties: being

---

[232] Dummett, 'The Two Faces of the Concept of Truth', 260.   [233] See p. 35.
[234] We encountered one of them in Brentano: see p. 378 above.

alarming, boring, disgusting, enchanting, fascinating, funny,[235] interesting, pleasing, shocking. It would be extremely implausible to claim that some truths in this region of discourse are in principle recognition-transcendent. But once again, this is something alethic realists can concede with equanimity.[236]

Is the fact that truth *is* locally constrained by epistemic properties a good reason for the contention that we have a *plurality of truth predicates*? I think the following Mixed Premisses Argument delivers the answer.[237] Suppose that I argue (A) 'I have a headache now: whoever has a headache now will sooner or later grope for an aspirin; therefore, I will sooner or later grope for an aspirin.' Let us assume that the first premiss has the 'privileged access' property specified above. Now (A) is valid, so the truth of the premisses necessitates the truth of the conclusion. Hence *both* premisses, if true at all, must be true in the *same* sense.

Furthermore, the principle that a conjunction is true if and only if its conjuncts are true is not negotiable.[238] Now the truth-value of one conjunct may be recognition-transcendent, whereas that of the other is not. So application of the conjunction platitude to such cases would be open to the charge of equivocation if the conjuncts were not true in the *same* sense.

In what sense? Well, in the sense that the modest account, like many others, tries to capture. This is a truth-concept that we need in any case, and I do not think we need any other. No matter which declarative sentence is substituted for the prosentence: if you think or say that things are thus-and-so, and things *are* thus, then what you think or say is true. This formula is, to use Strawson's words, 'no less hospitable to moral judgements and mathematical propositions than it is to records of common observation or history or propositions of natural science', and this is as it should be, for otherwise it would fail to register 'the coverage of the concept of truth that we actually have'.[239] True propositions of any one of those diverse types can join forces with true propositions of other types to guarantee the truth of a conclusion. The philosophical endeavour to determine the differences between those diverse kinds of propositions is not served by a fragmentation of our workaday concept of truth.

---

[235] Wright's favourite example in this connection: see *T&O*, *passim*, esp. 7–8, 58.

[236] Compare (*LocCon*) with (BASIC*) on p. 447.

[237] See Christine Tappolet, 'Mixed Inferences' and 'Truth Pluralism and Many-Valued Logic'. (She is wrong, though, in suggesting that Wright overlooked the point: cf. his *T&O*, 74–5 and his 'Response to Commentators', 923–5.)

[238] The right-to-left half of this truism is one of Wiggins's Marks of Truth: cf. 'Substantial', 211–12; 'Moral', 148, 152; 'Indefinibilist', 329; and 'Postscript 3', 339 n. for its critical potential. Cf. Wright, *T&O*, 73.

[239] Strawson, *Analysis and Metaphysics*, 90.

Bibliography

Almog, J., 'The Subject-Predicate Class I', *Noûs*, 25 (1991), 591–619.

Almog, J., Perry, J., and Wettstein, H. (eds.), *Themes from Kaplan*. New York: Oxford University Press, 1989.

Alston, W. P., *A Realist Conception of Truth* [*RCT*]. Ithaca, NY: Cornell University Press, 1996.

—— 'Truth: Concept and Property'. In R. Schantz (ed.), *What is Truth?* Berlin: de Gruyter, 2002, 11–26.

Altmann, A., and Stern, S. M., *Isaac Israeli: His Works Translated with Comments*. London: Oxford University Press, 1958.

Ammonius, *In Aristotelis De Interpretatione commentarium* [*c.* 500]. In *Commentaria in Aristotelem Graeca*, IV. 5. Berlin: Reimer, 1895.

Anscombe, E., ' "Making true" ' (1982). In R. Teichmann (ed.), *Logic, Cause and Action: Essays in Honour of Elizabeth Anscombe*. Cambridge: Cambridge University Press, 2000, 1–8.

Apel, K.-O., '*Fallibilismus, Konsenstheorie der Wahrheit und Letztbegründung*'. In Forum für Philosophie (ed.), *Philosophie und Begründung*. Frankfurt/M: Suhrkamp, 1987, 116–211.

Aquinas, *Expositio super librum Boethii De trinitate*. Leiden: Brill, 1965 [*c.*1257–8].

—— *Quaestiones disputatae de veritate*. Turin: Marietti, 1949 [*c.*1256–9]. (Trans. as *Disputed Questions on Truth*, Chicago: Regnery, 1952.)

—— *Sententia super Peri hermeneias*. Turin: Marietti, 1955 [*c.*1270–1].

—— *Summa contra gentiles*, Liber Primus. Turin: Marietti, 1934 [*c.*1259–65]. (Trans. as *Summa contra gentiles, Book One: God*, Notre Dame, IN: Notre Dame University Press, 1975.)

—— *Summa theologiae Ia*. Turin: Marietti, 1950 [*c.*1266–8]. (Relevant part trans. as *Summa theologiae, Vol. 4: Knowledge in God*, London: Eyre and Spottiswoode, 1964.)

Aristotle, *Categoriae et Liber de interpretatione*. Oxford: Clarendon Press, 1961. (Trans. with notes by J. L. Ackrill, Oxford: Oxford University Press, 1963.)

—— *De anima*. Oxford: Clarendon Press, 1961.

—— *Ethica Nicomachea*. Oxford: Clarendon Press, 1894.

—— *Metaphysics*. Oxford: Clarendon Press, 1923. (*Books* Γ, Δ, ϵ, trans. with notes by C. Kirwan, Oxford: Oxford University Press, 1971.)

—— *Prior and Posterior Analytics*. Oxford: Clarendon Press, 1949.

—— *Topica et Sophistici Elenchi*. Oxford: Clarendon Press, 1958.

Armstrong, D. M., *Belief, Truth and Knowledge*. Cambridge: Cambridge University Press, 1973.

—— 'Difficult Cases in the Theory of Truthmaking', *Monist*, 83 (2000), 150–60.

—— *A Theory of Universals*. Cambridge: Cambridge University Press, 1978.

—— *A World of States of Affairs* [*WSA*]. Cambridge: Cambridge University Press, 1997.

Austin, J., *How To Do Things with Words*. Oxford: Oxford University Press, 1962.

—— 'How to Talk' (1953). In his *Philosophical Papers*, 134–53.

Austin, J., *Philosophical Papers*, 2nd edn. Oxford: Oxford University Press, 1970.

—— *Sense and Sensibilia*. Oxford: Oxford University Press, 1962.

—— 'Truth' (1950). In his *Philosophical Papers*, 117–33.

—— 'Unfair to Facts' (1954). In his *Philosophical Papers*, 154–74.

Ayer, A. J., *Language, Truth and Logic*. Harmondsworth: Penguin, 1971 [1936; 2nd rev. edn., 1946].

—— *The Origins of Pragmatism*. London: Macmillan, 1968.

—— *Part of my Life*. Oxford: Oxford University Press, 1977.

—— *Russell and Moore, The Analytical Heritage*. London: Macmillan, 1971.

Bach, K., 'You Don't Say?', *Synthèse*, 128 (2001), 15–44.

Bacon, F., *Essays*, I. 'Of Truth' (1625). In *The Works of Francis Bacon*, London: Longman, 1861, VI. 377–9.

Baldwin, T., 'The Identity Theory of Truth', *Mind*, 100 (1991), 35–52.

Barcan Marcus, R., *Modalities*. New York: Oxford University Press, 1993.

Barwise, J., and Perry, J., *Situations and Attitudes*. Cambridge, MA: MIT Press, 1983.

Beckermann, A., '*Wittgenstein, Neurath und Tarski über Wahrheit*'. In *Zeitschrift für philosophische Forschung*, 49 (1995), 529–52.

Bell, D., and Cooper, N. (eds.), *The Analytic Tradition*. Oxford: Blackwell, 1990.

Berlin, I., 'Logical Translation' (1950). In his *Concepts and Categories*. Oxford: Oxford University Press, 1980, 56–80.

Bigelow, J., *The Reality of Numbers*. Oxford: Clarendon Press, 1988.

Black, M., 'The Semantic Definition of Truth' (1948). In M. Macdonald (ed.), *Philosophy and Analysis*. Oxford: Blackwell, 1954, 245–60.

Blackburn, S., *Spreading the Word*. Oxford: Clarendon Press, 1984.

——, and Simmons, K. (eds.), *Truth*. Oxford: Oxford University Press, 1999.

Blanshard, B., *The Nature of Thought* [*NTh*], II. London: Allen & Unwin, 1939.

Bobzien, S., 'Logic: The Stoics'. In K. Algra et al. (eds.), *The Cambridge History of Hellenistic Philosophy*. Cambridge: Cambridge University Press, 1999, 92–157.

Bochvar, D., 'On a Three-Valued Logical Calculus and its Application to the Analysis of the Paradoxes of the Classical Extended Functional Calculus', *History and Philosophy of Logic*, 2 (1981), 87–112. (Orig. Russian, 1937.)

Boghossian, P., 'The Status of Content', *Phil. Review*, 99 (1990), 157–84.

Bolzano, B., *Beyträge zu einer begründeteren Darstellung der Mathematik*. Darmstadt: Wissenschaftliche Buchgesellschaft, 1974 [1810]. (Trans. as 'Contributions to a Better-Grounded Presentation of Mathematics'. In W. Ewald (ed.), *From Kant to Hilbert: A Sourcebook in the Foundations of Mathematics*, I. Oxford: Clarendon Press, 1996, 174–224.

—— *Der Briefwechsel Bernard Bolzanos mit Michael Josef Fesl 1822–1848*. Berlin: Akademie-Verlag, 1965.

—— *Paradoxien des Unendlichen*. Leipzig: Reclam, 1849. (Trans. as *Paradoxes of the Infinite*, London: Routledge 1950.)

—— '*Verbesserungen und Zusätze zur Logik*'. In *Gesamtausgabe*, Vol. 2A12/2. Stuttgart: Frommann-Holzboog, 1977, pp. 53–184.

—— *Wissenschaftslehre* [*WL*]. 4 vols. Sulzbach: Seidel, 1837. In *Gesamtausgabe*, vols. I.11–I.14. Stuttgart: Frommann-Holzboog, 1985 ff. (Partially trans. as *Theory of Science*, Oxford: Blackwell, 1972; Dordrecht: Reidel 1973.)

BonJour, L., *The Structure of Empirical Knowledge*. Cambridge, MA: Harvard University Press, 1985.

Boolos, G., 'On Second-Order Logic', *Journ. Phil.*, 72 (1975), 509–27.

Bradley, F. H., *Appearance and Reality*. London: Swan Sonnenschein, 1893.

——— *Essays on Truth and Reality*. Oxford: Clarendon Press, 1914.

——— 'On Truth and Coherence' (1909). In his *Essays on Truth and Reality*, 202–18.

——— 'On Truth and Copying' (1907). In his *Essays on Truth and Reality*, 107–26.

Brandom, R., 'Explanatory vs. Expressive Deflationism about Truth'. In R. Schantz (ed.), *What is Truth?* Berlin: de Gruyter, 2002, 103–19.

——— 'From Truth to Semantics', and 'Reply to Tomberlin', *Phil. Issues*, 8 (1997), 141–54, 199–205.

——— *Making It Explicit [MIE]*. Cambridge, MA: Harvard University Press, 1994.

——— (ed.), *Rorty and his Critics*. Oxford: Blackwell, 2000.

Brentano, F., *Die Lehre vom richtigen Urteil [LRU]*. Bern: Francke, 1956.

——— '*Über den Begriff der Wahrheit*' (1889). In his *Wahrheit und Evidenz*, 3–29. (Trans. as 'On the Concept of Truth'. In *The True and the Evident*. London: Routledge, 1966, 3–25.)

——— *Versuch über die Erkenntnis*. Hamburg: Meiner, 1970.

——— *Von der mannigfachen Bedeutung des Seienden nach Aristoteles*. Darmstadt: Wissenschaftliche Buchgesellschaft, 1960 [1862].

——— *Wahrheit und Evidenz*. Leipzig: Meiner, 1930. (Trans. as *The True and the Evident*. London: Routledge 1966.)

Burge, T., 'Belief and Synonymy', *Journ. Phil.*, 75 (1978), 119–38.

——— 'Frege on Knowing the Foundations', *Mind*, 107 (1998), 305–47.

——— 'Frege on Truth'. In L. Haaparanta and J. Hintikka (eds.), *Frege Synthesized*, Dordrecht: Reidel, 1986, 97–154.

——— 'On Davidson's "Saying That" '. In E. Lepore (ed.), *Truth and Interpretation*. Oxford: Blackwell, 1986, 190–208.

Burgess, J., 'What Is Minimalism about Truth?', *Analysis*, 57 (1997), 259–67.

Buridanus, J., *Sophismata*. Stuttgart: Frommann, 1977 [c.1340].

——— *Sophismata*, ch. VIII, ed. and trans. in G. E. Hughes, *John Buridan on Self-Reference*. Cambridge: Cambridge University Press, 1982.

Carnap, R., *Der logische Aufbau der Welt*. Berlin: Weltkreis, 1928. (Trans. as *The Logical Structure of the World*. Berkeley and Los Angeles: University of California Press, 1969.)

——— *Die logische Syntax der Sprache*. Vienna: Springer, 1934. (Trans. as *The Logical Syntax of Language*. London: Routledge, 1937.)

——— 'Intellectual Autobiography'. In P. Schilpp (ed.), *The Philosophy of Rudolf Carnap*. LaSalle, ILL: Open Court, 1963, 3–84.

——— *Introduction to Semantics [IS]*. Cambridge, MA: Harvard University Press, 1942.

——— *Logical Foundations of Probability*. Chicago: Chicago University Press, 1950.

——— *Meaning and Necessity*. Chicago: University of Chicago Press, 1947.

——— 'Truth and Confirmation', enlarged trans. of '*Wahrheit und Bewährung*'. In H. Feigl and W. Sellars (eds.), *Readings in Philosophical Analysis*. New York: Appleton-Century-Crofts, 1949, 119–27.

Carnap, R., '*Wahrheit und Bewährung*' (1935). In G. Skirbekk (ed.), *Wahrheitstheorien*. Frankfurt/M: Suhrkamp, 1977, 89–95.

Carruthers, P., 'Eternal Thoughts', *Phil. Quart.*, 34 (1984), 186–204.

—— 'Frege's Regress', *Proc. Aristotelian Soc.*, 82 (1982), 17–32.

Cartwright, R., 'Negative Existentials' (1960). In his *Philosophical Essays*, 21–31.

—— 'A Neglected Theory of Truth' (1987). In his *Philosophical Essays*, 71–93.

—— *Philosophical Essays*. Cambridge, MA: MIT Press, 1987.

—— 'Propositions' (1962). In his *Philosophical Essays*, 33–53.

—— 'Propositions of Pure Logic' (1982). In his *Philosophical Essays*, 217–36.

Castañeda, H.-N., 'Indicators and Quasi-Indicators'. In *American Phil. Quart.*, 4 (1967), 85–100.

Chisholm, R., *Theory of Knowledge*. Englewood Cliffs, NJ: Prentice Hall, 1966; 2nd rev. edn., 1977; 3rd rev. edn., 1988.

—— 'William James's Theory of Truth', *Monist*, 75 (1992), 569–79.

Church, A., *Introduction to Mathematical Logic*. Princeton: Princeton University Press, 1956.

—— 'Review of Carnap's *Introduction to Semantics*', *Phil. Review*, 52 (1943), 298–304.

Clark, A. J., 'Why Kant Couldn't Be an Anti-Realist', *Analysis*, 45 (1985), 61–3.

Clark, P., and Hale, B. (eds.), *Reading Putnam*. Oxford: Blackwell, 1994.

Clark, R., 'Facts, Fact-Correlates, and Fact-Surrogates'. In P. Welsh (ed.), *Fact, Value and Perception*. Durham, NC: Duke University Press, 1975, 3–18.

Cohen, L. J., 'The Individuation of Proper Names'. In Z. van Straaten (ed.), *Philosophical Subjects, Essays Presented to P. F. Strawson*. Oxford: Clarendon Press, 1980, 140–63.

Copeland, J. (ed.), *Logic and Reality: Essays on the Legacy of Arthur Prior*. Oxford: Clarendon Press, 1996.

Costello, T. H., 'Royce's Encyclopaedia Articles', *Journ. Phil.*, 53 (1956), 311–12.

Cozzo, C., 'What Can We Learn from the Paradox of Knowability?', *Topoi*, 13 (1994), 71–8.

David, M., 'Analyticity, Carnap, Quine, and Truth', *Phil. Perspectives*, 10 (1996), 281–96.

—— *Correspondence and Disquotation [C&D]*. Oxford: Oxford University Press, 1994.

—— 'Minimalism and the Facts about Truth'. In R. Schantz (ed.), *What is Truth?* Berlin: de Gruyter, 2002, 161–75.

Davidson, D., 'Afterthoughts' (1987). In his *Subjective, Intersubjective, Objective*, 154–7.

—— 'The Centrality of Truth'. In J. Peregrin (ed.), *Truth and its Nature (if any)*. Dordrecht: Kluwer, 1999, 105–15.

—— 'A Coherence Theory of Truth and Knowledge' (1981). In his *Subjective, Intersubjective, Objective*, 137–53.

—— 'Empirical Content' (1982). In his *Subjective, Intersubjective, Objective*, 159–75.

—— 'Epistemology and Truth' (1988). In his *Subjective, Intersubjective, Objective*, 177–91.

—— *Essays on Actions and Events*. New York: Oxford University Press, 1980.

—— 'The Folly of Trying to Define Truth' ['Folly'], *Journ. Phil.*, 93 (1996), 263–78.

—— 'In Defence of Convention T' (1973). In his *Inquiries into Truth and Interpretation*, 65–75.

—— *Inquiries into Truth and Interpretation [ITI]*. New York: Oxford University Press, 1984.

—— 'Is Truth a Goal of Inquiry? Discussion with Rorty'. In U. Żegleń (ed.), *Donald Davidson: Truth, Meaning and Knowledge*. London: Routledge, 1999, 17–19.

—— 'Moods and Performances' (1979). In his *Inquiries into Truth and Interpretation*, 109–21.

—— 'On Saying That' (1968). In his *Inquiries into Truth and Interpretation*, 93–108.

—— 'On the Very Idea of a Conceptual Scheme' (1974). In his *Inquiries into Truth and Interpretation*, 183–98.

—— 'Pursuit of the Concept of Truth'. In P. Leonardi and M. Santambrogio (eds.), *On Quine*. New York: Cambridge University Press, 1995, 7–21.

—— 'Quotation' (1979). In his *Inquiries into Truth and Interpretation*, 79–92.

—— 'Reply to Foster' (1976). In his *Inquiries into Truth and Interpretation*, 171–9.

—— 'Reply to Wolfgang Künne'. In R. Stoecker (ed.), *Reflecting Davidson*. Berlin: de Gruyter, 1993, 21–3.

—— 'Reply to Stephen Neale'. In L. Hahn (ed.), *The Philosophy of Donald Davidson*. Chicago: Open Court, 1999, 667–9.

—— 'Reply to W. V. Quine'. In L. Hahn (ed.), *The Philosophy of Donald Davidson*. Chicago: Open Court, 1999, 80–6.

—— 'Reply to J. J. C. Smart'. In L. Hahn (ed.), *The Philosophy of Donald Davidson*. Chicago: Open Court, 1999, 123–5.

—— 'The Structure and Content of Truth' ['Structure'], John Dewey Lectures, *Journ. Phil.*, 87 (1990), 279–328.

—— *Subjective, Intersubjective, Objective*. Oxford: Clarendon Press, 2001.

—— 'Thought and Talk' (1975). In his *Inquiries into Truth and Interpretation*, 155–70.

—— 'True to the Facts' (1969). In his *Inquiries into Truth and Interpretation*, 37–54.

—— 'Truth and Meaning' (1967). In his *Inquiries into Truth and Interpretation*, 17–36.

—— 'Truth Rehabilitated'. In R. Brandom (ed.), *Rorty and his Critics*. Oxford: Blackwell, 2000, 65–74.

—— 'What is Quine's View of Truth?'. *Inquiry*, 37 (1994), 437–40.

Davies, M., *Meaning, Quantification, Necessity*. London: Routledge, 1981.

Descartes, R., Letter to Mersenne (16 Oct. 1639). In *Œuvres*, II. 587–99. (Trans. (in part) in *Philosophical Writings*, III. 138–40.)

—— *Meditationes de prima philosophia* (1641). In *Œuvres*, VII. 1–90. (Trans. as *Meditations on First Philosophy*, in *Philosophical Writings*, I. 1–62.)

—— *Œuvres*. Paris: Vrin, 1964–76.

—— *Philosophical Writings*. Cambridge: Cambridge University Press, 1985/91.

—— *Regulae ad directionem ingenii* (1628). In *Œuvres*, X. 359–472. (Trans. as *Rules for the Direction of the Mind*, in *Philosophical Writings*, I. 7–78.)

Dewey, J., *Essays in Experimental Logic*. Chicago: University of Chicago Press, 1916. (Quoted chs. also in *The Middle Works*, IV (1977), 78–90, 98–115; X (1980), 320–65.)

—— *Logic: The Theory of Inquiry* (1938). *The Later Works*, XII (1986).

—— *The Later Works*. Carbondale: Southern Illinois University Press, 1984 ff.

—— *The Middle Works*. Carbondale: Southern Illinois University Press, 1977 ff.

—— 'The Problem of Truth' (1911). In *The Middle Works*, VI (1978), 12–68.

—— *Reconstruction in Philosophy* (1920). In *The Middle Works*, XII (1982), 77–201.

—— 'Rejoinder to Russell'. In P. A. Schilpp (ed.), *The Philosophy of John Dewey*. LaSalle, ILL: Open Court, 1939, 544–49, 568–74. (Repr. in *The Later Works*, XIV (1988), 29–34, 52–8.)

Dodd, J., *An Identity Theory of Truth* [*ITT*]. London: Macmillan Press, 2000.

Donnellan, K., 'Reference and Definite Descriptions', *Phil. Review*, 75 (1966), 281–304.

Douven, I., 'Minimalism and the "Correspondence Intuition"'. In U. Meixner and P. Simons (eds.), *Papers of the 22nd International Wittgenstein Symposium*. Kirchberg a. W.: Wittgenstein-Gesellschaft, 1999, 167–72.

Ducasse, C., 'Propositions, Truth, and the Ultimate Criterion of Truth' (1944). In his *Truth, Knowledge and Causation*. London: Routledge, 1968, 150–78.

Dummett, M., 'Comments on Wolfgang Künne's Paper'. In W. Künne, M. Siebel, and M. Textor (eds.), *Bolzano and Analytic Philosophy*. Amsterdam: Rodopi, 1997, 241–8.

—— *Elements of Intuitionism*. Oxford: Oxford University Press, 1977.

—— *Frege and Other Philosophers*. Oxford: Clarendon Press, 1991.

—— *Frege—Philosophy of Language* [*FPL*]. London: Duckworth, 1973.

—— *Frege—Philosophy of Mathematics* [*FPM*]. London: Duckworth, 1991.

—— *The Interpretation of Frege's Philosophy* [*IFP*]. London: Duckworth, 1981.

—— 'Is the Concept of Truth Needed for Semantics?'. In C. Martínez, U. Rivas, and L. Villegas-Forero (eds.), *Truth in Perspective*. Aldershot: Ashgate, 1998, 3–22.

—— *The Logical Basis of Metaphysics* [*LBM*]. Cambridge, MA: Harvard University Press, 1991.

—— 'More about Thoughts' (1989). In his *Frege and Other Philosophers* (1991), 289–314.

—— 'Of What Kind of Thing Is Truth a Property?'. In S. Blackburn and K. Simmons (eds.), *Truth*. Oxford: Oxford University Press, 1999, 264–81.

—— *Origins of Analytical Philosophy* [*OAP*]. Cambridge, MA: Harvard University Press, 1993.

—— 'Realism' (1963). In his *Truth and Other Enigmas* (1978), 145–65.

—— 'Realism' (1982). In his *The Seas of Language* (1993), 230–76.

—— 'The Reality of the Past' (1969). In his *Truth and Other Enigmas*, 358–74.

—— 'Reply to McGuinness'. In B. McGuinness and G. Olivieri (eds.), *The Philosophy of Michael Dummett*. Dordrecht: Kluwer, 1994, 229–39.

—— *The Seas of Language*. Oxford: Clarendon Press, 1993.

—— 'Sentences and Propositions'. In R. Teichmann (ed.), *Logic, Cause and Action, Essays in Honour of Elizabeth Anscombe*. Cambridge: Cambridge University Press, 2000, 9–24.

—— 'The Source of the Concept of Truth' ['Source']. In his *The Seas of Language*, 188–201.

—— 'Truth' (1959), with 'Postscript (1972)'. In his *Truth and Other Enigmas*, 1–24.

—— *Truth and Other Enigmas* [*TOE*]. London: Duckworth, 1978.

—— 'The Two Faces of the Concept of Truth'. In R. Schantz (ed.), *What is Truth?* Berlin: de Gruyter, 2002, 249–62.

—— 'Victor's Error', *Analysis*, 61 (2001), 1–2.

—— 'What Is a Theory of Meaning? (II)' ['Meaning'] (1976). In his *The Seas of Language*, 34–93.

—— 'Wittgenstein on Necessity' (1990). In his *The Seas of Language*, 446–61.

Duncan-Jones, A., 'Fugitive Propositions' (1949). In M. Macdonald (ed.), *Philosophy and Analysis*. Oxford: Blackwell, 1954, 166–8.

Dunn, J. M., and Belnap, N. D., 'The Substitution Interpretation of the Quantifiers', *Noûs*, 8 (1968), 177–85.

Edgington, D., 'Meaning, Bivalence and Realism', *Proc. Aristotelian Soc.*, 81 (1981), 153–73.

—— 'The Paradox of Knowability', *Mind*, 94 (1985), 557–68.

Elias [?], *In Aristotelis Categorias commentarium* [c. 570]. In *Commentaria in Aristotelem Graeca* XVIII 1. Berlin: Reimer, 1900.

Ellis, B., *Truth and Objectivity*. Oxford: Blackwell, 1990.

Etchemendy, J., 'Tarski on Truth and Logical Consequence' ['Tarski'], *Journ. Symbolic Logic*, 53 (1988), 51–79.

Evans, G., *Collected Papers*. Oxford: Clarendon Press, 1985.

—— 'Does Tense Logic Rest on a Mistake?' ['Tense Logic'] (1979). In his *Collected Papers*, 343–63.

—— 'Pronouns, Quantifiers, and Relative Clauses (I)' (1977). In his *Collected Papers*, 76–152.

—— 'Understanding Demonstratives' (1981). In his *Collected Papers*, 291–321.

—— *The Varieties of Reference*. Oxford: Clarendon Press, 1982.

—— and McDowell, J. (eds.), *Truth and Meaning*. Oxford: Clarendon Press, 1976.

Ezorsky, G., 'Truth in Context', *Journ. Phil.*, 60 (1963), 113–35.

Field, H., 'The Deflationary Conception of Truth' ['Truth']. In G. Macdonald and C. Wright (eds.), *Fact, Science and Morality*. Oxford: Blackwell, 1986, 55–117.

—— 'Deflationist Views of Meaning and Content' ['Deflationist'] (1994), with a new 'Postscript'. In his *Truth and the Absence of Fact*, 104–40, 141–56.

—— 'Disquotational Truth and Factually Defective Discourse' ['Disquotational'] (1994). In his *Truth and the Absence of Fact*, 222–58.

—— 'Tarski's Theory of Truth' ['Tarski'] (1972), with a new 'Postscript'. In his *Truth and the Absence of Fact*, 3–26, 27–9.

—— *Truth and the Absence of Fact*. Oxford: Oxford University Press, 2001.

Fine, K., 'First Order Modal Theories III—Facts', *Synthèse*, 53 (1982), 43–122.

Fitch, F. B., 'A Logical Analysis of Some Value Concepts', *Journ. Symbolic Logic*, 28 (1963), 135–42.

Fitch, G. W., 'Tense and Contents', *Phil. Studies*, 94 (1999), 151–8.

Fodor, J., 'Fodor's Guide to Mental Representation' (1985). In his *A Theory of Content and Other Essays*, 3–30.

—— 'Substitution Arguments and the Individuation of Beliefs' (1990). In his *A Theory of Content and Other Essays*, 161–76.

—— *A Theory of Content and Other Essays*. Cambridge, MA: MIT Press, 1990.

Foley, R., 'Justified Inconsistent Belief', *American Phil. Quart.*, 16 (1979), 247–57.

—— *The Theory of Epistemic Rationality*. Cambridge, MA: Harvard University Press, 1986.

Forbes, G., 'Truth, Correspondence and Redundancy'. In G. Macdonald and C. Wright (eds.), *Fact, Science and Morality*. Oxford: Blackwell, 1986, 27–54.

Fox, J., 'Truthmaker', *Australasian Journ. Phil.*, 65 (1987), 188–207.

Frede, D., '*Wahrheit: Vom aufdeckenden Erschließen zur Offenheit der Lichtung*'. In D. Thomä (ed.), *Heidegger-Handbuch*. Metzler: Stuttgart, 2003.

Frede, M., *Die stoische Logik*. Göttingen: Vandenhoeck and Ruprecht, 1974.

Frege, G., *Collected Papers on Mathematics, Logic, and Philosophy*. Oxford: Blackwell, 1984.

—— *Grundgesetze der Arithmetik*, Bk. I. Hildesheim: Olms, 1962 [1893]. (Trans. as *The Basic Laws of Arithmetic*. Berkeley and Los Angeles: University of California Press, 1964.)

—— *Die Grundlagen der Arithmetik*. Hamburg: Meiner, 1986 [1884]. (Trans. as *The Foundations of Arithmetic*. Oxford: Blackwell 1950.)

—— *Kleine Schriften*. Hildesheim: Olms, 1967.

462   Bibliography

Frege, G., *Nachgelassene Schriften* [*NS*]. Hamburg: Meiner, 1969. (Trans. as *Posthumous Writings*. Oxford: Blackwell, 1979.)

—— *Wissenschaftlicher Briefwechsel* [*WB*]. Hamburg: Meiner, 1976. (Trans. as *Philosophical and Mathematical Correspondence*. Oxford: Blackwell, 1979.)

García-Carpintero, M., 'A Paradox of Truth Minimalism'. In C. Martínez, U. Rivas, and L. Villegas-Forero (eds.), *Truth in Perspective*. Aldershot: Ashgate, 1998, 37–62.

—— 'What Is a Tarskian Definition of Truth?', *Phil. Studies*, 82 (1996), 113–44.

García-Carpintero, M., and Pérez Otero, M., 'Davidson, Correspondence Truth and the Frege-Gödel-Church Argument', *History and Phil. of Logic*, 19 (1998), 63–81.

Geach, P., 'Aristotle on Conjunctive Propositions' (1963). In his *Logic Matters*, 13–27.

—— 'Ascriptivism' (1960). In his *Logic Matters*, 250–4.

—— 'Good and Evil'. In *Analysis*, 17 (1956), 33–42.

—— *Logic Matters*. Oxford: Blackwell, 1992.

—— 'On What There Is', *Proc. Aristotelian Soc.*, SV 25 (1951), 137–48.

—— *Reference and Generality*. Rev. edn. Ithaca, NY: Cornell University Press, 1968.

—— 'Russell's Theory of Descriptions' (1950), in M. Macdonald (ed.), *Philosophy and Analysis*. Oxford: Blackwell, 1954, 32–6.

—— 'Truth and God', *Proc. Aristotelian Soc.*, 82 (1982), 83–97.

—— 'What Actually Exists' (1968). In his *God and the Soul*. London: Routledge, 1969, 65–74.

Glock, H. J., 'Does Ontology Exist?', *Philosophy*, 77 (2002), 235–60.

Gödel, K., 'Russell's Mathematical Logic'. In P. A. Schilpp (ed.), *The Philosophy of Bertrand Russell*. Evanston: Northwestern University Press, 1944, 125–53.

Gomperz, H., *Weltanschauungslehre*, ii.1. Jena: Diederichs, 1908.

Goodman, N., *Fact, Fiction, and Forecast*. 2nd edn. Indianapolis: Bobbs-Merrill, 1965.

—— 'Notes on the Well-Made World'. In W. Leinfellner, E. Kraemer, and J. Schank (eds.), *Language and Ontology*. Wien: Hölder-Pichler-Tempsky, 1982, 31–8.

—— *Of Mind and Other Matters*. Cambridge, MA: Harvard University Press, 1984.

—— 'On Starmaking', *Synthèse*, 45 (1980), 211–15.

—— *Ways of Worldmaking*. Indianapolis, IN: Hackett, 1978.

Grice, P., 'Logic and Conversation' (1967). In his *Studies in the Way of Words*. Cambridge, MA: Harvard University Press 1989.

Grover, D. *A Prosentential Theory of Truth* [*PrTh*]. Princeton: Princeton University Press, 1992.

Grover, D., Camp, J., and Belnap, N., 'A Prosentential Theory of Truth' ['Prosentential'] (1975). In D. Grover, *A Prosentential Theory of Truth*. Princeton: Princeton University Press, 1992, 70–120.

Gupta, A., 'A Critique of Deflationism' ['Critique'], *Phil. Topics*, 21 (1993), 57–81.

—— 'An Argument Against Tarski's Convention T' ['Convention T']. In R. Schantz (ed.), *What is Truth?* Berlin: de Gruyter, 2002, 225–37.

—— 'Minimalism'. In *Phil. Perspectives*, 7 (1993), 359–69.

——, and Belnap, N., *The Revision Theory of Truth* [*RTT*]. Cambridge, MA: MIT Press, 1993.

—— 'Tarski's Definition of Truth'. In E. Craig (ed.), *Routledge Encyclopedia of Philosophy*. London: Routledge, 1998.

Guttenplan, S., *The Languages of Logic*. Oxford: Blackwell, 1986.

Haack, S., 'Is it True What They Say about Tarski?', *Philosophy*, 51 (1976), 323–36.
—— 'The Pragmatist Theory of Truth', *Brit. Journ. Phil. Sci.*, 27 (1976), 231–49.
Habermas, J., '*Wahrheit und Rechtfertigung*'. In his *Wahrheit und Rechtfertigung*. Frankfurt: Suhrkamp, 1999, 230–70. (Trans. as 'Richard Rorty's Pragmatic Turn'. In R. Brandom (ed.), *Rorty and his Critics*. Oxford: Blackwell, 2000, 31–55.)
—— '*Wahrheitstheorien*' (1973). In his *Vorstudien und Ergänzungen zur Theorie des kommunikativen Handelns*. Frankfurt/M: Suhrkamp, 1984, 127–83.
Hacker, P. M. S., 'On Davidson's Idea of a Conceptual Schema', *Phil. Quart.*, 46 (1996), 289–307.
—— *Wittgenstein: Mind and Will. Part I: Essays*. Oxford: Blackwell, 2000.
Hahn, H., '*Logik, Mathematik und Naturerkennen*' (1932). In his *Empirismus, Logik, Mathematik*. Frankfurt/M: Suhrkamp, 1988, 141–72.
Hahn, L. (ed.), *The Philosophy of Donald Davidson*. Chicago: Open Court, 1999.
—— *The Philosophy of P. F. Strawson*. Chicago: Open Court, 1998.
Hale, B., and Wright, C. (eds.), *Companion to the Philosophy of Language*. Oxford: Blackwell, 1997.
Hallett, G., *A Companion to Wittgenstein's 'Philosophical Investigations'*. Ithaca, NY: Cornell University Press, 1977.
Harcourt, E., 'A Reply to Wolfgang Künne', *Mind*, 102 (1993), 301–13.
Hart, W., 'Access and Inference', *Proc. Aristotelian Soc.*, SV 53 (1979), 153–65.
Hegel, G. W. F., *Die Phänomenologie des Geistes*. Hamburg: Meiner, 1952 |1807|. (Trans. as *Phenomenology of Spirit*, Oxford: Oxford University Press, 1977.)
—— *Enzyklopädie der philosophischen Wissenschaften im Grundrisse, 1. Teil: Wissenschaft der Logik*. Heidelberg: Oswald, 1830. (Trans as *The Encyclopaedia Logic*, Indianapolis, IN: Hackett, 1991.)
Heidegger, M., *Basic Writings*. New York: Harper & Row, 1977.
—— '*Das Ende der Philosophie und die Aufgabe des Denkens*' (1964). In his *Zur Sache des Denkens*. Tübingen: Max Niemeyer, 1969, 61–80, 92. (Trans as 'The End of Philosophy and the Task of Thinking', in his *Basic Writings*, 369–92.)
—— '*Der Ursprung des Kunstwerks*' (1936). In his *Holzwege*. Frankfurt: Klostermann, 1963, 7–68. (Trans. as 'The Origin of the Work of Art', in his *Basic Writings*, 143–87.)
—— *Sein und Zeit*. Tübingen: Max Niemeyer, 1927. (Trans. as *Being and Time*. New York: Harper & Row, 1962.)
—— '*Vom Wesen der Wahrheit*' (1930). In his *Wegmarken*. Frankfurt: Klostermann, 1967, 73–97. (Trans. as 'On the Essence of Truth', in his *Basic Writings*, 113–41.)
Heidelberger, H., 'The Indispensability of Truth', *American Phil. Quart.*, 5 (1968), 212–17.
Hempel, C. G., 'On the Logical Positivist Theory of Truth', *Analysis*, 2 (1935), 49–59.
Hintikka, J., 'Time, Truth and Knowledge in Aristotle and Other Greek Philosophers' (1967). In his *Time and Necessity*. Oxford: Clarendon Press, 1973, 62–92.
Hobbes, T., *De Corpore* (1655). Paris: Vrin, 1999. (Trans. as *Concerning Body*, in *The English Works of Thomas Hobbes*, I. London: Bohn, 1839.)
Hofweber, T., 'Inexpressible Properties and Propositions', forthcoming.
Hookway, C., *Truth, Rationality, and Pragmatism: Themes from Peirce*. Oxford: Clarendon Press, 2000.
Hornsby, J., 'Truth: The Identity Theory', *Proc. Aristotelian Soc.*, 97 (1997), 1–24.

Horwich, P., 'Davidson on Deflationism'. In U. Żegleń (ed.), *Donald Davidson: Truth, Meaning and Knowledge*. London: Routledge, 1999, 20–4.

——'A Defense of Minimalism' ['Defense']. In M. Lynch (ed.), *The Nature of Truth*. Cambridge, MA: MIT Press, 2001, 559–77.

—— *Meaning*. Oxford: Clarendon Press, 1998.

——'Theories of Truth'. In J. Kim and E. Sosa (eds.), *A Companion to Metaphysics*. Oxford: Blackwell, 1995, 491–6.

—— *Truth*. Oxford: Blackwell, 1990; 2nd rev. edn., Oxford: Clarendon Press, 1998 (references are to the 2nd edn., unless otherwise stated).

Hugly, P., and Sayward, C., *Intensionality and Truth: An Essay on the Philosophy of A. N. Prior* [*I&T*]. Dordrecht: Kluwer, 1996.

Hülser, K., *Die Fragmente zur Dialektik der Stoiker*. 4 vols. Stuttgart: Frommann-Holzboog, 1987–8.

Husserl, E., *Logische Untersuchungen* [*LU*] (1900/01). 2nd rev. edn. Halle: Niemeyer 1913/21. (Trans. as *Logical Investigations*. London: Routledge, 1970.)

Jackson, F., *From Metaphysics to Ethics: A Defence of Conceptual Analysis*. Oxford: Oxford University Press, 1998.

James, W., *The Meaning of Truth: A Sequel to 'Pragmatism'. The Works of William James*, II. Harvard: Harvard University Press, 1975 [1909].

—— *Pragmatism, A New Name for Some Old Ways of Thinking. The Works of William James*, I. Harvard: Harvard University Press, 1975 [1907].

——'Professor Pratt on Truth'. In his *The Meaning of Truth, A Sequel to 'Pragmatism'*, 90–8.

——'Two English Critics'. In his *The Meaning of Truth, A Sequel to 'Pragmatism'*, 146–53.

Joachim, H. H., *The Nature of Truth* [*NT*]. Oxford: Clarendon Press, 1906.

Johnson, W. E., *Logic*. Cambridge: Cambridge University Press, 1921–4.

Johnston, M., 'The End of the Theory of Meaning', *Mind and Language*, 3 (1988), 28–42.

——'Objectivity Refigured: Pragmatism without Verificationism'. In C. Wright and J. Haldane (eds.), *Reality, Representation, and Projection*. Oxford: Oxford University Press, 1993, 85–130.

——'Verificationism as Philosophical Narcissism', *Phil. Perspectives*, 7 (1993), 307–30.

Juškevič, A., and Winter, E. (eds.), *Leonhard Euler und Christian Goldbach, Briefwechsel 1729–1764*. Berlin: Akademie-Verlag, 1965.

Kahn, C., *The Verb 'Be' in Ancient Greek*. Dordrecht: Kluwer, 1973.

Kalderon, M. E., 'The Transparency of Truth', *Mind*, 106 (1997), 475–97.

Kamitz, R., 'Franz Brentano: Wahrheit und Evidenz'. In J. Speck (ed.), *Grundprobleme der großen Philosophen: Neuzeit III*. Göttingen: Vandenhoeck, 1983, 160–97.

Kant, I., *De mundi sensibilis atque intelligibilis forma et principiis* (1770). (Trans. as 'Inaugural Dissertation', in his *Selected Pre-Critical Writings*. Manchester: Manchester University Press, 1968.)

—— *Kritik der reinen Vernunft* (1781). 2nd rev. edn. 1787. (Trans. London: Macmillan, 1929.)

—— *Logik* (1800) (compiled by Jäsche). (Trans. as *Kant's Logic*, Indianapolis, IN: Bobbs-Merrill, 1974.)

Kaplan, D., 'Afterthoughts'. In J. Almog, J. Perry, and H. Wettstein (eds.), *Themes from Kaplan*. New York: Oxford University Press, 1989, 565–614.

——'Demonstratives' (1977). In J. Almog, J. Perry, and H. Wettstein (eds.), *Themes from Kaplan*. 481–563.

——'Words'. In *Proc. Aristotelian Soc.*, SV 64 (1990), 93–119.

Kapus, J., 'The Liar and the Prosentential Theory of Truth', *Logique et Analyse*, 34 (1991), 283–91.

Kemmerling, A., '*Die Objektivität der Glaubenssätze*'. In U. Haas-Spohn (ed.), *Intentionalität zwischen Wahrnehmung und Weltbezug*. Paderborn: Mentis, 2002, 147–202.

Kenny, A., *The Metaphysics of Mind*. Oxford: Oxford University Press, 1989.

Kirkham, R., *Theories of Truth [ThT], A Critical Introduction*. Cambridge, MA: MIT Press, 1992.

Kneale, M., and Kneale, W., 'Propositions and Time'. In A. Ambrose and M. Lazerowitz (eds.), *G. E. Moore: Essays in Retrospect*. London: Allen & Unwin, 1970, 228–41.

Kneale, W., 'Propositions and Truth in Natural Languages', *Mind*, 81 (1972), 225–43.

——'Russell's Paradox and Some Others', *Phil. of Science*, 22 (1971), 321–38.

Kokoszyńska, M., '*Bemerkungen über die Einheitswissenschaft* [Remarks on the Unity of Science]', *Erkenntnis*, 7 (1938), 325–35.

——'*Über den absoluten Wahrheitsbegriff und einige andere semantische Begriffe*', *Erkenntnis*, 6 (1936), 143–65.

——'*W sprawie wzglednosci i bezwzglednosci prawdy* [On the Relativity and Non-Relativity of Truth]', *Przegląd Filozoficzny*, 39 (1936), 424–5.

Kotarbiński, T., *Elementy teorii poznania, logiki formalnej i metodologii nauk* [*Elements of the Theory of Knowledge, Formal Logic and the Methodology of Sciences*], 2nd enlarged edn., Wroclaw: Ossolineum, 1961 [1929].

——'Franz Brentano as Reist'. In L. McAlister (ed.), *The Philosophy of Franz Brentano*. London: Duckworth, 1966, 194–203.

——*Gnosiology, The Scientific Approach to the Theory of Knowledge*. Oxford: Pergamon Press, 1966. (Trans. of the 2nd edn. of his *Elementy teorii poznania, logiki formalnej i metodologii nauk*.)

——'*Grundgedanken des Pansomatismus*' (1935). Part trans. of '*Zasadnicze myśli pansomatyzmu*'. In D. Pearce and J. Wolenski (eds.), *Logischer Rationalismus—Philosophische Schriften der Lemberg-Warschauer Schule*. Frankfurt/M: Athenäum, 1988, 246–52.

——'*W sprawie pojęcia prawdy* [On the Concept of Truth]', *Przegląd Filozoficzny*, 37 (1934), 85–91. (Review of Tarski, *Pojęcie prawdy w językach nauk dedukcyjnych* [*The Concept of Truth in the Languages of Deductive Sciences*], 1933.)

——'*Zagadnienie istnienia przyszłości* [The Problem of the Existence of the Future]', *Przegląd Filozoficzny*, 16 (1913), 74–92. (Trans. in *The Polish Review* (New York), 13 (1968), 7–22.)

——'*Zasadnicze myśli pansomatyzmu* [The Fundamental Ideas of Pansomatism]', *Przegląd Filozoficzny*, 38 (1935), 283–94. (Trans. (slightly enlarged) in *Mind*, 64 (1955), 488–500.)

Kripke, S., 'Is There a Problem about Substitutional Quantification?' ['Substitutional']. In G. Evans and J. McDowell (eds.), *Truth and Meaning*. Oxford: Clarendon Press, 1976, 325–419.

——*Naming and Necessity*, with a new Preface. Oxford: Blackwell, 1980 [1972].

——'Outline of a Theory of Truth', *Journ. Phil.*, 72 (1975), 690–716.

——'A Puzzle About Belief', In A. Margalit (ed.), *Meaning and Use*. Dordrecht: Reidel, 1979, 239–83.

Künne, W., *Abstrakte Gegenstände*. Frankfurt/M: Suhrkamp, 1983.

Künne, W., 'Bolzanos blühender Baum [. . .]' (1989). In *Forum für Philosophie* (ed.), *Realismus und Anti-Realismus*. Frankfurt/M: Suhrkamp, 1992, 224–44.

—— 'Constituents of Concepts: Bolzano vs. Frege'. In A. Newen et al. (eds.), *Building on Frege*. Stanford: CSLI Publications, 2001, 267–86.

—— 'Fiktion ohne fiktive Gegenstände'. In J. Brandl, A. Hieke, and P. Simons (eds.), *Metaphysik—Neue Zugänge zu alten Fragen*. Sankt Augustin: Academia, 1995, 141–62.

—— 'First Person Propositions'. In W. Künne, A. Newen, and M. Anduschus (eds.), *Direct Reference, Indexicality, and Propositional Attitudes*. Stanford: CSLI Publications, 1997, 49–68.

—— 'Hegel als Leser Platos', *Hegel-Studien*, 15 (1979), 109–46.

—— 'Hybrid Proper Names', *Mind*, 101 (1992), 721–31.

—— 'Indexikalität, Sinn und propositionaler Gehalt', *Grazer Philosophische Studien*, 18 (1982), 41–74.

—— 'The Intentionality of Thinking'. In K. Mulligan (ed.), *Speech Act and Sachverhalt: Reinach and the Foundations of Realist Phenomenology*. Dordrecht: Nijhoff, 1987, 175–87.

—— 'The Nature of Acts: Moore on Husserl'. In D. Bell and N. Cooper (eds.), *The Analytic Tradition*. Oxford: Blackwell, 1990, 104–16.

—— 'Propositions in Bolzano and Frege'. In Künne et al., *Bolzano and Analytic Philosophy*, 203–40.

—— 'Some Varieties of Thinking: Reflections on Meinong and Fodor', *Grazer Philosophische Studien*, 50 (1995), 365–95.

—— 'Substanzen und Adhärenzen. Zur Ontologie in Bolzanos Athanasia', *Logical Analysis and History of Philosophy*, 1 (1998), 233–50.

—— 'Truth and a Kind of Realism' (1997). In J. Nida-Rümelin (ed.), *Rationality, Realism, Revision*. Berlin: de Gruyter, 1999, 17–41.

—— 'Truth, Meaning and Logical Form'. In R. Stoecker (ed.), *Reflecting Davidson*. Berlin: de Gruyter, 1993, 1–20.

—— 'Truth, Rightness, and Permanent Acceptability', *Synthèse*, 95 (1993), 107–17.

—— 'Ultraminimal Realism. Alston on Truth', *Ratio*, 11 (1998), 193–9.

——, Siebel, M., and Textor, M. (eds.), *Bolzano and Analytic Philosophy*. Amsterdam: Rodopi, 1997.

Kvanvig, J., 'The Knowability Paradox and the Prospects for Anti-Realism', *Noûs*, 21 (1995), 501–15.

—— 'Truth and Superassertibility', *Phil. Studies*, 93 (1999), 1–19.

——, and Hand, M., 'Tennant on Knowability', *Australasian Journ. Phil.*, 77 (1999), 422–8.

Lambert, J. H., *Anlage zur Architectonic*. Riga: Hartknoch, 1771.

Lazerowitz, M., 'Strong and Weak Verification II' (1950). In his *The Structure of Metaphysics*. London: Routledge, 1955, 130–43.

Leeds, S., 'Theories of Reference and Truth'. In *Erkenntnis*, 13 (1978), 111–29.

Lehrer, K., *Theory of Knowledge*. London: Routledge, 1990.

Leibniz, G. W., *Nouveaux essais sur l'entendement humain* (1705). In *Sämtliche Schriften und Briefe*, vol. A VI, 6. Berlin: Akademie-Verlag, 1962. (Trans. as *New Essays on Human Understanding*. Cambridge: Cambridge University Press, 1996.)

Lemmon, E. J., *Beginning Logic*. London: Nelson, 1965.

Lepore, E. (ed.), *Truth and Interpretation*. Oxford: Blackwell, 1986.

Leśniewski, S., '*Czy prawda jest tylko wieczna czy też i wieczna i odwieczna?* [. . .] [Is a truth only true for ever, or has it always been true as well?]', *Nowe Tory*, 10 (1913), 493–528. (Trans. in his *Collected Works*, I. Dordecht: Kluwer, 1992, 86–114.)

Lewis, C. I., *Mind and the World Order*. New York: Dover, 1929.

Lewis, D., 'Armstrong on Combinatorial Possibility' (1992). In his *Papers in Metaphysics and Epistemology*, 196–214.

—— 'Finkish Dispositions' (1997). In his *Papers in Metaphysics and Epistemology*, 133–51.

—— 'Forget about the "Correspondence Theory of Truth" ' ['Correspondence'], *Analysis*, 61 (2001), 275–80.

—— *Papers in Metaphysics and Epistemology*. Cambridge: Cambridge University Press, 1999.

—— 'Truthmaking and Difference-Making', *Noûs*, 35 (2001), 602–15.

—— 'A World of Truthmakers?' (1998). In his *Papers in Metaphysics and Epistemology*, 215–20.

Lewy, C., *Meaning and Modality*. Cambridge: Cambridge University Press, 1976.

Loar, B., *Mind and Meaning*. Cambridge: Cambridge University Press, 1981.

Locke, J., *An Essay concerning Human Understanding* (1690). Harmondsworth: Penguin, 1997.

Lombard, L., *Events, A Metaphysical Study*. London: Routledge, 1986.

Lotze, H., *System der Philosophie, I. Logik* (1880), *II. Metaphysik* (1879). Leipzig: Meiner, 1912.

Lowe, J., *The Possibility of Metaphysics*. Oxford: Clarendon Press, 2001.

Lucretius, *De Rerum Natura*. Loeb Classical Library, Cambridge, MA: Harvard University Press, 1992 [c. 60 BC].

Łukasiewicz, J., '*O Determinizmie* [On Determinism]' (1922/3, 1961), trans. in his *Selected Works*. Amsterdam: North-Holland, 1970, 110–28. (Also trans. as '*Über den Determinismus*', *Studia Leibnitiana*, 5 (1973), 5–25.)

Lynch, M. (ed.), *The Nature of Truth*. Cambridge, MA: MIT Press, 2001.

McDermid, D., 'Pragmatism and Truth: The Comparison Objection to Correspondence', *Review of Metaphysics*, 51 (1998), 775–811.

Macdonald, G., and Wright, C. (eds.), *Fact, Science and Morality*. Oxford: Blackwell, 1986.

Macdonald, M. (ed.), *Philosophy and Analysis*. Oxford: Blackwell, 1954.

McDowell, J., *Meaning, Knowledge and Reality*. Cambridge, MA: Harvard University Press, 1998.

—— *Mind and World*. Cambridge, MA: Harvard University Press, 1994.

—— 'On "The Reality of the Past" ' (1978). In his *Meaning, Knowledge and Reality*, 295–313.

—— 'Physicalism and Primitive Denotation: Field on Tarski' (1978). In his *Meaning, Knowledge and Reality*, 132–54.

—— 'Truth-Conditions, Bivalence and Verificationism' (1976). In his *Meaning, Knowledge and Reality*, 3–28.

McGee, V., 'A Semantic Conception of Truth?', *Phil. Topics*, 21 (1993), 83–111.

—— 'Semantic Paradoxes and Theories of Truth'. In E. Craig (ed.), *Routledge Encyclopedia of Philosophy*. London: Routledge, 1998.

McGinn, C., *Logical Properties: Identity, Existence, Predication, Necessity, Truth*. Oxford: Clarendon Press, 2000.

Mackie, J., 'Truth and Knowability', *Analysis*, 40 (1980), 90–3.

—— *Truth, Probability, and Paradox*. Oxford: Clarendon Press, 1973.

McTaggart, J. E. M., 'Critical Notice [of James's *Pragmatism*]', *Mind*, 17 (1908), 104–9.

—— *The Nature of Existence*, 2 vols. Cambridge: Cambridge University Press, 1921/1927.

Makinson, D., 'The Paradox of the Preface', *Analysis*, 25 (1965), 205–7.

Martin, R. L. (ed.), *Recent Essays on Truth and the Liar Paradox*. Oxford: Clarendon Press, 1984.

Martínez, C., Rivas, U., and Villegas-Forero, L. (eds.), *Truth in Perspective*. Aldershot: Ashgate, 1998.

Marty, A., *Untersuchungen zur Grundlegung der allgemeinen Grammatik und Sprachphilosophie*. Halle: Niemeyer, 1908.

Mates, B., 'Synonymy', *University of California Publications in Philosophy*, 25 (1950), 201–26.

Meinong, A., *Über Annahmen* (1910). 2nd rev. edn. In *Gesamtausgabe*, vol. 4, Graz: Akademische Druck- und Verlagsanstalt, 1977. (Trans. as *On Assumptions*. Berkeley and Los Angeles: University of California Press, 1983.)

Melia, J., 'Anti-Realism Untouched', *Mind*, 100 (1991), 341–2.

Mellor, D. H., *The Facts of Causation*. London: Routledge, 1995.

—— and Oliver, A. (eds.), *Properties*. Oxford: Oxford University Press, 1997.

Mill, J. S., *System of Logic* (1843). In *Collected Works*, VII, VIII. London: Routledge, 1973.

Misak, C. J., *Truth and the End of Inquiry: A Peircean Account of Truth*. Oxford: Clarendon Press, 1991.

Moore, G. E., *Common Place Book 1919–1953*. London: Allen & Unwin, 1962.

—— 'External and Internal Relations' (1919). In his *Philosophical Studies*, 276–309.

—— 'Facts and Propositions' (1927). In his *Philosophical Papers*, 60–88.

—— 'Is Existence a Predicate?' (1936). In his *Philosophical Papers*, 115–26.

—— *Lectures on Metaphysics* (1934–5) (from the Notes of A. Ambrose and M. Macdonald). Peter Lang: New York, 1992.

—— *Philosophical Papers*. London: Allen & Unwin, 1959.

—— *Philosophical Studies*. London: Routledge, 1922.

—— *Principia Ethica*, Cambridge: Cambridge University Press, 1903.

—— 'A Reply to My Critics'. In P. Schilpp (ed.), *The Philosophy of G. E. Moore*. Evanston, ILL: Northwestern, 1942, 533–687.

—— *Selected Writings*. London: Routledge, 1993.

—— *Some Main Problems in Philosophy* [*SMPP*]. London: Allen & Unwin, 1953 [1910].

—— 'Truth' (1902). In his *Selected Writings*, 20–2.

—— 'William James' *Pragmatism*' (1908). In his *Philosophical Studies*, 97–146.

Morscher, E., 'Propositions and States of Affairs in Austrian Philosophy before Wittgenstein'. In C. Nyiri (ed.), *From Bolzano to Wittgenstein*. Vienna: Hölder-Pichler-Tempsky, 1986, 75–85.

Mulligan, K., Simons, P., and Smith, B., 'Truth-Makers', *Phil. and Phenomenological Research*, 44 (1984), 287–321.

Müller, V., and Stein, C., 'Epistemic Theories of Truth: The Justifiability Paradox Investigated'. In L. Villegas-Forero (ed.), *Verdad: Lógica, Representación y Mundo*, Santiago de Compostela: Universidad de Santiago de Compostela, 1996, 95–104.

Nagel, T., *The View from Nowhere*. New York: Oxford University Press, 1986.

Neale, S., *Descriptions*. Cambridge, MA: MIT Press, 1990.

—— *Facing Facts* [*FF*]. Oxford: Clarendon Press, 2001.

Neurath, O., *Gesammelte philosophische und methodologische Schriften*. 2 vols. Vienna: Hölder-Pichler-Tempsky, 1981.

—— *Philosophical Papers*. Dordrecht: Reidel, 1983.

—— '*Physikalismus* [Physicalism]' (1931). In his *Gesammelte philosophische und methodologische Schriften*, 417–21. (Trans. in his *Philosophical Papers*, 52–7.)

—— '*Protokollsätze* [Protocol Statements]' (1932). In his *Gesammelte philosophische und methodologische Schriften* (1981), 577–85. (Trans. in his *Philosophical Papers*, 91–9.)

—— '*Radikaler Physikalismus und "Wirkliche Welt"* [Radical Physicalism and the "Real World"]' (1934). In his *Gesammelte philosophische und methodologische Schriften* (1981), 611–23. (Trans. in his *Philosophical Papers*, 100–14.)

—— '*Soziologie im Physikalismus* [Sociology in the Framework of Physicalism]' (1931). In his *Gesammelte philosophische und methodologische Schriften*, 533–62. (Trans. in his *Philosophical Papers*, 58–90.)

Nozick, R., *Philosophical Explanations*. Oxford: Clarendon Press. 1981.

Nuchelmans, G., *Theories of the Proposition*. Amsterdam: North-Holland, 1973.

O'Leary-Hawthorne, J., and Oppy, G., 'Minimalism and Truth', *Noûs*, 31 (1997), 170–96.

Olson, K., *An Essay on Facts*. Stanford: CSLI Publications, 1987.

Parsons, T., 'On Denoting Propositions and Facts', *Phil. Perspectives*, 7 (1993), 441–60.

Peacocke, C., *Being Known*. Oxford: Clarendon Press, 1999.

—— 'How Are A Priori Truths Possible?', *European Journ. Phil.*, 1 (1993), 175–99.

—— 'Introduction', to Peacocke (ed.), *Understanding and Sense*, 1. Aldershot: Dartmouth, 1993, xi–xxiii.

—— *A Study of Concepts*. Cambridge, MA: MIT Press, 1992.

—— 'Truth Definitions and Actual Languages'. In G. Evans and J. McDowell (eds.), *Truth and Meaning*. Oxford: Clarendon Press, 1976, 162–88.

Pearce, D., and Woleński, J. (eds.), *Logischer Rationalismus–Philosophische Schriften der Lemberg-Warschauer Schule*. Frankfurt/M: Athenäum, 1998.

Peirce, C. S., *Collected Papers [CP]* (1931–5). Cambridge, MA: Harvard University Press, 1958.

Percival, P., 'Knowability, Actuality, and the Metaphysics of Context-Dependence', *Australasian Journ. Phil.*, 69 (1991), 82–97.

Peregrin, J. (ed.), *Truth and its Nature (if any)*. Dordrecht: Kluwer, 1999.

Perry, J., 'Evading the Slingshot'. In A. Clark (ed.), *Philosophy and Cognitive Science*. Dordrecht: Kluwer, 1996, 95–114.

—— *The Problem of the Essential Indexical and Other Essays*. New York: Oxford University Press, 1993.

Philoponus, J., *In Aristotelis Categorias commentarium*. In *Commentaria in Aristotelem Graeca* XIII 1. Berlin: Reimer, 1898 [c. 515].

Plantinga, A., 'How to Be an Anti-Realist', *Proc. and Addresses of the American Phil. Association*, 56 (1982), 47–70.

Plato, *Res publica. Theaetetus. Sophistes*. In *Opera*. Oxford: Clarendon Press, 1899–1907.

Platts, M. (ed.), *Reference, Truth, and Reality*. London: Routledge, 1980.

Plotinus, *Enneades I–III*. In *Opera*. Oxford: Clarendon Press, 1964 [c. 250].

Popper, K., 'Is it True What She Says about Tarski?', *Philosophy*, 54 (1979), 98.

Popper, K., 'Philosophical Comments on Tarski's Theory of Truth'. In his *Objective Knowledge*. Oxford: Clarendon, 1972, 319–40.

—— 'Truth, Rationality, and the Growth of Scientific Knowledge' (1960). In his *Conjectures and Refutations*. London: Routledge, rev. edn., 1972, 215–50.

Pratt, J. B., 'Truth and its Verification' (1907). In D. Olin (ed.), '*William James: Pragmatism In Focus*'. London: Routledge, 1992, 156–60.

Prior, A. N., 'Berkeley in Logical Form' (1955). In his *Papers in Logic and Ethics*, 33–8.

—— 'Correspondence Theory of Truth'. In P. Edwards (ed.), *The Encyclopedia of Philosophy*, II. London: Routledge, 1967, 223–32.

—— 'Definitions, Rules and Axioms' (1955). In his *Papers in Logic and Ethics*, 39–55.

—— *The Doctrine of Propositions and Terms*. London: Duckworth, 1976.

—— 'Entities' (1954). In his *Papers in Logic and Ethics*, 25–32.

—— 'The Formalities of Omniscience' (1962). In his *Papers on Time and Tense*. Oxford: Clarendon Press, 1968, 26–44.

—— 'Fugitive Truth', *Analysis*, 29 (1968), 5–8.

—— *Objects of Thought* [OT]. Oxford: Clarendon Press, 1971.

—— 'Oratio Obliqua' (1963). In his *Papers in Logic and Ethics*, 147–58.

—— *Papers in Logic and Ethics*. London: Duckworth, 1976.

—— 'Some Problems of Self-Reference in John Buridan' (1962). In his *Papers in Logic and Ethics*, 130–46.

—— 'Two Essays on Temporal Realism'. In J. Copeland (ed.), *Logic and Reality: Essays on the Legacy of Arthur Prior*. Oxford: Clarendon Press, 1996, 43–51.

Proclus, *The Elements of Theology*. 2nd rev. edn. Oxford: Clarendon Press, 1963 [c. 450].

—— *In Platonis Timaeum commentaria*. II. Leipzig: Teubner, 1904 [c. 450].

Putnam, H., 'Comment on Wolfgang Künne's Paper'. In J. Conant and U. Żegleń (eds.), *Pragmatism and Realism*. London: Routledge, 2002, 166.

—— 'A Comparison of Something with Something Else' (1985). In his *Words and Life*, 330–50.

—— 'A Defence of Internal Realism' (1982). In his *Realism with a Human Face*, 30–42.

—— 'Does the Disquotational Theory Really Solve All Philosophical Problems?' (1991). In his *Words and Life*, 264–78.

—— 'James' Theory of Truth'. In R. A. Putnam (ed.), *The Cambridge Companion to William James*. Cambridge: Cambridge University Press, 1997, 166–85.

—— 'Logical Positivism and the Philosophy of Mind' (1969). In his *Mind, Language and Reality*. Cambridge: Cambridge University Press, 1975, 441–51.

—— *Meaning and the Moral Sciences*. London: Routledge, 1978.

—— 'Michael Dummett on Realism and Idealism'. In P. Clark and B. Hale (eds.), *Reading Putnam*. Oxford: Blackwell, 1994, 256–62.

—— 'On Properties' (1970). In his *Mathematics, Matter and Method*. Cambridge: Cambridge University Press, 1975, 305–22.

—— 'On Truth' (1983). In his *Words and Life*, 315–29.

—— 'On Wittgenstein's Philosophy of Mathematics', *Proc. Aristotelian Soc.*, SV 70 (1996), 243–64.

—— 'The Permanence of William James' (1992). In his *Pragmatism: An Open Question*. Cambridge, MA: Blackwell, 1995, 5–26.

—— 'Pragmatism', *Proc. Aristotelian Soc.*, 95 (1995), 291–306.

—— *Realism and Reason*. Cambridge: Cambridge University Press, 1983.

—— *Realism with a Human Face*. Cambridge, MA: Harvard University Press, 1990.

—— *Reason, Truth and History*. Cambridge: Cambridge University Press, 1981.

—— 'Reply to David Anderson', *Phil. Topics*, 20 (1992), 361–9.

—— 'Reply to Gary Ebbs', *Phil. Topics*, 20 (1992), 347–58.

—— 'Reply to Terry Horgan', *Erkenntnis*, 43 (1991), 419–23.

—— 'Reply to Richard Miller', *Phil. Topics*, 20 (1992), 369–74.

—— *Renewing Philosophy*. Cambridge, MA: Harvard University Press, 1992.

—— *Representation and Reality*. Cambridge, MA: MIT Press, 1988.

—— 'Sense, Nonsense, and the Senses', John Dewey Lectures 1994. In his *The Threefold Cord: Mind, Body, and World*, 1–70.

—— 'Simon Blackburn on Internal Realism'. In P. Clark and B. Hale (eds.), *Reading Putnam*. Oxford: Blackwell, 1994, 242–54.

—— *The Threefold Cord: Mind, Body, and World*. New York: Columbia University Press, 1999.

—— 'Why Is a Philosopher?' (1989). In his *Realism with a Human Face*, 105–19.

—— *Words and Life*. Cambridge, MA: Harvard University Press, 1994.

Pyne Parsons, K., 'Ambiguity and the Truth Definition', *Noûs*, 7 (1973), 379–94.

Quine, W. V. O., 'Existence and Quantification' (1968). In his *Ontological Relativity and Other Essays*, 91–113.

—— *From a Logical Point of View*, 2nd edn. New York: Harper & Row, 1961.

—— 'The Limits of Knowledge' (1973). In his *The Ways of Paradox and Other Essays*, 59–67.

—— 'A Logistical Approach to the Ontological Problem' (1939). In his *The Ways of Paradox and Other Essays*, 197–202.

—— *Mathematical Logic*, rev. edn. Cambridge, MA: Harvard University Press, 1951.

—— 'Meaning and Existential Inference' (1953). In his *From a Logical Point of View*, 160–7.

—— 'Notes on the Theory of Reference' [Notes]. In his *From a Logical Point of View*, 130–8.

—— 'On the Very Idea of a Third Dogma'. In *Theories and Things*. Cambridge, MA: Harvard University Press, 1981, 38–42.

—— 'Ontological Relativity' (1968). In his *Ontological Relativity and Other Essays*, 26–68.

—— *Ontological Relativity and Other Essays*. New York: Columbia University Press, 1969.

—— *Philosophy of Logic* [PL]. Englewood Cliffs, NJ: Prentice Hall, 1970.

—— *Pursuit of Truth* [PT], rev. 2nd edn. Cambridge, MA: Harvard University Press, 1992

—— *Quiddities*. Cambridge, MA: Harvard University Press, 1987.

—— 'Reply to Davidson'. In D. Davidson and J. Hintikka (eds.), *Words and Objections*. Dordrecht: Reidel, 1969, pp. 333–5.

—— Review of Evans, G. and McDowell, J. (eds.), *Truth and Meaning, Journ. Phil.*, 74 (1977), 225–41, 415–16.

—— *The Roots of Reference*. La Salle, ILL: Open Court, 1973.

—— 'The Scope and Language of Science' (1954). In his *The Ways of Paradox and Other Essays*, 228–45.

—— 'Two Dogmas of Empiricism' (1951). In his *From a Logical Point of View*, 20–46.

Quine, W. V. O., *The Ways of Paradox and Other Essays*, rev. and enlarged edn. Cambridge, MA: Harvard University Press, 1976.

—— *Word and Object* [*W&O*]. Cambridge, MA: MIT Press, 1960.

Quinton, A., *The Nature of Things*. London: Routledge, 1973.

Ramsey, F. P., 'Facts and Propositions' (1927). In his *Philosophical Papers*. Cambridge: Cambridge University Press, 1990, 34–51.

—— *On Truth*. Dordrecht: Kluwer, 1991 [1928].

Rand, R., 'Kotarbinskis [...] "Elemente der Erkenntnistheorie, der Logik und der Methodologie der Wissenschaften" ', *Erkenntnis*, 7 (1937–8), 92–120.

Recanati, F., 'What Is Said', *Synthèse*, 128 (2001), 75–91.

Reichenbach, H., *Elements of Symbolic Logic*. New York: Free Press, 1947.

Reinach, A., *Sämtliche Werke*, I. Munich: Philosophia, 1989.

—— 'Zum Begriff der Zahl' (1914). In his *Sämtliche Werke*, 515–29.

—— 'Zur Theorie des negativen Urteils [On the Theory of Negative Judgements]' (1911). In his *Sämtliche Werke*, 95–140. (Trans. in B. Smith (ed.), *Parts and Moments*. Munich: Philosophia, 1982, 315–76.)

Rescher, N., *The Coherence Theory of Truth*. Oxford: Clarendon Press, 1973.

Resnik, M., 'Immanent Truth', *Mind*, 99 (1990), 405–24.

Restall, G., 'Truthmakers, Entailment and Necessity', *Australasian Journ. Phil.*, 74 (1996), 331–40.

Richard, M., 'Propositional Attitudes'. In B. Hale and C. Wright (eds.), *Companion to the Philosophy of Language*. Oxford: Blackwell, 1997, 197–226.

—— 'Propositional Quantification'. In J. Copeland (ed.), *Logic and Reality: Essays on the Legacy of Arthur Prior*. Oxford: Clarendon Press, 1996, 437–60.

—— 'Temporalism and Eternalism', *Phil. Studies*, 39 (1981), 1–13.

—— 'Tense, Propositions, and Meanings', *Phil. Studies*, 41 (1982), 337–51.

Rojszczak, A., 'Why Should a Physical Object Take on the Role of Truth-Bearer?'. In J. Woleński and E. Köhler (eds.), *Alfred Tarski and the Vienna Circle*. Dordrecht: Kluwer, 1999, 115–25.

Rorty, R., 'Is Truth a Goal of Enquiry? Davidson vs. Wright', *Phil. Quart.*, 45 (1995), 281–300.

—— 'Life at the End of Inquiry' (rev. of Putnam, *Realism and Reason*). In *London Review of Books*, 2 Aug. 1984, 6–7.

—— 'Pragmatism, Davidson, and Truth'. In E. Lepore (ed.), *Truth and Interpretation*. Oxford: Blackwell, 1986, 333–55.

—— 'Universality and Truth'. In R. Brandom (ed.), *Rorty and his Critics*. Oxford: Blackwell, 2000, 1–30.

Ross, D., *The Foundations of Ethics*. Oxford: Clarendon Press, 1939.

Routley [Sylvan], R., 'Necessary Limits to Knowledge: Unknowable Truths'. In E. Morscher, O. Neumaier, and G. Zecha (eds.), *Philosophie als Wissenschaft*. Bad Reichenhall: Comes, 1981, 93–115.

—— 'Relevant Logics'. In H. Burkhardt and B. Smith (eds.), *Handbook of Metaphysics and Ontology*. Munich: Philosophia, 1991, 787–9.

——, and Goddard, L., *The Logic of Significance and Context*. Edinburgh: Scottish Academy Press, 1973.

Ruben, D.-H., 'A Puzzle about Posthumous Predication', *Phil. Review*, 97 (1988), 211–36.

Rumfitt, I., 'Content and Context: The Paratactic Theory Revisited and Revised', *Mind*, 102 (1993), 429–54.

—— 'Unilateralism Disarmed: A Reply to Dummett and Gibbard', *Mind*, 111 (2002), 305–21.

Rundle, B., *Grammar in Philosophy [GP]*. Oxford: Clarendon Press, 1979.

Russell, B., 'Dewey's New *Logic*'. In P. A. Schilpp (ed.), *The Philosophy of John Dewey*. LaSalle, ILL: Open Court, 1939, 137–56.

—— *Human Knowledge: Its Scope and its Limits*. London: Allen & Unwin, 1948.

—— *An Inquiry into Meaning and Truth [IMT]*. Harmondsworth: Penguin, 1967 [1940].

—— *Introduction to Mathematical Philosophy*. London: Allen & Unwin, 1919.

—— 'Meinong's Theory of Complexes and Assumptions (III)' (1904). In his *Essays in Analysis*. London: Allen & Unwin, 1973, 59–76.

—— 'The Monistic Theory of Truth' (1907). In his *Philosophical Essays*, 131–46.

—— *My Philosophical Development*. London: Allen & Unwin, 1959.

—— *Our Knowledge of the External World*. London: Allen & Unwin, 1969 [1914].

—— *Philosophical Essays*. London: Allen & Unwin, 1966.

—— 'The Philosophy of Logical Atomism' *[PLA]* (1918). In his *Logic and Knowledge*. London: Allen & Unwin, 1956, 177–281.

—— *The Principles of Mathematics*. London: Allen & Unwin, 1964 [1903].

—— *The Problems of Philosophy*. Oxford: Oxford University Press, 1912.

—— 'Review of *Symbolic Logic and its Applications* by Hugh MacColl', *Mind*, 15 (1906), 255–60.

—— 'Transantlantic "Truth" ' (1908). In his *Philosophical Essays*, 112–30.

Russell, B., and Whitehead, A. N., *Principia Mathematica*, 1. Cambridge: Cambridge University Press, 1910.

Ryle, G., *Collected Papers*, 2 vols. London: Hutchinson, 1971.

—— *The Concept of Mind*. London: Hutchinson, 1949.

—— 'Heterologicality' (1950). In his *Collected Papers*, II. 250–7.

—— 'Plato's Parmenides' (1939). In his *Collected Papers*, I. 1–44.

—— 'Systematically Misleading Expressions' (1932). In his *Collected Papers*, II. 39–62.

—— 'Theory of Meaning' (1957). In his *Collected Papers*, II. 350–72.

Sainsbury, R. M., *Russell*. London: Routledge, 1979.

—— 'Philosophical Logic'. In A. C. Grayling (ed.), *Philosophy, A Guide Through the Subject*. Oxford: Oxford University Press, 1995, 61–122.

Salmon, N., *Frege's Puzzle*. Cambridge, MA: MIT Press, 1986.

—— 'Tense and Singular Propositions' ['Tense']. In J. Almog, J. Perry, and H. Wettstein (eds.), *Themes from Kaplan*. New York: Oxford University Press, 1989, 331–92.

Saul, J., 'Substitution and Simple Sentences', *Analysis*, 57 (1997), 102–8.

Schantz, R., *Wahrheit, Referenz und Realismus*, Berlin: de Gruyter, 1996.

—— (ed.), *What is Truth?* Berlin: de Gruyter, 2002.

Scheffler, I., 'On Synonymy and Indirect Discourse', *Phil. of Science*, 22 (1955), 39–44.

Schiffer, S., 'A Paradox of Meaning', *Noûs*, 28 (1994), 279–324.

—— 'Pleonastic Fregeanism'. In *The Proceedings of the Twentieth World Congress of Philosophy*, VI. Phil. Documentation Center: Bowling Green State University, 2000, 1–15.

474   Bibliography

Schiffer, S., *The Things We Mean* [*TWM*]. Oxford: Oxford University Press, forthcoming.

Schilpp, P. A. (ed.), *The Philosophy of John Dewey*. LaSalle, ILL: Open Court, 1939.

Schlick, M., 'Facts and Propositions' (1935). In M. Macdonald (ed.), *Philosophy and Analysis*. Oxford: Blackwell, 1954, 232–7; and in his *Philosophical Papers*, II. 400–4.

—— *Gesammelte Aufsätze*. Wien: Gerold and Co., 1938

—— *Philosophical Papers*, 2 vols. Dordrecht: Reidel, 1979.

—— '*Über das Fundament der Erkenntnis* [On the Foundation of Knowledge]' ['*Fundament*'] (1934). In his *Gesammelte Aufsätze*, 289–310. (Trans. in his *Philosophical Papers*, II. 370–87.)

—— 'Unanswerable Questions?' (1935). In his *Gesammelte Aufsätze*, 369–75, and *Philosophical Papers*, II. 414–19.

—— '*Das Wesen der Wahrheit nach der modernen Logik*' (1910). In his *Philosophische Logik*. Frankfurt/M.: Suhrkamp, 1986, 31–109. (Trans. as 'The Nature of Truth in Modern Logic'. In his *Philosophical Papers*, I. 41–103.)

Searle, J., *The Construction of Social Reality*. New York: Free Press, 1995.

—— *Intentionality*. Cambridge: Cambridge University Press, 1983.

—— 'Meaning and Speech Acts', *Phil. Review*, 71 (1962), 423–32.

—— 'Truth: A Reconsideration of Strawson's Views'. In L. Hahn (ed.), *The Philosophy of P. F. Strawson*. Chicago: Open Court, 1998, 385–401.

Sellars, W., 'Truth and "Correspondence"' (1962). In his *Science, Perception, and Reality*. London: Routledge, 1963, 197–224.

Sextus Empiricus, *Adversus Mathematicos*, Books VII–VIII. In *Sextus Empiricus*, vol. 2, Loeb Classical Library. Cambridge, MA: Harvard University Press, 1997 [fl. c. 200].

Simons, P., 'Aristotle's Concept of States of Affairs'. In M. Fischer and O. Gigon (eds.), *Antike Rechts- und Sozialphilosophie*. Frankfurt/M: Lang, 1988, 97–112.

—— 'How the World Can Make Propositions True: A Celebration of Logical Atomism' ['World']. In M. Omyła (ed.), *Skłonności Metafizyczna* (Metaphysical Inclinations). Warsaw: Warsaw University, 1998, 113–35.

—— 'Logical Atomism and Its Ontological Refinement: A Defense'. In K. Mulligan (ed.), *Language, Truth, and Ontology*. Dordrecht: Kluwer, 1992, 157–79.

—— '*Tatsache II*'. In J. Ritter, K. Gründer, and G. Gabriel (eds.), *Historisches Wörterbuch der Philosophie*, vol. 10. Darmstadt: Wissenschaftliche Buchgesellschaft, 1998, 913–16.

——, and Woleński, J., '*De Veritate*: Austro-Polish Contributions to the Theory of Truth from Brentano to Tarski'. In K. Szaniawski (ed.), *The Vienna Circle and the Lvov-Warsaw School*. Dordrecht: Kluwer, 1989, 391–442.

Sklar, L., 'Semantic Analogy', *Phil. Studies*, 38 (1980), 217–34.

Skorupski, J., 'Critical Study [of Wright, *Realism, Meaning, and Truth* (1st edn., 1993)]', *Phil. Quart.*, 38 (1988), 500–25.

—— 'The Intelligibility of Scepticism' ['Intelligibility']. In D. Bell and N. Cooper (eds.), *The Analytic Tradition*. Oxford: Blackwell, 1990, 1–29.

—— 'Meaning, Use and Verification'. In B. Hale and C. Wright (eds.), *Companion to the Philosophy of Language*. Oxford: Blackwell, 1997, 29–59.

Smart, J. J. C., 'Realism vs Idealism', *Philosophy*, 61 (1986), 295–312.

—— 'Review [of Putnam, *Realism and Reason*]', *Australasian Journ. Phil.*, 63 (1985), 533–5.

Smiley, T., 'Sense Without Denotation', *Analysis*, 20 (1960), 125–35.

Smith, B., *Austrian Philosophy. The Legacy of Franz Brentano*. Chicago: Open Court, 1994.

—— '*Sachverhalt*'. In J. Ritter, K. Gründer, and G. Gabriel (eds.), *Historisches Wörterbuch der Philosophie*, vol. 8. Darmstadt: Wissenschaftliche Buchgesellschaft, 1992, 1102–13.

Smith, P., 'Approximate Truth for Minimalists', *Phil. Papers*, 27 (1998), 119–28.

Soames, S., 'Semantics and Semantic Competence', *Phil. Perspectives*, 3 (1989), 575–96.

—— 'T-Sentences'. In W. Sinnott-Armstrong, D. Raffman, and N. Asher (eds.), *Modality, Morality, and Belief*. Cambridge: Cambridge University Press, 1995, 250–70.

—— *Understanding Truth* [*UT*]. Oxford: Oxford University Press, 1999.

—— 'What Is a Theory of Truth?', *Journ. Phil.*, 81 (1984), 411–29.

Sobel, J. H., 'Lies, Lies, and More Lies: A Plea for Propositions', *Phil. Studies*, 67 (1992), 51–69.

Sommers, F. (1969). 'On Concepts of Truth in Natural Languages', *Review of Metaphysics*, 23: 259–86.

Sorensen, R., *Blindspots*. Oxford: Clarendon Press, 1988.

Sosa, E., 'Epistemology and Primitive Truth'. In M. Lynch (ed.), *The Nature of Truth*. Cambridge, MA: MIT Press, 2001, 641–62.

—— 'Epistemology, Realism and Truth', *Phil. Perspectives*, 7 (1993), 1–16.

Spinoza, B., *Cogitata Metaphysica* (1663). In *Opera*, I. 231–81. (Trans. as *Metaphysical Thoughts*. In *Collected Works*, I. 299–346.)

—— *Collected Works*. Princeton: Princeton University Press, 1985.

—— *Korte Verhandeling* [. . .] (c. 1661). In *Opera*, I. 1–121. (Trans. as *Short Treatise on God, Man, and His Well-Being*. In *Collected Works*, I. 46–156.)

—— *Opera*. Heidelberg: Winter, 1924–5.

—— *Tractatus de intellectus emendatione* (c. 1661). In *Opera*, II. 5–40. (Trans. as *Treatise on the Emendation of the Intellect*. In *Collected Works*, I. 3–45.)

Stalnaker, R., *Inquiry*. Cambridge, MA: MIT Press, 1984.

Stegmüller, W., *Das Wahrheitsproblem und die Idee der Semantik*. Wien: Springer, 1957.

Stepanians, M., *Frege und Husserl über Urteilen und Denken*. Paderborn: Schöningh, 1998.

—— *Gottlob Frege zur Einführung*. Hamburg: Junius, 2001.

Stevenson, L., and Walker, R., Symposium on 'Empirical Realism and Transcendental Anti-Realism', *Proc. Aristotelian Soc.*, SV 57 (1983), 131–77.

Stoecker, R. (ed.), *Reflecting Davidson*. Berlin: de Gruyter, 1993.

Strawson, P. F., *Analysis and Metaphysics*. Oxford: Oxford University Press, 1992.

—— *The Bounds of Sense*. London: Methuen, 1966.

—— 'Categories' (1970). In his *Freedom and Resentment and Other Essays*, 108–32.

—— 'Causation and Explanation' (1985). In his *Analysis and Metaphysics*, 109–31.

—— 'Concepts and Properties' (1987). In his *Entity and Identity, and Other Essays*, 85–91.

—— 'Direct Singular Reference: Intended Reference and Actual Reference' (1986). In his *Entity and Identity, and Other Essays*, 92–9.

—— *Entity and Identity, and Other Essays*. Oxford: Clarendon Press, 1997.

—— *Freedom and Resentment, and Other Essays*. London: Methuen, 1974.

—— *Individuals*. London: Methuen, 1959.

Strawson, P. F., 'Intellectual Autobiography'. In L. Hahn (ed.), *The Philosophy of P. F. Strawson*. Chicago: Open Court, 1998, 1–21.

—— 'Is Existence Never a Predicate?' (1967). In his *Freedom and Resentment and Other Essays*, 189–97.

—— 'Knowledge and Truth', *Indian Phil. Quart.*, 3 (1976), 273–82.

—— *Logico-Linguistic-Papers*. London: Methuen, 1971.

—— 'Meaning and Truth' (1969). In his *Logico-Linguistic-Papers*, 170–89.

—— 'On Referring' (1950). In his *Logico-Linguistic-Papers*, 1–27.

—— 'Positions for Quantifiers' (1974). In his *Entity and Identity, and Other Essays*, 64–84.

—— 'A Problem about Truth' (1964). In his *Logico-Linguistic-Papers*, 214–33.

—— 'Propositions, Concepts, and Logical Truths' (1957). In his *Logico-Linguistic-Papers*, 116–29.

—— 'Reply Mauricio Beuchot'. In C. C. Caorsi (ed.), *Ensayos sobre Strawson*. Montevideo: Universidad de la Republica, 1992, 28–30.

—— 'Reply to Geach'. In Z. van Straaten (ed.), *Philosophical Subjects, Essays Presented to P. F. Strawson*. Oxford: Clarendon Press, 1980, 292–4.

—— 'Reply to Grover', *Philosophia* (Israel), 10 (1980), 325–6.

—— 'Reply to John Searle'. In L. Hahn (ed.), *The Philosophy of P. F. Strawson*. Chicago: Open Court, 1998, 402–4.

—— 'Singular Terms and Predication' (1961). In his *Logico-Linguistic-Papers*, 53–74.

—— *Skepticism and Naturalism: Some Varieties*. London: Methuen, 1985.

—— *Subject and Predicate in Logic and Grammar*. London: Methuen, 1974.

—— 'Truth' (1949). In M. Macdonald (ed.), *Philosophy and Analysis*. Oxford: Blackwell, 1954, 260–77.

—— 'Truth' (1950). In his *Logico-Linguistic-Papers*, 190–213.

—— 'Universals' (1979). In his *Entity and Identity, and Other Essays*, 53–63.

Stumpf, C., *Erkenntnislehre*, I. Leipzig: Ambrosius Barth, 1939.

Tappolet, C., 'Mixed Inferences: A Problem for Pluralism about Truth Predicates', *Analysis*, 57 (1997), 209–10.

—— 'Truth Pluralism and Many-Valued Logics', *Phil. Quart.*, 50 (2000), 382–385.

Tarski, A., *Collected Papers*, I–IV. Basel-Boston-Stuttgart: Birkhäuser, 1986.

—— '*Drei Briefe an Otto Neurath* [Three Letters to Neurath]' ['*Briefe*'] (1930/1936) (with trans.) *Grazer Philosophische Studien*, 43 (1992), 1–32.

—— '*Grundlegung der wissenschaftlichen Semantik* ['*Grundlegung*'] [The Establishment of Scientific Semantics]' (1936), In his *Collected Papers*, II. 259–68. (Trans. in his *Logic, Semantics, Metamathematics*, 401–8. Polish version: '*O ugruntowaniu naukowej semantyki*', *Przegląd Filozoficzny*, 39 (1936), 50–7.)

—— *Logic, Semantics, Metamathematics*, Papers from 1923 to 1938. 2nd edn. Indianapolis: Hackett, 1983.

—— *Pojęcie prawdy w językach nauk dedukcyjnych* [*The Concept of Truth in the Languages of Deductive Sciences*] (1933). Acta Societatis Scientiarum ac Litterarum Varsoviensis, fasc. 34.

—— Remarks on M. Kokoszyńska, (1936), in Polish. In his *Collected Papers*, IV. 701.

—— 'The Semantic Conception of Truth and the Foundations of Semantics' ['Semantic'] (1944). In his *Collected Papers*, II. 661–99, quoted by section number.

——— 'Sur les ensembles définissables de nombres réels I. [On Definable Sets of Real Numbers]' (1931). In his *Collected Papers*, I. 517–48. (Trans. in his *Logic, Semantics, Metamathematics*, 110–42.)

——— 'Truth and Proof' ['Proof'] (1969). In his *Collected Papers*, IV. 399–423.

——— *Der Wahrheitsbegriff in den formalisierten Sprachen* [*WB*] [*The Concept of Truth in Formalized Languages*] (1935). Enlarged German trans. of his *Pojęcie prawdy w językach nauk dedukcyjnych*. In his *Collected Papers*, II. 51–198, quoted by original pagination of the separatum (Lwów 1935). (Trans. in his *Logic, Semantics, Metamathematics*, 152–278.)

——— '*Der Wahrheitsbegriff in den Sprachen der deduktiven Disziplinen* [The Concept of Truth in the Languages of Deductive Sciences]' ['*Wahrheit*'] (1932). In his *Collected Papers*, I. 613–17.

Tarski, J., 'Philosophy in the Creativity of Alfred Tarski', *Dialogue and Universalism*, 1–2 (1996), 157–9.

Taylor, B., 'Truth-Theory for Indexical Languages'. In M. Platts (ed.), *Reference, Truth, and Reality*. London: Routledge, 1980, 182–98.

Teichmann, R. (ed.), *Logic, Cause and Action, Essays in Honour of Elizabeth Anscombe*. Cambridge: Cambridge University Press, 2000.

Tennant, N., 'Reply to Hand and Kvanvig', *Australasian Journ. Phil.*, 79 (2001), 107–13.

——— 'Reply to Williamson', *Ratio*, 14 (2001), 263–80.

——— *Taming the True*. Oxford: Clarendon Press, 1997.

Tichý, P., *The Foundations of Frege's Logic*. Berlin: de Gruyter, 1988.

——— 'The Transiency of Truth', *Theoria*, 46 (1980), 165–82.

Tugendhat, E., '*Tarskis semantische Definition der Wahrheit und ihre Stellung innerhalb der Geschichte des Wahrheitsproblems im logischen Positivismus*' (1960). In his *Philosophische Aufsätze*. Frankfurt/M: Suhrkamp, 1992, 179–213.

——— *Vorlesungen zur Einführung in die sprachanalytische Philosophie*. Frankfurt/M: Suhrkamp, 1976.

——— *Der Wahrheitsbegriff bei Husserl und Heidegger*. Berlin: de Gruyter, 1967.

———, and Wolf, U., *Logisch-semantische Propädeutik*. Stuttgart: Reclam, 1983.

Twardowski, K., '*O czynnościach i wytworach* [Actions and Products' (1912). Trans. in his *On Actions, Products and Other Topics in Philosophy*, 103–32. (German version, '*Funktionen und Gebilde*', *Conceptus*, 29 (1996), 157–86.)

——— '*O tak zwanych prawdach względnych* [On So-Called Relative Truths]' (1900). Trans. in his *On Actions, Products and Other Topics in Philosophy*, 147–69. (Also trans. as '*Über sogenannte relative Wahrheiten*' in D. Pearce and J. Woleński, J. (eds.), *Logischer Rationalismus—Philosophische Schriften der Lemberg-Warschauer Schule*. Frankfurt/M: Athenäum, 1988, 38–58.

——— *On Actions, Products and Other Topics in Philosophy*. Amsterdam: Rodopi, 1999.

——— '*Wykłady z teorii poznania* [Theory of Knowledge. A Lecture Course]' (1925). Trans. in his *On Actions, Products and Other Topics in Philosophy*, 181–239.

Vallicella, W., 'Three Conceptions of States of Affairs', *Noûs*, 34 (2000), 237–59.

van Inwagen, P., 'Generalizations of Homophonic Truth-Sentences' ['Truth-Sentences']. In R. Schantz (ed.), *What is Truth?* Berlin: de Gruyter, 2002, 205–22.

——— 'Why I Don't Understand Substitutional Quantification', *Phil. Studies*, 39 (1981), 281–5.

van Straaten, Z. (ed.), *Philosophical Subjects, Essays Presented to P. F. Strawson*. Oxford: Clarendon Press, 1980.

Vendler, Z., 'Facts and Events'. In his *Linguistics and Philosophy*. Ithaca, NY: Cornell University Press, 1967, 122–46.

Vision, G., *Modern Anti-Realism and Manufactured Truth*. London: Routledge, 1988.

Waismann, F., 'How I See Philosophy' (1956). In his *How I See Philosophy*. London: Macmillan, 1968, 1–38.

Walker, R., 'Bradley's Theory of Truth'. In G. Stock (ed.), *Appearance versus Reality*. Oxford: Clarendon Press, 1998, 93–109.

—— *The Coherence Theory of Truth*. London: Routledge, 1989.

—— 'Theories of Truth'. In B. Hale and C. Wright (eds.), *Companion to the Philosophy of Language*. Oxford: Blackwell, 1997, 309–30.

Warnock, G. J., 'A Problem about Truth'. In G. Pitcher, *Truth*. Englewood Cliffs, NJ: Prentice Hall, 1964, 54–67.

White, A., 'Propositions and Sentences'. In G. W. Roberts (ed.), *Bertrand Russell Memorial Volume*. London: Allen & Unwin, 1979, 22–33.

—— ' "True" and "Truly" ', *Noûs*, 2 (1968), 247–51.

—— *Truth*. London: Macmillan, 1970.

—— 'What We Believe'. In N. Rescher (ed.), *Studies in the Philosophy of Mind*. Oxford: Blackwell, 1972, 69–84.

Whitehead, A. N., *The Concept of Nature*. Cambridge: Cambridge University Press, 1920.

—— *Process and Reality* (1929). Corrected edn. New York: Free Press, 1978.

Wiggins, D., 'C. S. Peirce: Belief, Truth, and Going from the Known to the Unknown', *Canadian Journ. Phil.*, SV 24 (1999), 9–29.

—— 'An Indefinibilist cum Normative View of Truth and the Marks of Truth' ['Indefinibilist']. In R. Schantz (ed.), *What is Truth?* Berlin: de Gruyter, 2002, 316–32.

—— 'Meaning and Truth Conditions: From Frege's Grand Design to Davidson's' ['Meaning']. In B. Hale and C. Wright (eds.), *Companion to the Philosophy of Language*. Oxford: Blackwell, 1997, 3–28.

—— *Needs, Values, Truth*, 3rd edn. Oxford: Clarendon Press, 1998.

—— 'Objective and Subjective in Ethics, with Two Postscripts on Truth', *Ratio*, 8 (1995), 243–58.

—— 'Postscript 3' (1998). In his *Needs, Values, Truth*, 329–50.

—— 'Replies'. In S. Lovibond (ed.), *Identity, Truth and Value*. Oxford: Blackwell, 1996, 219–84.

—— 'The Sense and Reference of Predicates: A Running Repair to Frege's Doctrine and a Plea for the Copula', *Phil. Quart.*, 34 (1984), 311–28.

—— 'Truth, and Truth as Predicated of Moral Judgments' ['Moral'] (1987). In his *Needs, Values, Truth*, 139–84.

—— 'What Would be a Substantial Theory of Truth?' ['Substantial']. In Z. van Straaten (ed.), *Philosophical Subjects, Essays Presented to P. F. Strawson*. Oxford: Clarendon Press, 1980, 189–221.

Williams, C. J. F., *Being, Identity, and Truth* [*BIT*]. Oxford: Clarendon Press, 1992.

—— 'What does "X is true" say about X?', *Analysis*, 29 (1969), 113–24.

—— *What is Truth?* [*WIT*] Cambridge: Cambridge University Press, 1976.

Williams, M., 'Do We (Epistemologists) Need a Theory of Truth?', *Phil. Topics*, 14 (1986), 223–42.

—— 'On Some Critics of Deflationism'. In R. Schantz (ed.), *What is Truth?* Berlin: de Gruyter, 2002, 146–58.

Williamson, T., 'Anthropocentrism and Truth', *Philosophia* [Israel], 17 (1987), 33–53.

—— 'Knowability and Constructivism', *Phil. Quart.*, 33 (1988), 422–32.

—— *Knowledge and its Limits [KL]*. Oxford: Oxford University Press, 2000.

—— 'Tennant on Knowable Truth', *Ratio*, 13 (2000), 99–114.

Wilson, K., 'Some Reflections on the Prosentential Theory of Truth'. In J. Dunn and A. Gupta (eds.), *Truth or Consequences*. Dordrecht: Kluwer, 1990, 19–32.

Wittgenstein, L., *Bemerkungen über die Grundlagen der Mathematik/Remarks on the Foundations of Mathematics*, 3rd edn. Oxford: Blackwell, 1978.

—— *Bemerkungen über die Philosophie der Psychologie/Remarks on the Philosophy of Psychology*, I. Oxford: Blackwell, 1980.

—— *Notebooks 1914–1916*. Rev. 2nd edn. Oxford: Blackwell, 1979.

—— 'Notes Dictated to G. E. Moore in Norway' (1914). In his *Notebooks 1914–1916*, 108–19.

—— 'Notes on Logic' (1913). In his *Notebooks 1914–1916*, 93–107.

—— *Philosophische Bemerkungen/Philosophical Remarks*. Oxford: Blackwell 1964.

—— *Philosophische Grammatik/Philosophical Grammar*. Oxford: Blackwell, 1974.

—— *Philosophische Untersuchungen/Philosophical Investigations*, 3rd edn. Oxford: Blackwell, 1958.

—— *Tractatus Logico-Philosophicus*. London: Routledge 1961 [1921].

—— *Zettel*. Oxford: Blackwell, 1967.

Woleński, J., *Essays in the History of Logic and Logical Philosophy*. Kraków: Jagiellonian University Press, 1999.

Wolff, C., *Philosophia rationalis sive Logica* (1728); 3rd edn. 1740. In *Gesammelte Werke*, II/1: 1–3. Hildesheim: Olms, 1962 ff.

Wright, C., 'Anti-Realism, Timeless Truth and [Orwell's] *1984*' ['Timeless'] (1987). In his *Realism, Meaning, and Truth*, 176–203.

—— 'Can a Davidsonian Meaning-Theory be Construed in Terms of Assertibility?' ['Assertibility'] (1987). In his *Realism, Meaning, and Truth*, 403–32.

—— 'Introduction [to 1st edn. of his *Realism, Meaning, and Truth*]' (1987). In his *Realism, Meaning, and Truth*, 1–43.

—— *Truth and Objectivity [T&O]*. Cambridge, MA: Harvard University Press, 1992.

—— *Realism, Meaning, and Truth*, 2nd edn. Oxford: Blackwell, 1993.

—— 'Critical Study [of Walker, *The Coherence Theory of Truth*]', *Synthèse*, 103 (1995), 279–302.

—— 'Truth in Ethics', *Ratio*, 8 (1995), 209–27.

—— 'Précis of *Truth and Objectivity*' and 'Response to Commentators', *Phil. and Phenomenological Research*, 56 (1996), 863–8, 911–41.

—— 'Truth: A Traditional Debate Reviewed' ['Debate']. In S. Blackburn and K. Simmons (eds.), *Truth*. Oxford: Oxford University Press, 1999, 203–38.

—— 'Truth as Sort of Epistemic: Putnam's Peregrinations' ['Epistemic'], *Journ. Phil.*, 97 (2000), 335–64.

—— 'Minimalism, Deflationism, Pragmatism, Pluralism' ['Minimalism']. In M. Lynch (ed.), *The Nature of Truth*. Cambridge, MA: MIT Press, 2001, 751–87.

Wright, G. H. von, 'Demystifying Propositions'. In his *Truth, Knowledge and Modality*, 14–25.

—— 'Determinism and Future Truth'. In his *Truth, Knowledge and Modality*, 1–13.

—— *Logical Studies*. London: Routledge, 1957.

—— *Truth, Knowledge and Modality*. Oxford: Blackwell, 1984.

Żegleń, U. (ed.), *Donald Davidson: Truth, Meaning and Knowledge*. London: Routledge, 1999.

Name Index

Reference to pages may also cover footnotes, and reference to footnotes may cover more than one per page.

Subject Index

Italicized page numbers refer to flow charts in Chapter 1. Reference to pages may also cover footnotes, and reference to footnotes may cover more than one per page.

Made in the USA
San Bernardino, CA
31 March 2014